RXpert SERIES
Student's Companion

# Pharmacology - I

Rxpert SERIES
Student's Companion

# Pharmacology - I

**Dr. K. Ravi Shankar**
M.Pharm, Ph.D.

Professor, Department of Pharmacology, Faculty of Pharmacy,
Aditya University, Surampalem.

**G.V.N. Kiranmayi**
M.Pharm, Ph.D.

Professor, Department of Pharmacology, Faculty of Pharmacy,
Dr. M.G.R Educational and Research Institute, Chennai.

Pharma Med PRESS
An Imprint of BSP Books Pvt. Ltd.

**PharmaMed Press**
*An imprint of BSP Books Pvt. Ltd*
4-4-309/316, Giriraj Lane,
Sultan Bazar, Hyderabad - 500 095.

**Pharmacology - I**

***by Dr. K. Ravishankar and G.V.N. Kiranmayi***



***Published by:***

Pharma Med PRESS
An Imprint of
BSP Books Pvt. Ltd.

**PharmaMed Press**

*An imprint of BSP Books Pvt. Ltd.*

4-4-309/316, Giriraj Lane, Sultan Bazar, Hyderabad - 500 095.

Phone: 040-23445688; Fax: 91+40-23445611

e-mail: info@pharmamedpress.com

www.pharmamedpress.com/pharmamedpress.net

**ISBN: 978-93-48734-74-7 (Hardback)**

**Dedication to,**

To our mentors, who inspired the journey of discovery, championed the passions and exposed the frontiers. To our colleagues, who enriched the path, multiplying the dimensions beyond imagination. To our institutions, which nurtured the nascent trajectory and fostered the ultimate destination. To our families, who shared the ideals and enabled this extraordinary journey to progress every day.

*Dr. K. Ravishankar*

*G. V. N. Kiranmayi*

# Preface

Pharmacology is a very dynamic branch of medicine marked by continual development and marketing of new drugs and simultaneous withdrawal of older products.

The major difficulty in teaching pharmacology and therapeutics is that the subject matter stretches from fundamental studies to details of clinical management. The main objective kept in view while preparing this text book is to provide sound pharmacological basis and detailed information to the reader for rational drug use in therapeutics,

This text book is divided in 29 chapters and each chapter indicates all important and detailed information. The text is supported by background, neat diagrams, tables knowledge of physiology, chemistry and medicine related to drug action is provided. We have rendered our level best to make the text book readable and interesting.

This book Pharmacology is oriented to reflect the contemporary advancements. All the chapters have been updated and special emphasis is given. This book provides valuable substantial information and can be considered as a book of choice for under graduate students of pharmacy, medical and dental students.

*Dr. K. Ravishankar*

*G. V. N. Kiranmayi*

# Acknowledgements

We owe to express our utmost gratefulness to the Almighty for bestowing upon us the patience, courage and abundant blessings to complete the book. Indeed, without his help and will, nothing is accomplished.

At the outsight we express our sincere pranams to our esteemed Professor and Pharmacologist **Late Prof. Dr. D.Visweswaram, University College of Pharmaceutical Sciences, Andhra University, Viskhapatnam** and **Retd. Prof. Dr. M.C. Prabhakara, Pharmacologist, Kakatiya University** for giving us valuable education and what we are today is because of them.

We would like to extend our heartiest gratitude to **Mrs. M. Sridevi**, Associate Professor for extending her help in preparing this text book. We are also thankful to **Mrs. K. Vedavathi**, Office Incharge for her efforts and help in preparing tables and figures.

We would like to express our special gratitude and thanks to our beloved Chairman **Dr. N. Sesha Reddy Garu** and Vice Chairman **Dr. N. Satish Reddy Garu**, Aditya Group of Institutions, Surampalem for their encouragement.

We would also like to thank **Dr. N. Harikrishnan**, Principal and Professor, Faculty of Pharmacy, Dr.MGR University and **Management** of Dr. MGR University for the support.

We would like to convey our special thanks to our publisher **PharmaMed Press** for accepting and publishing our book and extending their whole hearted cooperation, and also thanks to Dr. Mohammed Mazzuddin, for editorial input.

Our sincere thanks to all our well wishers who supported us.

*Dr. K. Ravishankar*

*G. V. N. Kiranmayi*

# Contents

## Chapter - 4
## Drug Biotransformation



## Chapter - 5
## Drug Discovery and Development



## Chapter - 6
## Pharmacovigilance

## Chapter - 7
## Essential Drugs



## Chapter – 8
## Abnormal Actions of Drugs



## Chapter – 9
## Drug Interactions



# PART - II
# DRUGS AFFECTING AUTONOMIC NERVOUS SYSTEM

## Chapter - 10
## General Considerations of Autonomic Nervous System

## Chapter - 11
## Cholinergic Drugs



## Chapter - 12
## Muscarinic Receptor Blocking Drugs



## Chapter - 13
## Adrenergic Drugs

**Chapter -14**

**Adrenergic Blocking Drugs**



**Chapter - 15**

**Ganglionic Stimulating and Blocking Agents**



**Chapter - 16**

**Skeletal Muscle Relaxants**

## PART - III
## DRUGS AFFECTING CENTRAL NERVOUS SYSTEM

### Chapter - 17
### General Considerations of Central Nervous System



### Chapter - 18
### Neurodegenerative Diseases



### Chapter - 19
### General Anaesthetics



### Chapter - 20
### Sedative Hypnotics and Anxiolytic Drugs

**Chapter - 21**
**Neuroleptics**



**Chapter - 22**
**Antidepressants**



**Chapter - 23**
**Antiepileptic Drugs**

## Chapter - 24

## Opioid Analgesics



## Chapter - 25

## CNS Stimulants



## Chapter - 26

## Drug Dependence and Drug Abuse

## Abbreviations

3-MT : 3-methoxytyramine
7TM : 7 transmembrane segment
AAT : Alpha-1-antitrypsin
AcCoA : Acetyl coenzyme A
ACE : Angiotensin converting enzyme
Ach : Acetylcholine
ACTH : Adrenocorticotropic hormone
AD : Alzheimer's disease
ADCC : Antibody-dependent cell-mediated cytotoxicity
ADHD : Attention deficit hyperactivity disorder
ADME : Absorption, distribution, metabolism and excretion
ADR : Adverse drug reaction
ADRB2 : beta-2 adrenergic receptor
ANA : Antinuclear antibodies
ANS : Autonomic nervous system
ATP : Adenosine triphosphate
AV : Atrioventricular
BBB : Blood brain barrier
BDZ : Benzodiazepines
BMD : Bone mineral density
BPH : Benign prostatic hyperplasia
BUN : Blood urea nitrogen
CAD : Coronary artery disease
CaM : Calmodulin
cAMP : Cyclic adenosine monophosphate
CAP : Communityacquired pneumonia
CCC : Cardiac control centre
CCK : Cholecystokinin
CDP : Cytidine diphosphocholine
CF : Cystic fibrosis
CFTR : Cystic fibrosis transmembrane conductance regulator
CHF : Congestive heart failure
CIAA : Chloramphenicol induced aplastic anaemia
CN : Cranial nerve
CO : Cardiac output
CoA : Coenzyme A
COMT : Catechol o-methyltransferase
COPD : Chronic obstructive pulmonary disease
COX : Cyclooxygenase
CPS : Complex partial seizure
CPT : Chest physiotherapy
CSF : Cerebrospinal fluid
CTZ : Chemoreceptor Trigger Zone
CYP : Cytochrome P450
DAG : Diacylglycerol
DB : Diazepam-binding inhibitor
DBS : Deep brain stimulation
DDC : Decarboxylase
DFP : Di-isopropyl Fluorophosphate
DHFR : Dihydrofolatereductase
DIOS : Distal intestinal obstruction syndrome
DKA : Diabetic ketoacidosis
dmnX : Dorsal motor nucleus of the vagus nerve
DMPP : Dimethyl-4-phenylpiperazinium iodide
DNA : Deoxyribonucleic acid
DOC : Deoxycorticosterone
DOPA : Dihydroxyphenylalanine
DOPAC : Dihydroxyphenylacetic acid
DOPEG : Dihydroxyphenylethylene glycol

| | | |
|---|---|---|
| DR | : | Drug receptor complex |
| DTH | : | Delayed-type hypersensitivity |
| EAA | : | Excitatory amino-acid |
| EAAs | : | Excitatory amino acids |
| ED | : | Emergency department |
| ED | : | Erectile dysfunction |
| EDRF | : | Endothelium derived relaxing factor |
| EGb | : | Extract of ginkgo |
| EP | : | Epinephrine |
| EPS | : | The extrapyramidal system |
| FAD | : | Flavin adenine dinucleotide |
| FDA | : | Food and drug administration |
| FMN | : | Flavin mononucleotide |
| G-6-PD | : | Glucose-6 phosphate dehydrogenase |
| GABA | : | Gamma-aminobutyric acid |
| GAD | : | Glutamic acid decarboxylase |
| GIT | : | Gastro intestinal tract |
| GLUT4 | : | Glucose transporters |
| GMP | : | Good manufacturing practices |
| GPCRs | : | G-protein-coupled receptors |
| GSH | : | Glutathione |
| GST | : | Glutathione-S-transferase |
| GTCS | : | Grand mal seizures |
| GVE | : | General visceral efferent |
| Hb | : | Hemoglobin |
| HCTZ | : | Hydrochlorothiazide |
| HD | : | Huntington disease |
| HFCC | : | High frequency chest compression |
| HT | : | Hydroxytryptamine |
| HTR | : | Haemolytic transfusion reactions |
| HVA | : | Homovanillic acid |
| IBS | : | Irritable bowel syndrome |
| ICP | : | Intra-cranial pressure |
| IFN | : | Interferon |
| IL | : | Interleukin |
| IND | : | Investigational new drug |
| INR | : | International normalized ratio |
| IOP | : | Intraocular pressure |
| IPV | : | Intrapulmonary percussive ventilation |
| IRB | : | Institutional review board |
| IVRA | : | Intravenous regional anaesthesia |
| JAK | : | Janus kinase |
| L-AAD | : | L-dopa is converted by L-amino acid decarboxylase |
| LMA | : | Laryngeal mask airway |
| LMWH | : | Low molecular weight heparin |
| LTCC | : | Low-threshold calcium current |
| M | : | Muscarinic receptors |
| MAB | : | Monoclonal antibodies |
| MAC | : | Mycobacterium avium complex |
| mAChRs | : | Muscarinic cholinergic receptors |
| MAO | : | Monoamine oxidase |
| MAOIs | : | Monoamine oxidase inhibitors |
| MCAF | : | Monocyte chemotactic and activating factor |
| MDA | : | Methylenedioxyaphetamine |
| MDAC | : | Multiple dose activated charcoal |
| MDI | : | Metered dose inhaler |
| MDMA | : | Methylene-dioxymethamphetamine |
| MDR | : | Multi drug resistance |
| MEC | : | Minimum effective concentration |
| MFOs | : | Microsomal mixed function Oxidases |
| MAC | : | Minimum alveolar concentration |
| MOA | : | Mechanism of Action |
| MPKK | : | MAP kinase kinase |
| MPPP | : | Methyl-4-propionoxy-4-phenylpiperidine |
| MPTP | : | Methyl,4-phenyl-1,2,3,6-tetrahydropyridine |
| NAD | : | Nicotinamide adenine dinucleotide |
| NADPH | : | Nicotinamide adenine dinucleotide phosphate |
| NE | : | Norepinephrine |
| NMDA | : | N-methyl-D aspartate |
| NMS | : | Neuroleptic malignant syndrome |
| NRTIs | : | Nucleoside reverse transcriptase Inhibitors |

| | | |
|---|---|---|
| NSAIDs | : | Non steroidal Anti inflammatory drugs |
| NSF | : | N-ethylmaleimidesensitive factor |
| NTS | : | Nucleus of the solitary tract |
| OATPs | : | Organic anion transporting polypeptides |
| OCD | : | Obsessive compulsive disorder |
| PABA | : | Para-amino benzoate |
| PC | : | Partition coefficient |
| PCP | : | Pneumocystis carinii pneumonia |
| PD | : | Parkinson's disease |
| PEG | : | Polyethylene glycol |
| PKA | : | Protein kinase |
| PKC | : | Protein kinase C |
| PLC | : | Phospholipase C |
| PM | : | Poor metabolizers |
| PNS | : | Peripheral nervous system |
| PRL | : | Prolactin |
| PSNS | : | Parasympathetic nervous system |
| PT | : | Prothrombin time |
| PZA | : | Pyrazinamide |
| RCC | : | Respiratory control centre |
| REM | : | Rapid eye movement |
| SHMT | : | Serine hydroxymethyltransferase |
| SNAP | : | Soluble NSF attachment protein |
| SNARE | : | Soluble NSF attachment protein receptor |
| SNS | : | Sympathetic nervous system |
| SOD | : | Superoxide dismutase |
| SPS | : | Simple partial seizure |
| SSRIs | : | Selective seratonin specific re-uptake inhibitors |
| STATs | : | Signal transducers and activators of transcription |
| SULTs | : | Sulfotransferases |
| SVR | : | Systemic vascular resistance |
| TBPS | : | t-butylbicyclo-phosphorothionate |
| TCAs | : | Tricyclic antidepressants |
| TEA | : | Tetraethylammonium |
| THB | : | Tetrahydrobiopterin |
| THC | : | Tetrahydrocannabinol |
| THDA | : | Tuberohypophysial dopaminergic |
| TIDA | : | Tuberoinfundibular dopaminergic |
| TMA | : | Tetramethylammonium |
| UGT | : | UDP-glucuronosyltransferase |
| URI | : | Upper respiratory infection |
| VC | : | Vomiting centre |
| Vd | : | Volume of distribution |
| VF | : | Ventricular fibrillation |
| VMAT | : | Vesicular monoamine transporter |
| VMC | : | Vasomotor centre or |
| WBI | : | Whole bowel irrigation |

# Part - I

# General Principles

CHAPTER

# Branches and Divisions of Pharmacology

# 1

## Introduction

**Pharmacology** (*pharmakon*,"drug" in Modern Greek; and *-logia*, "study of") is the branch of medicine and biology concerned with the study of drug action

Where a drug can be broadly defined as any man-made, natural, or endogenous (within the cell) molecule which exerts a biochemical and/or physiological effect on the cell, tissue, organ, or organism.

The two main areas of pharmacology are Pharmacodynamics and Pharmacokinetics. The former studies the effects of the drugs on biological systems, and the latter deals with the effects of biological systems on the drugs. In broad terms, pharmacodynamics discusses the actions of drugs with biological receptors and pharmacokinetics discusses the absorption, distribution, metabolism, and excretion of drugs from the biological systems.

| Pharmacokinetics Vs. | Pharmacodynamics |
|---|---|
| ⇓ | ⇓ |
| What the body does to the drug | What the drug does to the body |

**Dioscorides' De Materia Medica** is often said to be the oldest and most valuable work in the history of pharmacology. The origins of clinical pharmacology date back to the middle ages in Avicenna's ***The Canon of Medicine*, Peter of Spain's *Commentary on Isaac*, and John of St Amand's *Commentary on the Antedotary of Nicholas*.** Clinical pharmacology owes much of its foundation to the work of William Withering. Pharmacology as a scientific discipline did not further advance until the mid-19th century amid the great biomedical resurgence of that period. Before the second half of the nineteenth century, the remarkable potency and specificity of the actions of drugs such as morphine, quinine and digitalis were explained vaguely and with reference to extraordinary chemical powers and affinities to certain organs or tissues. The first pharmacology department was set up by **Rudolf Buchheim** in 1847, in recognition of the need to understand how therapeutic drugs and poisons produced their effects.

Early pharmacologists focused on natural substances, mainly plant extracts. Pharmacology developed in the 19th century as a biomedical science that applied the principles of scientific experimentation to therapeutic contexts.

## Drug

The word drug comes from a French word '*Drogue*' meaning a dry herb. It can be defined as:

Natural or synthetic substance which (when taken into a living body) affects its functioning or structure, and is used in the diagnosis, mitigation, treatment, or prevention of a disease or relief of discomfort in man or animals. According to WHO "Substance or material that is used or intended to be used to modify or explore physiological processes or pathological states, for the benefit of the recipient."

## Drug Sources

1. **Plant sources:** Obtained from plant parts or products. Seeds, stems, roots, leaves, resins, and other parts yield these drugs. Examples include digoxin from digitalis and morphine from opium.
2. **Animal sources:** Glandular products from animals are used, such as insulin and thyroid.
3. **From micro-organisms (fungi, bacteria):** Penicillin was discovered by Alexander Fleming in 1928 as a product of *Penicillium notatum* (a mold growing in his lab).
4. **Mineral sources:** Some drugs are prepared from minerals, for example, lithium carbonate (an antipsychotic), $MgSO_4$ (Magnesium Sulphate) (a laxative).
5. **Synthetic sources:** Laboratories duplicate natural processes, and may modify the products. Frequently this can eliminate side effects and increase the potency of the drug. Examples include sulfonamides, and aspirin.
6. **Recombinant proteins:** Proteins that are synthesized by expression of cloned genes in recombinant cells, such as interferon's (INF's), antibodies.
7. **Hybridoma technique:** E.g., monoclonal antibodies (MAB).

## Drug Nomenclature

**Chemical name:** Represents the exact description of the drug's chemical composition.

**Generic name (non-proprietary) :** Simpler than the chemical name and derived from the chemical name itself. Easier to remember.

***Example* 1:** The chemical name 2-methyl-5-nitroimidazole-1-ethanol is metronidazole. The word methylnitro is condensed to metro and nidazole is due to its imidazole ring.

***Example* 2:** Metoclopramide is the condensed form of the word methoxychloroprocainamide: where Me is retained and th is written as t; chloro is written as clo: and procainamide is written as pramide.

**Brand or trade name (proprietary):** It is developed by the company requesting approval for the drug and identifies it as the exclusive property of that company.

***Example* 1:** Metrogyl® is the trade name for Metronidazole.

***Example* 2:** Reglan® is the trade name for Metoclopramide.

***Example* 3:** Amoxil® is the trade name for Amoxycillin.

***Example* 4:** Celebrex® is the trade name for Celecoxib.

## The Nature of Drugs

A. **Size:** The great majority of drugs lie in the range from molecular weight 100 to 1,000. Drugs in this range are large enough to allow selectivity of action and small enough to allow adequate movement i.e., permeability within the various compartments in the body (Fig. 1-1).

B. **Chemistry and reactivity:** Drugs may be small, simple molecules (amino acids, simple amines, organic acids, alcohols, esters, ions, etc.), carbohydrates, lipids, or even proteins. Binding of drugs to their **receptors** the specific molecules in a biologic system that mediate drug effects, is usually by noncovalent bonds (hydrogen bonds, van der Walls attractions, and ionic bonds), and less commonly by covalent bonds. Weaker, noncovalent bonds require a better fit of the drug to the receptor binding site and, usually, a reversible type of action. Very strong bonding, e.g., covalent bonds, usually involves less selectivity and an irreversible interaction.

C. **Shape:** The overall shape of a drug molecule is important for the fit of the drug to its receptor. Between a quarter and a half of all drugs in use exist as stereoisomers. In most cases the stereoisomers are chiral **Enantiomers**. Enantiomers are mirrored image twin molecules that result from the presence of an asymmetric carbon, or in a few cases, other asymmetric atoms in their

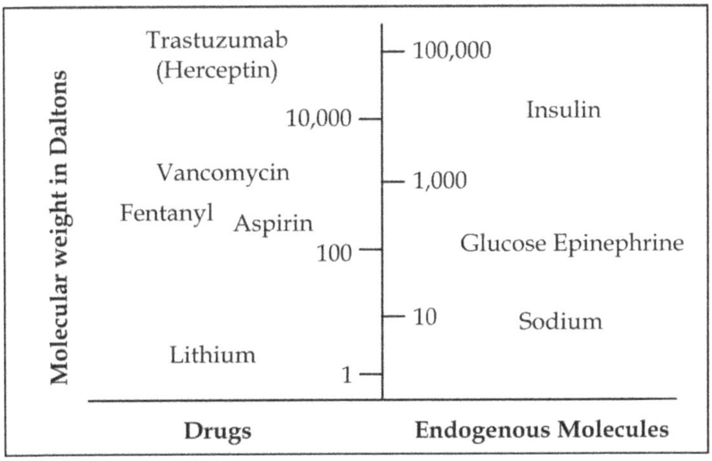


**Fig 1-1:** Molecular weights of several endogenous molecules and drugs. Lithium is used to treat people with psychiatric disorders, fentanyl is an opioid analgesic and *trastuzumab* is an antibody used to treat women with breast cancer.

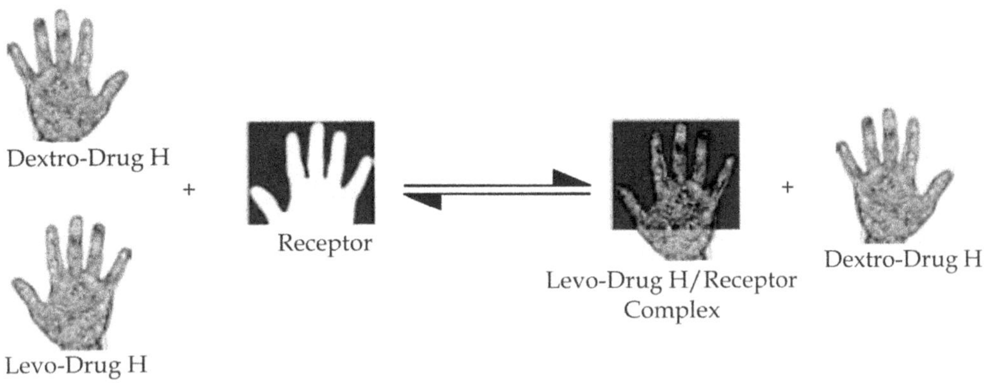


**Fig 1-2:** The two hands represent the enantiomer of Drug H. The shape of the Levo enantiomer allows it to bind tightly to the drug-binding site in the receptor.
**Note:** that this binding is reversible.

structures. Here drug action is based on the rotation of drug molecule, (Fig. 1-2) for example : Levo cetrizine and cetrizine actions for allergic reactions. Chiral enantiomers often differ in their ability to bind to and alter the function of receptors. They also can differ in their rates of elimination and in their toxicity. Most chiral drugs are still provided as **racemic mixtures** (mixtures of isomers) because it is expensive to separate the stereoisomers. In the past, little was known about the relative activity of stereoisomers. However, the Food and Drug Administration (FDA) now requires information about the structure and activity of each isomer present in a racemic mixture of a new medication.

## Branches of Pharmacology

Following are the important branches of Pharmacology:

1. Pharmacokinetics
2. Pharmacodynamics
3. Pharmacotherapeutics
4. Chemotherapy
5. Toxicology

6. Clinical pharmacology
7. Pharmacy
8. Pharmacognosy
9. Pharmacoeconomics
10. Pharmacogenetics
11. Pharmacogenomics
12. Pharmacoepidemiology
13. Comparative Pharmacology
14. Posology
15. Animal Pharmacology
16. Behavioural pharmacology
17. Environmental pharmacology
18. Neuropharmacology
19. Psychopharmacology

1. ***Pharmacokinetics:*** The word Pharmacokinetics is derived from two words, pharmacon meaning "drug" and kinetics meaning "putting in motion". It can be defined as:

   "The branch of pharmacology that deals with the absorption, distribution, metabolism and excretion of drugs and their relationship with the onset, duration and intensity of the drug effect". What the body does to the drug is pharmacokinetics.
2. ***Pharmacodynamics:*** Pharmacodynamics is the branch of pharmacology that deals with the mechanism of action of drug and the relation between the drug concentration and its effect, study of physical and chemical effects of drugs on body, parasites and microorganisms. What the drug does to the body is pharmacodynamics. For example, adrenaline acts on adrenal receptors, stimulates adenyl cyclase system producing effects such as cardiac stimulation and hyperglycemia was studied in pharmacodynamics.
3. ***Pharmacotherapeutics:*** The branch of pharmacology that deals with the art and science of treatment of disease. It is the application of pharmacological information together with the knowledge of disease, for the prevention and cure of the disease.
4. ***Chemotherapy:*** Chemotherapy refers to the treatment of diseases by chemicals that kill the cells, especially those of microorganisms and neoplastic cells. It is classified into two divisions:

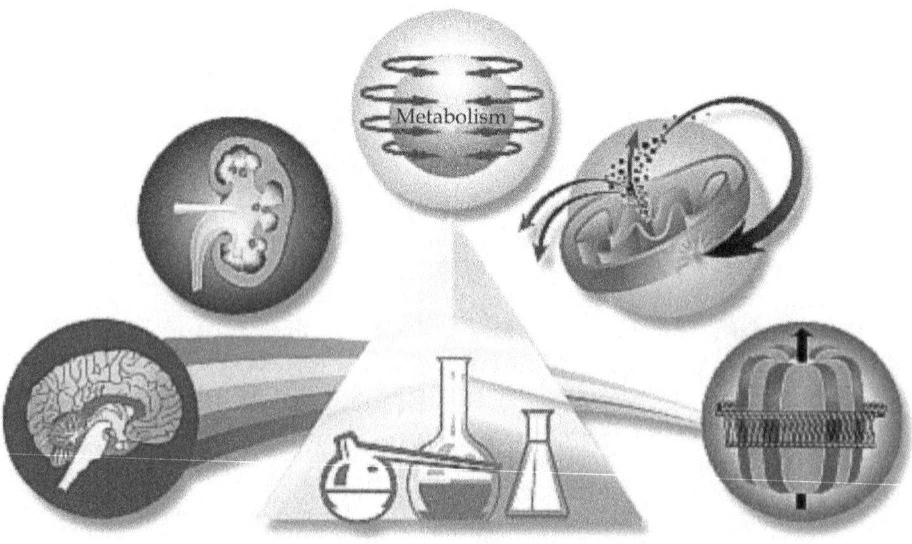


**Fig 1-3:** A variety of topics involved with pharmacology, including neuropharmacology, renal pharmacology, human metabolism, intracellular metabolism, and intracellular regulation.

(a) *Antibiotics:* Includes the choice of drugs most potent against the organism or least toxic. Examples include Erythromycin given for gram positive organisms and Aminoglycosides for gram negative organisms.

(b) *Antineoplastics*

***Examples include:***

**Methotrexate**, which is anticancer drug. It inhibits the dihydrofolate reductase and interferes with the DNA synthesis and repair.

**Vinca alkaloids**, which bind tubulin of microtubules and arrest mitosis in metaphase.

5. ***Toxicology:*** Toxicology is the branch of pharmacology which includes the study of adverse effects of drugs on the body. It deals with the symptoms, mechanisms, treatment and detection of poisoning caused by different chemical substances.

The main criterion is the dose. Essential medicines are poisons in high doses and some poisons are essential medicines in low doses.

6. ***Clinical pharmacology:*** Clinical pharmacology is the scientific study of drugs in man. It includes pharmacokinetic and pharmacodynamic investigations in healthy or diseased individuals. It also includes the comparison with placebos, drugs in the market and surveillance programmes.

*The main objectives are:*

1. Maximize the effect of drug
2. Minimize the adverse effects
3. Promote safety of prescription

*Aims include:*

1. Generate optimum data for use of drug.
2. Promote usage of evidence based medicine.

7. ***Pharmacy:*** Pharmacy is the branch of pharmacology and is the art and science of compounding by dispensing drugs, preparing suitable dosage form for administration to man and animals. The health profession blends health science with chemical science and effective use of drugs.

8. ***Pharmacognosy:*** Pharmacognosy is the identification of drugs by just seeing or smelling them. It is a crude method no longer used. Basically it deals with the drugs in crude or unprepared form and study of properties of drugs from natural sources or identification of new drugs obtained from natural sources.

9. ***Pharmacoeconomics:*** Pharmacoeconomics deals with the cost of drugs. In this discipline the cost of one drug is compared with another for same use. The cheap drugs are preferred.

10. ***Pharmacogenetics:*** Branch of pharmacology dealing with the genetic variations that cause difference in drug response among individuals or population. Example includes succinyl choline which is a skeletal muscle relaxant used in general anaesthesia. It is metabolized by pseudocholine esterase and has short duration of action. The presence of enzyme is determined by the gene and lack of this is recessively inherited. This may lead to respiratory paralysis, apnea and death.

11. ***Pharmacogenomics:*** Pharmacogenomics is the broader application of genomic technologies to new drug discovery and further characterization of older drugs.

Recombinant DNA technology involves the artificial joining of DNA of one species to another. *E. coli* is mostly used. In this way we can get huge amounts of drug in purified form which is less antigenic.

Examples include GH (Growth Hormone), inter interferon and vaccines.

12. ***Pharmacoepidemiology:*** Pharmacoepidemiology deals with the effects of drugs on a large population. The effects may be good or harmful. It is conducted in three ways:

(a) Observational cohort studies

(b) Case control studies

(c) Phase trials

(a) *Observational cohort studies:* Patients receiving drugs are collected and followed up to determine the outcomes. It is prospective (forward looking) research, however, is time consuming and lengthy.

(b) *Case control studies:* These are retrospective studies. They reverse the direction of scientific logic from forward looking to backward looking.

(c) *Phase trials:* These include different phases: (Fig. 1-4 ).

13. ***Comparative pharmacology:*** Branch of pharmacology dealing with the comparison of one drug to another belonging to the same or another group.
14. ***Posology:*** Posology deals with the dosage of drugs. Example includes paracetamol given as one tablet of 500 mg thrice a day for an adult.
15. ***Animal pharmacology:*** Animal pharmacology deals with the different properties of drugs in animals. A vast variety of animals are utilized including rabbits, mice guinea pigs, etc. Drugs are given to the animals and all parameters (their behaviour, activities, vital signs, physiological and anatomical changes etc.) are recorded. Any change is noted down. If any change was found to be useful in animals, then the drug is tested on humans.
16. ***Behavioural pharmacology:*** Behavioural pharmacology, also referred to as psychopharmacology, is an interdisciplinary field which studies about behavioural effects of psychoactive drugs. It incorporates approaches and techniques from neuropharmacology, animal behaviour and behavioural neuroscience, and is interested in the behavioural and neurobiological mechanisms of action of psychoactive drugs. Another goal of behavioural pharmacology is to develop animal behavioural models to screen chemical compounds with therapeutic potentials. People in this field (called behavioural pharmacologists) typically use small animals (e.g., rodents) to study

**Phases of Clinical Drug Development**

| | I | IIa | IIb | III | FDA | IV |
|---|---|---|---|---|---|---|
| Subjects | Healthy Normals | **First** time in Patients | Patients | Patients | | Patients |
| Number | 20 – 100 | 20 – 75 | 50 – 200 | > 300 | | > 1,000 |
| Measures | Asc. Dose, Kinetics, Equivalence, Safety | Dose range MOA, Efficacy, Safety | Efficacy, Safety | Efficacy, Safety | | Efficacy, Safety, New uses |
| **Value** | Kinetics, Dynamics | **Proof of Concept** | Confirm mechanism of action | Confirm usefulness | Review Approve or disapprove | Surveillance, extend patent expand market |
| **Where** | In-House (controlled) | In-House (controlled) | Ambulatory | Ambulatory | | Ambulatory |
| **Time** (Years) | 1 - 1.5 | 1 | 1 - 1.5 | 3 - 6 | 2 - 3 | 1 - 2 |

**Fig 1-4:** Phases of clinical drug development

psychotherapeutic drugs such as antipsychotics, antidepressants and anxiolytics, and drugs of abuse such as nicotine, cocaine, methamphetamine, etc.

17. ***Environmental pharmacology:*** Environmental pharmacology is a new discipline. Focus is being given to understand gene-environment interaction, drug-environment interaction and toxin-environment interaction. There is a close collaboration between environmental science and medicine in addressing these issues, as healthcare itself can be a cause of environmental damage or remediation. Human health and ecology is intimately related. Demand for more pharmaceutical products may place the public at risk through the destruction of species. The entry of chemicals and drugs into the aquatic ecosystem is a more serious concern today. In addition, the production of some illegal drugs pollutes drinking water supply by releasing carcinogens.
18. ***Neuropharmacology:*** Effects of medication on central and peripheral nervous system functioning.
19. ***Psychopharmacology:*** Effects of medication on the psycho; observing changed behaviours of the body and mind, and how molecular events manifest in a measurable behavioural form.

## Hypersensitivity

Hypersensitivity (or allergy) is an exaggerated response of the immune system to antigen challenge, harmful to the organism itself. Although the basic phenomenology of most types of hypersensitivity reactions was established at the end of the 19th century and in the early years of the 20th century (Koch's phenomenon, Richet and Portier's anaphylaxis, Arthus's phenomenon and serum sickness), it was only in 1963 that **Patrick Gell and Robin Coombs** produced a comprehensive classification of hypersensitivity reactions according to their underlying immune effector mechanism.

The Gell and Coombs classification distinguishes four types of reactions based on antibody (I-III) or cell-mediated (IV) effector mechanisms. Since the original classification, our understanding of the molecular and cellular immune reactions has considerably developed and several number of attempts have been made to revise or re-interpet the Gell and Coombs scheme but, to this time, the Gell and Coombs classification remains the most valid and useful frame work for understanding hypersensitivity.

There is a significant difference between Type I hypersensitivity and the other types of hypersensitivity caused by antibodies (Type II and III), namely the fact that Type I reactions occur only in a proportion of the subjects exposed to the agent in question (atopic individuals). Type II and III reactions, instead, occur in all individuals. For example, haemolytic transfusion reactions (HTR) occur whenever a blood transfusion between ABO incompatible individuals is carried out, the haemolytic disease of the newborn occurs whenever a Rh- mother produce an antibody response to Rh+, foetal RBC and serum sickness occurs whenever repeated and substantial doses of foreign serum is injected in patients for therapeutic purposes, as it occurred in the early days of serotherapy (Injections of a serum obtained especially from an immune animal). The common feature of Type I, II and III is that in all cases the antibody reactions induce cell or tissue damage (hence it appears justified that Gell and Coombs define all these reactions Hypersensitivity) but in the majority of Type II and III reactions there is no individual susceptibility or exaggerated response and, in the case of the HTR due to ABO incompatibility, there is not even a first sensitisation phase.

### Type I Hypersensitivity

Antigens causing Type I hypersensitivity reactions (or **immediate-type hyper-sensitivity**) are defined as **allergens** and induce the formation of antibodies of the IgE isotype in certain individuals. IgE-based antibody responses are common physiologically in parasitic infections but **atopic**

**individuals** produce IgE responses against a number of non-parasitic antigens that induce either no antibody response or antibody response of a different isotype, typically IgG, in normal individuals. Atopic individuals thus are susceptible to either generalised anaphylaxis local tissue reactions that involve a similar pathogenetic mechanism, namely asthma, hay fever, eczema or food allergies.

The tissue response caused by type I hypersensitivity reactions is now well understood and is determined by the binding of IgE antibodies to a high affinity receptor which binds the Fc portion of IgEs with subnanomolar affinity and located on the membrane of mast cells and basophils. As a result, a significant fraction of the IgE produced following initial contact with antigen, becomes 'fixed' on the surface of these cells and, in case of a second contact with antigen, the antigen-antibody reactions occurs not only in solution but also or predominantly on the mast cell and basophil membrane .

The IgE-antigen reaction occurring on the surface of basophils and mast cells leads to receptor cross-linking and **degranulation**, i.e., release of vasoactive amines (histamine and serotonin) and other agents (heparin, eosinophil and neutrophil chemotactic factors, platelet-activating factor, a variety of cytokines and prostaglandins and leukotrienes) from the cytoplasmic granules, which collectively cause contraction of smooth muscle cells, vasodilation, increased vascular permeability and platelet aggregation and degranulation. These reactions can affect a single tissue or organ (as in asthma, hay fever or eczema) or multiple ones (as in generalised anaphylaxis) depending on local or general re-exposure to the allergen.

## Type II Hypersensitivity

Unlike Type I reactions, Type II hypersensitivity is caused by direct antibody-mediated cell damage or lysis. The actual mechanisms underlying cell destruction are multiple (*Type II hypersensitivity - antibody-dependent cytotoxicity*):

(i) Complement-dependent red blood cell lysis, for example, as a result of haemolytic transfusion reactions (HTR) caused by ABO incompatibility and in other forms of haemolytic anaemias.

(ii) Antibody-dependent red blood cell degradation occurs, for example, as the result of binding of antibodies to the red cell membrane which fail to activate complement but promote macrophage uptake and RBC degradation. This occurs for example, in the haemolytic disease of the newborn (HDN) caused by Rh incompatibility.

(iii) Antibody-dependent cell-mediated cytotoxicity (ADCC), which occurs when cytotoxic antibodies become fixed on the surface of cytotoxic T cells and subsequent antigen binding induce perforin-dependent cell lysis of the cell bearing the antigen.

## Type III Hypersensitivity

Type III hypersensitivity reactions are caused by antibody-antigen complexes. When significant quantities of such immune complexes are formed, they can deposit in tissues and lead to a tissue reaction which is initiated by complement activation and leads to mast cell degranulation, leukocyte, predominantly neutrophil, chemotaxis and an inflammatory reactions caused by the activation of these cells.

There are systemic forms of type III hypersensitivity reactions, such as serum sickness, a disease which is now of pure historic interest but was a common occurrence in patients receiving repeated injections of anti-diphtheric horse serum and in which immune complex deposition occurred in a variety of tissues and organs leading to fever, generalised vasculitis with edema and erythema, arthritis and glomerulonephritis.

There are also local forms of immune complex diseases, such as the Arthus phenomenon . In both systemic and local forms of Type III hypersensitivity reactions, the emergence as well as the resolution of the tissue lesions and clinical symptoms follow strictly the formation of the immune complexes, the cause of tissue damage (see Fig 1-5). The principal mechanism responsible for tissue damage as a result of deposition of immune complexes is mediated by complement components, mainly the C3a and C5a anaphylotoxins, that attract phagocytes and mast cells and, following binding to complement receptors on the surface of such cells, lead to degranulation causing a local inflammatory reaction (vasodilation, increased vascular permeability, etc.)

## Type IV Hypersensitivity

The prototypical Type IV (or delayed-type hypersensitivity, DTH) tissue reaction is Koch's phenomenon. Type IV hypersensitivity reactions are caused by activated $TH_1$ cells that are activated by intracellular pathogens, including bacteria, fungi and protozoa, as well certain chemicals (hair dyes, nickel salts) leading to clonal expansion and differentiation of antigen-specific cells into $TH_1$ clones. This corresponds to the sensitisation phase of DTH.

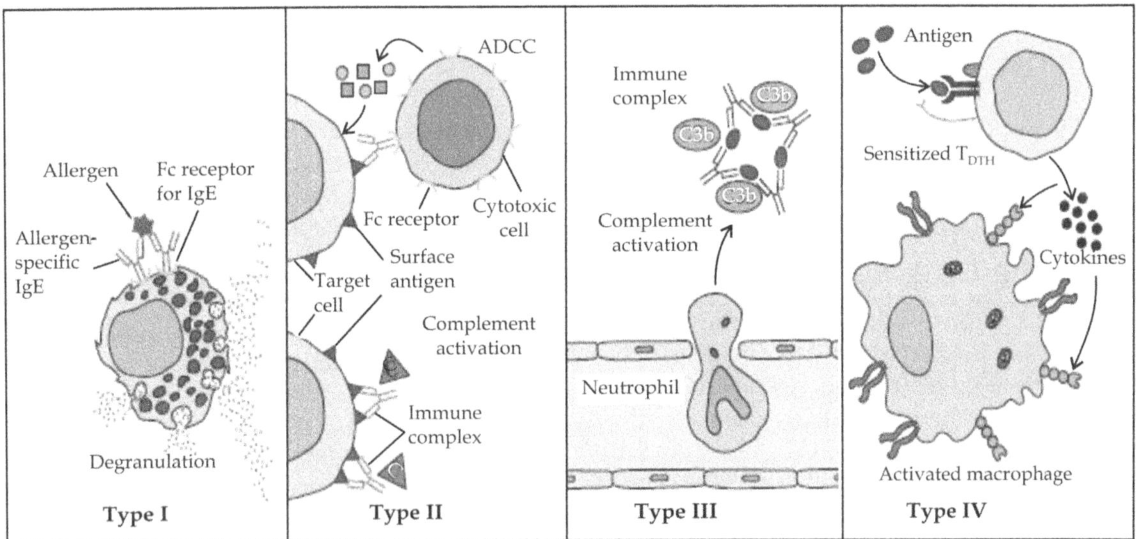


| IgE-Medicated Hypersensitivity | IgE-Medicated Cytotoxic Hypersensitivity | Immune Complex-Mediated Hypersensitivity | Cell-Mediated Hypersensitivity |
|---|---|---|---|
| Ag induced crosslinking of IgE bound to mast cells and basophils with release of vasoactive mediators | Ab directed against cell surface antigens meditates cell destruction via complement activation or ADCC | Ag-Ab complexes deposited in various tissues induce complement activation and an ensuing inflammatory response mediated by massive infiltrtation of neutrphils | Sensitized $T_H1$ cells release cytokines that activate macrophages or $T_C$ cells which mediate direct cellular damage |
| Typical manifestations include systemic anaphylaxis and localized anaphylaxis such as hay fever, asthma, hives, food allergies, and eczema | Typical manifestations include blood transfusion reactions, erythroblastosis fetalis, and autoimmune hemolytic anemia | Typical manifestations include localized Arthus reaction and generalized reactions such as serum sickness, necrotizing vasculitis, glomerulnephritis, rheumatoid arthritis, and systemic lupus erythematosus | Typical manifestations include contact dermatitis, tubercular lesions and graft rejection |

**Fig 1-5:** Types of hypersensitivity reactions

Upon re-encounter with antigen, in the so-called effector phase, the antigen-specific $TH_1$ clones undergo further clonal expansion and secretion of a variety of effector molecules. These include both cytokines (such as IFN-gamma, TNF-beta, IL-2 and IL-3) and chemokines such as IL-8, Monocyte chemotactic and activating factor (MCAF) and a migration inhibiting factor (MIF) that collectively lead to macrophage activation and to the development of a local tissue reaction.

Thus DTH is ultimately mediated by the macrophages recruited and activated by the products of antigen-specific $TH_1$ clones. Unlike Type I, II and III reactions that can be transferred by serum (i.e., serum antibodies), passive transfer of type IV requires the transfer of antigen-specific $TH_1$ clones that orchestrate the macrophage response.

## Drug Response and Factors Affecting Drug Response

Variations in the response to the same dose of a drug between different patients and even in the same patient on different occasions have been observed. The range of variability is more marked with drugs disposed by metabolism than with drugs excreted unchanged in urine. The dose of drug is generally expressed in the range, which gives therapeutic effect in majority of patients. The dose range usually based on the average requirements of an adult and is not strictly applicable under all circumstances.

### Important Factors Modifying Drug Action are:

- Body Weight/Size
- Age
- Sex
- Environmental factors
- Route of drug administration
- Time of drug administration
- Emotional factors
- Genetic factors
- Pathological states or presence of disease
- Metabolic disturbances
- Cumulative effect of drugs
- Other drug therapy
- Additive effect or summation
- Synergism
- Potentiation
- Tachyphylaxis/desensitization
- Tolerance
- Antagonism

**Body weight/size:** Obese (overweight) patients may require more medication than thin patients because of the drug has more tissue to which it can go. The dosage of many drugs is calculated on a weight basis. For example, a person might be prescribed a drug that has a dosage of 5 milligrams of drug per pound of patient body weight i.e., 5 mg × 5 pounds = 25 mg.

**Age:** As a rule, the very young and the elderly require less than the normal adult dose of most medications. Part of this requirement for less medication is due to the altered metabolism of the drug. Since body enzyme systems greatly influence drug metabolism, considering the differences in these enzyme systems based upon age is important especially CYP Enzyme. In the infant, some enzyme systems are not yet fully developed. On the other hand, the enzyme systems of the elderly may not function as well as in the past. Although several formulas are available for calculating a child's dose of medication, the two most accepted methods are those based upon the patient's weight (that is, milligrams per kilogram of body weight) or body surface area (that is, milligrams per square meter of surface area). Many examples of age-related differences in the response of individuals to a particular drug have been documented. In many cases these differences can be related to modified distribution, metabolism or excretion of the drug. There is evidence that in neonates and the elderly, the extent and rate of these processes are less than those in older children and young adults.

*Anatomical changes:* Age-related changes in the kidneys, liver, and other organs will influence the way many medications work. Nutritional status, multiple chronic diseases, and functional and cognitive deficits are other age-related factors that may have an impact on drug therapy. In general, because of a loss of muscle mass, elderly persons are physically smaller than younger adults. In addition, the percentage of body fat increases, and body water decreases. Cardiac output (the amount of blood that the heart pumps in one minute) decreases in most elderly persons as well. Kidney function gradually declines, and the effectiveness of the immune system decreases. These changes require a decrease in the dose of some medications to optimize their benefits and avoid toxicity and adverse reactions.

*Physiologic changes:* Physiologic changes that normally occur with aging may affect the way drugs work within the body. However, in a given age group there is no consistent trend for all drugs. In some cases the increased plasma concentration of the drug would be regarded as an advantage as it prolongs the response, but it is certainly not true for drugs such as streptomycin, warfarin and the hypoglycemic agents. Two points which emerge from the results of many studies with neonates and the elderly are that interindividual variations in plasma half-lives, metabolite and drug excretion and protein binding are significantly larger than those in young adults and that in the case of the elderly, chronological age does not necessarily reflect biological age. In combination these factors emphasise the importance of individual drug monitoring of plasma levels and hence of knowing the pharmacokinetic constants of the drug in the individual patient. In clinical practice, the dose of a drug is most commonly calculated on the basis of body weight or surface area. This is generally perfectly acceptable for older children and adults, but is not always a reliable formula for neonates and the very old. Simple changes in such parameters as urine pH can override calculations based upon body size.

**Sex:** Physiological differences between the sexes may influence the dose or the requirement for drugs. Since females have proportionately more fat tissue than males, drugs, which have a high affinity (likeness) for fat, may require larger doses in females. Moreover, estrogen and testosterone, two sex hormones, can affect the patient's rate of metabolism which can, in turn, influence the rate at which a drug is absorbed, metabolized, or excreted from the body. The requirement for iron is much higher in the female than in the male, because of the loss of blood in each menstural cycle. In women consideration must be given to mensturation, pregnancy and lactation. Drugs given during pregnancy may affect the fetus. Marked physiological changes occur during pregnancy that can alter the drug disposition. For example, G.I.T motility is decreased that results in delayed absorption of drug, plasma protein concentration and consequently binding of drug to proteins is increased during pregnancy, enzyme induction is observed and renal blood flow increases that cause rapid elimination of drug. The overall effect on drug disposition is complex and difficult to predict; drugs should be carefully given during pregnancy. A number of drugs like clonidine, methyldopa, and α-blockers interfere with sexual function in males but not in females. Gynecomastia produced by drugs like Digitalis, Cimetidine, Ketoconazole, Metoclopramide, Spironolactone and Chlorpromazine occur in males not in females.

**Environmental factors:** Drug metabolism is slow at high altitude due to oxygen deficiency. Cigarette smokers and industrial workers exposed to some pesticides metabolize drugs rapidly due to enzyme induction. Metabolism is low in hot and humid climate. Purgatives act better in summer while diuretics act better in winters. Oxidation of drugs is low at higher altitudes.

**Route drug of Administration:** Some drugs are incompletely absorbed after oral intake, when given intravenously; their dose has to be reduced. Examples include morphine and magnesium sulphate. Magnesium sulphate when given orally is osmotic purgative, but its 20% solution is injected intravenously to control the convulsions in eclampsia of pregnancy. Aminoglycosides like streptomycin when given intravenously cause neuromuscular blockage, which is not observed after intramuscular injection.

**Time of drug Administration:** Hypnotics (producing sleep) act better when administered at night and smaller doses are required. There is delayed drug absorption when drug is given orally after meals, which slows down the effects of drug. Drugs are usually given after meals to prevent gastric irritation. Under certain circumstances drugs must be given before meals.

***To prevent mixing of drug with food:*** Anthelmintics.

***To get immediate effect:*** Drugs used for prevention of motion sickness.

***To prevent formation of insoluble complexes:*** Tetracyclines.

To prevent specific side effects, for example, to prevent hypoglycemia, insulin and sulfonylureas are given before meals.

**Emotional factors:** Personality of physician and patient may influence the effects of drug. Sometimes inert dosage forms can relieve the symptoms this is called "PLACEBO". Placebo resembles the actual medicine in physical characteristics; it works by psychological rather than pharmacological effects and often produces response equivalent to the actual drug. Placebo is used to compare the therapeutic effects of various drugs during therapeutic trials of the drugs. Personality of patient also affects the drug response, nervous and anxious patients require more general anesthetics than normal persons do. Word placebo means "I SHALL PLEASE". Placebo resembles the actual medicine in physical characteristics. Placebo can be given orally as well as parenterally. It does not produce drug - drug interactions. Substances used as placebo are lactose, distilled water and dextrose.

**Genetic factors:** Genetic abnormalities influence the dose of a drug and response to drugs. It affects the drug response in individuals at 2 levels. At the level of receptors and at the level of drugs metabolizing enzyme. Thus, interfering with the functions such as rate of plasma drug clearance. Pharmacogenetics is the study of the relationship between genetic factors and drug response. Idiosyncrasy is the abnormal drug reaction due to genetic disorder. It is the unpredictable response seen on first dose of drug on hereditary basis. This may be due to Acetylation, Oxidation, Succinylcholine apnea and Glucose 6-phosphate dehydrogenase deficiency.

All individuals do not respond in similar way to same drug. Idiosyncrasy is used to describe abnormal drug response on administration of first dose.

***Genetic polymorphism:*** The existence in a population of two or more phenotypes with respect to the effect of a drug. E.g., Acetylation enzymes deficiency-Acetyl transferase (non-microsomal) affects isoniazid, sulphonamides, etc.

Slow acetylator phenotype may show peripheral neuropathy.

Rapid acetylator phenotype may show hepatitis.

***Pseudocholinesterase deficiency:*** Succinyl choline is a skeletal muscle relaxant. Succinylcholine apnea may occur due to paralysis of respiratory muscles.

***Malignant hyperthermia:*** Occurs by succinyl choline due to inherited inabilityto chelate calcium by sarcoplasmic reticulum resulting in $Ca^{+2}$ release, muscle spasm and rise in temperature.

***Oxidation polymorphism:*** In case of Debrisoquine.

Extensive metabolizers (EM) - need larger dose.

Poor metabolizers (PM) – need smaller dose.

**Deficiency of Glucose-6 phosphate dehydrogenase (G-6-PD):** G-6-PD Deficiency in RBCs leads to haemolytic anaemia upon exposure to some oxidizing agents like

Antimalarial drug, primaquine

Long acting sulphonamides

Fava beans (favism)

**Pathological states/ Presence of disease:** Diseases cause individual variation in drug response.

In liver diseases, prolonged duration of action occurs because of increased half life. Plasma protein binding for warfarin, tolbutamide is decreased leading to adverse effects, If hepatic blood flow is reduced; clearance of morphine, propranolol may be affected. Impaired liver microsomal enzymes may lead to toxic levels of diazepam, rifampicin and theophylline.

In renal disease GFR, tubular function and plasma albumin may be affected leading to abnormal effects of digoxin, lithium, gentamycin and penicillin. In **Malnutrition** plasma protein binding of drugs is reduced along with the amount of microsomal enzymes, leading to increased portion of free, unbound drug e.g., warfarin

**Metabolic disturbances:** Changes in water and electrolyte balance, body temperature and acid base balance may modify the effects of drug. For example, aspirin reduces body temperature only in presence of fever and have no effect on body temperature when it is normal. Iron is well absorbed in states of iron deficiency. Vasoconstrictor effect of norepinephrine is reduced in presence of metabolic acidosis.

**Cumulative effect of drugs:** Cumulative effect of drugs is

1. Due to many frequent doses.
2. Due to prolonged continued administration.

By cumulative effect is meant the unexpected, intense action of a drug after it has been given for some time, as differing from an immediate intense action of a drug which would show an idiosyncrasy.

1. The too frequent administration of a drug which is slow of excretion will cause it to accumulate and sooner or later produce a poisonous effect. Therefore, "the duration of the action of a drug", it is very important to remember how long it ordinarily takes a given drug to be excreted. For instance, if a drug that is excreted in eight hours was administered every two hours, at the end of eight hours five doses will have been taken, only the first of which has been completely excreted, leaving three doses acting and one beginning to act in the system.
2. Cumulative action from too long continued administration of a drug means the development of symptoms which show an over-action of the drug. This is of frequent occurrence and is sometimes accidental, but is often caused deliberately by pushing a drug to its full physiologic effect. In cases in which this action occurs unexpectedly and is undesired, the drug should be immediately stopped, and not again given in doses that could cause such an effect. Some drugs give notice of such an impending action by premonitory symptoms; such is true of digitalis.

In some diseases such cumulative physiologic action of certain drugs is desired. The drug is then stopped temporarily, and then again pushed to the point of tolerance, the best way to combat such over-action, and which drugs will produce an over-action without danger to the patient, can be learned only by the study of the pharmacology of the drugs.

**Other drug therapy:** Drugs may modify the response to each other by pharmacokinetic or pharmacodynamics interaction between them. Drug interaction does not necessarily mean that their concurrent use is contraindicated; many drugs can be used beneficially with dosing schedule adjustment.

**Additive effect or Summation:** When total pharmacological effect produced by concomitant use of two or more drugs is equal to the sum of their individual effects, it is called "Additive effect".

$$1 + 1 = 2$$

*Example:* Combination of ephedrine and theophylline in the treatment of asthma. The individual side effects of an additive pair may be different, and may not add up. The combination is better tolerated than higher dose of one component.

Aspirin + paracetamol as analgesic/antipyretic

Nitrous oxide + ether as general anaesthetic

Antihypertensive drugs

Cardiac stimulants

**Synergism:** When total pharmacological effect produced by concomitant use of two or more drugs is higher than the sum of their individual effects, it is called "Synergism".

$$1 + 1 = > 2.$$

*Example:* Codeine + Aspirin > Analgesia

Sulphonamide + Trimethoprim > Antibacterial effect

**Potentiation:** Enhancement of effect of one agent by another; so that the combined effect is more than the sum of their individual effects is called "Potentiation." In case of potentiation one agent has no effect when give alone but increases the effects of other co-administered drug.

$$0 + 1 \geq 2$$

*Example:* Acetylcholine + physostigmine. Physostigmine inhibits the action of esterase prolonging the effect of acetylcholine.

Levodopa (Parkinsonism) + carbidopa/benserazide. Levo/dopa is decarboxylated peripherally, carbidopa inhibits the decarboxylase.

Sulphonamide (effective against some microorganisms) when combined with trimethoprim is effective against a wider range of microorganisms.

Levodopa + Carbidopa = Parkinsonism.

Ampicillin + Clavulanic acid = ≥ Antibacterial effect.

The action is more than the normal therapeutic effect.

**Tachyphylaxis and Desensitization:** Repeated administration of a drug at short intervals of time leads to decrease in pharmacological response. Desensitization and tachyphylaxis are synonymous terms used to describe this phenomenon which often develops in course of few minutes. This occurs with indirectly acting drugs like amphetamine, ephedrine, MDMA (3,4-methylenedioxy-N-methylamphetamine). On repeated administration, depletion of endogenous receptors occurs. It is also known as acute tolerance. Example includes ephedrine, which acts by releasing noradrenaline from adrenergic stores. After repeated administration, these stores are exhausted and pharmacological action is not restored even on increasing the dose.

**Characteristics***:* Tachyphylaxis is characterized by the rate sensitivity: The response of the system depends on the rate with which a stimulus is presented. To be specific, a high-intensity prolonged stimulus or often-repeated stimulus may bring about a diminished response also known as desensitization. (Fig. 1-6)

**Molecular interaction:** In biological sciences, molecular interactions are the physical basis of the operation system. The control of the operation, in general, involves interaction of a stimulus molecule with a receptor/enzyme subsystem by, typically, binding to the macromolecule A and causing an activation or an inhibition of the subsystem by forming an

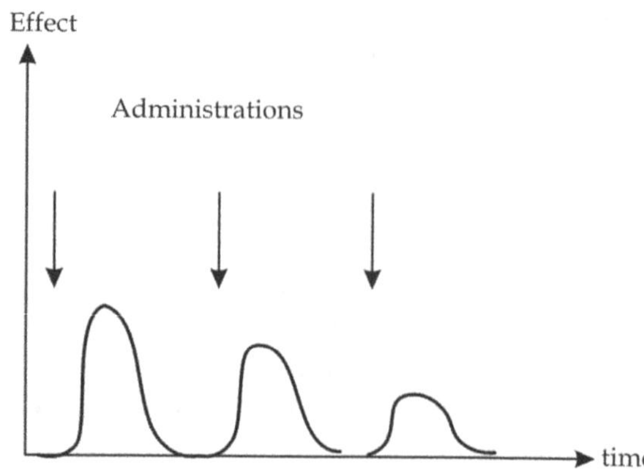


**Fig 1-6:** Tachyphylaxis

activated form of the macromolecule B. The following schematic represents the activity:

$$A \xrightarrow{p} B$$

where p is the activation rate coefficient. It is customary that p is called a rate constant, but, since p stands for measure of the intensity of the stimulus causing the activation, p may be variable (non-constant).

The above scheme is only the necessary condition for the rate sensitivity phenomenon, and other pathways of deactivation of B may be considered, with the subsequent return to the inactive form of the receptor/enzyme A.

*Examples:*

**Calcitonin:** Calcitonin demonstrates tachyphylaxis in 2–3 days when being used to treat hypercalcemia of malignancy. This reaction is anticipated and calcitonin is given along with bisphosphonates, which have their maximum effect in 2–3 days.

**Hormone replacement:** Hormone replacement when used in menopausal women in the form of estrogen and progesterone implants is cited as having potential to lead to tachyphylaxis, but that citation is based on a single study done in 1990 and no follow-up research is available to support this interpretation.

**Psychedelics:** Psychedelics such as LSD-25 and psilocybin containing mushrooms demonstrate very rapid tachyphylaxis. In other words, one may be unable to 'trip' two days in a row. Some people are able to 'trip' by taking up to three times the dosage, yet some users may not be able to negate tachyphylaxis at all until a period of days has gone by.

**Centrally-acting analgesics:** In a patient fully withdrawn from centrally-acting analgesics, *viz.*, opioids, going back to an intermittent schedule or maintenance dosing protocol, a fraction of the old tolerance level will rapidly develop, usually starting two days after opioid therapy is resumed and, in general, levelling off after day 7. Whether this is caused directly by opioid receptors modified in the past or effecting a change in some metabolic set-point is unclear. Increasing the dose will usually restore efficacy; relatively rapid opioid rotation may also be of use if the increase in tolerance continues.

**Beta-2 adrenergic receptor gene:** Gene encoding the beta-2 adrenergic receptor (ADRB2) is situated on chromosome 5q31. Individuals who are homozygous for the Gly16 form of the beta-2 adrenergic receptor gene have attenuated responses and more rapid tachyphylaxis to adrenergic bronchodilator medications than do those with the wild type, homozygous Arg16 form of the gene.

**Nicotine:** Nicotine may also show tachyphylaxis over the course of a day, although the mechanism of this action is unclear.

***Other examples:*** Nitroglycerine demonstrates tachyphylaxis, requiring drug-free intervals when administered transdermally.

Repeated doses of ephedrine may display tachyphylaxis, since it is an indirectly acting sympathomimetic amine, which will deplete noradrenaline from the nerve terminal. Thus, repeated doses result in less noradrenaline released than the initial dose.

Hydralazine displays tachyphylaxis if given as a monotherapy for antihypertensive treatment. It is administered with a beta-blocker with or without a diuretic.

Metoclopramide is another example.

Dobutamine, a direct-acting beta agonist used in congestive heart failure, also demonstrates tachyphylaxis.

Desmopressin used in the treatment of type 1 von Willebrand disease is, in general, given every 12–24 hours in limited numbers due to its tachyphylactic properties.

Mechanisms that give rise to this phenomenon are :

1. Change in receptors (Rapid desensitization)
2. Loss of receptors (down-regulation)
3. Exhaustion of mediators
4. Increased metabolic degradation
5. Physiological adaptation

*Change in receptors (Rapid desensitization):* A slow conformational change in the receptor, resulting in tight binding of the agonist molecule without the opening of the ionic channel (e.g., ligand-gated ion channels such as nicotinic receptors at the neuromuscular junction) → rapid and reversible.

Phosphorylation of intracellular region of the receptor protein, leading to:

Desensitization of ion channel, or interference with the receptor's (e.g., GPCR) ability to activate second messenger cascade, though it can still bind the agonist molecule → slow and reversible.

*Loss of receptors (down-regulation):* Prolonged exposure to agonists often results in a gradual decrease in the actual number of receptors expressed on the cell surface. The vanishing receptors are taken into the cell by endocytosis of patches of the membrane; a process that also depends on phosphorylation. It occurs more slowly than rapid desensitization and is less readily reversible. This is because down-regulation involves a net degradation of receptors present in the cell, requiring new receptor biosynthesis for recovery, in contrast to rapid desensitization which involves reversible phosphorylation of existing receptors. Many G protein–coupled receptors and many hormone receptors are down-regulated by undergoing ligand-induced endocytosis and delivery to lysosomes. Down-regulation generally occurs only after prolonged or repeated exposure of cells to agonist (over hours to days).

*Example:* Chronic administration of salbutamol ($\beta_2$ agonist) can cause internalization of receptors → less receptors available for stimulation → decreased bronchodilation.

*Exhaustion of mediators:* Depletion of a signaling molecule or an essential intermediate substance required for biological response.

*Example* **1:** prolonged stimulation of G-protein coupled receptors can lead to depletion of intracellular secondary messengers.

*Example* **2:** Indirectly acting sympathomimetics (e.g. amphetamine) act by releasing tissue stores of adrenaline and noradrenaline and other amines from the nerve terminal → tachyphylaxis occurs because the amine stores become depleted.

*Increased metabolic degradation:* Increase in the rate of metabolism and/or elimination of drug. Lowers plasma drug concentrations.

*Example:* barbiturates and ethanol induce the expression of metabolic enzymes (cytochrome P450s) that degrade the drug → low plasma drug concentration.

*Physiological adaptation:* A drug's decreasing effects may occur because it is nullified by a homeostatic response. These homeostatic mechanisms are very common and if they occur slowly the result will be a very gradually developing tolerance.

*Example* **1:** The blood pressure-lowering effect of thiazide diuretics is limited because of a gradual activation of the renin-angiotensin system.

*Example* **2:** It is a common experience that many side effects of drugs such as nausea and sleepiness tend to subside even though administration is continued.

*Tolerance:* Resistance to normal therapeutic dose of drug, producing lesser response to normal therapeutic dose is known as tolerance. This is acquired character. Examples include morphine, person is initially responsive, if continued, changes occur at cellular and pharmacokinetic level, reducing the action. Thus one has to increase the dose of drug to overcome. Alcoholics do not respond to hypnotics and analgesics, dose of which has to be increased many folds. In fact they may even tolerate toxic levels.

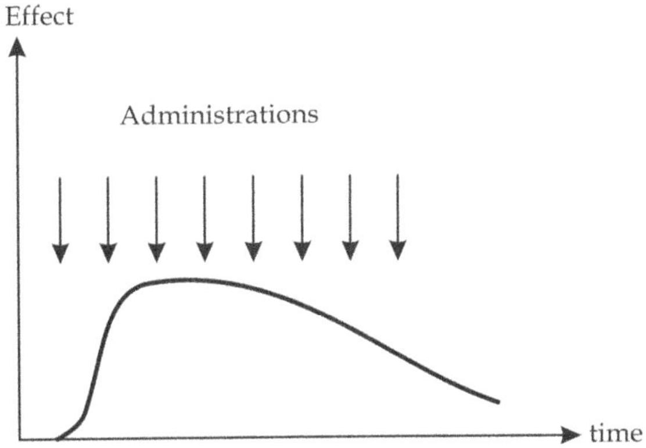


**Fig 1-7:** Tolerance

"Reduced responses to repeated administration of the same dose or increase in the dose are required to produce the same magnitude of response is called tolerance".

**Types of Tolerance**

**True Tolerance:** It is seen on both oral and parenteral administration of drug, and is divided into: Natural and Acquired.

***Natural Tolerance:*** This is seen in various animal species and also among the human races. It includes.

- *Species tolerance:* Certain animal species can tolerate certain drugs in quantities that are lethal to man.

  ***Example:*** Rabbits can tolerate large quantities of belladona than humans due to presence of an enzyme atropine esterase that detoxifies it.
- *Racial tolerance:* Ephedrine solution when incorporated in to conjunctival sac in Caucasians it may produce pupil dilatation but not in Negros.

***Acquired Tolerance:*** This type of tolerance unlike the racial and species tolerance develops only on repeated administration of drug. Many drugs like opiates, barbiturates, nitrites, and CNS depressants frequently develop tolerance. An uninterrupted presence of drug in the body favours the development of tolerance. However significant tolerance does not develop to atropine, digitalis, sodium nitroprusside and NSAIDs.

- ***Tissue tolerance:*** Tissue tolerance refers to the changes that occur on the tissue or cell that is affected by the drug.

  Example is barbiturates.
- ***Cross-tolerance:*** It refers to a pharmacological phenomenon, in which a patient being treated with a drug exhibits a physiological resistance to that medication as a result of tolerance to a pharmacologically similar drug. In other words, there is a decrease in response to one drug due to exposure to another similar acting drug. It is observed in treatment with antivirals, antibiotics and especially with opiate analgesics and many other medications including benzodiazepines.

  Cross-tolerance is particularly frequent amongst users of illicit drugs. For example, users with a high tolerance to the stimulant amphetamine may also exhibit a high tolerance to the structurally similar methamphetamine or other amphetamine-like stimulants. The phenomenon is also observed in cigarette smokers, in whom there is a demonstrably lessened sensitivity to the effects of caffeine. Cross-tolerance is also frequent in response to use of hallucinogens (e.g., LSD). General tolerance to the effects of tryptamines such as psilocybin, may be dramatic in response to repeated use, and this often translates into a tolerance to effects of other drugs such as mescaline. This is also true of benzodiazepines such as alprazolam and clonazepam, even opiates as well.

**Pseudo Tolerance:** It is confined to oral administration of drug. Example is feudal kings taking of small amounts of arsenic poison by mouth.

**Mechanism of tolerance development**

***Pharmacokinetic tolerance:*** Pharmaco-kinetic tolerance - Also known as dispositional tolerance occurs because of a decreased quantity of the substance reaching the site it affects. This may be caused by an increase in induction of the enzymes required for degradation of the drug e.g., CYP450 enzymes.

*Pharmacodynamic tolerance:* Also known as reduced responsiveness, the response to the substance is decreased by cellular mechanisms. This may be caused by a down regulation of receptor numbers.

**Antagonism:** When two drugs, administered simultaneously, oppose the action of each other on the same physiological system, the phenomenon is called antagonism. It can be of following types.

**Chemical antagonism:** It involves reduction of the biological activity of a drug by a chemical reaction with another agent e.g., between acids and alkalis: BAL (British anti lewisite) and arsenic. Antacids, used for dyspepsia involve administration of sodium bicarbonate to react with hydrochloric acid. In cases of heavy metal poisoning chelating agents are used like dimercaprol.

In iron poisoning deferoxamine is given which binds sulfhydryl groups forming insoluble complexes which can be easily detoxified.

**Pharmacological antagonism:** Pharmacological antagonism is of two types:

*Competitive or reversible antagonism:* In this type of antagonism the agonist and antagonist compete with each other for the same receptors. The extent of antagonism will depend on the relative number of receptors occupied by the two compounds. Other features are:

(a) Antagonist has chemical resemblance with agonist.
(b) Antagonism can be overcome by increasing the concentration of the agonist at receptor site. It means the maximal response to agonist is not impaired.
(c) Antagonist shifts the dose response curve to right.
(d) $E_{max}$ of agonist is obtained with high concentration of agonist.
(e) Duration of action is short. It depends on drug clearance.

Example is of acetylcholine and atropine antagonism on muscarinic receptors. In presence of antagonist, log dose response curve of agonist shifts to right, indicating a higher concentration of agonist is required for same response. Maximum height of the curve can be attained by overcoming the action of antagonist. This leads to a parallel shift of log dose response curve towards right.

*Non competitive antagonism:* Here an antagonist inactivates the receptor(R) in such a way so that the effective complex with agonist cannot be formed irrespective of the concentration of the agonist. This can happen by various ways:

The antagonist might combine at the same site in such a way that even higher concentration of the agonist cannot displace it.

The antagonist might combine at a different site of R in such a way that agonist is unable to initiate characteristic biological response.

The antagonist might itself induce a certain change in R so that the reactivity of the receptor site where agonist should interact is abolished.

*Other features of this antagonism are:*

1. Antagonist has no chemical resemblance with agonist.
2. Maximum response is suppressed.
3. Although antagonist shifts the dose response curve to right, the slope of the curve is reduced.
4. The extent of antagonism depends on the characteristics of antagonist itself and agonist has no influence upon the degree of antagonism or its reversibility.
5. $E_{max}$ of agonist is decreased even with high concentration of agonist.
6. Duration of action is long which depends upon new receptor synthesis.
7. Example is of phenoxybenzamine and adrenaline at alpha adrenergic receptors.

**Physiological antagonism:** In this interaction of two drugs, both are agonists, so they act at different receptor sites. They antagonize the action of each other because they produce opposite actions. Classical example of physiological antagonism is adrenaline and histamine. Former causes bronchodilatation while later bronchoconstriction. So adrenaline is a life saving drug in anaphylaxis. Acetylcholine slows the heart, and epinephrine accelerates it. Acetylcholine stimulates intestinal movement, and epinephrine inhibits it. Acetylcholine constricts the pupil, and epinephrine dilates it; and so on.

**Pharmacokinetic antagonism:** The situation in which the drug which may be termed the "antagonist" effectively reduces the concentration of the active drug (the "agonist") at its site of action. This may be due to an increase in metabolism or renal excretion of the "agonist" drug or to decreased absorption of the drug from the gastro-intestinal tract.

Example is warfarin and phenobarbital

**Clinical significance of drug antagonism:**

1. It helps to correct adverse effects of a drug e.g., ephedrine and phenobarbitone.
2. It is useful to treat drug poisoning e.g., morphine with naloxone.
3. It guides to avoid drug combinations with reduced drug efficacy such as penicillin and tetracycline combination.

CHAPTER 2

# Pharmacokinetics of Drugs

Pharmacokinetics deals with the absorption, distribution, metabolism and excretion of drugs in the body.

## Biotransport of Drug

It is translocation of a solute from one side of the biological barrier to the other side of the biological barrier.

1. **Structure of biological membrane:** The outer surface of the cell covered by a very thin structure known as plasma membrane. It is composed of lipid and protein molecules. The membrane proteins have many functions like
   (a) Contributing structure to the membrane
   (b) Acting as enzyme
   (c) Acting as carrier for transport of substances
   (d) Acting as receptors

   The plasma membrane is a semipermeable membrane allowing certain chemical substances to pass freely e.g., it allows water, glucose, etc., but it won't allow sucrose until it is converted into glucose and fructose.
2. **Passage of drug across membrane:** Before studying the passage of drugs across membranes it is necessary to recall the composition and structure of the membrane.

## Composition and Structure of Membranes

Plasma membrane which surrounds each cell consists of approximately 60% of phospholipids and 40% of protein.

### Lipids

The lipids entering the composition of membranes are amphipathic; they consist of molecules containing a polar head and a non polar or hydrophobic tail. They are primarily:

1. Glycerophospholipids (substituted glycerol).
2. Sphingolipids (i.e., derived from sphingosine which is an alcohol substituted by a fatty acid and a polar group). The sphingolipids are divided into three groups: sphingomyelins, cerebrosides and gangliosides.
3. Cholesterol consisting of a sterane nucleus substituted by a polar group (OH) and a non polar flexible chain. Cholesterol, intercalated between other lipids, reinforces the membrane structure.

These amphipathic lipids (glycerophospholipids and sphingolipids) Fig 2-1 are naturally oriented to form a bilayer polar groups located on both sides and the non polar tails in the middle.

The fluidity of the bilayer not only depends on temperature and but also on its composition. The unsaturated fatty acids which form less linear chains than the saturated fatty acids increase membrane fluidity.

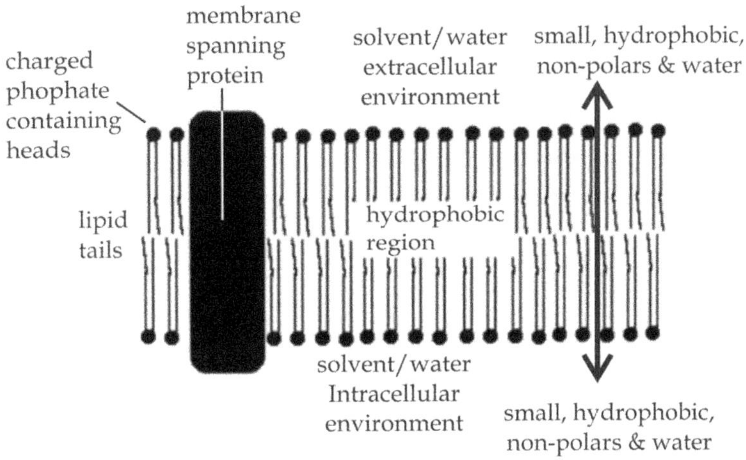


**Fig 2-1:** Amphipathic lipids

## Proteins

Proteins are large biological molecules, or macromolecules, consisting of one or more chains of amino acid residues.

The proteins found in membranes are either inserted in the lipid bilayer, inside or outside, or transmembrane on both sides,

These proteins constitute:

- Cell-surface receptors (generally glycoproteins, which ensure the intercellular communications).
- Structures which ensure the exchange of ions and certain molecules between the cell and its environment: pumps such as $Na^+/K^+$ ATPase, ion channels.

Transfer of molecules and drugs across membranes.

To penetrate into the cell, the drug must cross the cytoplasmic membrane. To pass from a compartment to another, the drug must cross one or several membranes. The membranes consist of cells bound to each other more or less tightly. These cells are located on a basement membrane, itself more or less permeable to molecules. One distinguishes:

1. **Transcellular transfer:** When the cells are tightly against each other, as in the endothelium of the cerebral capillaries, the drug must cross the cells themselves, i.e., the cytoplasmic membrane, to pass from one compartment to the other.
2. **Paracellular transfer:** When the epithelial cells are separated from each other by looser junctions, the molecules can pass through these junctions called "*gap junctions*". The paracellular transfer of a molecule depends primarily on its molecular weight and its flexibility.
3. **Porous filter:** Certain epithelia, like that of the renal glomerulus, bear pores permeable to molecules smaller than the pores. At the level of the renal glomerulus, the molecules whose molecular weight is lower than 68,000 daltons can theoretically pass, but the more molecular weight of a molecule approaches 68,000 daltons, its transfer becomes difficult. Other parameters than the molecular weight (directly linked to the size), such as charges or flexibility, are also to be taken into consideration.

## Transfer through the Lipid Bilayer

### Passive diffusion

The transfer Fig 2-2 through a lipid bilayer is passive without requiring energy. The lipid bilayer membrane constitutes a barrier.

- Impermeable to ions such as $Na^+$, $K^+$, $Cl^-$, to polar molecules even non charged, i.e., non-ionic, like glucose, and proteins.
- Permeable to non polar molecules (liposoluble or hydrophobic) of low or middle molecular weight, and to molecules at the gas state and small molecules of low polarity.

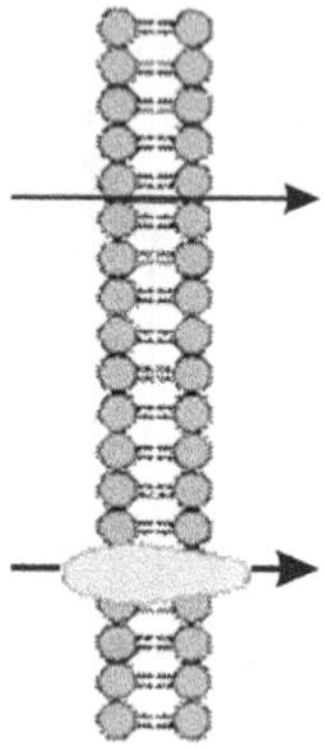


**Fig 2-2:** Passive diffusion through a lipid bilayer

The passage through the membrane is directed from the most concentrated solution towards the least concentrated solution until obtaining equilibrium. The rate of transfer (v) depends on the area, surface area S of the membrane, on the concentrations $C_1$ and $C_2$ on both sides of the membrane and on a diffusion constant K linked to the liposolubility and the size of the molecule (the smaller the molecule, the easier the transfer).

$$V = K.S. (C_2 - C_1)$$

where V = rate of transfer

The liposoluble character of a molecule is determined by the measurement of its partition coefficient between an aqueous solvent and an organic solvent like hexane. The liposoluble or non-polar molecules accumulate in organic solvent and the polar molecules in water.

The polarity of a drug depends on its ionization and one distinguishes three categories:

1. Permanently ionized molecules, whatever the pH, for example those with a quaternary ammonium. These molecules, in theory, do not cross the lipid bilayer by passive diffusion.
2. Neutral molecules, not ionized, whatever the pH. It is the case of the organic solvents which cross the lipid bilayer easily. This rule has limitations, in particular concerning intestinal absorption because it takes place from an aqueous medium. A very lipophilic molecule but almost insoluble in water can be poorly absorbed. A low availability can be the consequence of a low solubility in water.
3. Molecules whose ionization depends on pH in a neutral state, they cross the lipid bilayer, but not in the ionized state. The acid drugs dissociate in a basic medium and the bases in an acidic medium, to give ionized molecules. The pKa of an acid is the pH at which it is 50% dissociated. For example, an acid drug R-COOH partially dissociated in $R\text{-}COO^- + H^+$, neutral form R-COOH crosses membranes but not the ionized form $R\text{-}COO^-$. (Fig. 2-3)

Consequently, when two compartments at different pH are separated by a membrane, the equilibrium of the concentrations of a drug R-COOH on both sides of the membrane will be moved and drug R-COOH will accumulate in the basic compartment where it dissociates.

Binding of the drugs to plasma proteins, in particular to albumin, which can go from 0% to 99%, modifies their transfer through the membranes. In the free state, i.e., unbound to plasma proteins, the liposoluble drugs, if there is a gradient of favourable concentration, cross the lipid membrane, where as the fraction bound to plasma or tissue proteins does not cross it. (Fig. 2-4)

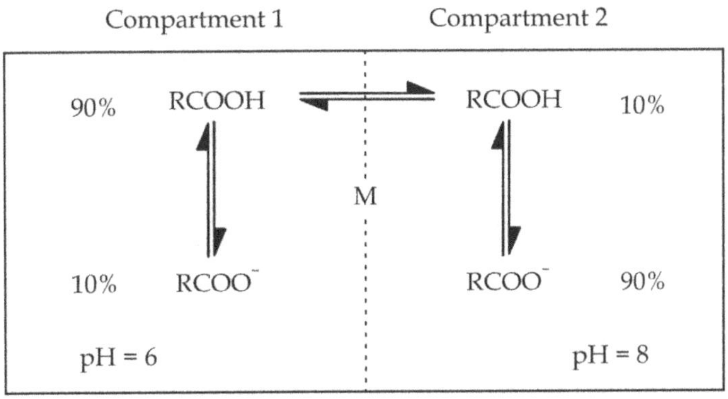


Distribution of a drug whose pKa = 7 between 2 compartments at different pH, 6 and 8, M = membrane

**Fig 2-3:** Transmembrane transfer of an acid drug according to pH

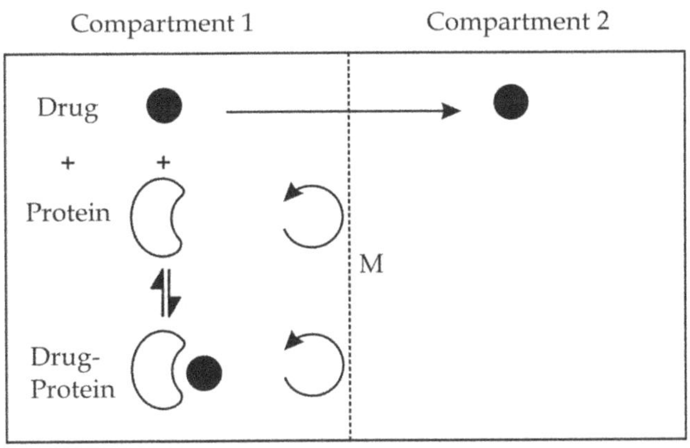


**Fig 2-4:** Transmembrane transfer of a drug according to its protein binding

Albumin is a protein with a molecular weight of 68,000 daltons, present in plasma at a concentration approximately 50 g/L. It is synthesized by the liver and degraded primarily by the vascular endothelium. Its plasma half-life is approximately 20 days. In addition to its role in oncotic pressure, it binds various endogenous molecules and drugs. There are six different types of sites on a molecule of albumin with different affinities for drugs.

The equilibrium for a drug between the free fraction, D, and the bound fraction, DP, is reversible and non-static in the body because the blood circulation causes dynamic changes.

Blood cells, mainly red cells, can play a role comparable to that of albumin for drugs that they bind or incorporate.

## Transfer through Membrane Protein Structures

The transfer through the protein structures of membranes is carried out by active transport, i.e., using energy provided by cellular metabolism.

**Direct active transport by pumps:** The active transport requires energy, generally provided by ATP hydrolysis. The $Na^+/K^+$-ATPase pump, $Mg^{2+}$ dependant, uses the energy of ATP to polarise the cell by extruding three $Na^+$ ions and incorporating two $K^+$ ions, which creates a potential difference between the intracellular medium and the extracellular medium. There are other pumps: a $Ca^{2+}$-ATPase pump localized on the level of the cytoplasmic membrane and at the level of the endoplasmic reticulum and an $H^+/K^+$-ATPase pump.

A particular membrane protein, P-glycoprotein, or P170 because its molecular weight is 170 Kd, uses, like the $Na^+/K^+$-ATPase pump , the energy supplied by the hydrolysis of ATP to drive certain drugs out of the cell. This glycoprotein, also called multi drug transporter, protects the cell against xenobiotics but, as it is expressed in the majority of cancerous cells, it also expel antineoplastic drugs out of cancerous cells, thus explaining their resistance to chemotherapy which is called MDR "Multi drug resistance". Drugs such as verapamil or quinidine inhibit P-glycoprotein but have other properties making their use as inhibitors of P-glycoprotein difficult. P-glycoprotein present in the blood-brain barrier reduces penetration of certain drugs into the brain. It can also reduce their digestive absorption.

Various microorganisms have in their plasma membrane, in addition to P-glycoprotein, proton-dependent pumps which drive toxic molecules out of their cytoplasm.

**Indirect active transport:** The energy necessary for facilitated diffusion, or secondary active transport, is supplied by the ion gradients on both sides of the membrane. It is not carried out through the lipid bilayer but through the protein structures.

It relates to only a small number of compounds:

1. Molecules implicated in metabolism, like glucose, amino acids, certain transmitters and drugs of close chemical structure. The energy necessary for their transport can be supplied by the sodium gradient.
   The kinetics of transfer is of Michaelis Menten type with maximum rate and possibility of competition between molecules. When sodium and the substrate cross the membrane in the same direction, the transport is called "symport" and "antiport" when they cross in opposite directions.
2. Peptides formed of 2 or 3 aminoacids are partially absorbed by the digestive tract and reabsorbed in the nephron by specific carriers using the $H^+$ gradient as source of energy. These carriers are involved in the digestive absorption of drugs with a chemical peptide-like structure such as beta-lactamines. A polypeptide such as insulin can cross the blood-brain barrier but the responsible mechanisms are poorly understood.
3. Ions like $Na^+$, $K^+$, $Ca^{2+}$, $Cl^-$, whose membrane transporters are channels and exchangers:
   - o Channels whose opening and closure depend either on the intra/extracellular potential difference (opening during depolarization), or on the presence of receptors which can be activated or inhibited by various transmitters.
   - o Exchangers, $Na^+/Ca^{2+}$ for example.

## Transport by Exocytosis and Endocytosis

Exocytosis consists of the exit out of the cell of molecules contained in vesicles which fuse with the plasma membrane and release their contents outside. It is the mode of release of transmitters.

Endocytosis consists of the absorption by a cell of an extracellular molecule. After its inclusion in a vesicle formed by an invagination of the plasma membrane, the molecule penetrates into the cytoplasm. It is, for example, the process used by hepatocytes to take up lipoproteins and transferrin,.

Oligonucleotides of 10 to 20 units, such as those used in antisense therapy (oligonucleotides complementary to the mRNA on which they bind) penetrate into cells by various mechanisms but primarily by endocytosis. In fact, an oligonucleotides penetrates better into cells that an isolated nucleotide.

## Drug Absorption

Absorption is the process by which the drug enters in to the systemic circulation from the site of administration through biological barrier. In case of intravenous or intra-arterial administration the drug bypasses absorption processes and it enters into the circulation directly.

1. **Routes of drug administration:**
   (a) **From the alimentary tract:**
      (i) *Buccal cavity:* Drugs can be absorbed through the oral cavity. Buccal (between the gums and cheek) and sublingual (underneath the tongue) can be effective means of drug administration. In both cases, drugs can enter the blood circulation without first pass metabolism in the liver. E.g., nitrates six different types of sites.
      (ii) *Stomach:* E.g., aspirin, alcohol.
      (iii) *Intestine:* E.g., most of non ionized and ionized drugs.
      (iv) *Rectum:* Rectal administration of a drug may be applied when the patient is unable to take the drug orally and some other routes are impractical. The drug administered *via* the rectum is absorbed and partially bypasses the liver. However, the absorption of drugs may be unreliable incertain cases. E.g., rectal suppositories, Bisacodyl laxatives.

   *Advantages of oral route:* This route is safe, convenient and economical.

   *Disadvantages of oral route:* Onset of drug action is slow, irritant drugs cannot be administered and it is not useful in vomiting and severe diarrhea, gastric acid and digestive enzymes may destroy some drugs, and water soluble drugs are absorbed poorly.

   (b) **From the parenteral route:**
      (i) *Intradermal:* This is given into the layers of the skin. E.g., B.C.G. vaccine.
      (ii) *Subcutaneous:* Non-irritant substances are given into subcutaneous tissue. E.g., insulin
      (iii) *Intramuscular:* Soluble substances, mild irritants, suspensions and colloids can be injected by this route. These injections can be given to deltoid or gluteal muscle. This route is one of the more common routes. E.g., multivitamins, streptomycin, etc.

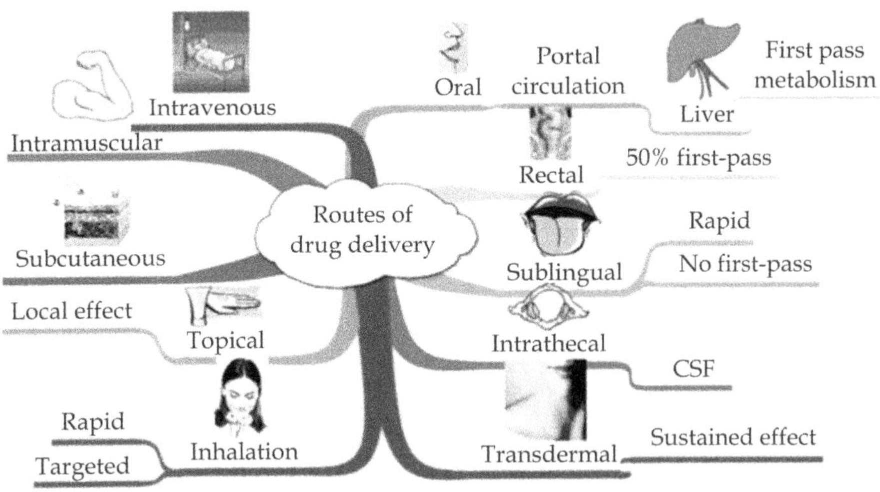


**Fig 2-5:** Routes of drug administration

*Advantages:* Rate of absorption is uniform, onset of action is faster than oral and it can be given in diarrhoea or vomiting. Subcutaneous and intramuscular administration can be used to deliver protein - based drugs.

*Disadvantages:* Pain at local site of injection, the volume of injection should not exceed 10 ml.

(iv) *Intravenous:* Drugs directly given into a vein, produce rapid action, no need of absorption as they enter directly into blood, can be given as bolus. E.g., furosemide, morphine, dopamine or as continuous infusion. E.g., fluids during shock or dehydration.

*Advantages:* It can be given in large volumes, production of desired blood concentration can be obtained with a well designed dose.

Intravenous injection is the normal route for administration of protein - based drugs, as they are likely to be destroyed if taken orally because of the pH conditions in the gastrointestinal tract.

The onset of drug action with intravenous injection is quick, and this method is especially useful for emergency cases.

The dosage can be controlled, unlike with other routes of administration, where the bioavailability of the drug may be unpredictable because of diffusion processes.

*Disadvantages:* Drug effect cannot be halted if once the drug is injected, expertise is needed to give injection.

Intravenous injection is potentially the most dangerous. Once a drug is injected, there is no means to stop it from circulating throughout the body. The complete circulation of blood in the body takes about a minute, and hence an adverse reaction can occur almost instantaneously.

(v) *Intrathecal:* Injected into subarachnoid space of spinal cord. E.g., spinal anaesthetics.

(vi) *Intraperitonial:* Injections given into the abdominal cavity. E.g., infant saline, glucose.

(vii) *Intra-articular:* Injected directly into a joint. E.g., hydrocortisone.

**(c) Transcutaneous route:**

(i) *Iontophoresis:* Galvanic current is used for bringing about the penetration of drugs into the deeper tissue. E.g., salicylates.

(ii) *Inunctions:* Absorbed when rubbed in to the skin. E.g., nitroglycerin ointment in angina pectoris.

(iii) *Jet injection:* With help of high velocity jet produced through a micro fine orifice; No need of needle and therefore painless. E.g., mass inoculation programmes.

(iv) *Adhesive units:* A transdermal therapeutic system produce prolonged systemic effect. E.g., scopolamine for motion sickness, nicotine transdermal patches for nicotine addiction patients.

**(d) Topical/ local route:**

The absorption through skin is a passive process. The absorption occurs more easily through the cell lining. E.g., dusting powder, paste, lotion, drops, ointment, suppository for vagina and rectum.

*Advantages:* The first pass metabolism is circumvented. Topical administration is used to apply the drug for local effects. The typical areas for topical application are the skin, eyes, throat, nose, and vagina.

**(e) Inhalation:**

Drugs may be administered as dry powders, and nebulised particles when sprayed as fine droplets get deposited over the mucous membrane producing local effects and may be absorbed for systemic effects. E.g., salbutamol spray used in bronchial asthma and volatile general anaesthetics.

*Advantages:* Aerosol particles of drug can be inhaled into the lungs. Because of the large surface area of the alveoli, absorption is rapid and effective. As the lungs are richly supplied with capillaries, distribution of inhalational drugs is very quick.

2. **Bioavailability:**

It is the rate and amount of drug that is absorbed from a given dosage form and reaches the systemic circulation following non-vascular administration. When the drug is given I.V. the bioavailability is 100%. It is important to know the manner in which a drug is absorbed. The route of administration largely determines the latent period between administration and onset of action. Drugs given by mouth may be inactive for the following reasons:

(a) Enzymatic degradation of polypeptides within the lumen of the gastrointestinal tract. E.g., insulin, ACTH.

(b) Poor absorption through gastrointestinal tract. E.g., aminoglycoside antibiotic.

(c) Inactivation by liver. E.g., testosterone during first passage through the liver before it reaches systemic circulation.

3. **Factors affecting drug absorption and bioavailability:**

(a) Physico-chemical properties of drug
(b) Nature of the dosage form
(c) Physiological factors
(d) Pharmacogenetic factors
(e) Disease states.

**(a) Physico-chemical properties of drug:**

(i) *Physical state:* Liquids are absorbed better than solids and crystalloids absorbed better than colloids.

(ii) *Lipid or water solubility:* Drugs in aqueous solution mix more readily than those in oily solution. However at the cell surface, the lipid soluble drugs penetrate into the cell more rapidly than the water soluble drugs.

(iii) *Ionization:* Most of the drugs are organic compounds. Unlike inorganic compounds, the organic drugs are not completely ionized in the fluid. Unionized component is predominantly lipid soluble and is absorbed rapidly and an ionized is often water soluble component which is absorbed poorly. Most of the drugs are weak acids or weak bases. It may be assumed for all practical purposes, that the mucosal lining of the G.I.T is impermeable to the ionized form of a weak organic acid or a weak organic base. These drugs exist in two forms.

*Acidic drugs:* Rapidly absorbed from the stomach. E.g., Salicylates and barbiturates.

*Basic drugs:* Not absorbed until they reach to the alkaline environment i.e., small intestine when administered orally. E.g., pethidine and ephedrine.

**(b) Nature of the dosage forms:**

(i) *Particle size:* Small particle size is important for drug absorption. Drugs given in a dispersed or emulsified state are absorbed better. E.g., vitamin D and vitamin A.

(ii) Disintegration time and dissolution rate.

*Disintegration time:* The rate of breakup of the tablet or capsule into the drug granules.

*Dissolution rate:* The rate at which the drug goes into solution.

(iii) *Formulation:* Usually substances like lactose, sucrose, starch and calcium phosphate are used as inert diluents in formulating powders or tablets. Fillers may not be totally inert but may affect the absorption as well as stability of the medicament. Thus a faulty formulation can render a useful drug totally useless therapeutically.

**(c) Physiological factors:**

(i) *Gastrointestinal transit time:* Rapid absorption occurs when the drug is given on empty stomach. However certain irritant drugs like salicylates and iron preparations are deliberately administered after food to minimize the gastrointestinal irritation. But some times the presence of food in the G.I tract aids the absorption of certain drugs. E.g., griseofulvin, propranolol and riboflavin.

(ii) *Presence of other agents:* Vitamin C enhances the absorption of iron from the G.I.T. Calcium present in milk and in antacids forms insoluble complexes with the tetracycline antibiotics and reduces their absorption.

(iii) *Area of the absorbing surface and local circulation:* Drugs can be absorbed better from the small intestine than from the stomach because of the larger surface area of the former. Increased vascular supply can increase the absorption.

(iv) *Enterohepatic cycling:* Some drugs move in between intestines and liver before they reach the site of action. This increases the bioavailability. E.g., phenolphthalein.

(v) *Metabolism of drug/first pass effect:* Rapid degradation of a drug by the liver during the first pass (propranolol) or by the gut wall (isoprenaline) also affects the bioavailability. Thus a drug though absorbed well when given orally may not be effective because of its extensive first pass metabolism.

**(d) Pharmacogenetic factors:**

Individual variations occur due to the genetically mediated reason in drug absorption and response.

Enzymes influencing metabolic reactions are under genetic control. A study of variability of action of drug in different human is called as pharmacogenetic.

Differences observed in the metabolism of the drug among different races are called ethnic variation.

For example, alcohol dehydrogenase enzyme, present in gastric mucosa, converts the alcohol into acetaldehyde, which is not intoxicating.

- Females have less quantity of this enzyme. So they often develops more adverse effect of alcohol than man.
- Asian males also have less level of this enzyme.

Some time, the drug is pseudotolerated by the patient, which can't be pseudotolerated by another one.

**(e) Disease states:**

Some diseases like mal absorption, thyrotoxicosis, achlorhydria, cirrhosis of liver and billiary obstruction can affect he absorption & bioavailability of drugs.

In case of mal absorption the pseudotolerance is developed and drug can't be absorbed.

In thyrotoxicosis (hyperthyroidism), the weight loss occurs due to less appetite.

In achlorhydria (decrease in HCL level in stomach), acidic drug can't be absorbed.

In cirrhosis of liver the drug is more metabolized and produces toxic effect.

**4. Bioavailability curves:**

Single dose bioavailability test involves an analysis of plasma or serum concentration of the drug at various time intervals after its oral administration and plotting a serum concentration time curve Fig 2-6.

## Distribution of Drugs

**Definition:** Penetration of a drug to the sites of action through the walls of blood vessels from the administered site after absorption is called drug distribution. Drugs distribute through various body fluid compartments such as (a) plasma (b) interstitial fluid compartment (c) trans-cellular compartment.

***Apparent Volume of Distribution (VD):*** The volume into which the total amount of a drug in the body would have to be uniformly distributed to provide the concentration of the drug actually measured in the plasma. It is an apparent rather than real volume.

$$\text{Bioavailability (F)} = \frac{\text{AUC after oral dose}}{\text{AUC after I.V. dose}}$$

AUC = Area under curve – which provides information about the amount of drug absorbed.

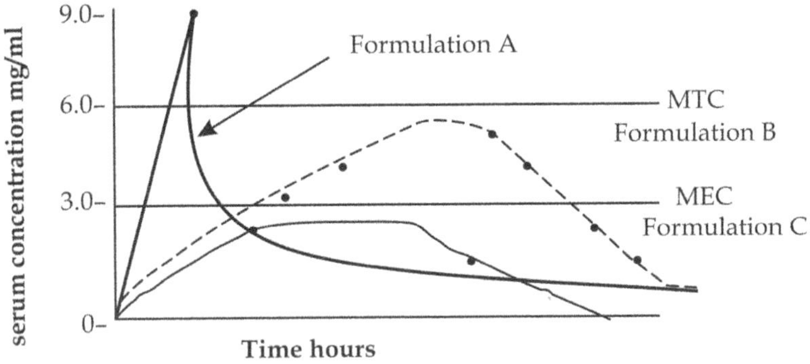


MTC: Minimum Toxic Concentration

MEC: Minimum Effective Concentration

Formulation A = Would produce quick onset and short duration of action, produce toxic effects

Formulation B = Effect would last much longer and nontoxic

Formulation C = Gives inadequate plasma level so therapeutically ineffective

**Fig 2-6:** The plasma drug level curves following administration of three formulations (A, B and C) of the same basic drug

## Drug Distribution from Blood

### Drug in blood and equilibrium between compartments

At equilibrium, a given plasma concentration of a drug corresponds to a given tissue concentration, i.e., blood mirrors what occurs in the whole body, although the concentrations in various tissues are generally different.

The measurement of the plasma concentration allows a monitoring of the treatments for avoiding toxic or ineffective concentrations, provided that sample of blood for the determination is performed at one well defined time after the administration of the drug to obtain comparable results.

Only the free fraction of the drug, i.e., the diffusible fraction is responsible for the equilibrium plasma/tissue concentrations. However, the ratio bound on free form is generally constant and the measurement of the total concentration of the drug is sufficient for therapeutic monitoring.

The desired plasma concentrations of a certain number of drugs, lower than their toxic and higher than their minimum effective concentration, called therapeutic windows, are known.

## Binding to Proteins

In blood drugs can bind reversibly to proteins. The concentration of proteins in plasma is normally 60 to 70 g/L. Certain plasma proteins play a part in the binding of the drugs:

- Albumin whose molecular weight is 65,000, Daltons, is made of a polypeptide chain with many disulfide bonds. Its half-life is about three weeks. It binds especially to acidic drugs such as nonsteroidal anti-inflammatory drugs, lipid-lowering drugs and endogenous molecules like fatty acids, thyroxine and estradiol. In addition to its role in the transport of endogenous compounds and drugs, it ensures the intravascular oncotic pressure and opposes extravascular water escape. In patients with hypo-albuminemia, lower than 20 g/L, it is necessary to correct the deficiency by administration of albumin which, at present, is obtained from human blood.
- Alpha-1 acid glycoprotein, also called *orosomucoid*, very rich in carbohydrates and sialic acid which gives it an acid property. It binds especially basic molecules like lidocaine, prazosin.
- Lipoproteins which bind certain drugs like chlorpromazine and imipramine.
- Immunoglobulins such as IgG whose plasma concentration is around 15 gm per litre.

Blood cells, in particular erythrocytes when they bind or take up certain drugs, play a role of temporary reservoir.

Binding of drugs to proteins depends on several factors:

1. The affinity of the drug for the binding sites on proteins. The binding can go from 0 to nearly 100%. The binding of anti-inflammatory drugs like indomethacin, certain antidepressants like imipramine, is higher than 95%. The binding of phenobarbital, of theophylline is about 50%. The binding of isoniazid, of acetaminophen is negligible.
2. The quantity of proteins which can vary according to the physiological or pathological state. For example, immobilization, bed rest, traumatisms, burns, pregnancy, cirrhosis decrease it whereas nephrotic syndromes, anxiety increase it.
3. *Concentration of the drug:* If a drug is present in sufficient concentration to saturate its binding sites, all new intake occurs as if the binding did not exist.
4. *The competition between a drug and another molecule:*
   1. Competition between two drugs for a same site, one drug can displace the other, salicylic acid displaces indomethacin, Clofibrate anti vitamin K. The freed drug can act and cause effects but it is also quickly metabolized and eliminated.
   2. Competition between a drug and an endogenous product, fatty acids and bilirubin which are also bound to albumin enter in competition with acid drugs.

The essential feature of the binding of drugs to proteins is to be reversible according to the following reaction where D indicates the drug, P for protein, the protein and DP the drug bound to protein.

[Drug + Protein] <=> [Drug - Protein]

- There is equilibrium between the free form and the bound form: when the concentration of D increases, the reaction is carried out in direction 1 and when it decreases, in direction 2.
- Only the free form [D] is active. It diffuses through membranes and the equilibrium between compartments is established according to its concentration. It is also the form which is eliminated and metabolized.
- The bound form [DP] can be regarded as a buffer, a form of store which does not cross the membranes.
- The binding of a drug to proteins reduces its dialysance and consequently the efficacy of dialysis used as mean of detoxification during poisoning.

## Tissue Distribution of Drugs

The drug diffuses from the plasma in the whole body. The distribution depends on the drug and tissues.

- *Drug:*Its plasma concentration in free form and of its physicochemical characteristics, in particular of its liposolubility.
- *Tissue or organ:* Existence of specific membranes, importance of the irrigation (blood flow rate) and tissue composition

giving more or less affinity for a particular compound. Thus, the cerebral tissue rich in lipids has a great affinity for liposoluble molecules.

These features explain why the drug is distributed in a non-homogeneous manner in the different organs. For example, chloroquine concentration is 700 times higher in the liver than in plasma.

**Transfer into the central nervous system and the cerebrospinal fluid**

The central nervous system weighs 2% of the weight of the body, receives 16% of the cardiac output (brain: 0.5 ml blood/g/minute, muscle at rest: 0.05 ml blood/g/minute). The white compound is less better irrigated than the gray one.

In spite of this excellent irrigation, a certain number of compounds do not penetrate into the brain. The membrane of the cerebral capillaries is doubled by a tissue of glial support, the astrocytes, thus creating a double barrier - capillary endothelium and glial membrane - not very permeable to the non-liposoluble molecules. Alterations of the barrier, in case of anoxia in particular, are likely to deteriorate its permeability.

Liposoluble molecules and gases, for example, inhalational anesthetics, penetrate easily in the brain by passive diffusion.

The polar molecules (ionized) do not penetrate or little by passive diffusion. Atropine, for example, crosses, but its positively charged quaternary form does not penetrate. Penicillin does not penetrate.

Various polar compounds, ions, sugars, amino acids and even certain peptides like insulin, cross the blood-brain barrier by using endogenous carriers. It is a secondary active transport. One can quote some of these carriers:

- Glut-1, glucose carrier non-dependant on insulin, which can also transfer some glycopeptides
- LNA system (large neutral amino acids) which allows the influx of certain amino acids and drugs having a similar structure, such as L-dopa, melphalan, gabapentin, baclofen
- Peptide carriers
- Receptors, such as those of transferrin which are internalized by endocytosis

In addition, certain compounds such as bradykinin distend intercellular tight junctions and facilitate the transfer of various compounds through the blood-brain barrier.

The transfer of a drug from brain into blood and peripheral organs is called redistribution. A drug such as thiopental which is very liposoluble, after intravenous administration penetrates very quickly into the brain, rich in lipids and well irrigated, where its concentration is quickly maximum. In a second time, the other fat tissues less irrigated than the brain accumulate thiopental, inducing a displacement of the product from the brain towards blood and peripheral fat tissues. This redistribution explains why thiopental acts very quickly and that its duration of action is short.

The cerebrospinal fluid secreted by the choroid plexus has a volume of approximately 150 to 200 ml. Its rate of renewal is approximately 0.5 ml/minute. Normally, it does not contain proteins. The concentration of a drug which diffuses passively in the cerebrospinal fluid is approximately equal to the concentration of its free form in plasma.

**Modifications of tissue distribution**

The distribution of a drug in certain parts of the body or of a tissue can be modified under pathological conditions, in particular in patients with circulatory disorders.

The distribution can also be voluntarily modified by electroporation. The electroporation is a technique which consists in subjecting tissues to impulses of electric field which increase the permeability of the plasma membrane by opening pores. It is called electrochemotherapy when it is used in cancerology.

**Factors determining the rate of distribution of drugs:**

1. **Protein binding of drug**: A variable and other significant portion of absorbed drug may become reversibly bound to plasma proteins. The active concentration of the drug is that part which is not bound, because it is only this fraction which is free to leave the plasma protein and site of action. (a) Free drug leave plasma protein to site of action (b) binding of drugs to plasma proteins assists absorption (c) protein binding acts as a temporary store of a drug and tends to prevent large fluctuations in concentration of unbound drug in the body fluids (d) protein binding reduces diffusion of drug into the cell and there by delays its metabolic degradation. E.g., high protein bound drug like phenylbutazone is long acting. Low protein bound drug like thiopental sodium is short acting.
2. **Plasma concentration of drug (PC):** It represents the drug that is bound to the plasma proteins (albumins and globulins) and the drug in free form. It is the free form of drug that is distributed to the tissues and fluids and takes part in producing pharmacological effects Fig. 2.7.

   The concentration of free drug in plasma does not always remain in the same level. E.g.,

   (i) After I.V. administration plasma concentration falls sharply

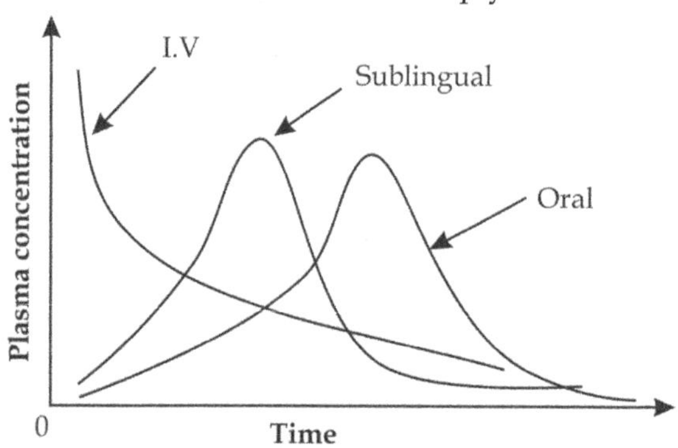


**Fig 2-7:** Plasma concentration of drug after different routes of administration

   (ii) After oral administration plasma concentration rises and falls gradually.

   (iii) After sublingual administration plasma concentration rise sharply and falls gradually.
3. **Clearance:** Volume of plasma cleared off the drug by metabolism and excretion per unit time.

   Protein binding reduces the amount of drug available for filtration at the glomeruli and hence delays the excretion, thus the protein binding reduces the clearance.
4. **Physiological barriers to distribution:** There are some specialized barriers in the body due to which the drug will not be distributed uniformly in all the tissues. These barriers are:

   (a) *Blood brain barrier (BBB):* Through which thiopental sodium is easily crossed but not dopamine. The reason for this is the highly lipoidal drug thiopental can easily penetrate through the blood brain barrier rather than dopamine.

   (b) *Placental barrier:* This allows non-ionized drugs with high lipid/water partition coefficient by a process of simple diffusion to the foetus. E.g., alcohol, morphine.
5. **Affinity of drugs to certain organs:** The concentration of a drug in certain tissues after a single dose may persist even when its plasma concentration is reduced to low. Thus the hepatic concentration of mepacrine is more than 200 times that of plasma level. Their concentration may reach a very high level on chronic administration. Iodine is similarly concentrated in the thyroid tissue.

## Excretion of Drugs

Excretion of drugs means the transportation of unaltered or altered form of drug out of the body. The major processes of excretion include renal excretion, hepatobiliary excretion and pulmonary excretion. The minor routes of excretion are saliva, sweat, tears, breast milk, vaginal fluid, nails and hair.

The rate of excretion influences the duration of action of drug. The drug that is excreted slowly, the concentration of drug in the body is maintained and the effects of the drug will continue for longer period.

## Different Routes of Drug Excretion

Drugs and their metabolites are eliminated primarily in urine and bile. Pulmonary excretion concerns volatile products.

The insufficiency of the excretion of a drug causes a lengthening of its half-life and a risk of accumulation with possible toxic effects. This is particularly true in cases of renal impairment.

**Renal Excretion:** The kidney which receives with high pressure approximately 1400 ml/min of blood, about a quarter of the cardiac output, eliminates drugs and various other compounds from the body. From the physiological point of view, the nephron, basic unit of the kidney, acts by three different mechanisms: glomerular filtration, tubular secretion and tubular reabsorption. There are approximately 1 million nephrons per kidney.

**Glomerular filtration:** The glomerulus can be regarded as a nonselective filter permeable to all the compounds whose molecular weight is lower than approximately 65000 Daltons. Albumin whose molecular weight is 65000 Daltons passes only in negligible quantity, called microalbuminuria.

The filtration needs a blood pressure sufficient to allow the flow of the filtrate and to counterbalance the oncotic pressure exerted by plasma proteins, in particular albumin.

The volume filtered per minute is approximately 140 ml, about a tenth of renal blood flow rate.

The composition of the glomerular filtrate is, for the majority of components, identical to that of plasma. As the molecular weight of drugs is usually lower than 65000 Daltons, one should always find an identical concentration of the drug in the filtrate and the plasma. But this is true only for the drugs for which the percentage of plasma protein binding is negligible. The concentration of a drug in the filtrate which is normally deprived of proteins is actually identical to the concentration of its free form in plasma.

Since the molecular weight of drugs is not generally the limiting factor, their glomerular filtration depends on their binding to plasma proteins: the more bound they are, the less they are filtered.

**Tubular secretion:** Tubular secretion consists of compound transport from the peritubular fluid into the tubular lumen. It should be recalled that the peritubular fluid consists of blood which was already filtered at the level of the glomerulus where it was impoverished in various low-weight compounds.

The tubular secretion which is carried out at the level of the proximal tubule is an active process which requires normal cellular operation to supply the energy necessary.

A general feature of this secretion, well highlighted for organic acids such as para-aminohippuric acid, is that it is limited by a maximum transport: when the concentration increases, tubular secretion increases until a threshold then remains constant, unlike what occurs for filtration which is proportional to the plasma concentration of unbound compounds.

Molecules, whose affinity for the carrier is high, like para-aminohippuric acid, are eliminated from the peritubular fluid in only one transfer. The tubular secretion of drugs is, essentially, independent of their binding to proteins, because it is reversible. This important difference from glomerular filtration can be explained as follows at the level of the glomerulus, when the concentrations of the free molecules on both sides of the membrane are equalized, by a passive process, the filtration stops. In the tubule, as the free fraction in the peritubular fluid is secreted, there is a dissociation of the complex drug-protein and the free form is actively eliminated. Thus, tubular secretion is overall independent of the binding of the drug to proteins.

When two or several drugs eliminated by the same process are present simultaneously in the body, they enter into competition for their tubular secretion. Thus the excretion of penicillin is delayed by the administration of probenecid.

There are two secretion types:

1. **Secretion of organic acids:** In addition to various endogenous organic acids and to para-aminohippuric acid used to explore renal blood flow rate, various drugs having an acid function are secreted in urine as anions: penicillin, beta-lactamines, salicylic acid, indomethacin, probenecid, diuretic thiazides, the majority of ACE inhibitors and various conjugated molecules. The phenomenon of competition between two molecules explains why the majority of thiazide diuretics tend to raise the level of blood uric acid by reducing its tubular secretion.
2. **Secretion of organic bases:** In addition to the physiological organic bases like thiamine, choline and histamine, a certain number of basic drugs are secreted by the tubule for example, quinine, morphine, procaine, neostigmine, amiloride and triamterene.

**Tubular reabsorption:** Tubular reabsorption involves the transfer of molecules from the lumen of the nephron into the blood. It can be done according to two mechanisms: one active and the other passive. But certain molecules are not reabsorbed, like the para-aminohippuric acid, mannitol, insulin.

The active reabsorption concerns primarily endogenous compounds such as sodium, potassium, uric acid, glucose and amino acids, and products whose structure is very similar to that of amino acids, for example alpha-methyl-dopa. This active reabsorption which requires an intake of energy, occurs primarily in the proximal tubule. It induces secondarily a passive reabsorption of water, to maintain Iso-osmolality between tubular filtrate and peritubular fluid.

Because of this passive water reabsorption, a certain number of compounds will be in the tubular fluid at higher a concentration than in the peritubular fluid. Consequently, these compounds are passively reabsorbed if they can cross the membrane, i.e., they are neutral and liposoluble.

The neutral character, i.e., not ionized, of acids and bases depends on their pKa and the pH of the medium, hence the importance for the excretion of certain drugs of modifications of pH of the urine. To accelerate the urinary excretion of acids, it is necessary to alkalize the urine and to acidify it for bases.

Thus, the urinary excretion of phenobarbital, an acid with pKa = 7.2, is induced by the alkalization of the urine, bicarbonate administration for example, the alkalization of the tubular fluid increases the percentage of ionized molecules not reabsorbed.

On the contrary, the urinary excretion of amphetamine, a basis with pKa = 5, is increased by the acidification of the urine, ammonium chloride administration for example, which increases its percentage of ionization.

As pH of urine is between 4, 5 and 8, the molecules most sensitive to pH modifications are those whose pKa is between 5 and 7.5. Modifications of urinary pH can be used for treatment of poisoning when the physicochemical characteristics of the poison are known.

**Pathological damage:** The renal excretion of a drug, i.e., its renal clearance, is reduced during renal impairment and decreases with age. The knowledge of the plasma clearance of creatinine makes it possible to evaluate the degree of renal impairment and to reduce the dosage of the drugs predominantly eliminated in urine, like antibiotics such as aminoglycosides.

**Digestive excretion of drugs:** The digestive tract is a location of exchanges where, of course, absorption is predominant after oral administration, but secretion is far from being negligible. Actually, very often absorption is followed by secretion, itself followed by reabsorption. The entero-hepatic cycle of biliary salts and of a certain number of drugs is a particular case of this general process.

The secretion of the drugs can occur along the digestive tract in saliva, gastric fluid, bile, intestinal secretions. This secretion is not necessarily an excretion, because the secreted drugs can be reabsorbed. The final excretion in stools results from the difference between secretion into the intestinal lumen and reabsorption. Moreover, during their transfer in the digestive tract, drugs can undergo biotransformations under the effect of digestive or microbial enzymes or because of their instability according to pH.

To study the fecal excretion of a drug, the drug must be administered by parenteral route because, after administration by oral route, it is difficult to differentiate between what was excreted and what was not absorbed.

**Salivary excretion:** Salivary secretion is far from being negligible because it can reach one to two liters daily. This secretion, variable during the day, particularly stimulated by meals, is almost non-existent during sleep.

The salivary excretion of various compounds, such as mercury derivatives, has been known for a long time and it is admitted generally that the salivary concentration of liposoluble drugs is the reflection of their plasma concentration in free form. But certain compounds such as iodide and spiramycin, reach salivary concentrations higher than those in plasma.

The determination of drugs in saliva, whose principal interest is to avoid the sampling of blood, could be used in therapeutic control. There is a rather good statistical correlation between blood and salivary concentrations, but with important and unpredictable individual variations. In practice, the determination of drugs in saliva is not used for therapeutic monitoring.

It should be recalled that drugs with atropinic properties inhibit salivary secretion and disturb the excretion of compounds by this route.

**Gastric secretion:** The study of the gastric secretion of drugs administered by parenteral route was carried out especially in animals. In fact the basic drugs such as quinine are secreted in the gastric fluid. On the other hand, the acid drugs practically do not pass, which is understood rather well if one looks at the phenomena of dissociations according to pH.

**Biliary secretion:** The drugs reach the liver by two different routes:

- The venous and the lymphatic system after digestive absorption and, in this case, the totality of the absorbed drug passes through the liver before being distributed in the whole body.
- The hepatic artery after parenteral administration. In this case, the drug is distributed to the whole body and only a fraction passes through the liver.

The liver binds drugs with more or less affinity and, after possible biotransformations, can excrete them in bile.

The uptake of molecules by hepatocytes occurs at a variable rate. Certain molecules are very quickly fixed by the liver: it is the case of bromosulfophthalein whose plasma decrease is a test of assessment of hepatic function. It is the same for iodized contrast agents used for radiological exploration of the biliary tract.

The liver is the principal organ of drug biotransformations with reactions of phase I, oxidations and of phase II, conjugations. These biotransformations produce more polar and of higher molecular weight molecules, two features which facilitate their excretion in bile.

The concentration of drugs or their metabolites in the bile can be higher, equal or lower than that of the plasma. The drugs whose concentration is much higher in bile than in plasma are secreted by active processes with a maximum rate of transport ($T_m$) and possible competition between transported compounds. These compounds have molecular weights equal to or higher than 300 and have polar groups. Among the drugs secreted in high concentration in bile, there are antibiotics: erythromycin, novobiocin, ampicillin, rifampin, and other compounds such as chlorothiazide, ergot derivatives.

A certain number of practical consequences result from these facts:

1. For the treatment of biliary infections, it is necessary to choose antibiotics which enter into bile in an active form and which have a suitable spectrum of activity.
2. Drugs can be in competition with bilirubin for active transport into bile, which explains the advent of jaundices "with free bilirubin".
3. In patients with hepatic insufficiency or obstruction of the biliary tract, the risk of accumulation of these drugs is raised.

**Intestinal secretion:** The importance of intestinal secretion itself, apart from biliary or pancreatic secretion, was well highlighted for metals, in particular zinc.

The importance of intestinal secretion in the excretion of drugs is generally low and not well known.

**Pulmonary excretion:** The pulmonary excretion (in expired air) concerns only a low number of drugs, but for which it can represent the main route of excretion. The concerned drugs are volatile products like some general anesthetics, halothane for example, from which 60% is eliminated in the expired air.

The excretion of ethyl alcohol by the pulmonary route is used to measure its plasma concentration. The expired air constitutes also a route of excretion of volatile solvents (ether, hexane, benzene, trichloroethylene, etc.) which can be at the origin of poisoning by pulmonary absorption. Absorption or excretion depends on the relative concentrations of these products in the expired air and blood.

## Other Routes of Excretion

### Milk Excretion

The excretion of drugs in milk constitutes only a secondary route of excretion for the woman, but can constitute a danger for the neonate. When it is necessary to prescribe drugs to the mother, the problem is to know if it is necessary to stop breast feeding, either transitorily, or definitively.

In general, the percentage of the dose given passing into milk in 24 hours is lower than 1%, except for some products like iodine 131 and thiouracil where it can reach 5%. The mechanisms of transfer of drugs in milk are complex: both active and passive and influenced by the variations of the composition of milk.

In spite of the low passage of drugs in milk, and partly as inactive metabolites, accidents can be observed in the new-born baby.

The excretion in the cow's milk of various drugs used in veterinary medicine or of various compounds like insecticides and weed killers posses an important problem of hygiene and control.

### Sweat Excretion

Sweat can contain traces of compounds such as iodine, bromine, ethanol, salicylic acid, sulphamides and various trace elements. But the sweat excretion appears secondary compared to the renal, hepatic and pulmonary excretion.

### Mammary Excretion

Many drugs mostly weak basic drugs are accumulated into the milk. Therefore lactating mothers should be cautious about the intake of these drugs because they may enter into baby through breast milk and produce harmful effects in the baby. E.g., ampicillin, aspirin, chlordiazepoxide, coffee, diazepam, furosemide, morphine, streptomycin etc.

### Excretion by various Secretions

One can find drugs, at least traces of them, in practically all secretions, lacrimal, nasal, bronchial or genital. These routes are secondary for the excretion of drugs but have therapeutic importance, in particular for the treatment of localized infections of microbial or parasitic origin.

## Artificial Methods of Excretion

Artificial methods of excretion are used in the case of poisoning by drugs or compounds which endanger the life of patients. One then seeks to eliminate them as fast as possible.

## Digestive Excretion

The digestive excretion can be increased by various processes:

1. Gastric lavage used frequently because it can withdraw a considerable quantity of poison, even several hours after intake.
2. Induced diarrhea, or enema, when the poison is present in large amounts in the intestine.
3. Activated charcoal administration known for a long time for its capacity to adsorb a great number of molecules, in particular drugs. It is used, in oral administration or by gastric probe, to reduce the digestive absorption and the bioavailability of toxic products and drugs taken in excess by oral route. The activated charcoal must be given as soon as possible after ingestion of the supposed poison.

This digestive excretion concerns primarily the not yet absorbed drug, but part of the eliminated drug can come from secretion.

## Accelerated Renal Excretion

To accelerate the renal excretion of toxic compounds there are two possibilities primarily: modification of pH of the urine (alkalization to induce the excretion of the acids and acidification for the bases) and osmotic diuresis by the perfusion of hyperosmolar solutions (mannitol for example). These two processes can be combined to obtain an alkalizing osmotic diuresis (sodium bicarbonate for example) or acidifying (ammonium chloride for example).

The maintenance of an high diuresis during treatments by drugs which are eliminated primarily by the kidney and can damage it, such as methotrexate and cisplatin, prevents their renal accumulation and toxicity.

## Artificial Excretion

Peritoneal dialysis, hemodialysis and sometimes exsanguino transfusion are used to compensate for renal impairment.

**Clearance of a drug:** It is the volume of plasma cleared of the drug by metabolism (hepatic) and excretion (renal) and other organs.

Total clearance will be calculated by $C_t = C_h + C_r$ + C others

$C_t$ = Total clearance

$C_h$ = Hepatic clearance

$C_r$ = Renal clearance

# Theoretical Pharmacokinetics

Information about the time course of drug absorption, distribution and excretion (pharmacokinetics) can be expressed in mathematical terms and has contributed to our understanding and planning of drug regimens. Pharmacokinetic principles aid in the selection and adjustment of drug-dose schedules.

**Half life:** Half life ($t_{1/2}$) of a drug is the time taken for the concentration of drug in the blood or plasma to decline to half of original value or the amount of drug in the body to be reduced by 50%. It has two phases, i.e., half-life of distribution and half-life of excretion. A half-life value can be readily determined for most drugs by administering a dose of the drug to a subject, taking blood samples at various time intervals and then assaying the samples. For example, if a blood level of drug A is 8.6 mg/ ml at 10 minutes and 4.3 mg/ ml at 60 minutes, so the half - life of that drug is 50 minutes. In most of the cases the rate of disappearance of a drug from the body is reflected in the rate of lowering of its plasma concentration following a single intravenous dose, the plasma concentration of the drug is focused to fall exponentially. With drugs whose excretion is exponential, the biological half - life is independent of the dose, the route of administration and the plasma concentration. It depends on VD as well as on the metabolism and renal excretion of the drug.

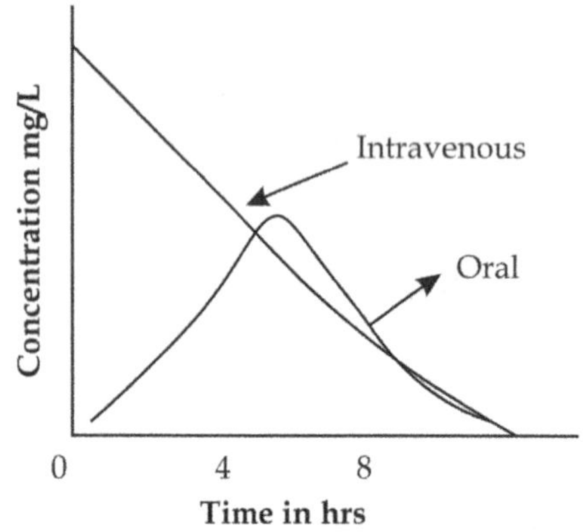


**Fig 2-8:** Exponential curves of plasma concentration following oral and intravenous drug administration

**Order of kinetics:** Drugs are used for the treatment of diseases but the modes of administration of drugs are different. For example, atenolol is administered once daily where as paracetamol needs 3-4 times administration daily. Morphine is more effective in intramuscular route, and insulin is in subcutaneous route. The mode of administration is designed on the basis of absorption, distribution, metabolism and excretion (ADME) of drugs. Drugs usually follow two processes for their pharmacokinetic behaviour in the body. These are first order and zero order process.

**First order kinetics:** This is the most common process for many drugs. The rate at which absorption, distribution, metabolism and excretion occur are proportional to the concentration of drugs, i.e., constant fraction of this drug in the body disappears in each equal interval of time.

**Zero order kinetics:** It is independent of the amount of drug present at the particular sites of drug absorption or excretion. Few drugs follow this process. E.g., ethanol, phenytoin. Here constant amount of the drug is eliminated in each equal interval of time. On repeated administration of drug after certain stage it goes on accumulating in the body and leads to toxic reactions.

**Steady state plasma concentration:** When a drug dose is given repeatedly over a given period, a steady state is eventually reached, at which point the amount of drug absorbed is in equilibrium with that eliminated from the body. Fig 2-9.

For some drugs, the effects are difficult to measure, toxicity and lack of efficacy are both potential dangers, and/or the therapeutic window is narrow. In these circumstances doses must be adjusted carefully to a desired steady-state concentration by giving loading and maintenance doses.

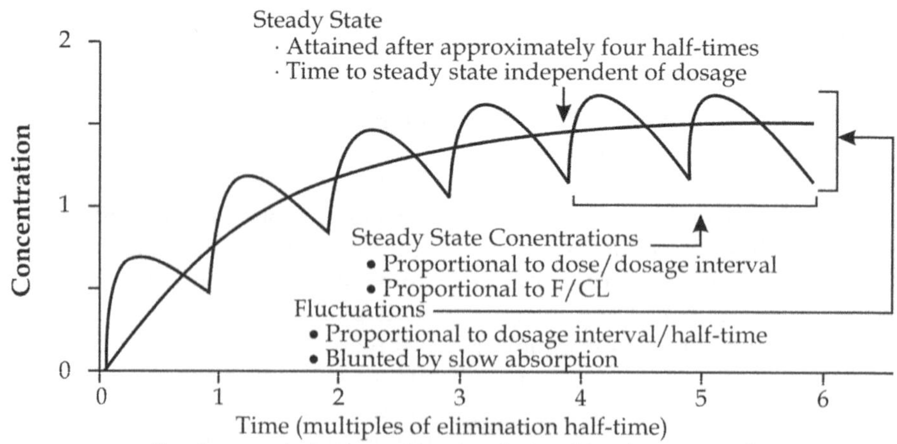


Fundamental pharmacokinetic relationships for repeated administration of drugs.

**Fig 2-9:** Steady state plasma concentration of a drug after repeated administrations

**Loading dose:** The loading dose is one or a series of doses that may be given at the onset of therapy with the aim of achieving the target concentration rapidly.

**Maintenance dose:** To maintain the chosen steady-state or target concentration, the rate of drug administration is adjusted such that the rate of input equals to rate of loss.

## References

Holford NHG: Pharmacokinetic and pharmacodynamic principles. 2003; http://www.health.auckland.ac.nz/courses/Humanbio251/.

Holford NHG, Sheiner LB (1981): Understanding the dose-effect relationship. *Clin Pharmacokinet* **6:** 429.

Holford NHG (1999): Target concentration intervention: Beyond Y2K. *Br J Clin Pharmacol* **48:** 9.

CHAPTER

# Drug Receptors and Pharmacodynamics 3

## Introduction

The concept of proteins as drug targets is not novel and was suggested at the end of the19$^{th}$ and the beginning of the 20$^{th}$ centuries. Ehrlich and Langley both contributed the idea that compounds displayed biological activity by binding to cellular constituents that were soon named 'receptors' (Langley: 'receptive substances'). One could consider that every protein that acts as the molecular target for a certain drug should be called a receptor. A receptor is a component of a cell or organism that interacts with a drug and initiates the chain of biochemical events leading to the drug's observed effects.

## Drug-Receptor Complex Nomenclature

1. **Agonist:** A drug that activates a receptor is known as agonist, which has following properties;
   - Agonists can differ in both affinity and efficacy for the receptor
   - High efficacy agonists are full agonists because they elicit maximal effects
   - Low efficacy agonists are partial agonists because they cannot elicit a maximal effect at receptors even at high concentrations (false transmitters)
   - Direct agonists act on receptors, while indirect agonists facilitate the actions of the endogenous agonist (the neuro-transmitter, itself)
2. **Antagonist:** A drug that does not activate the receptor is antagonist, which possess the following features;
   - Antagonists also prevent the activation of the receptor by an agonist, thus antagonists are essentially zero efficacy drugs
   - Competitive antagonists bind to the same binding site as the agonist and therefore compete with the agonist for that binding site
   - Non-competitive antagonists have a different binding site to the agonist and therefore do not compete with the agonist. Some non-competitive antagonists have a binding site within the ion channel associated with the receptor complex.
3. **Functional antagonism:** An antagonist may act at a completely separate receptor, initiating effects that are functionally opposite those of the agonist. A classic example is the antagonism by epinephrine to histamine-induced bronchoconstriction. Histamine binds to $H_1$ histamine receptors on bronchial smooth muscle, causing contraction and narrowing of the bronchial tree. Epinephrine is an agonist at $\alpha_2$-adrenoceptors on bronchial smooth muscle, which causes the muscles to actively relax. This functional antagonism is also known as "physiologic antagonism" which leads to hypotension.
4. **Partial agonists:** Partial agonists have efficacies (intrinsic activities) greater than zero, but less than that of a full agonist. Even

if all the receptors are occupied, partial agonists cannot produce an $E_{max}$ of as great a magnitude as that of a full agonist. However, a partial agonist may have an affinity that is greater than, less than, or equivalent to that of a full agonist. A unique feature of these drugs is that, under appropriate conditions, a partial agonist may act as an antagonist of a full agonist. Consider what would happen to the $E_{max}$ of an agonist in the presence of increasing concentrations of a partial agonist. As the number of receptors occupied by the partial agonist increases, the $E_{max}$ would decrease until it reached the $E_{max}$ of the partial agonist. This potential of partial agonists to act both agonistically and antagonistically may be therapeutically exploited.

For example, aripiprazole, an atypical neuroleptic agent, is a partial agonist at selected dopamine receptors. Dopaminergic pathways that were overactive would tend to be inhibited by the partial agonist, whereas pathways that were underactive may be stimulated. This might explain the ability of aripiprazole to improve many of the symptoms of schizophrenia, with a small risk of causing extrapyramidal adverse effects.

## Some Characteristics of Receptors

A. **Spare receptors:** A characteristic of many receptors, particularly those that respond to hormones, neurotransmitters, and peptides, is their ability to amplify signal duration and intensity. The family of G protein–linked receptors exemplifies many of the possible responses initiated by ligand binding to a receptor. Specifically, two phenomena account for the amplification of the ligand–receptor signal. First, a single ligand–receptor complex can interact with many G proteins, thereby multiplying the original signal many-folds. Second, the activated G proteins persist for a longer duration than the original ligand–receptor complex. The binding of albuterol, for example, may only exist for a few milliseconds, but the subsequent activated G proteins may last for hundreds of milliseconds. Further prolongation and amplification of the initial signal is mediated by the interaction between G proteins and their respective intracellular targets. Because of this amplification, only a fraction of the total receptors for a specific ligand may need to be occupied to elicit a maximal response from a cell. Systems that exhibit this behaviour are said to have spare receptors. Spare receptors are exhibited by insulin receptors, where it has been estimated that 99 percent of the receptors are "spare". This constitutes an immense functional reserve that ensures adequate amounts of glucose enter the cell. On the other end of the scale is the human heart, in which about five to ten percent of the total α-adrenoceptors are spare. An important implication of this observation is that little functional reserve exists in the failing heart; most receptors must be occupied to obtain maximum contractility.

B. **Desensitization of receptors:** Repeated or continuous administration of an agonist (or an antagonist) may lead to changes in the responsiveness of the receptor. To prevent potential damage to the cell (for example, high concentrations of calcium, initiating cell death), several mechanisms have evolved to protect a cell from excessive stimulation. When repeated administration of a drug results in a diminished effect, the phenomenon is called tachyphylaxis. The receptor becomes desensitized to the action of the drug. In this phenomenon, the receptors are still present on the cell surface but are unresponsive to the ligand. Other types of desensitization occur when receptors are down-regulated. Binding of the agonist results in molecular changes in the membrane-bound receptors, such that the receptor undergoes endocytosis and is sequestered from further agonist interaction. These receptors may be recycled to the cell surface, restoring sensitivity, or alternatively, may be further processed and degraded, decreasing the total number of receptors available. Some receptors, particularly voltage-gated channels, require a finite time (rest period) following stimulation before they can be activated again. During this recovery phase they are said to be "refractory" or "unresponsive".

C. **Importance of the receptor concept:** It is important that we understand the roles and functions of receptors because most drugs interact with receptors that will determine selective therapeutic and toxic effects of the drug. Moreover, receptors largely determine the quantitative relations between dose of a drug and pharmacologic effect.

### Chemical Nature of Receptors

For many years' receptors, remained hypothetical structures, until in the 1970s the development of radioactive ligand led to the visualization and quantification of binding sites for drugs in tissues or isolated cells. Nowadays, structural information (X-ray, NMR) of a variety of receptor proteins is known and this has led to the development of detailed insights in the molecular processes involved in drug–receptor interactions. Receptors are no longer hypothetical. Hundreds of receptor proteins have been isolated, purified, cloned, and their primary amino acid sequence has been established. It has been possible to study the receptor by binding assay, biochemical characterization, immunological characterization and molecular biological characterization. Most of the receptors like regulatory enzymes (dihydrofolate reductase enzyme) acetylcholinestrase transport proteins and structural proteins (Tubulin) are protein in nature and some are glycoprotein's (G-protein coupled receptors) or nucleic acids.

### General Principles of Drug Action

- Variety of receptor proteins is known and this has led to the development of detailed insights in the molecular processes involved in drug–receptor interactions.
- Receptors are no longer hypothetical. Hundreds of receptor proteins have been isolated, purified, cloned, and their primary amino acid sequence has been established. It has been possible to study the receptor by binding assay, biochemical characterization, immunological characterization and molecular biological characterization.

### Classes of drug receptors

Drug receptors are mostly proteins. Most of these fall into one of the following categories:

1. Enzymes
2. Ion channels:
   1. Ligand-gated channels: Ion channels that open upon binding of a mediator.
   2. Voltage-gated channels: Ion channels that are not normally controlled by ligand binding but by changes to the membrane potential.
3. 'Metabolic' receptors – hormone and neurotransmitter receptors that are coupled to biochemical secondary messengers and effector mechanisms. Most metabolic receptors that are drug targets belong to the family of G protein-coupled receptors.
4. Cytoskeletal proteins that are involved in cell motility – e.g., actin or tubulin.

**Drug target sites that are not proteins include:**

- *DNA:* This is very common with cytotoxic drugs used in cancer therapy, e.g. Alkylating agents. These are generally of very poor selectivity and therefore highly toxic. This degree of toxicity is only acceptable in the treatment of life-threatening diseases such as cancer.
- *RNA:* Although not yet important in clinical practice, antisense oligonucleotides are a very important topic in experimental drug development. These are short, synthetic sequences of DNA (or modified versions of DNA), designed to bind and inactivate RNA transcribed from specific genes. While this is a theoretically extremely elegant and versatile approach, it has so far remained largely experimental, despite considerable efforts in the last 10-15 years.

- *Membranes:* Inhalation anaesthetics (diethyl ether, chloroform, and their more modern replacements). The mode of action of these was enshrouded in mystery for a long time, but accumulating evidence now supports direct interaction with several ion channels. Nevertheless, there is a remarkably close correlation between the ability of these agents to partition into lipid membranes, as measured by their oil-water partition coefficients, and their narcotic activity; so, in a sense, cell membranes may be considered the targets of these agents.
- *Fluid compartments:* Osmotically active solutes. These are in fact the only clear exceptions that can think of to the principle that a drug has to bind before acting. Applications include:
  - o Plasma volume expanders. If blood is lost during trauma, the loss of volume is more immediately threatening than the loss of red blood cells. Replacement with salt solutions does not work well because small solutes get rapidly filtrated into the interstitial fluid compartment. Only macromolecules are retained in the intravascular space and can prevent filtration of the diluted plasma due to their osmotic activity. Commonly used plasma expanders are metabolically inert polysaccharides such as dextran and hydroxyethyl-starch.
  - o Osmotically acting diuretic agents. These are applied in the treatment of intoxication in order to increase the urine volume and accelerate elimination of the poison ('forced diuresis). The classical example is mannitol. This sugar is quite similar to glucose in structure but does not get metabolized nor reabsorbed from the primary glomerular filtrate in the kidneys.
  - o Laxatives. Example: Sodium sulfate effective but obsolete.

However, again, most drugs act directly on receptors that are proteins.

### Types of Receptors

However, the overall structure of receptor proteins is often not so divergent, suggesting that signal transmission *via* receptor proteins is governed by a limited number of basic mechanisms that are utilised in an extremely efficient way. One distinguishes four superfamilies of receptor proteins, which cover most of the relevant receptor proteins. These four receptor families are:

1. **Ion Channel Receptors:** There are two main types of ion channel receptors: ligand gated and voltage gated. In addition, some ion channels are regulated through GPCRs or via activation by amino acids.
   A. *Ligand Gated Ion Channels:* The ligand gated family consists of receptors of the so called cys - loop superfamily/ receptors (nicotinic receptors, gamma - aminobutyric acid (GABA- A and GA BA- C) receptors, glycine receptors, 5-$HT_3$ receptors and some glutamate activated anionic channels (Fig. 3.1)). The common feature is that they are made up of five subunits (designated as two $\alpha$ , one $\beta$ , one $\gamma$ , and one $\delta$ subunits). Natural ligands for this family of ion channels include acetylcholine, GABA, glycine, and aspartic acid. They are, in general, synaptic transmitters. Normally, in the resting state, the channel is impermeable to ions. When a ligand binds to the receptor, it becomes activated and opens a channel to a diameter of about 6.5 Å ($6.5 \times 10^{-10}$ m). This action allows the migration, for example, extracellular sodium ions to the interior of the cell. A cascade of further changes then proceed within the cell to amplify the signal. Voltage - gated ion channels depend on changes of transmembrane voltage to regulate the opening and closing of

channel gates. A common feature of this type of receptor is the presence of four domains, where each domain consists of six membrane - spanning regions. Some of these channels are the sodium, calcium, and potassium channels, and they regulate the influx of these ions into the cell interior to propagate the signal. Diseases mediated through ion channel receptors include cardiovascular disease, hypertension, and central nervous system dysfunctions. A voltage - gated ion channel is a key to the treatment of cystic fibrosis.

*Example:* Nicotinic Acetylcholine Receptor

**The nicotinic acetylcholine receptor** best studied examples of a **ligand - gate receptor channel**.

The receptor opens in response to the neurotransmitter acetylcholine (and also nicotine) and found in the postsynaptic membrane of neurons at certain synapses and in muscle fibers (myocytes) at neuromuscular junctions. Acetylcholine released by an excited neuron diffuses a few micrometers across the synaptic cleft or neuromusclular junction to the postsynaptic neuron or myocyte, where

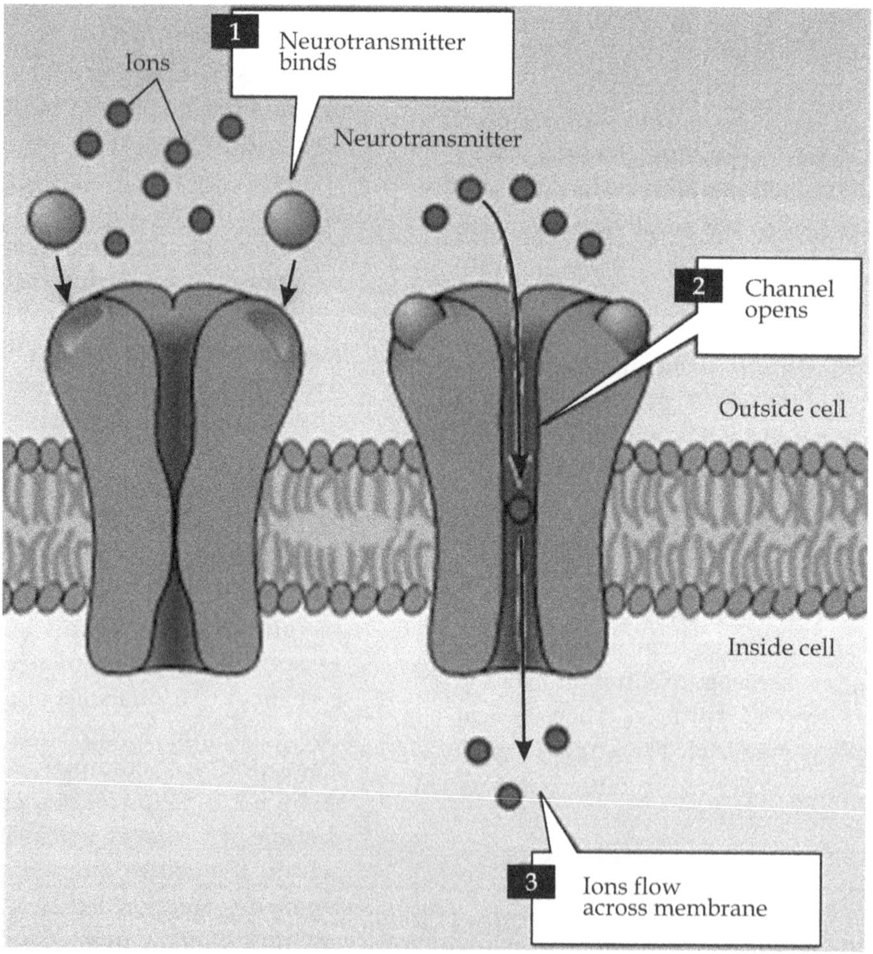


**Fig 3-1:** Ligand gated ion channels

it interacts with the acetylcholine receptor and triggers electrical excitation (depolarization) of the receiving cell. The acetylcholine causes a change from the closed to the open conformation. The process is positively cooperative. Binding of acetylcholine to the first site increases the acetylcholine-binding affinity of the second site. When the presynaptic cell releases a brief pulse of acetylcholine, both sites on the postsynaptic cell receptor are occupied briefly and the channel opens for either $Na^+$, or $Ca^{2+}$ and the inward flux of these ions depolarizes the plasma membrane, initiating subsequent events that vary with the type of tissue. In a postsynaptic neuron, **depolarization** initiates **an action potential** at a neuromuscular junction, depolarization of the muscle fibre triggers **muscle contraction**. The acetylcholine concentration in the synaptic cleft is immediately lowered by the enzyme **acetylcholinesterase**, present in the cleft. When acetylcholine levels remain high for more than a few milliseconds, the receptor is **desensitized.** The desensitized receptor channel is converted to a third conformation, in which the channel is closed and the acetylcholine is very tightly bound. The slow release of acetylcholine from its binding sites eventually allows the receptor to return to its resting state closed and resensitized to acetylcholine levels.

**B.** ***Voltage Gated Ion Channel:*** A network of neurons involved in the signalling in the nervous system, which are specialized cells that carry an electrical impulse (action potential) from one end of the cell ( the cell body) through an elongated cytoplasmic extension (the axon). The electrical signal triggers release of neurotransmitter molecules at the synapse, earning the signal to the next cell in the circuit.

There are three types of **voltage - gated ion channels that** are essential to this signalling mechanism. When the nucleotide binding to $G_s$, (on the α subunit) is occupied by GDP, it is inactive. Along the entire length of the axon are **voltage gated $Na^+$ channels,** Fig 3-2, which are closed when the membrane is at rest ($V_m$ = -60 mV) but open briefly when the membrane is depolarized locally in response to acetylcholine ( or some other neurotransmitter). The depolarization induced by the opening of **$Na^+$** channels causes voltage - gated $K^+$ Channels to open, and the resulting efflux of $K^+$, repolarizes the membrane locally. A brief pulse of **depolarization transverses the axon** as local depolarization triggers the brief opening of neighbouring $Na^+$ channels, then $K^+$ channels. After each opening of a $Na^+$ channel (a short refractory period follows during which that channel cannot open again), thus **a unidirectional wave of depolarization** sweeps from the nerve cell body toward the end of the axon.

**The voltage-gated $Ca^{2+}$** channels are present at the distal tip. When the wave of depolarization reaches these channels they open, and **influx of $Ca^{2+}$** from the extracellular space. The rise in cytoplasmic [$Ca^{2+}$] then triggers release of acetylcholine by exocytosis into the synaptic cleft. Acetylcholine diffuses to the postsynaptic cell (another neuron or a myocyte), where it binds to acetylcholine receptors and triggers depolarization. Thus the message is passed to the next cell in the circuit. So, the gated ion channels convey signals in either of two ways, by changing the cytosolic concentration of an ion (such as $Na^+$), which then serves as an intracellular **second messenger** (the hormone or neurotransmitter is the first messenger), or by changing Vm (Membrane potential) and affecting other membrane proteins that are sensitive to Vm.

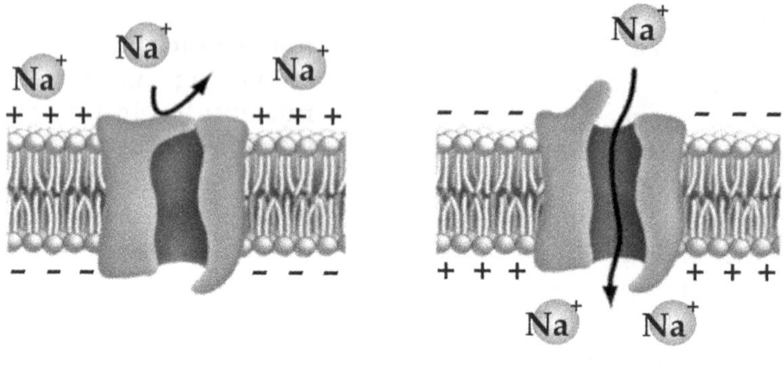


At the resting potential, voltage-gated $Na^+$ channels are closed.

When the membrane is depolarized, conformational changes open the voltage-gated channel.

**Fig 3-2:** Voltage gated ion channel

2. **G-protein (Guanine nucleotide-regulatory protein) coupled receptors:** G-protein coupled receptors, which are membrane-bound receptors coupled to G-proteins. G-protein-coupled receptors (GPCRs) constitute a large and diverse family of proteins whose primary function is to transduce extracellular stimuli into intracellular signals. They are among the largest and most diverse protein families in mammalian genomes. On the basis of homology with rhodopsin, they are predicted to contain seven membrane-spanning helices, an extracellular N-terminus and an intracellular C-terminus. This gives rise to their other names, the 7-TM receptors or the heptahelical receptors. GPCRs transduce extracellular stimuli to give intracellular signals through interaction of their intracellular domains with heterotrimeric G proteins, and the crystal structure of one member of this group, bovine rhodopsin, has recently been solved.

   The presence of GPCRs in the genomes of bacteria, yeast, plants, nematodes and other invertebrate groups argues in favour of a relatively early evolutionary origin of this group of molecules. The diversity of GPCRs is dictated both by the multiplicity of stimuli to which they respond, as well as by the variety of intracellular signalling pathways they activate. These include light, neurotransmitters, odorants, biogenic amines, lipids, proteins, amino acids, hormones, nucleotides, chemokines and undoubtedly, many others. In addition, there are at least 18 different human Gα proteins to which GPCRs can be coupled . These Gα proteins form heterotrimeric complexes with Gβ subunits, of which there are at least 5 types, and Gδ subunits, of which there are at least 11 types. The first step in signal transduction is ligand binding. The nature of GPCR ligand-binding sites is best studied by a combination of site-directed mutagenesis, molecular modelling of the receptors and screening of large numbers of potential ligands. Agonist binding is followed by a change in the conformation of the receptor that may involve disruption of a strong ionic interaction between the third and sixth transmembrane helices which facilitates activation of the G-protein heterotrimer. Depending on the type of G protein to which the receptor is coupled, a variety of downstream signalling pathways can be activated. Signalling is then attenuated (desensitized) by GPCR internalization, which is facilitated by arrestin binding. Signalling, desensitization and eventual resensitization are regulated by complex interactions of various intracellular domains of the GPCRs with numerous intracellular proteins .

What are the changes that occur when drug binds to GPCR......?

*Example:* **The β - Adrenergic Receptor System**

The hormone **epinephrine** action begins, it binds to a protein receptor in the plasma membrane.

The **adrenergic receptors** are of four general types ( $\alpha_1$, $\alpha_2$, $\beta_1$, and $\beta_2$) differ in their affinities and responses to a group of agonists and antagonists. The four types of adrenergic receptors are found in different target tissues and mediate different responses to epinephrine. Adrenergic receptors of the $\beta_1$ and $\beta_2$ subtypes act through the same mechanism. Antagonists are analogs that bind without triggering the normal effect and there by block the effects of agonists.

The β-adrenergic receptor is an integral protein of membrane protein with seven **hydrophobic regions of** 20 to 28 amino acid residues. This protein also belongs to a very large family of receptors, all with seven transmembrane helices, that are commonly called **serpentine receptors, G protein - coupled receptors (GPCR), or 7 trans membrane segment (7TM) receptors.**

The **binding of epinephrine to a site on the receptor deep within the membrane promotes a conformation change** in the receptor's intracellular domain that affects its interaction with the second protein in the signal - transduction pathway, a heterotrimeric GTP-bindings **stimulatory G protein, or Gs,** on the cytosolic side of the plasma membrane.

When GTP is bound to Gs, Gs stimulate the production of cAMP by adenylyl cyclase in the plasma membrane. The Gs functions as a molecular switch resembles that of another class of G proteins typified by Ras (the insulin receptor).

Structurally, Gs and Ras are quite distinct; G Proteins of the Ras type are monomers (Mr 20,000), whereas the G Proteins that interest with serpentine receptors are trimers of three different submits α ( Mr 43,000 ), β (Mr 37,000) and γ (Mr 7,500 to 10,000). When the nucleotide - binding to Gs, (on the a submit) is occupied by GDP, it is inactive. The Gs with GTP bounds is active and activate adenylyl cyclise. Binding of epinephrine enables the receptor to catalyze displacement of bound GDP by GTP, converting Gs to its active form. At this occurs, the β and γ subunits of Gs dissociate from the a subunit, and Gsα, with its bound GTP, moves in the plasma of the membrane from the receptor to a nearby molecule of adenylyl cyclase.

The Gs∝ is held to the membrane by a covalently attached palmitoyl group.

Adenylyl cyclase is an integral protein of the plasma membrane, with active site on the cytosolic face. It catalyzes the synthesis of cAMP from ATP. With association of Gs∝, adenylyl cyclase stimulates the cyclase to catalyze cAMP synthesis and raising the cytosolic [cAMP].

This stimulation by Gs is self-limiting, Gs∝ is a GTP as that turns itself off by convering its bound GTP to GDP.

The now inactive by Gs dissociates from adenylyl cyclase, rendering the cyclase inactive. After Gs∝ reassociates with β and γ subunits and again ready for the interaction with a hormone - bound receptor. One downstream effect of epinephrine is to activate glycogen phosphorylase b.

This conversion is promoted by the enzyme phosphorylase b kinase, which catalyzes the phosphorylation of two specific Ser residues in phosphorylase b, converting it to phosphorylase A.

Cyclec AMP activates cAMP-dependent protein kinase, also called protein kinase A or PKA, which catalyzes the phosphorylation of inactive phosphorylase b kinase to yield the active form.

The **inactive form of PKA** contains two catalytic subunits (C) and two regulatory subunits (R), which are similar in sequence to the catalytic and regulatory domains of PKG (cGMP-dependent protein kinase).

The tetrameric $R_2C_2$ complex is catalytically inactive, because an auto inhibitory domain of each R subunit occupies the substrate binding site of each subunit.

When cAMP binds to two sites on each R subunit, the R subunits undergo a conformational change and the $R_2C_2$ complex dissociates to yield two free, catalytically active C sub units.

The pKA regulates a number of enzymes, although the proteins regulated by cAMP-dependent phosphorylation have diverse functions, they share a region of sequence similarity around the Ser or Thr.

Signal transduction by adenylyl cyclase have several steps that amplify the original hormone signal.

Methyl xanthenes such as caffeine and theophylline (a component of tea) inhibit the phosphodiesterase, increasing the half-life of cAMP and thereby potentiating agents that act by stimulating adenylyl cyclase.

***Cycle AMP – Second Messenger:*** Apart from epinephrine, many hormones, growth factors, and other regulatory molecules that act by changing the intracellular [cAMP] and thus the activity of PKA.

***Examples:*** The glucagon binds to its receptors in the plasma membrane of adipocytes, activating (*via* a Gs protein) adenylyl cyclase. PKA, stimulated by the resulting rise in [cAMP], phosphorylates and activates two proteins critical to the conversion of stored fat to fatty acids (perilipin and hormone-sensitive triacylglycerol lipase), leading to the mobilization of fatty acids.

The adrenocorticotropic hormone (ACTH, also called corticotrophin), produced by the anterior pituitary, binds to specific receptors in the adrenal cortex, activating adenylyl cyclase and raising the intracellular [cAMP]. PKA then phosphorylate and activates several of the enzymes required for the synthesis of cortisol and other steroid hormones. The catalytic subunit of PKA can also move into the nucleus, where it phosphorylates a protein that alters the expression of specific genes.

Some hormones act by **inhibiting adenylyl cyclase, lowering cAMP levels**, and suppressing protein phosphorylation. For example, the binding of somatostatin to its receptor leads to activation of an **inhibitory G protein** (Gi) structurally homologous to Gs, that inhibits adenylyl cyclase and lowers [cAMP].

***Phosphatidylinositol – Secondary Messengers:*** **A Second class of serpentine receptors** are coupled through a G protein to plasma membrane **Phospholipase C (PLC)** that is specific for the plasma membrane lipid phosphatidylinsitol 4,5-bisphosphate in the plasma membrane.

This hormone-sensitive enzyme catalyzes the formation of two potent second messengers:

***Diacylglycerol and Inositol 1,4,5-Trisphosphate ($IP_3$):*** When a hormone binds its specific receptor in the plasma membrane, the receptor – hormone complex catalyzes GTP-GDP exchange on an associated G protein **(Gq)** activating it exactly as the β-adrenergic receptor activates Gs.

The activated Gq in turn activates a specific membrane-bound PLC, which catalyzes the production of the two second messengers **diacylglycerol** and **$IP_3$** by hydrolysis of phosphatidylinositol 4,5-bisphosphate in the plasma membrane.

**$IP_3$** a water-soluble compound, diffuses from the plasma membrane to the endoplasmic reticulum, where it binds to specific **$IP_3$ receptors and causes** $Ca^{2+}$ channels within the ER to open, $Ca^{2+}$ is thus released into the cytosol. One effect of elevated [$Ca^{2+}$] is the activation of **Protein kinase (PKC).**

**Diacylglycerol** cooperates with $Ca^{2+}$ in activating PKC, thus also acting as a second messenger. PKC phosphorylates Ser or Thr residues of specific target proteins, changing their catalytic activities.

***Calcium – Second Messenger:*** In many cells, $Ca^{2+}$ acts as as a second messenger that triggers intracellular responses, such as exocytosis in neurons and endocrine cells, contraction in muscle, and cytoskeletal rearrangement during amoeboid movement.

Normally, cytosolic [$Ca^{2+}$] is kept very low by the action of $Ca^{2+}$ pumps in the ER, mitochondria, and plasma membrane.

Hormonal, neural, or other stimuli causes either an influx of $Ca^{2+}$ into the cell through specific $Ca^{2+}$ channels in the plasma membrane or the release of sequestered $Ca^{2+}$ from the ER or mitochondria, in either case raising the cytosolic [$Ca^{2+}$] and triggering a cellular response.

Changes in intracellular [$Ca^{2+}$] are detected by $Ca^{2+}$- binding proteins that regulate a variety of $Ca^{2+}$- dependent enzymes.

**Calmodulin (CaM) (Mr 17,000) is protein with four high -** $Ca^{2+}$ binding sites. When intracellular [$Ca^{2+}$] rises, the binding of $Ca^{2+}$ to calmodulin leads to conformational change in the protein and bound state it modulates their activities of other proteins.

3. **Tyrosine Kinase-linked Receptors:** Tyrosine kinase -linked receptors are membrane bound receptors and contain an intrinsic enzymatic function (tyrosine kinase activity) in their intracellular domain. Upon combination with ligand like insulin, the receptor is activated and is able to phosphorylate tyrosine residues of other intracellular proteins. Protein phosphorylation is one of the underlying mechanisms of the regulation of protein function. E.g., Receptors for insulin and various cytokines and growth factors.

*Example:* Insulin Receptor .

The insulin receptor (Fig. 3.4) consists of two identical α chains protruding from the outer face of the plasma membrane and two transmembrane α subunits with their carboxyl termini protruding into the cytosol. The α chains contain the insulin binding domain, and the intracellular domains of the β chains contains the protein kinase activity that transfers a phosphoryl group from ATP to the hydroxyl group of Tyrosine residues in specific target proteins.

*In step 1,* binding of insulin to the chains activates the Tyrosine kinase activity of the β chains, and each αβ monomer phosphorylates three critical Tyr residues near the carboxyl terminus of the β of its partner in the dimer. This is known as autophosphorylation, opens up the active site so that the enzyme can phosphorylate Tyr residues of other target proteins.

*Step 2:* The target protein, insulin receptor substrate - 1 (IRS-1), Phosphorylated on its Tyr residues, IRS - 1 becomes the point of nucleation and that carry the message from

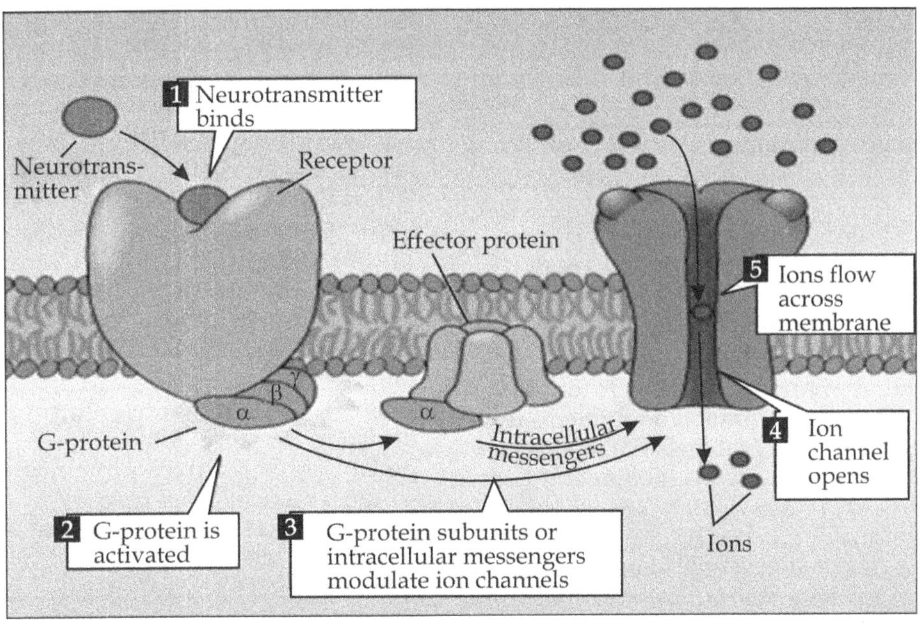


**Fig 3-3:** G protein coupled receptors

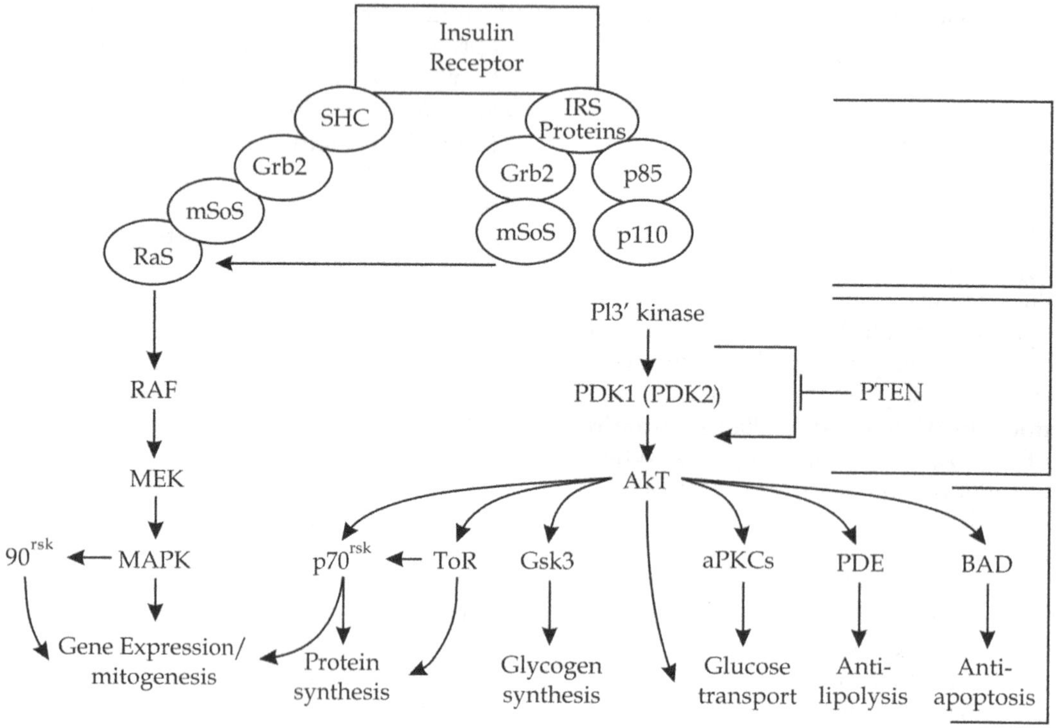


**Fig 3-4:** Insulin receptor

the insulin receptor to end targets in the cytosol and nucleus, through a long series of intermediate proteins.

*Step3:* At first, a P-Tyr residue in IRS-1 is bound by the $SH_2$ domain of the protein Growth factor receptor-bound protein 2 (Grb2).

A number of signalling proteins contain $SH_2$ domains, all of which bind P-Tyr residues in a protein partner.

The Grb2 also contains a second protein binding domains, $SH_3$, that binds to regions rich in Proline residues.

Grb2 binds to a Proline-rich region of Sos.

*Step4:* When bound to Grb2, Sos catalyzes the replacement of bund GDP by GTP on Ras, one of a family of guanosine nucleotide-binding, proteins (G proteins) that mediate a wide variety of signal transductions.

*Step5:* When GTP is bound, Ras can activate a protein kinase, Raf-1, MEK, Na ERK – that form a cascade in which each kinase activates the next byo phosphorylation.

*Step 6:* When activated, ERK mediates some of the biological effects of insulin by entering the nucleus and phosphorylating proteins such as ELK1, which modulates the transcription of insulin – regulated genes.

Extracellular Signal-Regulated Kinases (ERK) belong to MAPK family (mitogen-activated protein kinases involved in mitosis and cell division).

The MAPK, activated by another protein kinase, called MAP kinase kinase (MPKK) and again activated by another kinase, MAP kinase kinase kinase (MAPKKK).

The MAPK and MAPKKK families are specific for Ser or Thr residues, but MAPKKs ( here, MEk) Phosphorylate both a Ser and a Tyr residue in their substrate, a MAPK (here, ERK).

The target of phosphorylation is often another protein kinase, which then phosphorylates a third protein kinase, and so on. The result is a cascade of reactions that amplifies the initial signal by many orders of magnitude.

Cascades as discussed above are called MAPK cascades. Apart from Grb2 (see above), IRS-1 also associates with phosphoinositide

3- kinase (PI-3K) through $SH_2$ domain.

The activated, PI-3K converts the membrane lipid phosphatidylinositol 4,5-bisphosphate ( $PIP_2$) to phosphoinositide 3- kinase (PI-3K). The $PIP_3$ now associates with a protein kinase B ( PKB), phosphorylates it and activated by another protein kinase, $PDK_1$.

The activated PKB then phosphorylates Ser or Thr residues of glycogen synthase kinase 3 ($GSK_3$), in its active, non phosphorylated form, $GSK_3$ phosphorylates glycogen synthase, inactivating it and thereby contributing to the slowing of glycogen synthesis.

When phosphorylated by PKB, $GSK_3$ is inactivated. By thus preventing inactivation of glycogen synthase in liver and muscle the cascade of protein phosphorylates glycogen synthase, inactivating it and there by contributing to the slowing of glycogen synthesis.

In muscle, PKB triggers the movement of glucose transporters ( $GLUT_4$) from internal vesicles to the plasma membrane, stimulating glucose uptake from the blood.

PKB also triggered by $\Delta^9$ - tetrahydrocannabinol (THC) [active ingredient of marijuana and hashish] and activates the $CB_1$ receptor in the plasma membrane of neurons in the brain, triggering a signalling cascade that involves MAPKs. One consequence of $CB_1$ activation is the stimulation of appetite, one of the well - established effects of marijuana use.

*JAK-STAT System:* The erythropoietin (EPO), a 165 amino acid protein produced in the kidneys.

When EPO binds to its plasma membrane receptor, the receptor dimerizes and binds, activates a soluble protein kinase JAK ( Janus kinase).

The activated JAK, phosphorylates several Try residues in the cytoplasma domain of the EPO Receptor.

The STATs (signal transducers and activators of transcription) are family of transcription factors, also targets of the JAK kinase activity.

An $SH_2$ domain in $STAT_5$ binds P - Tyr residues in the EPO receptor positioning it for this phosphorylation by JAK.

The phosphoryalted $STAT_5$ undergo dimerisation, exposing a signal for its transport into the nucleus. There, $STAT_5$ causes the expression (transcription) of specific genes essential for **erythrocyte maturation.**

The similar JAK-STAT system operates in a number of other signalling pathways, including that for the hormone leptin.

Activated JAK can also trigger, through Grb2, the MAPK cascade, which leads to altered expression of specific genes.

Sre is another soluble protein Try kinase that associates with certain receptors when they bind their ligans. Sre was the first protein found to have the characteristic P -Tyr - binding domain that was subsequently named the **Sre homology ($SH_2$) domain**.

4. **Intracellular receptors regulating gene transcription:** Intracellular receptors regulating gene transcriptions, which are located in the cytosol. These are the receptors that are unique in the aspect that they are totally present inside the cell and they can only be activated by the ligands that can easily and considerably enter the cell membrane and reach the receptor. The ligand must have really good lipid solubility and it should also be non-ionized to enter the cells. Once the ligand enters the cell, it will attach with the receptor and do its required function. Function of these types of receptors is either to increase or to decreases the transcription and translation process in which the cells will produce proteins and DNA. The antibiotics like the aminoglycosides are used to decrease the growth of bacteria causing infection. These drugs enter the cells and cause the inhibition of cellular translation process.Upon binding of the appropriate chemical e.g. steroid hormones, the activated receptors translate to the nucleus and initiate gene transcription. These are also known as nuclear receptors. E.g., Receptors for steroid hormones, thyroid hormones and vitamin D.

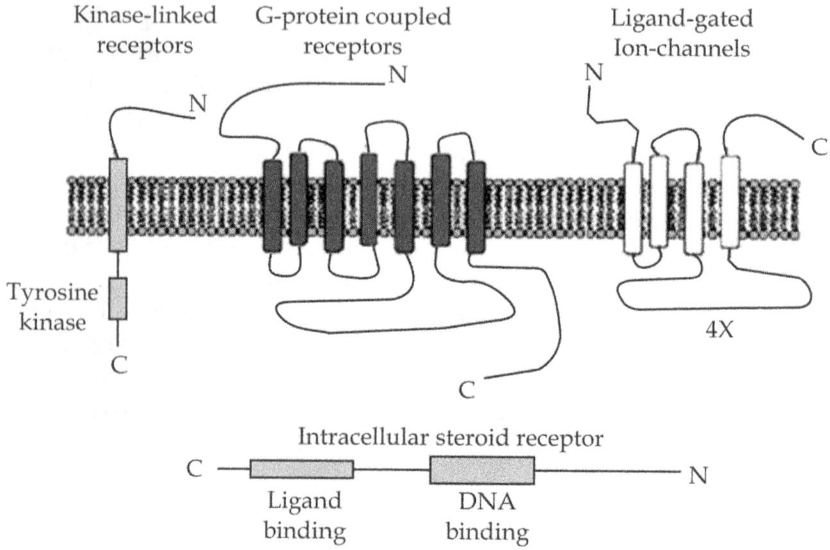


Schematic representation of the four major causes of receptor proteins. Except for the steroid receptors, the receptor proteins are localised in the cell membrane. The ligand-gated ion channels are made up of an assembly by 4–5 subunits, which each contain four transmembrane domains.

**Fig 3-5:** Types of receptors

**Table 3-1:** Properties of receptors

| Property | Ligand gated ion channels | GPCR G-protein coupled receptor | Enzyme linked receptors | Nucleic acid receptors |
|---|---|---|---|---|
| 1. Location | Membrane | Membrane | Membrane | Intracellular/ nucleus |
| 2. Site of drug Receptor interaction | Extracellular or intracellular | Extra or Intra cellular | Extracellular | Cytoplasm or nucleus |
| 3. Effector | Ion channel | Enzyme or Channel | Enzyme | Gene transcription |
| 4. Coupling | Direct | G-protein | Direct | Via DNA |
| 5. Time of response, Examples | Milliseconds nAchR, GABA, Glutamate, 5HT3 | Seconds Opiate, mAchR, 5HT, dopamine purine | Minutes Insulin, ANF, growth factor receptors | Hours Steroid thyroid retinoic acid receptors |
| 6. Structure | Oligomeric subunits | Monomeric having seven transmembrane helices | Single transmembrance helix | Monomeric structure and DNA binding domains |

## Drug Receptor Interactions

Majority of drugs show remarkably high correlation of structure and specificity to produce pharmacological effects. A minimum three-point attachment of a drug to a receptor site is required. In most cases specific chemical structure is required for the receptor site and a complementary drug structure. Slight changes in the molecular structure of the drug may drastically change specificity. To initiate a biological response, the drug must form bond with the receptor surface. Different types of binding forces that may exist in drug-receptor interactions are as follows:

**(i) Covalent interactions:** These chemical forces may result in a temporary binding of the drug to the receptor. Frequently, a covalent bond is firm and described as essentially "irreversible" under biological conditions. Since by definition the drug-receptor interaction is reversible, covalent bond formation is rather rare except in a toxic situation. Examples:

(a) A covalent bond is formed between the activated form of phenoxybenzamine (α-adrenergic receptor antagonist)

(b) Antineoplastic or antibiotic drugs act mainly through the formation of covalent bonds

(c) The DNA-Alkylating chemotherapeutic agents are chemically highly reactive, forming covalent bonds with DNA functional groups. Such covalently modified DNA may be incompatible with successful tumor cell division

**(ii) Ionic interactions:** Since many drugs contain acid or amine functional groups,

Which are ionized at physiological pH. Ionic bonds are formed by the attraction of opposite charges in the receptor site with the ionized groups of the drug molecule. They are strong electrostatic interactions (5-10 kcal/mol) and are responsible for relative orientation of the drug to its binding site. Electrostatic interactions tend to be much more common than the covalent bonding in drug-receptor interactions. Attraction between ions of opposite charge is inversely proportional to the square of the distance between them. Strong electrostatic interactions occur between permanently charged ionic molecules. The overall contribution of ionic interactions may be overemphasized due to desolvation. Ionic bonds have a relatively high stability.

*E.g.:* In acetylcholine molecule, the positively charged quaternary nitrogen may be attracted to the negative charged ionized carboxyl group present in the receptor site.

**(iii) Hydrogen bonding interactions (non-ionic/neutral):** Polar-polar interactions are the attraction of opposite charges. The drug-receptor reaction is essentially an exchange of the hydrogen bond between a drug molecule, surrounding water, and the receptor site. The hydrogen bond strength is distance dependent may range from 5 - 7 kcal/mol, depending on the binding environment.

**(iv) Vander Waals interaction:** These forces have the following characteristic features:

(a) Interactions at a close range

(b) The van der Waals interaction forces occur less frequently than hydrophobic forces

(c) Interactions are much weaker (~ 0.5-1 kcal/mol) than other electrostatic interactions

(d) Close contacts (attractive forces) over a large surface area i.e., at the interface of ligand and binding site, may contribute to binding

**(v) Hydrophobic/Lipophilic interactions:** Finally hydrophobic bonds are formed between non-polar hydrocarbon groups on the drug and those in the receptor site. These bonds are not very specific but the interactions do occur to exclude water molecules. Most of the drug molecules have a non-polar portion (alkyl or aryl groups) which may combine with non-polar portion of the receptor site through hydrophobic forces. Hydrophobic interactions are generally weak, but important. Hydrophobic interactions are probably significant in driving interactions

(a) Between lipophilic drugs and the lipid component of biological membranes

(b) Between drugs and relatively nonpolar (non charged) receptor regions

## Receptor Site Theories

After attachment of drug molecule to a receptor site, a drug may either initiate a response or prevent a response from occurring. This concept can be easily understood if one considers the 'lock-and-key' principle for ligand–receptor interaction. Only keys (Ligands) that fulfil all criteria for fitting into the lock (receptor) can open the door (produce an effect). Some keys can fit in the lock but not perfectly, consequently they cannot open the door yet. By fitting into the lock, these keys prevent the original key from fitting into the lock and opening the door. The concept of receptor antagonism is extremely important in medicinal chemistry and is very often the underlying mechanism of drug action e.g., to prevent the constriction of airway smooth muscle in asthmatic conditions one can administer receptor antagonists that prevent the actions of the signalling molecules causing muscle contraction (e.g., histamine and leukotriene antagonists) effects.

(i) **Occupation theory:** In fact, similar mathematical models have been applied to the receptor–ligand interaction. Clark's occupation theory was the first model that could describe the observations of drug action on isolated tissues. In this theory the receptor–ligand interaction is considered to be a bimolecular interaction, in which the receptor–ligand complex is responsible for the generation of the biological effect. Clark assumed that the effects of a drug were proportional to the fraction of receptors occupied by the drug. Consequently, for a maximal effect the drug has to occupy all receptors. In Clark's theory, the agonist (A) interacts in a reversible way with the receptor (R) and the formed complex (AR) gives rise to the effect:

$$A + R \rightleftharpoons AR \rightarrow \text{effect}$$

In equilibrium, the rate of the forward reaction of an agonist A reversibly bound to its receptor R is proportional to the concentration of A and R, and the proportionality constant is denoted by $k_1$

Rate of association $= k_1[A][R]$

Similarly, the rate of the backward reaction, in which the agonist–receptor complex dissociates again, is proportional to the concentration of the AR complex

Rate of dissociation $= k_2\,[AR]$

At equilibrium the rate of the forward reaction equals the rate at which existing AR complexes dissociate i.e., $k_1[A][R] = k_2[AR]$. In other words, within a certain period of time the same number of molecules A will bind to and dissociate from the receptor. At equilibrium the dissociation constant K can be described as follows:

$$K = \frac{k_1}{k_2} = \frac{[A][R]}{[AR]}$$

(ii) **Rate theory:** Rate theory was proposed by Paton and Rang in 1965. According to this theory the most important factor in determining drug action is the rate at which drug receptor combination takes place. The rate theory can be explained by the formula:

$$\text{Rate of receptor occupation} = \frac{k_2}{1 + \frac{KA}{[A]}}$$

(iii) **Induced-fit theory:** This theory states that after combination, the substrate induces a change in conformation of the enzyme, leading to an enzymatically active orientation of groups. E.g.: Acetylcholine may interact with the regulating protein and alter the normal forces. Macromolecular perturbation theory and activation-aggregation theories are the extension of induced fit theory.

Pharmacodynamics starts where pharmacokinetics left off – it assumes that the drug has managed to reach its target, and looks at the principles that govern the interaction between the two. Almost all drugs will trigger their effects by binding to a receptor. In physiology, the term 'receptor' is limited to the sites of action of hormones, neurotransmitters or cytokines. While many drugs do indeed bind to such receptors, in pharmacology the term is used in a more inclusive sense and is applied to other targets such as enzymes and Cytoskeletal proteins as well.

## Pharmacodynamics

Involves how the drugs act on target cells to alter cellular function.

A. **Receptor and non-receptor mechanisms:** Most of the drugs act by interacting with a cellular component called receptor. Some drugs act through simple physical or chemical reactions without interacting with any receptor.

   1. Receptors are protein molecules present either on the cell surface or within the cell e.g., adrenergic receptors, cholinoceptors, insulin receptors, etc.
   2. The endogenous neurotransmitters, hormones, autacoids and most of the drugs produce their effects by binding with their specific receptors.
   3. Aluminium hydroxide and magnesium trisilicate, which are used in the treatment of peptic ulcer disease act by non-receptor mechanism by neutralizing the gastric acid. Many drugs are similar to or have similar chemical groups to the naturally occurring chemical and have the ability to bind onto a receptor where one of two things can happen- either the receptor will respond or it will be blocked.

A drug, which is able to fit onto a receptor, is said to have affinity for that receptor. Efficacy is the ability of a drug to produce an effect at a receptor. An agonist has both an affinity and efficacy whereas antagonist has affinity but not efficacy or intrinsic activity. When a drug is able to stimulate a receptor, it is known as an agonist and therefore mimics the endogenous transmitter.

When the drug blocks a receptor, it is known as antagonist and therefore blocks the action of the endogenous transmitter (i.e., it will prevent the natural chemical from acting on the receptor).

However, as most drug binding is reversible, there will be competition between the drug and the natural stimulus to the receptor.

The forces that attract the drug to its receptor are termed chemical bonds and they are (a) hydrogen bond (b) ionic bond (c) covalent bond (d) van der Waals force. Covalent bond is the strongest bond and the drug-receptor complex is usually irreversible.

$$D + R \underset{K_2}{\overset{K_1}{\rightleftharpoons}} DR \xrightarrow{K_3} \text{Biological effect}$$

Where

D = Drug

R = Receptor

DR = Drug receptor complex (affinity)

$K_1$ = Association constant

$K_2$ = Dissociation constant

$K_3$ = Intrinsic activity

When first messengers like neurotransmitters, hormones, autacoids and most of drugs bind with their specific receptors, the drug receptor complex is formed which subsequently causes the synthesis and release of another intracellular regulatory molecule termed as second messengers e.g., cyclic AMP, calcium, cyclic GMP, inositol triphosphate (IP3), diacylglycerol and calmodulin which in turn produce subcellular or molecular mechanism of drug action.

B. **Site of drug action:**

   - A drug may act:

   1. Extracellularly e.g.: Osmotic diuretics, plasma expanders.
   2. On the cell surface e.g.: Digitalis, penicillin, catecholamines.

3. Inside the cell e.g.: Anti-cancer drugs, steroid hormones.

C. **Dose response relationship:** The exact relationship between the dose and the response depends on the biological object under observation and the drug employed.

When a logarithm of dose as abscissa and responses as ordinate are constructed graphically, the "S" shaped or sigmoid type curve is obtained (Fig. 3-6).

The lowest concentration of a drug that elicits a response is minimal dose, and the largest concentration after which further increase in concentration will not change the response is the maximal dose.

1. ***Graded dose effect:*** As the dose administered to a single subject or tissue increases, the pharmacological response also increases in graded fashion up to ceiling effect.

- It is used for characterization of the action of drugs. The concentration that is required to produce 50% of the maximum effect is termed as $EC_{50}$ or $ED_{50}$.

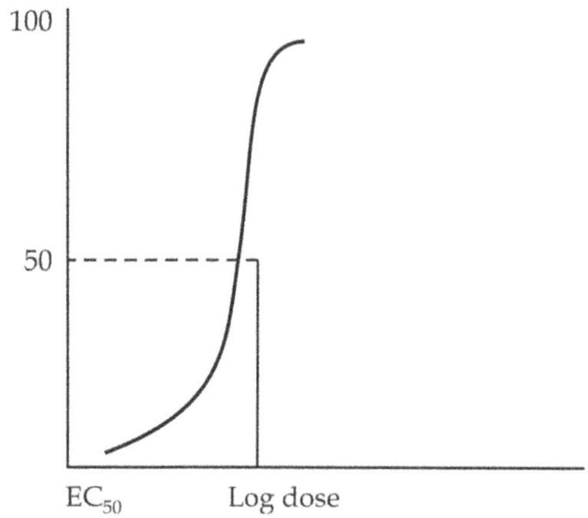


**Fig 3-6:** Log dose response relationship

2. ***Quantal dose effect:*** It is all or none response, the sensitive objects give response to small doses of a drug while some will be resistant and need very large doses. The quantal dose effect curve is often characterized by stating the median effective dose and the median lethal dose.

***Median lethal dose or $LD_{50}$:*** This is the dose (mg/kg), which would be expected to kill one half of a population of the same species and strain.

***Median effective dose or $ED_{50}$:*** This is the dose (mg/kg), which produces a desired response in 50% of test population.

***Therapeutic index:*** It is an approximate assessment of the safety of the drug. It is the ratio of the median lethal dose and the median effective dose. Also called as therapeutic window or safety.

Therapeutic index (T. I) = The larger the therapeutic index, the safer is the drug. Penicillin has a very high therapeutic index, while it is much smaller for the digitalis preparation.

D. **Structural activity relationship:** The activity of a drug is intimately related to its chemical structure. Knowledge about the chemical structure of a drug is useful for:

Synthesis of new compounds with more specific actions and fewer adverse reactions

Synthesis of competitive antagonist and understanding the mechanism of drug action.

Slight modification of structure of the compound can change the effect completely.

1. ***Synthesis of new compounds***

(a) To increase or decrease the duration of action of the original drug or to get a more parent compound.

- Tetracaine was found to be fifty times more active than Procaine.This marked and pronounced potentiation of local anaesthetic profile offered by tetracaine may be attributed to the distinct electron releasing activity of the n-butyl function *via* the inductive effect,the preferrentially increase in the prevailing electron density of the para amino moiety, which subsequently enhances the creation of the resonance form readily available for enabling to get bound to the viable receptor proteins. So it is easily absorbed than procaine.

For the above reasons Tetracaine has quick onset of action and less duration of action compared to Procaine which has low onset of action and more duration of action.

- The diuretics Polythiazide and bendroflumethiazide are as effective as the parent compound, Chlorthiazide, in which smaller doses.
- Thiobarbiturates has quick onset of action compared to other barbiturates due to the presence of Sulphur atom on 2nd carbon of thiobarbiturate so the lipophilicity increases and produces quick onset of action.

(b) To restrict the drug action to a particular system of the body

- Chlorpromazine has pharmacological actions such as antipsychotic, anticholinergic (extrapyramidal side effects), sedative and hypotensive. By structural modifications of the chlorpromazine molecule, compounds have been synthesized which have a more potent antipsychotic effect but less extrapyramidal side effects. E.g., Clozapine.

(c) To reduce the adverse reactions, and other disadvantages associated with the available drugs.

- Ketoconazole used in the treatment of fungal infections may produce Gyanacomastia, several drug interactions. A related compound Flucanozole has the same efficacy against fungal infections but does not produce Gyanacomastia and drug interactions.

2. *Synthesis of competitive antagonists*
   - Folic acid is an important substituent in the synthesis of DNA. Methotrexate which shows a structural similarity to Folic acid probably acts by competing with it for the binding of dihydrofolate reductase (DHFR). Non availability of DHFR to folic acid and arrests the synthesis of DNA.
3. ***Understanding the basic chemical groups responsible for drug action***
   - Adrenaline stimulates both $\alpha_1$ and $\alpha_2$ adrenergic receptors. A related compound, Noradrenaline selectively stimulates the beta adrenergic receptors while a very closely similar compound Propranolol blocks the beta adrenergic receptors.
   - Halogenated Sulphomoyl group present on the benzene ring was responsible for causing diuretic effect of Furosemide.
4. ***Based on isomerism the pharmacological activity also changed***
   - Quinidine and Quinine were stereoisomer's where Quinidine has antiarrythmic effect and quinine has antimalarial effect.

## References

Allesteros J. A, Jensen A. D, Liapakis G, Rasmussen S. G, Shi L, Gether U and Javitch J. A (2001). Activation of the beta 2-adrenergic receptor involves disruption of an ionic lock between the cytoplasmic ends of transmembrane segments 3 and 6. *J. Biol. Chem.* **276:** 29171-29177.

Arteaga CL, Moulder SL, Yakes FM (2002). HER (erbB) tyrosine kinase inhibitors in the treatment of breast cancer. *Semin Oncol* **29:** 4.

Berridge MJ, Bootman MD, Roderick HL (2003). Calcium signalling: Dynamics, homeostasis and remodelling. *Nat Rev Mol Cell Biol* **4:** 517.

Bhatnagar A, Willins D. L, Gray J. A, Woods J, Benovic J. L and Roth B. L (2001). The dynamin-dependent, arrestin-independent internalization of 5-hydroxytryptamine 2A (5-HT2A) serotonin receptors reveals differential sorting of arrestins and 5-HT2A receptors during endocytosis. *J. Biol. Chem.* **276:** 8269-8277.

Bockaert J, Marin P, Dumuis A and Fagni L (2003). The 'magic tail' of G protein-coupled receptors: an anchorage for functional protein networks. *FEBS Lett.* **546:** 65-72.

Cabrera-Vera TM *et al.*, (2003). Insights into G protein structure, function, and regulation. *Endocr Rev* **24:** 765.

Civelli O (2005). GPCR deorphanizations: The novel, the known and the unexpected transmitters. *Trends Pharmacol Sci* **26:** 15.

Dancey JE (2004). Predictive factors for epidermal growth factor receptor inhibitors - The bull's-eye hits the arrow. *Cancer Cell* **5:** 411.

Derynck R, Akhurst RJ, Balmain A (2001). TGF-beta signaling in tumor suppression and cancer progression. *Nat Genet* **29:** 117.

Ginty DD, Segal RA (2002). Retrograde neurotrophin signaling: Trk-ing along the axon. *Curr Opin Neurobiol* **12:** 268.

Gouaux E, MacKinnon R (2005). Principles of selective ion transport in channels and pumps. *Science* **310:** 1461.

CHAPTER

# Drug Biotransformation

4

## Introduction

Biotransformation of drug is defined as **"the conversion from one chemical form to another"**. The term is used synonymously with **metabolism**.

**Xenobiotics:** All chemical substances that are not nutrients for the body and enter the body through ingestion, inhalation, or absorption are called xenobiotics.

**Biotransformation leads to**
**Pharmacologic Inactivation of Drug**

**E.g: Active Drug → Inactive Drug**

Salicylic Acid → Salicyluric Acid

**Active Metabolite from an Inactive Drug**

**E.g: Inactive (Prodrug) → Active**

Aspirin → Salicylic Acid

**No Change in Pharmacologic Activity**

**E.g: Active → Active Drug**

Codeine → Morphine

Isoniazid → Iproniazid

## Sites of Drug Metabolism

Xenobiotic metabolizing enzymes are found in most tissues in the body with the highest levels located in the tissues of the gastrointestinal tract (liver, small and large intestines). Drugs that are orally administered, absorbed by the gut, and taken to the liver, can be extensively metabolized. The liver is considered the major "metabolic clearing house" for both endogenous chemicals (e.g., cholesterol, steroid hormones, fatty acids, and proteins), and xenobiotics. The small intestine plays a crucial role in drug metabolism since most drugs that are orally administered are absorbed by the gut and taken to the liver through the portal vein. The high concentration of xenobiotic metabolizing enzymes located in the epithelial cells of the GI tract is responsible for the initial metabolic processing of most oral medications. This should be considered the initial site for first pass metabolism of drugs. The absorbed drug then enters the portal circulation for its first pass through the liver, where metabolism may be prominent, as it is for adrenergic receptor antagonists, for example. While a portion of active drug escapes this first-pass metabolism in the GI tract and liver, subsequent passes through the liver result in more metabolism of the parent drug until the agent is eliminated. Thus, drugs that are poorly metabolized remain in the body for longer periods of time and their pharmacokinetic profiles show much longer elimination half-lives than drugs that are rapidly metabolized. Other organs that contain significant xenobiotic-metabolizing enzymes include the tissues of the nasal mucosa and lung, which play important roles in the first-pass metabolism of drugs that are administered through aerosol sprays. These tissues are also the first line of contact with hazardous chemicals that are airborne. Within the cell, xenobiotic-metabolizing enzymes are found in the intracellular membranes and in the cytosol. The phase 1 CYPs, FMOs, and EHs, and some phase 2 conjugating enzymes, notably the UGTs, are all located in the endoplasmic reticulum of the cell. The endoplasmic reticulum consists of phospholipid bilayers organized as tubes and sheets throughout the cytoplasm of the cell. This network has an inner lumen that is physically distinct from the rest of the cytosolic components of the cell and has connections to the plasma membrane and nuclear envelope. This membrane localization is ideally suited for the metabolic function of these enzymes: hydrophobic molecules enter the cell and become embedded in the lipid bilayer where they come into direct contact with the phase I enzymes. Once subjected to oxidation, drugs can be conjugated in the membrane by the UGTs or by the cytosolic transferases such as GST and SULT. Then the metabolites can be transported out of the cell through the plasma membrane where they are deposited into the bloodstream. Hepatocytes, which constitute more than 90% of the cells in the liver, carry out most drug metabolism and can produce conjugated substrates that can also be transported though the bile canalicular membrane into the bile from which they are eliminated into the gut.

## Drug Metabolizing Enzymes

**Microsomal:** Found predominately in the smooth endoplasmic reticulum of liver.

**Other areas:** Kidney, Lungs, Intestinal mucosa

**Undergone reactions:**

Non-synthetic/Phase I reactions

Most oxidation and reduction

Some hydrolysis

Synthetic/Phase II reactions

Only Glucuronide conjugation

**Non - Microsomal:** Found in the cytoplasm and mitochondria of hepatic cells.

Other tissues including plasma.

**Undergone reactions:**

Non-synthetic/Phase I reactions

Mostly hydrolysis

Some oxidation and reduction

Synthetic/Phase II reactions

All except Glucuronide conjugation

**Need for biotransformation:** Most drugs are excreted by the kidneys.

**For renal excretion drugs should:**

Have small molecular mass

Be polar in nature

Not be fully ionised at body pH

Most drugs are complex and do not have these properties and thus have to be broken down to simpler products.

Drugs are lipophilic in nature.

Strongly bound to plasma proteins.

This property also stops them from getting eliminated.

They have to be converted to simpler hydrophilic compounds so that they are eliminated and their action is terminated.

Biotransformation occurs between absorption and elimination from kidneys.

Drugs administered orally can biotransform in the intestinal wall.

**Classification of Biotransformation:** These are classified into two types:

Phase I

Phase II

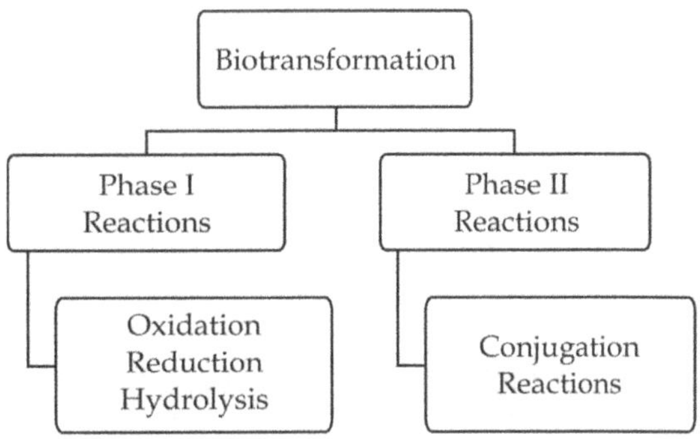


**Fig 4-1:** Classification of Biotransformation

**Phase I:** A polar functional group is either introduced or unmasked if already present on the otherwise lipid soluble substrate Fig 4-2.

E.g. -OH, -COOH, $-NH_2$ and -SH.

Thus, phase I reactions are called as **functionalization reactions**.

Phase I reactions are Non-synthetic in nature.

The majority of phase I metabolites are generated by a common hydroxylating enzyme system known as Cytochrome P450.

**Phase II:** Phase II - combines functional group of compound with endogenous substance.

E.g., Glucuronicacid, Sulfuric acid, Amino Acid, Acetyl.

Products usually very hydrophilic.

Phase II reactions are synthetic in nature.

The final compounds have a larger molecular weight.

## Phase I Reactions

1. **Oxidative reactions:** Oxidation of aromatic carbon atoms.

   Oxidation of olefins.

   Oxidation of benzylic, allylic carbon atoms and carbon atoms alpha to carbonyl and imines.

   Oxidation of aliphatic carbon atoms.

   Oxidation of alicylic carbon atoms.

   Oxidation of carbon – heteroatom systems.

   Carbon – nitrogen systems.

   N-Dealkylation.

**Phase 1** (addition or uncovering of a reactive group)

- Oxidation
- Reduction
- Hydrolysis

→ Makes the molecule more susceptible to Phase 2 reactions

**Phase 2** (conjugation of endogenous molecule with drug)

- Glucuronide
- Sulphate
- Amino acids, GSH
- Acetylation/methylation

→ Makes the molecule more polar, ideal substrates for active transport, and excretion

**Fig 4 -2:** Phase I and Phase II reactions

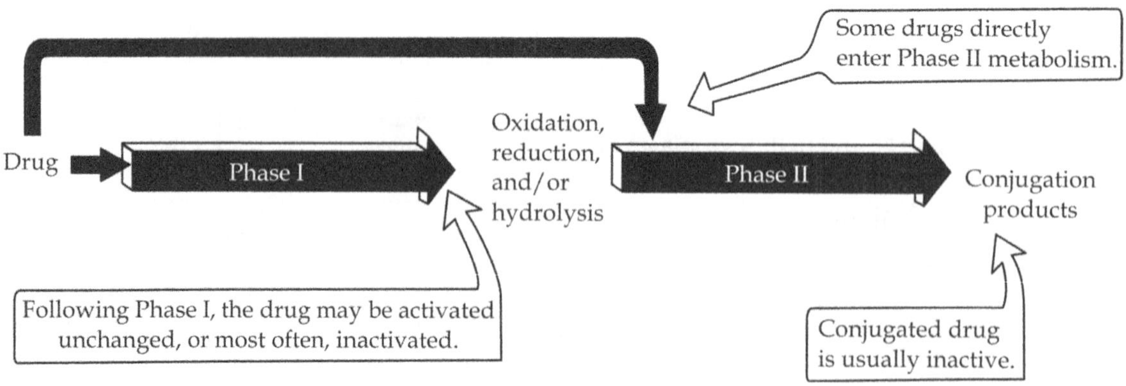


**Fig 4-3:** Drug biotransformation

Oxidative deamination.

N-Oxide formation.

N-Hydroxylation.

*Carbon-sulfur systems*:

S-dealkylation.

Desulfuration.

S- oxidation.

*Sulfur- Oxygen systems*:

Oxidation of alcohol, carboxyl and carboxylic acid.

Miscellaneous oxidative reactions.

2. **Reductive reactions:** Reduction of carbonyl functions (Aldehydes and Ketones).

   Reduction of alcohols and Carbon-Carbon double bonds.

   Reduction of N-compounds (nitro and azo N-oxide).

   Miscellaneous reductive reactions.

3. **Hydrolytic reactions:**Hydrolysis of esters and ethers.

   Hydrolysis of amides (C-N cleanage).

   Hydrolytic cleavage of non aromatic heterocycles.

   Hydrolytic dehalogenation.

   Miscellaneous hydedytic reactions

   - Alkylation (Methylation)
   - Dealkylation
   - Ring cyclization
   - N-carboxylation
   - Dimerization

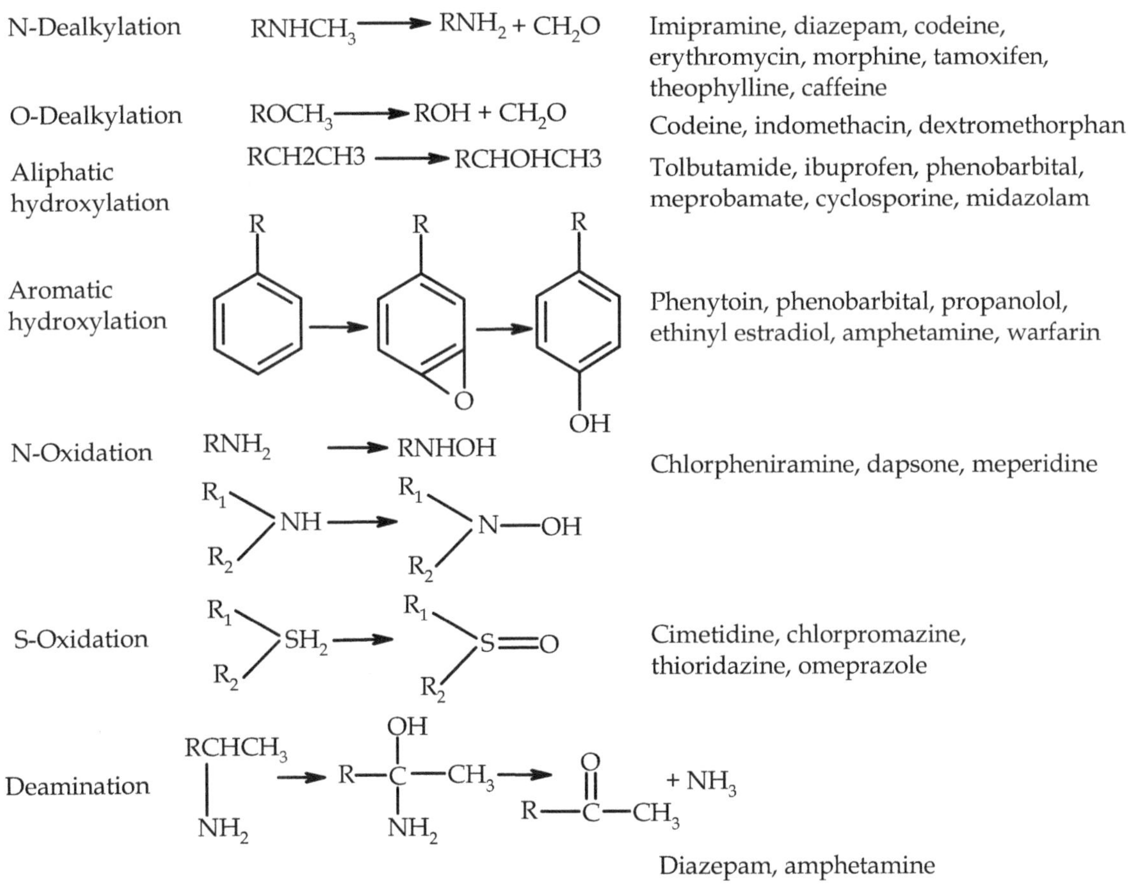


**Fig 4 -4:** Oxidative reactions

Isomerization
Decarboxylation

## Oxidative Reactions

Two types of oxidation reactions:

1. Oxygen is incorporated into the drug molecule (e.g., Hydroxylation)
2. Oxidation causes the loss of part of the drug molecule

(E.g., oxidative deamination, Dealkylation)

***Microsomal Mixed Function Oxidases (MFOs):***

"Microsomes" form *in vitro* after cell homogenization and fractionation of ER.

Rough microsomes are primarily associated with protein synthesis.

Smooth microsomes contain a class of oxidative enzymes called "Mixed Function Oxidases" or "Monooxygenases".

These enzymes require a reducing agent (NADPH) and molecular oxygen (one oxygen atom appearing in the product and the other in the form of water).

**MFO consists of two enzymes:** Flavoproteins, NADPH-cytochrome c reductase. One mole of this enzyme contains one mole each of flavin mononucleotide (FMN) and flavin adenine dinucleotide (FAD), Enzyme is also called NADPH-cytochrome P450 reductase.

**Cytochrome P450**

Named based on its light absorption at 450 nm and it emits pink color when complexed with carbon monoxide. Is a haemoprotein containing an iron atom which can alternate between the ferrous ($Fe^{++}$) and ferric ($Fe^{+++}$) states.

**Electron acceptor**

***Serves as terminal oxidase:*** Its relative abundance compared to NADPH-cytochrome P450 reductase makes it the rate-limiting step in the oxidation reactions.

**Cytochromes**

The CYPs are a superfamily of enzymes, all of which contain a molecule of heme that is noncovalently bound to the polypeptide chain. Many other enzymes that use $O_2$ as a substrate for their reactions contain heme. Heme is the oxygen-binding moiety, also found in hemoglobin, where it functions in the binding and transport of molecular oxygen from the lung to other tissues. Heme contains one atom of iron in a hydrocarbon cage that functions to bind oxygen in the CYP active site as part of the catalytic cycle of these enzymes. CYPs use $O_2$, plus $H^+$ derived from the cofactor-reduced nicotinamide adenine dinucleotide phosphate (NADPH), to carry out the oxidation of substrates. The H is supplied through the enzyme NADPH-cytochrome P450 oxidoreductase. Metabolism of a substrate by a CYP consumes one molecule of molecular oxygen and produces an oxidized substrate and a molecule of water as a by-product. However, for most CYPs, depending on the nature of the substrate, the reaction is "uncoupled", consuming more $O_2$ than substrate metabolized and producing what is called activated oxygen or $O_2^-$. The $O_2^-$ is usually converted to water by the enzyme superoxide dismutase. Among the diverse reactions carried out by mammalian CYPs are *N* -dealkylation, *O* -dealkylation, aromatic hydroxylation, *N*-oxidation, *S*-oxidation, deamination, and dehalogenation. More than 50 individual CYPs have been identified in humans. As a family of enzymes, CYPs are involved in the metabolism of dietary and xenobiotic agents, as well as the synthesis of endogenous compounds such as steroids and the metabolism of bile acids, which are degradation by-products of cholesterol. In contrast to the drug-metabolizing CYPs, the CYPs that catalyze steroid and bile acid synthesis have very specific substrate preferences. For example, the CYP that produces estrogen from testosterone, CYP19 or aromatase, can metabolize only testosterone and does not metabolize xenobiotics. Specific inhibitors for aromatase, such as anastrozole, have been developed for use in the treatment of estrogen-dependent tumors. The synthesis of bile acids from cholesterol occurs in the liver, where, subsequent to CYP-catalyzed oxidation, the bile acids are conjugated and transported through the bile duct and gallbladder into the small intestine. CYPs involved in bile acid production have strict substrate requirements and do not participate in xenobiotic or drug metabolism. The CYPs that carry out xenobiotic metabolism have a tremendous capacity to metabolize a large number of structurally diverse chemicals. This is due both to multiple forms of CYPs and to the capacity of a single CYP to metabolize many structurally distinct chemicals. A single compound can also be metabolized, albeit at different rates, by different CYPs. In addition, CYPs can metabolize a single compound at different positions on the molecule. In contrast to enzymes in the body that carry out highly specific reactions involved in the biosynthesis and degradation of important cellular constituents in which there is a single substrate and one or more products, or two simultaneous substrates, the CYPs are considered promiscuous in their capacity to bind and metabolize multiple substrates. This property, which is due to large and fluid substrate binding sites in the CYP, sacrifices metabolic turnover rates; CYPs metabolize substrates at a fraction of the rate of more typical enzymes involved in intermediary metabolism and mitochondrial electron transfer. As a result, drugs have, in general, half lives of the order of 3 to 30 hours, while endogenous compounds have half-lives of the order of seconds or minutes (dopamine and insulin). Even though CYPs have slow catalytic rates, their activities are sufficient to metabolize drugs that are administered at high concentrations in the body. This unusual feature of extensive overlapping substrate specificities by the CYPs is one of the underlying reasons for the predominance of drug-drug interactions. When two coadministered drugs are both metabolized by a single CYP, they compete for binding to the enzyme's active site. This can result in the inhibition of metabolism of one or both of the drugs, leading to elevated plasma levels. If there is a narrow therapeutic index for the drugs, the elevated serum levels may elicit unwanted toxicities.

**Drug oxidation requires:** Cytochrome P450

Cytochrome P450 reductase

NADPH

Molecular oxygen

The cycle involves four steps (Fig 4-5):

1. Oxidized ($Fe^{3+}$) cytochrome P-450 combines with a drug substrate to form a binary complex.
2. NADPH donates an electron to the cytochrome P-450 reductase, which in turn reduces the oxidized cytochrome P-450-drug complex.
3. A second electron is introduced from NADPH *via* the same cytochrome P-450 reductase, which serves to reduce molecular

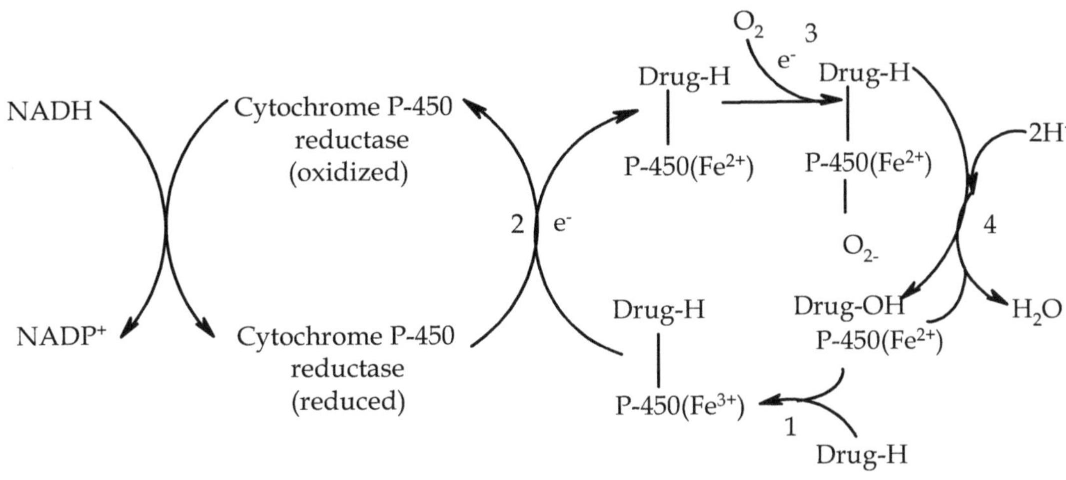


**Fig 4-5:** Cytochrome P450 oxidation reduction cycle

oxygen and forms "activated oxygen-cytochrome P-450-substrate complex".

4. This complex in turn transfers "activated oxygen" to the drug substrate to form the oxidized product. The potent oxidizing properties of this activated oxygen permit oxidation of a large number of substrates.

**Oxidation of aromatic carbon atoms:** Mono substituted benzene derivatives can be hydroxylated at ortho meta or para positions but para hydroxylated product is most common.

*Example*: Conversion of Acetanilide to Paracetamol.

**Oxidation of olefins:** Non aromatic C=C is analogous to aromatic.

Hydroxylation that is it proceeds via formation of epoxides to 1,2 dihydrodiols.

*Example*: Carbamazepine → Carbamazepine 11 epoxide → trans10, 11-dihydroxy carbamazepine.

**Oxidation of Benzylic carbon atoms:** Drug is oxidised to aldehydes and then to carboxylic acids.

*Example*:

Tolbutamide → Primary carbinol → Corresponding aldehyde + corresponding carboxylic acid.

Secondary carbonyl is converted to ketones.

**Oxidation of Aliphatic carbon atoms:** Alkyl or aliphatic carbon atoms can be hydroxylated at two positions at a terminal methyl group called α- Oxidation and the penultimate carbon atoms called as β-1 oxidation.

*Example*: Ibuprofen.

**Oxidation of alicylic carbon atoms:** Cyclohexane and piperidine rings are commonly found in number of molecules.

*Example*: Acetohexamide.

Minoxidil.

Such rings are generally hydroxylated at c-3 positions or c-4 positions .

**Oxidation of carbon-heteroatom system:** Bio transformation of C-N, C-O and C-S systems proceeds in one of the two ways

**Hydroxylation:** Hydroxylation of carbon atom attached to the heteroatom and subsequence cleavage at carbon hetero atom bond.

*Example*: N-, O-, and S- dealkylation, oxidative deamination and desulfuration.

**Oxidation:** Oxidation of the heteroatom itself.

*Example:* N- and S- oxidation

**Oxidative of carbon nitrogen systems :** N-dealkylation see in Fig 4-6.

Alkyl groups attached directly to nitrogen atom in nitrogen bearing compounds are capable of undergoing N- alkylation reactions

*Example:* Secondary and tertiary aliphatic and aromatic amines, tertiary alicylic amines and N- substituted amides and hydrazines.

Imipramine

Hexobarbitol

Diazepam

**Oxidative Deamination see in Fig 4-7**

Like N- dealkylation, these reactions also proceed, *via* the carbinolamine pathways but

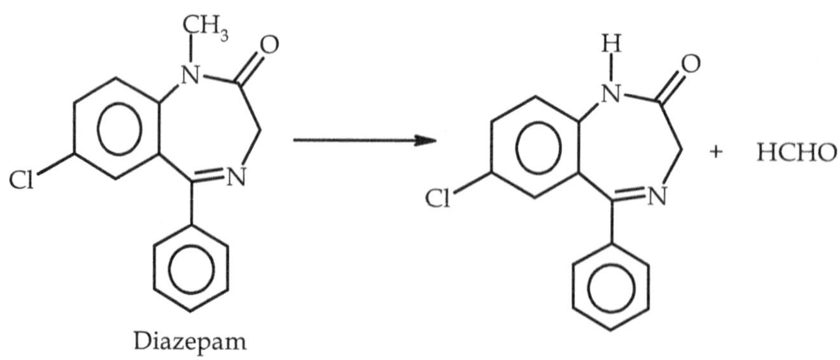


**Fig 4-6:** N- dealkylation of diazepam

Amphetamine

**Fig 4-7:** Oxidative deamination of Amphetamine

here the C-N bond cleavage occurs at the bond that links amino group to the larger portion of the drug molecule.

*Example*: Primary aliphatic amines

Amphetamine

Secondary and tertiary amines

Propranolol

**N-oxide formation**

N- oxides are formed only by nitrogen atoms having basic properties. Thus amines can form N- oxides amides cannot generally the tertiary amines yield, N- oxides.

*Example*: Nicotine

Trimethoprim

**N- hydroxylation**

Converse to basic compound that form N- oxides N- hydroxyl formation is usually displayed by non basic nitrogen atoms such as amide nitrogen

*Example*: Lidocaine

**Oxidation of carbon sulpur systems:** S- dealkylation.

The mechanism of S- dealkylation (Fig 4-8) of thio ether is analogues to N- dealkylation. That is it proceeds *via* α- carbon hydroxylation

*Example*: 6-methyl mercaptopurine

**Desulfuration**

This reaction also involves cleavage of carbon sulpur bond [C=S] .It also occurs with compound containing P=S bonds such as the organo phosphate pesticides.

*Example*: Parathion

**S- oxidation**

It can oxidized to sulfones [ $RSO_2S$ ] several phenothiazines.

**Example:** Chlorpromazine, undergo S- oxidation.

**Oxidation of carbon oxygen systems:** O- dealkylation Fig 4-9:

This reaction is similar to N- alkylation to form unstable hemiacetal or hemiketal intermediate undergoes C-O bond cleavage to form alcohol and carbonyl moiety.

*Example*: Phenacetin to Paracetamol

Codeine to Morphine

S-dealkylation

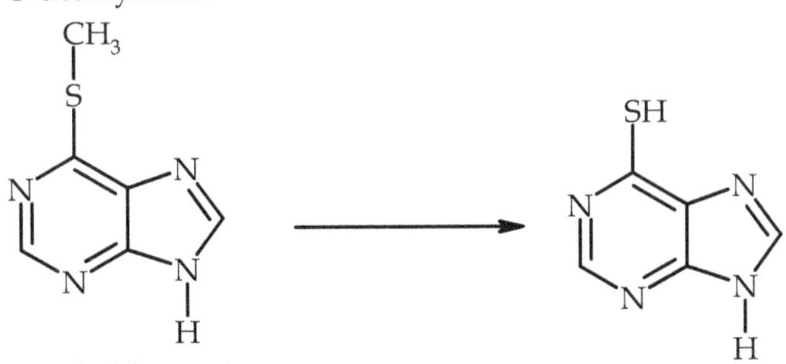

S-methylthiopurine

**Fig 4-8:** S-Dealkylation of 6-methyl mercaptopurine

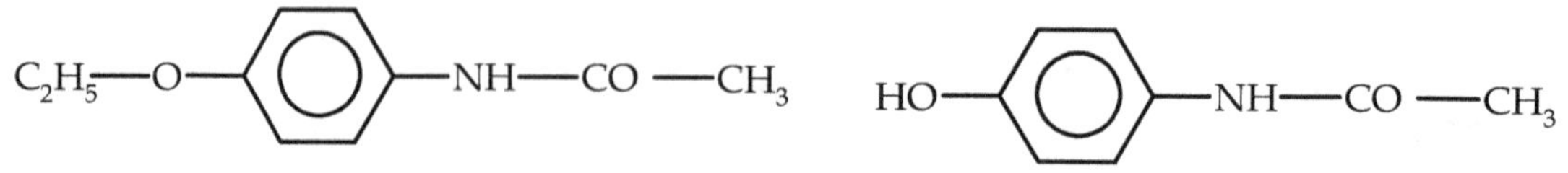


Phenacetin

**Fig 4-9:** O-Dealkylation of phenacetin

**Oxidation of alcohol, carboxyl and carboxylic acid:** These reactions are mainly catalyzed by non-microsomal enzymes dehydrogenases. Primary and secondary alcohols and aldehydes undergo oxidation relatively easily but tertiary alcohols, ketones and carboxylic acids are resistant as such a reaction involves cleavage of C-C bonds.

In case of ethanol, oxidation of acetaldehyde is reversible and further oxidation of the later to acetic acid is very rapid since acetaldehyde is highly toxic and should not accumulate in the body.

**Miscellaneous of oxidative reactions**

I(a) **Oxidative aromatization/dehydrogenation :** An example of metabolic aromatization of drug is nifedipine.

I(b) **Oxidative dehalogenation:** This reaction is common with halogen containing drugs such as chloroform.

Oxidative ring cleavage, oxidation of phenols to quinones is other oxidative reactions.

## Reductive Reactions

**Reduction of carbonyl functions (Aldehydes and Ketones):** Depending on the reactivity towards bio reduction, carbonyls can be divided in to 3 categories

The aliphatic aldehydes and ketones

The aromatic aldehydes and ketones

The esters, acids and amines

Aliphatic aldehydes - chloral hydrate

Aliphatic ketones - methadone

Alicyclic ketones - ketone

Aromatic ketone - acetophenone

(a) **Reduction of alcohols and carbon- carbon double bonds:** These two reductions are considered together because the groups are inter convertible by simple addition or loss of water molecule. Before an alcohol is reduced, it is dehydrated to C=C bond

Example - bencyclone (anti spasmodic)

**Reduction of N-compounds (nitro, azo and N- oxide):** The N containing functional groups that commonly undergo bio reduction are nitro, azo and N-oxide. It is important to note that such a reaction is reverse of oxidation. Reduction of nitro group proceeds via formation of nitro and hydroxylamine intermediates to yield amines

**Nitrazepam**

**Miscellaneous reduction reactions:** Reductive dehalogenation Fig 4-10.

This reaction involves replacement of halogen attached to the carbon with the H.atom.

*Example*: Halothane

Halothane

**Fig 4-10:** Reductive dehalogenation of halothane

The C-F bond is resistant to reduction.

(b) **Reduction of sulfur containing functional groups:** An example of S-S reductive cleavage is Disulfiram.

## Hydrolytic Reactions

The Hydrolytic Reactions are shown in Fig. 4.11.

**Hydrolysis of esters and ethers:** Esters on hydrolysis (Fig 4-12) yield alcohol and carboxylic acid, the reactions catalysed by esterease.

Organic acid esters

E.g. Clofibrate

Inorganic acid esters

E.g. Stilbestrol diphosphate

Esters undergoing hydrolysis are glycosides such as digoxin, digitoxin and O-glucuronides.

**Hydrolysis of amides (C-N cleavage):** Amides are hydrolyzed (Fig 4-13) slowly in comparison to esters.

Primary amides are rare

Secondary amides with aliphatic substituent

E.g. Procainamide

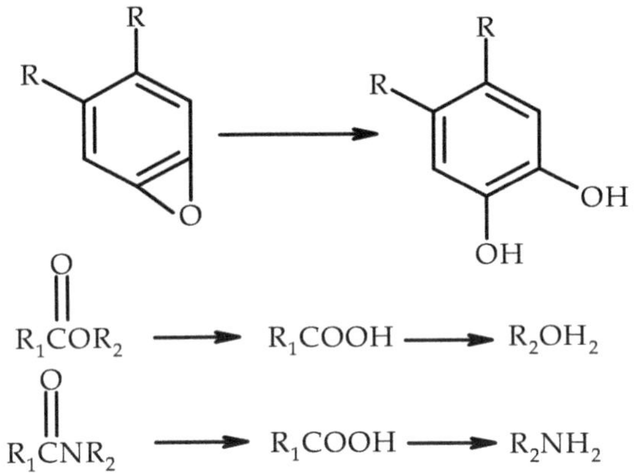


Carbamazepine

Procaine, aspirin, clofibrate, meperidine, enalapril, cocaine

Lidocaine, procainamide, indomethacin

**Fig 4-11:** Hydrolytic reactions

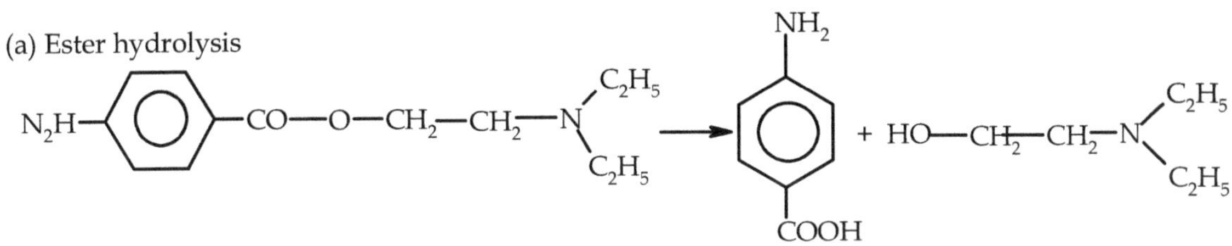


**Fig 4-12:** Ester Hydrolysis

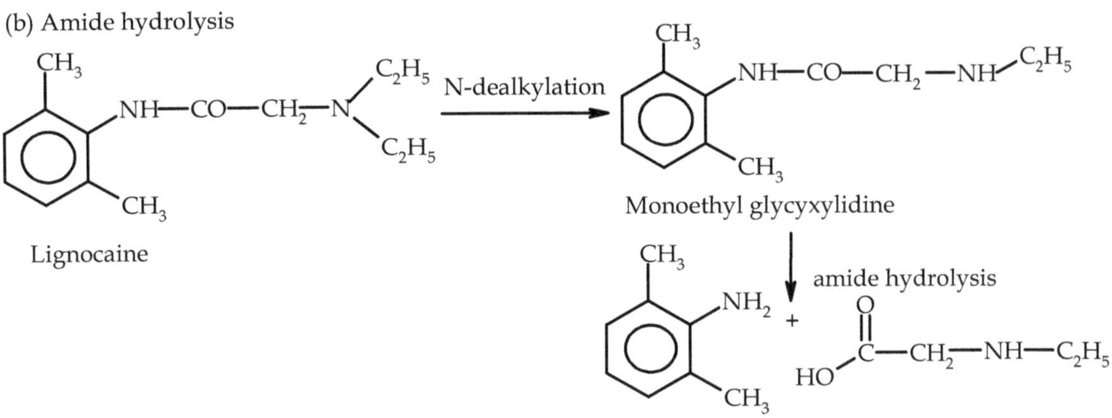


**Fig 4-13:** Amide hydrolysis

Secondary amides with aromatic substituents

E.g. Lidocaine

Tertiary amides

E.g. Carbamazepine

**Hydrolytic cleavage of non aromatic heterocycles:** Non aromatic heterocycles also contain amide functions

Lactams

Four membered lactams E.g: Penicillin

Five membered lactams E.g: Succinimides

Six membered lactams E.g: Thalidomide

Seven membered lactams E.g: - Chlordiazepoxide

**Hydrolytic dehalogenation:** Chlorine atom attached to aliphatic carbons is dehalogenated easily.

**Miscellaneous hydrolytic reactions:** Include hydration of epoxides and arene oxides, hydrolysis of sulphonyl ureas, carmates and hydroxamates of Glucuronide and sulphate conjugates.

## Phase II Reactions

### Conjugation Reactions

The Conjugation Reactions are shown in Fig 4.14.

1. Glucuronidation by UDP-glucuronosyltransferase (on -OH, -COOH, $-NH_2$, -SH groups)
2. Sulfation by sulfotransferase (on $-NH_2$, $-SO_2NH_2$, -OH groups)
3. Acetylation by acetyltransferases (on $-NH_2$, $-SO_2NH_2$, -OH groups)
4. Fatty acid conjugation (on -OH groups)
5. Amino acid conjugation (on -COOH groups)
6. Glutathione conjugation by Glutathione-S-transferase: (to epoxides or organic halides)
7. Condensation reactions

Glucuronidation

Glucuronidation

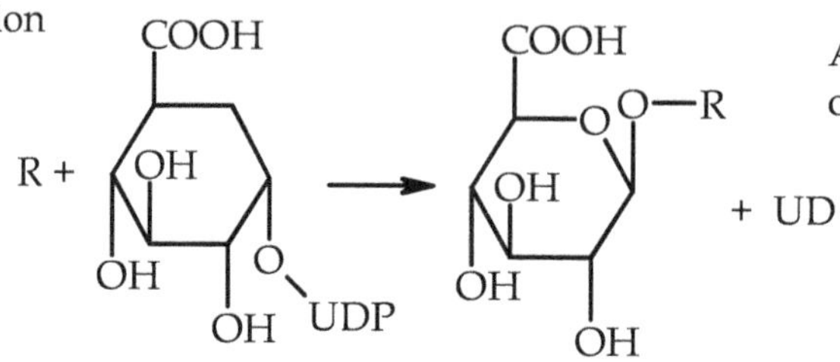


UDP-glucuronic acid

Acetaminophen, morphine, oxazepam, lorazepam

Sulfation PAPS + ROH ⟶ R—O—$SO_2$—OH + PAP

3'-phosphoadenosine-5 phosphosulfate 3'-phosphoadenosine-5'-phosphate

Acetaminophen, steroids, metholdopa

Acetylation CoAS—CO—$CH_3$ + $RNH_2$ ⟶ RNH—CO—$CH_3$ + CoA-SH

Sulfonamides, isoniazid, dapsone, clonazepam

Methylation RO— RS— RN— + AdoMet ⟶ RO—$CH_3$ + AdoHomCys

L-Dopa, methyldopa, mercaptopurine, captopril

Glutathione conjugation GSH + R ⟶ R—GSH

Adrimycin, fosfomycin, busulfan

**Fig 4-14:** Conjugation reactions

## Glucuronidation

The Glucuronidation are shown in Fig. 4-15 and 4-16.

**Glucuronidation (= conjugation to α-d-glucuronic acid):** Quantitatively the most important phase II pathway for drugs and endogenous compounds.

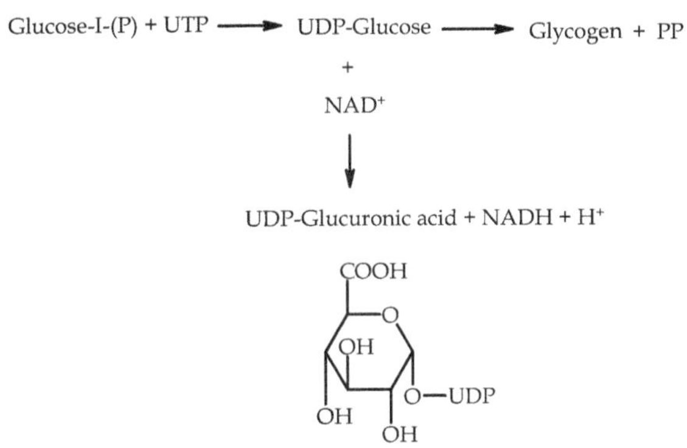


**Fig 4-15:** Synthesis of UDP-Glucouronic acid

Products are often excreted in the bile.

Enterohepatic recycling may occur due to gut glucuronidases.

*Requires enzyme UDP-glucuronosyltransferase (UGT):* Genetic family of enzymes, metabolizes a broad range of structurally diverse endogenous and exogenous compounds. Structurally related family with approximately 16 isoforms in man.

*Glucuronidation – requires creation of high energy intermediate:* UDP-Glucuronic Acid

**N-Glucuronidation (Fig 4-17):** Occurs with amines (mainly aromatic)

Occurs with amides and sulfonamides

**O-Glucuronidation (Fig 4-18):** Occurs by ester linkages with carboxylic acids.

Occurs by ether linkages with phenols and alcohols.

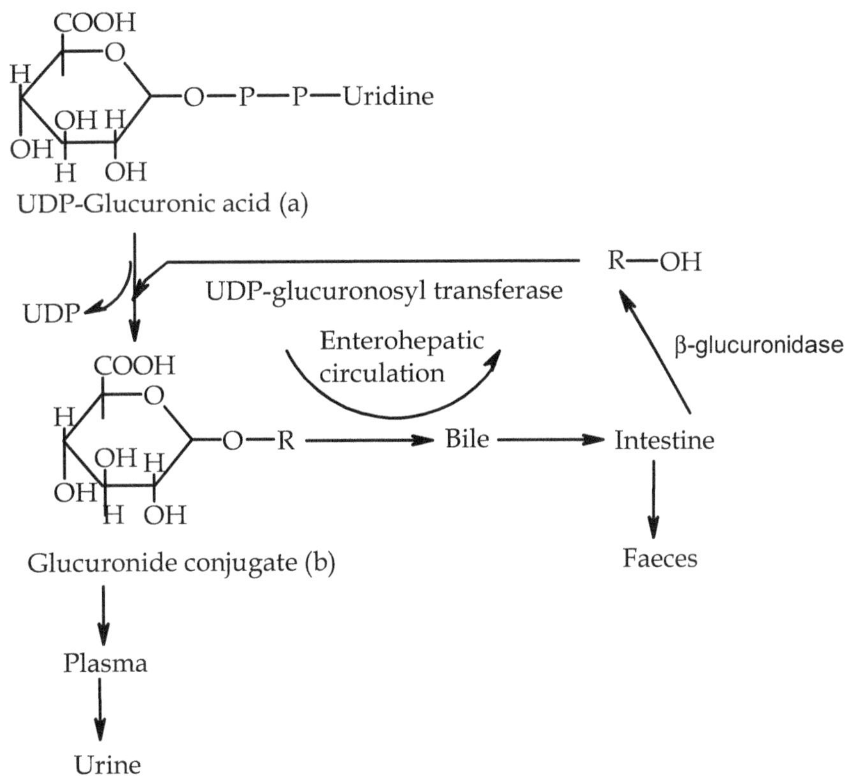


**Fig 4-16:** Glucuronidation Pathway and Enterohepatic Recirculation

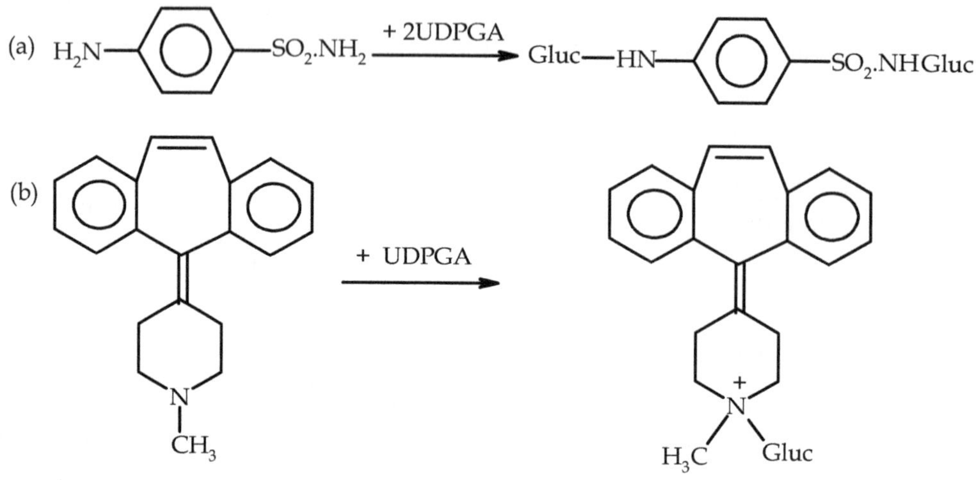


**Fig 4-17:** N-Glucuronidation of (a) sulfanilamide (b) cyproheptidine

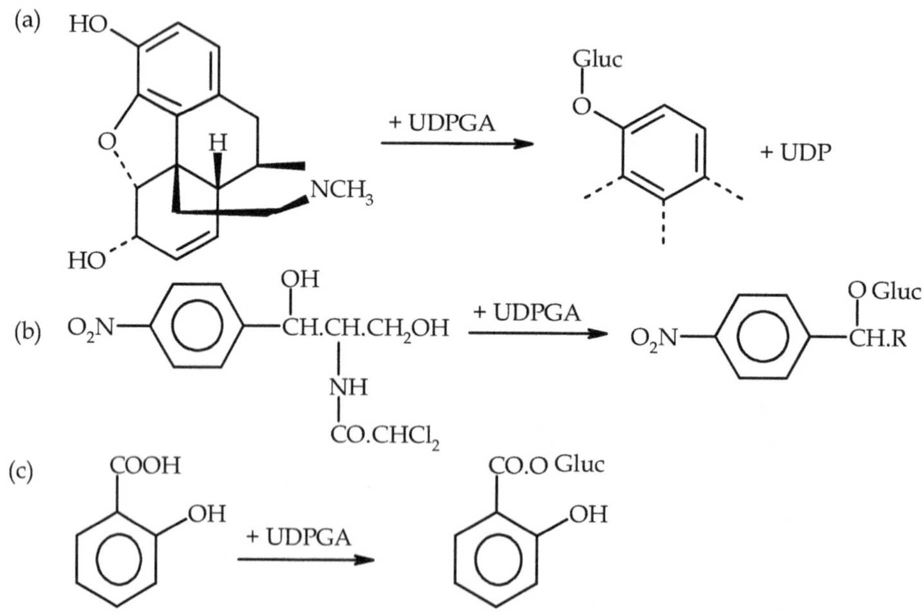


**Fig 4-18:** O-Glucuronidation of (a) morphine (b) chloramphenicol (c) salicylic acid

**Sulfation by Sulfotransferase:** Major pathway for phenols but also occurs for alcohols, amines and thiols

***Energy rich donor required:*** PAPS (3′-Phosphoadenosine-5′-phosphosulfate) Fig 4-19.

***Sulfation and Glucuronidation are competing pathways:*** Sulfation predominates at low substrate concentrations

Glucuronidation predominates at higher concentrations

There is relatively less PAPS in cell cytosol compared to UDPGA

***Sulfotransferases (=SULTs) catalyze transfer of sulfate to substrates:*** Phenol, alcohol and aryl amine Sulfotransferases are fairly non-specific

Steroid sulfotransferases are very specific

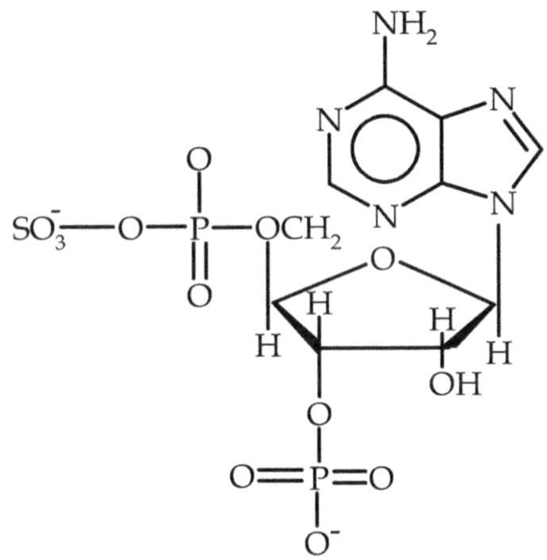


**Fig 4-19:** Structure of PAPS

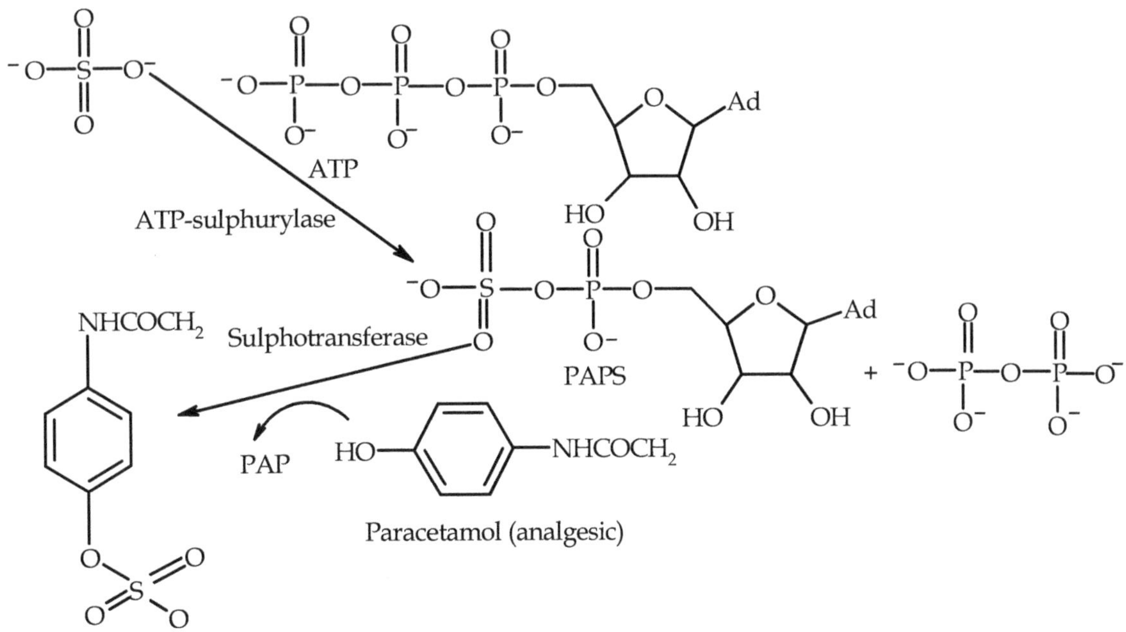


**Fig 4-20:** Sulfate conjugation of paracetamol

**General reaction:**

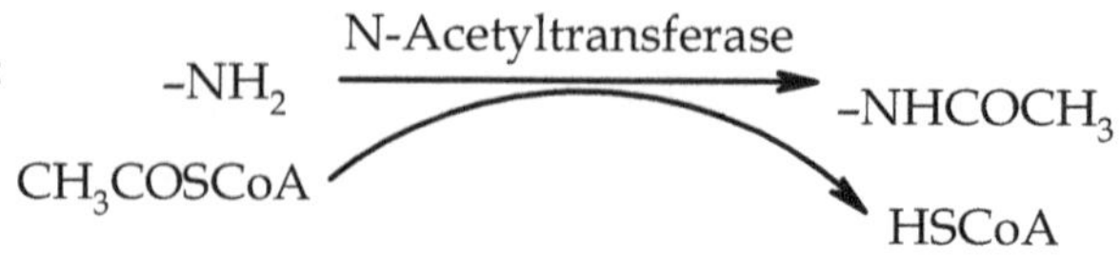


**Example:**

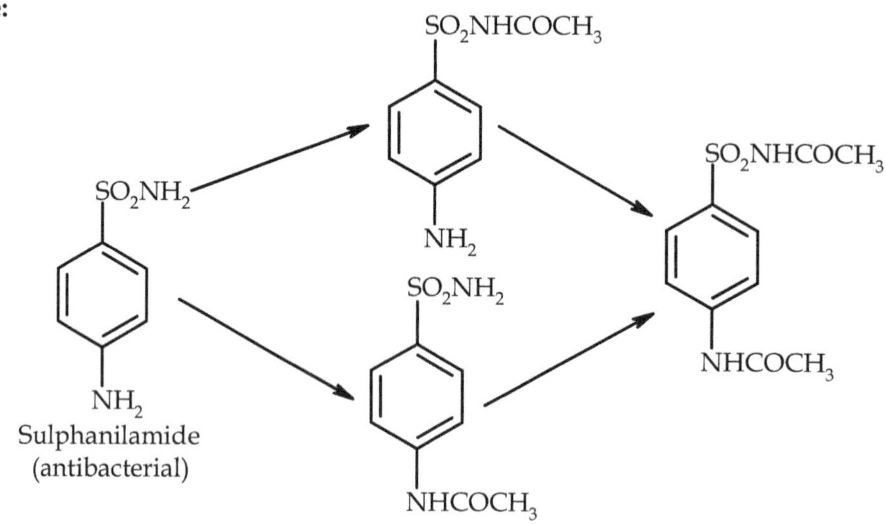


**Fig 4-21:** Acetylation of Sulphanilamide

**Acetylation by a Catyltransferase:** Common reaction for aromatic amines and sulfonamides

Requires co-factor acetyl-CoA

Responsible enzyme is N-acetyltransferase

Takes place mainly in the liver

Important in sulfonamide metabolism (Fig 4-21) because acetyl-sulfonamides are less soluble than the parent compound and may cause renal toxicity due to precipitation in the kidney.

**Fatty acid conjugation**

Stearic and palmitic acids are conjugated to drug by esterification reaction

Occurs in liver microsomal fraction.

(Cannabinols are metabolized in this fashion => long half-life)

**Amino acid conjugation (Fig 4-22)**

ATP-dependent acid:CoA ligase forms active CoA-amino acid conjugates which then react with drugs by N-Acetylation.

***Usual amino acids involved are:*** Glycine, Glutamine, Ornithine, Arginine

**Glutathione conjugation (Fig 4-23, 4-24, 4-25)**

Tripeptide Gly-Cys-Glu; conjugated by glutathione-S-transferase (GST)

Glutathione is a protective factor for removal of potentially toxic compounds.

Conjugated compounds can subsequently be attacked by Gamma -glutamyltranspeptidase and a peptidase to yield the cysteine conjugate .

Product can be further acetylated to N-acetylcysteine conjugate.

Paracetamol was metabolised through GSH conjugation . Due to genetic problems GSH was low in children who is affected genetically. In

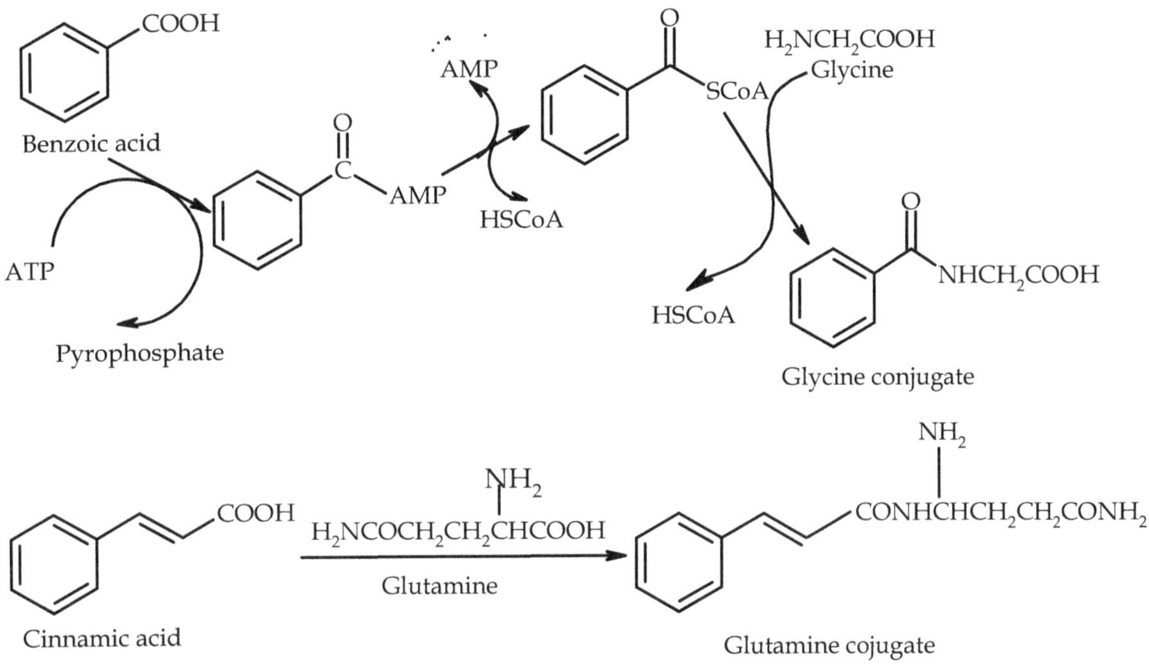


**Fig 4-22:** Amino acid conjugation

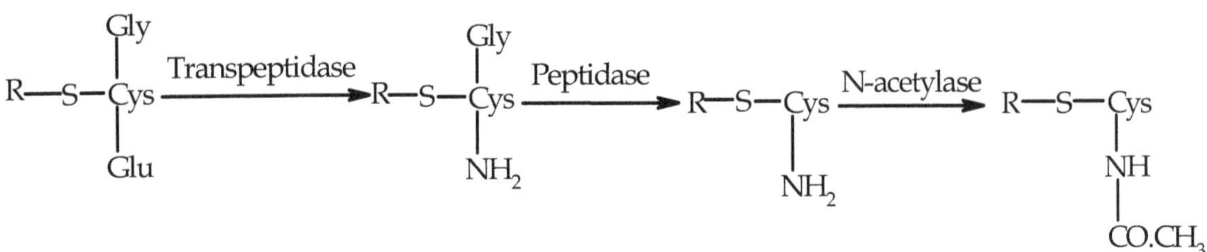


**Fig 4-23:** The further metabolism of glutathione conjugation

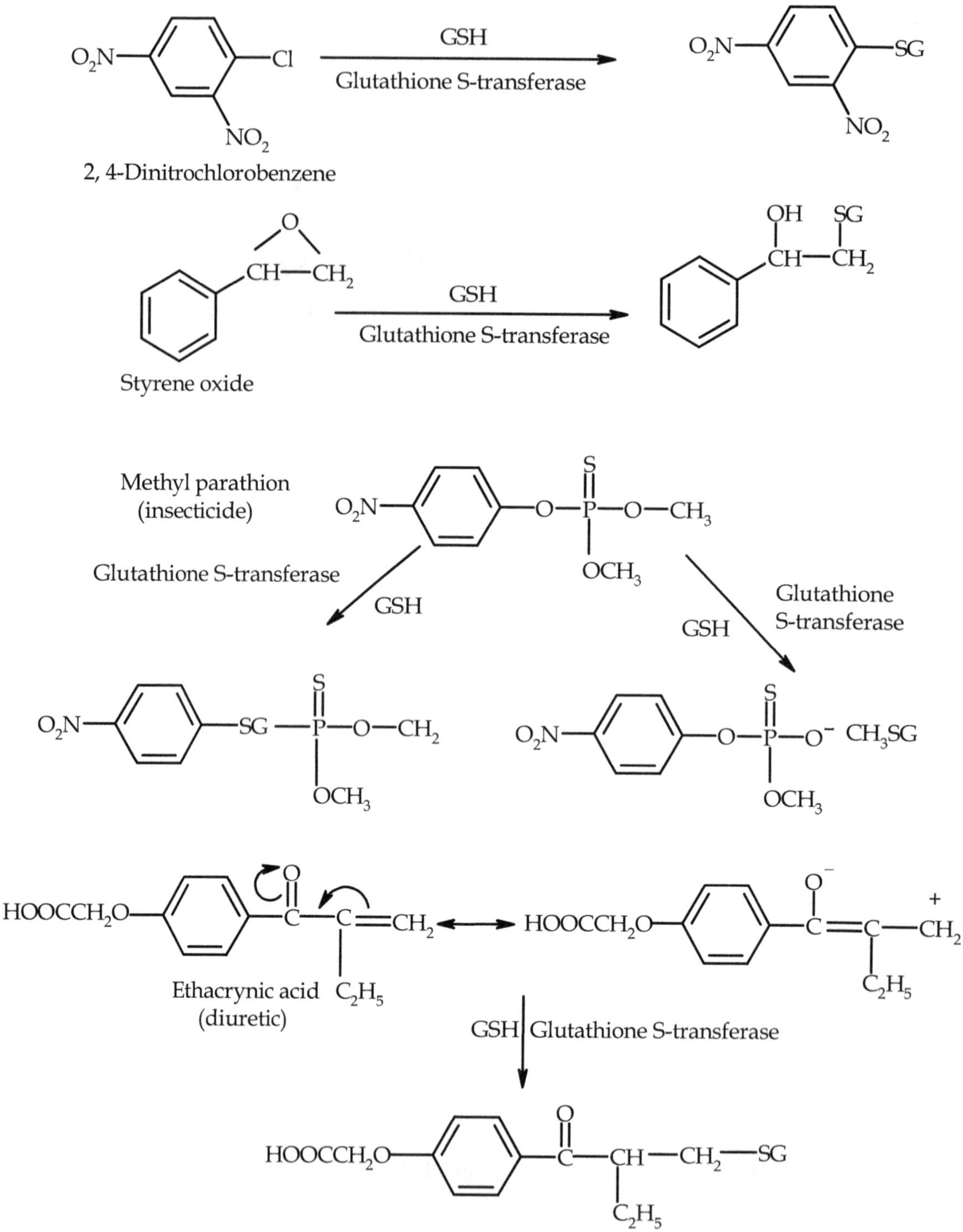


**Fig 4-24:** Example of glutathione conjugation

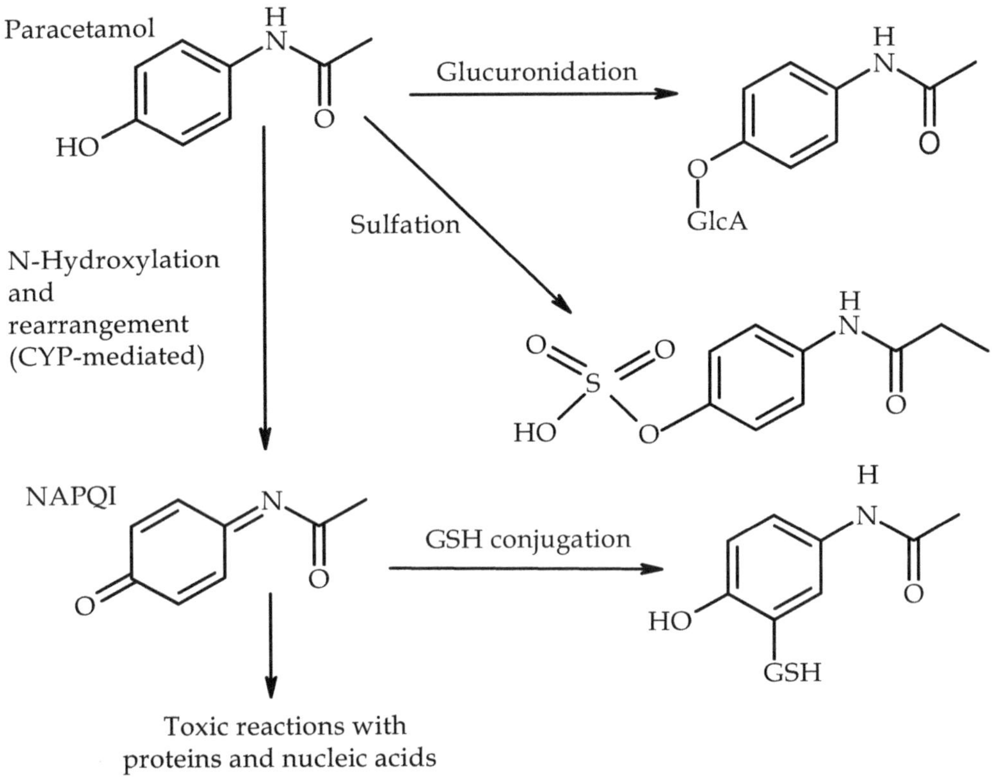


**Fig 4-25:** Paracetamol Metabolism

such affected ones paracetamol was metabolized very slowly, leads to the accumulation of toxic metabolite iminoquinone derivative which is highly reactive and less stable. It reacts with proteins of liver and denatures it. Finally leads to liver damage.

## Factors Affecting Biotransformation of Drug

Biotransformation is significantly affected by a number of factors, these include:

**Enzyme Induction:** When drugs are given over prolonged period of time, up regulation of enzymes takes place. Most of the time cytochrome P450 is involved leading to increased synthesis of new enzymes. The rate of metabolism increases as enzyme induction takes place. The drugs which bring about these changes are known as enzyme inducers. Some examples include anticonvulsants like phenytoin, carbomycin and chronic alcoholism. Others include various sedatives, hypnotics, tranquilizers and insecticides.

When drugs are taken together, sometimes drugs acting as enzyme inducers for others cause increased metabolism of themselves, which is known as **autometabolism.** Example includes artemether and carbamazepine when taken together.

Enzyme induction is brought about by gene transcription, which is enhanced. Enzyme induction leads to a decreased levels of the parent drug and increased levels of metabolites. Sometimes toxic metabolites are also produced. The rate of reaction increases and quicker conversion of parent drug takes place.

Drugs following first pass metabolism, have decreased bioavailability.

**Significance:** Care should be taken when enzyme inducers are given, especially when two drugs are given together, drug-drug interaction might occur, leading to therapeutic failure.

1. Rifampicin is an enzyme inducer. If it is taken by female patients taking contraceptives, decreased therapeutic effect of contraceptive might occur, leading to pregnancy. Therefore, the dose should be increased.
2. Phenobarbitone is used in seizures and epilepsy. It is also an enzyme inducer. If it is administered to patients taking warfarin, therapeutic failure of later might occur, leading to increased bleeding tendency.

**Some enzyme inducers include:**

1. Ethchlorvynol enhances metabolites of warfarin
2. Phenytoin enhances metabolism of cortisol and digitoxin
3. Rifampicin increases metabolism of digitoxin,ketoconazole
4. Barbiturates
5. Chloral hydrate
6. Erythromycin

**Drugs which are significantly affected by enzyme induction include:**

1. Phenytoin
2. Warfarin
3. Tolbutamide
4. Imipramine
5. Oral contraceptives
6. Chloramphenicol
7. Doxycycline
8. Theophylline
9. Griseofulvin
10. Phenylbutazone

**Consequences of microsomal enzyme induction:**

1. Decreased intensity and duration of action of drugs e.g., failure of contraceptives.
2. Increased intensity of action of drugs activated by metabolism. E.g., acute paracetamol toxicity is due to one of its metabolites.
3. If drug induces its own metabolism e.g., cicobarbitone it develops tolerance so effects are not produced.
4. Precipitation of acute intermittent porphyria. Enzyme induction might increase porphyrin synthesis.
5. Intermittent use of an inducer might interfere adjustment of dose of another drug e.g., oral anti coagulants, oral hypoglycemic, antiepileptics and antihypertensives.

**Auto induction**

The phenomenon in which a drug induces metabolism of other drugs as well as its own. E.g. carbamazepine-antiepileptic.

## Enzyme Inhibition

The process in which drug metabolizing capacity of cytochrome is decreased is known as enzyme inhibition. The rate of metabolism is decreased. Drugs bringing about these changes are known as enzyme inhibitors. Examples include ketoconazole- antifungal drug, cimetidine and verapamil-calcium channel blocker.

Enzyme inhibition is a rapidly occurring process, most critical for the drugs having a large therapeutic index. Competition for the active sites takes place between the enzymes and the given drugs. When enzyme inhibitor attaches, less metabolism occurs. As rate of metabolism is decreased, plasma levels of parent drugs are increased while that of metabolites are low. Serious drug-drug interactions might occur, as the plasma half life is also increased.

Sulfonamides decrease the metabolism of phenytoin so that its blood levels become toxic. Cimetidine decreases the metabolism of propranolol leading to enhanced bradycardia. Metabolism of tolbutamide is inhibited by phenylbutazone or coumarins, leading to prolonged hypoglycemia. Oral contraceptives inhibit metabolism of antipyrine. Astemizole decreases the metabolism of ketoconazole so that its blood levels becomes toxic leads to an important adeverse effect gynacomastia.

## Presystemic Metabolism/First Pass Effect/Route of Administration

Drugs following first pass metabolism have decreased bioavailability. Most of the drugs are metabolized within the liver. Changing the route of administration might change the first pass metabolism.

Propranolol is 80% metabolized before reaching systemic circulation.

Lidocaine is completely metabolised before reaching systemic circulation.

## Genetic Variations

Inter individual variations might occur, as drugs behave differently in different individuals due to genetic variations resulting in absent or malformed enzymes due to absent or malformed genes. Mostly non microsomal enzyme show genetic variations. Examples include succinyl choline, which is a skeletal muscle relaxant. It is metabolized by pseudocholine esterase. Some people lack this enzyme, due to which lack of metabolism of succinyl choline might occur. When administered in those individuals, prolonged apnea might result. Different groups of populations might be classified as fast metabolizers and poor metabolizers of drugs. For certain drugs, like Isoniazid, fast acetylators as well as slow acetylators are present. Fast acetylators cause rapid acetylation, while poor metabolizers metabolize less. Hepatic acetyl transferase catalyzes acetylation. Slow acetylation might occur due to genetic malformation leading to decreased production.

Fast metabolism may lead to hepatotoxicity while poor metabolism might result in peripheral neuropathy. Absence of catalase may lead to achalasia, while G6PD deficiency predisposes erythrocytes to hemolysis as a result of oxidative stress imposed by some commonly used drugs.

## Species Differences

Species differences are most established in animals. Some metabolize drugs rapidly. Rats and rabbits metabolize drugs more efficiently than humans. Certain species of rabbits feed on Belladonna, and have atropinase to tolerate the effects of atropine. Research on humans is still going on. Asians, Orientals, Blacks and Whites might have different drug metabolizing capacities. Examples include difference in drug metabolizing capacity of certain anti malarial, amongst the Eskimos and the Asians. Eskimos may metabolize drugs more efficiently than the Asians.

## Exposure to Pollutants from Environment or Industry

Cigarette smokers might act as enzyme inducers. Chronic alcoholism might lead to enzyme induction as well. Similarly, pesticides or insecticides may act as enzyme inducers.

In hot and humid climate biotransformation is decreased and vice versa. At high altitude, decreased biotransformation occurs due to decreased oxygen leading to decreased oxidation of drugs.

## Age

Age plays a very important role. Extreme age groups (very young and very old) behave almost the same. Drug metabolizing enzyme develops early but their capacity is low. Thus the rate of metabolism in infants is very low. Care should be taken in administering drugs in younger patients. True development of enzyme occurs in one to two months.

Chloramphenicol (antimicrobial drug) when administered in infant, does not have great efficacy. Toxic effects in the form of grey baby syndrome might occur. The baby may be cyanosed, hypothermic, flaccid and grey in color. Shock and even death might occur if toxic levels get accumulated.

Diazepam (sedative hypnotic) may result in floppy baby syndrome in which flaccidity of the baby is seen.

In elderly, most processes slow down which leads to decreased metabolism. Shrinkage of organs occurs as well along with decreased liver functions and decreased blood flow through the liver. All these factors decrease the metabolism. Old people are usually taking multiple drugs, so are more prone. The drug doses should be decreased in the elderly.

## Sex

Male have a higher BMR as compared to the females, thus can metabolize drugs more efficiently, e.g., Salicylates (others might include ethanol, propranolol, benzodiazepines). Females, during pregnancy, have an increased rate of metabolism. Thus, the drug dose has to be increased. After the pregnancy is over, the dosage is decreased back to normal levels. Example includes phenytoin, whose dose has to be increased during pregnancy (specially second and third trimester).

## Drug-Drug Interaction

Toxic effects might result when drug combinations act as enzyme inhibitors and inducers. The dose has to be adjusted accordingly.

## Nutrition

Malnutrition may also effect biotransformation. Depletion of amino acids and glycine may affect drug metabolizing capacity, especially during the phase II, which depends on the food stores. Synthesis of microsomal enzymes depends on nutritional status.

## Pathological Conditions

Most of the drugs are metabolized in the liver, any disease of which (cirrhosis, viral hepatitis, drugs induced hepatitis, hepatocarcinoma) may affect and slow down the metabolizing capacity. Jaundice depresses glucuronic acid conjugation and oxidative function of liver microsomes.

Cardiovascular diseases, although have no direct effect, decrease the blood flow, which may slow down biotransformation of drugs like isoniazid, morphine and propranolol. Similarly pulmonary conditions may decrease biotransformation.

***Example:*** Procaine and procainamide hydrolysis is impaired.

Hypothyroidism increases drug metabolizing capacity (increased half life of antipyrine, digoxin, methimazole, practolol) while hyperthyroidism decreases it.

## Circadian Rhythm

The rate of hepatic metabolism of certain drugs follow diurnal rhythm in rats and mice. This may be true in humans as well.

# References

Dr. Shobha Rani R. Hiremath (2000). Text book of Biopharmaceutics & Pharmacokinetics, Prism Books Pvt Ltd, Bangalore, Pg.no. 157-166.

Dutton G.J (1980). Glucuronidation of drugs and other compounds. *CRC Press, Inc.*, Boca Raton.

Milo Gibaldi. Biopharmaceutics & Pharmacokinetics, 4th edition, Pg.no. 203.

CHAPTER

# Drug Discovery and Development 5

## Introduction

Discovering and bringing one new drug to the public typically costs a pharmaceutical or biotechnology company from $800 million to more than $1 billion and takes an average of 10 to 15 years. The drug discovery and development process is designed to ensure that only those pharmaceutical products that are both safe and effective are brought to market. It is the mission of pharmaceutical research companies to take the path from understanding a disease to bringing a safe and effective new treatment to patients. Scientists work to piece together the basic causes of disease at the level of genes, proteins and cells. Out of this understanding emerge "targets," which potential new drugs might be able to affect

Researchers work to:

- Validate these targets,
- Discover the right molecule (potential drug) to interact with the target chosen,
- Test the new compound in the lab and clinic for safety and efficacy and
- Gain approval and get the new drug into the hands of doctors and patients.

This whole process takes an average of 10-15 years.

## The Discovery Process

### Pre Discovery

**Understand the disease**

Before any potential new medicine can be discovered, scientists work to understand the disease to be treated as well as possible and to unravel the underlying cause of the condition. They try to understand how the genes are altered, how that affects the proteins they encode and how those proteins interact with each other in living cells, how those affected cells change the specific tissue they are in and finally how the disease affects the entire patient. This knowledge is the basis for treating the problem. Researchers from government, academia and industry all contribute to this knowledge base. However, even with new tools and insights, this research takes many years of work and too often, leads to frustrating dead ends. And even if the research is successful, it will take many more years of work to turn this basic understanding of what causes a disease into a new treatment.

### Target Identification

Drugs usually act on either cellular or genetic chemicals in the body, known as targets, which are believed to be associated with disease. Scientists use a variety of techniques to identify and isolate individual targets to learn more about their functions and how they influence disease. Compounds are then identified that have various interactions with the drug targets that might be helpful in treatment of a specific disease.

### Target Prioritization/Validation

To select targets most likely to be useful in the development of new treatments for disease, researchers analyze and compare each drug target to others based on their association with a specific disease and their ability to regulate biological and chemical compounds in the body. Tests are conducted to confirm that interactions with the drug target are associated with a desired change in the behaviour of diseased cells. Research scientists can then identify compounds that have an effect on the target selected.

## Lead Identification

A lead compound or substance is one that is believed to have potential to treat disease. Laboratory scientists can compare known substances with new compounds to determine their likelihood of success. Leads are sometimes developed as collections or libraries, of individual molecules that possess properties needed in a new drug. Testing is then done on each of these molecules to confirm its effect on the drug target.

**There are a few ways to find a lead compound:**

**Nature:** Until recently, scientists usually turned to nature to find interesting compounds for fighting disease. Bacteria found in soil and moldy plants both led to important new treatments, for example. Nature still offers many useful substances, but now there are other ways to approach drug discovery.

**De novo:** Thanks to advances in chemistry, scientists can also create molecules from scratch. They can use sophisticated computer modeling to predict what type of molecule may work.

**High-throughput Screening:** This process is the most common way that leads are usually found. Advances in robotics and computational power allow researchers to test hundreds of thousands of compounds against the target to identify any that might be promising. Based on the results, several lead compounds are usually selected for further study.

**Biotechnology:** Scientists can also genetically engineer living systems to produce disease-fighting biological molecules.

## Lead Optimization

Lead optimization compares the properties of various lead compounds and provides information to help biopharmaceutical companies select the compound or compounds with the greatest potential to be developed into safe and effective medicines. Often during this same stage of development, lead prioritization studies are conducted in living organisms (*in vivo*) and in cells in the test tube (*in vitro*) to compare various lead compounds and how they are metabolized and affect the body.

## Early Safety Tests

Perform initial tests on promising compounds.

Lead compounds go through a series of tests to provide an early assessment of the safety of the lead compound. Scientists test Absorption, Distribution, Metabolism, Excretion and Toxicological (ADME/Tox) properties or "pharmacokinetics," of each lead.

Successful drugs must be:

- Absorbed into the bloodstream,
- Distributed to the proper site of action in the body,
- Metabolized efficiently and effectively,
- Successfully excreted from the body and
- Demonstrated to be not toxic.

These studies help researchers prioritize lead compounds early in the discovery process. ADME/Toxicology studies are performed in living cells, in animals and via computational models.

## Lead Optimization

Alter the structure of lead candidates to improve properties

Lead compounds that survive the initial screening are then "optimized" or altered to make them more effective and safer. By changing the structure of a compound, scientists can give it different properties. For example, they can make it less likely to interact with other chemical pathways in the body, thus reducing the potential for side effects.

Hundreds of different variations or "analogues" of the initial leads are made and tested. Teams of biologists and chemists work together closely: The biologists test the effects of analogues on biological systems while the chemists take this information to make additional alterations that are then retested by the biologists. The resulting compound is the candidate drug.

Even at this early stage, researchers begin to think about how the drug will be made, considering formulation (the recipe for making a drug, including inactive ingredients used to hold it together and allow it to dissolve at the right time), delivery mechanism (the way the drug is taken - by mouth, injection, inhaler) and large-scale manufacturing (how you make the drug in large quantities).

### Preclinical Testing

Lab and animal testing to determine if the drug is safe enough for human testing with one or more optimized compounds in hand, researchers turn their attention to testing them extensively to determine if they should move on to testing in humans. Scientists carry out in vitro and in vivo tests. In vitro tests are experiments conducted in the lab, usually carried out in test tubes and beakers ("vitro" is "glass" in Latin) and invivo studies are those in living cell cultures and animal models ("vivo" is "life" in Latin). Scientists try to understand how the drug works and what its safety profile looks like. The U.S. Food and Drug Administration (FDA) requires extremely thorough testing before the candidate drug can be studied in humans. During this stage researchers also must work out how to make large enough quantities of the drug for clinical trials. Techniques for making a drug in the lab on a small scale do not translate easily to larger production. This is the first scale up. The drug will need to be scaled up even more if it is approved for use in the general patient population. At the end of several years of intensive work, the discovery phase concludes. After starting with approximately 5,000 to 10,000 compounds, scientists now have winnowed the group down to between one and five molecules, "candidate drugs," which will be studied in clinical trials.

## The Development Process

Investigational New Drug (IND) Application and Safety File IND with the FDA before clinical testing can begin; ensure safety for clinical trial volunteers through an Institutional Review Board

Before any clinical trial can begin, the researchers must file an Investigational New Drug (IND) application with the FDA. The application includes the results of the preclinical work, the candidate drug's chemical structure and how it is thought to work in the body, a listing of any side effects and manufacturing information. The IND also provides a detailed clinical trial plan that outlines how, where and by whom the studies will be performed.

The FDA reviews the application to make sure people participating in the clinical trials will not be exposed to unreasonable risks. In addition to the IND application, all clinical trials must be reviewed and approved by the Institutional Review Board (IRB) at the institutions where the trials will take place. This process includes the development of appropriate informed consent, which will be required of all clinical trial participants.

Statisticians and others are constantly monitoring the data as it becomes available. The FDA or the sponsor company can stop the trial at any time if problems arise. In some cases a study may be stopped because the candidate drug is performing so well that it would be unethical to with hold it from the patients receiving a placebo or another drug. Finally, the company sponsoring the research must provide comprehensive regular reports to the FDA and the IRB on the progress of clinical trials.

## Clinical Trial Design

An incredible amount of thought goes into the design of each clinical trial. To provide the highest level of confidence in the validity of results, many drug trials are placebo controlled, randomized and double-blinded.

- **Placebo controlled:** Some subjects will receive the new drug candidate and others will receive a placebo. (In some instances, the drug candidate may be tested against another treatment rather than a placebo).
- **Randomized:** Each of the study subjects in the trial is assigned randomly to one of the treatments.
- **Double blinded:** Neither the researchers nor the subjects know which treatment is being delivered until the study is over. This method of testing provides the best evidence of any direct relationship between the test compound and its effect on disease because it minimizes human error. The number of subjects enrolled in a trial (the "power" of the trial) also has to be carefully considered: In general, enrolling more subjects results in greater statistical significance of the results, but is also more expensive and difficult to undertake.

### Phase 1 Clinical Trial

Perform initial human testing in a small group of healthy volunteers.

In Phase 1 trials the candidate drug is tested in people for the first time. These studies are usually conducted with about 20 to 100 healthy volunteers. The main goal of a Phase 1 trial is to discover if the drug is safe in humans. Researchers look at the pharmacokinetics of a drug: How is it absorbed? How is it metabolized and eliminated from the body? They also study the drug's pharmacodynamics: Does it cause side effects? Does it produce desired effects? These closely monitored trials are designed to help researchers determine what the safe dosing range is and if it should move on to further development.

### Phase 2 Clinical Trial

Test in a small group of patients

In Phase 2 trials researchers evaluate the candidate drug's effectiveness in about 100 to 500 patients with the disease or condition under study and examine the possible short term side effects (adverse events) and risks associated with the drug. They also strive to answer these questions: Is the drug working by the expected mechanism? Does it improve the condition in question? Researchers also analyze optimal dose strength and schedules for using the drug. If the drug continues to show promise, they prepare for the much larger Phase 3 trials.

### Phase 3 Clinical Trial

Test in a large group of patients to show safety and efficacy

In Phase 3 trials researchers study the drug candidate in a larger number (about 1,000-5,000) of patients to generate statistically significant data about safety, efficacy and the overall benefit risk relationship of the drug. This phase of research is key in determining whether the drug is safe and effective. It also provides the basis for labeling instructions to help ensure proper use of the drug (e.g., information on potential interactions with other medicines).

Phase 3 trials are both the costliest and longest trials. Hundreds of sites around the United States and the world participate in the study to get a large and diverse group of patients. Coordinating all the sites and the data coming from them is a monumental task.

During the Phase 3 trial (and even in Phases 1 and 2), researchers are also conducting many other critical studies, including plans for fullscale production and preparation of the complex application required for FDA approval.

## New Drug Application (NDA) and Approval

### Submit Application for Approval to FDA

Once all three phases of the clinical trials are complete, the sponsoring company analyzes all of the data. If the findings demonstrate that the experimental medicine is both safe and effective, the company files a New Drug Application (NDA) – which can run 100,000 pages or more – with the FDA requesting approval to market the drug.

The NDA includes all of the information from the previous years of work, as well as the proposals for manufacturing and labeling of the new medicine.

FDA experts review all the information included in the NDA to determine if it demonstrates that the medicine is safe and effective enough to be approved (see sidebar – "How does the FDA decide to approve a new drug?"). Following rigorous review, the FDA can either 1) approve the medicine, 2) send the company an "approvable" letter requesting more information or studies before approval can be given or 3) deny approval.

Review of an NDA may include an evaluation by an advisory committee, an independent panel of FDA-appointed experts who consider data presented by company representatives and FDA reviewers. Committees then vote on whether the FDA should approve an application and under conditions. The FDA is not required to follow the recommendations of the advisory committees, but often does.

## Benefit Vs. Risk

After close to a decade of testing, the company files a New Drug Application (NDA) with the FDA. Reported in the NDA are all the data gathered from all studies of the potential new drug, including the preclinical as well as clinical findings. The FDA then scrutinizes all the data carefully to determine if the medicine should be approved. In particular, it uses the information in the NDA to try to address three major concerns:

1. Because no drug has zero risk, the FDA must determine whether the benefits of the drug outweigh the risks, i.e., is the drug effective for its proposed use, and has an acceptable balance between benefits and risks been achieved.
2. Based on its assessment of risk and benefit, the FDA must decide what information the package insert should contain to guide physicians in the use of the new drug.
3. Finally, the FDA must assess whether the methods used to manufacture the drug and ensure its quality are adequate to preserve the drug's identity, strength and purity.

## Manufacturing

Going from small scale to large scale manufacturing is a major undertaking. In many cases, companies must build a new manufacturing facility or reconstruct an old one because the manufacturing process is different from drug to drug. Each facility must meet strict FDA guidelines for Good Manufacturing Practices (GMP).

Making a high quality drug compound on a large scale takes great care. Imagine trying to make a cake, for example, on a large scale making sure the ingredients are evenly distributed in the mix, ensuring that it heats evenly. The process to manufacture most drugs is even more complicated than this. There are few, if any, other businesses that require this level of skill in manufacturing.

## Ongoing Studies and Phase 4 Trials

Research on a new medicine continues even after approval. As a much larger number of patients begin to use the drug, companies must continue to monitor it carefully and submit periodic reports, including cases of adverse events, to the FDA. In addition, the FDA sometimes requires a company to conduct additional studies on an approved drug in "Phase 4" studies. These trials can be set up to evaluate long term safety or how the new medicine affects a specific subgroup of patients.

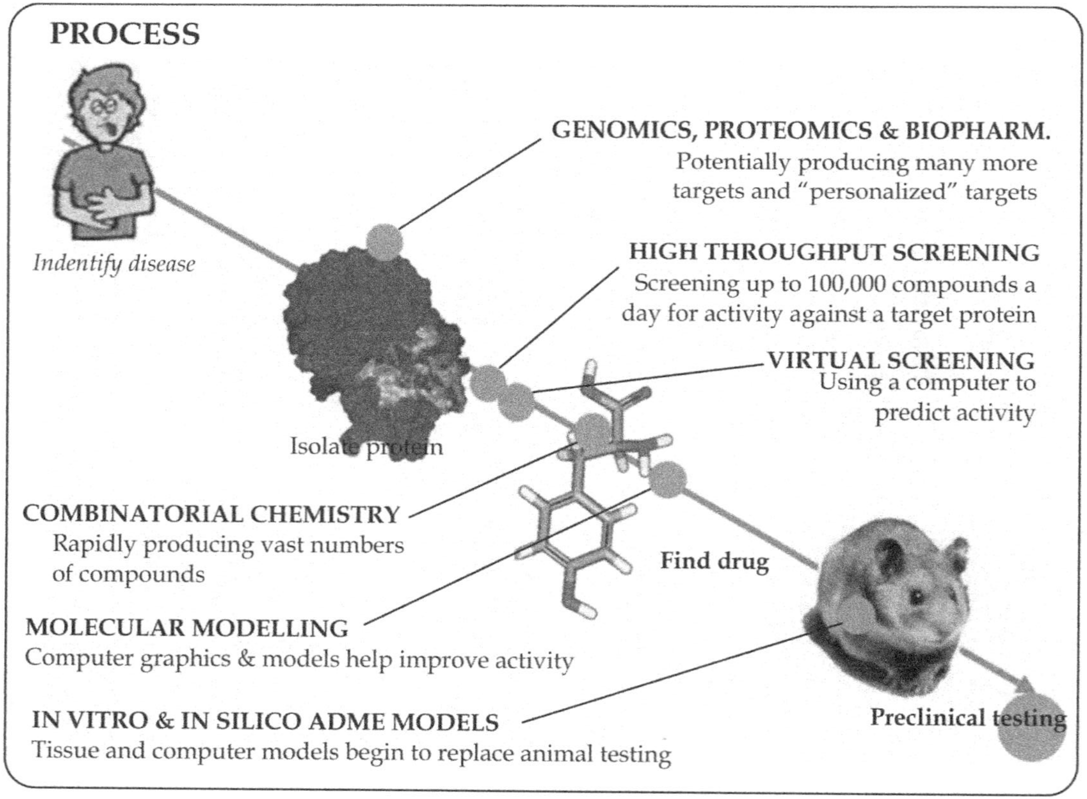
PROCESS
Indentify disease
Isolate protein
GENOMICS, PROTEOMICS & BIOPHARM.
Potentially producing many more targets and "personalized" targets
HIGH THROUGHPUT SCREENING
Screening up to 100,000 compounds a day for activity against a target protein
VIRTUAL SCREENING
Using a computer to predict activity
COMBINATORIAL CHEMISTRY
Rapidly producing vast numbers of compounds
Find drug
MOLECULAR MODELLING
Computer graphics & models help improve activity
IN VITRO & IN SILICO ADME MODELS
Tissue and computer models begin to replace animal testing
Preclinical testing

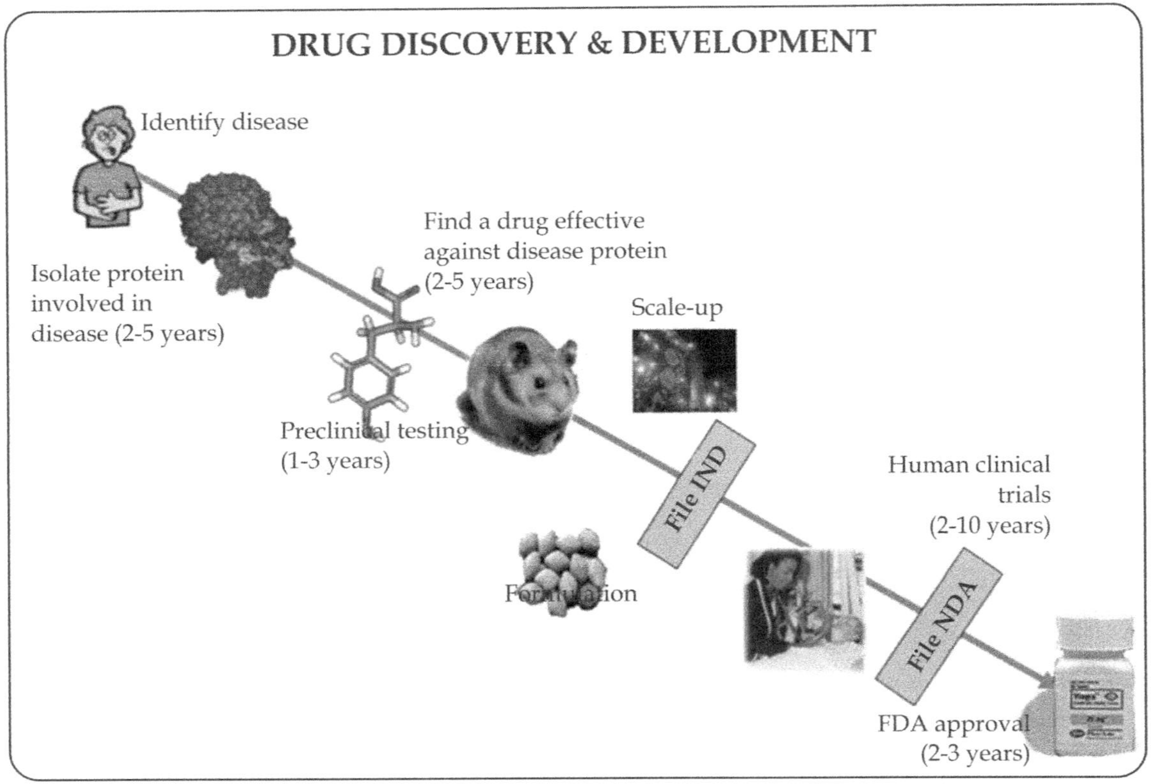


**Fig 5-1 :** Drug discovery and development

## Conclusion

The discovery and development of new medicines is a long, complicated process. Each success is built on many, many prior failures. Advances in understanding human biology and disease are opening up exciting new possibilities for breakthrough medicines. At the same time, researchers face great challenges in understanding and applying these advances to the treatment of disease. These possibilities will grow as our scientific knowledge expands and becomes increasingly complex. Research based pharmaceutical companies are committed to advancing science and bringing new medicines to patients.

## References

J.A. DiMasi (2001). "New Drug Development in the United States from 1963-1999," *Clinical Pharmacology and Therapeutics* **69(5):** 286-296.

J.A. DiMasi, R.W. Hansen and H.G. Grabowski (2003). "The Price of Innovation: New Estimates of Drug Development Costs," *Journal of Health Economics* **22:** 151-185.

Pharmaceutical Research and Manufacturers of America, based on data from Tufts University, Tufts Center for the Study of Drug Development (1995).

CHAPTER

6

# Pharmacovigilance

## Definition

The science and activities relating to the Detection, Assessment, Understanding and Prevention of adverse effects or any other medicine-related problem –WHO.

## Vigilance

Vigilare = to watch
–alert watchfulness
–forbearance of sleep; wakefulness
–watchfulness in respect of danger; care;
Caution; circumspection
–the process of paying close and
Continuous attention

## History.....

- Registration of New Chemical Entities was very much dependant on the status of products in the reference countries.
- Changes to product information was mainly industry driven.
- Few pre-clinical studies conducted in the region and hardly any Phase IV studies.
- Adverse drug reaction reporting was very minimal and mainly involved reports submitted by health care professionals.
- Most reports were for known reactions involving older drugs which were used in government-run hospitals.
- Signal detection not possible as there were too few reports.
- Only able to detect some quality defects of generics which manifested as adverse drug reactions (ADRs).
- Pharmacovigilance was mainly about getting ADR reports and submitting them to WHO.
- No significant regulatory changes made based on these reports.

## Current Scenario

- Increased awareness and interest amongst doctors and pharmacists to report ADRs as they have seen some benefit in reporting.
- Increasing number of clinical trials being conducted especially in Singapore, Thailand and Malaysia.
- Good clinical practice (GCP) training for investigators served to increase awareness of serious adverse event (SAE) and ADR reporting amongst health care professionals and the industry.
- More hospitals and companies using on-line reporting system – less hassle than submitting hard copy reports.
- Increasing involvement by hospital pharmacists in Pharmacovigilance– during clinical ward rounds and when counseling patients.

## Major Aims

- Early detection of unknown safety problems.
- Identification of risk factors.
- Quantifying risks.
- Preventing patients from being affected unnecessarily.
- To improve patient care and safety.
- To improve public health and safety.
- To contribute to the assessment of benefit, harm, effectiveness and risk of medicines.
- To promote understanding, education and clinical training.
- Rational and safe use of medicines.

## Common ADRs

- Constipation after Codeine; Sedation with Antihistamine;
- Nausea with Fluoxetine; GIT upset with NSAIDs.
- 1959 / 61–Thalidomide 4.000 –10.000 cases (Phocomelia).

***"Medicines are supposed to save lives."***

***Dying from a disease is sometimes unavoidable; dying from a medicine is unacceptable. WHO. Geneva 2005.***

## Why Pharmacovigilance?

### Risk

No medicinal product is entirely or absolutely safe for all people, in all places, at all times.

We must always live with some measure of uncertainty.

Humanitarian concern.

- Insufficient evidence of safety from clinical trials.
- Animal experiments.
- Phase 1 – 3 studies prior to marketing authorization.

Drug discovery and clinical trails

(Fig. 6.1, 6.2) indicates stages of drug development, preclinical and clinical studies.

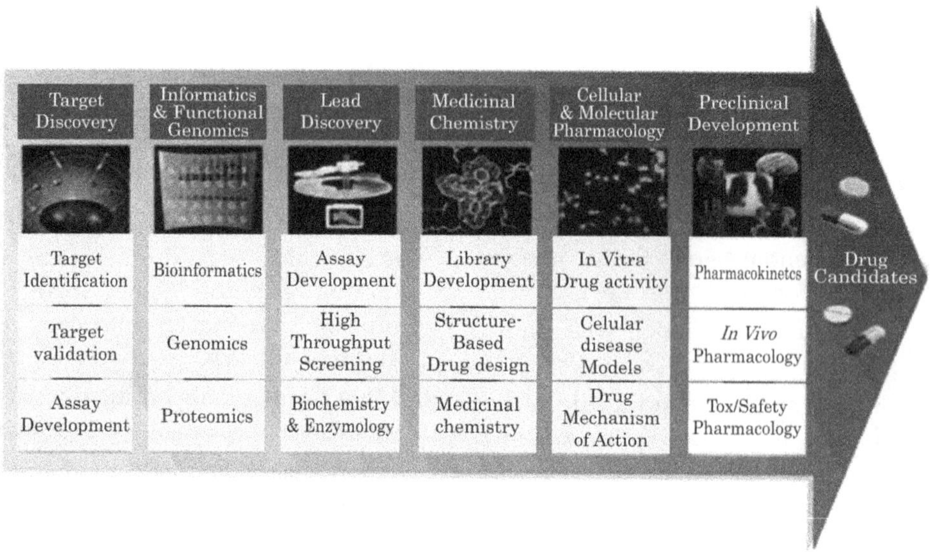


**Fig 6-1:** Drug development

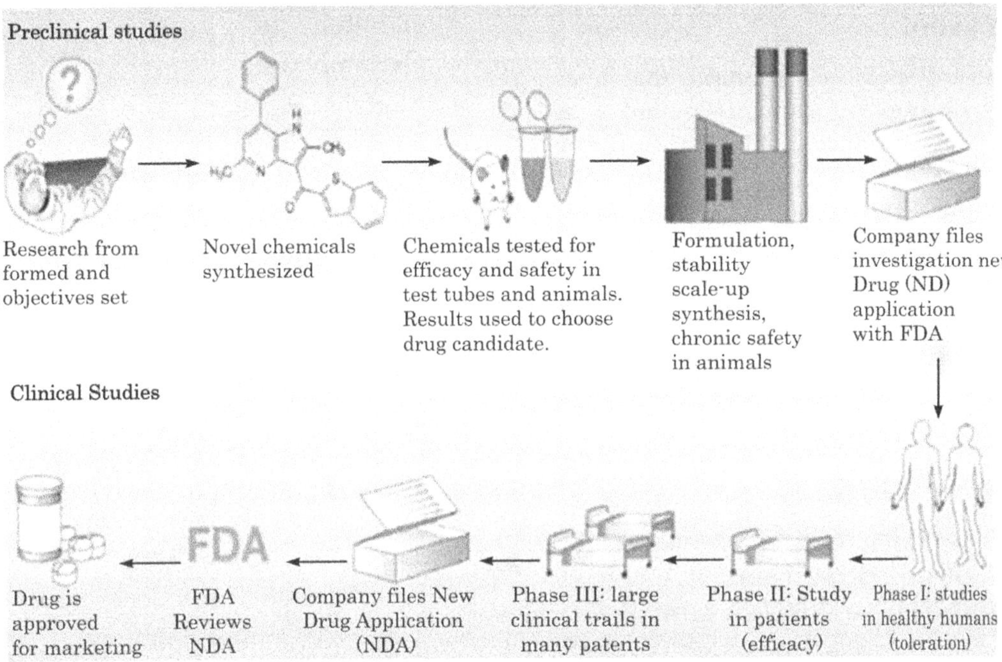


**Fig 6-2:** Preclinical and clinical studies

## Limitations of Phase 1-3 Clinical Trials

- limited size: no more than 5000 and often as little as 500 volunteers.
- narrow population: age and sex specific.
- narrow indications: only the specific disease studied.
- short duration: often no longer than a few weeks.

## Withdrawn Drugs (in the US, Since 2000)

| | |
|---|---|
| Thalidomide (1961) | Congenital limb defects |
| Benoxaprofen (1982) | Hepatotoxicity |
| Phenformin (1982) | Lactic acidosis |
| Fenfluramine (1997) | Heart-valve abnormalities |
| Astemizole | Many drug interactions |
| Phenylpropanolamine (2000) | Hemorrhagic stroke |
| Kava kava | Liver abnormalities |
| Cerivastatin | Rhabdomyolysis |
| Cisapride | Cardiac arrhythmias |
| Rofecoxib (2004) | Cardiovascular events |
| Valdecoxib (2005) events, | Cardiovascular |
| | Serious skin reactions |
| Comfrey, Senecio | Nephrotoxicity |
| Tegaserod (2007) | Cardiovascular events |
| Clobutinol (2007) | Cardiac arrhythmia |

## Definitions

### Adverse drug reaction (Table 7.1)

"A response to a drug which is noxious and unintended, and which occurs at doses normally used in man for the prophylaxis, diagnosis, or therapy of disease, or for the modification of physiological function."

### Adverse event

Any untoward medical occurrence that may present during treatment with a pharmaceutical product but which does not necessarily have a causal relationship with this treatment.

### Side effect

Any unintended effect of a pharmaceutical product occurring at doses normally used in man which is related to the pharmacological properties of the drug.

## Outcome of PVG

- Contribute to the regulatory assessment of benefit, harm, effectiveness and risk of medicines, encouraging their safe, rational and more effective (including cost effective) use.
- Improve patient care and safety in relation to use of medicines and all medical and paramedical interventions.
- Improve public health and safety in relation to use of medicines.
- Promote understanding, education and clinical training in pharmacovigilance and its effective communication to the public.
- The results of pharmacoepidemiological studies would confirm or disprove the license.
- Effectiveness of the drug in clinical practice (confirmation of the therapeutic effect), determine whether approved uses should be expanded or restricted.

## Drug Outcomes

- Outcomes:
- Effects (Pharmacological, therapeutic)
- Side effects (Unintended)
- Interactions (Expected, unexpected)
- Impact:
- Beneficial
- Harmful
- Harmful Effects
- Mortality
- Morbidity
- Hospitalization
- Prolonged stay
- Extra treatment
- Cost

## WHO Programme for International Drug Monitoring

The WHO Programme, which was established in 1968, consists of a network of

- The National Centre's
- WHO Headquarters, Geneva and
- The WHO Collaborating Centre for International Drug Monitoring, the Uppsala Monitoring Centre (UMC), in Uppsala, Sweden.

## WHO Collaborating Centre (Uppsala Monitoring Centre)

- Collection and processing of data: maintaining and developing the international adverse drug reaction database > 4 million reports.
- Regular screening of data to issue signals.
- Research
  - New ADR findings, new methodology, technology, methods of communication
- Information centre.
- Training centre.

## Subsequently Aims to

- Generate broad based ADR data on the Indian population and share the information with global health-care community through WHO-UMC.
- Ensure optimum safety of drug products in the Indian market.

- Provide technical expertise for evaluating statutory AE reports furnished by sponsors conducting clinical trials in India.

## National Pharmacovigilance Policy

### Milestones

- Short-term objectives: To foster a culture of notification.
- Medium-term objectives: To engage several healthcare professionals and NGOs in the drug monitoring and information dissemination processes.
- Long-term objectives: To achieve such operational efficiencies that would make Indian National Pharmacovigilance Programme a benchmark for global drug monitoringendeavors'.

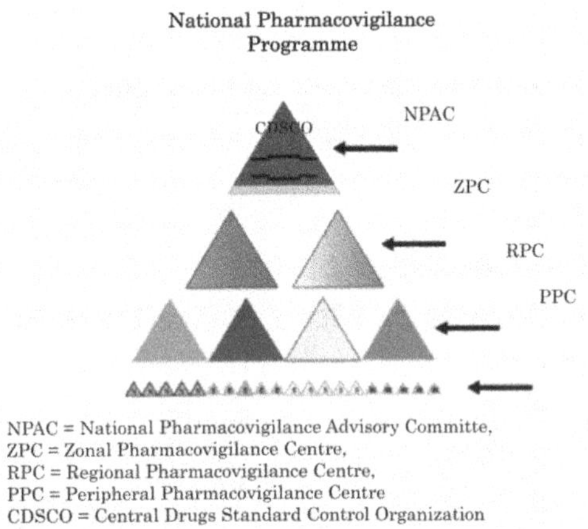


**Fig 6-3:** National pharmacovigilance programme

### Expected and Unexpected Events

Expected are those adverse events that were observed during clinical trials or post-approval observations and are mentioned in Summary of Product Characteristics (SPC).

- Unexpected are those adverse events that were not previously observed and are not documented (in SPC)
- Based on frequency of occurrence there are following categories of adverse events:

**Table 6-1:** Types of adverse reactions (rawlins and thompson classification)

| Type | Type of effect | Features | Examples |
|---|---|---|---|
| A | Augmented | Common, predictable, low mortality | Bradycardia–β-blockers |
| B | Bizarre | Uncommon, unpredictable, high morbidity and high mortality | Anaphylaxis - Penicillin |
| C | Chronic | Dose related and time related | Dyskinesia - Levodopa |
| D | Delayed | Time Related | Teratogenesis |
| E | End of use | Withdrawal of chronic therapy abruptly | Corticosteroids |
| F | Failure | Unexpected failure of therapy | Oral contraceptive failure - Rifampin |

### Key Facts

- No medicine is risk free. Vigilant assessment of the risks and benefits of medicines promotes patient safety.
- People in every country of the world are affected by ADRs. In some countries ADR-related costs, such as hospitalization, surgery and lost productivity, exceed the cost of the medications.
- Unintended, harmful reactions to medicines (known as adverse drug reactions) are among the leading causes of death in many countries.

The Majority of Adverse Drug Reactions (ADR) is Preventable and can be due to:

1. Wrong diagnosis of the patient's condition;
2. Prescription of the wrong drug or wrong dosage of the right drug;
3. An undetected medical, genetic or allergic condition that might cause a patient reaction;
4. Self-medication with prescription medicines;
5. Not following the instructions for taking the medication;
6. Reactions with other drugs (including traditional medicines)and certain foods;
7. Use of a sub-standard medication whose composition and ingredients do not meet the correct scientific requirements, and can be ineffective and often dangerous;
8. Use of counterfeit medicines with no active ingredients or the wrong ingredients, which can be dangerous or fatal.

   Prescribing and transcription –60%;

   Administration –30%;

   Dispensing –10%

   Causality Assessment

To determine likelihood of a causal relationship between drug exposure and adverse events it is necessary to evaluate:

- Association in time/place between drug use and event
- Pharmacology (including current knowledge of nature and frequency of adverse reactions)
- Medical or pharmacological plausibility (signs and symptoms, tests, pathological findings, mechanism)
- Likelihood or exclusion of other causes (Case reports describe suspected ADRs)

There are more than 34 types of assessment scales for causality evaluation which include:

- Karch and Lasagna scale
- Naranjo's scale
- The literature (9 points of consideration – Morges, Switzerland, 1981)
- WHO probability scale
- Aetiological– Diagnostic Systems (Bénchiou's group method)
- French imputation systems
- Kramer's scale
- Jones scale
- European ABO system
- Bayesian system.

## Karch and Lasagna

- Uses three categories of causality

  A – causality is highly probable

  B – not adequate proof of causality

  0 – data are not adequate to assess causality

## The literature (9 points of consideration –Morges, Switzerland, 1981)

1. Drug given prior to event?
2. Reaction at site of application?
3. Drug/ADR interval compatible with the event?
4. ADR immediately follows drug administration and is of acute onset?
5. Rechallenge positive?
6. Dechallenge positive?
7. Were concomitant drugs stopped the same time?
8. Same adverse reaction to this drug before?
9. Adverse reaction known with the suspected drug?

## Methods used in Pharmacovigilance

The activities undertaken in the name of Pharmacovigilance can be roughly divided into three groups: regulatory, industry, and academia. Regulatory Pharmacovigilance is driven by the aim to provide drugs with a positive benefit–harm profile to the public. Some of the problems related to regulatory post-marketing surveillance will be discussed in this context, followed by a description of the methods used to detect new ADRs and a discussion of the pros and cons of each method.

1. **Clinical trial data insufficient to evaluate drug risk**

The main method currently used to gather information on a drug in the pre-marketing phase is to conduct a clinical trial. Pre-marketing clinical trials can be divided into three phases. Phase III studies are often double blind randomized controlled trials; these are considered to be the most rigorous approach to determining whether a cause-effect relationship exists between a treatment and an outcome. However, when it comes to monitoring the safety of a drug, this study design is not optimal. Due to the limited number of patients participating, it is generally not possible to identify ADRs that occur only rarely. The relatively short duration of clinical trials makes it difficult to detect ADRs with a long latency. Another limitation of clinical trials is the population in which a drug is tested. The characteristics of the participants do not always correspond to the characteristics of the population in which it will later be used; consequently, it may be difficult to extrapolate the results obtained from clinical trials to the population at large. This is especially true for the elderly, for women or for people belonging to a minority ethnic group. In order to study rare ADRs, ADRs with a long latency and ADRs in specific populations, careful monitoring of the drug in the post-marketing phase is essential. Post-marketing studies can be descriptive or analytical. Descriptive studies generate hypotheses and attempt to describe the occurrence of events related to drug toxicity and efficacy. Analytical studies test hypotheses and seek to determine associations or causal connections between observed effects and particular drugs, and to measure the size of these effects. Descriptive studies are widely used in post-marketing surveillance because they are able to generate hypotheses that will become starting points for analytical studies. Two forms of descriptive studies—spontaneous reporting and intensive monitoring—will be discussed. Analytical studies can be conducted using a variety of approaches, including case-control studies, cohort studies and clinical trials. In order to be able to conduct retrospective cohort and case-control studies, data which have been collected in a reliable and routine manner needs to be available.

2. **Spontaneous reporting**

Spontaneous reporting systems (SRS) were created, and these have become the primary method of collecting post marketing information on the safety of drugs. The main function of SRS is the early detection of signals of new, rare and serious ADRs. A spontaneous reporting system enables physicians and, increasingly more often, pharmacists and patients to report suspected ADRs to a Pharmacovigilance centre. The task of the Pharmacovigilance centre is to collect and analyse the reports and to inform stakeholders of the potential risk when signals of new ADRs arise. Spontaneous reporting is also used by the pharmaceutical industry to collect information about their drugs. By means ofa SRS it is possible to monitor all drugs on the market throughout their entire life cycle at a relatively low cost. The main criticism of this approach is the potential for selective reporting and under reporting.

### 3. Data mining in spontaneous reporting

In the past, signal detection in spontaneous reporting has mainly occurred on the basis of case-by-case analyses of reports. In recent years, however, data mining techniques have become more important. The term 'data mining' refers to the principle of analyzing data from different perspectives and extracting the relevant information. Algorithms are often used to determine hidden patterns of associations or unexpected occurrences—i.e. signal—in large databases. Although the methodology of the various data mining methods applied in Pharmacovigilance differ, they all share the characteristic that they express to what extent the number of observed cases differs from the number of expected cases. Several approaches of data mining are currently in use. Proportional reporting ratios (PPRs), compare the proportion of reports for a specific ADR reported for a drug with the proportion for that ADR in all other drugs.

### 4. Intensive monitoring

These intensive monitoring systems use prescription data to identify users of a certain drug. The prescriber of the drug is asked about any adverse event occurring during the use of the drug being monitored. These data are collected and analyzed for new signals. The basis of intensive monitoring is a non-interventional observational cohort, which distinguishes it from spontaneous reporting because the former only monitors selected drugs during a certain period of time. Through its non-interventional character, intensive monitoring provides real world clinical data involving neither inclusion nor exclusion criteria throughout the collection period. It is unaffected by the kind of selection and exclusion criteria that characterize clinical trials, thereby eliminating selection bias. Strength of the methodology is that it is based upon event monitoring and is therefore capable of identifying signals for events that were not necessarily suspected as being ADRs of the drug being studied. Intensive monitoring programmes also enable the incidence of adverse events to be estimated, thus enabling quantification of the risk of certain ADRs. This approach, however, also has recognized limitations. The proportion of adverse effects that go unreported to doctors is unknown. The studies also produce reported event rates rather than true incident rates. This is the same for all studies based on medical record data, including computer databases and record linkage.

### 5. Database studies

In order to test a hypothesis, a study has to be performed. The study can be conducted using a variety of methods, including case-control studies and cohort studies. The limitations of these methods include power considerations and study design. In order to be able to conduct retrospective cohort and case-control studies, data which have been collected in a reliable and routine fashion needs to be available. The General Practice Research Database (GPRD) and the PHARMO Record Linkage System, which will be described in further detail in the following sections, were chosen here because they represent two different types of European databases.

### 6. General Practice Research Database

Virtually all patient care in the UK is coordinated by the general practitioner (GP), and data from this source provide an almost complete picture of a patient, his illnesses and treatment. In any given year, GPs, who are members of the GPRD, collect data from about 3 million patients (about 5% of the UK population). These patients are broadly representative of the general UK population in terms of age, sex and geographic distribution. The data collected include demographics (age and sex), medical diagnoses that are part of routine care or resulting from hospitalizations, consultations or emergency care, along with the date and location of the event. There is also an option of adding free text, referral to hospitals and specialists, all prescriptions, including date of prescription, formulation strength, quantity and dosing instructions, indication for treatment for all new prescriptions and events leading to withdrawal of a drug or a treatment. Data on vaccinations and miscellaneous information, such as smoking, height, weight, immunizations, pregnancy, birth, death, date entering the practice, date leaving the practice and laboratory results, are also collected.

**7. PHARMO**

In the early 1990s, the PHARMO system of record linkage was developed in The Netherlands. PHARMO links community pharmacy and hospital data within a specific region on the basis of patient birth date, gender and GP code. The system now includes drug-dispensing records from community pharmacies and hospital discharge records of about 2 million people in the Netherlands. The data collection is longitudinal and goes back to 1987. More recently, PHARMO has also been linked to other data, such as primary care data, population surveys, laboratory and genetic data, cancer and accident registries, mortality data and economic outcomes. The system has well-defined denominator information that allows incidence and prevalence estimates and is relatively cheap because existing databases are used and linked. The PHARMO database is used for follow-up studies, case-control studies and other analytical epidemiological studies for evaluating drug induced effects. In the past the database has been used for studies on drug utilisation, persistence with treatment, economic impact and ADRs

## Who Should Report Safety Data

- Health care professional (Physicians, Pharmacists, Dentists and nurses)
- Pharmaceutical companies qualified persons – (Pharmacovigilance/Regulatory manager)
- Investigational products (clinical trials)
- Post-approval reporting – Individual Case Safety Report (ICSR), Periodic Safety Update Report (PSUR)

## What to Report – WHO Recommendations

- All adverse events related to the use of a drug.
- All suspected adverse reactions
- Reactions to any other drugs which are suspected of significantly affecting a patient's management, including reactions suspected of causing:
- Death
- Life-threatening (real risk of dying)
- Hospitalization(initial or prolonged)
- Disability (significant, persistent or permanent)
- Congenital anomaly
- Required intervention to prevent permanent impairment or damage

## Where to Report

- The prescribed 'Adverse Drug Event Reporting Form' shall be used for the purpose of National Pharmacovigilance Programme (Fig. 7.4).
- After completion the form shall be returned/ forwarded to the same Pharmacovigilance Centre from where it was received.
- Only those forms which meet the following criteria shall be analyzed:
- Authenticity (including reporter's and patient's traceability).
- Completeness (at least with respect to point no.'s 1, 5, 8, 11, 20 and 22 on the ADE Reporting Form).

## ADVICE ABOUT REPORTING

- **Report adverse experiences with medications**
- **Report serious adverse reactions. A reaction is serious when the patient outcome is:**
    - death
    - life-threatening (real risk of dying)
    - hospitalization (initial or prolonged)
    - disability (significant, persistent or permanent)
    - congenital anomaly
    - required intervention to prevent permanent impairment or damage
- **Report even if:**
    - You're not certain the product caused adverse reaction
    - You don't have all the details although point nos. 1, 5, 7, 8, 11, 15, 16 & 18 (see reverse) are essentially required.
- **Who can report:**
    - Any health care professional (Doctors including Dentists, Nurses and Pharmacists).
- **Where to report:**
    - After completing, please return this form to the same Pharmacovigilance centre from where you received.
    - A list of countrywide Pharmacovigilance Centres is available at: www.cdsco.nic.in
- **What happens to the submitted information:**
    - Information provided in this form is handled in strict confidence. Peripheral Pharmacovigilance Centres will forward this form to the Regional Pharmacovigilance Centres, where the causality analysis is carried out and the information is forwarded to the Zonal Pharmacovigilance Centres. Finally the data is statistically analysed and forwarded to the Global Pharmacovigilance Database managed by WHO Uppsala Monitoring Center in Sweden.
    - Data is periodically reviewed by the National Pharmacovigilance Advisory Committee constituted by the Ministry of Health and Family Welfare. The Committee is entrusted with responsibility to review the data and suggest any interventions that may be required.

## Suspected Adverse Drug Reaction Reporting Form

For VOLUNTARY reporting
of suspected adverse drug reactions by
health care professionals

CDSCO

Central Drugs Standard Control Organization

Directorate General of Health Services,
Ministry of Health & Family Welfare, Government of India.
Nirman Bhawan, New Delhi-110011
www.cdsco.nic.in

**ATTENTION**
**HEALTH CARE PROFESSIONALS**
**Your 5 Minutes Can Help Us Ensure Safer Medications**

**Please return this form to:**

**Confidentiality:** The patient's identity is held in strict confidence and protected to the fullest extent. Programme staff is not expected to and will not disclose the reporter's identity in response to a request from the public. Submission of a report does not constitute an admission that medical personnel or manufacturer or the product caused or contributed to the reaction.

# SUSPECTED ADVERSE DRUG REACTION REPORTING FORM

**CDSCO**
**Central Drugs Standard Control Organization**
Directorate General of Health Services,
Ministry of Health & Family Welfare, Government of India,
Nirman Bhawan, New Delhi - 110011
www.cdsco.nic.in

For VOLUNTARY reporting of Adverse Drug Reactions by health care professionals

Report #

To be filled in by Pharmacovigilance centres receiving the form.

**A. Patient Information**

1. Patient identifier initials ______ In confidence
2. Age at time of event: or ______ Date of Birth:
3. Sex ☐ M ☐ F
4. Weight ______ Kgs

**B. Suspected Adverse Reaction**

5. Date of reaction started (dd/mm/yy):
6. Date of recovery (dd/mm/yy):
7. Describe reaction or problem

12. Relevant tests/ laboratory data, including dates

13. Other relevant history, including pre-existing medical conditions (e.g., allergies, race, pregnancy, smoking alcohol use, hepatic/ renal dysfunction, etc.)

14. Seriousness of the reaction
☐ Death (dd/mm/yy) ______
☐ Life threatening
☐ Hospitalization-initial or prolonged
☐ Disability
☐ Congenital anomaly
☐ Required intervention to prevent permanent impairment/ damage
☐ Other (specify) ______

15. Outcomes
☐ Fatal ☐ Recovering ☐ Unknown
☐ Continuing ☐ Recovered ☐ Other (specify) ______

**C. Suspected medication(s)**

| Sl. No. | 8. Name (brand and / or generic name) | Manufacturer (if known) | Batch No. / Lot No. (if known) | Exp. Date (if known) | Dose used | Route used | Frequency | Therapy dates (if unknown, give duration) | | Reason for Use or prescribed for |
|---|---|---|---|---|---|---|---|---|---|---|
| | | | | | | | | Date started | Date stopped | |
| i | | | | | | | | | | |
| ii | | | | | | | | | | |
| iii | | | | | | | | | | |
| iv | | | | | | | | | | |

| Sl. No. As per C | 9. Reaction abated after drug stopped or dose reduced | | | | | 10. Reaction reappeared after reintroduction | | | | |
|---|---|---|---|---|---|---|---|---|---|---|
| | Yes | No | Unknown | NA | Reduced dose | Yes | No | Unknown | NA | If reintroduced, dose |
| i | | | | | | | | | | |
| ii | | | | | | | | | | |
| iii | | | | | | | | | | |
| iv | | | | | | | | | | |

11. Concomitant medical products and therapy dates including self medication and herbal remedies (exclude those used to treat reaction)

**D. Reporter (see confidentiality section in first page)**

16. Name and Professional Address: ______
Pin code: ______ E-mail: ______
Cell No. / Tel. No. with STD Code: ______
Speciality: ______ Signature:

17. Occupation

18. Date of this report (dd/mm/yy)

**Fig 6.4** Adverse effect reporting form

## Role of NPV Centre

1. Shall monitor the ADRs to identify previously unexpected or indicate that certain reactions occur more commonly than previously.
   - This will include the collation, review and evaluation of all spontaneous ADR reports received by the unit on a nation-wide basis.
   - Information will then be keyed into the ADR database for use in aggregate analysis.
   - These reports shall also be submitted to the WHO International Drug Monitoring Programme for international collaboration on drug safety.
1. Shall review Periodic Safety Update Reports (PSURs)Pharmaceutical companies are required to submit the PSURs of all new chemicals drugs and expected to be submitted every 6monthly for the first 2 years of marketing in India, and annually for the subsequent 2 years.
2. Shall maintain contacts with international regulatory bodiesworking in pharmaco-vigilance and exchange information on drug safety.
3. Based on the available data, the Advisory Committee shall make recommendations on product label amendments, product withdrawals and suspension.
4. Shall provide information to end-users through adverse drug reaction news bulletins, drug alerts and seminars.

## Limitations

- Too many patients: no time for filling the forms
- Lack of trained manpower
- Lack of responsibility regarding ADR
- Lack of institutional commitment
- Lack of pharmaceutical care service in hospital

## Future Strategies and Proposals

- Building and maintaining a Robust Pharmacovigilance system
- Strengthen the programme with trained scientific and medical assessors for Pharmacovigilance
- Health care professionals being communicated through internet facilities
- Education and training of medical students, pharmacists and nurses in the area of Pharmacovigilance
- Collaborating with Pharmacovigilance organizations in enhancing drug safety.

## So...What is Our Role?

Send Not Only Quantity But.... Quality Reports

## References


1. Source: The Importance of Pharmacovigilance, WHO 2002
2. *Pharmacovigilance*. Mann RD, Andrews EB, eds. John Wiley and Sons Ltd, Chichester, 2002. spontaneous reports are very useful.
3. Rahman, SZ; Khan, RA; Gupta, V; Uddin, Misbah(July2007)."Pharmacoenvironmentolo gy -A Component of Pharmacovigilance". *Environmental Health* 6(20).
4. Rahman, SZ; Khan RA, Gupta V, Misbah Uddin (2008). "Chapter2: Pharmacoenvironmentology – Ahead of

Pharmacovigilance". In Rahman SZ, Shahid M and Gupta A.*An Introduction to Environmental Pharmacology* (1st ed.). Aligarh: Ibn Sina Academy. pp. 35–52.

5. Ilene Sue Ruhoy, Christian G. Daughton. Beyond the medicine cabinet: An analysis of where and why medications accumulate. Environment International 2008, Vol. 34 (8): 1157-1169
6. WHO guidelines on safety monitoring of herbal medicines in pharmacovigilance systems, World Health Organization, Geneva, 2004
7. S Z Rahman and K C Singhal, Problems in pharmacovigilance of medicinal products of herbal origin and means to minimize them, Uppsala Reports, WHO Collaborating Center for ADR monitoring, Uppsala Monitoring Centre, Sweden, Issue 17 January 2002: 1-4.

CHAPTER

# Essential Drugs 7

## Definition

In 1975, world health organization (WHO) has come to know about the drug problems faced by developing country. There is the concept of essential drugs. Each country has its own essential drug policy it is given by experts from pharmacology and other branches.

1st essential drug list prepared in 1977 and 10th - 1998.

### The Concept of Essential Medicines

A limited range of carefully selected essential medicines leads to better health care, better drug management, and lower costs.

## Definition

"Those drugs that satisfy the health care needs of the majority of the population; they should therefore be available at all times in adequate amounts and in appropriate dosage forms, at a price the community can afford."

### History of the WHO Model List of Essential Drugs

- 1977 First Model list published, ± 200 active substances.
- List is revised every two years by WHO Expert Committee.
- 2002 Revised procedures approved by WHO.
- April revision 2003 contains 315 active substances.

The first list was a major breakthrough in the history of medicine, pharmacy and public health.

## Purpose

Essential medicines are intended to be available within the context of functioning health systems at all times, in adequate amounts, in the appropriate dosage forms, with assured quality, and at a price the individual and the community can afford. Fig. 7.1 shows the essential medicines target.

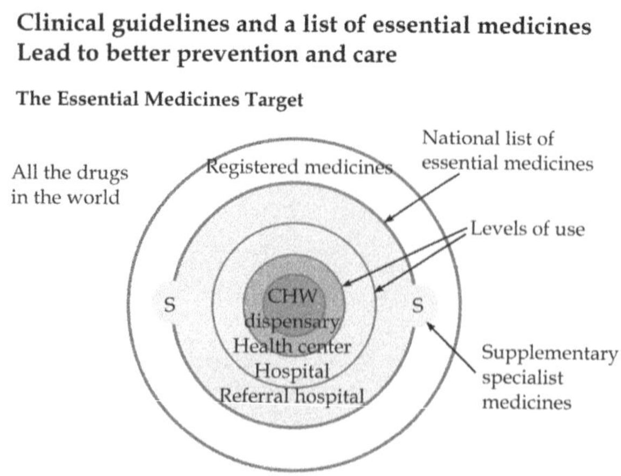


**Fig 7-1** Essential medicines target

## Implementation

The implementation of the concept of essential medicines is intended to be flexible and adaptable to many different situations; exactly which medicines are regarded as essential remains a national responsibility.

**Fig 7-2** Clinical guidelines

These should be available in all times in adequate amounts in appropriate dosage forms. Model list of essential drugs is of great importance due to following reasons

1. Development of treatment guidelines (Fig. 7.2).
2. Development of National formulary.
3. Measure to use drug information to patient and public.

### Choice of Essential Drug

1. Prevalence of disease in the country.
2. Treatment facilities available.
3. Financial status of the country.
4. Level of training and experience by personnel, who handle these drugs.
5. Based on genetic, environmental and demographic factors.

### Seven Steps to Get a New Medicine on

1. Identification of public-health need for a medicine.
2. Development of the medicine; phase I-II-III trials.
3. Regulatory approval in a number of countries.
4. Effective and safe medicine on the market
5. More experience under different field circumstances; post-marketing surveillance.
6. Price indication for public sector use.
7. Review by WHO disease programme; define comparative effectiveness and safety in real-life situations, comparative cost-effectiveness and public health relevance.
8. Medicine included in WHO treatment guideline.
9. Submission to WHO Expert Committee on Essential Drugs.
10. Medicine included in WHO Model List.

### Systematic and Transparent Process

- Guideline development group with wide representation.
- Careful consideration of conflict of interest.
- Systematic computer search for evidence.
- Evaluation of strength of evidence.
- Systematic cost-effectiveness analysis.
- For WHO: evaluation of public health considerations.
- Graded recommendations with linked references.
- External review of draft recommendations.
- If there is insufficient evidence: consensus expert opinion.

### Steps in Review of Applications to the Model List

1. Summary of application posted on WHO Medicines web site.
2. Specialist assessment of comparative efficacy, safety and cost effectiveness.
3. Review of assessments by Expert Committee member ("presenter"); formulation of draft.

4. Recommendation.
5. Review of draft recommendation by relevant Expert Advisory Panel members; and posted on WHO Medicines web site.
6. Review by presenter, prepares final draft recommendation.
7. Discussion of draft recommendation and proposed text for WHO Model Formulary by the Expert Committee.

## Role of Treatment Cost and Global Cost-effectiveness Analyses

- High cost alone should not exclude an essential medicine.
- Cost-effectiveness (C/E) comparisons will be made among alternative medicines within the same therapeutic group.
- Price information from existing UN sources will be used; all information sources will be identified.
- Simple indicators will be used: cost per unit, cost per treatment/month, cost per cure, cost per case prevented.
- Emphasis on usual outcome measures, and use of existing and published comparative cost-effectiveness analyses.
- New C/E calculations will be transparent and can be adapted.

## Presentation of Recommendations, Report Presentation of Recommendations

- Summary of reasons for each recommendation.
- Reference to underlying evidence and systematic reviews.
- Reference to existing clinical guidelines.
- Inclusion in WHO Essential Medicines Library

## Report, web site, translations

- Report of the meeting published on WHO Medicines web site.
- Report issued in WHO Technical Report Series.
- List and recommendations translated into other languages.

The WHO Model List of Essential Drugs (Fig. 7.3) Selection of Essential Drugs Depends on Following Factors:

1. It should be evidence based, not situation based.
2. Selected drugs should have sound and adequate data on efficacy and quality based on clinical studies.
3. Performance of drug as general use in variety of medical settings.
4. Based on bioavailability and stability of drug.
5. Whether the drug is available in particular or appropriate dosage form approved by National Drug and Therapeutics Committee (NDTC).
6. If two drugs having similarity in bioavailability stability then we go into consideration for efficacy, safety, quality and availability of drug.
7. Cost effectiveness --- cost / benefit ratio only unit cost should not be taken into consideration. The cost that will happen for entire treatment is taken into consideration. For this Pharmacoeconomics come into consideration.
8. Based on pharmacokinetics of the drug.
9. Local storage is applicable (or) not and is taken into consideration. Generally single drug is preferred.
10. If combination of the drugs is taken then each ingredient should have its own efficacy, economy and patient compliance.

    E.g., T.B. drugs Isoniazid, rifampicin and pyrazinamide as drugs.

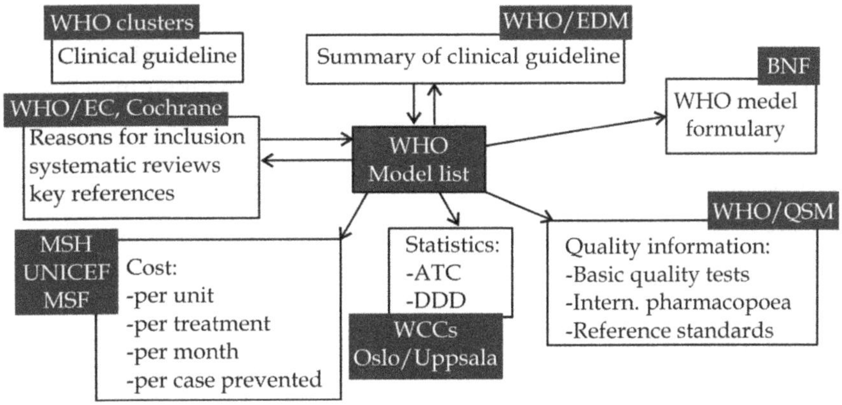


**Fig 7-3** WHO essential medicines model list

## Pharmaceutical Dosage Forms – Guidelines for in the List of Essential Drugs

1. The dosage form should have general utility and wider availability.
2. Tablets are having wider acceptability.
3. Establish local preference.
4. Stability under ambient temperature conditions.
5. Consideration of pharmacokinetic and bioavailability parameters.
6. Salt forms of the drug also should be taken into consideration. E.g., Chloramphenicolpalmitate, Erythromycin estolate.
7. Sustained / controlled release dosage forms having low t½should be included into this essential drug list on the basis of advice given by the expert. E.g., Theophylline

## 1998-10th List Model List of Essential Drugs Salient Features

1. Drugs included as therapeutic need not be mentioned as pharmacological classification, there are 27 classes from anesthesia drugs to vitamins
2. Anaesthetics
   (i) Local anesthetics
   (ii) General anesthetics
   (iii) Pre-operative medication
   (iv) Cardiovascular drugs
   (v) Anti hypertensive's
   (vi) Anti arrythmics
   (vii) Thrombolytics
   (viii) Hypolipidemics

1. Dosage forms as well as dose also will be mentioned in the righth and corner
2. Most commonly used drugs having wider availability are included. Again 2-4 drugs are included in each class.
3. Some of the drugs are indicated by a square preceeding which indicates it as a therapeutic drug.
4. For some of the drugs numbers are included in parenthesis (brackets)
   (i) Drugs which are under international control narcotics and psychotropics.
   (ii) Drugs which improves patient compliance (for E.g., T.B drugs)
   (iii) Drugs having renal impairment. E.g., Ethambutol
   (iv) Drugs having narrow therapeutic index. E.g., Digitalis, theophylline)
   (v) Drugs that require therapeutic drug monitoring. E.g., Digoxin.

Tasks that has to be carried out after preparation of essential drugs list.

1. Updating the essential drugs list: in the one year mean time it should be updated for new disease.
2. Model list of essential drugs for primary health care centers: There will not be adequate amount of medicines due to inadequate diagnostic equipments the persons. They should be educated and proper supply of drugs.
3. Specialist control for drug usage: Should have specialist for control of Antineoplastics, T.B drugs, Antiviral drugs. Educate the patients.
   (a) Antiviral drugs
   (b) Antineoplastics
   (c) Immunosuppressive drugs
   (d) T.B.drugs
1. Research and development: Consider the Q.A and research activity is done after the preparation of essential drug list.
2. Drug information and health education: Educate the patient and also the prescribes should know the knowledge of drugs.
3. List of reserves antibiotic drugs: E.g., Ampicillin, cephalexin, cephatriazone, amoxicillin. These are included in essential drug list.
4. Post registration drug studies:
   (a) In clinical trials not done on children, pregnant women and elderly people.
   (b) Some of the genetic and environmental factors
   (c) If there is any misuse or over usage of drug is not reveled in clinical trials.
   (d) Unexpected use of the drug is not revealed.
   (e) Any poor manufacturing process deviation is not revealed in clinical trials.

## Conclusion

- The concept of essential medicines is a global concept
- WHO clinical guidelines are the foundation for the Model List of Essential Drugs; the Model List remains a strong public health tool

The WHO Essential Medicines Library is a valuable information base for all Member States, international organisations, drugs and therapeutic committees and health insurance organisations.

CHAPTER

# Abnormal Actions of Drugs 8

### Adverse Drug Reaction (ADR)

An *adverse drug reaction* is a "response to a drug which is noxious and unintended and which occurs at doses normally used in man for prophylaxis, diagnosis or therapy of disease or for the modification of physiologic function."

There is a causal link between a drug and an adverse drug reaction.

In sum, an *adverse drug reaction* is harm **directly caused by the drug at normal doses, during normal use.**

## Adverse Drug Event (Abbreviated ADE)

It refers to any injury caused by the drug (at normal dosage and/or due to overdose) and any harm associated with the use of drug (e.g. discontinuation of drug therapy). ADRs are a special type of ADEs.

## The Risk to Benefit Ratio

When prescribing drugs a doctor must assess risk to benefit ratio in the individual patient by

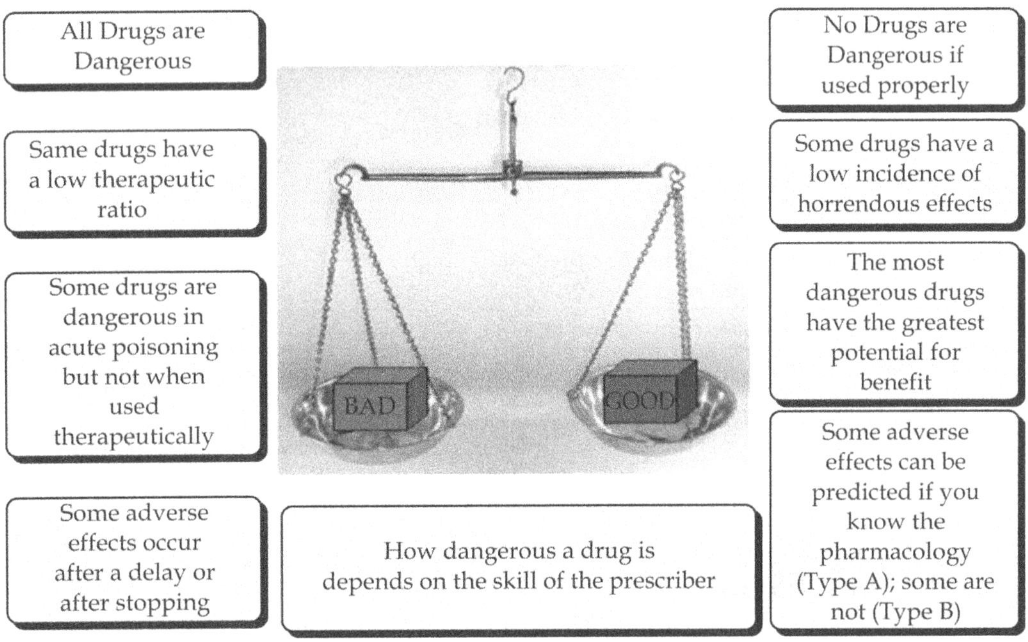


**Fig 8-1:** Adverse drug effects

- Choosing an appropriate class of drug then an appropriate individual agent
- Is it effective?
- What are the chances of adverse effect?
- Are there features in this patient which affect choice E.g., other drugs, organ failure, aged
- Tailoring the dose
- Considering duration of treatment

The Risks when prescribing drugs with a low therapeutic ratio are greatly increased if

1. Pharmacokinetic process is complicated E.g., high hepatic extraction or zero order elimination
2. Wide interindividual variation in kinetics and/or response
3. Pharmacokinetics sensitive to drug interaction, disease or ageing.

## Classification

### Predictable Reactions (Type A)

1. Can be predicted from the known pharmacology of the drug.
2. May be common within the pharmacological groups
3. Are due either to excessive action at the target receptor or to action at a non-target receptor.
4. Are related closely to the amount of drug in the body.
5. Are determined by dose and by pharmacokinetic and pharmacodynamic factors (E.g., greatly reduced dose of Warfarin needed in liver disease).
6. Are common, accounting for 75% or more of all adverse effects.
7. Are largely avoidable with care.

### Unpredictable Reactions (Type B)

1. The effect is unrelated to established pharmacological effects.
2. The effect may not be shared with in pharmacological groups
3. The effect may be serious organ damage (E.g., Pulmonary Fibrosis with sulphasalazine)
4. There is a poor relationship to dose.
5. They are uncommon and difficult to detect in drug development.
6. They cannot be avoided if the drug is used.
7. Patient idiosyncrasy is a major factor.

**Table 8-1:** Classification of adverse effects

| Type | Type of effect | Features | examples |
|---|---|---|---|
| A | Augmented | Common, predictable, low mortality | Bradycardia–β-blockers |
| B | Bizarre | Uncommon, unpredictable, high morbidity and high mortality | Anaphylaxis - Penicillin |
| C | Chronic | Dose related and time related | Dyskinesia - Levodopa |
| D | Delayed | Time Related | Teratogenesis |
| E | End of use | Withdrawal of chronic therapy abruptly | Corticosteroids |
| F | Failure | Unexpected failure of therapy | Oral contraceptive failure - Rifampin |

## Seriousness and Severity

The American Food and Drug Administration define a serious adverse event as one when the patient outcome is one of the following:

- Death
- Life threatening
- Hospitalization (initial or prolonged)

- Disability significant, persistent or permanent change, impairment, damage or disruption in the patient's body function/ structure, physical activities or quality of life.
- Congenital anomaly
- Requires intervention to prevent permanent impairment or damage

Severity is a point on an arbitrary scale of intensity of the adverse event in question. The terms "severe" and "serious" when applied to adverse events are technically very different. They are easily confused but cannot be used interchangeably, requiring care in usage.

A headache is severe, if it causes intense pain. There are scales like "visual analog scale" that help us assess the severity. On the other hand, a headache is not usually serious (but may be in case of subarachnoid hemorrhage, subdural bleed, even a migraine may temporally fit criteria), unless it also satisfies the criteria for seriousness listed above.

## Overall Drug Risk

While no official scale exists yet to communicate overall drug risk, the Guard Drug Risk Rating System is a five color rating scale similar to the Homeland Security Advisory System:

- Red (high risk)
- Orange (elevated risk)
- Yellow (guarded risk)
- Blue (general risk)
- Green (low risk)

## Location

Adverse effects may be local, i.e., limited to a certain location or systemic, where a medication has caused adverse effects throughout the systemic circulation.

For instance, some ocular antihypertensives cause systemic effects, although they are administered locally as eye drops, since a fraction escapes to the systemic circulation

## Mechanisms

As research better explains the biochemistry of drug use, fewer ADRs are Type B and more are Type A. Common mechanisms are:

- Abnormal pharmacokinetics due to
  - genetic factors
  - comorbid disease states
- Synergistic effects between either
  - a drug and a disease
  - two drugs

## Abnormal Pharmacokinetics

### Co - morbid disease states

Various diseases, especially those that cause renal or hepatic insufficiency, may alter drug metabolism. Resources are available that report changes in a drug's metabolism due to disease states.

### Genetic factors

Abnormal drug metabolism may be due to inherited factors of either Phase I oxidation or Phase II conjugation. Pharmacogenomics is the study of the inherited basis for abnormal drug reactions.

### Phase I reactions

Inheriting abnormal alleles of cytochrome P450 can alter drug metabolism. Tables are available to check for drug interactions due to P450 interactions.

Inheriting abnormal butyryl cholinesterase (pseudocholinesterase) may affect metabolism of drugs such as succinylcholine

### Phase II reactions

Inheriting abnormal N-acetyltransferase which conjugated some drugs to facilitate excretion may affect the metabolism of drugs such as isoniazid, Hydralazine and procainamide.

### Interactions with other drugs

The risk of drug interactions is increased with polypharmacy.

### Protein binding

These interactions are usually transient and mild until a new steady state is achieved. These are mainly for drugs without much first pass liver metabolism. The principal plasma proteins for drug binding are:

1. albumin
2. $\alpha_1$-acid glycoprotein
3. lipoproteins

Some drug interactions with warfarin are due to changes in protein binding.

### Cytochrome P450

Patients have abnormal metabolism by cytochrome P450 due to either inheriting abnormal alleles or due to drug interactions. Tables are available to check for drug interactions due to P450 interactions.

### Synergistic effects

An example of synergism is two drugs that both prolong the QT interval.

**Table 8-2:** Examples of adverse effects as associated with specific medications

| Condition | Substance |
|---|---|
| Abortion, miscarriage or uterine hemorrhage | Misoprostol (Cytotec), a labor-inducing drug (this is a case where the adverse effect has been used legally and illegally for performing abortions) |
| Addiction | Many sedatives and analgesics such as diazepam, morphine, etc. |
| Birth defects | Thalidomide and Accutane |
| Bleeding of the intestine | Aspirin therapy |
| Cardiovascular disease | COX-2 inhibitors (i.e., Vioxx) |
| Deafness and kidney failure | Gentamicin (an antibiotic) |
| Death, following sedation | Propofol (Diprivan) |
| Depression or hepatic injury | Interferon |
| Diabetes | Atypical antipsychotic medications (neuroleptic psychiatric drugs) |
| Diarrhea | Orlistat (Xenical) |
| Erectile dysfunction | Many drugs, such as antidepressants |
| Fever | Vaccination (in the past, imperfectly manufactured vaccines, such as BCG and poliomyelitis, have caused the disease they intended to fight). |
| Glaucoma | Corticosteroid-based eye drops |
| Hair loss and anemia | Chemotherapy against cancer, leukemia, etc. |
| Headache | Spinal anesthesia |
| Hypertension | Ephedrine users, which prompted FDA to remove the status of dietary supplement of ephedra extracts |
| Insomnia | Stimulants, Ritalin, Adderall, etc. |
| Lactic acidosis | Stavudine (Zerit, for anti-HIV therapy) or metformin (for diabetes) |
| Liver failure | Paracetamol |

*Table 8-2 Contd...*

| Condition | Substance |
|---|---|
| Melasma and thrombosis | Estrogen-containing hormonal contraception such as the combined oral contraceptive pill |
| Irreversible Peripheral neuropathy | Fluoroquinolone medications |
| Rhabdomyolysis | Statins (anti-cholesterol drugs) |
| Seizures | Withdrawal from benzodiazepine |
| Drowsiness or increase in appetite | Antihistamine use. Some antihistamines are used in sleep aids explicitly because they cause drowsiness. |
| Stroke or heart attack | Sildenafil (Viagra) when used with nitroglycerine; COX-2 inhibitors |
| Suicide, increased tendency | Fluoxetine and other SSRI antidepressants |
| Parkinsonism | MPTP a meperidine related drug considered highly neurotoxic |
| Tardive dyskinesia | Long-term use of metoclopramide and many antipsychotic medications |
| Spontaneous Tendon rupture | Fluoroquinolone drugs even occurring as late as 6 months after treatment had been terminated. |

## Detecting Adverse Effects

- If a new drug causes a bizarre effect in 1 in 6000 patients it would need 18000 patients to use the drug for it to occur in 3 patients.
- It would take twice as many before there was any suspicion that the effect was due to the drug.
- If the effect also occurs naturally then it would take many times more patients.
- Most early trials involve about 2000 patients.
- MHRA (Medicine and Healthcare products Regulatory Agency) free phone service for reporting and information about suspected ADRs.
- Self reporting by patients and relatives using Yellow cards available at pharmacies.
- Prescription event monitoring.
- New drugs - black triangles and yellow cards.

## Prevention of Adverse Drug Reactions

- Never use any drug unless there is good indication. If the patient is pregnant do not use the drug unless the need is imperative.
- Allergy and idiosyncrasy are important causes of ADRs. Ask if the patient had previous reactions.
- Ask if the patient is already taking other drugs including self medication
- Age, hepatic and renal disease may impair clearance of drugs so smaller doses may be needed. Genetic factors may also predispose to certain ADRs
- Prescribe as few drugs as possible and give clear instructions
- Where possible use familiar drugs. With new drugs be particularly alert for ADRs and unexpected event.
- If serious ADRs are liable to occur warn the patient.

## Hypersensitivity

Hypersensitivity refers to undesirable (damaging, discomfort producing and sometimes fatal) reactions produced by the normal immune system. Hypersensitivity reactions require a pre sensitized (immune) state of the host.

Hypersensitivity reactions can be divided into four types: type I, type II, type III and type IV, based on the mechanisms involved and time taken for the reaction. Frequently, a particular clinical condition (disease) may involve more than one type of reaction.

### Type I Hypersensitivity

It is also known as immediate or anaphylactic hypersensitivity. The reaction may involve skin (urticaria and eczema), eyes (conjunctivitis), nasopharynx (rhinorrhea, rhinitis), bronchopulmonary tissues (asthma) and gastrointestinal tract (gastroenteritis). The reaction may cause from minor inconvenience to death. The reaction takes 15-30 minutes from the time of exposure to the antigen. Sometimes the reaction may have a delayed onset (10-12 hours). Immediate hypersensitivity is mediated by IgE. The primary cellular component in this hypersensitivity is mast cell or basophil. The reaction is amplified and/or modified by platelets, neutrophils and eosinophils. A biopsy of the reaction site demonstrates mainly mast cells and eosinophils. The mechanism of reaction involves preferential production of IgE, in response to certain antigens, allergens. IgE has very high affinity for its receptor on mast cells and basophils. A subsequent exposure to the same allergen cross links the cell-bound IgE and triggers the release of various pharmacologically active substances. Cross-linking of IgE Fc-receptor is important in mast cell triggering. Mast cell degranulation is preceded by increased Ca++ influx, which is a crucial process; ionophores which increase cytoplasmic Ca++ also promote degranulation, whereas, agents which deplete cytoplasmic Ca++suppress degranulation. Mast cells may be triggered by other stimuli such as exercise, emotional stress, chemicals (e.g., photographic developing medium, calcium ionophores, codeine, etc.), anaphylotoxins (e.g., C4a, C3a, C5a, etc.). These reactions mediated by agents without IgE-allergen interaction are not hypersensitivity reactions, although they produce the same symptoms.

**Table 8-3:** Pharmacologic mediators of immediate hypersensitivity

| Mediator | |
|---|---|
| Preformed mediators in granules | |
| Histamine<br>Tryptase<br>Kininogenase<br>ECF-A<br>(tetrapeptides) | Bronchoconstriction, mucus, vasodialatation, vascular permeability proteolysis<br>Kinins and vasodialatation, vascular permeability, edema attract cosinophil and neutrophils. |
| Newly formed mediators | |
| Leukotriene $B_4$<br>Leukotriene $C_4$, $D_4$<br>Prostaglandins $D_2$<br>PAF | Basophil attractant same as histamine but 1000s more potent edema and pain platelet aggregation and heparin release microthrombin |

The reaction is amplified by PAF (platelet activation factor) which causes platelet aggregation and release of histamine, heparin and vasoactive amines. Eosinophil chemotactic factor of anaphylaxis (ECF-A) and neutrophil chemotactic factors attract eosinophils and neutrophils, respectively, which release various hydrolytic enzymes that cause necrosis. Eosinophil may also control the local reaction by releasing arylsulphatase, histaminase, phospholipase-D and prostaglandin-E, Cyclic nucleotides appear to play a significant role in the modulation of immediate hypersensitivity reaction, although their exact function is ill understood. Substances which alter cAMP and cGMP levels significantly alter the allergic symptoms. Thus, substances that increase intracellular cAMP seem to relieve allergic symptoms, particularly broncho-pulmonary ones, and are used therapeutically (Table 2). Conversely, agents that decrease cAMP or stimulate cGMP aggravate these allergic conditions.

Diagnostic tests for immediate hypersensitivity include skin (prick and intradermal) tests, measurement of total IgE and specific IgE antibodies against the suspected allergens. Total IgE and specific IgE antibodies are measured by a modification of enzyme immunoassay (ELISA). Increased IgE levels are indicative of atopic condition, although IgE may be elevated in some non atopic diseases (e.g., myelomas, helminthic infection, etc.).

Symptomatic treatment is achieved with antihistamines which block histamine receptors. Chromolyn sodium inhibits mast cell degranulation, probably, by inhibiting Ca++ influx. Late onset allergic symptoms, particularly bronchoconstriction which is mediated by leukotrienes are treated with leukotriene receptor blockers (Singulair, Accolate) or inhibitors of cyclooxygenase pathway (Zileutoin). Symptomatic, although short term relief from bronchoconstriction is provided by bronchodilators (inhalants) such as isoproterenol derivatives (Terbutaline, Albuterol). Thophylline elevates cAMP by inhibiting cAMP-phosphodiesterase and inhibits intracellular Ca++ release is also used to relieve broncho-pulmonary symptoms. There appears to be a genetic predisposition for atopic diseases and there is evidence for HLA (A2) association. Hyposensitization (immunotherapy or desensitization) is another treatment modality which is successful in a number of allergies, particularly to insect venoms and, to some extent, pollens. The mechanism is not clear, but there is a correlation between appearance of IgG (blocking) antibodies and relief from symptoms. Suppressor T cells that specifically inhibit IgE antibodies may play a role.

### Type II Hypersensitivity

It is also known as cytotoxic hypersensitivity and may affect a variety of organs and tissues. The antigens are normally endogenous, although exogenous chemicals (haptens) which can attach to cell membranes can also lead to type II hypersensitivity. Drug-induced hemolytic anemia, granulocytopenia and thrombocytopenia are such examples. The reaction time is minutes to hours. It is primarily mediated by antibodies of IgM or IgG class and complement. Phagocytes and K cells may also play a role (ADCC). The lesion contains antibody, complement and neutrophils. Diagnostic tests include detection of circulating antibody against tissues involved and the presence of antibody and complement in the lesion (biopsy) by immunofluorescence. The staining pattern is normally smooth and linear, such as that seen in Goodpasture's nephritis (renal and lung basement membrane) and pemphigus (skin intercellular protein, desmosome). Treatment involves anti inflammatory and immunosuppressive agents.

### Type III Hypersensitivity

It is also known as immune complex hypersensitivity. The reaction may be general (e.g., serum sickness) or may involve individual organs including skin (e.g., systemic lupus erythematosus, Arthus reaction), kidneys (e.g., lupus nephritis), lungs (e.g., aspergillosis), blood vessels (e.g., polyarteritis), joints (e.g., rheumatoid arthritis) or other organs. This reaction may be the pathogenic mechanism of diseases caused by many microorganisms. The reaction may take 3-10 hours after exposure to the antigen (as in Arthus reaction). It is mediated by soluble immune complexes. They are mostly of IgG class, although IgM may also be involved. The antigen may be exogenous (chronic bacterial, viral or parasitic infections), or endogenous (non organ specific autoimmunity: e.g., systemic lupus eythematosus, SLE). The antigen is soluble and not attached to the organ involved. Primary components are soluble immune complexes and complement (C3a, C4a and C5a). The lesion contains primarily neutrophils and deposits of immune complexes and complement. Macrophages infiltrating in later stages may be involved in the healing process. The affinity of antibody and size of immune complexes are important in production of disease and determining the tissue involved. Diagnosis involves examination of tissue biopsies for deposits of Ig and complement by immuno-fluorescence. The immunofluorescent staining in type III hypersensitivity is granular (as opposed to linear in type II: Goodpasture). Presence of immune complexes in serum and depletion in complement level are also diagnostic. Polyethylene glycol mediated turbidity (nephelometry), binding of C1q and Raji cell test are utilized to detect immune complexes. Treatment includes anti inflammatory agents.

### Type IV Hypersensitivity

It is also known as cell mediated or delayed type hypersensitivity. The classical example of this hypersensitivity is tuberculin (Montoux) reaction which peaks 48 hours after the injection of antigen (PPD or old tuberculin). The lesion is characterized by induration and erythema. Type IV hypersensitivity is involved in the pathogenesis of many autoimmune and infectious diseases (tuberculosis, leprosy, blastomycosis,histoplasmosis, toxoplasmosis, leishmaniasis, etc.) and granulomas due to infections and foreign antigens. Another form of delayed hypersensitivity is contact dermatitis (poison ivy, chemicals, heavy metals, etc.) in which the lesions are more papular. Type IV hypersensitivity can be classified into three categories depending on the time of onset and clinical and histological presentation. Mechanisms of damage in delayed hyper-sensitivity include T lymphocytes and monocytes and/or macrophages. Cytotoxic T cells (Tc) cause direct damage whereas helper T (TH1) cells secrete cytokines which activate cytotoxic T cells and recruit and activate monocytes and macrophages, which cause the bulk of the damage (Table 8-4). The delayed hypersensitivity lesions mainly contain monocytes and a few T cells.

Major lymphokines involved in delayed hypersensitivity reaction include monocyte chemotactic factor, interleukin-2, interferon TNF, etc.

**Table 8-4:** Delayed hypersensitivity reactions

| Type | Reaction time | Clinical Appearance | Histology | Antigen and size |
|---|---|---|---|---|
| Contact | 48-72 hr | Eczema | Lymphocytes, followed by macrophages; edema of epidermis | Epidermal (organic chemicals, poison ivy, heavy metals etc.) |
| Tuberculin | 48-72 hr | Local induration | Lymphocytes, monocytes, macrophages | Intradermal (tuberculin, lepromin, etc.) |
| Granuloma | 21-28 days | Hardening | Macrophages, epitheloid and giant cells, fibrosis | Persistent antigen or foreign body presence (tuberculosis, leprosy, etc.) |

**Table 8-5:** Comparision of different types of hypersensitivity

| Characteristics | Type-I (Anaphylactic) | Type-II (Cytotoxic) | Type-III (Immune complex) | Type-IV (Declayed type) |
|---|---|---|---|---|
| Antibody | IgE | IgG, IgM | IgG, IgM | None |
| Antigen | Exogenous | Cell surface | Soluble | Tissues and Organs |
| Response time | 15-30 minutes | Minutes-hours | 3-8 hours | 48-72 hours |
| Appearance | Weal an flare | Lysis and Necrosis | Erythema and edema, necrosis | Erythema and induration |
| Histology | Basophils and Eosinophil | Antibody and complement | Complement and neutrophils | Monocytes and lymphocytes |
| Transferred with | Antibody | Antibody | Antibody | T-cells |
| Examples | Allergic asthma, hay fever | Erythroblastosis fetalis, Good pasture's nephritis | SLE, farmer's lung disease | Tuberculin test, poison ivy, granuloma |

## Drug Habituation

Drug habituation (habit) is a condition resulting from the repeated consumption of a drug. Its characteristics include:

1. A desire (but not a compulsion) to continue taking the drug for the sense of improved well- being which it engenders;
2. Little or no tendency to increase the dose; Some degree of psychic dependence on the effect of the drug, but absence of physical dependence and hence of an abstinence syndrome;
3. Detrimental effects, if any, primarily on the individual.

## Drug Allergy

An allergic reaction is caused by the body's immune overreacting to the drug, which is viewed as a chemical "invader," or antigen. This overreaction is often called a hypersensitivity reaction.

- The body produces antibodies to the antigen and stores the antibodies on special cells.
    - The antibody in an allergic reaction is called immunoglobulin E, or IgE.
    - When the body is exposed to the drug again, the antibodies signal the cells to release chemicals called "mediators." Histamine is an example of a mediator.
    - The effects of these mediators on organs and other cells cause the symptoms of the reaction.
- The most common triggers of drug allergies are the following:
    - Painkillers (called analgesics) such ascodeine, morphine, nonsteroidal antiinflammatory drugs (NSAIDs, such as ibuprofen or indomethacin), and aspirin
    - Antibiotics such as penicillin, sulfa drugs and tetracycline
    - Antiseizure medications such as phenytoin (Dilantin) or carbamazepine (Tegretol)
- Risk factors for drug allergies include the following:
    - Frequent exposure to the drug
    - Large doses of the drug
    - Drug given by injection rather than pill

- o Family tendency to develop allergies and asthma
- o Certain food allergies such as to eggs, soybeans, or shellfish

**Drug Allergy Symptoms**

Drug allergies may cause many different types of symptoms depending on the drug and the degree of exposure to the drug (how often you have taken it). These are the most common reactions:

- Skin reactions:
    - o A measles-like rash
    - o Hives-Slightly red, itchy and raised swellings on the skin, which have an irregular shape
    - o Photo allergy Sensitivity to sunlight, an itchy and scaly rash that occurs following sun exposure
    - o Erythema multiforme Red, raised and itchy patches on the skin that sometimes look like bull's-eye targets and which may occur together with swelling of the face or tongue
- Fever
- Muscle and joint aches
- Lymph node swelling
- Inflammation of the kidney
- Unlike most allergic reactions, which occur fairly quickly after exposure to the allergen, allergic reactions to drugs tend to occur days or weeks after the first dose of the drug.
- Anaphylaxis or anaphylactic reaction; this is a serious allergic reaction that can be life threatening. A person with anaphylaxis must be treated in a hospital emergency department. Characteristics of anaphylaxis (sometimes referred to as anaphylactic shock) include:
    - o Skin reaction - Hives, redness/flushing, sense of warmth, itching
    - o Difficulty breathing - Chest tightness, wheezing, throat tightness
    - o Fainting - Light-headedness or loss of consciousness due to drastic decrease in blood pressure ("shock")
    - o Rapid or irregular heart beat
    - o Swelling of face, tongue, lips, throat, joints, hands, or feet
- Almost all anaphylactic reactions occur within four hours of the first dose of the drug. Most occur within one hour of taking the drug and many occur within minutes or even seconds.

**When to Seek Medical Care**

Always contact the health-care provider who prescribed the medication for advice.

- If the symptoms are mild, such as itching and localized hives, the provider may switch you to a different type of medication, recommend that you stop the medication, or, if appropriate, prescribe antihistamines to relieve your symptoms.
- If you cannot reach this provider for advice quickly, play it safe and go to a hospital emergency department.
- If you are having any "systemic" symptoms such as fever or vomiting, you should stop taking the medication and be seen immediately by a medical professional.
- If you are having difficulty breathing, your throat is swelling, or you are feeling faint, you may be having an anaphylactic reaction. Go immediately to a hospital emergency department. Do not attempt to drive yourself. If no one is available to drive you right away, call for an ambulance. While waiting for the ambulance, start self-treatment.

**Medical Treatment**

Generally, treatment of a drug allergy falls into three categories:

- Mild allergy (localized hives and itching)
    - o Treatment is aimed at caring for the symptoms and stopping the reaction caused by the drug.
    - o Medications prescribed may include antihistamines, such as Diphenhydramine (Benadryl)

- o You may be advised to stop taking the medication that caused the allergy.
- Moderately severe allergy (all-over hives and itching)
  - o Treatment is aimed at caring for the symptoms and stopping the reaction.
  - o Usually the offending medication is stopped.
  - o Medications prescribed may include antihistamines such as diphenhydramine (Benadryl)), oral steroids (prednisone), or histamine blockers such as cimetidine (Tagamet), famotidine (Pepcid), or ranitidine (Zantac).
- Severe allergy(shortness of breath, throat tightness, faintness, severe hives, involvement of many organ systems)
  - o Treatment includes strong medications to quickly reverse the dangerous chain of events.
  - o The offending medication is stopped immediately.
  - o Medications prescribed may include antihistamines such as diphenhydramine (Benadryl), oral or IV steroids such as prednisone or methylprednisolone (SoluMedrol), or histamine blockers such as cimetidine (Tagamet), famotidine (Pepcid), or ranitidine (Zantac).

**Potentiation**

- Potentiation occurs when two drugs are taken together and one of them intensifies the action of the other. This could be expressed by a +b= B. As an example, Phenergan(R), an antihistamine, when given with a painkilling narcotic such as Demerol(R) intensifies its effect, there by cutting down on the amount of the narcotic needed.

**Synergism**

- Synergism is similar to potentiation. If two drugs are taken together that are similar in action, such as barbiturates and alcohol, which are both depressants, an effect exaggerated out of proportion to that of each drug taken separately at the given dose may occur. This could be expressed by 1+1= 5. An example might be a person taking a dose of alcohol and a dose of a barbiturate. Normally, taken alone, neither substance would cause serious harm, but if taken together, the combination could cause coma or death.

**Table 8-6:** Additive, synergistic or summation interactions

| Drugs | Result of Interaction |
|---|---|
| Antipsychotics + Antimuscarinics | Increased antimuscarinic effects; heart stroke in hot and humid conditions, toxic psychosis |
| Antihypertensives + drugs that cause hypotension (e.g. Phenothiazines, Sildenafil) | Increased antihypertensive effects |
| Beta-agonist bronchodilators + Potassium-depleting drugs | Hypokalemia |
| CNS depressants + Alcohol + Antihistamines Benzodiazepines + Anaesthetics, general Opiods + Benzodiazepines | Impaired psychomotor skills, reduced alertness, drowsiness, stupor, respiratory depression, coma, death |
| Drugs that prolong the QT interval + Other drugs that prolong the QT interval Amiodarone + Disopyramide | Additive prolongation of QT interval, increased risk of torsade depointes |
| Methotrexate + CO-trimoxazole | Bone marrow megaloblastosis due to folic acid antagonism. |

*Table 8-6 Contd...*

| Drugs | Result of Interaction |
|---|---|
| Nephrotoxic drugs + Nephrotoxic drugs (e.g. Aminoglycosides, Ciclosporin, Cisplatin, Vancomycin) | Increased nephrotoxicity |
| Neuromuscular blockers + Drugs with neuromuscular blocking effects (e.g. Aminoglycosides) | Increased neuromuscular blockade; delayed recovery, prolonged apnoea. |
| Potassium supplements + Potassium-sparing drugs (e.g. ACE inhibitors, Angiotensin II receptor antagonists, Potassium-sparing diuretics) | Hyperkalemia |

## References

"Adverse Drug Events, Adverse Drug Reactions and Medication Errors". VA Center for Medication Safety. Retrieved 3 February 2012.

"Drug-Interactions.com". Archived from the original on 30 August 2007. Retrieved 2007-09-18.

"MedWatch - What Is A Serious Adverse Event?". Archived from the original on 29 September 2007. Retrieved 2007-09-18.

"Clinical Drug Use". Archived from the original on 1 November 2007. Retrieved 2007-09-18.

Aronson JK. Drug therapy. In: Haslett C, Chilvers ER, Boon NA, Colledge NR, Hunter JAA, eds. Davidson's principles and practice of medicine 19th ed. Edinburgh: Elsevier Science, 2002:147-

Barriaux, Marianne (2007-10-02). "'Traffic-light' medicine risk website to launch". London: The Guardian. Retrieved 2010-04-23.

DeVane CL (2002). "Clinical significance of drug binding, protein binding, and binding displacement drug interactions". *Psychopharma-cology bulletin.* **36** (3): 5–21.

Evans WE, McLeod HL (2003). "Pharmacogenomics—drug disposition, drug targets, and side effects". *N. Engl. J. Med.* **348** (6): 538–49.

Goldstein DB (2003). "Pharmacogenetics in the laboratory and the clinic". *N. Engl. J. Med.* **348** (6): 553–6.

Nebeker JR, Barach P, Samore MH (2004). "Clarifying adverse drug events: a clinician's guide to terminology, documentation, and reporting". *Ann. Intern. Med.* **140** (10): 795–801.

Phillips KA, Veenstra DL, Oren E, Lee JK, Sadee W (2001). "Potential role of pharmacogenomics in reducing adverse drug reactions: a systematic review". *JAMA* **286** (18): 2270–9.

Rang, H. P. (2003). *Pharmacology*. Edinburgh: Churchill Livingstone. ISBN 0-443-07145-4. Page 146

Rawlins MD, Thompson JW. Pathogenesis of adverse drug reactions. In: Davies DM, ed. Textbook of adverse drug reactions. Oxford: Oxford University Press, 1977:10.

Weinshilboum R; Collins, Francis S.; Weinshilboum, Richard (2003). "Inheritance and drug response". *N. Engl. J. Med.* **348** (6): 529–37.

CHAPTER

# Drug Interactions 9

## Definition

An interaction is said to occur when the effects of one drug are changed by the presence of another drug, herbal medicine, food, drink or by some environmental chemical agent.

### Prevalence

Among US adults older than 55, 4% are taking medication and or supplements that put them at risk of a major drug interaction. Potential drug drug interactions have increased over time and are more common in the low educated elderly even after controlling for age, sex, place of residence and co morbidity.

### Factors Contributing to Drug Interactions

Some of the more important risk factors that lead to drug interactions include-

1. **Multiple drug therapy:** This is very common in most acute and chronic care settings, for e.g., therapy in patient suffering from hypertension and congestive heart failure includes antihypertensives as Concurrent use of non prescription drugs, for e.g. aspirin as well as herbal medications also lead to drug interactions. Theoretically, the possibility for drug interactions to occur is over 50% when a patient is receiving five medications and the probability increases to 100% when seven drugs are used.
2. **Multiple prescribers:** Some individuals go to more than one physician and it is common for a patient to be treated by one or more specialists in addition to family doctors. It is frequently difficult for one prescriber to become aware of all the medications that have been prescribed by others for a particular patient and many difficulties arise for a patient while another prescribe an antihistamine having sedative properties with the possible consequence of an excessive depressant effect.
3. **Multiple pharmacological effects of drug:** Most drugs used in current therapy exhibit more than one type of pharmacological action and have the capacity to influence many physiological systems. Therefore, two concomitantly administered drugs will often affect some of the same systems for e.g., antihistamines (secondary effect is sedation) enhance the sedative effect of tranquillizers.
4. **Multiple diseases/predisposing illness:** Some patients take several drugs owing to their suffering from more than one disease, for e.g., a patient with both diabetes and hypertension. Multiple therapies in such individuals generally result in drug interactions, for e.g., oral Hypoglycemics and beta-blockers can result in decreased response to antidiabetic drug resulting in elevated blood sugar levels.
5. **Poor patient compliance :** This result when a patient does not take medication in the manner intended by the doctor; which may be due to inadequate instructions from the doctor or pharmacist, confusion regarding taking several medicines, etc. all of which of may lead to either under dosing or Overdosing and a consequent drug interaction.

6. **Advancing age patient:** Increased tendency of drug interaction episodes in elderly is generally due to decrease in liver function in such individuals.
7. **Drug-related factors:** Clinically significant interactions are most likely to occur between drugs that have potent effects, a narrow therapeutic index and a steep dose response curve (e.g., cytotoxic, antihypertensive and hypoglycemic drugs, digoxin, warfarin, etc.).

## Mechanisms of Drug Interaction

Some drugs interact together in totally unique ways, but as the many examples amply illustrate, there are certain mechanisms of interaction that are encountered time and time again. Some of these common mechanisms are discussed here in greater detail. Mechanisms that are unusual or peculiar to particular pairs of drugs are detailed within the monographs. Very many drugs that interact do so, not by a single mechanism, but often by two or more mechanisms acting in concert, although for clarity most of the mechanisms are dealt with here as though they occur in isolation.

For convenience, the mechanisms of interactions can be subdivided into those that involve the pharmacokinetics of a drug and those that are pharmacodynamic.

**I. Pharmacokinetic interactions:** Pharmacokinetic interactions are those that can affect the processes by which drugs are absorbed, distributed, metabolized and excreted (the so called ADME interactions). Fig 9-1.

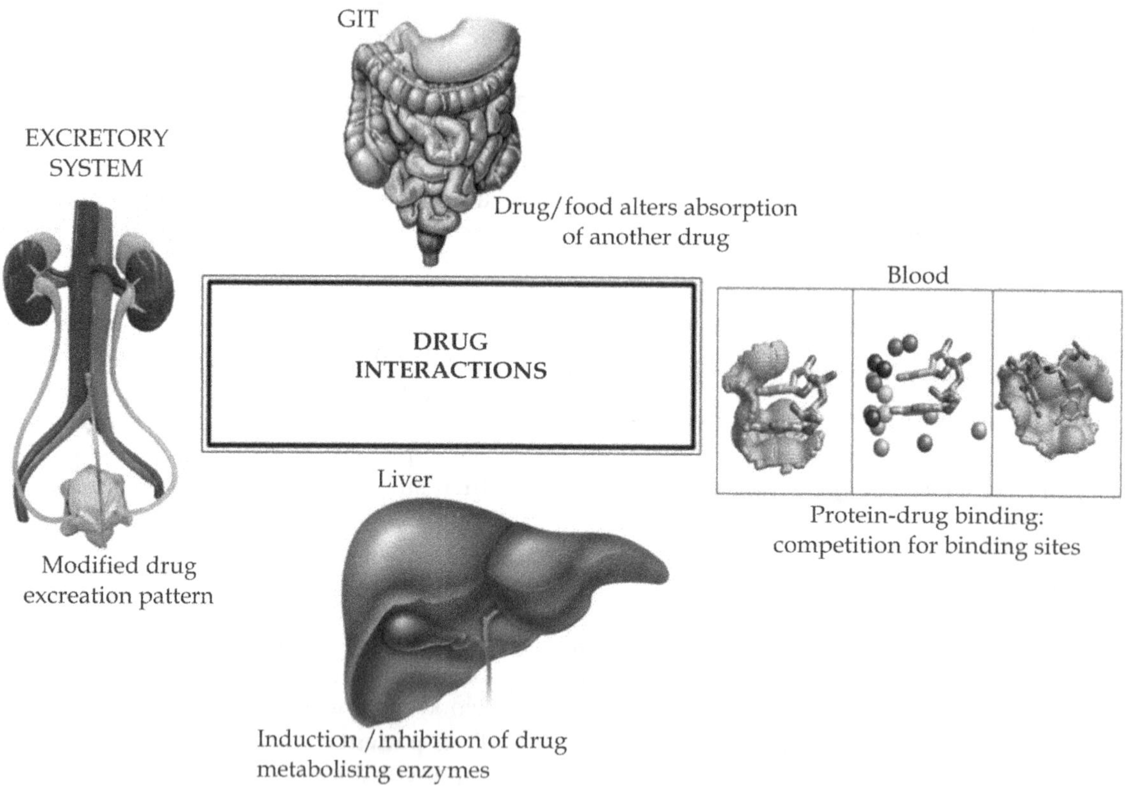


**Fig 9-1:** Pharmacokinetic interactions

### Drug absorption interactions

Most drugs are given orally for absorption through the mucous membranes of the gastrointestinal tract and the majority of interactions that go on within the gut result in reduced rather than increased absorption. A clear distinction must be made between those that decrease the *rate* of absorption and those that alter the *total amount* absorbed. For drugs that are given long-term, in multiple doses (e.g., the oral anticoagulants) the rate of absorption is usually unimportant, provided the total amount of drug absorbed is not markedly altered. On the other hand for drugs that are given as single doses, intended to be absorbed rapidly (e.g., hypnotics or analgesics), where a rapidly achieved high concentration is needed, a reduction in the rate of absorption may result in failure to achieve an adequate effect.

(a) **Effects of changes in gastrointestinal pH:** The passage of drugs through mucous membranes by simple passive diffusion depends upon the extent to which they exist in the non ionised lipid soluble form. Absorption is therefore governed by the pKa of the drug, its lipid-solubility, the pH of the contents of the gut and various other parameters relating to the pharmaceutical formulation of the drug. Thus the absorption of salicylic acid by the stomach is much greater at low pH than at high. On theoretical grounds it might be expected that alterations in gastric pH caused by drugs such as the H2-receptor antagonists would have a marked effect on absorption, but in practice the outcome is often uncertain because a number of other mechanisms may also come into play, such as chelation, adsorption and changes in gut motility, which can considerably affect what actually happens. However, in some cases the effect can be significant. Rises in pH due to 'proton pump inhibitors', 'H2-receptor antagonists', can markedly reduce the absorption of ketoconazole.

(b) **Adsorption, chelation and other complexing mechanisms:** Activated charcoal is intended to act as an adsorbing agent within the gut for the treatment of drug overdose or to remove other toxic materials, but inevitably it can affect the absorption of drugs given in therapeutic doses. Antacids can also adsorb a large number of drugs, but often other mechanisms of interaction are also involved. For example, the tetracycline antibacterials can chelate with a number of divalent and trivalent metallic ions, such as calcium, aluminum, bismuth and iron, to form complexes that are both poorly absorbed and have reduced antibacterial effects .These metallic ions are found in dairy products and antacids. Separating the dosages by 2 to 3 hours goes some way towards reducing the effects of this type of interaction. The marked reduction in the bioavailability of penicillamine caused by some antacids seems also to be due to chelation, although adsorption may have some part to play. Cholestyramine, an anionic exchange resin intended to bind bile acids and cholesterol metabolites in the gut, binds to a considerable number of drugs (e.g. digoxin, warfarin, levothyroxine), thereby reducing their absorption.

(c) **Changes in gastrointestinal motility:** Since most drugs are largely absorbed in the upper part of the small intestine, drugs that alter the rate at which the stomach empties can affect absorption. Propantheline, for example, delays gastric emptying and reduces 'paracetamol (acetaminophen)' absorption, whereas 'metoclopramide', has the opposite effect. However, the total amount of drug absorbed remains unaltered. Propantheline also increases the absorption of 'hydrochlorothiazide'. Drugs with antimuscarinic effects decrease the motility of the gut, thus the tricyclic antidepressants can increase the absorption of 'dicoumarol', probably because they increase the time available for dissolution and absorption but in the case of 'levodopa', they may reduce the absorption, possibly because the exposure time to intestinal mucosal metabolism is increased. The same reduced levodopa absorption has also been seen with 'homatropine'. These examples illustrate that what actually happens is sometimes very unpredictable because the final outcome may be the result of several different mechanisms.

(d) **Malabsorption caused by drugs:** Neomycin causes a malabsorption syndrome. The effect is to impair the absorption of a number of drugs including 'digoxin', and 'methotrexate'.

# Drug Distribution Interactions

## Protein-binding Interactions

Following absorption, drugs are rapidly distributed around the body by the circulation. Some drugs are totally dissolved in the plasma water, but many others are transported with some proportion of their molecules in solution and the rest bound to plasma proteins, particularly the albumins. The extent of this binding varies enormously but some drugs are extremely highly bound. For example, dicoumarol has only four out of every 1000 molecules remaining unbound at serum concentrations of 0.5 mg%. Drugs can also become bound to albumin in the interstitial fluid, and some, such as digoxin, can bind to the heart muscle tissue. The binding of drugs to the plasma proteins is reversible, an equilibrium being established between those molecules that are bound and those that are not. Only the unbound molecules remain free and pharmacologically active, while those that are bound form a circulating but pharmacologically inactive reservoir which, in the case of drugs with a low-extraction ratio, is temporarily protected from metabolism and excretion. As the free molecules become metabolized, some of the bound molecules become unbound and pass into solution to exert their normal pharmacological actions, Depending on the concentrations and their relative affinities for the binding sites; one drug may successfully compete with another and displace it from the sites it is already occupying. The displaced (and now active) drug molecules pass into the plasma water where their concentration rises. So for example, a drug that reduces the binding from 99 to 95% would increase the unbound concentration of free and active drug from 1 to 5% (a fivefold increase). This displacement is only likely to raise the number of free and active molecules significantly if the majority of the drug is within the plasma rather than the tissues, so that only drugs with a low apparent volume of distribution (Vd) will be affected. Examples include the sulphonylureas, such as tolbutamide (96 per cent bound, $V_d$ 10 litres), oral anticoagulants, such as warfarin (99 percent bound, $V_d$ 9 litres), and phenytoin (90 percent bound, Vd 35 liters). However, another important factor is clearance. Clinically important protein-binding interactions are unlikely if only a small proportion of the drug is eliminated during a single passage through the eliminating organ (low extraction ratio drugs), since any increase in free fraction will be effectively cleared. Most drugs that are extensively bound to plasma proteins and subject to displacement reactions (e.g., warfarin, sulphonylureas, phenytoin, methotrexate and valproate) have low extraction ratios and drug exposure is therefore independent of protein binding. Before they, in their turn are metabolized and excreted.

### Drug Metabolism (Biotransformation) Interactions

Although a few drugs are cleared from the body simply by being excreted unchanged in the urine, most are chemically altered within the body to less lipid soluble compounds, which are more easily excreted by the kidneys. If this were not so, many drugs would persist in the body and continue to exert their effects for a long time. This chemical change is called 'metabolism', 'biotransformation', 'biochemical degradation' or sometimes 'detoxification'. Some drug metabolism goes on in the serum, the kidneys, the skin and the intestines, but the greatest proportion is carried out by enzymes that are found in the membranes of the endoplasmic reticulum of the liver cells. If liver is homogenized and then centrifuged, the reticulum breaks up into small sacs called microsomes which carry the enzymes, and it is for this reason that the metabolizing enzymes of the liver are frequently referred to as the 'liver microsomal enzymes'. Drugs are metabolized by two major types of reaction. The first, so-called phase I reactions (involving oxidation, reduction or hydrolysis), turn drugs into more polar compounds, while phase II reactions involve coupling drugs with some other substance (e.g., Glucuronic acid, known as Glucuronidation) to make usually inactive compounds. The majority of phase I oxidation reactions are carried out by the haem containing enzyme cytochrome P450. Cytochrome P450 is not a single entity, but is in fact a very large family of related isoenzymes, about 30 of which have been found in human liver tissue. However, in practice, only a few specific subfamilies seem to be responsible for most (about 90%) of the metabolism of the commonly used drugs. The most important isoenzymes are: CYP1A2, CYP2C9, CYP2C19, CYP2D6, CYP2E1 and CYP3A4. Other enzymes involved in phase I metabolism include monoamine oxidases and epoxide hydrolases. Less is known about the enzymes responsible for phase II conjugation reactions. However, UDP-glucuronyltransferases (UGT), methyl-transferase and N-acetyltransferases (NAT) are examples.

**(a) Changes in first pass metabolism**

(i) *Changes in blood flow through the liver:* After absorption in the intestine, the portal circulation takes drugs directly to the liver before they are distributed by the blood flow around the rest of the body. A number of highly lipid-soluble drugs undergo substantial biotransformation during this first-pass through the gut wall and liver and there is some evidence that some drugs can have a marked effect on the extent of first pass metabolism by altering the blood flow through the liver. However, there are few clinically relevant examples of this, and many can be explained by other mechanisms, usually altered hepatic metabolism. One possible example is the increase in rate of absorption of dofetilide with 'verapamil', which has resulted in an increased incidence of torsade de pointes. Another is the increase in bioavailability of high-extraction beta blockers with 'Hydralazine', possibly caused by altered hepatic blood flow, or altered metabolism.

(ii) *Inhibition or induction of first-pass metabolism:* The gut wall contains metabolizing enzymes, principally the cytochrome P450 isoenzymes. In addition to the altered metabolism caused by changes in hepatic blood flow, there is evidence that some drugs can have a marked effect on the extent of first pass metabolism by inhibiting or inducing the cytochrome P450 isoenzymes in the gut wall or in the liver. An example is the effect of grapefruit juice, which seems to inhibit the cytochrome P450 isoenzyme CYP3A4, mainly in the gut, and therefore reduces the metabolism of oral calcium channel blockers. Although altering the amount of drug 'absorbed', these interactions are usually considered drug metabolism interactions. The effect of grapefruit on the metabolism of other drugs is discussed further under 'Drug-food interactions'.

**(b) Enzyme induction:** When barbiturates were widely used as hypnotics it was found necessary to keep increasing the dosage as time went by to achieve the same hypnotic effect, the reason being that the barbiturates increase the activity of the microsomal enzymes so that extent of metabolism and excretion increases. This phenomenon of enzyme stimulation or 'induction' not only accounts for the need for an increased barbiturate dose but if another drug that is metabolized by the same range of enzymes is also present, its enzymatic metabolism is similarly increased and larger doses are needed to maintain the same therapeutic effect. However, note that not all enzyme inducing drugs induce their own metabolism (a process known as auto induction). The metabolic pathway that is most commonly induced is phase I oxidation mediated by the cytochrome P450 isoenzymes. The extent of the enzyme induction depends on the drug and its dosage, but it may take days or even 2 to 3 weeks to develop fully, and may persist for a similar length of time when the enzyme inducer is stopped. This means that enzyme induction interactions are delayed in onset and slow to resolve. Enzyme induction is a common mechanism of interaction and is not confined to drugs; it is also caused by the chlorinated hydrocarbon insecticides such as Dicophane and Lindane, and smoking tobacco. If one drug reduces the effects of another by enzyme induction, it may be possible to accommodate the interaction simply by raising the dosage of the drug affected, but this requires good monitoring, and there are obvious hazards if the inducing drug is eventually stopped without remembering to reduce the dosage again. The raised drug dosage may be an overdose when the drug metabolism has returned to normal.

(c) **Enzyme inhibition:** More common than enzyme induction is the inhibition of enzymes. This results in the reduced metabolism of an affected drug, so that it may begin to accumulate within the body, the effect usually being essentially the same as when the dosage is increased. Unlike enzyme induction, which may take several days or even weeks to develop fully, enzyme inhibition can occur within 2 to 3 days, resulting in the rapid development of toxicity. The metabolic pathway that is most commonly inhibited is phase I oxidation by the cytochrome P450 isoenzymes. For example a marked increase occurred in the plasma levels of a single dose of sildenafil after Ritonavir had also been taken for 7 days, probably because Ritonavir inhibits the metabolism of sildenafil by CYP3A4 .An example of inhibition of phase I hydrolytic metabolism, is the inhibition of epoxide hydrolase by valpromide, which increases the levels of 'carbamazepine'. Phase II conjugative metabolism can also be inhibited. Examples are the inhibition of carbamazepine Glucuronidation by 'sodium valproate' and the inhibition of methyltransferase by aminosalicylates causing raised levels of 'azathioprine'.The clinical significance of many enzyme inhibition interactions depends on the extent to which the serum levels of the drug rise. If the serum levels remain within the therapeutic range the interaction may not be clinically important.

(d) **Cytochrome P450 isoenzymes and predicting drug interactions:** It is interesting to know which particular isoenzyme is responsible for the metabolism of drugs because by doing *in vitro* tests with human liver enzymes it is often possible to explain why and how some drugs interact. For example, cyclosporin is metabolized by CYP3A4 and we know that Rifampicin (rifampin) is a potent inducer of this isoenzyme, whereas ketoconazole inhibits its activity, so that it comes as no surprise that Rifampicin reduces the effects of cyclosporin and ketoconazole increases it.

What is very much more important than retrospectively finding out why two drugs interact, is the knowledge such *in vitro* tests can provide about forecasting which other drugs may possibly also interact. This may reduce the numbers of expensive clinical studies in subjects and patients and avoids waiting until significant drug interactions are observed in clinical use. A lot of effort is being put into this area of drug development. However, at present such prediction is, like weather forecasting, still a somewhat hit-and-miss business because we do not know all of the factors that may modify or interfere with metabolism. It is far too simplistic to think that we have all the answers just because we know which liver isoenzymes are concerned with the metabolism of a particular drug, but it is a very good start.

## Drug Excretion Interactions

With the exception of the inhalation anesthetics, most drugs are excreted either in the bile or in the urine. Blood entering the kidneys along the renal arteries is, first of all, delivered to the glomeruli of the tubules where molecules small enough to pass through the pores of the glomerular membrane (e.g., water, salts, some drugs) are filtered through into the lumen of the tubules. Larger molecules, such as plasma proteins and blood cells are retained within the blood. The blood flow then passes to the remaining parts of the kidney tubules where active energy-using transport systems are able to remove drugs and their metabolites from the blood and secrete them into the tubular filtrate. The renal tubular cells additionally possess active and passive transport systems for the reabsorption of drugs. Interference by drugs with renal tubular fluid pH, with active transport systems and with blood flow to the kidney can alter the excretion of other drugs. Fig 9-2.

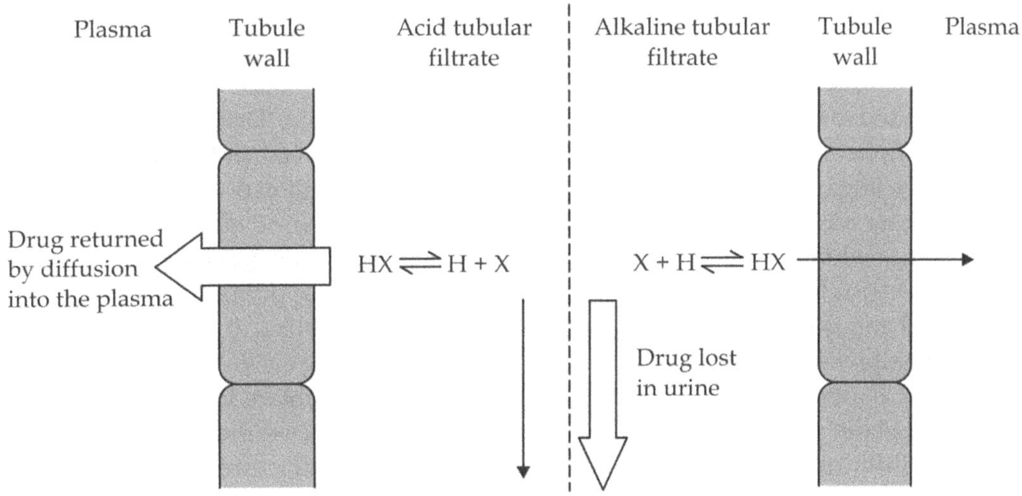


**Fig. 9-2:** An excretion interaction. If the tubular filtrate is acidified, most of the molecules of weakly acid drugs (HX) exist in an un-ionised lipid-soluble Form and are able to return through the lipid membranes of the tubule cells by Simple diffusion. Thus they are retained. In alkaline urine most of the drug Molecules exist in an ionised non-lipid soluble form (X). In this form the molecules are unable to diffuse freely through these membranes and are therefore lost in the urine.

(a) **Changes in urinary pH:** As with drug absorption in the gut, passive reabsorption of drugs depends upon the extent to which the drug exists in the non ionised lipid-soluble form, which in its turn depends on its pKa and the pH of the urine. Only the non ionised form is lipid-soluble and able to diffuse back through the lipid membranes of the tubule cells. Thus at high pH values (alkaline), weakly acid drugs (pKa 3 to 7.5) largely exist as ionised lipid insoluble molecules, which are unable to diffuse into the tubule cells and will therefore remain in the urine and be removed from the body. The converse will be true for weak bases with pKa values of 7.5 to 10.5. Thus pH changes that increase the amount in the ionized form (alkaline urine for acidic drugs, acid urine for basic drugs) increase the loss of the drug, whereas moving the pH in the opposite direction will increase their retention.

(b) **Changes in active renal tubular excretion:** Drugs that use the same active transport systems in the renal tubules can compete with one another for excretion. For example, probenecid reduces the excretion of penicillin and other drugs. With the increasing understanding of drug transporter proteins in the kidneys, it is now known that probenecid inhibits the renal secretion of many other anionic drugs by organic anion transporters (OATs). Probenecid possibly also inhibits some of the ABC transporters in the kidneys. The ABC transporter, P-glycoprotein, is also present in the kidneys and drugs that alter this may alter renal drug elimination.

(c) **Changes in renal blood flow:** The flow of blood through the kidney is partially controlled by the production of renal vasodilatory prostaglandins. If the synthesis of these prostaglandins is inhibited the renal excretion of some drugs may be reduced. An interaction where this is the suggested mechanism is the rise in serum lithium seen with some NSAIDs.

(d) **Biliary excretion and the entero-hepatic shunt**

(i) ***Enterohepatic recirculation:*** A number of drugs are excreted in the bile, either unchanged or conjugated (e.g., as the Glucuronide) to make them more water soluble. Some of the conjugates are metabolised to the parent compound by the gut flora and are then reabsorbed. This recycling process prolongs the stay of the drug within the body, but if the gut flora are diminished by the presence of an antibacterial, the drug is not recycled and is lost more quickly. This may possibly explain the rare failure of the oral contraceptives that can be brought about by the concurrent use of penicillin's or Tetracyclines. Anti-microbial-induced reductions in gut bacteria may reduce the activation of 'Sulfasalazine'.

**(ii)** ***Drug transporters:*** Increasing research shows that numerous drug transporter proteins (both from the ABC family and SLC family, 'Drug transporter proteins', are involved in the hepatic extraction and secretion of drugs into the bile. The relevance of many of these to drug interactions is still unclear, but the bile salt export pump (ABCB11) is known to be inhibited by a variety of drugs including cyclosporine, Glibenclamide, and Bosentan. Inhibition of this pump may increase the risk of cholestasis and the manufacturer of Bosentan says that they should be avoided in patients taking Bosentan.

**Table 9-1:** List of some of the important pharmacokinetic (ADME) interactions

| Object Drug (s) | Precipitant Drug (s) | Influence on Object Drug (s) |
|---|---|---|
| | **Absorption Interactions** | |
| **1. Complexation and Adsorption** | | |
| Tetracycline, fluoroquinolones like ciprofloxacin, Penicillamine | Antacids, food and mineral supplements containing Al,Mg,Fe,Zn, Bi and Ca ions | Formation of poorly soluble and unabsorbable complex with such heavy metal ions |
| Cephalexin, sulphamethoxazole, trimethoprim, warfarin and thyroxine | Cholestyramine | Reduced absorption due to adsorption and binding |
| **2. Alteration of G1 PH** | | |
| Sulphonamides, aspirin | Antacids | Enhanced dissolution and absorption rate |
| Ferrous sulphate | Sodium bicarbonate, calcium carbonate | Decreased dissolution and hence absorption |
| Ketoconazole, tetracycline, Atenolol | Antacids | Decreased dissolution and bioavailability |

*Table 9-1 Contd...*

| Object Drug (s) | Precipitant Drug (s) | Influence on Object Drug (s) |
|---|---|---|
| **Absorption Interactions** | | |
| **3. Alteration of Gut Motility** | | |
| Aspirin, diazepam, levodapa, lithium carbonate, paracetamol, mexiletine. | Metoclopramide | Rapid gastric emptying; increased rate of absorption |
| Levodapa, lithium carbonate, mexiletine | Anticholinergic (Atropine) | Delayed gastric emptying: decreased rate of absorption |
| 4. Alteration of GI Microflora | | |
| Digoxin | Antibiotics (erythromycin, tetracycline) | Increased bioavailability due to destruction of bacterial flora that inactivates digoxin in lower intestine. |
| Oral contraceptives | Antibiotics (ampicillin) | Decreased reabsorption of drugs secreted as conjugates via bile in the intestine. |
| 5. Malabsorption Syndrome | | |
| Vitamin A, B12, digoxin | Neomycin and colchicines | Inhibition of absorption due to malabsorption/steatorrhoea caused by neomycin |
| **Distribution Interactions** | | |
| **Competitive Displacement Interactions** | | |
| ***Displaced drug(s)*** | ***Displacer(s)*** | |
| Anticoagulants (warfarin) | Phenylbutazone, chloral hydrate, salicylates | Increased clotting, time; increased risk of hemorrhage. |
| Tolbutamide | Sulphonamides | Increased hypoglycemic effect |
| Methotrexate | Sulphonamides, salicylic acid | Increased methotrexate toxicity |
| Phenytoin | Valproic acid | Phenytoin toxicity |
| **Metabolism Interactions** | | |
| **1. Enzyme Induction** | | |
| Corticosteroids, oral contraceptives, coumarins, phenytoin, tolbutamide, tricyclic antidepressants | Barbiturates | Decreased plasma levels; decreased efficacy of object drugs |
| Corticosteroids, oral contraceptives, theophylline, cyclosporin | Phenytoin | Decreased plasma levels; decreased efficacy of object drugs |
| Oral contraceptives, oral hypoglycemics, coumarins | Rifampicin | Decreased plasma levels; decreased efficacy of object drugs |

*Table 9-1 Contd...*

| Object Drug (s) | Precipitant Drug (s) | Influence on Object Drug (s) |
|---|---|---|
| | **Absorption Interactions** | |
| **2. Enzyme Inhibition** | | |
| Tyramine rich food (cheese, liver, yeast prodcuts) | MAO Inhibitors (phenelzine , pargyline) | Enhanced absorption of unmetabolised tyramine; increased pressor activity; potentially fatal risk of hypertensive crises |
| Drugs that undergo extensive first-pass hepatic metabolism (e.g., Propranolol, calcium channel blockers, etc.) | Grape fruit juice | Enhanced absorption of drugs; increased risk of toxicity. |
| Folic acid | Phenytoin | Decreased absorption of folic acid due to inhibition of an enzyme responsible for its absorption |
| Tricyclic antidepressants | Chlorpromazine, haloperidol | Increased plasma half-life of tricyclics; increased risk of sudden death from cardiac disease in such patients. |
| Coumarins | metronidazole, Phenylbutazone | Increased anticoagulant activity; risk of hemorrhage |
| Oral hypoglycemics | Phenylbutazone, sulphaphenazole, chloramphenicol | Hypoglycemia may be precipitated |
| Alcohol | Disulphiram, metronidazole, tinidazole | Disulphiram like reactions due to increase in plasma acetaldehyde levels |
| AZT, mercaptopurine | Xanthine oxidase inhibitors (Allopurinol) | Increased toxicity of antineoplastics |
| Alcohol, benzodiazepines, warfarin, phenytoin, theophylline, phenobarbital | Cimetidine | Increased blood levels of object drugs |
| | **Excretion Interactions** | |
| **1. Changes in Active Tubular Secretion** | | |
| Penicillin, cephalosporin, Nalidixic acid, PAS, Methotrexate, Dapsone | Probenecid (acid) | Elevated plasma levels of acidic drugs; risk of toxic reactions |
| Procainamide | Cimetidine (base) | Increased plasma levels of basic object drugs; risk of toxicity |
| Acetohexamide | Phenylbutazone | Increased hypoglycemic effect |

*Table 9-1 Contd...*

| Object Drug (s) | Precipitant Drug (s) | Influence on Object Drug (s) |
|---|---|---|
| **Absorption Interactions** | | |
| **2. Changes in Urine PH** | | |
| Amphetamine, tetracycline, quinidine | Antacids, thiazides, Acetazolamide | Increased passive reabsorption of basic drugs; increased risk of toxicity |
| **3. Changes in Renal Blood Flow** | | |
| Lithium bicarbonate | NSAIDS (inhibitors of prostaglandin synthesis; the latter control renal blood flow partially by vasoconstriction) | Decreased renal clearance of lithium; risk of toxicity |

**II. Pharmacodynamic interactions:** Pharmacodynamic interactions are those where the effects of one drug are changed by the presence of another drug at its site of action. Sometimes the drugs directly compete for particular receptors (e.g. beta2 agonists, such as salbutamol and beta blockers, such as propranolol) but often the reaction is more indirect and involves interference with physiological mechanisms. These interactions are much less easy to classify neatly than those of a pharmacokinetic type.

1. **Drugs Having Similar Pharmacological Effects:** An excessive response attribute to the concurrent use of drugs having similar actions is the type of interaction that occurs most often and these potential problems warrant particular attention.

   *CNS Depressants* - An excessive CNS depressant effect resulting from the concurrent use of two or more drugs exhibiting a depressant action represents one of the most dangerous drug-related problems. Older patients should be viewed as being especially susceptible to this type of response, and patients experiencing effects such as sedation and dizziness are at increased risk of falls and injuries, such as hip fractures. Patients also must be advised of the risks of operating motor vehicles or machinery. In considering multiple drug regimens, recognition must be taken of the large number of agents (e.g., sedative hypnotics, antipsychotics, tricyclic antidepressants, opioid analgesics and most antihistamines) than can exhibit a depressant effect that will be at least additive to the effect contributed by other drugs. If it is considered necessary to use agents with a CNS depressant action concurrently, it should be anticipated that a lower dosage of at least one of the agents should be used.

   *Alcohol-Other CNS Depressants* - The increased CNS depressant effect that is experienced by individuals being treated with depressant drugs when they consume alcoholic beverages is among the best known interactions. However, this interaction also illustrates the difficulties in trying to predict the magnitude of the response that will be experienced by a particular patient; a response will depend on many variables, including the patient's tolerance to alcohol. How then should the patient be instructed when he or she is to take a depressant medication? Certainly it would be most desirable not to consume alcoholic beverages during the period the medication is being taken. However, there should be a realistic recognition that many patients if faced with amandate not to drink while on drug therapy will decide not to take the drug. Every patient should be alerted to the fact that the depressant effect of the drug prescribed may be increased by alcohol. If it is anticipated that a patient would not completely avoid alcoholic beverages, that patient should be urged to use them in moderation, particularly when therapy is initiated or the dosage is increased and cautioned to observe his or her own tolerance when such combinations are employed. The fact that many individuals can take depressant drugs and consume relatively large amounts of alcoholic beverages with no apparent difficulty should not be cause to forget that such combinations have been lethal in some individuals and the cause of injury in others. Thus, there is an important need to caution all patients for whom such drugs are prescribed.

**Drugs Having Anticholinergic Activity:** Drugs that differ considerably in their primary pharmacological actions may exhibit the same secondary effects. Some patients being treated with antipsychotic agents such as chlorpromazine also the given an antiparkinson agent such as trihexyphenidyl to control the extrapyramidal effects of the former. In addition, a number of these patients experience symptoms of depression and a tricycle antidepressant such as amitriptyline might be added to the therapy. Each of these three agents possesses anticholinergic activity and the additive effect could result in side effects such as dryness of the mouth, blurred vision, urinary retention, constipation and elevation of intraocular pressure.

Even an effect such as dryness of the mouth, which most health professionals would consider as a minor problem, could be troublesome in certain patients. For example, persistent dryness of the mouth could make the use of dentures more difficult and also cause other dental complications. In addition, there may be increased difficulty in chewing and swallowing, an important factor with respect to the problem of malnutrition in many elderly individuals. Dryness of the mouth also may result in other problems as illustrated by a case report of a patient treated with imipramine. The patient experienced persistent dryness of the mouth and when nitroglycerin tablets were administered sublingually for the management of exertional angina, the relief of the symptoms was delayed because of the slower dissolution of the sublingual tablets.

It has been observed that an excessive anticholinergic effect can cause an atropine-like delirium, particularly in geriatric patients. This effect could be misinterpreted as an increase in psychiatric symptoms, which might be treated by increasing the dosage of the therapeutic agents that the actually responsible for causing the problem. This example points out the difficulty that often can exist in distinguishing between the symptoms of the conditions(s) being treated and the effects of the drug(s) being employed as therapy.

Several studies call attention to other potential problems associated with the use of drugs having anticholinergic activity. In one investigation using volunteers aged 60 to 72, trihexyphenidyl was found to cause substantial memory impairment. In another study of 22 demented nursing-home patients, it was noted that those with high serum anticholinergic concentrations had greater impairment in elf care capacity than patients with low concentrations.

The blurring of vision, which also may be associated with the use of drugs having anticholinergic activity, may be especially distressing for older patients, particularly those whose physical activities may be limited and for whom reading is a favorite activity.

Several reports have described the development of severe hyperpyrexia in patients taking phenothaizine antiparkinson combinations who were exposed to high environmental temperature and humidity. These investigations call attention to the ability of these combinations to interfere with the thermoregulatory system of the body and recommend that physicians treating patients in hot and humid climates should minimize outdoor exposure of patients receiving high doses of these agents.

**Drugs Exhibiting Hypotensive Effects:** Certain antihypertensive drugs as well as some other classes of medications e.g., tricyclic antidepressants) can cause orthostatic hypotension, resulting in symptoms such as dizziness, lightheadedness and in more severe cases, syncope. Older patients are most susceptible to this type of response and the associated risks such as falls and injuries and appropriate precautions should be exercised whether these agents are given alone or in combination.

The use of sildenafil, tadalafil and vardenafil in the treatment of erectile dysfunction is contraindicated in patients treated with nitrates because these agents may potentiate the hypotensive effect of the nitrates.

**NSAIDS:** Several situations exist in which a patient unknowingly may be taking several different products that contain the same NSAID. An arthritic patient whose conditions has been managed with ibuprofen obtained via prescription (often at dosage levels at or near the recommended maximum) may purchase an ibuprofen product available without a prescription for pain/ discomfort not associated with the arthritis, without recognizing that the two products contain the same drug and that there is an increased risk of adverse effects.

**Table 9-2:** Additive, synergistic or summation interactions

| Drugs | Result of Interaction |
|---|---|
| Antipsychotics + Antimuscarinics | Increased antimuscarinic effects; heart stroke in hot and humid conditions, toxic psychosis |
| Antihypertensives + drugs that cause hypotension (e.g., Phenothiazines, Sildenafil) | Increased antihypertensive effects |
| Beta-agonist bronchodilators + Potassium-depleting drugs | Hypokalemia |
| CNS depressants + Alcohol + Antihistamines Benzodiazepines + Anaesthetics, general Opiods + Benzodiazepines | Impaired psychomotor skills, reduced alertness, drowsiness, stupor, respiratory depression, coma, death |
| Drugs that prolong the QT interval + Other drugs that prolong the QT interval Amiodarone + Disopyramide | Additive prolongation of QT interval, increased risk of torsade depointes |
| Methotrexate + CO-trimoxazole | Bone marrow megaloblastosis due to folic acid antagonism. |
| Nephrotoxic drugs + Nephrotoxic drugs (e.g., Aminoglycosides, Cyclosporin, Cisplatin, Vancomycin) | Increased nephrotoxicity |
| Neuromuscular blockers + Drugs with neuromuscular blocking effects (e.g., Aminoglycosides) | Increased neuromuscular blockade; delayed recovery, prolonged apnoea. |
| Potassium supplements + Potassium-sparing drugs (e.g., ACE inhibitors, Angiotensin II receptor antagonists, Potassium-sparing diuretics) | Hyperkalemia |

2. **Drugs Having Opposing Pharmacological Effects:** Interactions resulting from the use of two drugs with opposing effects should be among the easiest to detect. However, these sometimes are due to the secondary effects of certain drugs and this and other factors may preclude early identification of such situations.

*Diuretics* – The ability of the thiazides and certain other diuretics to elevate blood glucose concentrations is well known. When the diuretic is prescribed for a diabetic patient being treated with insulin or one of the oral antidiabetic agents, this action may partially counteract the glucose-lowering action of the anti diabetic drug, necessitating an adjustment in dosage. Similarly, many diuretics may produce a hyperuricemic effect. Therapy in patients with gout should be monitored closely, as the hyperuricemic action of a diuretic may necessitate an adjustment in dosage of the agent being used in the treatment of gout.

**Table 9-3:** Opposing or antagonistic interactions

| Drugs affected | Interacting drugs | Results of interaction |
|---|---|---|
| ACE inhibitors or Loop diuretics or Loop diuretics | NSAIDs | Antihypertensive effects opposed |
| Anticoagulants | Vitamin K | Anticoagulant effects opposed |
| Antidiabetics | Glucocorticoids | Blood glucose-lowering effects opposed |
| Antineoplastics | Megestrol | Antineoplastic effects possibly opposed |
| Levodopa | Antipsychotics (those with dopamine antagonist effects) | Antiparkinsonian effects opposed |
| Levodopa | Tacrine | Antiparkinsonian effects opposed |

3. **Alteration of Electrolyte Concentrations:** Several important drug interactions occur as a result of the ability of certain therapeutic agents to alter the concentration of electrolytes such as potassium and sodium. When these drugs are included in a therapeutic regimen, it is important that electrolyte concentrations be monitored periodically.

*Digoxin-Diuretics:* One of the problems associated with the use of most of the commonly employed diuretics (e.g., The Thiazide derivatives is that they can cause an excessive loss of potassium. Particular caution is necessary in patients also being treated with digoxin, many of whom would be candidates for diuretic therapy. If potassium depletion remains uncorrected, the heart may become more sensitive to the effects of the cardiac glycoside and arrhythmia may result.

Although potassium supplementation will be necessary in many individuals being treated with a potassium-depleting diuretic, the initiation of therapy with such a diuretic must not be viewed as a mandate also to provide potassium supplementation. This decision should be based on a consideration of the individual patient situation and the appropriate parameters should be monitored periodically. It must be recognized that dangers also exist if hyperkalemia occurs as a result of excessive supplementation. This risk of such complications is greatest in patients with diminished renal functions.

In addition to the diuretics, other agents also can cause potassium depletion. Prolonged therapy with cathartics and corticosteroids may cause potassium depletion, although this is not likely to occur as quickly or to the same extent as with diuretics.

Interest has developed also in the clinical implications of magnesium depletion. Concern has been expressed that this condition occurs much more commonly than is recognized and that some clinical problems may continue or worsen despite seemingly adequate electrolyte therapy because magnesium deficiency has not been identified and corrected.

Diuretic therapy may lead to development of magnesium depletion and as observed when potassium is depleted, the activity of digoxin may be increased and possibly result in toxicity. In some patients with digoxin toxicity, low serum-magnesium concentrations may coexist with normal potassium values.

Angiotensin Converting Enzyme Inhibitors-Potassium-Sparing Diuretics

The angiotensin converting enzyme (ACE) inhibitors (enalapril, lisinopril, ramipril) may cause an elevation of serum potassium concentrations. Potassium sparing diuretics (amiloride, spironolactone and triamterne) or potassium supplements should be used concurrently with caution, because of the risk of hyperkalemia and associated complications. Salt substitutes containing potassium also should be used with caution.

***Lithium-Diuretics:*** Sodium depletion is known to increase lithium toxicity, for which reason it generally has been recommended that lithium salts should not be used in patients on diuretic therapy or an a sodium-restricted diet. Even protracted sweating or diarrhea can cause sufficient depletion of sodium to result in decreased tolerance to lithium.

4. **Interactions at Receptor Sites:** MAOIs-Sympathomimetic Agents

MAO functions to breakdown catecholamines such as norepinephrine. When the enzyme is inhibited, the concentrations of norepinephrine within adrenergic neurons increase and a drug that can stimulate its release can bring about an exaggerated response. It is by this mechanism that interactions between MAOIs and indirectly acting sympathomimetic amines (e.g., amphetamine) develop. Thus, if amphetamine is administered to patients whose stores of norepinephrine have been increased by MAO inhibition, they may experience severe headache, hypertension (possible a hypertensive crisis) and cardiac arrhythmias. The serious consequences associated with these interactions contraindicate use of these agents in combination.

Although most sympathomimetic amines, such as amphetamine, are available only by prescription, others such as Phenylephrine, which also has been reported to interact similarly with MAOIs, are found in many nonprescription cold and allergy preparations. It is important that patients being treated with MAOIs avoid using products containing these agents.

***MAOIs - Tricyclic Antidepressants*** - Cautions in the product literature, as well as case reports, warn against concurrent use of an MAOI with a tricyclic antidepressant (e.g., amitriptyline, imipramine) because severe atropine-like reactions, tremors, convulsions, hyperthermia and vascular collapse have been reported to result from such use. It is recommended in the labeling for most of these products that therapy with an MAOI or a tricyclic antidepressant should not be initiated until at least 7 to 14 days after therapy with the other has been discontinued.

Although the labeling for most MAOIs and tricyclic antidepressants notes that concurrent use is contraindicated, there is debate as to the degree of risk involved.

Several studies of the combined use of these agents have revealed little evidence of interactions and the growing impression that serious interactions are uncommon, coupled with the reports of favorable results with such combinations in selected patients who did not respond to either agent given alone, have led some to conclude that these combinations can be employed cautiously. In patients who are refractory to single antidepressants and who are not candidates for alternative therapeutic approaches, the potential benefits of combination therapy may outweigh the risks. However, such therapy should be undertaken only by those who are thoroughly familiar with the risks involved and under circumstances in which therapy can be monitored closely.

***MAOIs - Selective Serotonin Reuptake Inhibitors*** – Serious consequences may result from the combined use of an MAOI and a selective serotonin reuptake inhibitor (SSRI, citalopram, escitalopram, fluoxetine, fluvoxamine, paroxetine, sertaline) and concurrent use of use within 14 days before or after most of these agents is contraindicated.

There have been several reports of deaths of patients in whom therapy with an MAOI was initiated shortly after discontinuation of fluoxetine. Because of the long half-lives of fluoxetine and its active metabolite, it is recommended that atleast 5 weeks should elapse between discontinuation of fluoxetine and initiation of therapy with an MAOI.

It should be noted that the antineoplastic procarbazine and the anti-infectives furazolidone and linezolid, also can inhibit MAO enzymes and warnings applying to the use of other MAOIs should be needed for these drugs also.

***Guanethidine-Tricyclic Antidepressants*** Guanethidine is transported to its site of action within adrenergic neurons by a transport system that also is responsible for uptake of nor epinephrine, as well as several indirectly acting sympathomimetic amines such as ephedrine and the amphetamines. Concentration of guanethidine in these neurons is necessary for its antihypertensive action. Tricyclic antidepressants can inhibit uptake of guanethidine into the neuron terminal, thereby preventing its concentration at these sites and reducing its activity. Other studies suggest that antipsychotic agents such as chlorpromazine and haloperidol can act similarly to the tricyclic antidepressants in reducing the antihypertensive effect of this agent.

Although other mechanisms may be involved in the development of drug interactions, the ones cited are the most important. As often stated, more than one mechanism may be responsible for certain interactions; these mechanisms may work in concert or in opposition as determinants of the resulting effect. Still other drug interactions develop by mechanisms yet to be identified.

However, an awareness of the factors predisposing to the development of drug interactions, as well as the mechanisms by which many of them occur, will be of value in the identification and prevention of potential problems.

It is evident that significant limitations still exist in trying to predict the results of combination therapy. In the following section, guidelines are provided to reduce the risk of the occurrence of drug interactions.

## Drug-food Interactions

It is well established that food can cause clinically important changes in drug absorption through effects on gastrointestinal motility or by drug binding, In addition, it is well known that tyramine (present in some foodstuffs) may reach toxic concentrations in patients taking 'MAOIs'. With the growth in understanding of drug metabolism mechanisms, it has been increasingly recognized that some foods can alter drug metabolism. Currently, grapefruit juice causes the most clinically relevant of these interactions,

(a) **Cruciferous vegetables and charcoal-broiled meats:** Cruciferous vegetables, such as Brussels sprouts, cabbage and broccoli, contain substances that are inducers of the cytochrome P450 isoenzyme CYP1A2. Chemicals formed by 'burning' meats additionally have these properties. These foods do not appear to cause any clinically important drug interactions in their own right, but their consumption may add another variable to drug interaction studies, so complicating interpretation. In drug interaction studies where alteration of CYP1A2 is a predicted mechanism, it may be better for patients to avoid these foods during the study.

(b) **Grape fruit juice:** By chance, grapefruit juice was chosen to mask the taste of alcohol in a study of the effect of alcohol on felodipine, which led to the discovery that grapefruit juice itself markedly increased felodipine levels; In general, grapefruit juice inhibits intestinal CYP3A4 and only slightly affects hepatic CYP3A4. This metabolized by CYP3A4 are not much affected, whereas oral preparations of the same drugs are. These interactions result in increased drug levels. Some drugs that are not metabolized by CYP3A4 show decreased levels with grapefruit juice, such as 'fexofenadine'. The probable reason for this is that grapefruit juice is an inhibitor of some drug transporters and possibly affects organic anion transporting polypeptides (OATPs), although inhibition of P-glycoprotein has also been suggested. The active constituent of grapefruit juice is uncertain. Grapefruit contains naringin, which degrades during processing to naringenin, a substance known to inhibit CYP3A4. Because of this, it has been assumed that whole grapefruit will not interact, but that processed grapefruit juice will however subsequently some reports have implicated the whole fruit. Other possible active constituents in the whole fruit include bergamottin and dihydroxy-bergamottin.

**Table 9-4:** Food drug interactions

| Specific Agents | Food-Drug Interaction | Comments |
|---|---|---|
| **Antibiotics** | | |
| Ciprofloxacin (Cipro, various) | • When the tablet formulation is given with food, there is a delay in the absorption of the drug resulting in peak concentrations that occur closer to 2 hours after dosing rather than 1 hour, but bioavailability is not affected<br>• Concurrent administration of antacids containing magnesium hydroxide or aluminium hydroxide may reduce the bioavailability by as much as 90%.<br>• Dairy products and other products containing calcium, magnesium, aluminium iron or zinc decrease the absorption. | • Take with food or on an empty stomach and drink fluids liberally.<br>• Avoid concurrent administration with magnesium/aluminum antacids or other products containing calcium, iron or zinc.<br>• Take 2 hours before or 6 hours after taking these products.<br>• Do not take with dairy products or calcium-fortified juices.<br>• Can be taken with a meal that contains these products. |

*Table 9-4 Contd...*

| Specific Agents | Food-Drug Interaction | Comments |
|---|---|---|
| | **Antibiotics** | |
| Clarithromycin (Biaxin, various) (Biaxin XL) | • Absorption of Biaxin XL tablets may be decreased by 30% under fasting conditions.<br>• Food delays the absorption of the immediate release tablets but does not affect the absorption. | • Biaxin can be taken with or without food.<br>• Take Biaxin XL tablets with food. |
| Erythromycin | • Food alters erythrocycin concentrations.<br>• Erythromycin base and stearate are absorbed better in the fasting state. | • To optimize erythromycin efficacy, take on an empty stomach at least 30 minutes before meals.<br>• Erythromycin ethylsuccinate, erythromycin estolate, and enteric-coated erythromycin may be administered without regard to meals. |
| Metronidazole (Flagyl, various) | • Concurrent administration with alcohol can cause a disulfiram-like reaction | • Avoid concurrent use with alcohol containing products. |
| Nitrofurantoin Monohydrate Macrocrystal (Macrobid) | • Bioavailability may be increased by 40% when given with food.<br>• Antacids containing magnesium trisilicate can decrease the rate and extent of absorption. | • Take with food<br>• Do not use antacids containing magnesium trisilicate while taking macrobid. |
| Tetracyclines Tetracycline (Sumycin, various Demeclocycline (Declomycin) Doxycycline (Vibramycin, various | • Milk and other dairy products may reduce the absorption of most tetracycline derivatives by 50% or more.<br>• Absorption may be decreased when given with iron and/or food.<br>• Products/foods containing calcium, magnesium, aluminium, iron or zinc decrease the absorption. | • Take 1 hour before or 2 hours after dairy foods and/or meals.<br>• Take 2 to 3 hours before or after taking any products containing magnesium, aluminium, calcium, iron or zinc. |
| | **Anticoagulants** | |
| Warfarin (Coumadin, various) | • Alcohol can increase or decrease PT/INR<br>• Vitamin E can increase PT/INR<br>• Vitamin K can decrease PT/INR | • Avoid alcohol consumption<br>• Patients initiated on vitamin E may require dosing adjustments downward to maintain a therapeutic INR.<br>• Eat a normal, balanced diet maintaining a consistent amount of vitamin K.<br>• Avoid drastic changes in dietary habits, such as eating large amounts of green leafy vegetables.<br>• See Table 1 for foods high in vitamin K.. |

*Table 9-4 Contd...*

| Specific Agents | Food-Drug Interaction | Comments |
|---|---|---|
| **Anticonvulsant Agents** | | |
| Phenytoin (Dilantin, various) | • Absorption may increase 27% when taken with a standard meal | • Administer phenytoin consistently with regard to meals.<br>• Do not administer phenytoin concomitantly with an enteral feeding preparation. Hold enteral feeding 2 hours before and after dosing (Dose adjustment may be necessary)<br>• Avoid alcohol consumption or dose adjust for patients who regularly ethanol. |
| **Antifungal Agents** | | |
| Griseofulvin (Grifulvin-V, various | • Concurrent administration with alcohol may produce a disulfiram-like reaction.<br>• Absorption can be increased when given with a fatty meal. | • Avoid alcohol and alcohol-containing products.<br>• Take after a high-fat content meal, if possible, to maximize absorption. |
| Itraconazole (Sporanox, various) | • Bioavailability of capsule formulation is maximal when taken with a full meal.<br>• Absorption of capsule formulation can be increased after coadministration with a cola beverage (AUC may increase by 75% and $C_{max}$ may increase by 95%).<br>• Absorption of the solution formulation can be decreased when taken with a meal. | • Take capsule formulation with a full meal.<br>• Take solution formulation on an empty stomach. |
| Ketoconazole (Nizoral, various) | • Concurrent administration with alcohol may produce a disulfiram-like reaction | • Avoid alcohol or alcohol-containing products |
| **Antineoplastic Agents** | | |
| Procarbazine (Matulane) | • Hypertensive urgency or emergency may result when combined with foods containing tyramine.<br>• Concurrent administration with alcohol may produce a disulfiram-like reaction. | • Avoid tyramine containing foods (see MAOI section)<br>• Avoid alcohol and alcohol-containing products, |
| **Antipsychotic Agents** | | |
| Ziprasidone (Geodon) | • Absorption can increase as much as 2 times with food | • Take with food |
| Theophylline | • Excessive caffeine intake can increase serum concentrations and toxicities (nausea, vomiting, palpitations, seizures.<br>• Food may alter the bioavailability of some sustained-release preparations. | • Avoid caffeine or maintain daily intake relatively constant.<br>• Take theophylline preparations consistently with regard to meals. |
| **Gastrointestinal Stimulants** | | |
| Tegaserod (Zelnorm) | • Food may reduce bioavailability by 40 to 65% and reduce $C_{max}$ by 20 to 40%. | • Take on an empty stomach 30 minutes before meals. |

*Table 9-4 Contd...*

| Specific Agents | Food-Drug Interaction | Comments |
|---|---|---|
| | **Grapefruit Juice** | |
| Grapefruit juice interactions with multiple drugs | • Grapefruit juice significantly increases the bioavailability of the following medications:<br>• Amiodarone (Cardarone Pacerone, various)<br>• Amlodipine (Norvasc)<br>• Atorvastatin (Lipitor)<br>• Buspirone (Buspar)<br>• **Grapefruit juice significantly increase the bioavailability of the following medications (continued);**<br>• Carbamazepine (Tegretol, Carbatrol)<br>• Cyclosporine (Gengral, Neoral, Sandimmune)<br>• Diazepam (Valium various)<br>• Digoxin (Lanoxin, various)<br>• Diltiazem (Cardezem, various)<br>• Estrogens (various)<br>• Felodipine (Plendil)<br>• Itraconazole (Sporanox)<br>• Losartan (Diovan)<br>• Methylprednisolone (Medrol)<br>• Midazolam (Versed)<br>• Nicardipine (Cardene)<br>• Nifedipine (Adalat, Procardia, various)<br>• Nimodipine (Nimotop)<br>• Quinidine (various)<br>• Sildenafil (Viagara, Revotio)<br>• Simvastatin (Zocor)<br>• Sirolimus (Rapamune)<br>• Tacrolimus (Prograf)<br>• Triazolam (Halcion)<br>• Verapamil (Calan, various)<br>• Warfarin (Coumadin, various) | • Avoid grapefruit juice with these medications. |
| | **Non-nucleoside Reverse Transcriptase Inhibitors (NNRTI)** | |
| Efavirenz (Sustiva) | • High-fat/high-calorie can increase bioavailability by 50%. | • Take on an empty stomach preferably at bedtime |
| | **Nucleoside Reverse Transcriptase Inhibitors (NRTIs)** | |
| Abacavir (Ziagen) | • Alcohol can increase AUC by 41% and increase $t_{1/2}$ by 26%. | • Avoid alcohol |
| Didanosine (Videx) | • Food can decrease AUC by 19% and decrease $C_{max}$ by 46%. | • Take on an empty stomach 30 minutes before or 2 hours after meals. |
| Tenofovir (Viread) | • High-fat meal can increase bioavailability and can increase AUC by 40% and increase $C_{max}$ by 14%. | • Take with or without food, however oral bioavailability is increased following a high-fat meal. |

*Table 9-4 Contd...*

| Specific Agents | Food-Drug Interaction | Comments |
|---|---|---|
| | **Protease Inhibitors** | |
| Atazanovir (Reyataz) | • A light meal can increase AUC by 70% and Cmax by 57%. | • Take with food |
| Lopinavir/Ritonavir (Kaletra) | • High-fat meal taken along with capsule formulation can increase AUC by 97% and increase $C_{max}$ by 43%.<br>• High-fat meal taken along with solution formulation can increase AUC by 130% and increase $C_{max}$ by 56%.<br>• No clinically significant changes have been observed following administration of the tablet formulation with food. | • Capsule or oral solution may be taken with food.<br>• Tablets may be taken with or without food. |
| Nelfinavir (Viracept) | • High-fat meal can increase AUC by 5.1% fold and increase $C_{max}$ by 3, 8-fold. | • Take with food<br>• Increase exposure of drug by increasing fat or calorie content of food. |
| Ritonavir (Norvir) | • Food can increase the extent of absorption of the capsule formulation by 13%. | • Take with food |
| Alendronate (Fosamax) | • Dairy products can reduce absorption<br>• Food can decrease bioavailability by 40%<br>• Orange juice or coffee can decrease bioavailability by 60%<br>• Calcium supplements and antacids may interfere with absorption | • Take with a full glass of water upon arising for the day on an empty stomach at least 30 minutes.<br>• Avoid concurrent administration with orange juice or coffee |

## Reducing the Risk of Drug Interactions – Principles of Drug Interactions Management

The consequences of drug interactions may be:

- **Major:** Life threatening
- **Moderate:** Deteriorations of patient's status
- **Minor:** Bothersome or little effect.

The risk of drug interactions is a challenge that embraces a number of considerations. The following are guidelines to reduce and manage drug interactions.

1. Identify patient risk factors such as age, the nature of the patient's medical problem (e.g., impaired renal Function), dietary habits, smoking and problems such as alcoholism influence the effect of certain drugs.
2. Take thorough drug history and maintain complete patient medication records.
3. Impart knowledge about actions (both primary and secondary pharmacological actions) of drugs being utilized.
4. Consider therapeutic alternatives.
5. Avoid complex therapeutic regimens where possible.
6. Educate the patient to comply with instructions for administering medications. They should be encouraged to ask questions about their therapy and to report any excessive or unexpected responses.
7. Monitor therapy: priority should be suspected as drug related until that possibility is excluded.
8. Individualize therapy: priority should be assigned to the needs and clinical response

of the individual patient, rather than to the usual dosage recommendations, standard treatment and monitoring guidelines.

9. Involve the patient as a partner in health care. If the optimal benefits of therapy are to be achieved with minimal risk, each participant must be knowledgeable about and diligent in fulfilling his responsibilities.

## References


Bachmann KA and Ghosh R (2001). The use of *in vitro* methods to predict *in vivo* pharmacokinetics and drug interactions. *Curr Drug Metab* **2:** 299–314.

Bjornsson TD, Callaghan JT, Einolf HJ, Fischer V, Gan L, Grimm S, Kao J, King SP, MiwaG, Ni L, Kumar G, McLeod J, Obach RS, Roberts S, Roe A, Shah A, Snikeris F, Sullivan JT, Tweedie D, Vega JM, Walsh J and Wrighton SA (2003). The conduct of in vitro and in vivo drug-drug interaction studies: a PhRMA perspective. *J Clin Pharmacol* **43**: 443–69.

Fugh-Berman A (2000). Herb-drug interactions. *Lancet* **355**: 134–8. Correction. ibid. 1020.

Henderson L, Yue QY, Bergquist C, Gerden B, 8Arlett P (2002). St John's wort (*Hypericum perforatum*):drug interactions and clinical outcomes. *Br J Clin Pharmacol* **54:** 349–56.

Miller LG (1998). Herbal medicinals. Selected clinical considerations focusing on known or potential drug-herb interactions. *Arch Intern Med* **158:** 2200–11.

Phillips KA, Veenstra DL, Oren E, Lee JK and Sadee W (2001). Potential role of Pharmacogenomics in reducing adverse drug reactions: a systematic review. *JAMA* **286**: 2270–79.

Venkatakrishnan K, von Moltke LL, Obach RS and Greenblatt DJ (2003). Drug metabolism and drug interactions:application and clinical value of *in vitro* models. *Curr Drug Metab* **4**: 423–59.

Wang Z, Gorski JC, Hamman MA, Huang S M, Lesko LJ and Hall SD (2001). The effects of St John's wort *(Hypericum perforatum)* on human cytochrome P450 activity. *Clin Pharmacol Ther* **70:** 317–26.

Williamson EM (2003). Drug interactions between herbal and prescription medicines. *Drug Safety* **26:** 1075–92.

Worboys PD and Carlile DJ (2001). Implications and consequences of enzyme induction on preclinical and clinical drug development. *Xenobiotica* **31**: 539–56.

Yao C and Levy RH (2002). Inhibition-based metabolic drug-drug interactions: predictions from *in vitro* data. *J Pharm Sci* **91:** 1923–35.

# Part - II

# Drugs Affecting Autonomic Nervous System

CHAPTER

# General Considerations of Autonomic Nervous System 10

The autonomic nervous system (ANS or visceral nervous system or involuntary nervous system) is the part of the peripheral nervous system that acts as a control system functioning largely below the level of consciousness, and controls visceral functions. The ANS affects heart rate, digestion, respiratory rate, salivation, perspiration, pupillary dilation, micturition (urination), and sexual arousal. Most autonomous functions are involuntary but a number of ANS actions can work alongside some degree of conscious control. Everyday examples include breathing, swallowing, and sexual arousal, and in some cases functions such as heart rate.

Within the brain, the ANS is located in the medulla oblongata in the lower brainstem. The medulla's major ANS functions include respiration (the respiratory control centre, or "rcc"), cardiac regulation (the cardiac control centre, or "ccc"), vasomotor activity (the vasomotor centre or "vmc"), and certain reflex actions (such as coughing, sneezing, vomiting and swallowing). These then subdivide into other areas and are also linked to ANS subsystems and nervous systems external to the brain. The hypothalamus, just above the brain stem, acts as an integrator for autonomic functions, receiving ANS regulatory input from the limbic system to do so.

The ANS is classically divided into two subsystems: the parasympathetic nervous system (PSNS) and sympathetic nervous system (SNS) which operate independently in some functions and interact co-operatively in others. In many cases the two have "opposite" actions where one activates a physiological response and the other inhibits it. An older simplification of the sympathetic and parasympathetic nervous systems as "excitory" and "inhibitory" was overturned due to the many exceptions found. A more modern characterisation is that the sympathetic nervous system is a "quick response mobilising system" and the parasympathetic is a "more slowly activated damping system", but even this has exceptions, such as in sexual arousal and orgasm where both play a role. The enteric nervous system is also sometimes considered part of the autonomic nervous system, and sometimes considered an independent system.

## Anatomy

ANS innervation is divided into sympathetic nervous system and parasympathetic nervous system divisions (Fig. 10.1). The sympathetic division has thoracolumbar "outflow", meaning that the neurons begin at the thoracic and lumbar (T1-L2) portions of the spinal cord. The parasympathetic division has craniosacral "outflow", meaning that the neurons begin at the cranial nerves (CN 3, CN7, CN 9, and CN10) and sacral (S2-S4) spinal cord.

The ANS is unique in that it requires a sequential two-neuron efferent pathway; the preganglionic neuron must first synapse onto a postganglionic neuron before innervating the target organ. The preganglionic, or first, neuron will begin at the "outflow" and will synapse at the postganglionic, or second, neuron's cell body. The post ganglionic neuron will then synapse at the target organ.

## Sympathetic Division

The sympathetic division (thoracolumbar outflow) consists of cell bodies in the lateral horn of spinal cord (intermediolateral cell columns) from T1 to L2. These cell bodies are GVE (general visceral efferent) neurons and are the preganglionic neurons. There are several locations upon which preganglionic neurons can synapse for their postganglionic neurons:

Paravertebral ganglia (3) of the sympathetic chain (these run on either side of the vertebral bodies)

1. Cervical ganglia (3)
2. Thoracic ganglia (12) and rostral lumbar Ganglia (2 or 3)
3. Caudal lumbar ganglia and pelvic ganglia
4. Prevertebral ganglia (celiac ganglion, aorticorenal ganglion, superior mesenteric ganglion, inferior mesenteric ganglion)
5. Chromaffin cells of adrenal medulla (this is the one exception to the two-neuron pathway rule: synapse is direct onto the target cell bodies)
6. These ganglia provide the postganglionic neurons from which innervation of target organs follows.

Examples of splanchnic (visceral) nerves are:

(a) Cervical cardiac nerves & thoracic visceral nerves which synapse in the sympathetic chain
(b) Thoracic splanchnic nerves (greater, lesser, least) which synapse in the prevertebral ganglion
(c) Lumbar splanchnic nerves which synapse in the prevertebral ganglion
(d) Sacral splanchnic nerves which synapse in the inferior hypogastric plexus

7. These all contain afferent (sensory) nerves as well, known as GVA (general visceral afferent) neurons.

## Parasympathetic Division

The parasympathetic division (craniosacral outflow) consists of cell bodies from one of two locations: Brainstem (Cranial Nerves III, VII, IX, X) or sacral spinal cord (S2, S3, S4). These are

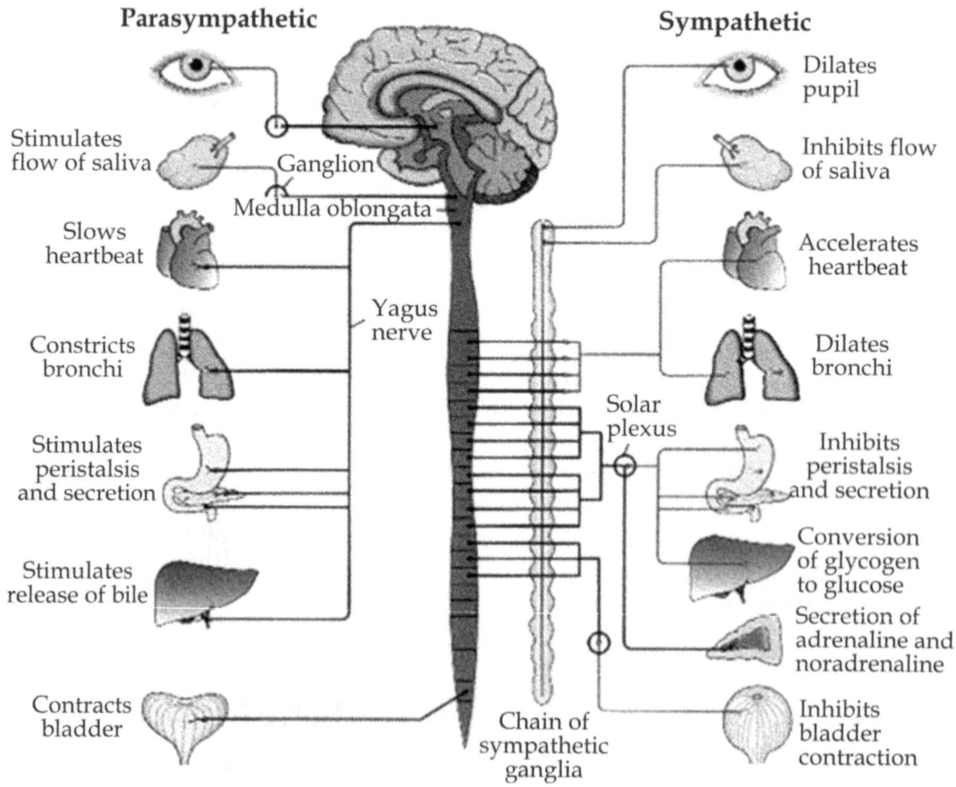


**Fig 10-1**: Sympathetic and para sympathetic divisions

the preganglionic neurons, which synapse with postganglionic neurons in these locations:

1. Parasympathetic ganglia of the head [Ciliary (CN III), Sub mandibular (CN VII), Pterygopalatine (CN VII), Otic (CN IX)]
2. In or near wall of organ innervated by Vagus (CN X), Sacral nerves (S2, S3, S4)
3. These ganglia provide the postganglionic neurons from which innervations of target organs follows.

   Examples are:

   (a) The preganglionic parasympathetic splanchnic (visceral) nerves

   (b) Vagus nerve, which wanders through the thorax and abdominal regions innervating, among other organs, the heart, lungs, liver and stomach

## Sensory Neurons

The sensory arm is made of "primary visceral sensory neurons" found in the peripheral nervous system (PNS), in "cranial sensory ganglia": the geniculate, petrosal and nodosa ganglia, appended respectively to cranial nerves VII, IX and X. These sensory neurons monitor the levels of carbon dioxide, oxygen and sugar in the blood, arterial pressure and the chemical composition of the stomach and gut content. (They also convey the sense of taste and smell, a conscious perception). Blood oxygen and carbon dioxide are in fact directly sensed by the carotid body, a small collection of chemosensors at the bifurcation of the carotid artery, innervated by the petrosal (IX) ganglion. Primary sensory neurons project (synapse) onto "second order" or relay visceral sensory neurons located in the medulla oblongata, forming the nucleus of the solitary tract (NTS), that integrates all visceral information. The NTS also receives input from a nearby chemosensory center, the area postrema, that detects toxins in the blood and the cerebrospinal fluid and is essential for chemically induced vomiting or conditional taste aversion (the memory that ensures that an animal which has been poisoned by a food never touches it again).

## Motor Neurons

Motor neurons of the ANS are also located in ganglia of the PNS, called "autonomic ganglia". They belong to three categories with different effects on their target organs (see below "Function"): sympathetic, parasympathetic and enteric.

Sympathetic ganglia are located in two sympathetic chains close to the spinal cord: the prevertebral and pre-aortic chains. Parasympathetic ganglia, in contrast, are located in close proximity to the target organ: the submandibular ganglion close to salivary glands, paracardiac ganglia close to the heart etc. Enteric ganglia, which as their name implies innervate the digestive tube, are located inside its walls and collectively contain as many neurons as the entire spinal cord, including local sensory neurons, motor neurons and interneuron's. It is the only truly autonomous part of the ANS and the digestive tube can function surprisingly well even in isolation. For that reason the enteric nervous system has been called "the second brain".

The activity of autonomic ganglionic neurons is modulated by "preganglionic neurons" (also called improperly but classically "visceral motoneurons") located in the central nervous system. Preganglionic sympathetic neurons are in the spinal cord, at thoraco-lumbar levels. Preganglionic parasympathetic neurons are in the medulla oblongata [forming visceral motor nuclei: the dorsal motor nucleus of the vagus nerve (dmnX), the nucleus ambiguus, and salivatory nuclei] and in the sacral spinal cord. Enteric neurons are also modulated by input from the CNS, from preganglionic neurons located, like parasympathetic ones, in the medulla oblongata (in the dmnX).

The feedback from the sensory to the motor arm of visceral reflex pathways is provided by direct or indirect connections between the nucleus of the solitary tract and visceral motorneurons.

## Function

Sympathetic and parasympathetic divisions typically function in opposition to each other. The sympathetic division typically functions in actions requiring quick responses. The parasympathetic division functions with actions that do not require immediate reaction. Consider sympathetic as "fight or flight" and parasympathetic as "rest and digest" or "feed and breed".

However, many instances of sympathetic and parasympathetic activity cannot be ascribed to "fight" or "rest" situations. For example, standing up from a reclining or sitting position would entail an unsustainable drop in blood pressure if not for a compensatory increase in the arterial sympathetic tonus. Another example is the constant, second to second modulation of heart rate by sympathetic and parasympathetic influences, as a function of the respiratory cycles. More generally, these two systems should be seen as permanently modulating vital functions, in usually antagonistic fashion, to achieve homeostasis. Some typical actions of the sympathetic and parasympathetic systems are listed below.

### Sympathetic Nervous System

1. Promotes a "fight or flight" response, corresponds with arousal and energy generation, and inhibits digestion.
2. Diverts blood flow away from the gastro-intestinal (GI) tract and skin *via* vasoconstriction.
3. Blood flow to skeletal muscles and the lungs is enhanced (by as much as 1200% in the case of skeletal muscles).
4. Dilates bronchioles of the lung, which allows for greater alveolar oxygen exchange.
5. Increases heart rate and the contractility of cardiac cells (myocytes), thereby providing a mechanism for the enhanced blood flow to skeletal muscles.
6. Dilates pupils and relaxes the ciliary muscle to the lens, allowing more light to enter the eye and far vision.
7. Provides vasodilation for the coronary vessels of the heart.
8. Constricts all the intestinal sphincters and the urinary sphincter.
9. Inhibits peristalsis.
10. Stimulates orgasm.

### Parasympathetic Nervous System

Promotes a "rest and digest" response, promotes calming of the nerves return to regular function, and enhances digestion.

Dilates blood vessels leading to the GI tract, increasing blood flow. This is important following the consumption of food, due to the greater metabolic demands placed on the body by the gut.

1. The parasympathetic nervous system can also constrict the bronchiolar diameter when the need for oxygen has diminished.
2. Dedicated cardiac branches of the vagus and thoracic spinal accessory nerves impart parasympathetic control of the heart or myocardium.
3. During accommodation, the parasympathetic nervous system causes constriction of the pupil and contraction of the ciliary muscle to the lens, allowing for closer vision.
4. The parasympathetic nervous system stimulates salivary gland secretion, and accelerates peristalsis, so, in keeping with the rest and digest functions, appropriate PNS activity mediates digestion of food and indirectly, the absorption of nutrients.
5. Is also involved in erection of genitals, *via* the pelvic splanchnic nerves 2–4.
6. Stimulates sexual arousal.

## Neurotransmitters and Pharmacology

At the effector organs, sympathetic ganglionic neurons release noradrenaline (norepinephrine), along with other co-transmitters such as ATP, to act on adrenergic receptors, with the exception of the sweat glands and the adrenal medulla.

Acetylcholine is the preganglionic neurotransmitter for both divisions of the ANS, as well as the postganglionic neurotransmitter of parasympathetic neurons. Nerves that release acetylcholine are said to be cholinergic. In the parasympathetic system, ganglionic neurons use acetylcholine as a neurotransmitter, to stimulate muscarinic receptors.

At the adrenal medulla, there is no postsynaptic neuron. Instead the presynaptic neuron releases acetylcholine to act on nicotinic receptors. Stimulation of the adrenal medulla releases adrenaline (epinephrine) into the bloodstream which acts on adrenoceptors, producing a widespread increase in sympathetic activity.

**Table 10-1:** The actions of these neurotransmitters as a function of their receptors

**Circulatory system**

| Target | Sympathetic (Adrenergic) | Parasympathetic (Muscarinic) |
|---|---|---|
| **1. Heart** | | |
| cardiac output | $\beta_1$, ($\beta_2$): increases | $M_2$: decreases |
| SA node: heart rate (chronotropic) | $\beta_1$, ($\beta_2$): increases | $M_2$: decreases |
| Atrial cardiac muscle: contractility (inotropic) | $\beta_1$, ($\beta_2$): increases | $M_2$: decreases |
| at AV node | $\beta_1$: increases conduction, increases cardiac muscle automaticity | $M_2$: decreases conduction Atrioventricular block |
| Ventricular cardiac muscle | $\beta_1$, ($\beta_2$): increases contractility (inotropic) increases cardiac muscle automaticity | --- |
| **2. Blood Vessels** | | |
| Vascular smooth muscle in general | $\alpha_1$: contracts; $\beta_2$: relaxes | $M_3$: relaxes |
| Renal artery | $\alpha_1$: constricts | --- |
| Larger coronary arteries | $\alpha_1$ and $\alpha_2$: constricts | --- |
| Smaller coronary arteries | $\beta_2$:dilates | --- |
| Arteries to viscera | $\alpha$: constricts | --- |
| Arteries to skin | $\alpha$: constricts | --- |
| Arteries to brain | $\alpha_1$: constricts | --- |
| Arteries to erectile tissue | $\alpha_1$: constricts | $M_3$: dilates |
| Arteries to salivary glands | $\alpha$: constricts | $M_3$: dilates |
| Hepatic artery | $\beta_2$: dilates | --- |
| Arteries to skeletal muscle | $\beta_2$: dilates | --- |
| Veins | $\alpha_1$ and $\alpha_2$: constricts<br>$\beta_2$: dilates | --- |
| **3. Other** | | |
| Platelets | $\alpha_2$: aggregates | --- |
| Mast cells - histamine | $\beta_2$: inhibits | --- |

## Respiratory System

The bronchioles have no sympathetic innervation, but are instead affected by circulating adrenaline

| Target | Sympathetic (adrenergic) | Parasympathetic (muscarinic) |
|---|---|---|
| Smooth muscles of bronchioles | $\beta_2$: relaxes (major contribution)<br>$\alpha_1$: contracts (minor contribution) | $M_3$: contracts |

## Nervous System

| Target | Sympathetic (adrenergic) | Parasympathetic (muscarinic) |
|---|---|---|
| Pupil dilator muscle | $\alpha_1$: dilates (causes mydriasis) | |
| Iris sphincter muscle | - | $M_3$: contracts (causes miosis) |
| Ciliary muscle | $\beta_2$: relaxes (causes long-range focus) | $M_3$: contracts (causes short-range focus) |

## Digestive System

| Target | Sympathetic (adrenergic) | Parasympathetic (muscarinic) |
|---|---|---|
| Salivary glands: secretions | β: stimulates viscous, amylase secretions<br>$\alpha_1$: stimulates potassium secretions | $M_3$: stimulates watery secretions |
| Lacrimal glands (tears) | β: stimulates protein secretion | --- |
| Juxtaglomerular apparatus of kidney | $\beta_1$: renin secretion | --- |
| Parietal cells | --- | $M_1$: gastric acid secretion |
| Liver | $\alpha_1$, $\beta_2$: glycogenolysis, gluconeogenesis | --- |
| Adipose cells | $\beta_1$, $\beta_3$: stimulates lipolysis | --- |
| GI tract (smooth muscle) motility | $\alpha_1$, $\alpha_2$, $\beta_2$: decreases | $M_3$, ($M_1$): increases |
| Sphincters of GI tract | $\alpha_1$, $\alpha_2$, $\beta_2$: contracts | $M_3$: relaxes |
| Glands of GI tract | no effect | $M_3$: secretes |

## Endocrine System

| Target | Sympathetic (adrenergic) | Parasympathetic (muscarinic) |
|---|---|---|
| Pancreas (islets) | $\alpha_2$: decreases insulin secretion from beta cells, increases glucagon secretion from alpha cells | $M_3$: increases secretion of both insulin and glucagon |
| Adrenal medulla | N (nicotinic ACh receptor): secretes epinephrine and norepinephrine | --- |

### Urinary System

| Target | Sympathetic (adrenergic) | Parasympathetic (muscarinic) |
|---|---|---|
| Detrusor muscle of bladder wall | $\beta_2$, $\beta_3$: relaxes | $M_3$: contracts |
| Internal urethral sphincter | $\alpha_1$: contracts | $M_3$: relaxes |

### Reproductive System

| Target | Sympathetic (adrenergic) | Parasympathetic (muscarinic) |
|---|---|---|
| Uterus | $\alpha_1$: contracts (pregnant)<br>$\beta_2$: relaxes (non-pregnant) | --- |
| Genitalia | $\alpha_1$: contracts (ejaculation) | $M_3$: erection |

## References

Elliott J (1997). Alpha-adrenoceptors in equine digital veins: Evidence for the presence of both alpha1 and alpha2-receptors mediating vasoconstriction. *Journal of Veterinary Pharmacology & Therapeutics* (Blackwell Publishings) **20(4):** 308-317. doi:10.1046/j.1365-2885.1997.00078.x .PMID 9280371.

Kullmann FA, *et al.*, (2009). Effects of beta3-adrenergic receptor activation on rat urinary bladder hyperactivity induced by ovariectomy. *J Pharmacol Exp Ther.* **330(3):** 704-17. *Epub* 2009 Jun 10.

P. Mauduit, G. Herman and B. Rossignol (1984). Protein secretion induced by isoproterenol or pentoxifylline in lacrimal gland. *American Journal of Physiology and Cell Physiology* **246:** C37-C44.

Sagrada A, Fargeas MJ, Bueno L A, Fargeas MJ, Bueno L (1987). Involvement of alpha-1 and alpha-2 adrenoceptors in the postlaparotomy intestinal motor disturbances in the rat. *Gut* **28(8):** 955-959. doi:10.1136/gut.28.8.955. PMC 1433140. PMID 2889649.

CHAPTER

# 11 Cholinergic Drugs

## The Cholinergic Neuron

The preganglionic fibers terminating in the adrenal medulla, the autonomic ganglia (both parasympathetic and sympathetic), and the postganglionic fibers of the parasympathetic division use acetylcholine as a neurotransmitter. In addition, cholinergic neurons innervate the muscles of the somatic system and also play an important role in the central nervous system (CNS).

### Neurotransmission at Cholinergic Neurons

Neurotransmission in cholinergic neurons involves sequential six steps. The first four synthesis, storage, release, and binding of acetylcholine to a receptors are followed by the fifth step, degradation of the neurotransmitter in the synaptic gap (that is, the space between the nerve endings and adjacent receptors located on nerves or effector organs), and the sixth step, the recycling of choline (Figure 11-1).

**Synthesis of acetylcholine:** Acetylcholine is synthesized in two steps:

Choline is transported from the extra-cellular fluid into the cytoplasm of the cholinergic neuron by an energy-dependent carrier system that co transports sodium and that can be inhibited by the drug hemicholinium. Choline has a quaternary nitrogen and carries a permanent positive charge, and thus, cannot diffuse through the membrane. The uptake of choline is the rate-limiting step in acetylcholine synthesis. Choline acetyltransferase catalyzes the reaction of choline with acetyl coenzyme A (CoA) to form acetylcholine an ester in the cytosol. Acetyl CoA is derived from the mitochondria and is produced by the Krebs cycle and fatty acid oxidation. Choline present in tissues has two origins: exogenous, in food, and endogenous, by biosynthesis from glycine through many steps: serine, ethanolamine, Phosphatidyl-ethanolamine, Phosphatidyl-choline and choline. The trimethylation of Phosphatidyl-ethanolamine needs the presence of vitamin $B_{12}$, folic acid and methionine.

**Storage of acetylcholine in vesicles:** The acetylcholine is packaged into presynaptic vesicles by an active transport process coupled to the efflux of protons. The mature vesicle contains not only acetylcholine but also adenosine triphosphate (ATP) and proteoglycan. ATP has been suggested to be a cotransmitter acting at prejunctional purinergic receptors to inhibit the release of acetylcholine or norepinephrine. Co-transmission from autonomic neurons is the rule rather than the exception. This means that most synaptic vesicles will contain the primary neurotransmitter, here acetylcholine, as well as a cotransmitter that will increase or decrease the effect of the primary neurotransmitter. The neurotransmitters in vesicles will appear as bead-like structures, known as varicosities, along the nerve terminal of the presynaptic neuron.

**Release of acetylcholine:** In presynaptic terminations, acetylcholine is contained in vesicles. Nervous impulse, i.e., action potential, induces migration of vesicles towards the membrane and release of acetylcholine into the synaptic cleft. The stimulation of presynaptic muscarinic receptors inhibits acetylcholine release and, conversely, their inhibition increases it. Botulinum toxin is an inhibitor of the acetylcholine release.

**Binding to the receptor:** Acetylcholine released from the synaptic vesicles diffuses across the synaptic space, and it binds to either of two postsynaptic receptors on the target cell or to presynaptic receptors in the membrane of the neuron that released the acetylcholine. The postsynaptic cholinergic receptors on the surface of the effector organs are divided into two classes muscarinic and nicotinic. Binding to a receptor leads to a biologic response within the cell, such as the initiation of a nerve impulse in a postganglionic fiber or activation of specific enzymes in effector cells as mediated by second-messenger molecules.

**Degradation of acetylcholine:** Tissues which contain acetylcholine and enzymes involved in its synthesis, contain also cholinesterases which hydrolyze acetylcholine, which explains the fugacious activity of acetylcholine. Two types of cholinesterases have been distinguished according to their affinities for different substrates, endogenous such as acetylcholine, and exogenous such as acetyl-β-méthylcholine, butyrylcholine and benzoylcholine. Acetylcholinestrase, present in nervous tissue and erythrocytes, very quickly hydrolyzes acetylcholine and acetyl-β-méthylcholine, but does not hydrolyze butyrylcholine. It is called true cholinesterase. Butyrylcholinesterase, present in tissues such as heart and plasma, hydrolyzes acetylcholine, benzoylcholine, butyrylcholine but not acetyl-β-méthylcholine. It is called pseudo-cholinesterase. Choline resulting from the hydrolysis of acetylcholine is reuptaken by the cholinergic terminations by an active mechanism, $Na^+$ and $Cl^-$ dependent channel, inhibited by hemicholinium. An enzymatic deficiency or an enzyme inhibition is detected by determination of activity of pseudo-cholinesterase in serum and of cholinesterase in red blood cells.

**Recycling of choline:** Choline may be recaptured by a sodium-coupled, high-affinity uptake system that transports the molecule back into the neuron, where it is acetylated into acetylcholine that is stored until released by a subsequent action potential.

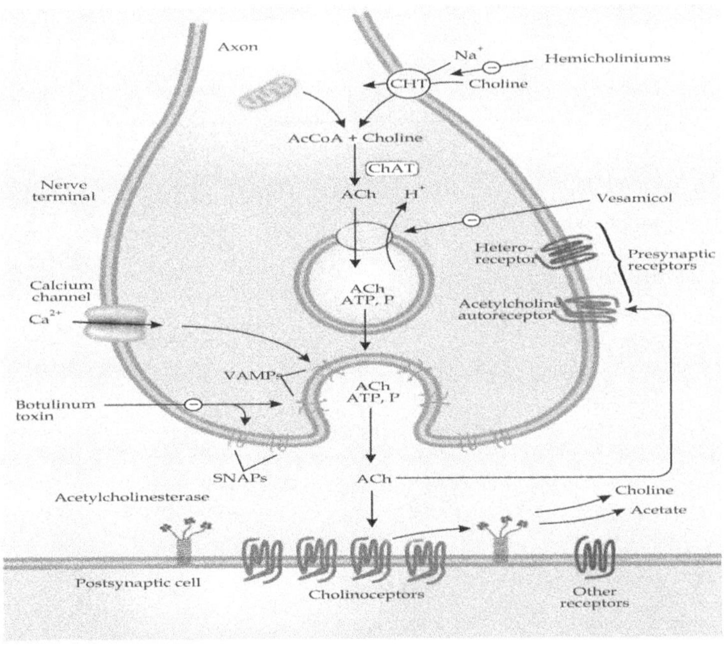


**Fig 11-1:** Synthesis and release of acetylcholine from the cholinergic neuron. AcCoA = acetyl coenzyme A

# Cholinergic Receptors (Cholinoceptors)

Two families of cholinoceptors, designated muscarinic and nicotinic receptors, can be distinguished from each other on the basis of their different affinities for agents that mimic the action of acetylcholine (cholinomimetic agents or parasympathomimetics).

Muscarinic receptors (M) G-Protein coupled receptors.

Nicotinic receptors (N) Ligand gated ion channel

## Muscarinic Receptors (M)

They are activated by Ach, muscarine and other agonists.

Antagonist: Atropine

**Locations:** Plasma membranes of the cells of tissues innervated by parasympathetic nerves in heart, smooth muscles, exocrine glands and uninnervated endothelial receptors.

CNS; brain is richer in M receptors and spinal cord in N receptors

5 types : $M_1$, $M_2$, $M_3$, $M_4$, $M_5$

G-Protein coupled receptors contain 7 transmembrane domains, whose third loop is coupled to G-Protein that acts as a transducer.

## Molecular Mechanism at Muscarinic Receptors

**At $M_1$, $M_3$ and $M_5$:** Binding of ACh to receptor site. Conformational change occurs. Interaction with G protein– Gq. Coupling of Gq *via* α subunit to phospholipase C (effector enzyme). Hydrolysis of Phosphatidyl inositol(4, 5) biphosphate-($PIP_2$). Formation of second messengers– increase in $IP_3$, DAG– Increased cytosolic $Ca^{2+}$. Increased cytosolic $Ca^{2+}$, stimulates or inhibits enzymes – response.

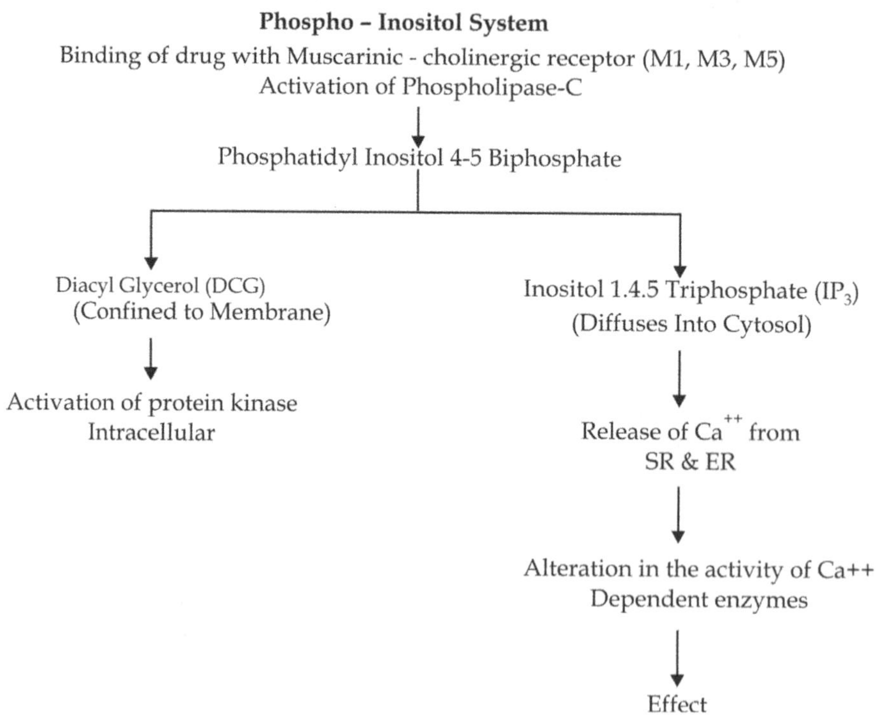


**Fig 11-2:** Phospho – inositol system

**$M_2$ Receptors:** Coupling of $G_{i/o}$ *via* β γ subunit with adenylyl cyclase and decrease cAMP in the heart. Coupling of Gi via βγsubunit and opening of $K^+$ channels in the heart.

**$M_4$ Receptors (like $M_2$):** Moreover, muscarinic agonist attenuates activation of adenylyl cyclase and modulate the increase in cAMP by catecholamines.

## Nicotinic Receptors

**Agonists:** Acetylcholine, Nicotine and other nicotinic agonists

**Locations**

$N_N$: Autonomic ganglia, adrenal medulla, brain and spinal cord.

*Antagonist:* Ganglion blockers-Trimethaphan

$N_M$: Skeletal muscles motor end plate-Neuromuscular Junction.

*Antagonist:* Neuromuscular junction blockers – d-tubocurarine

*Nicotinic receptor:* It is a ligand-gated ion channel

It is composed of 5 sub units – 2 α, β, δ, γ

They enclose a central ion channel. The receptor sites at 2 α subunits. When Ach binds to the receptor sites, there is conformational change and opening of the channel. Influx of sodium ions leads to depolarization and action potential is generated.

## Molecular Mechanisms / Signal Transduction at Nicotinic Receptors

**Nicotinic receptors**

**Subtypes:**

$N_M$: Composed of 2 α, β, δ, γ

***Location:*** Skeletal muscles: Neuromuscular junction

***Binding of agonist:*** Ach, Nicotine at binding sites on 2 α subunits.

***Molecular mechanism:*** Opening of sodium channel, there is conformational change - opening of the channel.

***Responses:*** End-plate depolarization, skeletal muscle contraction.

*Neuronal (Peripheral& central)* $N_N$

Ion channel, pentamer, composed of 2 α, 3β subunits

Binding of Ach, Nicotine at binding sites on 2α subunits.

*Molecular mechanisms:* Opening of sodium channel.

*Responses:*

- In automomic ganglia, adrenal medulla, depolarization and firing of post ganglionic neuron; depolarization of the medullary cell and secretion of catecholamines
- *In CNS:* Prejunctional control of neurotransmitter release

## Parasympathomimetic Drugs or Cholinergic Drugs or Cholinomimetic Drugs

Parasympathomimetic/cholinergic drugs can be defined as a group of drugs whose effects resemble those of stimulating the parasympathetic nerves/acetylcholine. They include direct acting cholinergic receptor agonists and indirect acting drugs which are anticholinesterases. Anticholinesterases inhibit the enzyme that terminates the action of endogenously released Ach so concentration of Ach in the synapse is increased so the response is enhanced.

**Classification of Cholinomimetic/Cholinergic/ Parasympathomimetic drugs**

- Direct Acting
- Indirect Acting

**Direct Acting Cholinergic Drugs**

**(a)** ***Choline esters***

Acetylcholine
Carbachol
Methacholine
Bethanechol

**Table 11-1:** Subtypes/locations and characteristics of cholinoceptors

| Receptor | Location | Mechanism | Result of ACh. binding |
|---|---|---|---|
| $M_1$ | CNS Neurons, some presynaptic sites, sympathetic postgang-lionic neurons | Gq-coupled via α subunit | Stimulation of phospholipase C increase $IP_3$, DAG, increase intracellular $Ca^{++}$ |
| $M_2$ | Myocardium, smooth muscles, some presynaptic sites, CNS Neurons | Gi-coupled via βγ subunit | Inhibition of Adenylyl cyclase decrease cAMP, activates $K^+$ channel |
| $M_3$ | Smooth muscle, exocrine glands, endothelium, CNS Neurons | Gq-coupled | Like $M_1$ |
| $M_4$ | CNS Neurons; possibly vagal nerve endings | Gi-coupled | Like $M_2$ |
| $M_5$ | Vascular endothelium of cerebral BV, CNS Neurons | Gq-coupled | Like $M_1$ |
| $N_N$ | Post ganglionic neurons of ANS ganglia, Adrenal medulla, CNS mainly spinal cord. Some presynptic cholinergic terminals | Ion channel | Opening of channel, $Na^+$. Influx, depolarization-- AP generation |
| $N_M$ | Skeletal muscle neuromuscular end plate | Ion channel | Opening of channels, $Na^+$. Influx, depolarization--AP generation |

(b)*Cholinomimetic Alkaloids*

1. Mainly muscarinic Agonists

   ***Natural alkaloids:*** Muscarine, Pilocarpine, Arecholine

   ***Synthetic alkaloid:*** Cevimeline, Oxotramorine

2. Mainly nicotinic agonists

   ***Natural alkaloids:*** Nicotine, Lobeline

   *Synthetic:* Varenicline, Dimethylphenyl piperazinium (DMPP)

**Indirect Acting Cholinergic Drugs or Anticholinesterases**

***Reversible***

Carbamates

*Tertiary amines:* Physostigmine

*Quaternary ammonium compounds:* Neostigmine, Pyridostigmine, Distigmine, Ambenonium, Demecarium

*Alcohols:* Edrophonium

*Miscellaneous:* Donepezil, Galantamine, Rivastigmine , Tacrine

***Irreversible anticholinesterases/ (Organophosphorous compounds)***

*Therapeutically useful:* Ecothiophate

*War gases:* Sarin, Tuban, Soman

*Insecticides:* Parathion , Malathion

Di-isopropyl Fluorophosphate (DFP)

## Acetylcholine Effects

Acetylcholine has muscarinic and nicotinic effects by stimulation of the corresponding receptors. Fig 6-3.

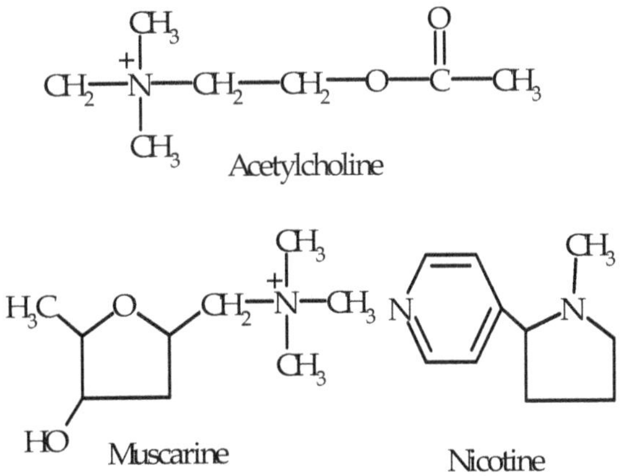


**Fig 11-3:** Structures of ach, muscarine and nicotine

## Muscarinic Effects

Muscarinic effects thus called because they resemble those of muscarine, compound extracted from a mushroom, and result from stimulation of muscarinic receptors.

There are several types of muscarinic receptors $M_1$, $M_2$, $M_3$, $M_4$ and $M_5$, coupled to G proteins. Schematically, $M_1$ and $M_3$ receptors are coupled to phospholipase C which induces a rise of inositol-triphosphate, $IP_3$, diacylglycerol, DAG, and of $Ca^{2+}$; $M_2$ receptors are coupled to $K^+$ channels and to adenylcyclase whose activity they reduce.

Endogenous acetylcholine has peripheral muscarinic effects, the best known, and central ones. Muscarinic effects are inhibited by atropine.

## Cardiac Effects

The cholinergic innervation of auricles is much more important than that of the myocardium. An injection of acetylcholine or the stimulation of the parasympathetic induces. Bradycardia, even transitory discontinuation of heart beats (vagal escape) by sinus effect. Decrease of atrioventricular conduction. Decrease of the strength of atrium contractions. Cardiac slowing is explained at least partly by cellular hyperpolarisation resulting from opening of potassium channels linked to the G proteins and potassium exit out of the cell, inducing an increase in polarization. The decrease of the force of contraction comes from a decrease of $Ca^{2+}$ entry in the cell, probably by inhibition of adenylcyclase. Intravenous injection of very low doses of acetylcholine in animals or in human beings causes immediate and fugacious fall of the arterial pressure resulting from cardiac slowing and vasodilation.

## Vascular Effects

Vessels have muscarinic receptors but do not receive cholinergic innervation. Acetylcholine injection induces an arteriolar vasodilation by release by the endothelium of a vasodilator compound, called initially EDRF (endothelium derived relaxing factor) then identified as nitric oxide, (NO). The paradoxical vasoconstriction induced by acetylcholine on coronary vessels presenting atherosclerotic lesions is explained by absence of *Endothelium-derived relaxing factor* (EDRF) release by damaged or absent endothelial cells and direct stimulation of the smooth muscles.

## Effects on Smooth Muscles (Except Vascular)

By stimulation of phospholipase C, acetylcholine elicits:

**Intestine:** An increase in tone with sometimes an increase in the peristaltic contractions. Nausea and vomiting testify to this stimulative action.

**Ureter:** Increase in tone.

**Bronchi:** bronchoconstriction. An aerosol of acetylcholine can cause an attack of asthma.

## Effects on Secretions (Receptors $M_3$)

Acetylcholine increases, by activation of phospholipase C, digestive (abundant saliva), bronchial, cutaneous (sweat) and lacrimal secretions.

## Effects on the Eye (Receptors $M_3$)

Acetylcholine induces a decrease of iris diameter or miosis, which facilitates the flow of aqueous humour and tends to lower the intra-ocular pressure. Miosis (decreases size of pupil) due to contraction of sphincter muscle of iris. Cyclospasm/accommodation for near vision due to contraction of ciliary muscle. Decrease in intraocular pressure. Increase lacrimation due to stimulation of lacrimal glands. Conjunctival congestion due to dilation of BV.

**Spasm of Accommodation:** Stimulation of $M_3$ receptors in ciliary muscle. Contraction of muscle pulls ciliary body forwards and inwards. Relaxation of suspensory ligament of the lens. The lens bulges more, and its focal length is decreased. Eye accommodated for near vision. Decrease in intraocular pressure. Contraction of sphincter pupillae pulls the iris away from the angle of anterior chamber. Contraction of ciliary muscle pulls the scleral spur, opens up the trabecular mesh work at the base of the muscle. Both these effects facilitate the out flow of aqueous humor into the canal of schlemm, which drains the anterior chamber. So there is decrease in the IOP in glaucoma.

## Central Effects

Muscarinic effects in the central nervous system are complex and not well characterized. According to conditions, the stimulation of the post-synaptic muscarinic receptors elicits a depolarization or an hyperpolarisation. In animals, their stimulation induces facilitation of training but also hypothermia, tremors, seizures.

## Nicotinic Effects

The nicotinic effects of acetylcholine resemble those of nicotine and result from activation of acetylcholine nicotinic receptors, receptor-channels, which, in an activated state, let sodium and calcium enter into cells, thus creating a depolarization. Nicotinic receptor-channels are members of the ligand-gated ion-channel family, also called ionotropic receptors. Nicotinic receptors have a pentameric structure forming a central channel which can be open or closed and are activated by acetylcholine. Two molecules of acetylcholine are needed for activation of one receptor and opening the channel. They have a fast response.

However, nicotinic receptors are not strictly identical in ganglia of the autonomic nervous system, in the neuromuscular junction and in brain. One distinguishes those which are inhibited by bungarotoxin A, polypeptide extracted from a snake venom and those which are not. But their way of operating is similar, leading to a depolarization mainly by sodium entry in the cell.

Acetylcholine, by its nicotinic effects, is responsible for synaptic transmission. The principal steps of synaptic transmission are represented as follows Fig 11-4.

## Autonomic Ganglia Effects

Acetylcholine is responsible of transmission in the autonomic nervous system. The presynaptic nerve releases acetylcholine which, by activating nicotinic receptors, induces a depolarization at the origin of a new impulse in the postsynaptic nerve. This ganglionic stimulation elicits in its turn a release of acetylcholine by the parasympathetic terminations and noradrenaline by the adrenergic terminations.

## Neuromuscular Junction Effects

The stimulation of nicotinic receptors by acetylcholine is responsible of neuromuscular transmission. In the vicinity of the muscle, the motor nerve covered with its myelin sheath is divided into a bouquet of final branches deprived of myelin. These final branches are very rich in mitochondria and small synaptic vesicles (300 to 500 Å) containing acetylcholine. The stimulation of the motor nerve induces acetylcholine release in the synaptic cleft of the neuromuscular junction. On the other hand

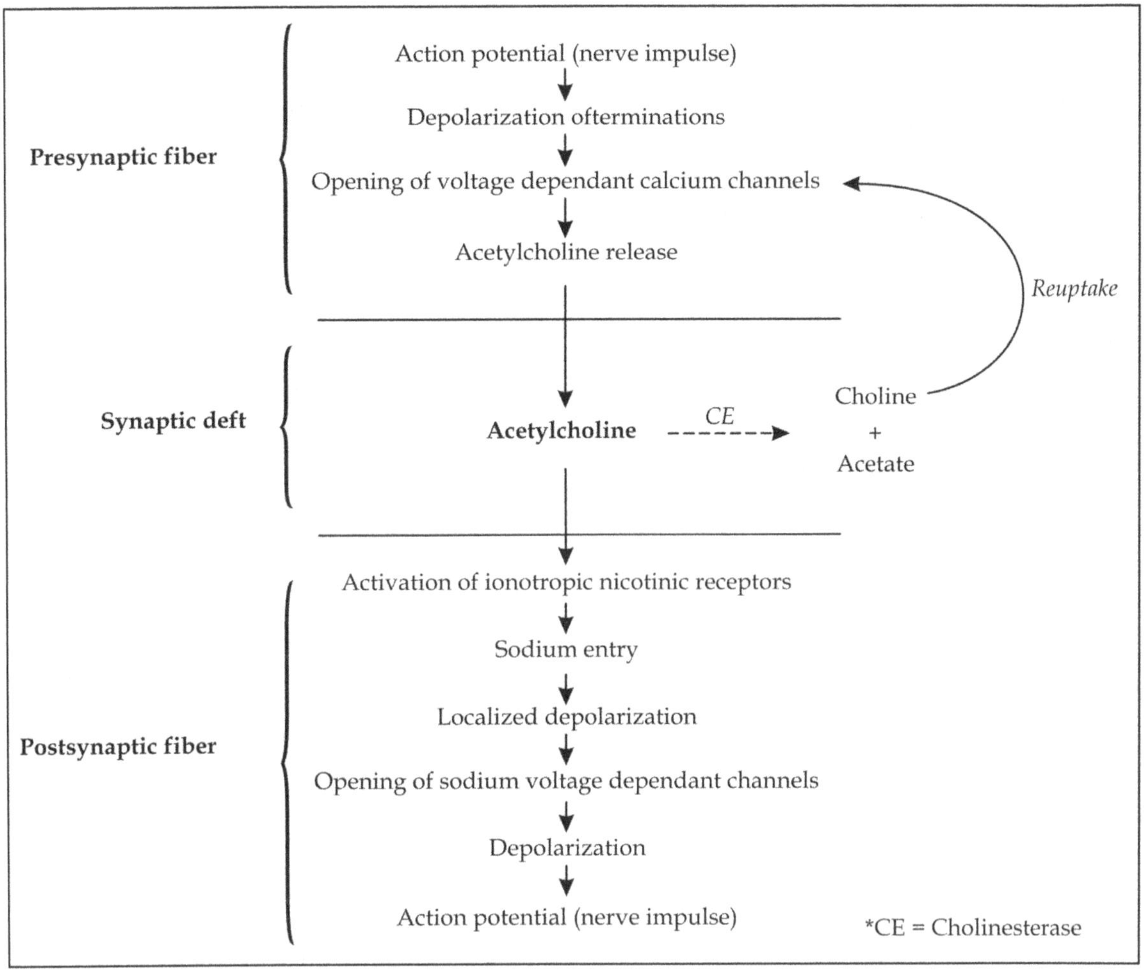


**Fig 11-4:** Cholinergic synaptic transmission by activation of nicotinic receptors

direct stimulation of the muscle, even if it causes contractions, does not induce acetylcholine release.

**Acetylcholine acts selectively on the neuromuscular junction:** Applied to the junction, in low quantity acetylcholine elicits a muscular contraction, in large quantity acetylcholine can inhibit the muscular contractions resulting from the stimulation of the nerve. Applied to the nerve or the muscle apart from the junction, it does not cause any effect. The nerve action potential elicits a localized postjunctional depolarization called end-plate potential. When this depolarization reaches a sufficient threshold, it appears, by opening of the voltage-dependant cation channels, a postsynaptic potential appears which propagates in muscular fibers. The ions $Ca^{2+}$ and $Mg^{2+}$ are involved in this transmission, $Ca^{2+}$ facilitates this transmission whereas $Mg^{2+}$ has an inhibiting effect. Myasthenia (Myasthenia gravis) results in a muscular weakness. It is generally an acquired disease, of immunological origin, due to damage of neuromuscular nicotinic receptors by antibodies. There are also forms of genetic origin, resulting from a defect of acetylcholine synthesis or release or from damage to neuromuscular receptors.

## Central Nervous System Effects

Stimulation of nicotinic receptors of the central nervous system induces, by opening of cation channels, a depolarization whose consequences are difficult to systematize. The respective roles of muscarinic and nicotinic receptors in the central effects of acetylcholine are difficult to distinguish. There is a brain cholinergic deficiency in Alzheimer disease and directly and indirectly acting cholinomimetic agents are used for its treatment.

# Parasympathomimetic Drugs

## Directly acting Cholonergic Drugs

### Choline esters

*Methacholine:* Methacholine acts as a non-selective muscarinic receptor agonist to

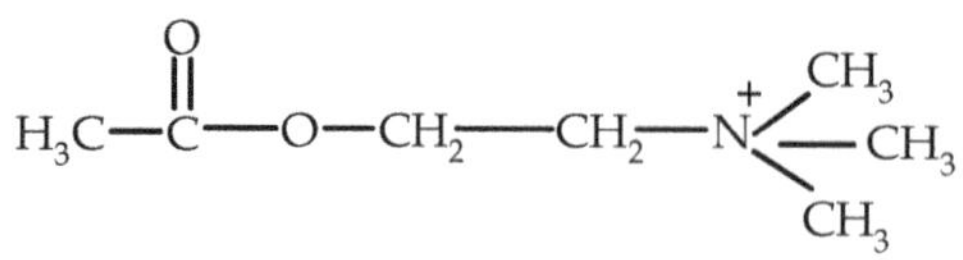

Acetylcholine

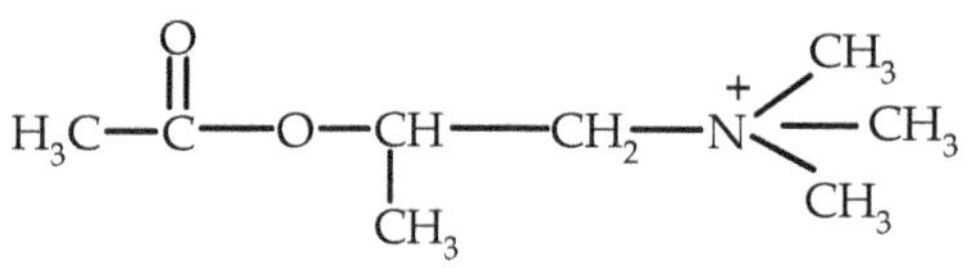

Methacholine
(acetyl-β-methylcholine)

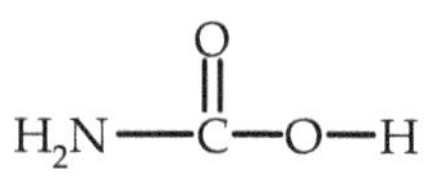

Carbamic acid

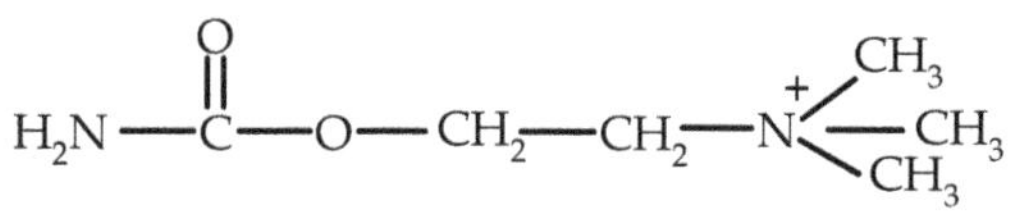

Carbachol
(carbamoylcholine)

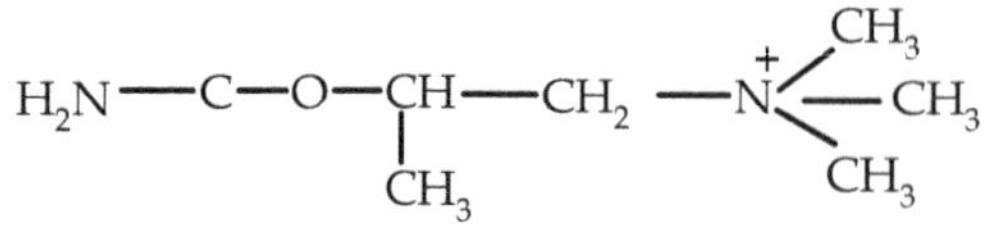

Bethanechol
(carbamoyl-β-methylcholine

**Fig 11-5:** Choline esters

stimulate the parasympathetic nervous system. It is most commonly used for diagnosing bronchial hyperreactivity, using the bronchial challenge test. Through this test, the drug causes bronchoconstriction and people with pre-existing airway hyperreactivity, such as asthmatics, will react to lower doses of drug. Acetate is replaced by carbamate and choline is methylated. It is Acetyl, β Methyl choline. Negligible metabolism by cholinesterase. Duration of action longer than Ach. No nicotinic effects. Muscarinic effects are more prominent on CVS. Methacholine acts as a non-selective muscarinic receptor agonist to stimulate the parasympathetic nervous system. It is highly active at all of the muscarinic receptors. By agonizing the muscarinic receptors, this drug induces bronchoconstriction.

Beta-Blockers like betaxolol may worsen bronchoconstriction and decrease the effectiveness of agents used to treat the resulting bronchoconstriction. Use of betaxolol and methacholine concomitantly is contraindicated.

***Carbachol:*** It is carbamoylcholine carbamic acid ester of choline. Poor substrate for AChE. Slowly metabolized by other esterases. Duration of action longer than Ach. Have both muscarinic and nicotinic effects. Muscarinic effects are more prominent on smooth muscles of GIT, UB and eye. A slowly hydrolyzed cholinergic agonist that acts at both muscarinic and nicotinic receptors. Carbachol is a potent cholinergic (parasympathomimetic) agent which produces constriction of the iris and ciliary body resulting in reduction in intraocular pressure. The exact mechanism by which carbachol lowers intraocular pressure is not precisely known. In the cat and rat, carbachol is well-known for its ability to induce rapid eye movement (REM) sleep when microinjected into the pontine reticular formation. Carbachol elicits this REM sleep-like state *via* activation of postsynaptic muscarinic cholinergic receptors (mAChRs). Carbachol is a parasympathomimetic that stimulates both muscarinic and nicotinic receptors. In topical ocular and intraocular administration its principal effects are miosis and increased aqueous humour outflow.

***Therapeutic uses:*** Rarely used due to high potency, receptor non- selectivity.

Primarily used in the treatment of Glaucoma used as eye drops, but is also used during ophthalmic surgery.

**Bethanechol:** A choline ester poor lipid solubility. Does not enter CNS , not active in eye after topical application. It is Carbamoyl α Methyl choline carbamic acid ester of choline. Bethanechol is a synthetic ester structurally and pharmacologically related to acetylcholine. A slowly hydrolyzed muscarinic agonist with no nicotinic effects, bethanechol is generally used to increase smooth muscle tone, as in the GI tract following abdominal surgery or in urinary retention in the absence of obstruction. Bethanechol is a parasympathomimetic (cholinergic) used for the treatment of acute postoperative and postpartum nonobstructive (functional) urinary retention and for neurogenic atony of the urinary bladder with retention. Bethanechol, a cholinergic agent, is a synthetic ester which is structurally and pharmacologically related to acetylcholine. It increases the tone of the detrusor muscle, usually producing a contraction sufficiently strong to initiate micturition and empty the bladder. It stimulates gastric motility, increases gastric tone, and often restores impaired rhythmic peristalsis. Bethanechol chloride is not destroyed by cholinesterase and its effects are more prolonged than those of acetylcholine. Bethanechol directly stimulates cholinergic receptors in the parasympathetic nervous system while stimulating the ganglia to a lesser extent. Its effects are predominantly muscarinic, inducing little effect on nicotinic receptors and negligible effects on the cardiovascular system. Negligible metabolism by cholinesterase. Duration of action longer than Ach i.e., 0.3-2 hr. No nicotinic effects. Muscarinic effects are more prominent on smooth muscles of GIT, UB and eye. It may cause hypotension, cardiac rate changes, and bronchial spasms.

***Therapeutic uses of Bethanechol*:** Depression of SM activity without obstruction.

Post operative Ileus-Abdominal distention.

Congenital megacolon

Urinary retention

Post operative, post partum, after SC injury (Neurogenic bladder)

Reflux esophagitis

*Dose:* Bethanechol 10-20 mg TDS

## Cholinomimetic Alkaloids

### Mainly Muscarinic Agonists

***Natural alkaloids***

- *Muscarine and Arecholine:* Used as a research tool, muscarine poisoning may occur due to certain mushroom (Inocybe)
- *Pilocarpine:* Used in glaucoma & as Sialagouge
- *Sialagouge:* A drug which increases salivary secretion.

**Table 11-2:** Properties of choline esters

| Choline Ester | Susceptibility to cholinesterase | Muscarinic action | Nicotinic action |
|---|---|---|---|
| Acetylcholine chloride | ++++ | +++ | +++ |
| Methacholine chloride | + | ++++ | None |
| Carbachol chloride | Negligible | ++ | +++ |
| Bethanechol chloride | Negligible | ++ | None |

*Synthetic alkaloids*

- *Cevimeline:* Derivative of Ach. Used as Sialagouge
- *Oxotramorine:* Used as a research tool, mostly affects $M_5$ receptors in CNS.

**Mainly Nicotinic Agonists**

*Natural alkaloids:* Nicotine , Lobeline

*Synthetic:* Varenicline– used in the smoking deaddiction.

Dimethylphenylpiperazinium (DMPP)

Varenicline–Partial agonist at N receptors. Orally effective. High lipid solubility.

Duration of action is 12 hr. Used to stop smoking.

**Pilocarpine:** A natural alkaloid tertiary amine. Obtained from *Pilocarpus jaborandi* leaves.

Well absorbed from most sites of administration. Topically in eye, orally and I.M. Stable to hydrolysis by AchE.

**Mechanism of action:** It is a direct agonist at cholinergic receptors mainly muscarinic receptors.

**Effects:** like Ach, Nicotinic effects are mild.

The most important effect is on eye and exocrine glands.

*Eye*: Activates $M_3$ receptors. Miosis/decrease size of pupil- contraction of sphincter muscle of iris. Cyclospasm/accommodation for near vision due to contraction of ciliary muscle. Conjunctival hyperemia is due to dilatation of blood vessels via EDRF. Increase lacrimation due to stimulation of lacrimal glands. Decrease in intraocular pressure. Spasm Of accommodation lasts for 2 hours. Stimulation of $M_3$ receptors in ciliary muscle. Contraction of muscle pulls ciliary body forwards and inwards. Relaxation of suspensory ligament of the lens.

The lens bulges more and its focal length is decreased. Eye accommodated for near vision. *I.O.P:* Decreased in glaucoma, in normal individual, little effect.

Contraction of sphincter pupillae pulls iris away from angle of anterior chamber. Contraction of ciliary muscle pulls the scleral spur, opens up the trabecular mesh work at the base of the muscle. Also restores alignment if distorted.

Both these effects facilitate the out flow of aqueous humor in to the canal of schlemm, decreasing IOP.

*Effects of pilocarpine on CVS*: Given IV, a brief initial hypotension , then may produce longer-lasting hypertension. Hypertension is due to vasoconstriction *via* Ganglionic effect.

*Effects on exocrine glands*: Marked increase in salivary and other exocrine secretions.

**Therapeutic uses**

*Route of administration*: Pilocarpine is used Topically in eye, orally or S.C.

Never given through IV because pulmonary edema can occur. Used in glaucoma (raised IOP) as eye drops 0.5-4% or plastic film reservoir of drug. Better tolerated than anti-cholinesterases. Duration of action 4-6 hours. Open angle glaucoma, standard treatment lifelong. Secondary glaucoma- some cases for life long. Angle-closure glaucoma prior to surgery. To counteract the mydriasis produced by atropine. To break up adhesions between iris and lens, alternatively with atropine .

*Xerostomia*: 5-10 mg orally or S.C as sialagogue to increase salivary secretion in xerostomia due to Sjogren's syndrome. Head and neck radiation therapy and parkinsonism.

**Aceclidine**

Aceclidine is a cholinomimetic obtained by chemical synthesis, used in the form of ophthalmic solution in the treatment of glaucoma.

**Cevimeline**

Cevimeline is a cholinergic agonist with muscarinic effect. It is used for the treatment of symptoms of dry mouth with Sjögren's syndrome. Indirectly acting cholinomimetic agents do not themselves activate acetylcholine receptors. They exert their effects by increasing the concentration of endogenous acetylcholine in contact of the cholinergic receptors. Acetylcholine stimulates the receptors and is responsible for the elicited effects.

**This rise in the acetylcholine level can result either from an increase in its synthesis and of its release, or of an inhibition of its destruction.**

### Increase of Synthesis

The diet of an adult supplies approximately 0.5 to 1 gm of choline per day in free and esterified form. Attempts to increase acetylcholine synthesis by choline administration, in Alzheimer's disease for example, did not give convincing results. Choline acts as a methyl donor and its absence in diet induces hepatic steatosis. Choline is present in many multi-ingredient proprietary medical preparations. Other compounds, involved directly or indirectly in acetylcholine synthesis are: betaine, phosphorylcholine, phosphatidylcholine and cytidine diphosphocholine, called citicoline or CDP-choline. The latter has been proposed in the treatment of strokes and cranial traumatisms.

### Indirectly Acting Cholinomimetic Agents - Increase of Release

The principal drug which acts by releasing acetylcholine is cisapride.

Cisapride induces acetylcholine release by cholinergic fibers of the digestive tract, which increases motricity of the esophagus, stomach, duodenum, small intestine and colon. It increases, moreover, the pressure of the lower sphincter of the esophagus, thus opposing gastroesophageal reflux. Contrary to metoclopramide, cisapride does not have an antidopamine effect but it has an agonist effect on serotonin $5HT_4$ receptors, which reinforces its prokinetic effect.

The essential therapeutic indication of cisapride is gastroesophageal reflux. It is, of course, contraindicated if there is an organic obstacle to the progression of the bolus. It can give intestinal pains, diarrhea, and modify the kinetics of absorption of other drugs. Atropine prevents the effects of cisapride by inhibiting muscarinic receptors. Cisapride does not have central action because, in usual conditions, it does not cross the blood-brain barrier. Catabolism of cisapride by the P-450 cytochrome can be inhibited by the concomitant intake of other drugs such as ketoconazole, miconazole, itraconazole and macrolides. This type of interaction, induces an increase of cisapride concentration, which can lead to the lengthening of QT electrocardiogram space by slowing repolarization and risk of torsades de pointes, in particular in case of hypokalemia and hypomagnesemia. This risk of cardiac conduction disorders, sometimes fatal, led to the discontinuation of cisapride marketing in many countries and to restrictions of its prescription in other countries where reinforced warnings were introduced into the SPC of cisapride; they mention in particular the risk of interactions with many other drugs.

***Inhibition of Destruction***: Anticholinesterase agents (Fig 11-6).

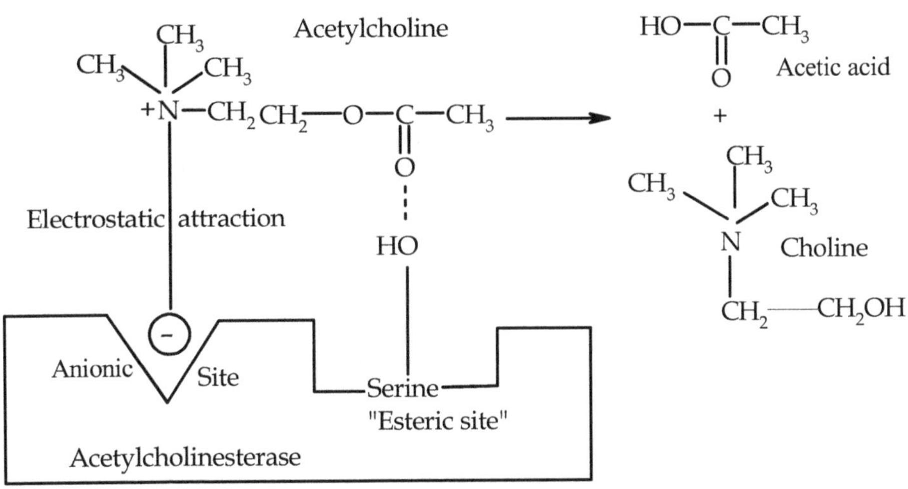


**Fig 11-6:** Acetylcholinestrase

## Acetylcholinestrase

This enzyme has two reactive sites which are used for hydrolysis of compounds like Ach. These sites are **anionic** and **esteratic** sites. Anionic site attaches to N portion of Ach and esteratic site attaches to carbon of Ach. So, complex is formed. After this, addition of water occurs and acetylated enzyme and choline detaches. In the last step, choline detaches from esteratic site.

Since acetylcholine is inactivated by cholinesterases, inhibition of cholinesterases leads to a rise in acetylcholine concentration. If this rise remains moderate, it can have beneficial effects but if is too high it causes toxic effects.

Cholinesterase inhibitors, also called anticholinesterase agents, are schematically classified, according to their intensity and duration of action and consequently of their toxicity, into reversible and irreversible inhibitors. In human beings, inhibition of cholinesterases induces, by accumulation of acetylcholine, muscarinic and nicotinic effects. These effects are predominately central or peripheral according to whether the inhibitor penetrates or not into the brain. Inhibition of cholinesterases of insects is a way to obtain their destruction.

## Reversible Inhibitors

The reversible inhibitors, Fig. 11-7 which inhibit enzyme in a transitory way, as long as their

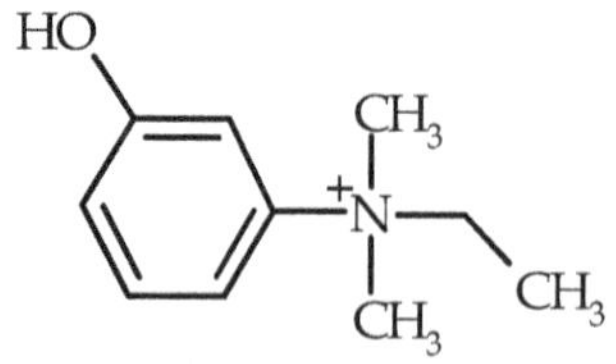

Edrophonium

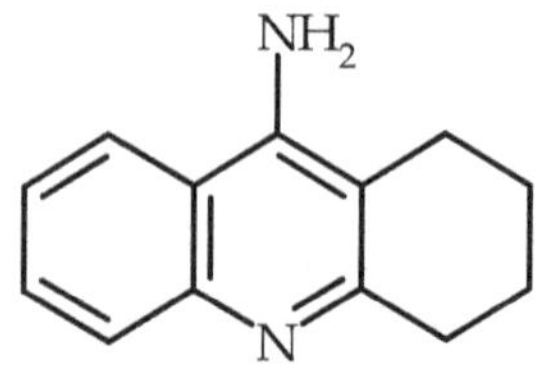

Tacrine (Cognex)

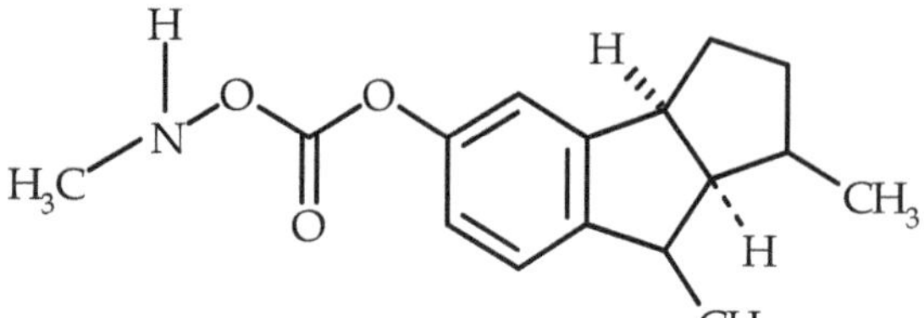

Physostigmine

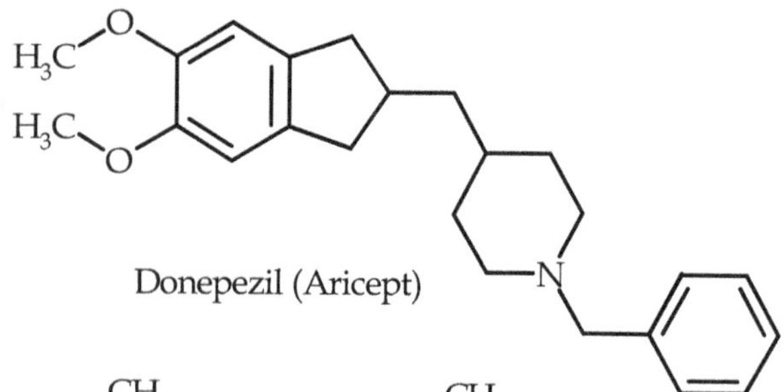

Donepezil (Aricept)

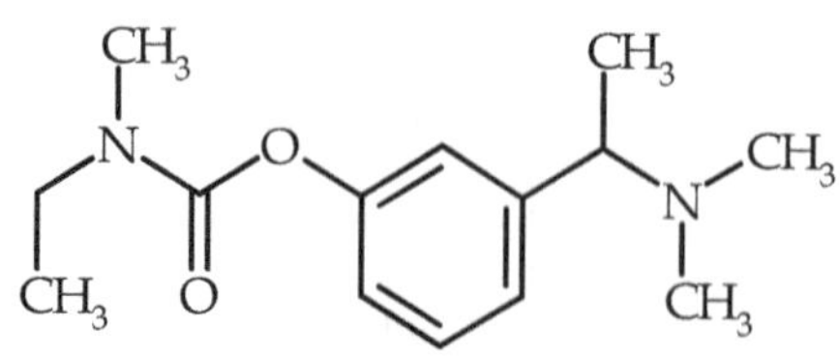

Rivastigmine (Exelon)

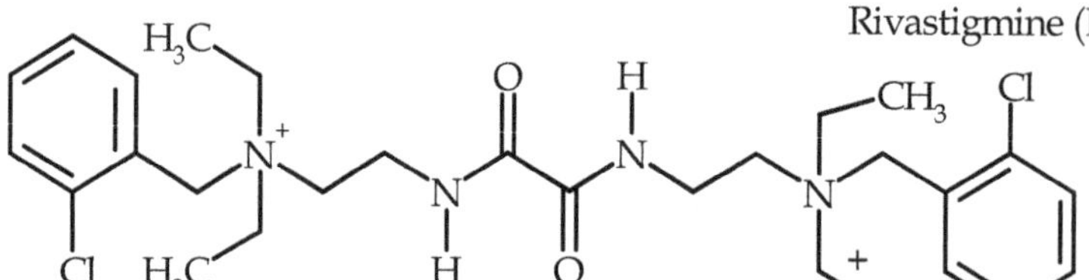

Ambenonium

**Fig 11-7:** Reversible anticholinesterase inhibitors

concentration is sufficient, are used in therapeutics and, for the majority of them, are known for a long time. Reversible cholinesterase inhibitors, as the name implies, form transient complexes with the cholinesterases. In essence, they compete for acetylcholine at the enzyme active site. For one group - quaternary alcohols - they act as simple competitive inhibitors, binding and blocking access to the active site. In the second group - carbamates- the compounds are actually slowly hydrolyzed substrates, which both block access and tie up the active site serine.

Edrophonium forms ionic bond with acetylcholinesterase for this reason it is used in the diagnosis of myasthenia gravis.

**Physostigmine or Eserine**

Physostigmine, also called Eserine, alkaloid obtained from calabar bean, gives primarily muscarinic effects and crosses the blood-brain barrier. The tertiary amine used in the treatment of wide-angle glaucoma, often together with Pilocarpine; acts to facilitate efflux of aqueous humour *via* canal of schlemm. It increases the gastric and intestinal peristalsis and induces bronchoconstriction and contraction of ureter. It increases bronchial and digestive secretions (gastric, intestinal, salivary), as well as lacrimal secretion. Its cardiovascular action is complex but, in general, it has a muscarinic action bradycardia and decrease of the force of cardiac contractions. Eserine elicits miosis, spasm of accommodation, fall of intraocular pressure, hyperemia of conjunctiva and lacrymation. Generally, it stimulates neuromuscular transmission, what results in muscle fasciculations. In addition to its indirect action by inhibition of cholinesterases, it could directly stimulate neuromuscular nicotinic receptors. It does not have an action on the uterus. Eserine is indicated in treatment of paralytic ileus, intestinal atonicity, glaucoma, myasthenia, post-anesthetic long-lasting curarization. It was tested in the treatment of Alzheimer's disease using transdermal preparations which make possible to obtain relatively stable plasma concentrations. The multiplicity of effects of Eserine is often a disadvantage in therapeutics where only an effect is generally sought.

***Adverse effect*:** Can facilitate formation of cataracts.

**Neostigmine**

Quaternary amine having a short duration of action (0.5-2 hr). Neostigmine, better tolerated than Eserine, acts less on eye, cardiovascular system and central nervous system, but it is more active on digestive tract and bladder. Neostigmine is used in the treatment of the postoperative atonicity (intestine, bladder), and of myasthenia in high dose combined or not with atropine. It accelerates decurarization as an indirect antidote of competitive neuromuscular inhibitors. The drug of choice for use in paralytic loss of tone in the GI tract and bladder. Standard drug for use in myasthenia gravis (though oral absorption is poor).

**Pyridostigmine**

Pyridostigmine has pharmacological properties close to those of neostigmine, with perhaps a more progressive and more durable action. It is used in the treatment of intestinal atonicity and myasthenia.

**Ambenonium**

Ambenonium is a long-acting inhibitor of cholinesterase, about five to six hours after oral intake, used in the treatment of myasthenia gravis.

**Tacrine**

Tacrine or 9 amino-1,2,3,4-tétrahydroacridine is an anticholinesterase agent which penetrates into the brain and has been used in the treatment of Alzheimer's disease. It was successively proposed as a disinfectant, as antagonist of morphine respiratory depression and finally used in the treatment of Alzheimer's disease for which it attenuates certain symptoms.

Tacrine has various adverse effects of muscarinic type but its major disadvantage is its hepatic toxicity which usually results in a rise of transaminases. A metabolite of Tacrine could be responsible for this hepatic toxicity.

### Donepezil

Donepezil is a selective and reversible inhibitor of acetylcholinesterase, having little effect on Butyryl-cholinesterase and penetrating well into brain. Its half-life of plasma elimination is about 70 hours and just a once-daily intake is enough. Donepezil is indicated in the supportive care of Alzheimer's disease.

The most frequent adverse effects of the Donepezil are digestive disorders (diarrhea, nausea, vomiting, abdominal pains). It can also induce dizziness and bradycardia but without hepatic toxicity, the major undesirable effect of Tacrine.

### Rivastigmine

Rivastigmine is a new anticholinesterase, quite well absorbed by oral route and crossing well the blood-brain barrier. It is used twice daily in the supportive care of Alzheimer's disease. It does not present hepatic toxicity.

### Galantamine

Galantamine, also written galanthamine, is a product known for about fifty years. Recent studies showed that it could have an interest in the treatment of Alzheimer's disease. It is metabolized by cytochromes CYP2D6 and CYP3A4 and interactions with drugs inhibiting these cytochromes were described.

Huperzine is an alkaloid of vegetable origin, known for many years, which inhibits cholinesterases reversibly and penetrates into the brain. It was proposed as a dietary supplement of vegetable origin intended to reduce memory disorders.

## Mechanisms of Action of Indirect (Reversible) Cholinergic Agonists

## Irreversible Inhibitors Fig 11-8

Irreversible inhibitors (Fig 11-8) of cholinesterases, while being fixed at enzymes by

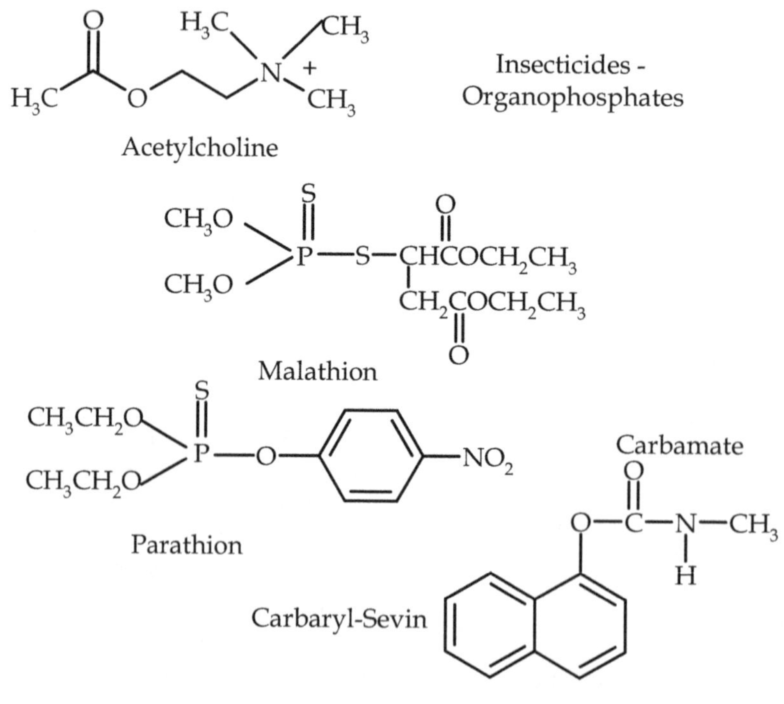


**Fig 11-8:** Irreversible anticholinesterase inhibitors

covalent bonds, inhibit them irreversibly. In fact they are mainly organophosphorus compounds which, because of their toxicity, are only exceptionally used in therapeutics. One of the least toxic among more than 50,000 derivatives which were prepared, diisopropyl fluorophosphates or D.F.P., was tested in treatment of myasthenia, paralytic ileus and of glaucoma as an ophthalmic solution. It was at the origin of poisonings and is not released on the market any more.

'Irreversible' cholinesterase inhibitors are termed organophosphates and form highly stable (covalent) phospho-intermediates. The organophosphates bind to and undergo initial hydrolysis by AChE, but the acyl intermediate is replaced by a phosphoryl moiety which is cleaved extremely slowly because of covalent bond formation (requiring upto hundreds of hours) and is, hence, effectively 'irreversible'. For most of the organophosphates, full recovery of the cholinesterase activity in the tissue would require *de novo* biosynthesis of AChE to occur. It is possible, however, to reactivate the phosphoryl enzyme using a strong nucleophile, atleast at an early stage of inhibition. This is accomplished using an oxime, such as pralidoxime (2-PAM). At later stages of inhibition, the phosphoryl group on the enzyme will undergo aging, wherein an alkyl group is lost from the phosphoryl moiety rendering it resistant to oxime attack because oximes are more nucleophilic compared to carbamyl groups.

The sulfur organophosphorus compound ecothiopate, was used in therapeutics in the form of an ophthalmic solution, in the treatment of glaucoma. It has very long action and its use has to be very spaced (once-daily to twice a week).

Malathion is the active product of certain preparations intended for the treatment of lice of the scalp (lice). When it is applied strictly to the hair, the scalp being intact, one does not observe general effects.

Metrifonate and dichlorvos are organophosphorus compounds inhibitors of cholinesterases, having antihelminthic activity against *Schistosoma mansoni* and haematobium. In the body metrifonate is partly converted to dichlorvos which is considered as the active product.

Irreversible inhibitors of cholinesterases are largely used in agriculture as insecticides and some of them, because of their very great toxicity, were retained as chemical warfare agents, also called nerve gases.

**Tetra-ethyl-pyrophosphate or T.E.P.P.**

Liquid product, of pleasant odour soluble in water where it is quickly hydrolyzed and in several organic solvents, T.E.P.P. is used as an insecticide.

**Parathion or Thiophos**

This is brown, viscous yellow fluid at ordinary temperature, practically insoluble in water, soluble in ethanol, used in insecticide preparations. By itself, this product is not very toxic, but in the body, it is transformed into paraoxon, metabolite much more toxic.

Other derivatives such as formathion, diethion, malathion and diazinon are very much used as insecticides.

Generally, the substitution of the phosphorus atom by a fluorine atom or a cyanide group increases toxicity and one obtains compounds such as tabun, sarin and soman classified as nerve gas.

## Anticholinesterase / Organophosphorus Poisoning and Treatment

The symptoms of poisoning by organophosphorus compounds depend on the conditions of poisoning and more particularly on its severity.

Between latent forms, detected by cholinesterases determination, and forms quickly fatal, there are many intermediate forms. The following symptomatology is generally observed:

**Muscarinic signs:** Miosis, nausea, salivation, vomiting, diarrhea, sweats, bradycardia, bronchial obstruction.

**Nicotinic signs:** Neuromuscular (twitchings, fasciculations, cramps, paralysis in the case of severe poisoning) and cardiac (tachycardia, rise in arterial pressure).

**Central signs:** Headache, drowsiness, disorientation, coma or generalized convulsions.

In severe forms where the disorders appear very quickly, death, preceded by a loss of consciousness and seizures, comes from a respiratory arrest by central inhibition and paralysis of the neuromuscular transmission phrenic nerve/diaphragm. The bronchial hypersecretion worsens moreover the respiratory failure.

Persistence of various neuropsychiatric disorders a long time after an acute poisoning or following a chronic poisoning by irreversible anticholinesterases is possible.

**Treatment** of poisoning by anticholinesterases consists of discontinuation of the poison, administration of atropine and possibly of pralidoxime, a cholinesterase reactivator. It acts as antidote.

Atropine which inhibits muscarinic effects is administered by parenteral route in doses higher than in its usual indications (1 mg possibly renewed).

Pralidoxime, which reactivates inhibited cholinesterases, is administered by parenteral route, generally intravenous, at renewable dose of 0.5 gm in adult. It acts by detaching the phosphate group of the inhibitors from the esteratic site. It should be noticed that in animal experiments, pralidoxime in large dose can partially inhibit cholinesterases and may cause transient neuromuscular blockade. Thus, it should not be administered as an antidote in too high doses. Obidoxime is another reactivator of cholinesterases.

Recent data shows that, during severe poisonings by organophosphorus compounds, the stimulation of acetylcholine receptors by acetylcholine which accumulates induces glutamate release which makes sodium and calcium enter the cell inducing cellular damage. The use of antagonists of glutamate can thus be considered.

## References


Boehm S, Kubista H (2002). Fine tuning of sympathetic transmitter release *via* ionotropic and metabotropic presynaptic receptors. *Pharmacol Rev* **54:** 43.

Brodde OE *et al.,* (2001). Presence, distribution and physiological function of adrenergic and muscarinic receptor subtypes in the human heart. *Basic Res Cardiol* **96:** 528.

Celie PH *et al.,* (2004). Nicotine and carbamylcholine binding to nicotinic acetylcholine receptors as studied in AChBP crystal structures. *Neuron* **41:** 907.

Eglen RM, Choppin A, Watson N (2001). Therapeutic opportunities from muscarinic receptor research. *Trends Pharmacol Sci* **22:** 409.

Ehlert FJ (2003). Contractile role of M2 and M3 muscarinic receptors in gastrointestinal, airway and urinary bladder smooth muscle. *Life Sci* **74:** 355.

Fox RI, Konttinen Y, Fisher A (2001). Use of muscarinic agonists in the treatment of Sjögren's syndrome. *Clin Immunol* **101:** 249.

Furchgott RF, Zawadzki JV (1980). The obligatory role of endothelial cells in the relaxation of arterial smooth muscle by acetylcholine. *Nature* **288:** 373.

Gerthoffer WT (2005). Signal-transduction pathways that regulate visceral smooth muscle function. III. Coupling of muscarinic receptors to signaling kinases and effector proteins in gastrointestinal smooth muscles. *Am J Physiol* **288:** G849.

CHAPTER

# Muscarinic Receptor Blocking Drugs

# 12

Muscarinic receptor antagonists, Fig. 12-1, called previously parasympatholytic and now cholinolytic, antimuscarinic, atropinic drugs, inhibit the muscarinic effects of acetylcholine. The drugs of this group are atropine, scopolamine and their derivatives.

Atropine is an alkaloid extracted from the leaves of a shrub called *Atropa belladonna*, which acts primarily at the peripheral level.

## Classification

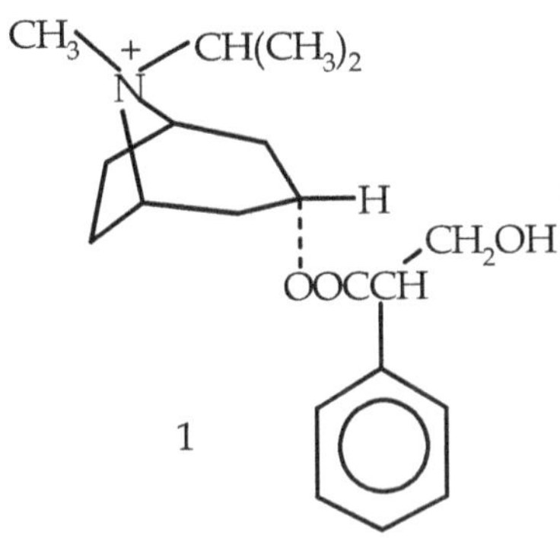


1

Ipratropium

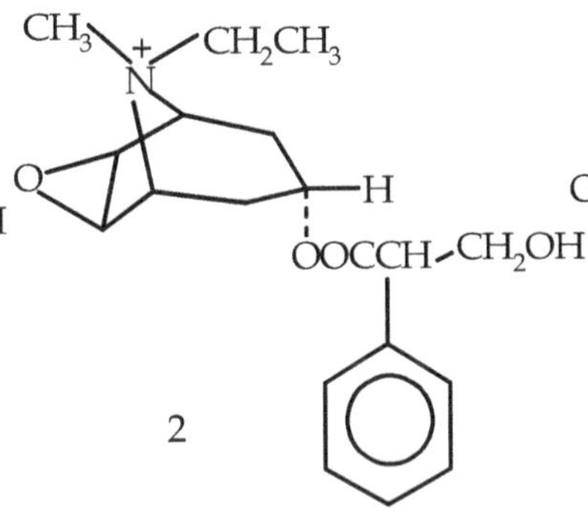


2

Oxitropium

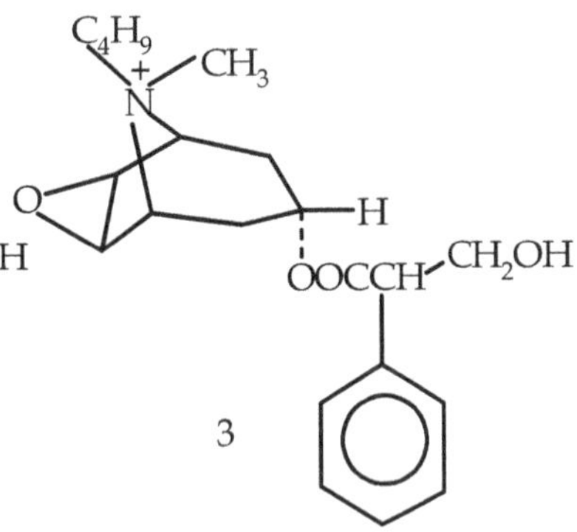


3

N-Butylscopolamine

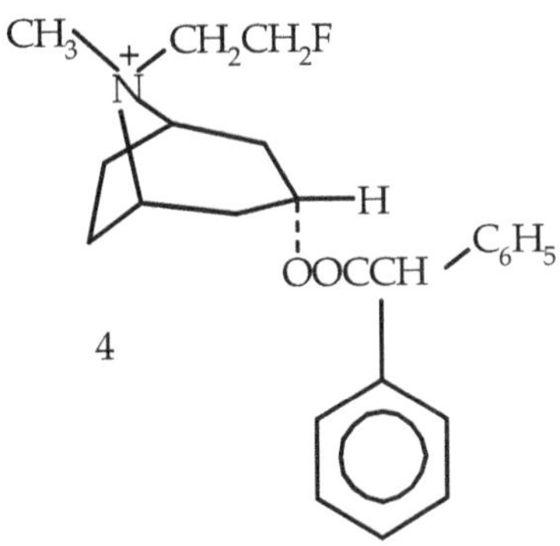


4

Flutropium

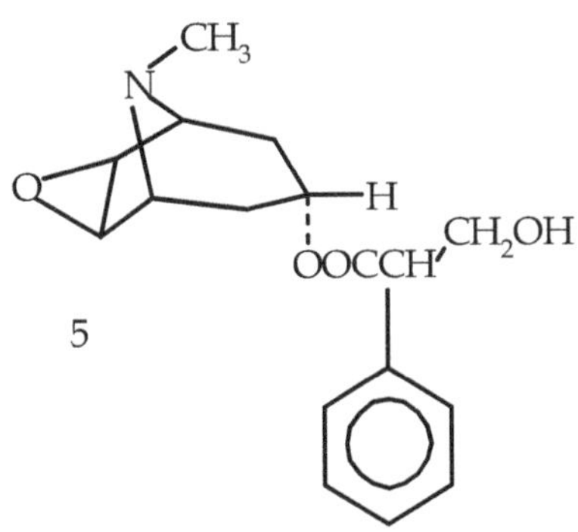


5

Scopolamine

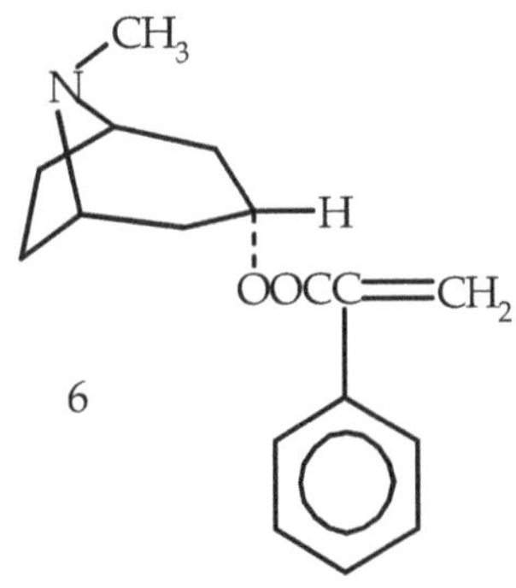


6

Apoatropine

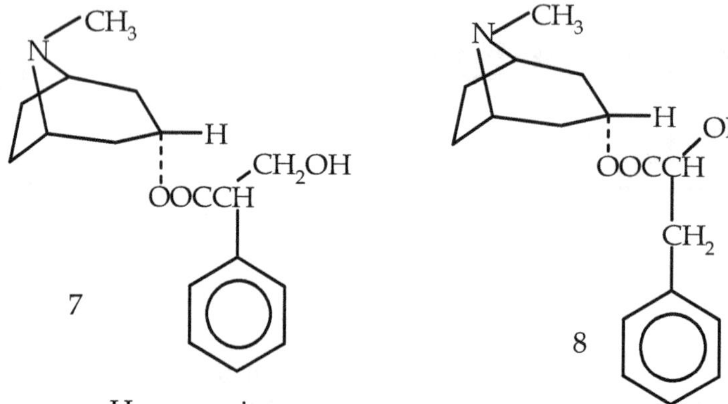


7 Hyoscyamine

8 Littorine

**Fig 12-1:** Muscarinic receptor blocking drugs

## Basic Pharmacology of Muscarinic Receptor Blocking Drugs

### Pharmacokinetics

**Chemistry:**

*Tertiary:* Atropine, hyoscine, hyoscyamine

*Quaternary:* Propantheline, glycopyrrolate, pirenzepine, dicyclomine, tropicamide, ipratropium, benztropine

**Absorption:** Natural alkaloids and tertiary antimuscarinic drugs well absorbed from GIT (lipid soluble) and conjunctival membrane.

Scopolamine absorbed from skin.

Quaternary (less lipid soluble) only 10-30% of a dose is absorbed from the oral administration.

**Distribution:** Natural alkaloids and tertiary antimuscarinic drugs well distributed.

Significant levels are achieved within 30 min-1 hr.

**Metabolism and Excretion:**

Atropine disappears from the blood after administration with a $T_{1/2}$ of 2 hr.

60% excreted unchanged in the urine.

Remaining is metabolized by hydrolysis and conjugation.

In all organs except eye the drug declines rapidly.

Effects on iris and ciliary muscles persist for hours.

### Mechanism of Action

Antimuscarinic drugs are competitive antagonists of the binding of ACh to muscarinic receptors. The seven trans- membrane helices of these receptors have a ring like organization in the cell membrane that forms a narrow central cleft where ACh binds. At least seven amino acids from four transmembrane helices have been implicated in agonist binding to the muscarinic receptors. Some of these residues, particularly a negatively charged aspartate, interact electrostatically with the positively charged quaternary ammonium moiety of ACh, whereas other residues are required for binding to the ester moiety. Although the tertiary amine and quarternary ammonium groups of antimuscarinic drugs bind to the same anionic site on the receptor that agonists occupy, these drugs do not fit into the narrow cleft and consequently cannot activate the receptor.

### Effects

The effects of application, mechanism of antimuscarinic drugs are listed in Table 12-1.

**Central nervous system:** Longer lasting sedation by action on parasympathetic medullary centres. Scopolamine has marked central effects include drowsiness and amnesia in sensitive individuals in recommended doses. Used in Parkinson's disease as adjunctive therapy with levodopa.

Although atropine and scopolamine share many properties, an important difference is the easier entry of scopolamine into the CNS. Typical doses of atropine (0.2–2 mg) have minimal central effects, while larger doses can produce a constellation of responses collectively termed the central anticholinergic syndrome. At intermediate doses (2–10 mg), memory and concentration may be impaired, and the patient may be drowsy. If doses of 10 mg or more are used, the patient may exhibit confusion, excitement, hallucinations, ataxia, a synergia, and possibly coma.

Even low doses of scopolamine have central effects. Sedation, amnesia, and drowsiness are common during the clinical use of this drug. Large doses of scopolamine can produce all of the responses seen with atropine. Other tertiary amine compounds with muscarinic receptor blocking activity have similar central effects.

**Eye and Ophthalmogical Disorders:** Muscarinic cholinergic activation on pupillary constrictor muscle is blocked by topical atropine and other antimuscarinic drugs. This results in unopposed sympathetic dilator activity and mydriasis. Second effect is weakening of contraction of ciliary muscles or *Cyclopegia* i.e., loss of accommodation for near vision. Third effect is reduction of lacrimal secretion, patients complains of dry or sandy eyes, when receiving large dose of antimuscarinic drug. Accurate measurement of refractive error in uncooperative patients e.g., young children requires ciliary paralysis. Ophthalmologic examination of retina is facilitated by mydriasis. Antimuscarinic agents are administered as eye drops or ointment. For adults and older children the shorter acting drugs are preferred e.g., are tertiary amines having good penetration after conjunctival application. Glycopyrrolate a quaternary agent is as rapid and as long acting as atropine. Antimuscarinic drugs should never be used in mydriasis unless cyclopegia or prolonged action is required. Alpha adrenoceptor stimulant drug e.g., Phenylephrine is sufficient for fundoscopic examination. Another use is to prevent Synechia (adhesion) formation in uveitis and iritis longer lasting antimuscarinic drug especially homatropine is valuable.

**The Cardio vascular system:**

(a) ***Heart:*** SA node is very sensitive to Muscarinic receptor blockade. Moderate to high therapeutic doses of atropine causes Blockade of vagal slowing relative tachycardia. Lower dose causes Initial bradycardia before tachycardia. This slowing maybe due to the block of presynaptic muscarinic receptors on vagal postganglionic fibers. These presynaptic muscarinic receptors normally limit the release of Ach in the SA node and other tissues. Because of presynaptic muscarinic block there is unlimited release of Ach leading to bradycardia. The same mechanism operates in the control of AV node function in the presence of high vagal tone. Atropine can significantly reduce the PR interval of the ECG by blocking muscarinic receptors in the AV node. Muscarinic effects on the atrial muscles are similarly blocked.

(b) ***Blood vessels:*** Blood vessels receive no direct innervation from parasympathetic nervous system. Parasympathetic nerve stimulation dilates coronary Arteries and parasympathetic cholinergic nerves cause vasodilation in the skeletal muscle vascular bed. Atropine can block this dilation. Almost all vessels contain endothelial muscarinic receptor that mediates vasodilation. These receptors are readily blocked by antimuscarinic drugs. At toxic doses and in some individuals at normal doses, antimuscarinic drugs cause cutaneous vasodilation, especially in the upper portion of the body.

Tachycardia and little effects on blood pressure. Cardiovascular effects of direct acting muscarinic innervation are easily prevented. Marked reflex vagal discharge sometimes accompanies the pain of MI and may result in sufficient depression of SA- and AV- nodal functions to impair cardiac output. In this condition parenteral atropine and a similar antimuscarinic agent is appropriate therapy. Circulating antibodies against the second extracellular loop of cardiac muscarinic receptors have been detected; these antibodies have parasympathomimetic action on heart. Their action is prevented by atropine.

**Respiratory system:** Both muscles and secretary glands receive vagal innervation and contain muscarinic receptors. Atropine causes bronchodilation and reduction of secretion. Effectiveness of unselective, antimuscarinic drugs in asthma and chronic obstructive pulmonary disease (COPD) is limited because of block of auto inhibitory $M_2$ receptors on postganglionic parasympathetic nerves can oppose the bronchodilation caused by block of $M_3$ receptors on airway smooth muscles. These antimuscarinic agents are frequently given prior to the administration of inhalant anaesthetics to reduce the accumulation of secretion in trachea and the possibility of laryngospasm. Atropine or scopolamine can reduce these hazards as preanesthetic medication.

***Post surgical effects of scopolamine are:***

Amnesia

Urinary retention

Intestinal hypomotility

Ipratropium (a synthetic analog of Atropine) is used as inhalation drug in Asthma and COPD.

Aerosol route of administration provides the advantage of maximal concentration at the bronchial target tissue with reduced systemic effects.

**Gastro Intestinal Tract (GIT):** Blockade of muscarinic receptors has dramatic effects on motility and some of the secretary functions of the gut. Even complete muscarinic blockade cannot abolish the activity in this organ system since local hormones and noncholinergic neurons in the enteric nervous system. Antimuscarinic drugs have marked effects on salivary secretion dry mouth in patients of Parkinson's disease or urinary conditions taking antimuscarinic drug. Gastric secretion is blocked less effectively the volume and amount of acid, pepsin, and mucin are reduced in large doses. The drugs like pirenzepine and telenzepine more selectively and potently reduce the gastric secretions but with fewer side effects than of atropine and other less selective agents. Pancreatic and intestinal secretions are less effectively blocked by atropine. These processes

**Table 12-1:** Organ/system effects, mechanisms, applications of antimuscarinic drugs

| Organ system | Drugs | Applications |
|---|---|---|
| CNS | Benztropine, trihexyphenidyl, biperiden | To treat Parkinson's disease manifestations |
| | Scopolamine | To prevent or reduce motion sickness |
| Eye | Atropine, homatropine, cyclopentolate, tropicamide | To produce mydriasis and cyclopegia. Cyclopentolate is well absorbed from conjunctival sac into the eye |
| Bronchi | Ipratropium | To cause bronchodilation in asthma and chronic obstructive pulmonary diseases |
| GIT | Glycopyrrolate, dicyclomine, methscopolamine | To reduce transient hypermotility |

*Table 12-1 Contd...*

| Organ system | Drugs | Applications |
|---|---|---|
| Genito-urinary tract | Oxybutynin, glycopyrrolate, dicyclomine, tolterodine | To treat transient cystitis, postoperative bladder spasm, or incontinence |
| **Organ** | **Effects** | **Mechanisms** |
| CNS | Sedation, anti motion sickness, Anti parkinson's, amnesia, delirum | Blockade of muscarinic receptor, Unknown subtype. |
| Eye | Cyclopegia, mydriasis | Blockade of $M_3$ receptors |
| Bronchi | Bronchodilation especially if constructed | Blockade of $M_3$ receptors |
| GIT | Relaxation, slowed peristalsis | Blockade of $M_1$, $M_3$ receptors |
| Genitourinary | Relaxation of bladder wall, urinary retention | Blockade of $M_3$ receptors |
| Heart | Initial bradycardia, especially at low doses; then tachycardia | Tachycardia from block of $M_3$ receptors in the heart |
| Blood vessels | Blockade of muscarinic vasodilatation; not manifested unless a muscarinic agonist is present | Blockade of $M_3$ receptors on endothelium of vessels |
| Glands | Reduction of salivation, lacrimation and sweating; less reduction of gastric secretion | Blockade of $M_1$, $M_3$ receptors |

are primarily under hormonal than vagal control. Walls of the viscera are relaxed, and both the tone and propulsive movements are diminished gastric emptying is prolonged intestinal transit time is lengthened. Diarrhea due to over dosage of parasym-pathomimetic drug is readily Stopped and even it is caused by non autonomic drug, which can temporarily be stopped. Used in the treatment of motion sickness or traveler's diarrhea. Clinically given in combination with the opioid antidiarrheal agents to enhance effectiveness. A classic example is LOMOTIL (tablet or liquid form) that is combination of atropine with diphenoxylate, a non analgesic congener of meperidine.

**Genito urinary tract:** Relaxes smooth muscles of ureter and bladder walls and slows voiding. Useful in the treatment of spasm caused by mild inflammation, surgery and certain neurological conditions. Anti muscarinic drugs have no significant action on the uterus. They are used for the symptomatic relief from the urinary urgency; however certain anti bacterial drugs are prescribed for the treatment of infections (bacterial cystitis). Oxybutynin is used for the relief of bladder spasm after the urologic surgery and prostectomy. Also valuable to reduce the involuntary voiding in patients with neurologic diseases e.g., in patients with meningomyelocele. In such conditions oral oxybutynin or instillation of the drug by catheter into the bladder improves bladder capacity and continence to reduce infection and renal damage. Imipramine a tricyclic antidepressant is used to reduce incontinence in institutionalized elderly patients. Proiverine is also used for this purpose. These antimuscarinic agents are also used in urolithiasis to reduce muscular spasm caused by passage of stone.

**Sweat gland:** Atropine reduces thermoregulatory sweating by muscarinic receptors Atropine Fever. Sympathetic cholinergic fibers innervate sweat glands and their muscarinic receptors are easily accessible by antimuscarinic drugs.

## Toxicity of Antimuscarinic Drugs

A traditional mnemonic for atropine toxicity is "Dry as a bone, red as a beet, Mad as a hatter".

### Predictable Toxicities

Blockade of thermoregulatory sweating hyperthermia or Atropine Fever. Tachycardia or arrhythmias (dry as bone). Most important toxicity in elderly patients include acute angle closure glaucoma and urinary retention particularly in parts of prostatic hyperplasia. Constipation, blurred vision.

### Unpredictable Toxicities

(a) **CNS:** Sedation, amnesia, delirium and hallucination, convulsions (mad as hatter).

(b) **Cardiovascular:** i.v conduction blockade.

Dilation of coetaneous vessels of arms, head, neck and trunk leading to "Atropine Flush" (red as beet).

*Cholinergic Poisoning:*

1. Antimuscarinic therapy
2. Cholinesterase regenerator compounds.
3. Pretreatment with reversible inhibitor of enzyme

1. ***Antimuscarinic Therapy:*** Large doses of atropine are needed to reverse the muscarinic effect of extremely potent agents.

   For parathion and chemical warfare nerve gases: 1-2 mg of atropine I.V every 5 min until signs of antimuscarinic effects are observed (dry mouth, reversal of miosis).

2. ***Cholinesterase Regenerator Compounds:*** Used for the treatment of organophosphorus poisoning.

   They are known as oxime agents and include pralidoxime (PAM) and diacetylmonoxime. The oxime group has a high affinity for binding with phosphorus atom and hydrolyze the phosphorylated enzyme. Pralidoxime I.V 1-2 g for over 15-30 min and for several days in severe poisoning. This drug may cause neuromuscular weakening. Pralidoxime is not recommended in reversal of inhibition of acetylcholine estrase by carbamate inhibitors. Diacetylmonoxime does cross the BBB.

3. ***Pretreatment with Reversible Inhibitor of Enzyme:*** To protect against excessive AchE inhibition, pretreatment with reversible inhibitors of the enzyme to prevent binding of the irreversible organophosphate inhibitors. This prophylaxis can be achieved with pyridostigmine or physostigmine, but is reserved for situations in which possibly lethal poisoning is anticipated e.g., chemical warfare. Simultaneous use of atropine is required to control muscarinic excess.

**Mushroom Poisoning:** Rapid onset: 15-30 min following ingestion. Parenteral atropine 1-2mg is effective in treatment. Signs are of muscarinic excess. Delayed onset :6-12 hr. Atropine is not used in such poisoning.

**Atropine Poisoning:** Manifestations are dry mouth, mydriasis, tachycardia, hot and flushed skin, agitation, delirium and hyperthermia.

## Clinical Uses

The clinical uses, MoA, Adverse effects of Antimuscarninic agents are listed in Table 7-2.

### Mydriatic Agents

Tropicamide is a muscarinic receptor antagonist used as a mydriatic. Tropicamide is different from atropine by its shorter duration of action which is approximately 1 hour and half. The effect appears in 10 minutes, is maximum in 15 or 20 minutes. The pupil finds its normal diameter in approximately 6 hours. Cyclopentolate is presented in the form of an ophthalmic solution with mydriatic effect of shorter duration than atropine.

### Gastric Acid Secretion Inhibitors

Numerous muscarinic receptor antagonists, including pirenzepine which has a quite specific action on the stomach, have been used in the management of peptic ulcer disease. Pirenzepine was withdrawn from the market after the introduction in therapeutics of $H_2$ antihistamines and proton pump inhibitors which are more effective and better tolerated.

## Bronchodilators

The two muscarinic receptor antagonists used as bronchodilators are oxitropium and ipratropium. They are given by pulmonary route, in the form of aerosol, in the preventive and curative treatment of asthma. Their efficacy is however lower than that of beta-mimetics. The advantage of these products compared to atropine result from a pharmacokinetic particularity as they involve a quaternary ammonium in their chemical formula, they are only little or not absorbed by bronchi and thus have a predominantly local effect. There is also a preparation for nasal use for rhinorrhea treatment. Tiotropium, anticholinergic of long duration of action, used in inhalation, is released on the market in Switzerland and Belgium but not in France.

## With Vesical Indications

Tolterodine is a cholinergic antagonist whose effect on the bladder prevails. It is used in the treatment of vesical instability with symptoms of pressing micturition or incontinence. Oxybutynin, which is a muscarinic receptor antagonist and has direct effects on smooth muscles, is proposed for the treatment of urinary incontinence of adults and could be used in the treatment of infantile enuresis. Trospium, an anticholinergic known for a long time, involving a quaternary ammonium group in its structure, was the subject of recent studies in urinary disorders.

## Used as Antispasmodics

Muscarinic receptor antagonists have antispasmodic properties, but all the antispasmodic agents are not necessarily muscarinic receptor antagonists. The antispasmodic effect of some of them results from a direct effect on smooth muscle, often by calcium-channel antagonism. Muscarinic receptor antagonists used as antispasmodics are, in addition to atropine itself, dihexyverine, prifinium and propantheline. Among antispasmodic drugs having at the same time a muscarinic receptor antagonist effect and a direct effect on smooth muscles one can quote tiemonium, although its effect on smooth muscle activity predominates over its muscarinic receptor antagonist activity. The antispasmodics with direct smooth muscle effect such as phloroglucinol, pinaverium, mebeverine and Trimébutine are also used in the treatment of hepatic and renal colics, colopathies and dysmenorrhea.

## Used as Antiparkinsonians

It is admitted that Parkinson's disease is the consequence of the destruction of the dopaminergic neurons, what induce an imbalance between dopaminergic and cholinergic effects, with cholinergic excess. Muscarinic receptor antagonists used as antiparkinsonians are trihexyphenidyl also called benzhexol, tropatepine and biperidene.

These drugs, in particular trihexyphenidyl, are used frequently for prevention and treatment of dyskinesia elicited by neuroleptic agents.

## Uses in Urology

Propantheline (Pro-Banthine), oxybutynin, dicyclomine, and several other agents have been used for uninhibited bladder syndrome, bladder spasm, enuresis, and urge incontinence. Tolterodine (Detrol), a nonselective muscarinic antagonist, exhibits functional specificity for blocking muscarinic receptors in the bladder, with fewer side effects than oxybutynin. However, total prevention of involuntary bladder contractions is difficult to achieve. The participation of noncholinergic, nonadrenergic nerves in bladder contraction may explain this apparent resistance to muscarinic blocking agents.

## Uses in Anaesthesiology

At one time, atropine or scopolamine was routinely administered before the induction of general anaesthesia to block excessive salivary and respiratory secretions induced by certain inhalation anesthetics (e.g., diethyl ether). With the newer, less irritating anaesthetics, antimuscarinic premedication is not routinely required as an antisialagogue (i.e., to counteract the formation of saliva). Sedation can occur following scopolamine administration, and preanaesthetic or postoperative agitation has been observed in some patients. High serum levels of drugs with antimuscarinic activity can

**Table 12-2:** Antimuscarinic agents mechanism of action, clinical uses and their adverse effects

| Substance | Mechanism | Clinical use | Adverse effects |
|---|---|---|---|
| Atropine (D/L-Hyoscyamine) | Non-selective antagonism, CNS stimulation | In anaesthesia, anticholinesterase (organophosphorous) poisoning, bradycardia, antispasmodic in gastrointestinal hypermotility | Urinary retention xerostomia blurred vision |
| Scopolamine (L-Hyoscine) | Non-selective antagonism, CNS depression | As atropine motion sickness | As atropine sedation |
| Ipratropium | Non-selective antagonism, without any mucociliary excretion inhibition. | In asthma and bronchitis | Oedema of legs in women |
| Tropicamide | Short acting non-selective antagonism, CNS depression | Produce mydriasis and cyclopegia in diagnostics | May cause ocular hypertension |
| Pirenzepine | $M_1$ receptor-selective antagonist, inhibits gastric secretion | In peptic ulcer (not much anymore) | (Fewer than non-selective ones) |
| Diphenhydramine | | For extrapyramidal symptoms from typical and a typical antipsychotic medications, antihistamine, sleep aid, antiparkinson agent | |
| Dimenhydrinate | | Motion sickness | |
| Dicyclomine | | Peptic diseases, morning sickness, motion sickness | |
| Flavoxate | | Urinary bladder antis-pasmodic | |
| Oxybutynin | | Overactive bladder urge incontinence | |
| Tiotropium | | Chronic obstructive pulmonary disease | |
| Cyclopentolate | Short acting non-selective antagonism, CNS depression | Produce mydriasis and cyclopegia in diagnostics | May cause ocular hypertension |

*Table 12-2 Contd...*

| Substance | Mechanism | Clinical use | Adverse effects |
|---|---|---|---|
| Atropine methonitrate | Non-selective antagonism, blocks transmission in ganglia. Lacks CNS effects | Antispasmodic in gastrointestinal hypermotility | |
| Trihexyphenidyl/ Benzhexol | Targets the $m_1$ Muscarinic receptor | Parkinson's disease | Drug at relative dose has 83% activity of atropine, thus has the same side-effects |
| Solifenacin | Competitive muscarinic acetylcholine receptor antagonist | Overactive bladder (OAB),<br><br>Urgency (urge incontinence) | |
| Darifenacin | Selective for $m_3$ receptors | Urinary incontinence | Few side effects |
| Benzatropine | Reduces the effects of the relative central cholinergic excess that occurs as a result of dopamine deficiency | Parkinson's disease | |
| Mebeverine | A muscolotropic spasmolytic with a strong and selective action on the smooth muscle spasm of the gastrointestinal tract, particularly of the colon. | Irritable bowel syndrome in its primary form (e.g., abdominal pain, bloating, constipation, and diarrohea).<br><br>Irritable bowel syndrome associated with organic lesions of the gastrointestinal tract. (e.g., diverticulosis and diverticulitis, etc.) | Skin rashes |
| Procyclidine | Antimuscarinic | Drug-induced park-insonism, akathisia and acute dystonia;<br><br>Parkinson disease; and Idiopathic or secondary dystonia | Overdose produces confusion, agitation and sleeplessness that can last up to or more than 24 hours. Pupils become dilated and unreactive to light. Tachycardia (fast heart beat), as well as auditory and visual hallucinations |

produce postoperative delirium. Glycopyrrolate bromide (Robinul) has also been given intramuscularly as a preanaesthetic medication with satisfactory results. This agent is a quaternary ammonium compound and therefore produces no central effects.

### Other Drugs

It is necessary to insist on the fact that numerous drugs whose principal property is not to be muscarinic receptor antagonists have antimuscarinic effects and the corresponding undesirable effects. It is the case of many neuroleptic agents and antidepressants.

## Contraindications and Cautions

Muscarinic blocking agents are contraindicated in angle-closure glaucoma. Caution also should be used in individuals with untreated open-angle glaucoma, cardiac disease, hyperthyroidism, or prostatic hypertrophy. Muscarinic antagonists can aggravate reflux oesophagitis by decreasing the tone of the lower oesophageal sphincter. Infants and children are especially sensitive to the hyperthermic action of muscarinic blockers. Elderly patients are especially sensitive to antimuscarinic effects in the CNS, such as impairment of memory. Phenothiazines and tricyclic antidepressants have antimuscarinic activity and can produce effects that are additive to those of the muscarinic blocking drugs. Antimuscarinics should not be given to patients with gastrointestinal infections because the drug will slow gastric motility and cause the patient to retain the infectious organisms in the gastrointestinal tract.

## References

Brodde OE *et al.,* (2001). Presence, distribution and physiological function of adrenergic and muscarinic receptor subtypes in the human heart. *Basic Res Cardiol* **96:**528.

Campbell SC (2001). Clinical aspects of inhaled anticholinergic therapy. *Respir Care* **46:** 275.

Casaburi R *et al.,* (2005). Improvement in exercise tolerance with the combination of tiotropium and pulmonary rehabilitation in patients with COPD. *Chest* **127:** 809.

Chapple CR *et al.,* (2005). A comparison of the efficacy and tolerability of solifenacin succinate and extended release tolterodine at treating overactive bladder syndrome: Results of the STAR trial. *Eur Urol* **48:** 464.

Chapple CR, Abrams P (2005). Comparison of darifenacin and oxybutynin in patients with overactive bladder: assessment of ambulatory urodynamics and impact on salivary flow. *Eur Urol* **48:**102.

Coulson FR, Fryer AD (2003). Muscarinic acetylcholine receptors and airway diseases. *Pharmacol Ther* **98:** 59.

Disse B (2001). Antimuscarinic treatment for lung diseases from research to clinical practice. *Life Sci* **68:** 2557.

Fukusaki M *et al.,* (1999). Effects of controlled hypotension with sevoflurane anesthesia on hepatic function of surgical patients. *Eur J Anaesthesiol* **16:** 111.

CHAPTER

# Adrenergic Drugs 13

## The Adrenergic Neuron

Adrenergic neurons release norepinephrine as the primary neurotransmitter. These neurons are found in the central nervous system (CNS) and also in the sympathetic nervous system, where they serve as links between ganglia and the effector organs. The adrenergic neurons and receptors located either Presynaptically on the neuron or Postsynaptically on the effector organ, are the sites of action of the adrenergic drugs.

### Neurotransmission at Adrenergic Neurons

Neurotransmission in adrenergic neurons closely resembles that already described for the cholinergic neurons, except that norepinephrine is the neurotransmitter instead of acetylcholine. Neurotransmission takes place at numerous bead-like enlargements called varicosities. The process involves five steps: synthesis, storage, release, and receptor binding of norepinephrine, followed by removal of the neurotransmitter from the synaptic gap (Figure 13-1).

**Synthesis of Norepinephrine:** Tyrosine is transported by a $Na^+$-linked carrier into the axoplasm of the adrenergic neuron, where it is hydroxylated to dihydroxy-phenylalanine (DOPA) by tyrosine hydroxylase. This is the rate-limiting step in the formation of norepinephrine. DOPA is then decarboxylated by the enzyme dopa decarboxylase (aromatic l-amino acid decarboxylase) to form dopamine in the cytoplasm of the presynaptic neuron.

**Storage of Norepinephrine in Vesicles:** Dopamine is then transported into synaptic vesicles by an amine transporter system that is also involved in the reuptake of preformed norepinephrine. This carrier system is blocked by reserpine. Dopamine is hydroxylated to form norepinephrine by the enzyme, dopamine $\beta^2$-hydroxylase. In the adrenal medulla, norepinephrine is methylated to yield epinephrine, both of which are stored in chromaffin cells. On stimulation, the adrenal medulla releases about 80 percent epinephrine and 20 percent norepinephrine directly into the circulation.

**Release of norepinephrine:** An action potential arriving at the nerve junction triggers an influx of calcium ions from the extracellular fluid into the cytoplasm of the neuron. The increase in calcium causes vesicles inside the neuron to fuse with the cell membrane and expel (exocytosis) their contents into the synapse. This release is blocked by drugs such as guanethidine.

**Binding to a receptor:** Norepinephrine released from the synaptic vesicles diffuses across the synaptic space and binds to either postsynaptic receptors on the effector organ or to presynaptic receptors on the nerve ending. The recognition of norepinephrine by the membrane receptors triggers a cascade of events within the cell, resulting in the formation of intracellular second messengers that act as links (transducers) in the communication between the neurotransmitter and the action generated within the effector cell. Adrenergic receptors use both the cyclic adenosine monophosphate (cAMP) second-messenger system, and the phosphatidylinositol cycle, to transduce the signal into an effect.

**Removal of norepinephrine:** Norepinephrine may 1) diffuse out of the synaptic space and enter the general circulation, 2) be metabolized to O-methylated derivatives by postsynaptic cell membrane associated catechol O-methyltransferase (COMT) in the synaptic space be recaptured by an uptake system that pumps the norepinephrine back into the neuron. The uptake by the neuronal membrane involves a sodium/potassium-activated ATPase that can be inhibited by tricyclic antidepressants, such as imipramine, or by cocaine. Uptake of norepinephrine into the presynaptic neuron is the primary mechanism for termination of nor epinephrine's effects.

**Potential fates of recaptured norepinephrine**: Once norepinephrine re-enters the cytoplasm of the adrenergic neuron, it may be taken up into adrenergic vesicles *via* the amine transporter system and be sequestered for release by another action potential, or it may persist in a protected pool. Alternatively, norepinephrine can be oxidized by monoamine oxidase (MAO) present in neuronal mitochondria. The inactive products of norepinephrine metabolism are excreted in the urine as vanillylmandelic acid, metanephrine, and normetanephrine.

## Synthesis, Storage and Release of Catecholamines

Five enzymes are involved in the pathway of the biosynthesis of adrenaline. The first enzyme is the iron containing phenylalanine-hydroxylase (also called phenylalanine-4monooxy-genases). The second enzyme, tyrosine-hydroxylase, contains iron, too, and catalyses the conversion of tyrosine to L-α-(3,4-dihydroxyphenyl)-β-alanine (DOPA). After decarboxylation of DOPA

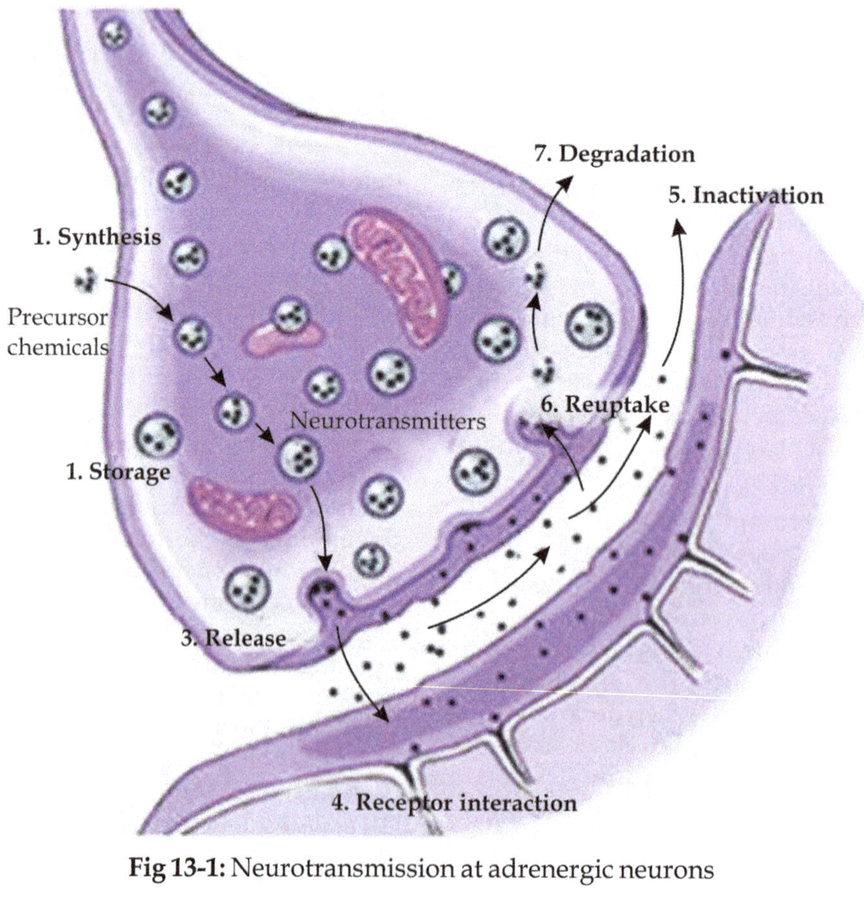


**Fig 13-1:** Neurotransmission at adrenergic neurons

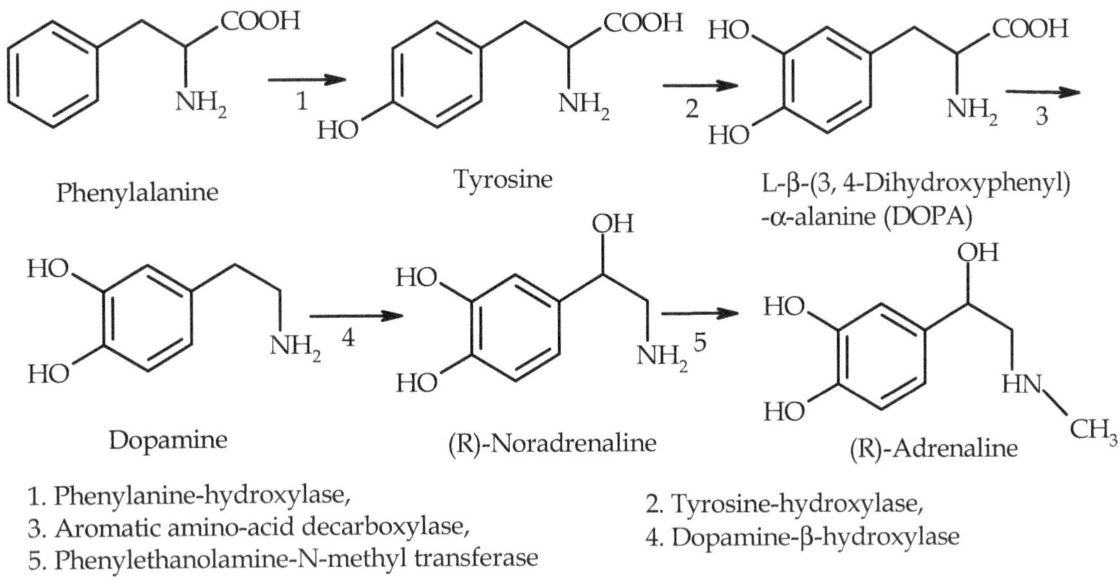


**Fig 13-2:** Biosynthesis of catecholamine

to dopamine (aromatic amino-acid decarboxylase) the copper-containing enzyme dopamine-β-hydroxylase converts dopamine to noradrenaline. The final enzyme noradrenaline N-methyltransferase then methylates noradrenaline to adrenaline. The noradrenaline formed in the adrenergic nerve endings remain stored in vesicles as its adenosine triphosphate complex. The adrenal medulla also synthesizes and stores noradrenaline and adrenaline. The neurotransmitters are released by increasing the permeability of nerve terminal membrane to $Ca^{++}$. The inflow of $Ca^{++}$ triggers the fusion of vesicle with the cell membrane, resulting in exocytosis.

## Metabolism and Distribution of Catecholamines

The actions of adrenaline and noradrenaline are (Fig 8-3) terminated by three processes;

1. Re-uptake into the nerve terminal
2. Dilution by diffusion from the junctional cleft and uptake at non-neuronal sites, and
3. Metabolic transformation

Two enzymes namely monoaminooxidase (MAO) and catechol-o-methyl transferase (COMT) are important in the biotransformations of catecholamines. COMT and MAO are distributed widely throughout the body, including the brain the highest concentrations of each are found in the liver and kidney. They differ in their cytosolic locations.

Norepinephrine (NE) released intraneurally is initially deaminated by MAO to 3,4-dihydroxyphenyl glycoaldehyde (DOPGAL). The aldehyde group is reduced to glycol by aldehyde reductase, yielding 3,4-dihydroxy-phenylethylene glycol (DOPEG). Aldehyde dehydrogenase converts 3,4-dihydroxyphenyl glycolaldehyde to 3,4-dihydroxy-mandelic acid (DOMA). The final common metabolites formed by the action of COMT are DOMA (3-methoxy-4-hydroxy mandelic acid) and VMA (3-methoxy-4-hydroxymandelic acid).

## Adrenergic Receptors

There are two main groups of adrenergic receptors, α and β, with several subtypes.

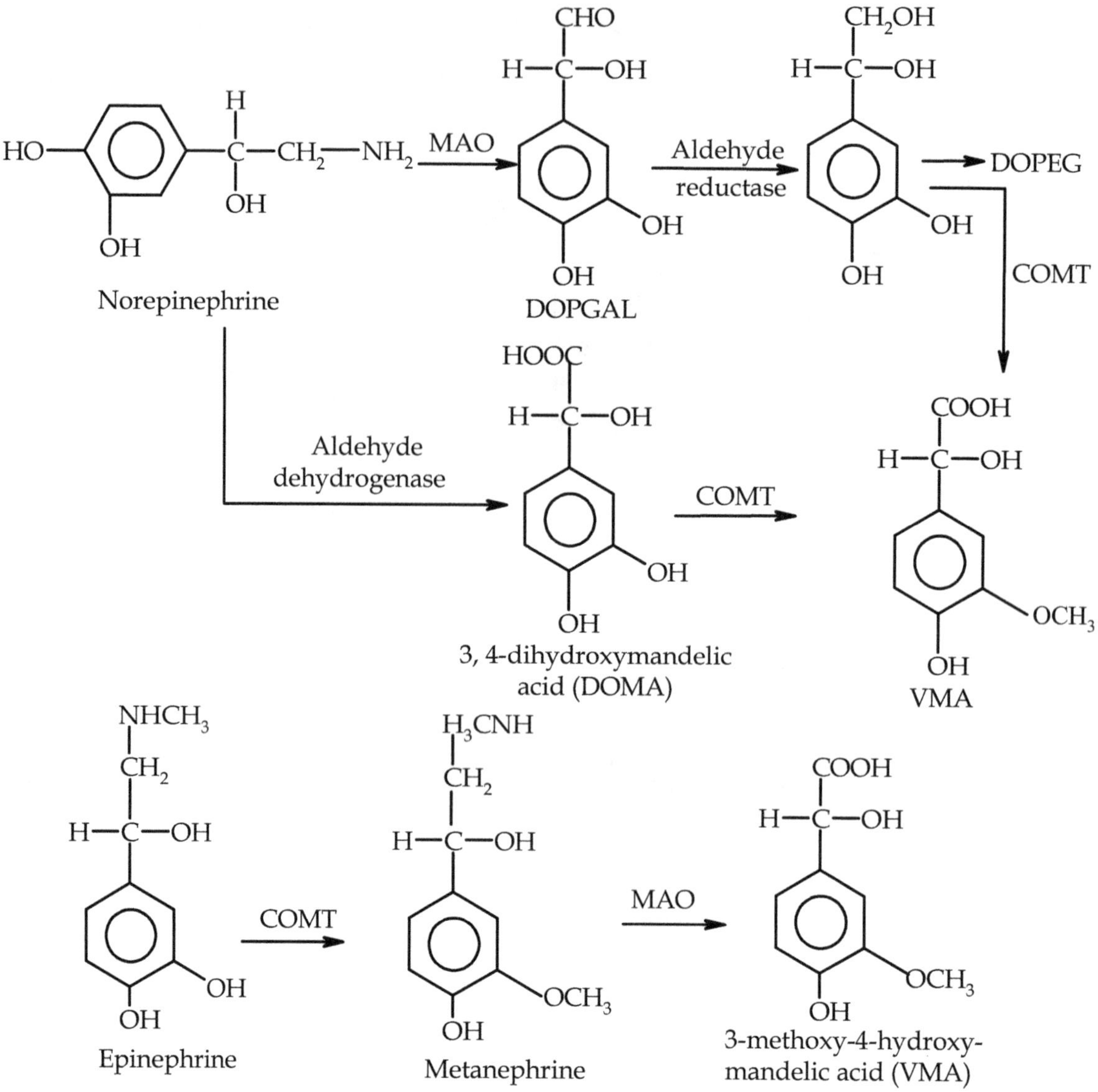


**Fig 13-3:** Metabolic pathways of catecholamines

α receptors have the subtypes $\alpha_1$ (a $G_q$ coupled receptor) and $\alpha_2$ (a $G_i$ coupled receptor). Phenylephrine is a selective agonist of the α receptor.

β receptors have the subtypes $\beta_1$, $\beta_2$ and $\beta_3$. All three are linked to $G_s$ proteins (although $\beta_2$ also couples to $G_i$), which in turn are linked to Adenylate cyclase. Agonist binding thus causes a rise in the intracellular concentration of the second messenger cAMP. Downstream effectors of cAMP include cAMP-dependent protein kinase (PKA), which mediates some of the intracellular events following hormone binding. Isoprenaline is a non-selective agonist.

## α Receptors

α receptors have several functions in common, but also individual effects. Common (or still unspecified) effects include:

- Vasoconstriction of arteries to heart (coronary artery).
- Vasoconstriction of veins.
- Decrease motility of smooth muscle in gastrointestinal tract.

### $\alpha_1$ Receptor

Alpha1-adrenergic receptors are members of the G protein-coupled receptor super family. Upon activation, a heterotrimeric G protein, $G_q$, activates phospholipase C (PLC). The PLC cleaves phosphatidylinositol 4,5-bisphosphate ($PIP_2$), which in turn causes an increase in inositol triphosphate ($IP_3$) and diacylglycerol (DAG). The former interacts with calcium channels of endoplasmic and sarcoplasmic reticulum, thus changing the calcium content in a cell. This triggers all other effects.

Specific actions of the $\alpha_1$ receptor mainly involve smooth muscle contraction. It causes vasoconstriction in many blood vessels, including those of the skin, gastrointestinal system, kidney (renal artery) and brain.

***Other areas of smooth muscle contraction are:***

- Ureter
- Vas deferens
- Uterus (when pregnant)
- Urethral sphincter
- Bronchioles (although minor to the relaxing effect of $\beta_2$ receptor on bronchioles)

### $\alpha_2$ Receptor

There are 3 highly homologous subtypes of $\alpha_2$ receptors: $\alpha_{2A}$, $\alpha_{2B}$, and $\alpha_{2C}$.

***Specific actions of the $\alpha_2$ receptor include:***

- Inhibition of insulin release in the pancreas.
- Induction of glucagon release from the pancreas.
- Contraction of sphincters of the gastrointestinal tract.
- Negative feedback in the neuronal synapses - presynaptic inhibition of noradrenalin release in CNS.
- Increased thrombocyte aggregation.

## β Receptors

### $\beta_1$ Receptor

***Specific actions of the $\beta_1$ receptor include:***

- Increase cardiac output, by raising heart rate (positive chronotropic effect), increasing impulse conduction (positive dromotropic effect), and increasing contraction (positive ionotropic effect), thus increasing the volume expelled with each beat (increased ejection fraction).
- Increase renin secretion from juxtaglomerular cells of kidney.

### $\beta_2$ Receptor

***Specific actions of the $\beta_2$ receptor include the following:***

- Smooth muscle relaxation, e.g., in bronchi, GI tract (decreased motility).
- Lipolysis in adipose tissue.
- Anabolism in skeletal muscle.
- Relax non-pregnant uterus.
- Dilate arteries to skeletal muscle.
- Glycogenolysis and gluconeogenesis.
- Stimulates insulin secretion.
- Contract sphincters of GI tract.
- Thickened secretions from salivary glands.
- Inhibit histamine-release from mast cells.
- Increase renin secretion from kidney.
- Relaxation of bronchioles (salbutamol, a beta 2 agonist relieves broncho constriction).
- Involved in brain - immune communication.

**Table 13-1:** Drugs acting at adrenergic receptors

| Tissue | Receptor subtype | Agonists | Antagonists |
|---|---|---|---|
| Heart | beta 1 | NE, dobutamine, xamoterol | EP, atenolol, metoprolol |
| Adipose tissue | beta 1, beta 3 | | |
| Vascular smooth muscle | beta 2 | EP, salbutamol, terbutaline, salmeterol | Butoxamine |
| Air way smooth muscle | beta 2 | Terbutaline, salbutamol, salmeterol and zinterol | Butoxamine |
| Smooth muscle contraction | alpha 1 | NE, EP, phenylephrine, oxymetazoline | Prazosin, doxazocin |
| Inhibition of transmitter release, hypotension, anaesthesia, vasoconstriction | alpha 2 | Clenbuterol, alphamethylnoradrenaline, dexmedetomidine, and mivazerol, clonidine | Yohimbine, idazoxan, atipamezole, efaroxan, and rauwolscine |

EP : Epinephrine; NE : Norepinephrine

### $\beta_3$ Receptor

*Specific actions of the $\beta_3$ receptor include:*

Enhancement of lipolysis in adipose tissue. Beta-3 activating drugs could theoretically be used as weight-loss agents, but are limited by the side effect of tremors.

## Classification of Adrenergic Agonists

Adrenergic agonists (Fig 13-4) are sub-divided into 3 classes, they are direct acting, indirect-acting and dual acting agonists. These agents act on sympathetic nervous system, activates it.

**Direct-acting agonists:** They bind to and activate $\alpha_1$, $\alpha_2$, $\beta_1$ and $\beta_2$ receptors. Naturally occurring molecules which bind to these receptors include norepinephrine (NE; a neurotransmitter which binds to $\alpha_1$, $\alpha_2$ and $\beta_1$ receptors), epinephrine (EP; a hormone produced in and secreted from the adrenal medulla which binds to $\alpha_1$, $\alpha_2$, $\beta_1$ and $\beta_2$ receptors – EP is a non-selective adrenergic agonist) and dopamine (DA; also a neurotransmitter which binds to DA receptors as well as $\alpha_1$, $\alpha_2$ and $\beta_1$ receptors).

Dopamine

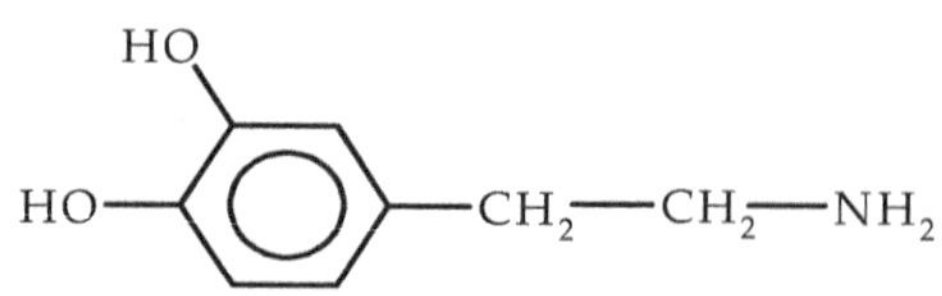

Norepinephrine

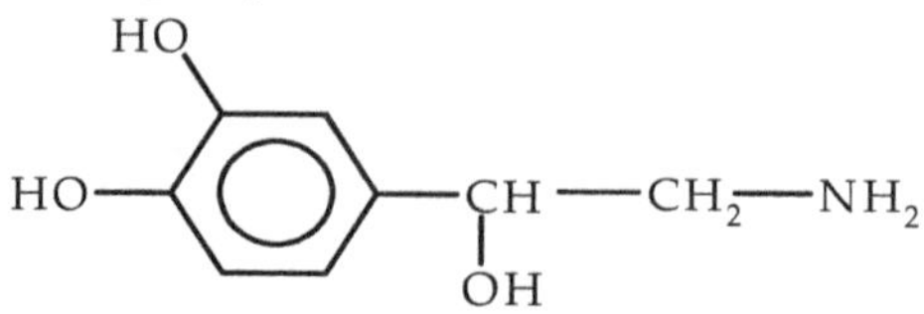

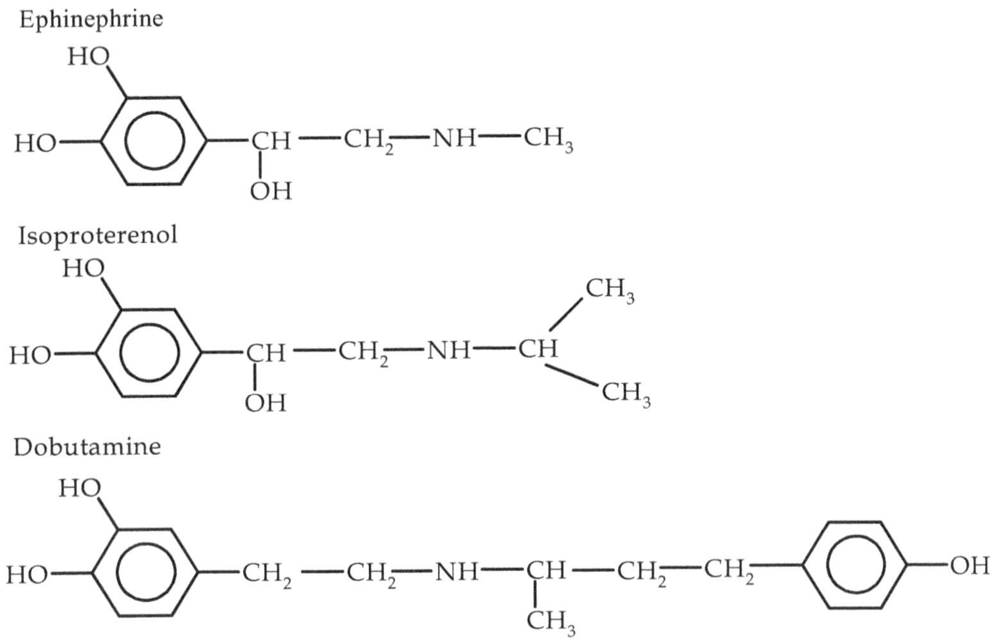


**Fig 13-4:** Catecolamines

**Indirect acting adrenergic agonists:** They (i.e., amphetamines and cocaine) produce NE-like actions by stimulating NE release and preventing its re-uptake and thus its inactivation.

**Dual-acting adrenergic agonists:** These agents (i.e., ephedrine) act as direct- and indirect-adrenergic agonists (hence dual-acting). They bind to adrenergic receptors and stimulate NE release.

## Structure Activity Relationship of Adrenergic Drugs

1. The sympathomimetic drugs may be divided into catechol and non-catechol amines.
2. All catecholamines, possess the catechol nucleus (O-dihydroxybenzene) .
3. Noncatecholamines consisting of a benzene ring and an ethylamine side chain. β-phenylethylamine can be viewed as the parent compound, consisting of a benzene ring and an ethylamine side chain.
4. Separation of the aromatic ring and the amino group by two carbon atom shows the greatest activity.
5. Substitution on the amino group, increasing the size of the alkyl substituent increases β receptor activity, e.g., Isoproterenol.
6. Substitution on the aromatic nucleus, specifically OH groups at the 3 and 4 positions of the ring are required for maximal α and β activity. When one or both of these groups is absent, without other aromatic substitution, the overall potency is reduced. Phenylephrine is thus less potent at both receptors than adrenaline, with β activity almost entirely absent.

   **NOTE**: Ephedrine and amphetamine are the two drugs doesn't contain OH groups at the 3 and 4 positions of the ring, but both drugs have sympathomimetic (Adrenergic stimulation) activity.
7. Hydroxyl (–OH) groups at the 3 and 5 positions, in compounds with large amino

substituents, confers $\beta_2$ selectivity, e.g., metaproterenol, terbutaline.

8. The response of non-catecholamines is largely determined by their ability to release NE, thus their effects are mainly on $\alpha$ and $\beta_1$.
9. Phenylethylamines lacking both aromatic –OH groups and the β-OH on the ethyl chain produce almost all of their effects by NA release. Catecholamines have only a brief duration of action, and are ineffective orally, due to degradation by COMT. Agents lacking –OH substitution, especially the compounds with 3-OH, are resistant to COMT and have a longer duration of action and oral effectiveness
10. Substitution with groups other than –OH, in general, reduces α-adrenergic activity and almost abolishes β-adrenergic activity.
11. Substitution on the β-C atom generally decreases central stimulant action, due to the lower lipid solubility of these agents. However, this also greatly enhances both α and β potency. Thus, ephedrine is less potent than methamphetamine as a CNS stimulant, but is more potent vaso-constrictor and bronchodilator. Absence of the benzene ring reduces the CNS stimulant action, without reducing peripheral effects, when replaced by a saturated, e.g., cyclopentamine the proportion of $\alpha : \beta$ activity varies with the compound. However, the absence of benzene confers greater activity and many of these agents are used as nasal decongestants.
12. Optical isomerism is conferred by substitution on either of the ethyl carbon atoms.

    *Levorotatory*: Substitution at the β-carbon atom produces naturally occurring NE and EP, both of which are over 10 times as potent as their isomers.

    *Dextrorotatory*: Substitution at the α-carbon atom generally confers greater potency in CNS stimulation, e.g. d-amphetamine.
13. Substitution of methyl group on -NH in epinephrine is responsible for stimulatory action of $\beta_2$ receptors in smooth muscle where as norepinephrine does not have stimulatory action of $\beta_2$ receptors in smooth muscle because of absence of methyl group.

# Direct-Acting Agonists

## Epinephrine (EP)

### Mechanism of Action

Epinephrine or adrenaline is a direct-acting sympathomimetic drug that acts as an agonist at alpha and beta-adrenergic receptors. It produces vasoconstriction to counteract the vasodilation and resulting hypotension associated with anaphylaxis. The bronchodilatory effects of epinephrine and its ability to reduce mucosal edema relieve bronchoconstriction and improve respiratory effort. Epinephrine also down-regulates the release of histamine, tryptase, and other inflammatory mediators from mast cells and basophils, improving respiratory function and reducing the pruritus, urticaria, angioedema, and gastrointestinal symptoms which occur after allergen exposure.

### Effects

(a) **Cardiovascular system:** Potent elevator of blood pressure. Intravenous injection causes dose dependent increases in blood pressure; systolic pressure is more affected than diastolic and so pulse pressure is increased. Effects are due to increased heart rate, increased contractions of the myocardium and vasoconstriction. Subcutaneous administration or intravenous infusion causes a lower increase in systolic blood pressure with decreased peripheral vascular resistance and diastolic blood pressure. Vasoconstriction of subcutaneous small vessels, increased blood flow to skeletal muscle. Stimulation of myocardium–increased pulse, arrhythmias, increased work and oxygen consumption, increased cardiac output.

(b) **Smooth muscle:** Increased blood flow, relaxation of GIT and bladder muscle, $\beta_2$ selective agonists relax uterine smooth muscle.

(c) **Respiratory system:** Epinephrine affects respiration primarily by relaxing bronchial muscle. It has a powerful bronchodilator action, most evident when bronchial muscle is contracted because of disease, as in bronchial asthma, or in response to drugs or various autacoids. In such situations, epinephrine has a striking therapeutic effect as a physiological antagonist to substances that cause bronchoconstriction.

The beneficial effects of epinephrine in asthma also may arise from inhibition of antigen-induced release of inflammatory mediators from mast cells, and to a lesser extent from diminution of bronchial secretions and congestion within the mucosa.

(d) **Metabolic effects:** Increased oxygen consumption, hyperglycemia, lactic acidosis, increased free fatty acids ($\beta$ receptors); effects on insulin depend on receptor – $\alpha_2$ inhibit secretion, $\beta_2$ stimulate it, the result is inhibition. A transient hyperkalemia is followed by a more persistent Hypokalemia.

(e) **Central nervous system:** Because of the inability of this rather polar compound to enter the CNS, epinephrine in conventional therapeutic doses is not a powerful CNS stimulant. While the drug may cause restlessness, apprehension, headache, and tremor in many persons, these effects in part may be secondary to the effects of epinephrine on the cardiovascular system, skeletal muscles, and intermediary metabolism; that is, they may be the result of somatic manifestations of anxiety. Some other sympathomimetic drugs more readily cross the blood–brain barrier.

(f) **Other effects:** Eosinopenia (a decrease in the number of eosinophils in the blood), increased coagulability of blood, decreased intraocular pressure, mydriasis (dilatation of the pupil), and tears.

**Pharmacokinetics**

Due to rapid oxidation and conjugation in the GIT mucosa and liver adrenaline is ineffective after oral administration. Absorption from subcutaneous tissues occurs slowly due to local vasoconstriction. Adrenaline is rapidly inactivated in the body, despite its stability in blood. The liver is rich in both COMT and MAO, however is not essential in the degradation process. The majority of an administered drug is excreted in the urine as metabolites.

**Clinical uses**

The oral intake of adrenaline has no effect. Therefore it has to be administered parenterally. It is used as sympathomimetic (drugs which support the beating of the heart), broncholytic (drugs which relax the bronchial muscles) and antiasthmatic (drugs against asthma). It is also used to prevent bleedings during surgery or in the case of inner organ bleeding. Because adrenaline leads to constriction of blood vessels, it is administered in combination with local anaesthetics. In this combination, anaesthetics have a longer lasting effect and can be administered in smaller doses.

**Adverse effects**

(a) May be transient – fear, anxiety, dizziness, pallor, tremors, headache and palpitations.

(b) More serious effects are arrhythmias and cerebral haemorrhage – due to rapid elevation of blood pressure.

(c) Worse in patients with psychiatric backgrounds, hypertension or hyper-thyroidism.

**Contraindications:** Patients receiving non-selective beta blockers (a effects unopposed), patients with both emphysema and heart disease.

**Dosing and administration**

Epinephrine auto-injectors should be administered intramuscularly into the anterolateral aspect of the thigh as soon as possible after exposure to the allergen. If necessary, the injection may be given through clothing. For adults and children > 30 kg, a dose of 0.3 mg is recommended. A lower dose, 0.15 mg, is recommended for children between 15 and 30 kg. The dose should be approximately 0.01 mg/kg, up to a maximum single dose of 0.3 mg. The dose may be repeated every 10 to 20 minutes as needed until the patient can be seen by a health care provider. Epinephrine should not be injected into the buttocks, as absorption may be significantly delayed. Administration into the hands or feet should also be avoided, as it may result in loss of blood flow and tissue necrosis. Inadvertent intravenous administration may result in profound hypertension or pulmonary edema.

### Drug Interactions

Epinephrine should used with caution in patients taking digoxin, quinidine, diuretics, or other alpha or beta-adrenergic agonists, as concomitant administration may lead to arrhythmias or hypertension. The effects of epinephrine may be increased when given with antihistamines, furazolidone, levothyroxine, methyldopa, Reserpine, tricyclic antidepressants, or monoamine oxidase inhibitors.

## Norepinephrine (NE)

Norepinephrine (or) noradrenaline administered to a normotensive adult either subcutaneously or by slow intravenous injection, constricts most blood vessels. Venules as well as arterioles are constricted. As a consequence, there is a net increase in the total peripheral resistance. The effects of norepinephrine on cardiac function are complex because of the dynamic interaction of the direct effects of norepinephrine on the heart and the initiation of powerful cardiac reflexes. Important considerations are as follows:

1. The direct effect of norepinephrine on the heart is stimulatory.
2. The reflexes initiated is inhibitory, that is, opposite to the direct effect.
3. The reflex varies with the level of sympathetic and parasympathetic activity just before the initiation of the reflex.
4. The distribution of sympathetic and parasympathetic nerves is not uniform in the heart.

The net effect of norepinephrine administration on heart rate and ventricular contractile force therefore varies with the dose of norepinephrine, the physical activity of the subject, any prior cardiovascular and baroreceptor pathology, and the presence of other drugs that may alter reflexes. In a normal resting subject who is receiving no drugs, there is a moderate parasympathetic tone to the heart, and sympathetic activity is relatively low. The ventricular muscle receives little, if any, parasympathetic innervation. As the blood pressure rises in response to norepinephrine, the baroreceptor reflex is activated, parasympathetic impulses (which are inhibitory) to the heart increase in frequency, and what little sympathetic outflow there is may be reduced. Heart rate is slowed so much that the direct effect of norepinephrine to increase the rate is masked and there is a net decrease in rate. Under the conditions described, however, the impact of the reflex on the ventricles is very slight because there is no parasympathetic innervation and the preexisting level of sympathetic activity is already low. A further decrease in sympathetic activity therefore would have little further effect on contractility in this subject. Thus, a decrease in heart rate and an increase in stroke volume will occur, and cardiac output will change very little. The reflex nature of the bradycardia induced by parenterally administered norepinephrine can readily be demonstrated by administration of atropine, a cholinoreceptor antagonist. Atropine abolishes the compensatory vagal reflexes. Under conditions of vagal blockade, the direct cardiac stimulatory effects of norepinephrine are unmasked. There is marked tachycardia, an increase in stroke volume, and as a consequence, a marked increase in cardiac output. *More potent than epinephrine on receptors, much less potent on $\beta_2$ receptors and the same on $\beta_1$ receptors.*

**Adverse effects:** As with epinephrine, but milder Severe hypertension, headache, photophobia, pallor, sweating and vomiting. Increased risk of arrhythmias.

**Contraindications:** pregnancy (will cause uterine contractions).

## Dopamine

Precursor of both epinephrine and norepinephrine

### Pharmacological effects

Dopamine is a naturally occurring catecholamine; it is the immediate biochemical precursor of the norepinephrine found in adrenergic neurons and the adrenal medulla.

It is also a neurotransmitter in the CNS, where it is released from dopaminergic neurons to act on specific dopamine receptors . Dopamine is a unique adrenomimetic drug in that it exerts its cardiovascular actions by

1. Releasing norepinephrine from adrenergic neurons,
2. Interacting with $\alpha$ and $\beta_1$ adrenoceptors, and
3. Interacting with specific dopamine receptors.

The cardiovascular response to dopamine in humans depends on the concentration infused. Low rates of dopamine infusion can produce vasodilation in the renal, mesenteric, coronary, and intercerebral vascular beds with little effect on other blood vessels or on the heart. The vasodilation produced by dopamine is not antagonized by the $\beta$ adrenoceptor blocking agent propranolol but is antagonized by haloperidol and other dopamine receptor-blocking agents.

Dopamine can exert pronounced cardiovascular and renal effects through the activation of both $D_1$ and $D_2$ receptor subtypes. Stimulation of the $D_1$ receptor, which is present on blood vessels and certain other peripheral sites, will result in vasodilation, natriuresis, and diuresis. $D_2$ receptors are found on ganglia, on sympathetic nerve terminals, on the adrenal cortex, and within the cardiovascular centers of the CNS; their activation produces hypotension, bradycardia, and regional vasodilation (e.g., renal vasodilation). The kidney appears to be a particularly rich source for endogenous dopamine in the periphery. The infusion of moderately higher concentrations of dopamine increases the rate and contractile force of the heart and augments the cardiac output. This action is mediated by $\beta_1$ adrenoceptors and norepinephrine release and is antagonized by propranolol. In contrast to isoproterenol, which has a marked effect on both the rate and the contractile force of the heart, dopamine has a greater effect on the force than on cardiac rate. The advantage of this greater inotropic than chronotropic effect of dopamine is that it produces a smaller increase in oxygen demand by the heart than does isoproterenol. Systolic blood pressure is increased by dopamine, whereas diastolic pressure is usually not changed significantly. Total peripheral resistance is decreased because of the vasodilator effect of dopamine. At still higher concentrations, dopamine causes $\alpha$ adrenoceptor-mediated vasoconstriction in most vascular beds and stimulates the heart. Total peripheral resistance may be increased. If the concentration of dopamine reaching the tissue is high enough, vasoconstriction of the renal and mesenteric beds also occurs. The vasoconstrictive action of dopamine is antagonized by $\alpha$ adrenoceptor blocking agents such as phentolamine.

### Clinical uses

Dopamine is used in the treatment of shock owing to inadequate cardiac output (cardiogenic shock), which may be due to myocardial infarction or congestive heart failure. It is also used in the treatment of septic shock, since renal circulation is frequently compromised in this condition. An advantage of using dopamine in the treatment of shock is that its inotropic action increases cardiac output while dilating renal blood vessels and thereby increasing renal blood Flow.

### Adverse effects

Nausea, vomiting, tachycardia, chest pain, headache, hypertension, vasoconstriction and arrhythmias.

**Contraindications** (relative) patients receiving monoamine oxidase inhibitors.

## Amphetamine

Amphetamine is an indirectly acting adrenomimetic amine that depends for its action on the release of norepinephrine from noradrenergic nerves. Its pharmacological effects are similar to those of ephedrine, however, its CNS stimulant activity is somewhat greater. Both systolic and diastolic blood pressures are increased by oral dosing with amphetamine. The heart rate is frequently slowed reflexively. Cardiac output may remain unchanged in the low- and moderate-dose range. The therapeutic uses of amphetamine are based on its ability to stimulate the CNS. The D-isomer (dextro-amphetamine) is three to four times as potent as the L-isomer in producing CNS effects. It has been used in the treatment of obesity because of its anorexic effect, although tolerance to this effect develops rapidly. It prevents or overcomes fatigue and has been used as a CNS stimulant. Amphetamine is no longer recommended for these uses because of its potential for abuse. Amphetamine is useful in certain cases of narcolepsy or minimal brain dysfunction, Attention deficit hyperactive disorder in children.

### Adverse effects

Increased errors in tasks performed, headache, palpitations, arrhythmias, depression, fatigue, dry mouth, increased sweating, nausea and vomiting, abdominal pain, confusion and psychomotor agitation. Chronic use may cause psychotic reactions. Toxic doses can cause convulsions, coma and death.

## Ephedrine

Ephedrine is a naturally occurring alkaloid that can cross the blood-brain barrier and thus exert a strong CNS-stimulating effect in addition to its peripheral actions. The latter effects are primarily due to its indirect actions and depend largely on the release of norepinephrine. However, ephedrine may cause some direct receptor stimulation, particularly in its bronchodilating effects. Because it resists metabolism by both COMT and MAO, its duration of action is longer than that of norepinephrine. As is the case with all indirectly acting adrenomimetic amines, ephedrine is much less potent than norepinephrine; in addition, tachyphylaxis develops to its peripheral actions. Unlike epinephrine or norepinephrine, however, ephedrine is effective when administered orally.

### Pharmacological actions

Ephedrine increases systolic and diastolic blood pressure; heart rate is generally not increased. Contractile force of the heart and cardiac output are both increased. Ephedrine produces bronchial smooth muscle relaxation of prolonged duration when administered orally. Aside from pupillary dilation, ephedrine has little effect on the eye.

### Clinical uses

Ephedrine is useful in relieving broncho-constriction and mucosal congestion associated with bronchial asthma, asthmatic bronchitis, chronic bronchitis, and bronchial spasms. It is often used prophylactically to prevent asthmatic attacks and is used as a nasal decongestant, as a mydriatic, and in certain allergic disorders. Although its bronchodilator action is weaker than that of Isoproterenol, its oral effectiveness and prolonged duration of action make it valuable in the treatment of these conditions. Because of their oral effectiveness and greater bronchiolar selectivity, terbutaline and albuterol are replacing ephedrine for bronchodilation.

### Adverse effects

Symptoms of overdose are related primarily to cardiac and CNS effects. Tachycardia, premature systoles, insomnia, nervousness, nausea, vomiting, and emotional disturbances may develop. Ephedrine should not be used in patients with cardiac disease, hypertension, or hyperthyroidism.

## Isoproterenol

Slow intravenous infusion of therapeutic doses of isoproterenol in humans produces a marked decrease in total peripheral resistance, owing to the predominance of vasodilation in skeletal muscle vascular beds. As a consequence, diastolic and mean blood pressures fall. The depressor action of isoproterenol is more pronounced than that of epinephrine because isoproterenol causes no vasoconstriction, whereas epinephrine does in some vascular beds. Systolic blood pressure may remain unchanged or may increase. When an increase in systolic blood pressure is seen, it is due to the marked increase in cardiac output produced by isoproterenol. Isoproterenol usually increases the heart rate and stroke volume more than dose epinephrine. This is partly due to its ability to decrease mean blood pressure, which then reflexively diminishes vagal activity, and partly to its action on the heart.

# Selective Adrenergic Agonists

## Phenylephrine, Metaraminol, and Methoxamine

These drugs are directly acting adrenomimetic amines that exert their effects primarily through an action on $\alpha$ adrenoceptors. Consequently, these agents have little or no direct action on the heart. All three drugs increase both systolic and diastolic blood pressures through their vasoconstrictor action. The pressor response is accompanied by reflex bradycardia, no change in the contractile force of the heart, and little change in cardiac output. They do not precipitate cardiac arrhythmias and do not stimulate the CNS.

Phenylephrine is not a substrate for COMT, while metaraminol and methoxamine are not metabolized by either COMT or MAO. Consequently, their duration of action is considerably longer than that of norepinephrine. Following intravenous injection, pressor responses to phenylephrine may persist for 20 minutes, while pressor responses to metaraminol and methoxamine may last for more than 60 minutes.

The clinical uses of these drugs are associated with their potent vasoconstrictor action. They are used to restore or maintain blood pressure during spinal anesthesia and certain other hypotensive states. The reflex bradycardia induced by their rapid intravenous injection has been used to terminate attacks of paroxysmal atrial tachycardia. Phenylephrine is commonly used as a nasal decongestant, although occasional nasal mucosal.

## Dobutamine

Dobutamine (*Dobutrex*), in contrast to dopamine, does not produce a significant proportion of its cardiac effects through the release of norepinephrine from adrenergic nerves; dobutamine acts directly on $\beta_1$ adrenoceptors in the heart. Dobutamine exerts a greater effect on the contractile force of the heart relative to its effect on the heart rate than does dopamine. Dobutamine increases the oxygen demands on the heart to a lesser extent than does dopamine. Like dopamine, although at higher doses, it produces vasodilation of renal and mesenteric blood vessels. Dobutamine may be more useful than dopamine in the treatment of cardiogenic shock because dopamine can be readily metabolised by intestinal decarboxylase and dobutamine can readily converted into noradrenaline in cardiac tissues and it stimulates $\beta_1$ adrenoceptors in the heart.

**Adverse Effects:** Hypertension, tachycardia.

## Terbutaline and Albuterol

Terbutaline and albuterol are relatively selective $\beta_2$ adrenoceptor agonists. Both have a longer duration of action than isoproterenol because they are not metabolized by COMT. Like isoproterenol, they are not metabolized by MAO and are not transported into adrenergic neurons.

Terbutaline and albuterol are effectively administered either orally or subcutaneously. Because of their selectivity for $\beta_2$ adrenoceptors, they produce less cardiac stimulation than does isoproterenol but are not completely without effects on the heart. Therapeutically, terbutaline and albuterol are used to treat bronchial asthma and bronchospasm associated with bronchitis and emphysema.

**Side Effects:** Include nervousness, tremor, tachycardia, palpitations, headache, nausea, vomiting, and sweating. The frequency of appearance of these adverse effects is minimized, however, when the drugs are given by inhalation.

## References

Burnstock G and Grifûth SG (1988). Nonadrenergic Innervation of Blood Vessels. Boca Raton, FL:CRC.9.

Gootman PM (ed.) 1986. Developmental Neurobiology of the Autonomic Nervous System. Clifton, NJ: Humana.

Holmes A, Lachowicz JE, Sibley DR (2004). Phenotypic analysis of dopamine receptor knockout mice; recent insights into the functional specificity of dopamine receptor subtypes. *Neuropharmacology* **47:**1117.

Koch WJ (2004). Genetic and phenotypic targeting of beta-adrenergic signaling in heart failure. *Mol Cell Biochem* **263:** 5.

Koshimizu T *et al.,* (2002). Recent progress in alpha1-adrenoceptor pharmacology. *Biol Pharm Bull* **25:** 401.

Lefkowitz RJ, Shenoy SK (2005). Transduction of receptor signals by beta-arrestins. *Science* **308:** 512.

Mitler MM, Hayduk R (2002). Benefits and risks of pharmacotherapy for narcolepsy. *Drug Saf* **25:**791.

Oldenburg O *et al.,* (2002). Treatment of orthostatic hypotension. *Curr Opin Pharmacol* **2:** 740.

Philipp M, Hein L (2004). Adrenergic receptor knockout mice: Distinct functions of 9 receptor subtypes. *Pharmacol Ther* **101:** 65.8.

CHAPTER

# Adrenergic Blocking Drugs 14

The adrenergic antagonists (also called blockers or sympatholytic agents) bind to adrenoceptors but do not trigger the usual receptor-mediated intracellular effects. These drugs act by either reversibly or irreversibly attaching to the receptor, thus preventing its activation by endogenous catecholamines.

Drugs block the actions of circulating catecholamine (EP and NE) on adrenergic receptors.

Also inhibit the effects of adrenergic nerve stimulation.

## Classification of Sympatholytic Drugs

A. Alpha ($\alpha$) Adrenoceptor Antagonists

B. Beta ($\beta$) Adrenoceptor Antagonists

C. Alpha ($\alpha$) and Beta ($\beta$) Adrenoceptor Antagonists

## Alpha-Adrenergic Antagonists (Blockers)

### Classification of $\alpha$ Antagonist

1. Non-specific $\alpha_1$ and $\alpha_2$ antagonists: Phentolamine and Phenoxybenzamine
2. Specific $\alpha_1$ antagonist: Prazosin, Doxazosin, Terazosin, Tamsulosin and Alfuzosin
3. Specific $\alpha 2$ antagonist: Yohimbine and Tolazoline

#### Introduction

The clinically important $\alpha$-blockers fall primarily into three chemical groups: The Haloalkylamines (e.g., phenoxybenzamine), the Imidazolines (e.g., phentolamine), and the Quinazoline derivatives (e.g., Prazosin). Of these three classes of $\alpha$-adrenoceptor antagonists, the quinazoline compounds are of greatest clinical utility. The use of the haloalkylamines and imidazolines has diminished in recent years because they lack selectivity for $\alpha_1$ and $\alpha_2$ receptors.

### Quinazoline Derivatives

The chief use of these drugs is in the management of primary hypertension. Examples of quinazoline $\alpha$-blockers include Prazosin (Minipress), Trimazosin (Cardovar), Terazosin (Hytrin), and Doxazosin (Cardura).

#### Mechanism of Action

The $\alpha$-antagonism produced by prazosin Fig 14-1 and the other quinazoline derivatives is of the equilibrium-competitive type. The drugs are selective for $\alpha_1$-adrenoceptors, so that at usual therapeutic concentrations there is little or negligible antagonism of $\alpha_2$-adrenoceptors. However, selectivity is only relative and can be lost with high drug concentrations. While most of the pharmacological effects of prazosin are directly attributable to $\alpha_1$-antagonism, at high doses the drug can cause vasodilation by a direct effect on smooth muscle independent of $\alpha$-receptors. This action appears to be related to an inhibition of phosphodiesterase that results in an enhancement of intracellular levels of cyclic nucleotides.

Prazosin Hydrochloride
$C_{19}H_{21}N_5O_4HCl$

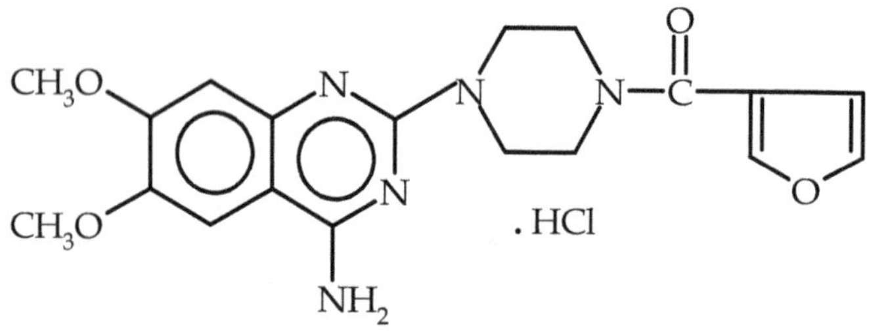

**Fig 14-1:** Prazosin

**Pharmacokinetics**

Prazosin is readily absorbed after oral administration, peak serum levels occur approximately 2 hours after a single oral dose, and the antihypertensive effect of Prazosin persists for up to 10 hours. Its half-life in plasma ranges from 2.5 to 4 hours, and elimination from plasma appears to follow first-order kinetics. The drug is extensively (perhaps as high as 97%) bound to plasma proteins; this observation partially explains the lack of correlation between plasma drug levels and persistence of antihypertensive effect.

Hepatic O-Dealkylation and Glucuronide formation appear to be major pathways of biotransformation. Only about 10% of orally administered prazosin is excreted in the urine. Plasma levels of prazosin are increased in patients with renal failure; the nature of this interaction is unknown.

**Pharmacological Actions**

The most important pharmacological effect of prazosin is its ability to antagonize vascular smooth muscle contraction that is caused by either sympathetic nervous activity or the action of adrenomimetics. Haemodynamically, the effects of prazosin differ from those of phenoxybenzamine and phentolamine in that venous smooth muscle is not as much affected by prazosin. Postural hypotension during chronic treatment is also less of a problem. Also, increases in heart rate, contractile force, and plasma renin activity, which normally occur after the use of vasodilators and α-blockers, are much less prominent following chronic treatment with prazosin.

Phenoxybenzamine and phentolamine, in addition to blocking postsynaptic α-receptors, also block $\alpha_2$- receptors on nerves and therefore can enhance the release of norepinephrine. When norepinephrine exerts a postsynaptic action by means of β-adrenoceptors (e.g., cardiac stimulation, renin release), blockade of presynaptic $\alpha_2$-receptors by phenoxybenzamine and phentolamine may actually potentiate the responses. Prazosin blocks responses mediated by postsynaptic $\alpha_1$-receptors but has no effect on the presynaptic $\alpha_2$-receptors. Thus, stimulation of the heart and renin release is less prominent with this drug.

**Clinical Uses**

Prazosin is effective in reducing all grades of hypertension. The drug can be administered alone in mild and (in some instances) moderate hypertension. When the hypertension is moderate or severe, prazosin generally is given in combination with a thiazide diuretic and a β-blocker. The antihypertensive actions of Prazosin are considerably potentiated by co administration of thiazides or other types of antihypertensive drugs.

Prazosin may be particularly useful when patients cannot tolerate other classes of antihypertensive drugs or when blood pressure is not well controlled by other drugs. Since prazosin does not significantly influence blood uric acid or glucose levels, it can be used in hypertensive patients whose condition is complicated by diabetes mellitus or gout.

Prazosin and other α-antagonists find use in the management of benign prostatic obstruction, especially in patients who are not candidates for surgery. Blockade of α-adrenoceptors in the base of the bladder and in the prostate apparently reduces the symptoms of obstruction and the urinary urgency that occurs at night.

## Imidazoline Derivative

### Phentolamine (Fig 14-2)

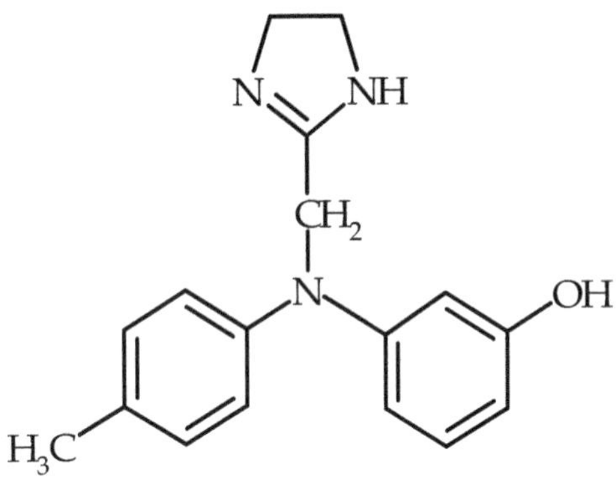


**Fig 14-2:** Phentolamine

*Mechanism of action:* Blocks both $\alpha_1$ and $\alpha_2$-receptors. Its primary action is vasodilation due to $\alpha_1$ blockade. It also can lead to reflex tachycardia because of hypotension and $\alpha_2$ inhibition, which increases sympathetic tone.

*Effects*

Antagonism of $\alpha_1$-receptors (possibly $\alpha_2$) of vascular smooth muscles leads to decrease in PVR and decrease in BP.

Cardiac stimulation in response to baroreflex mechanism.

Antagonism of presynaptic $\alpha_2$-receptors causes increase in release of NE from sympathetic nerves causing cardiac stimulation.

Inhibits response to serotonin, agonist of muscarinic, $H_1$ and $H_2$ histamine receptors.

*Pharmacokinetics:* Limited absorption after oral intake, other properties are not well known.

*Adverse effects:* Tachycardia, arrhythmias, myocardial ischemia, diarrhoea, increases gastric acid production.

*Therapeutic uses:* The primary application for Phentolamine is for the control of hypertensive emergencies, most notably due to erectile dysfunction (Pheochromocytoma).

It also has usefulness in the treatment of cocaine induced hypertension, where one would generally avoid beta blockers and where calcium channel blockers are not effective. Beta-blockers (i.e., Metoprolol) or combined alpha and beta adrenergic blocking agents (i.e., labetalol) should be avoided in patients with a history of cocaine abuse. They can cause an unopposed alpha-adrenergic mediated coronary vaso-constriction, causing the worsening of myocardial ischemia and hypertension.

Phentolamine also has diagnostic and therapeutic roles in complex regional pain syndrome (reflex sympathetic dystrophy).

Phentolamine has recently been introduced in the dental field as a local anesthetic reversal agent. Distributed by Novalar, OraVerse is a Phentolamine Mesylate injection designed to reverse the local vasoconstrictor properties used in many local anesthetics to prolong anesthesia.

## Haloalkylamines

### Phenoxybenzamine

**Mechanism of action:** Irreversible (covalent) binding to α-receptors (more selective for $\alpha_1$) long

Phenoxybenzamine Hydrochloride
$C_{10}H_{22}ClNO \cdot HCl$

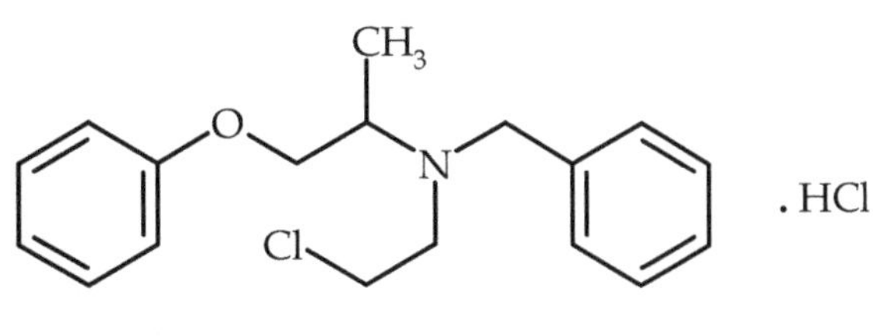


**Fig 14-3:** Phenoxybenzamine

duration (14-48 hr) blockade. Phenoxybenzamine produces its therapeutic actions by blocking alpha receptors, leading to a muscle relaxation and a widening of the blood vessels. This widening of the blood vessels results in a lowering of blood pressure.

Phenoxybenzamine is indicated for the control of episodes of hypertension and sweating that occur with a disease called pheochromocytoma. If tachycardia is excessive, it may be necessary to use a beta-blocking agent concomitantly. Phenoxybenzamine is a long-acting, adrenergic, alpha-receptor blocking agent which can produce and maintain "chemical sympathectomy" by oral administration. It increases blood flow to the skin, mucosa and abdominal viscera, and lowers both supine and erect blood pressures. It has no effect on the parasympathetic system. Phenoxybenzamine works by blocking alpha receptors in certain parts of the body. Alpha receptors are present in the muscle that lines the walls of blood vessels. When the receptors are blocked by Phenoxybenzamine, the muscle relaxes and the blood vessels widen. This widening of the blood vessels results in a lowering of blood pressure.

*Effects*

Inhibits reuptake of NE by pre-synaptic nerve terminals

Blocks $H_1$, ACh and 5-HT receptors

Blocks catechol-induced vasoconstriction and cause decrease in BP during high sympathetic tone (upright position)

*Pharmacokinetics*

Usually given orally, absorbed after oral intake with low starting dose of 10-20 mg/dl.

*Adverse Effects*

Postural hypotension, tachycardia, nasal stiffness, inhibition of ejaculation, fatigue, sedation and nausea.

*Therapeutic Uses*

An alpha-adrenergic antagonist with long duration of action. It has been used to treat hypertension and as a peripheral vasodilator. For the treatment of pheochromocytoma (malignant), benign prostatic hypertrophy and malignant essential hypertension.

**Terazosin** is another reversible $\alpha_1$-selective antagonist that is effective in hypertension; it is also approved for use in men with urinary symptoms due to benign prostatic hyperplasia (BPH). Terazosin has high bioavailability but is extensively metabolized in the liver, with only a small fraction of unchanged drug excreted in the urine. The half-life of terazosin is 9-12 hours.

**Doxazosin** is efficacious in the treatment of hypertension and BPH. It differs from prazosin and terazosin in having a longer half-life of about 22 hours. It has moderate bioavailability and is extensively metabolized, with very little parent drug excreted in urine or feces. Doxazosin has active metabolites, although their contribution to the drug's effects is probably small.

**Tamsulosin** is a competitive $\alpha_1$ antagonist with a structure quite different from that of most other $\alpha_1$-receptor blockers. It has high bioavailability and a long half-life of 9-15 hours. It is metabolized extensively in the liver. Tamsulosin has higher affinity for $\alpha_{1A}$ and $\alpha_{1D}$ receptors than for the $\alpha_{1B}$subtype. Evidence suggests that tamsulosin has relatively greater potency in inhibiting contraction in *prostate* smooth muscle versus *vascular* smooth muscle compared with other $\alpha_1$-selective antagonists. The drug's efficacy in BPH suggests that the $\alpha_{1A}$ subtype may be the most important $\alpha$ subtype mediating prostate smooth muscle contraction. Furthermore, compared with other antagonists, tamsulosin has less effect on standing blood pressure in patients. Nevertheless, "caution is appropriate in using any $\alpha$ antagonist in patients with diminished sympathetic nervous system function".

## Clinical Pharmacology of α-receptor Blocking Drugs

**1. Pheochromocytoma**

Tumor of adrenal medulla; releases mix of EP, NE; patients have increase BP, tachycardia, arrhythmia

Phenoxybenzamine used in

(a) Chronic treatment of inoperable or metastatic condition

(b) Phentolamine used to manage increased BP

2. **Hypertensive emergencies**

Limited use of α-antagonist, only labetalol is used

3. **Chronic hypertension**

Members of prazosin family are effective for mild to moderate systemic hypertension. Major advantageous effect is postural hypotension; dizziness.

4. **Peripheral vascular disease**

Phentolamine, prazosin, phenoxybenzamine used in Raynaud's phenomenon; excessive reversible vasospasm in peripheral circulation.

5. **Local vasoconstrictor excess**

Phentolamine reverses intense local vasoconstriction caused by infiltration of α-agonists into subcutaneous tissues.

6. **Urinary obstruction**

(a) Partial reversal of smooth muscle contraction in enlarged prostate and in bladder base

(b) Effect on cells in prostate and improve symptoms of BPH e.g., prazosin, doxazosin and terazosin useful for BPH + hypertensive patients

(c) Tamsulosin effective for those BPH patients having postural hypotension

7. **Erectile dysfunction**

E.g., Phentolamine

## β-Adrenergic Antagonists

### Introduction

β-adrenergic antagonists (Fig 14-4) are clinically important drugs, used in treatment of hypertension, coronary vascular disease and arrhythmias. Propranolol is an example of a non-selective β-adrenergic receptor blocker, i.e., capable of blocking both $\beta_1$ and $\beta_2$ receptor subtypes.

Metoprolol (Lopressor) and atenolol (Tenormin) are examples of $\beta_1$ selective drugs, having a greater affinity for $\beta_1$ compared to $\beta_2$ receptor subtypes. The selectivity is not absolute in that a "$\beta_1$ selective" drug will interact with $\beta_2$ sites.

$\beta_1$ selective antagonists are cardioselective receptor blockers exert most of their therapeutic actions on the cardiovascular system.

### Mechanism of Action

All of the β-blockers exert equilibrium-competitive antagonism of the actions of catecholamines and other adrenomimetics at β-receptors. Probably the best recognized action of these compounds that is not mediated by a β-receptor is depression of cellular membrane excitability. This effect has been described as a membrane-stabilizing action, a quinidine like effect, or a local anesthetic effect. This action is not too surprising in view of the structural similarities between β-blockers and local anesthetics. However, with the usual therapeutic doses, the actions of the β-receptor blocking agents appear to be almost entirely accounted for by their β-receptor antagonism. Because the β-receptors of the heart are primarily of the $\beta_1$ type and those in the pulmonary and vascular smooth muscle are $\beta_2$ receptors, $\beta_1$ -selective antagonists are frequently referred to as cardioselective blockers.

### Absorption, Metabolism, and Excretion

Propranolol (Inderal) is suitable for both parental and oral administration. Absorption from the gastrointestinal tract is extensive. The peak therapeutic effect after oral administration occurs in 1 to 1.5 hours. The plasma half-life of propranolol is approximately 3 hours. The drug is concentrated in the lungs and to a lesser extent in the liver, brain, kidneys, and heart. Binding to plasma proteins is extensive (90%). The liver is the chief organ involved in the metabolism of propranolol, and the drug is subject to a

**Table 14-1:** Comparative information about the three classes of α-adrenoceptor antagonists

| | Haloalkylamines | Imidazolines | Quinazolines |
|---|---|---|---|
| Prototype | Phenoxybenzamine (Dibenzyline) | Phentolamine (Regitine) | Prazosin (Minipress) |
| Others | | Tolazoline (Priscoline) | Terazosin (Hytrin)<br>Doxazosin (Cardura)<br>Trimazosin (Cardovar) |
| Antagonism | Irreversible (non-equilibrium) competitive | Equilibrium competitive | Equilibrium competitive |
| Selectivity<br>Hemodynamic effects | Somewhat selective for $\alpha_1$<br>Decreased peripheral vascular resistance and blood pressure<br>Venodilation is prominent<br>Cardiac stimulation occurs because of cardiovascular reflexes and enhanced release of norepinephrine | Nonselective similar to phenoxybenzamine | Selective for $\alpha_2$<br>Decreased peripheral vascular resistance and blood pressure<br>Veins seem to be less susceptible to antagonism than arteries; thus, postural hypotension is less of a problem<br>Cardiac stimulation is less because release of norepinephrine is not enhanced |
| Actions other than α -blockade | Some antagonism of responses to ACh, 5-HT, and histamine<br>Blockade of neuronal and extraneuronal uptake | Cholinomimetic, adrenomimetic, and histamine like actions<br>Antagonism of responses to 5-HT | At high doses some direct vasodilator action, probably due to phosphodiesterase inhibition |
| Routes | Intravenous and oral<br>Oral absorption incomplete and erratic | Similar to phenoxybenzamine | Oral |
| Adverse reactions | Postural hypotension, tachycardia, miosis, nasal stuffiness, failure of ejaculation | Same as phenoxybenzamine and in addition gastrointestinal disturbances | Some postural hypotension, especially with the first dose; less of a problem overall than with phenoxybenzamine or phentolamine |
| Therapeutic uses | Conditions of catecholamine excess such as pheochromocytoma<br>Peripheral vascular disease<br>Benign prostatic hypertrophy | Same as phenoxybenzamine | Primary hypertension<br>Benign prostatic hypertrophy |

*ACh, acetylcholine; 5-HT, 5-hydroxytryptamine.

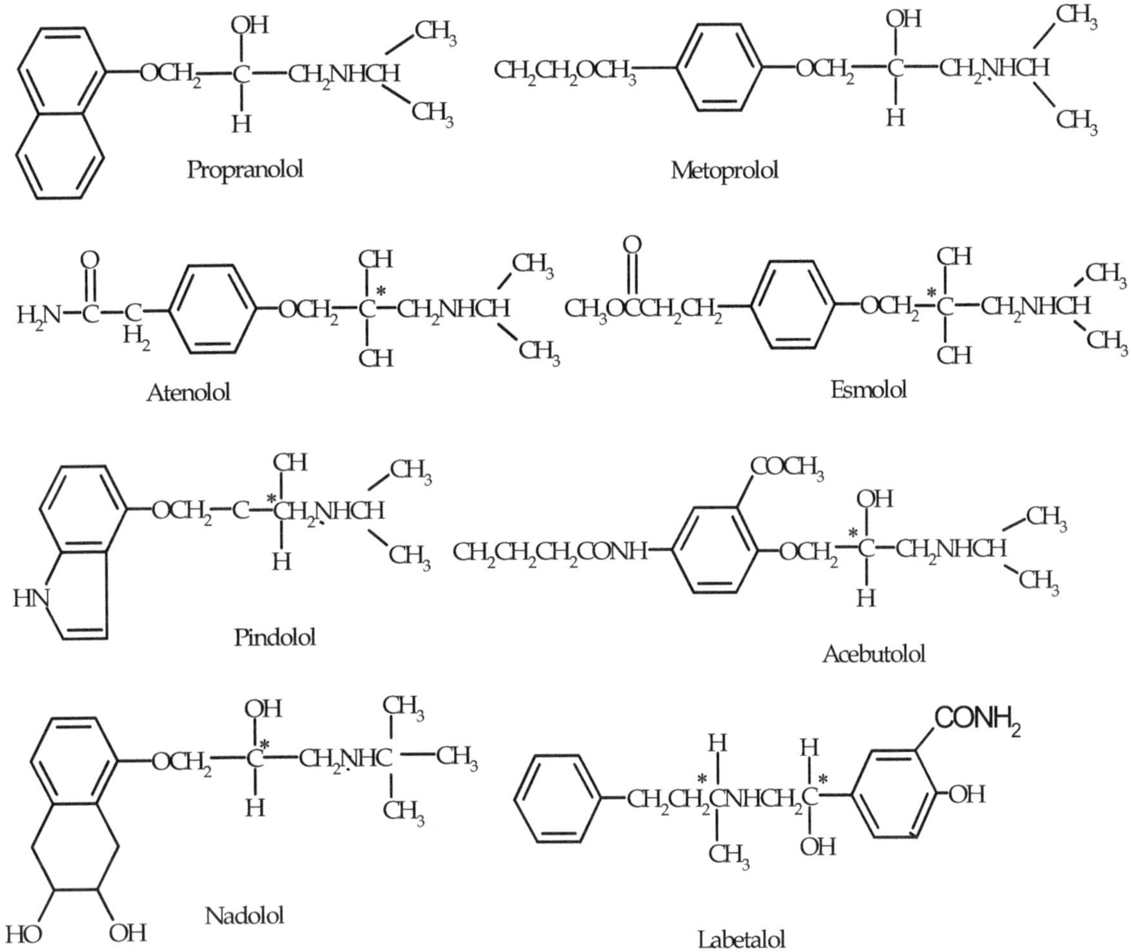


**Fig 14-4 :** Beta blockers

significant degree of first-pass metabolism. At least eight metabolites have been recovered from the urine, the major excretory route.

The pharmacokinetic profile of metoprolol (Lopressor) is similar to that of propranolol. Metoprolol is readily and rapidly absorbed after oral administration and is subject to a significant amount of first-pass metabolism by the liver. Curiously, the duration of metoprolol's action is longer than one would predict from its plasma half-life, which ranges from 0.5 to 2.5 hours. The degree of binding of metoprolol to plasma proteins is modest (10%). The extensive distribution of metoprolol to the lungs and kidney is typical of a moderately lipophilic drug. Metoprolol undergoes considerable metabolism; only 3 to 10% of an administered dose is recovered as unchanged drug. The metabolites are essentially inactive as β-receptor blocking agents and are eliminated primarily by renal excretion. Small amounts of the drug are present in the feces.

Timolol (Timoptic) is almost completely absorbed from the gastrointestinal tract. Peak plasma levels occur 2 to 4 hours after oral administration; the plasma half life of timolol is approximately 5.5 hours. The extensive tissue distribution of timolol into lung, liver, and kidney is similar to that of other β-blockers. Approximately70% of the drug is excreted in the urine within 24 hours, mostly as highly polar unconjugated metabolites. Only 6% of an administered dose is recovered in the feces. Although timolol is approved for the topical treatment of elevated intraocular pressure, there is limited information about its pharmacokinetics following administration by this route. The drug apparently can reach the systemic circulation after intraocular instillation, but plasma levels are only about 7% of those achieved in the aqueous humor. About half of an orally administered dose of acebutolol (Sectral) is absorbed. Approximately 25% of the drug is bound to plasma proteins, and its plasma half life is about 4 hours. Metabolism of acebutolol produces a metabolite with β-blocking activity whose half-life is 10 hours. Roughly half of an orally administered dose of atenolol (Tenormin) is absorbed. The drug is eliminated primarily by the kidney and unlike propranolol, undergoes little hepatic metabolism. Its plasma half-life is approximately 6 hours, although if it is administered to a patient with impaired renal function, its half-life can be considerably prolonged.

Absorption of an oral dose of betaxolol (Kerlone, Betoptic) is almost complete. The drug is subject to a slight first-pass effect such that the absolute bioavailability of the drug is about 90%. Approximately 50% of administered betaxolol binds to plasma proteins, and its plasma half-life is about 20 hours; it is suitable for dosing once per day. The primary route of elimination is by liver metabolism, with only 15% of unchanged drug being excreted.

Carteolol (Cartrol) is a long-acting β-blocker that is suitable for dosing once per day. It is almost completely absorbed and exhibits about 30% binding to plasma proteins. Unlike many β-blockers, carteolol is not extensively metabolized. Up to 70% of an administered dose is excreted unchanged.

The β-blocker esmolol (Brevibloc) is unusual in that 9 minutes. It is subject to hydrolysis by cytosolic esterases in red blood cells to yield methanol and an acid metabolite, the latter having an elimination half-life of about 4 hours. Only 2% of the administered esmolol is excreted unchanged. Because of its rapid onset and short duration of action, esmolol is used by the intravenous route for the control of ventricular arrhythmias in emergencies.

Nadolol (Corgard) is slowly and incompletely absorbed from the gastrointestinal tract, and only 30% of an orally administered dose is absorbed. Appreciable metabolism does not seem to occur; nadolol is excreted primarily unchanged in the urine and feces. The plasma half-life is quite long, approaching 24 hours, which permits dosing once per day.

Pindolol (Visken) is extensively absorbed from the gastrointestinal tract. First-pass metabolism is estimated at about 15%, and its plasma half-life is on the order of 3 to 4 hours. The binding of pindolol to plasma proteins is approximately 50%. The metabolic fate of pindolol is not completely understood, although 50% of an administered dose is recovered, primarily in the urine, as unchanged drug.

## Effects

### *Heart*

Decrease heart rate. Reduce contractility and decrease conduction velocity in atria and AV node. Decrease phase 4 depolarization reduce myocardial oxygen demand and increased refractory period of the AV node.

### *Antihypertensive Effects*

β receptor blockers reduce blood pressure in patients with hypertension (not in normal subjects) receptor blockers are effective in reducing blood pressure in both "high-renin" and "low-renin" patients. Renin release in response to sympathetic stimulation is blocked by β receptor blockers. A long-term reduction in peripheral resistance, in addition to a reduction in cardiac output, contributes to the antihypertensive effects of β receptor blockers. (Mechanism for reduction in peripheral resistance is unknown) Some antihypertensive β receptor blockers also exhibit α-receptor blocking properties, e.g., Labetalol. In this case, reduction in peripheral resistance is explained by α-receptor blocking properties

*Pulmonary Effects*

In asthmatic patients or patients with COPD (chronic obstructive pulmonary disease) β receptor blockers cause dangerous bronchiolar constriction. This effect is particularly prominent with nonselective β receptor blockers, such as propranolol.

*Metabolic Actions*

β adrenergic receptor antagonists influence carbohydrate and lipid metabolism. Catecholamine's increase glycogenolysis and glucose availability in hypoglycaemia: this response is reduced by β adrenergic receptor antagonists. In insulin-dependent diabetes, adrenergic receptor antagonists impede recovery from hypoglycaemia. Adrenergic receptor antagonists may mask symptoms of hypoglycaemia. This property interferes with the patient's ability to anticipate a hypoglycaemic episode. Circulating free fatty acids are utilized by exercising muscle. Increasing availability of free fatty acids may be mediated by $\beta_3$ adrenergic receptor subtypes. β adrenergic receptor antagonists interfere with this metabolic response. β adrenergic receptor agonists decrease plasma $K^+$ concentration by promoting transport into cells, primarily muscle. In exercise, serum $K^+$ increases. Catecholamines are involved in regulating serum levels. β adrenergic receptor antagonists' interfere with this $K^+$ regulation mechanism.

*Other Effects*

β adrenergic receptor antagonists block catecholamine-induced tremor and mast-cell degranulation.

## Nonselective-β Adrenergic Receptor Antagonists

**Propranolol (Inderal):** Lipophilic nonselective β adrenergic receptor antagonist.

Effective in treating essential hypertension, angina, certain arrhythmias.

Propranolol (Inderal) decreases amide local anesthetic clearance by decreasing hepatic blood flow and inhibiting hepatic metabolism.

**Bupivacaine (Marcaine):** 35% decrease in clearance probably due to metabolic effects since bupivacaine is a low extraction drug (not sensitive to hepatic blood flow changes). Possible increases in systemic toxicity of bupivacaine (Marcaine) (and other amide local anesthetics) when the anesthetics are administered concurrently with propranolol (Inderal).

Propranolol (Inderal) (after chronic administration) reduces pulmonary first-pass uptake of fentanyl (Sublimaze). As a consequence: immediately after fentanyl (Sublimaze) administration, 2X to 4X more injected fentanyl (Sublimaze) reaches into the systemic circulation as propranolol (a basic, lipophilic amine) inhibits the pulmonary uptake of a second basic lipophilic amine (fentanyl).

**Nadolol (Corgard):** Nonselective β adrenergic receptor antagonist having long half-life. May accumulate in patient with renal dysfunction.

**Timolol (Blocadren):** Nonselective β adrenergic receptor antagonist used for treatment of glaucoma. Systemic effects common after ocular application.

Bradycardia and hypotension, refractory to atropine, may occur during anesthesia in pediatric and adult patients receiving topical timolol (Blocadren).

May impair Neonatal Ventilation – An unexpected postoperative apnea may Ensue (Blood-Brain Barrier Immaturity in the neonate may facilitate CNS access and promote this effect). Contraindicated in patients with congestive heart failure .

## Selective-$\beta_1$ Adrenergic Receptor Antagonists

**Metoprolol (Lopressor)**

Cardioselective $\beta_1$ adrenergic receptor antagonist. Effective in treating essential hypertension. Effective in treating symptoms of coronary artery disease. Contraindicated in management of acute myocardial infarction if heart rates are < 45 bpm.

**Esmolol (Brevibloc)**

Cardioselective $\beta_1$ adrenergic receptor antagonist. Very short duration of action I.V. administration effective in rapid termination of paroxysmal supraventricular arrhythmias. Short duration of action (plasma esterases, not plasma cholinesterase's) is beneficial in management of intraoperative adverse BP/heart rate increases associated with noxious stimulation (e.g., during tracheal intubation). IV esmolol administration before direct laryngoscopy in tracheal intubation protects against heart rate in systolic blood pressure increases typically associated with tracheal intubation. Preoperative hypertension and tachycardia may also be generally prevented by esmolol (Brevibloc) administration over a 15 second period before anaesthesia induction.

Esmolol (Brevibloc), I.V, administered to patients undergoing electroconvulsive treatment and anesthetized with methohexital (Brevital) and succinylcholine (Anectine) have reduced positive chronotropic effects and reduced duration of electrically-induced seizures.

**Other uses:** Reduced catecholamine release during anaesthesia in patients with hypertrophic obstructive cardiomyopathy.

Reduced catecholamine release in patients experiencing hypercyanotic spells (associated with tetralogy of Fallot).

Esmolol (Brevibloc) reduces plasma propofol concentration needed to prevent patient movement upon surgical skin incision—unknown mechanism.

**Atenolol (Tenormin)**

Most cardioselective $\beta_1$ adrenergic receptor antagonist. Used in treating hypertension, somewhat longer action compared to metoprolol. Atenolol may have special benefit for patients undergoing noncardiac surgery but having significant underlying coronary artery disease: preoperative IV Atenolol (Tenormin), postoperative IV Atenolol (Tenormin), and oral therapy during hospitalization reduces mortality and incidence of cardiovascular complications.

Preoperative atenolol (Tenormin) for high-risk patients (CHD): reduces postoperative myocardial ischemia incidence.

## Therapeutic uses for Beta Adrenergic Receptor Antagonists (Blockers)

The β-receptor blocking agents have widespread and important uses in the management of cardiac arrhythmias, angina pectoris, and hypertension. Even though acute administration of β-blockers can precipitate congestive heart failure in patients who are largely dependent on enhanced sympathetic nerve activity to maintain sufficient cardiac output, the β-blockers have been shown to be quite useful in the long-term management of patients with mild to moderate heart failure. The β-blockers also offer proven benefit in preventing the recurrence of a myocardial infarction (MI). For this purpose, it is best if β-blocker therapy is instituted soon after the MI and continued for the long term.

## Hyperthyroidism

The β-blockers significantly reduce the peripheral manifestations of hyperthyroidism, particularly elevated heart rate, increased cardiac output, and muscle tremors. Although the β -blockers can improve the clinical status of the hyperthyroid patient, the patient remains biochemically hyperthyroid. The β-blockers should not be used as the sole form of therapy in hyperthyroidism. They are most logically employed in the management of hyperthyroid crisis, in the preoperative preparation for thyroidectomy, and during the initial period of administration of specific antithyroid drugs.

## Glaucoma

β-Blockers can be used topically to reduce intraocular pressure in patients with chronic open-angle glaucoma and ocular hypertension. The mechanism by which ocular pressure is reduced appears to depend on decreased production of aqueous humor. Timolol has a somewhat greater ocular hypotensive effect than do the available cholinomimetic or adrenomimetic drugs. The β-blockers also are beneficial in the treatment of acute angle-closure glaucoma.

## Anxiety States

Patients with anxiety have a variety of psychic and somatic symptoms. The peripheral manifestations of anxiety may include a number of symptoms (e.g., palpitations) that are due in part to overactivity of the sympathetic nervous system.

## Migraine

The β-blockers may offer some value in the prophylaxis of migraine headache, possibly because a blockade of craniovascular β-receptors results in reduced vasodilation. The painful phase of a migraine attack is believed to be produced by vasodilation.

## Angina Pectoris

The primary goal of beta-blocking agent therapy is to reduce cardiac responses to sympathetic nervous system activation by exertion, emotion, and other types of stress. Limiting or preventing sympathetically induced increases in heart rate, contractility, and systolic blood pressure minimizes increases in myocardial oxygen demand. Doses required to achieve these goals often reduce resting heart rate. This effect may slightly increase ventricular end-systolic volume and myocardial oxygen demand, but this concern is not a clinically important problem. Also, nonselective beta-blocking agents risk coronary vasospasm owing to unopposed alpha-adrenergic receptor responses, but this too is not a clinically important problem, possibly because of routine use of coronary vasodilators (e.g., nitroglycerin). Side-effects of antianginal therapy with beta-blocking agents are considered in the following, but the most common complaints from chronic ingestion are mental depression, fatigue, limited work capacity, and impotence.

## Acute Myocardial Infarction

Clinical trials of intravenous beta-adrenergic blockers in the early phases of acute myocardial infarction suggest that mortality decreases 10 percent. Following myocardial infarction, chronic oral beta-blocking agents reduce the incidence of recurrent myocardial infarction. The major risk of beta-blocking agents after acute myocardial infarction is congestive heart failure, since the heart may be dependent on sympathetic tone to maintain cardiac output.

## Supraventricular Tachycardias and Ventricular Dysrhythmias

Adrenergic beta-blocking agents are Class II antidysrhythmics that primarily block cardiac responses to catecholamines. Beta-blocking agents decrease spontaneous depolarization in the sinus and atrioventricular (AV) nodes, decrease automaticity in Purkinje fibers, increase AV nodal refractoriness, increase the threshold for fibrillation (but not for depolarization), and decrease ventricular slow responses that are dependent on catecholamines. There is evidence that beta-blocking agents also decrease intramyocardial conduction in ischemic tissue and reduce the risks of dysrhythmias, to the extent that they decrease myocardial ischemia. Beta-adrenergic blockers are not particularly effective in controlling dysrhythmias that are not induced or maintained by catecholamines. Membrane stabilizing effects of beta-adrenergic blockers occur at doses much higher than those tolerated by patients.

## Hypertension

The mechanisms for the antihypertensive effects of beta-adrenergic receptor blockers is incomplete, yet it is clear that these effects are caused by beta blockade. During the early phases of therapy there is a decrease in cardiac output, a rise in systemic vascular resistance (SVR), and relatively little change in mean arterial blood pressure. Within hours to days SVR normalizes and blood pressure declines. In addition, the release of renin from the juxtaglomerular apparatus in the kidney is inhibited ($beta_1$ blockade). Presumably, beta-blocking agents with intrinsic agonistic activity reduce systemic vascular resistance below pretreatment levels, presumably by activating $beta_2$ receptors in vascular smooth muscle. In addition, labetalol has the ability to block alpha-adrenergic receptors on vascular smooth muscle. Most often beta-adrenergic receptor blockers are used with other drugs in the treatment of chronic hypertension. When combined with a vasodilator, beta-blocking agents limit reflex tachycardia. When propranolol is combined with intravenous nitroprusside, the beta-blocking agent prevents reflex release of renin and reflex tachycardia induced by the vasodilator.

## Adverse Effects of β Adrenergic Receptor Antagonists

The most prominent side effects associated with the administration of the β-blockers are those directly attributable to their ability to block β-receptors. Although β-blockers prevent an increase in heart rate and cardiac output resulting from an activation of the autonomic nervous system, these effects may not be troublesome in patients with adequate or marginal cardiac reserve. However, they can be life threatening for a patient with congestive heart failure. Also, because conduction of impulses in the heart may be slowed by β-blockers, patients with conduction disturbances, particularly through the atrioventricular node, should not be treated with β-blockers.

Caution must be exercised in the use of β-blockers in obstructive airway disease, since these drugs promote further bronchoconstriction. Cardioselective β-blockers have less propensity to aggravate bronchoconstriction than do nonselective β-blockers.

β-Blockers potentiate hypoglycemia by antagonizing the catecholamine-induced mobilization of glycogen. The use of β-blockers in hypoglycemic patients is therefore dangerous and must be undertaken with caution. If β-blocker therapy is required, a cardioselective β-blocker is preferred.

Whenever β-blocker therapy is employed, the period of greatest danger for asthmatics or insulin- dependent diabetics is during the initial period of drug administration, since the greatest disruption of the autonomic balance will occur at this time. If marked toxicity does not occur during this period, further doses are less likely to cause problems.

Although the β-blockers produce a number of central effects, it is not clear whether these effects are due to blockade of central β-receptors. After high doses, patients may have hallucinations, nightmares, insomnia, and depression.

Topical application of timolol to the eye is well tolerated, and the incidence of side effects, which consist of burning or dryness of the eyes, is reported to be 5 to 10%.

In spite of the potential seriousness of some of their side effects, β-blockers as a class are well tolerated and patient compliance is good.

## Drugs with Combined α- and β-Blocking Activity

## Labetalol

Labetalol (Normodyne, Trandate) Fig 9-5 possesses both α-blocking and β-blocking activity and is approximately one-third as potent as propranolol as a β-blocker and one-tenth as potent as phentolamine as a α-blocker. The ratio of β- to α-activity is about 3:1 when Labetalol is administered orally and about 7: 1 when it is administered intravenously. Thus the drug can be most conveniently thought of as a β-blocker with some α-blocking properties.

### Mechanism of Action

Labetalol produces equilibrium-competitive antagonism at β-receptors but does not exhibit selectivity for $\beta_1$- or $\beta_2$-receptors. Like certain other β-blockers (e.g., pindolol and timolol), labetalol possesses some degree of intrinsic activity. This intrinsic activity, or partial

Labetalol Hydrochloride
$C_{19}H_{24}N_2O_3.HCl$

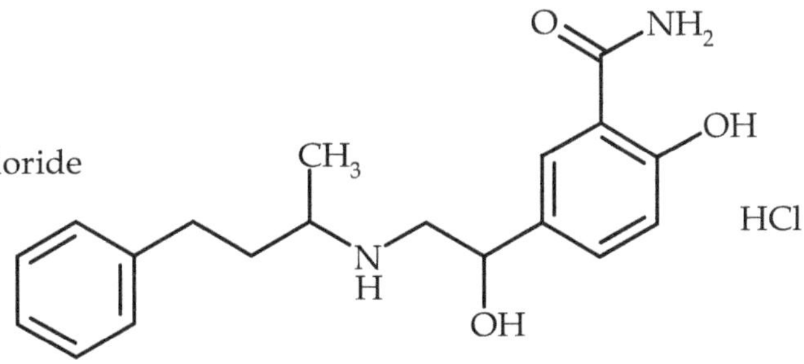

**Fig 14-5:** Structure of labetalol

agonism, especially at $\beta_2$-receptors in the vasculature, has been suggested to contribute to the vasodilator effect of the drug. The membrane-stabilizing effect, or local anesthetic action, of propranolol and several other β- blockers, is also possessed by labetalol, and in fact the drug is a reasonably potent local anesthetic.

The α-blockade produced by labetalol is also of the equilibrium-competitive type. In a manner similar to prazosin, labetalol exhibits selectivity for $\alpha_1$-receptors. Presynaptic α-receptors, which are of the $\alpha_2$ subclass, are not antagonized by labetalol. The drug also has some intrinsic activity at α-receptors, although this action is less than its intrinsic β-receptor–stimulating effects.

Labetalol appears to produce relaxation of vascular smooth muscle not only by α-blockade but also by a partial agonist effect at $\beta_2$-receptors. In addition, labetalol may produce vascular relaxation by a direct non–receptor-mediated effect.

Labetalol can block the neuronal uptake of norepinephrine and other catecholamines. This action, plus its slight intrinsic activity at α-receptors, may account for the seemingly paradoxical, although infrequent, increase in blood pressure seen on its initial administration.

**Pharmacokinetics**

Labetalol is almost completely absorbed from the gastrointestinal tract. However, it is subject to considerable first-pass metabolism, which occurs in both the gastrointestinal tract and the liver, so that only about 25% of an administered dose reaches the systemic circulation. While traces of unchanged labetalol are recovered in the urine, most of the drug is metabolized to inactive glucuronide conjugates. The plasma half-life of labetalol is 6 to 8 hours, and the elimination kinetics are essentially unchanged in patients with impaired renal failure.

**Pharmacological Actions**

Although capable of antagonizing a variety of responses in a number of effectors that are mediated by both α- and β-receptors, the most important actions of labetalol are on the cardiovascular system. These effects vary from individual to individual and depend on the sympathetic and parasympathetic tone at the time of drug administration.

The most common hemodynamic effect of acutely administered labetalol in humans is a decrease in peripheral vascular resistance and blood pressure without an appreciable alteration in heart rate or cardiac output.

This pattern differs from that seen following administration with either a conventional α- βor β-blocker. Acute administration of α-blocker produces a decrease in heart rate and cardiac output with little effect on blood pressure, while acute administration of an - blocker leads to a decrease in peripheral vascular resistance and a reflexively initiated increase in cardiac rate and output. Thus, the pattern of cardiovascular responses observed after labetalol administration combines the features of α- and β-blockade, that is, a decrease in peripheral vascular resistance (due to α-blockade and direct vascular effects) without an increase in cardiac rate and output (due to β-blockade).

Prolonged oral therapy with Labetalol results in cardiovascular responses similar to those obtained following conventional β-blocker administration, that is, decreases in peripheral vascular resistance, blood pressure, and heart rate. Generally, however, the decrease in heart rate is less pronounced than after administration of propranolol or other β-blockers.

### Clinical Uses

Labetalol is useful for the chronic treatment of primary hypertension. It can be used alone but is more often employed in combination with other antihypertensive agents. Labetalol also has been used intravenously for the treatment of hypertensive emergencies. Like conventional β-blockers, labetalol may be useful for patients with coexisting hypertension and anginal pain due to ischemia. It is also being investigated as a possible therapeutic modality for ischemic heart disease, even in the absence of hypertension. The benefit derives from its β-blocking activity, which decreases cardiac work, and from its ability to decrease afterload by virtue of its α-blocking activity.

Labetalol, because it possesses both α- and β-blocking activity, is useful for the preoperative management of patients with a pheochromocytoma.

### Adverse Effects

There have been reports of excessive hypotension and paradoxical pressor effects following intravenous administration of labetalol. These latter effects may be due to a labetalol-induced blockade of neuronal amine uptake, which increases the concentrations of norepinephrine in the vicinity of its receptors.

Approximately 5% of the patients who receive labetalol complain of side effects typical of noradrenergic nervous system suppression. These include postural hypotension, gastrointestinal distress, tiredness, sexual dysfunction, and tingling of the scalp. Most of these effects are related to α-blockade, although the tingling of the scalp may be due to the drug's intrinsic activity at α-receptors. Side effects associated with α-blockade, such as induction of bronchospasm and congestive heart failure, may also occur, but generally at a lower frequency than α-receptor–associated effects.

Skin rashes have been reported, as has an increase in the titer of antinuclear antibodies. Despite the latter observation, the appearance of a systemic lupus syndrome is rare. Labetalol also has been reported to interfere with chemical measurements of catecholamines and metabolites.

## Other Compounds

Several other β-adrenoceptor antagonists, similar to labetalol, exhibit some degree of α-receptor antagonism. These include bucindolol, carvedilol, and medroxalol.

## References

Blumenthal M, Goldberg A, and Brinckmann J. (eds.) (2000). Herbal Medicine: Expanded Commission E Monographs. Newton, MA: Integrative Medicine Communications.

Cupp MJ. (ed.) (2000). Toxicology and Clinical Pharmacology of Herbal Products. Totowa, NJ: Humana.

Fetrow CW and Avila JR (eds.) (1999). Professional's Handbook of Complementary and Alternative Medicines. Springhouse, PA: Springhouse.

CHAPTER

# Ganglionic Stimulating and Blocking Agents 15

## Introduction

Two natural alkaloids, *nicotine* and *lobeline*, exhibit peripheral actions by stimulating autonomic ganglia (Fig 10-1). Nicotine was first isolated from leaves of tobacco, *Nicotiana tobacum*, Langley and Dickinson painted the superior cervical ganglion of rabbits with nicotine and demonstrated that its site of action was the ganglion rather than the preganglionic or postganglionic nerve fiber. Lobeline, from *Lobelia inflata*, has many of the same actions as nicotine but is less potent.

A number of synthetic compounds also have prominent actions at ganglionic receptor sites. The actions of the "onium" compounds, of which *tetramethylammonium* (TMA) is the simplest prototype, were explored.

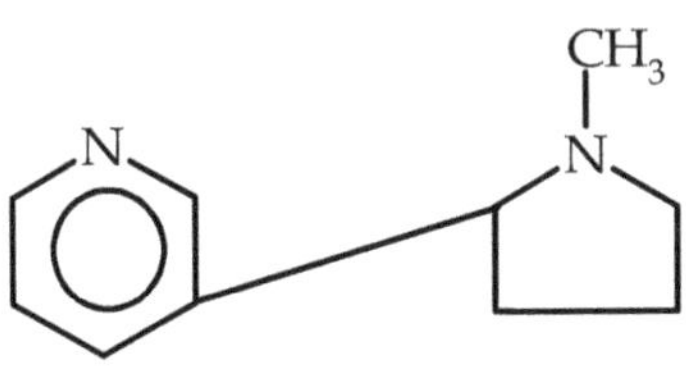

Nicotine

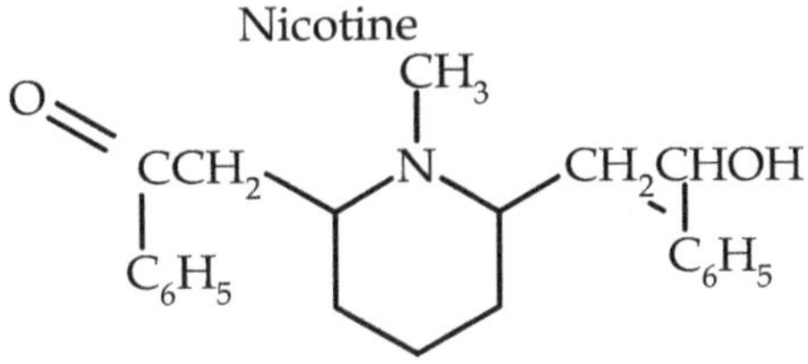

Lobeline

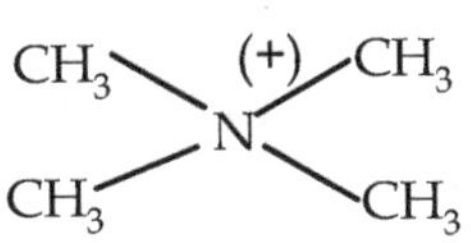

Tetramethylammonium (TMA)

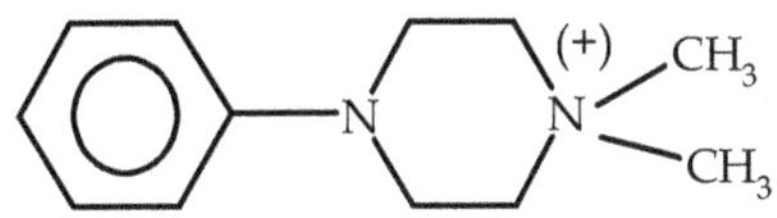

1,1-Dimethyl-4-Phenylpiperazinium (DMPP)

**Fig 15-1:** Ganglionic stimulants

## Mechanism of Action

Nicotine's actions are complex.

At low dosages it stimulates ganglionic nicotinic receptors (cause marked activation of these nicotinic receptors and initiate action potentials in postganglionic neurons) thus enhancing both sympathetic and parasympathetic neuro-transmission

- The initial response therefore often resembles simultaneous discharge of both the parasympathetic and the sympathetic nervous systems.
- In the case of the cardiovascular system, the effects of nicotine are chiefly sympathomimetic on blood vessels, and parasympathomimetic on the heart.
- In the GI and urinary tracts, the effects are largely parasympathomimetic.
- As nicotine dosages increase, there is stimulation of nicotinic receptors in many other sites.

  At high dosages, nicotine possesses some antagonist effect at nicotinic receptors.
- Prolonged exposure results in depolarizing blockade of the ganglia.

## Pharmacological Actions

The complex and often unpredictable changes that occur in the body after administration of nicotine are due not only to its actions on a variety of neuroeffector and chemosensitive sites but also to the fact that the alkaloid can stimulate and desensitize receptors. The ultimate response of any one system represents the summation of stimulatory and inhibitory effects of nicotine. For example, the drug can increase heart rate by excitation of sympathetic or paralysis of parasympathetic cardiac ganglia, and it can slow heart rate by paralysis of sympathetic or stimulation of parasympathetic cardiac ganglia. In addition, the effects of the drug on the chemoreceptor's of the carotid and aortic bodies and on brain centers influence heart rate, as do also the cardiovascular compensatory reflexes resulting from changes in blood pressure caused by nicotine. Finally, nicotine elicits a discharge of epinephrine from the adrenal medulla, which accelerates heart rate and raises blood pressure.

### Peripheral Nervous System

The major action of nicotine consists initially of transient stimulation and subsequently of a more persistent depression of all autonomic ganglia. Small doses of nicotine stimulate the ganglion cells directly and may facilitate impulse transmission. When larger doses of the drug are applied, the initial stimulation is followed very quickly by a blockade of transmission. Whereas stimulation of the ganglion cells coincides with their depolarization, depression of transmission by adequate doses of nicotine occurs both during the depolarization and after it has subsided. Nicotine also possesses a biphasic action on the adrenal medulla, small doses evoke the discharge of catecholamines, and larger doses prevent their release in response to splanchnic nerve stimulation.

The effects of nicotine on the neuromuscular junction are similar to those on ganglia. However, with the exception of avian and denervated mammalian muscle, the stimulant phase is obscured largely by the rapidly developing paralysis. In the latter stage, nicotine also produces neuromuscular blockade by receptor desensitization.

Nicotine, like ACh, is known to stimulate a number of sensory receptors. These include mechanoreceptors that respond to stretch or pressure of the skin, mesentery, tongue, lung, and stomach, chemoreceptors of the carotid body; thermal receptors of the skin and tongue, and pain receptors. Prior administration of hexamethonium prevents stimulation of the sensory receptors by nicotine but has little, if any effect on the activation of sensory receptors by physiological stimuli.

### Central Nervous System

Nicotine markedly stimulates the CNS. Low doses produce weak analgesia, with higher doses, tremors leading to convulsions at toxic doses are evident. The excitation of respiration is a prominent action of nicotine, although large doses act directly on the medulla oblongata, smaller doses augment respiration reflexly by excitation of the chemoreceptors of the carotid and aortic bodies. Stimulation of the CNS with large doses is followed by depression and death results from failure of respiration owing to both central paralysis and peripheral blockade of muscles of respiration.

Nicotine induces vomiting by both central and peripheral actions. The central component of the vomiting response is due to stimulation of the emetic chemoreceptor trigger zone in the area postrema of the medulla oblongata. In addition, nicotine activates vagal and spinal afferent nerves that form the sensory input of the reflex pathways involved in the act of vomiting. Studies in isolated higher centers of the brain and spinal cord reveal that the primary sites of action of nicotine in the CNS are prejunctional, causing the release of other transmitters. Accordingly, the stimulatory and pleasure-reward actions of nicotine appear to result from release of excitatory amino acids, dopamine, and other biogenic amines from various CNS centers. Release of excitatory amino acids may account for much of nicotine's stimulatory action.

## Cardiovascular System

When administered intravenously to dogs, nicotine characteristically produces an increase in heart rate and blood pressure. The latter is usually more sustained. In general, the cardiovascular responses to nicotine are due to stimulation of sympathetic ganglia and the adrenal medulla, together with the discharge of catecholamines from sympathetic nerve endings. Also contributing to the sympathomimetic response to nicotine is the activation of chemoreceptor's of the aortic and carotid bodies, which reflexly results in vasoconstriction, tachycardia, and elevated blood pressure.

## Gastrointestinal Tract

The combined activation of parasympathetic ganglia and cholinergic nerve endings by nicotine results in increased tone and motor activity of the bowel. Nausea, vomiting, and occasionally diarrhea are observed following systemic absorption of nicotine in an individual who has not been exposed to nicotine previously.

## Exocrine Glands

Nicotine causes an initial stimulation of salivary and bronchial secretions that is followed by inhibition.

## Pharmacokinetics

Nicotine is readily absorbed from the respiratory tract, buccal membranes, and skin. Severe poisoning has resulted from percutaneous absorption. Being a relatively strong base, its absorption from the stomach is limited. Intestinal absorption is far more efficient. Nicotine in chewing tobacco, because it is absorbed more slowly than inhaled nicotine, has a longer duration of effect. The average cigarette contains 6 to 11 mg nicotine and delivers about 1 to 3 mg nicotine systemically to the smoker, bio-availability can increase as much as threefold with intensity of puffing and technique of the smoker. Nicotine is available in several dosage forms help to achieve abstinence from tobacco use. Efficacy results primarily from preventing a withdrawal or abstinence syndrome. Nicotine may be administered orally as a gum (*nicotine polacrilex,*NICORETTE), transdermal patch (NICODERM, HABITROL, others), a nasal spray (NICOTROL NS), and a vapor inhaler (NICOTROL INHALER ). The first two are used most widely, and the objective is to obtain a sustained plasma nicotine concentration lower than venous blood concentrations after smoking. Arterial blood concentrations immediately following inhalation can be as much as tenfold higher than venous concentrations.

Approximately 80% to 90% of nicotine is altered in the body, mainly in the liver but also in the kidney and lungs. Cotinine is the major metabolite, with nicotine-1'-*N*-oxide and 3-hydroxycotinine and conjugated metabolites found in lesser quantities. The profile of metabolites and the rate of metabolism appear to be similar in smokers and nonsmokers. The half-life of nicotine following inhalation or parenteral administration is about 2 hours. Nicotine and its metabolites are eliminated rapidly by the kidney. The rate of urinary excretion of nicotine diminishes when the urine is alkaline. Nicotine also is excreted in the milk of lactating women who smoke; the milk of heavy smokers may contain 0.5 mg/L.

## Acute Nicotine Poisoning

Poisoning from nicotine may occur from accidental ingestion of nicotine-containing insecticide sprays or in children from ingestion of tobacco products. The acutely fatal dose of nicotine for an adult is probably about 60 mg of the base. Smoking tobacco usually contains 1% to 2% nicotine. Apparently, the gastric absorption of nicotine from tobacco taken by mouth is delayed because of slowed gastric emptying, so vomiting caused by the central effect of the initially absorbed fraction may remove much of the tobacco remaining in the GI tract.

The onset of symptoms of acute, severe nicotine poisoning is rapid; they include nausea, salivation, abdominal pain, vomiting, diarrhea, cold, sweat, headache, dizziness, disturbed hearing and vision, mental confusion, and marked weakness. Faintness and prostration ensue; the blood pressure falls; breathing is difficult; the pulse is weak, rapid, and irregular; and collapse may be followed by terminal convulsions. Death may result within a few minutes from respiratory failure.

## Therapy

Vomiting may be induced, or gastric lavage should be performed. Alkaline solutions should be avoided. A slurry of activated charcoal is then passed through the tube and left in the stomach. Respiratory assistance and treatment of shock may be necessary.

### Lobeline

Source and Chemistry. Lobeline (α-lobeline ; l-lobeline; inflatine) is the principal alkaloid of the dried leaves and tops of *Lobelia inflata.*

**Effects on organ systems**

The actions of lobeline are in many respects similar to those of nicotine, but lobeline has a potency of one-fifth to one-twentieth that of nicotine. Like nicotine, lobeline is a primary stimulant and a secondary depressant to the sympathetic ganglia, parasympathetic ganglia, adrenal medulla, medullary centers (especially the emetic centers), neuromuscular junction, and chemoreceptors in the carotid and aortic bodies

**Preparations and doses**

Lobelia Tincture (formerly listed in the National Formulary): oral dose, 1 ml orally.

Lobeline hydrochloride (listed in the International Pharmacopeia) : ampule containing 3 mg or 10 mg per m*l*; subcutaneous dose, 10 mg ; intravenous dose, 3 mg.

**Therapeutic uses**

Tincture of lobeline enjoyed some popularity in the past as a nauseant expectorant, especially in bronchial spasm. Lobeline is available for intravenous injection to stimulate respiration. A transient nature of the hyperpnea, which lasts only for a few minutes, and an accompanying apnea, vomiting, bradycardia, and hypotension in some subjects. The use of lobeline to resuscitate the newborn has been recommended, but experimental studies emphasize its hazards more than its usefulness. An injection of lobeline in the newborn rabbit was ineffective in producing hyperpnea in some rabbits. When it was effective, there was a narrow margin of safety between the dose to produce hyperpnea and the dose leading to convulsions.

The uncertain respiratory action of lobeline is understandable if its multiple actions are considered . The most desirable action of lobeline is a stimulation of receptors in the carotid and aortic bodies. Hyperpnea from this reflex is clear in a normal adult in eupnoea.

However, in a person in apnoea, the sensitivity of chemoreceptors may be reduced, perhaps because of poor development in some newborn babies, or because of the narcotic effect of the accompanying hypercapnia, even though the receptors are fully developed. The respiratory center may be depressed from other causes even though the chemoreceptors are excited by lobeline. Lobeline acts in other areas important to respiratory control.

## Other Ganglionic Stimulants

Stimulation of ganglia by tetramethylammonium (TMA) or *1,1-dimethyl-4-phenylpiperazinium iodide* (DMPP) differs from that produced by nicotine in that the initial stimulation is not followed by a dominant blocking action. DMPP is about three times more potent and slightly more ganglion-selective than nicotine. Although parasympathomimetic drugs stimulate ganglia, their effects usually are obscured by stimulation of other neuroeffector sites. McN-A-343 represents an exception to this; in certain tissues its primary action appears to occur at muscarinic $M_1$ receptors in ganglia.

## Ganglion-Blocking Drugs

Prevent reflex changes in heart rate elicited by vasoconstriction ($\beta_1$) and Vasodilation ($\beta_2$).

Do not prevent changes in H.R elicited directly by the drug ($\beta_1$ and M2).

Block the action of ACh and similar agonists at nicotinic receptors of both parasympathetic and sympathetic autonomic ganglia.

Ganglion-blocking drugs (10-2) are important and used in pharmacologic and physiologic research because they can block all autonomic outflow.

Lack of selectivity confers such a broad range of undesirable effects that they have limited clinical use.

### Classification

(i) Quarternary compounds: Hexamethonium
(ii) Tertiary compounds e.g., Pempidine
(iii) Secondary amine e.g., Mecamylamine
(iv) Complex monosulphonium compound e.g., Trimethaphan camphor sulphonate

## Chemistry and Pharmacokinetics

All ganglion-blocking drugs of interest are synthetic amines.

***Tetraethylammonium (TEA):***

- o The first to be recognized as having this action.
- o Has a very short duration of action.

Hexamethonium ("C6") was developed and was introduced clinically as the first drug effective for management of hypertension.

Decamethonium, the "C10" analog of hexamethonium, is a depolarizing neuromuscular blocking agent.

There is an obvious relationship between the structures of the agonist acetylcholine and the nicotinic antagonists tetraethylammonium and hexamethonium.

The quaternary amine ganglion-blocking compounds were poorly and erratically absorbed after oral administration.

**Mecamylamine,** a secondary amine, was developed to improve the degree and extent of absorption from the GIT.

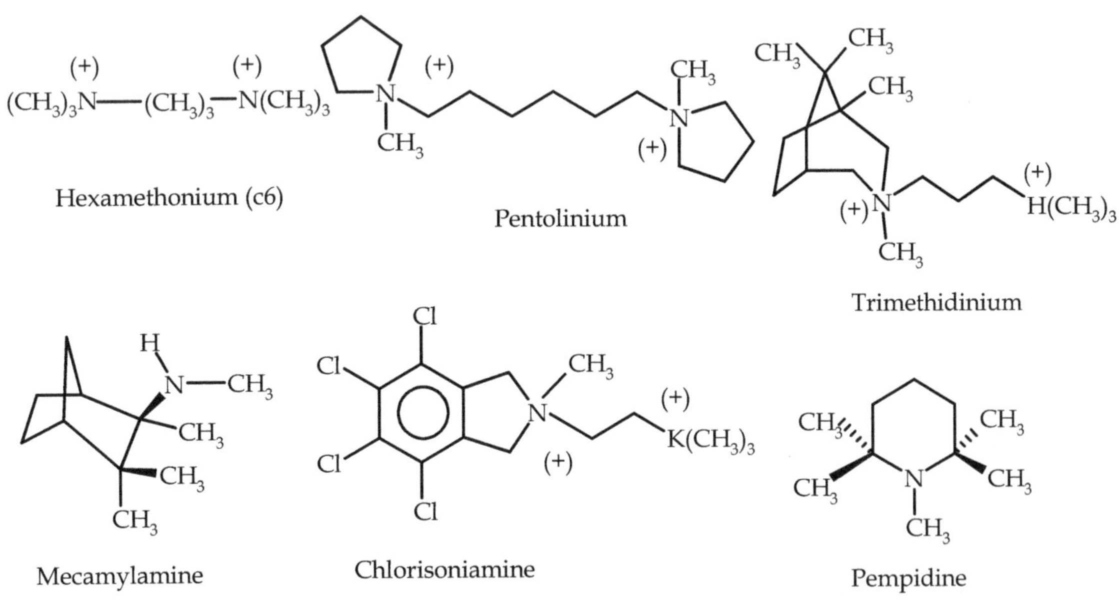


**Fig 15-2:** Ganglionic blockers

**Trimethaphan,** a short-acting ganglion blocker, is inactive orally and is given by intravenous infusion.

## Pharmacodynamics

### Mechanism of Action

Ganglionic nicotinic receptors are subject to both depolarizing and nondepolarizing blockade.

Nicotine and even acetylcholine (if amplified with Acetylcholinesterase inhibitor) can produce depolarizing ganglion block.

Drugs now used as ganglion blockers are classified as nondepolarizing competitive antagonists.

- o Hexamethonium actually produces most of its blockade by occupying sites in or on the nicotinic ion channel, not by occupying the cholinoceptor itself.
- o Trimethaphan appears to block the nicotinic receptor, not the channel.

Drugs can block autonomic ganglia by any one of several mechanisms. They may act presynaptically by affecting nerve conduction or neurotransmitter synthesis, release, or reuptake. Acting postjunctionally, drugs may affect the interaction between ACh and its receptor, or they may affect depolarization of the ganglion cell or initiation of a propagated action potential. The site of action of many blocking drugs has been shown to be at the associated ionic channel rather than at the receptor. Prolonged administration of ganglionic blocking drugs leads to the development of tolerance to their pharmacological effects.

## Organ System Effects

The effects of Ganglionic blockes are listed in Talbe 15-1.

### Central Nervous System

Mecamylamine, unlike the quaternary amine agents and trimethaphan, crosses the BBB and readily enters the CNS.

- o Sedation, tremor, choreiform movements, and mental aberrations.

### Eye

Cycloplegia with loss of accommodation because the ciliary muscle receives innervation primarily from the parasympathetic nervous system.

The effect on the pupil is not so easily predicted, moderate dilation of the pupil because parasympathetic tone usually dominates this tissue.

### Cardiovascular System

Blood vessels receive chiefly vasoconstrictor fibers from the sympathetic nervous system; therefore, ganglionic blockade causes a marked decrease in arteriolar and venomotor tone. Hypotension is marked in the upright position cardiac effects include diminished contractility and, sinoatrial node is usually dominated by the parasympathetic nervous system, a moderate tachycardia.

### Gastrointestinal Tract

Secretion is reduced, although not enough to effectively treat peptic disease. Motility is profoundly inhibited, and constipation can be marked.

### Genitourinary

Hesitancy in urination. Erection and ejaculation may be prevented by moderate doses.

## Clinical Applications and Toxicity

Use of the ganglion blockers is infrequent

Mecamylamine is being studied for possible use in reducing nicotine craving in patients

**Trimethaphan is occasionally used:**

- o Treatment of hypertensive emergencies and dissecting aortic aneurysm.
- o To produce controlled hypotension, which can be of value in neurosurgery to reduce bleeding in the operative field; and in patients undergoing electroconvulsive therapy.

### Hypertensive cardiovascular disease

Ganglionic blockers were once widely used in the management of essential hypertension, and they constituted an important advance in the treatment of that disease. Unfortunately, the development of tolerance to these drugs and their numerous undesirable side effects resulting from their nonselective ganglion-blocking properties led to a decline in their use. They have now been completely replaced by more effective and less toxic drugs. They do, however, retain some usefulness in the emergency treatment of hypertensive crisis.

### Controlled hypotension

Ganglionic blocking agents have been used to achieve controlled hypotension in plastic, neurological, and ophthalmological surgery. They are most commonly used in surgical procedures involving extensive skin dissection.

### Adverse effects

Many of these responses are undesirable effects that limit the therapeutic usefulness of these agents. Mild untoward responses include mydriasis, difficulty in vision accommodation, dry mouth, urinary hesitancy, constipation, diarrhea, abdominal discomfort, anorexia, and syncope. More serious but less frequent disturbances include marked hypotension, constipation, paralytic ileus, urinary retention, and anginal pain.

### Trimethaphan

Trimethaphan camsylate (Arfonad) is an extremely short-acting agent whose major therapeutic use is in the production of controlled hypotension in certain surgical procedures and in the emergency treatment of hypertensive crisis. Continuous infusion may be employed to maintain its antihypertensive effect, especially in patients with an acute dissecting aortic aneurysm. Much of the decrease in blood pressure following trimethaphan administration is thought to be due to its direct vasodilating properties. Trimethaphan can produce prolonged neuromuscular blockade in some patients, and therefore, it should be used with caution as a hypotensive agent during surgery. It also has been reported to potentiate the neuromuscular blocking action of tubocurarine, and because of its histamine-releasing properties, trimethaphan should be used with caution in patients with allergies.

### Mecamylamine

Mecamylamine hydrochloride (Inversine) is a secondary amine and can therefore easily penetrate cell membranes. Its absorption from

**Table 15-1:** Effects of ganglionic blockade

| Site | Predominant Tone | Effect of Ganglionic Blockade |
|---|---|---|
| Arterioles | Sympathetic (adrenergic) | Vasodilation; increased peripheral blood flow; hypotension |
| Veins | Sympathetic (adrenergic) | Dilation: peripheral pooling of blood; decreased venous return; decreased cardiac output |
| Heart | Parasympathetic (cholinergic) | Tachycardia |
| Iris | Parasympathetic (cholinergic) | Mydriasis |
| Ciliary muscle | Parasympathetic (cholinergic) | Cycloplegia-focus to far vision |
| Gastrointestinal tract | Parasympathetic (cholinergic) | Reduced tone and motility; constipation; decreased gastric and pancreatic secretions |
| Urinary bladder | Parasympathetic (cholinergic) | Urinary retention |
| Salivary glands | Parasympathetic (cholinergic) | Xerostomia |
| Sweat glands | Sympathetic (cholinergic) | Anhidrosis |
| Genital tract | Sympathetic and parasympathetic | Decreased stimulation |

the gastrointestinal tract is more complete than that of the quaternary ammonium compounds. Mecamylamine is well absorbed orally and crosses both the blood-brain and placental barriers, its distribution is not confined to the extracellular space. High concentrations of the drug accumulate in the liver and kidney, and it is excreted unchanged by the kidney. In contrast to most of the highly ionized ganglionic blocking agents, mecamylamine can produce central nervous system effects, including tremors, mental confusion, seizures, mania, and depression. The mechanism by which these central effects are produced is unclear. Mecamylamine is rarely used today as an antihypertensive drug because it blocks both parasympathetic and sympathetic ganglia.

## References

Benowitz, N.L (1998). In, Nicotine Safety and Toxicity. (Benowitz, N.L., ed.) Oxford University Press, New York, pp. 3-28.

Benowitz, N.L (1999). Nicotine addiction. *Primary Care,* **26:** 611-653.

Boni R, Kryden O.P, and Burg G (2000). Revival of the use of botulinum toxin: Application in dermatology. *Dermatology* **200:** 287-291.

Davis E, and Barnes M.P (2000). Botulinum toxin and spasticity. *J. Neurol. Neurosurg. Psychiatry* **68:**141-147.

Di Chiara G (2000). Behavioral pharmacology and neurobiology of nicotine reward and dependence. In, *Neuronal Nicotinic Receptors.* (Clementi F, Fornasari D, and Gotti C, eds.) Springer-Verlag, Berlin, pp. 603-750.

CHAPTER

# 16 Skeletal Muscle Relaxants

## Introduction

Drugs that affect skeletal muscle function as two very different therapeutic groups, those used during surgical procedures and in intensive care units to produce muscle paralysis for patients requiring ventilatory assistance (i.e., **neuromuscular blockers**) and those used to reduce spasticity in a variety of neurologic conditions (i.e., **spasmolytics**).

Neuromuscular blocking drugs interfere with transmission at the neuromuscular end plate and lack central nervous system activity. These compounds are used primarily as adjuncts during general anesthesia to facilitate tracheal intubation and optimize surgical conditions while ensuring adequate ventilation.

Drugs in the spasmolytic group have traditionally been called "centrally acting" muscle relaxants and are used primarily to treat chronic back pain and fibromyalgic conditions. Dantrolene, a spasmolytic agent that has no significant central effects and is used primarily to treat malignant hyperthermia.

## Neuromuscular Physiology

**The neuromuscular junction consists of (Fig 16-1):**

1. A motor nerve ending with mitochondria and acetylcholine vesicles (prejunctional)
2. A synaptic cleft of 20-30 nm in width containing extracellular fluid.

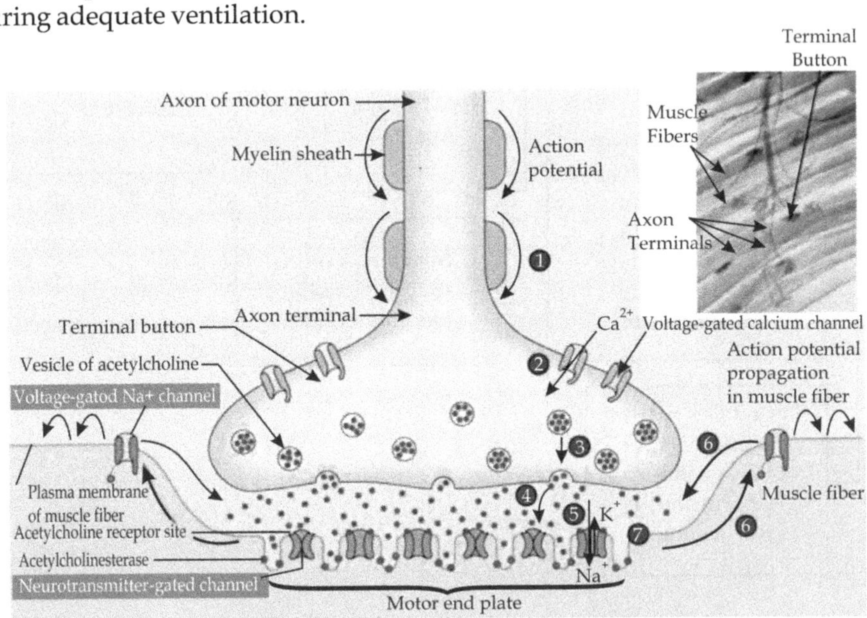


**Fig 16-1:** Neuromuscular junction

3. A highly folded skeletal muscle membrane (post junctional)
4. Nicotinic cholinergic receptors located on both the presynaptic and postsynaptic membranes.

Drugs, can block neuromuscular transmission/ or muscle contraction by acting.

**Presynaptically:** To inhibit acetylcholine synthesis or release (practically not used). As they may have whole body unspecific nicotinic as well as muscarinic effects

**Postsynaptically:** To block the receptor activity. To block ion channel at the end plate.

Clinically these drugs are only used as an adjuvant to general anesthesia, (only when artificial respiration is available). They interfere with the post synaptic action of acetylcholine.

## Classification (Fig 16-2)

## Mechanism of Skeletal Muscle Contraction

1. Initiation of impulse
2. Release of acetylcholine
3. Activation of nicotinic receptor at motor end plate
4. Opening of ion channel, passage of $Na^+$, depolarization of end plate
5. Muscle contraction

Neuromuscular blocking agents used in clinical practice interfere with this process.

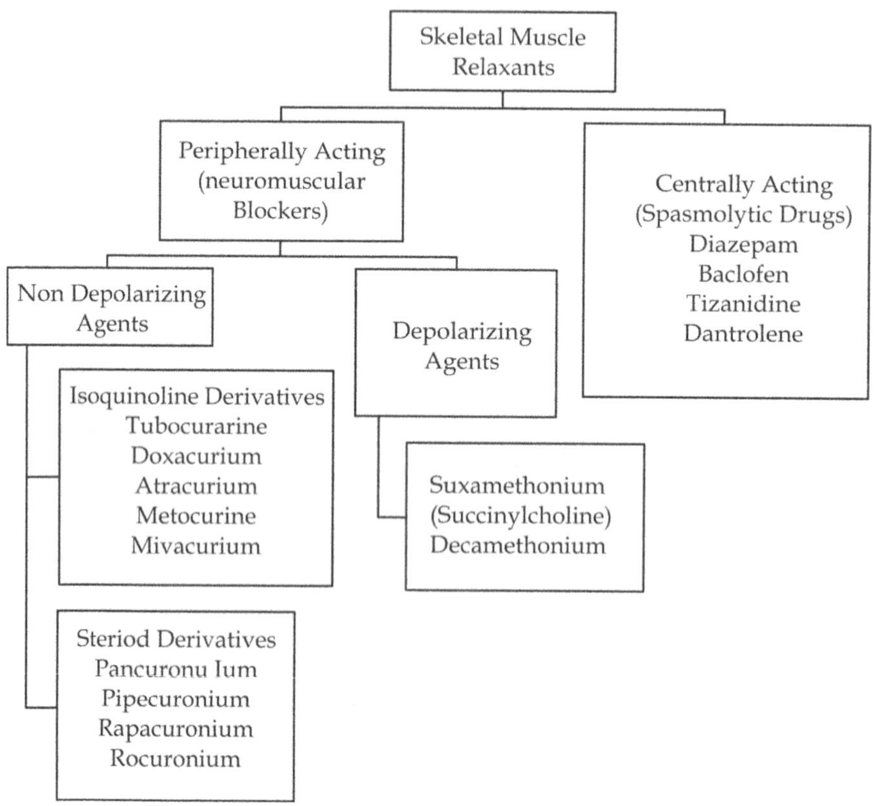


**Fig 16-2:** Classification of skeletal muscle relaxants

# Nondepolarizing Agents

## Mechanism of Action

With the exception of Succinylcholine, all neuromuscular blocking agents are nondepolarizing. These agents prevent excitation of end plate AChRs by acting as reversible competitive antagonists at the binding sites. The prototype for this group is d-tubocurarine, an alkaloid used as a South American arrow poison. In general, these compounds have two charged heads (e.g., quaternary ammonium) separated by a "thick" organic moiety (e.g., steroid nucleus). These heads enable attachment of the drug to the two AChR binding sites. However, because of the large intervening moiety, the channel is occluded such that the flow of cations is prevented. Because of the competitive nature of this blockade, the effect of nondepolarizing blockers can be reversed by anti-AChE agents and other procedures that increase the synaptic concentration of ACh.

## Pharmacological Actions

d-Tubocurarine blocks nicotinic AChRs in muscle end plates and autonomic ganglia but has no effect on muscarinic AChRs. It does not affect nerve or muscle excitability or conduction of action potentials. Because it is charged, it penetrates cells poorly and does not enter the CNS. However, if applied directly to brain or spinal cord, it will block nicotinic AChR in those tissues. In humans, d-tubocurarine has a moderate onset of action (34 minutes) followed by progressive flaccid paralysis. The head and neck muscles are affected initially, then the limb muscles, and finally the muscles of respiration. Recovery from paralysis is in the reverse order.

## Clinical Uses

Nondepolarizing blockers are used to relax skeletal muscle for surgical procedures, to prevent dislocations and fractures associated with electroconvulsive therapy, and to control muscle spasms in tetanus. They do not produce anesthesia or analgesia. The degree of blockade can be influenced by body pH and electrolyte balance. Hypokalemia due to diarrhea, renal disease, or use of potassium-depleting diuretics potentiates the effect of nondepolarizing blockers. By contrast, hyperkalemia may oppose the actions of d-tubocurarine but enhance the end plate response to succinylcholine. The effectiveness of d-tubocurarine is reduced by alkalosis. Newborn children are extremely sensitive to nondepolarizing muscle relaxants but may require three times as much depolarizing agent as an adult for an equivalent degree of block. Like newborn children, patients with myasthenia gravis are very sensitive to paralysis by d-tubocurarine but are resistant to succinylcholine. This altered responsiveness is probably due to the fewer number of functional AChRs at the end plate. Since neonates are very sensitive to d-tubocurarine, the dosage must be reduced and the degree of block closely monitored.

## Adverse Effects and Precautions

d-Tubocurarine may cause bronchospasms and hypotension by release of histamine from mast cells. This may be counteracted by prior treatment with antihistamines. d-Tubocurarine produces partial block of sympathetic ganglia and the adrenal medulla, which may also contribute to hypotension. Inhalation anesthetics, such as isoflurane, enflurane, halothane, and nitrous oxide, potentiate the action of nondepolarizing blockers, either through modification of end plate responsiveness or by alteration of local blood flow. The extent of potentiation depends on the anesthetic and the depth of anesthesia. The dose of muscle relaxant should be reduced when used with these anesthetics. Certain antibiotics (e.g., aminoglycosides, macrolides, polymyxins, lincomycin) enhance neuromuscular blockade by either decreasing Ach release or blocking the postjunctional response. Procainamide and phenytoin also increase the effects of d-tubocurarine-like drugs. The amount of neuromuscular blocker should be decreased accordingly.

## Other Nondepolarizing Blockers of Importance

The Nondepolarizing Blockers are shown Fig. 16-3

### Classification According to Duration of Action

1. Short acting : Mivacurium
2. Intermediate acting:
   Vecuronium
   Rocuronium
   Cisatracurium
3. Long acting: Pancuronium

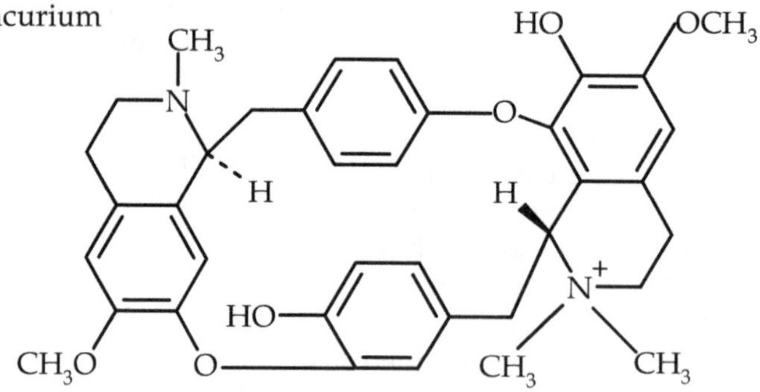

Tubocurarine

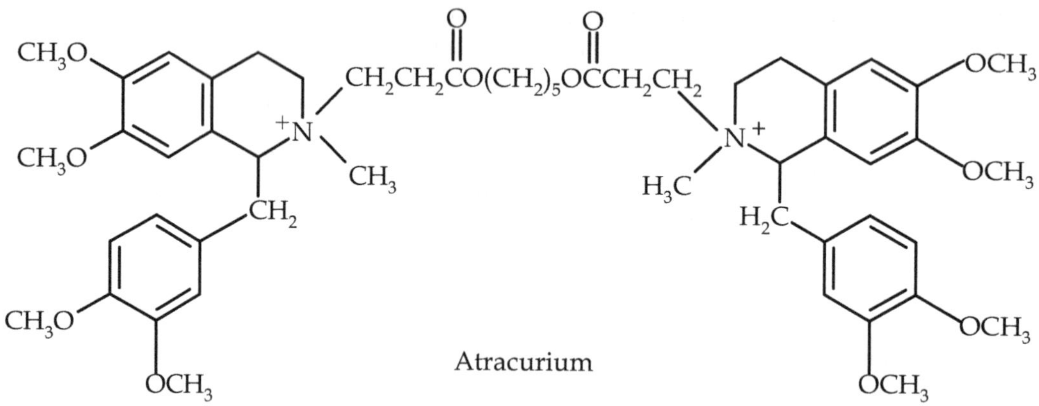

Atracurium

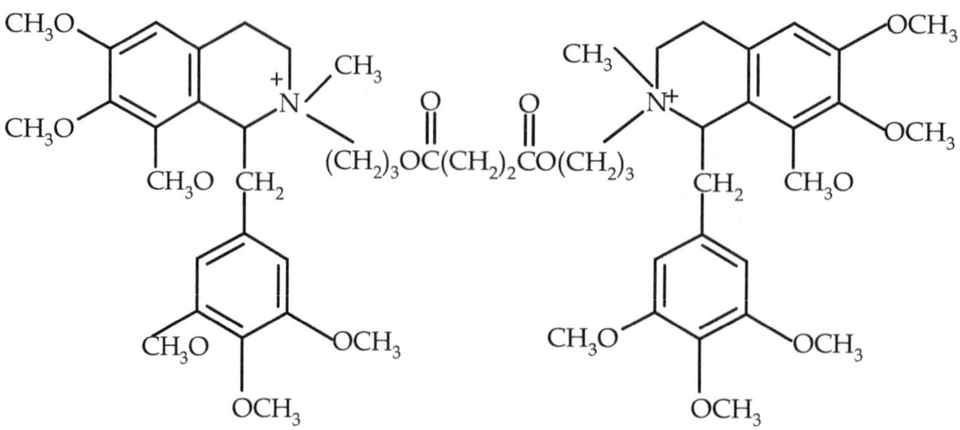

Doxacurium

**Fig 16-3:** Non depolarizing agents

*Atracurium besylate (Tracrium):* It is a benzylisoquinolinium compound like d-tubocurarine. Its actions are similar to those of d-tubocurarine, but its duration of action is shorter (45 minutes) because of spontaneous degradation of the molecule (Hofmann elimination). Because of this, atracurium is useful in patients with low or atypical plasma cholinesterase and in patients with renal or hepatic impairment.

*Mivacurium chloride (Mivacron):* It is a newer agent that is chemically related to atracurium. The primary mechanism of inactivation is hydrolysis by plasma cholinesterase. Although it is useful for patients with renal or hepatic disease, some caution is warranted, since these individuals may have reduced plasma cholinesterase as a result of the disease. Mivacurium has an onset of action (1.8 minutes) and duration of effect (20 minutes) only twice that of succinylcholine, and in this respect, it is the most similar to succinylcholine of all of the nondepolarizing agents.

*Pancuronium bromide (Pavulon):* It is a synthetic bisquaternary agent containing a steroid nucleus (amino steroid), as denoted by the -curonium suffix. It is five times as potent as d-tubocurarine. Unlike d-tubocurarine, it does not release histamine or block ganglionic transmission. Like d-tubocurarine, it has a moderately long onset (2.9 minutes) and duration of action (110 minutes). Pancuronium and its metabolite are eliminated in the urine. Aminosteroid compound. Onset 3-5 minutes, duration 60-90 minutes. Intubating dose 0.08-0.12 mg/kg. Elimination mainly by kidney (85%), liver (15%).

*Side effects:* Hypertension, tachycardia, dysrhythmia.

*Vecuronium bromide (Norcuron):* It is chemically identical to pancuronium except for a tertiary amine in place of a quaternary nitrogen. However, some of the drug will exist as the bisquaternary compound, depending on body pH. Vecuronium has a moderate onset of action (2.4 minutes) and a duration of effect of about 50 minutes. Like pancuronium, it does not block ganglia or vagal neuroeffector junctions, does not release histamine, and is eliminated by urinary excretion.

*Rocuronium bromide (Zemuron):* It is a recently approved amino steroid neuromuscular blocking agent. It has a rapid onset of action (1 minute), but its duration of action is intermediate (55 minutes), about that of vecuronium. On rare occasions, it may release histamine and cause cardiac irregularities. Rapacuronium bromide (Raplon) is the most recent neuromuscular blocking agent approved by the United States Food and Drug Administration (FDA). It is an analogue of vecuronium and is thus categorized as an amino steroid. It has a rapid onset of action (1.5 minutes) and a short to intermediate duration of action (20 minutes). This makes it a suitable alternative to mivacurium or succinylcholine for short procedures. It is eliminated mainly by the liver.

**Adverse Effects** are dose dependent; they include tachycardia, hypotension, and bronchospasm. These effects may be related to the ability of the drug to release a small amount of histamine.

(a) **At low doses:** These drugs combine with nicotinic receptors and prevent acetylcholine binding. As they compete with acetylcholine for receptor binding they are called competitive blockers. Thus prevent depolarization at end-plate. Hence inhibit muscle contraction, relaxation of skeletal muscle occurs. Their action can be overcome by increasing concentration of acetylcholine in the synaptic gap (by inhibition of acetylcholineestrase enzyme).

    E.g.: Neostigmine, Physostigmine, Edrophonium

    Anaesthetist can apply this strategy to shorten the duration of blockage or overcome the overdosage.

(b) **At high doses:** These drugs block ion channels of the end plate. Leads to further weakening of the transmission and reduces the ability of Ach-esterase inhibitors to reverse the action.

**Actions:** All the muscles are not equally sensitive to blockade. Small and rapidly contracting muscles are paralyzed first.

Respiratory muscles are last to be affected and first to recover.

**Pharmacokinetics:** Administered intravenously cross blood brain barrier poorly (they are poorly lipid soluble). Some are not metabolized in liver, their action is terminated by redistribution, excreted slowly and excreted in urine unchanged (tubocurarine, mivacurium, metocurine). They have limited volume of distribution as they are highly ionized.

Atracurium is degraded spontaneously in plasma by ester hydrolysis, it releases histamine and can produce a fall in blood pressure, flushing and bronchoconstriction. It is metabolized to laudanosine (which can provoke seizures), Cisatracurium with similar pharmacokinetics is more safer.

Non depolarizers are excreted *via* kidney, have long half life and duration of action than those which are excreted by liver. Some (vecuronium, rocuronium) are acetylated in liver. (there clearance can be prolonged in hepatic impairment).

**Uses:** As adjuvant to anesthesia during surgery. Control of ventilation (endotracheal intubation). Treatment of convulsion.

**Drug interactions**

Choline esterase inhibitors such as neostigmine, pyridostimine and edrophonium reduce or overcome their activity but with high doses they can cause depolarizing block due to elevated acetylcholine concentration at the end plate.

Halogenated hydrocarbons, aminoglycosides, calcium channel blockers synergize their effect.

**Adverse effects**

***Fall in arterial pressure*** chiefly a result to ganglion block, may also be due to histamine release this may give rise to bronchospasm (especially with tubocurarine, mivacurium and atracurium)

Gallamine and pancuronium block, muscarinic receptors also, particularly in heart which may results in to tachycardia.

**Factors that affect their duration of action:**

1. *pH:* Changes metabolic acidosis and to a lesser extent respiratory acidosis extend the blockage duration.
2. ***Body temperature:*** Hypothermia potentiate the blockage duration.
3. *Age:* Older patients have prolonged effect also.
4. *Electrolytes changes:* Decrease in serum potassium concentration potentiate the blockage decrease in ionized calcium concentration also potentiate the blockage

*Note:* Concomitant administration of potent inhalational agents potentiate the duration of blockage especially with isoflurane, enflurane and sevoflurane.

## Depolarizing Agents

### Drugs: Suxamethonium (succinylcholine) Decamethonium

**Mechanism of action:** These drugs act like acetylcholine but persist at the synapse at high concentration and for longer duration and constantly stimulate the receptor. First, opening of the $Na^+$ channel occurs resulting in depolarization, this leads to transient twitching of the muscle, continued binding of drugs make the receptor incapable to transmit the impulses, paralysis occurs. The continued depolarization makes the receptor incapable of transmitting further impulses.

**Pharmacokinetics:** Administered intravenously. Due to rapid inactivation by plasma cholinesterase, given by continued infusion.

**Therapeutic uses:** When rapid endotracheal intubations is required. Electroconvulsive shock therapy.

### Succinylcholine

**Mechanism of action:** Succinylcholine chloride (*Anectine*) is the only depolarizing-type blocker that is in widespread clinical use. ***It produces neuromuscular block by overstimulation, so that the end plate is unable to respond to further stimulation.***

Structurally, succinylcholine is equivalent to two ACh molecules joined back to back. The resulting 10 carbon atom spacing between the two quaternary ammonium heads is important for activation of the two binding sites on the AChR. Because the succinylcholine molecule is "thin", binding to the two sites does not sterically occlude the open channel, and cations are allowed to flow and depolarize the end plate. Neuromuscular block with succinylcholine occurs by two sequential events. An initial depolarization of the end plate produces muscle action potentials and fasciculation. Maintained depolarization past the threshold for firing produces $Na^+$ channel inactivation, so that muscle action potentials cannot be generated. This is called *phase I,* or *depolarization block.* In the continued presence of succinylcholine, the membrane becomes repolarized, $Na^+$ channel inactivation is reversed, and muscle membrane excitability is restored. Nonetheless, the neuromuscular block persists because of desensitization of the AChR. This is known as *phase II,* or *desensitization block.* Although the mechanism for phase II block is not completely understood, a series of allosteric transitions in the AChR is suspected. One model to describe this has the AChR in equilibrium among four conformations i.e., resting, active, inactive, and desensitized. Agonists stabilize the active and desensitized states, whereas antagonists tend to stabilize the resting and possibly the desensitized state.

**Absorption, metabolism, and excretion:** Succinylcholine is given systemically because the molecule is charged and does not easily cross membranes. It is rapidly hydrolyzed by plasma cholinesterase to succinylmonocholine, which is pharmacologically inactive. Because plasma cholinesterase is synthesized in the liver, neuromuscular block may be prolonged in patients with liver disease. About 10% of succinylcholine is excreted unchanged in the urine. The response to succinylcholine may also be prolonged in individuals with a genetic defect leading to atypical plasma cholinesterase (homozygous incidence of about 1 in 2,500). In this case, the enzyme has a decreased affinity for substrates such as succinylcholine that can be measured by the dibucaine test.

**Pharmacological actions:** Succinylcholine acts primarily at the skeletal neuromuscular junction and has little effect at autonomic ganglia or at postganglionic cholinergic (muscarinic) junctions. Actions at these sites attributed to succinylcholine may arise from the effects of choline. Succinylcholine has no direct action on the uterus or other smooth muscle structures. It does not enter the CNS and does not cross the placental barrier. It may, however, release histamine from mast cells. Because succinylcholine works by stimulating rather than blocking end plate receptors, anti AChEs will not reverse muscle paralysis and may actually prolong the block.

**Clinical uses:** The principal advantage of succinylcholine is its rapid and ultra short action. With intravenous (IV) administration, succinylcholine produces flaccid paralysis that occurs in less than 1 minute and lasts about 10 minutes. This makes it suitable for short-term procedures, such as endotracheal intubation, setting of fractures, and prevention of injury during electroconvulsive therapy. Apart from its rapid onset and brief action, succinylcholine has few benefits and many disadvantages.

**Adverse effects and contraindications:** Succinylcholine produces muscle fasciculation, which may result in myoglobinuria and postoperative muscle pain. The amount produced depends on the level of physical fitness. Succinylcholine causes contractions of extraocular muscles, posing the danger of transient elevated intraocular pressure. Succinylcholine may produce hyperkalemia in patients with large masses of traumatized or denervated muscle (e.g., spinal cord injury). Denervated muscle is especially sensitive to depolarizing drugs because of the increased number of AChRs on the sarcolemma (denervation supersensitivity). Succinylcholine also causes prolonged contraction of the diseased muscles of patients with myotonia or amyotrophic lateral sclerosis. Succinylcholine-induced hyperkalemia may lead to cardiac arrhythmia and arrest when plasma $K^+$ reaches 7 and 10 mM, respectively. The drug also may precipitate a fulminant attack of malignant hyperthermia in susceptible individuals (not to be confused with neuroleptic malignant hyperpyrexia, which involves dopamine and the CNS). Treatment in either case consists of cooling the body and administering oxygen and dantrolene sodium.

## Uses of Neuromuscular Blocking Drugs

**Surgical relaxation:** By far the most important application of the neuromuscular blockers is in facilitating intracavitary surgery. This is especially important in intra-abdominal and intrathoracic procedures.

**Tracheal intubation:** By relaxing the pharyngeal and laryngeal muscles, neuromuscular blocking drugs facilitate laryngoscopy and placement of the tracheal tube. Placement of a tracheal tube ensures an adequate airway and minimizes the risk of pulmonary aspiration during general anesthesia.

**Control of ventilation:** In critically ill patients who have ventilatory failure from various causes (e.g., severe bronchospasm, pneumonia, chronic obstructive airway disease), it may be necessary to control ventilation to provide adequate gas exchange and to prevent atelectasis. Muscle paralysis is produced by neuromuscular blocking drugs to reduce chest wall resistance (i.e., improve thoracic compliance) and ineffective spontaneous ventilation.

**Treatment of convulsions:** Neuromuscular blocking drugs are occasionally used to attenuate the peripheral manifestations of convulsions associated with status epilepticus or local anesthetic toxicity. Although this approach is effective in eliminating the muscular manifestations of the seizures, it has no effect on the central processes because neuromuscular blocking drugs do not cross the blood-brain barrier.

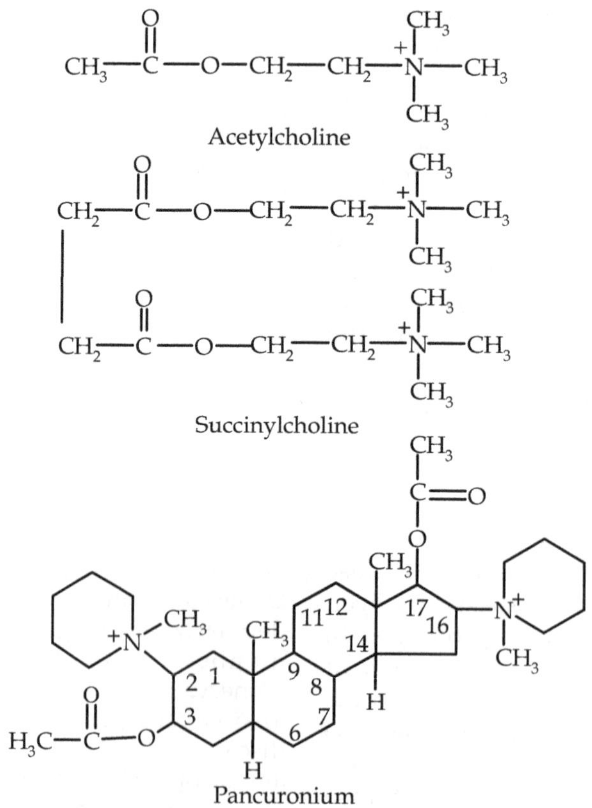


**Fig 16-4:** Structural relationship of succinylcholine, a depolarizing agent, and pancuronium, a nondepolarizing agent, to acetylcholine, the neuromuscular transmitter

## Central Acting Skeletal Muscle Relaxants (Spasmolytic Drugs)

Spasticity is characterized by an increase in tonic stretch reflexes and flexor muscle spasms (i.e., increased basal muscle tone) together with muscle weakness. It is often associated with cerebral palsy, multiple sclerosis, and stroke. These conditions often involve abnormal function of the bowel and bladder as well as skeletal muscle. The mechanisms underlying clinical spasticity appear to involve not only the stretch reflex arc itself but also higher centers in the central nervous system (i.e., upper motor neuron lesion), with damage to descending pathways in the spinal cord resulting in hyper excitability of the alpha motorneurons in the cord. Pharmacological therapy may ameliorate some of the symptoms of spasticity by modifying the stretch reflex arc or by interfering directly with skeletal muscle (i.e., excitation-contraction coupling).

- These produce selective action in the cerebrospinal axis – acts as skeletal muscle relaxants.
- These depress the spinal and supraspinal polysynaptic reflexes involved in the regulation of muscle tone.
- Polysynaptic reflex in the RAS - involved in the wakefulness also depressed - sedative action.

Examples of centrally acting skeletal muscle relaxants (Fig 16-5):

- Chlorzoxazone, Methocarbamol
- Diazepam
- Baclofen
- Tizanidine

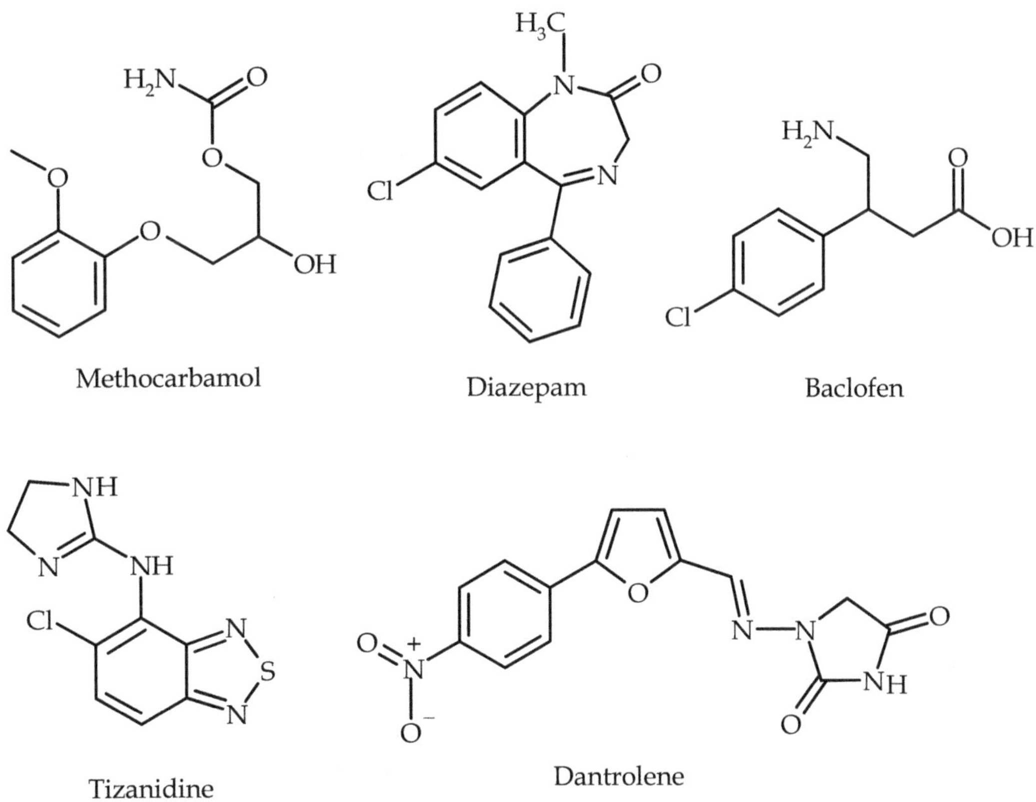


**Fig 16-5:** Central acting skeletal muscle relaxants

## Methocarbamol

Methocarbamol is structurally related to the expectorant guaifenesin and the muscle relaxants chlorphenesin and mephenesin. It is a centrally acting muscle relaxant that suppresses spinal polysynaptic reflexes and has no direct effect on skeletal muscle. It is extensively metabolized in the liver and is excreted through the kidneys, with a small amount excreted with feces. Acutely, Methocarbamol can be administered four times a day at a dose of 1500 mg. For maintenance therapy, 1500 mg can be given three times per day. This medication can also be administered *via* intravenous and intramuscular routes. Frequent side effects include drowsiness and dizziness, followed by nausea, anorexia, headache, blurred vision, muscular discoordination, and, in some instances, urine discoloration. Seizures have been reported with intravenous administration, especially with a history of epilepsy

## Baclofen

Structurally, baclofen is related to the centrally occurring inhibitory neurotransmitter GABA. Clinically, it has commonly been used for its muscle relaxant effects in the treatment of spasticity, as well as for its neuropathic analgesic properties in the treatment of trigeminal neuralgia pain, huntingtons disease. Baclofen is a GABA-B receptor agonist with presynaptic and postsynaptic effects leading to a decrease in the excitatory neurotransmitter release as well as in substance P, which is involved in transmission of Nociceptive impulses. It is metabolized in the liver and excreted in the urine. Baclofen can be administered orally as well as intrathecally *via* an implanted pump mechanism when significant adverse effects preclude further dose escalation to achieve therapeutic effect. Initial dosing of baclofen should be gradual, starting with 5 to 10 mg three times per day. The maximum recommended dose is 80 mg per day in divided doses; however, higher therapeutic doses in cases of refractory spasticity have been used without any significant untoward side effects. Common side effects are weakness, sedation, and dizziness. At higher doses, baclofen can cause seizures, ataxia, and hallucinations. Abrupt withdrawal should be avoided because it can precipitate seizures and hallucinations

## Dantrolene

Dantrolene reduces muscle spasms by inhibiting the release of calcium from the sarcoplasmic reticulum and does not directly affect the central nervous system. It is metabolized in the liver and excreted through the kidneys. Because dantrolene tends to produce greater muscle weakness than baclofen, it should not be the first-line agent for patients who are capable of ambulation. Typically, this medication should be started at a relatively low dose of 25 mg per day and slowly titrated on a weekly basis per effect or side effect up to the maximum of 100 mg three times per day.

### Adverse Effects

Such slow titration can obviate the development of some of the common side effects: drowsiness, weakness, dizziness, and diarrhea. Less frequently observed side effects are constipation, nausea, insomnia, diplopia, tachycardia, depressed mood, anxiety, muscle pain, dificult urination/frequency, erectile dysfunction, and respiratory depression. More serious but relatively rare adverse effects are hepatitis, seizure, heart failure, aplastic anemia, leukopenia, thrombocytopenia, respiratory depression, pleural effusion, and pericarditis.

### Contraindications

Dantrolene should be used with caution in patients with heart failure, chronic obstructive pulmonary disease, and liver disease.

## Botulinum Toxin Type A,B

*Clostridium botulinum* is a spore-forming anaerobic bacillus that produces seven distinct antigenic types of botulinum toxin named from A to G. Toxins type A, B, and F are the only neurotoxins that have been used in the clinical arena. These neurotoxins exert their pharmacological effect at the neuromuscular junction, where they prevent the calcium-dependent release of acetylcholine, producing a state of temporary drug-induced denervation. The therapeutic effect can take up to 1 week to take place fully and can last up to 3 months, at which point repeat injections can be considered. Injectable botulinum preparations are unstable and need to be stored and reconstituted with caution per the manufacturers' recommendations. Each unit of the respective clinically available neurotoxin carries a different level of biologic potency and cannot be reliably interconverted. Relative muscle weakness of the injected musculature as well as of adjacent muscle groups is to some degree expected from local spread of the neurotoxin. Caution should be exercised in using appropriate botulinum dosing to avoid functionally limiting muscle weakness. Headache, dizziness, fever, flulike symptoms, nausea, biliary colic, injection site pain, edema, and erythema are some of the **adverse effects** encountered. Dysphagia, dry mouth, and dysphonia can be observed with injections in the cervical area. Rare instances of arrhythmia, myocardial infarction, hypertension, and botulism like syndrome have been reported. Patients who receive repeated botulinum injections can develop antibodies and become resistant to the neurotoxin's therapeutic eûect.

## Benzodiazepines (Diazepam, Llorazepam, Clonazepam, etc.)

Diazepam has commonly been used in the treatment of muscle spasm, especially in the acute setting. It belongs to a group of compounds called benzodiazepines, known for their potent anxiolytic, sedative, as well as muscle relaxant effects. Their main mechanism of action is through central potentiation of the inhibitory γ-aminobutyric acid (GABA) effect through presynaptic facilitation of GABA release. Benzodiazepines are extensively metabolized in the liver into inactive and in some cases active metabolites. Compounds that lack active metabolites should be used as first-line agents in the elderly and in patients with liver or kidney insufficiency. Such compounds are lorazepam, clonazepam, temazepam, and oxazepam. Excretion principally occurs through the kidneys. Some of the common side effects are drowsiness, confusion, ataxia, cognitive impairment, memory loss, agitation, and disinhibition. Of note, withdrawal symptoms may occur after only 4 to 6 weeks of use, and their potential for abuse should be taken into consideration.

## Tizanidine

Tizanidine is a centrally acting muscle relaxant that, through its alpha-2 adrenergic agonist properties, is thought to prevent the release of excitatory amino acids by suppressing polysynaptic excitation of spinal cord interneurons. Metabolism is through the liver, and excretion is 60% through the kidneys and 20% through the feces. Tizanidine should be administered through a gradual upward titration from an initial dose of 2 to 4 mg at bedtime up to the maximum of 8 mg three times per day. The bedtime dose can provide an analgesic effect as well as improve quality of sleep owing to the commonly occurring sedating side effect.

*Adverse effects:* Other common side effects are daytime drowsiness, hypotension, weakness, and dry mouth. Even though tizanidine's pharmacological effect is similar to another alpha-2 agonist, clonidine, it possesses only a fraction of its blood pressure–lowering effect. Less commonly reported side effects of tizanidine are palpitations, bradycardia, dizziness, headache, nausea, elevated liver enzymes, and several rare cases of fulminant liver failure that led to death. Serial monitoring of liver enzymes is strongly recommended

## Drugs Used to Treat Acute Local Muscle Spasm

A large number of drugs (e.g., **carisoprodol, chlorphenesin, chlorzoxazone, cyclobenzaprine, metaxalone, methocarbamol,** and **orphenadrine**) (Fig 16-6) are promoted for the relief of acute muscle spasm caused by local tissue trauma or muscle strains. It has been suggested that these drugs act primarily at the level of the brainstem.

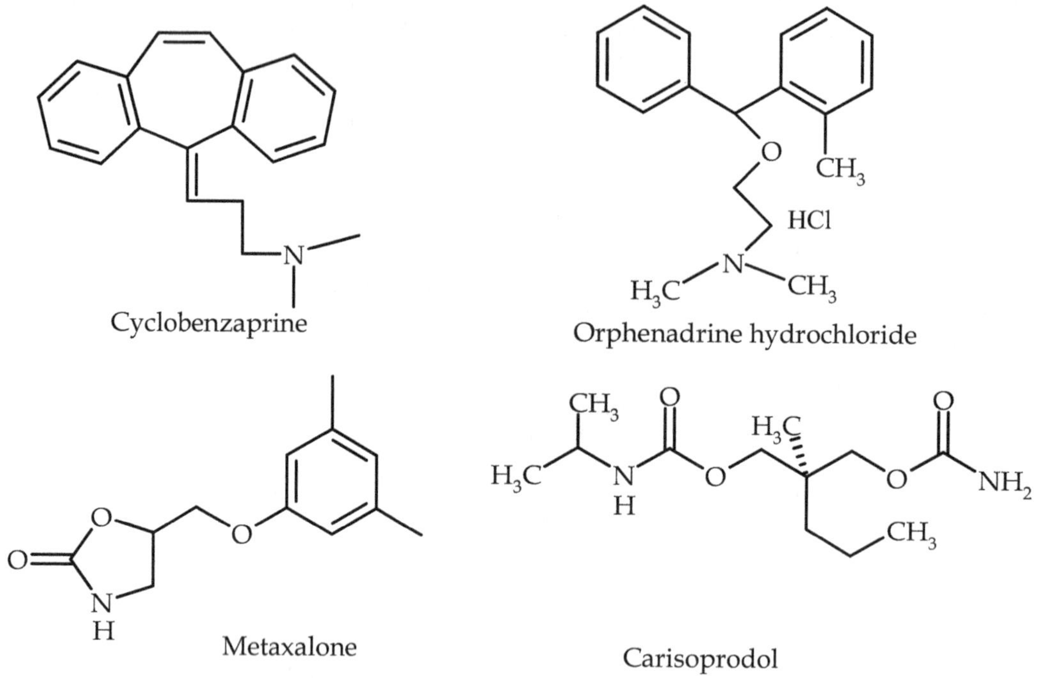


**Fig 16-6:** Drugs used to treat acute local muscle spasm

## Cyclobenzaprine

Cyclobenzaprine is probably the most commonly used muscle relaxant for nonspasticity-related muscle pain. Structurally, it resembles tricyclic antidepressants and differs from amitriptyline by only one double bond. Its therapeutic effect is centrally mediated and carries no direct peripheral action on the affected muscles. Its main pharmacological action occurs at the brainstem and spinal cord levels and is partially explained by a depressant effect on the descending serotonergic neurons. It is extensively metabolized in the liver and excreted as a glucuronated metabolite through the kidneys. It possesses a fairly long half-life of approximately 18 hours and can continue to accumulate for up to 4 days when administered at a frequency of three times per day. Given its structural similarity to tricyclic antidepressants as well as potent anticholinergic properties, caution should be exercised when considering its use in the elderly or in patients with heart disease. Likewise, concomitant use with monoamine oxidase inhibitors is absolutely contraindicated because this combination can cause a hyperpyretic crisis or even death. The initial starting dose should be 5 mg three times per day on as needed basis and can be titrated up to 10 mg three times per day per therapeutic effect or side effect. In patients with hepatic or renal insufficiency, it should initially be administered once per day given its relatively long half-life. Of note, one recent study showed equal eûcacy of 5 and 10 mg doses, with the smaller dose showing a lower level of sedation . The most common side effects are drowsiness, dry mouth, fatigue, and headache, followed by less often occurring adverse effects of diarrhea, dizziness, abdominal pain, nausea, nervousness, blurred vision, and confusion.

### Orphenadrine

Orphenadrine is structurally related to diphenhydramine and carries relatively stronger anticholinergic and weaker sedative properties. It does not produce any direct effect on skeletal muscle, and its exact mechanism of action is unknown. Orphenadrine is mostly excreted through the kidneys. The typical adult oral dose is 100 mg administered at the frequency of twice per day owing to its relatively long half-life. The drug can also be administered intravenously as well as intramuscularly. Common side effects include drowsiness and dizziness, followed by other central nervous system effects such as agitation, hallucinations, and euphoria. The following adverse effects have been reported owing to orphenadrine's anticholinergic properties: dry mouth, nausea, constipation, urinary retention, tachycardia, blurred vision, and mental confusion, especially in the elderly.

### Metaxalone

Metaxalone is a centrally acting muscle relaxant with an unknown mechanism of action. It is metabolized in the liver and excreted through the kidneys in the form of metabolites. Typical adult dosing consists of 800 mg three to four times per day. It is recommended to monitor liver function tests after initiation of this agent.

**Side Effects:** Include drowsiness, dizziness, nervousness, nausea, and headache. The following are, rare but serious adverse reactions have been reported: leukopenia, hemolytic anemia, jaundice, and hyper-sensitivity reactions.

### Carisoprodol

Carisoprodol is still a commonly prescribed muscle relaxant that should be dispensed with caution owing to the potentially addictive properties of its main metabolite, meprobamate. Carisoprodol produces its muscle relaxant effect by depressing the interneuronal activity at the spinal cord level as well as in the descending tracts of the reticular formation. It is not recommended for use in the pediatric age population. This drug is metabolized in the liver with meprobamate as its main metabolite. It is mainly excreted through the kidneys. The usual adult dosage is 350 mg four times per day. The most common side effect is drowsiness. Other central nervous system adverse effects that have been reported include ataxia, agitation, insomnia, and others. Adverse effects such as tachycardia, postural hypotension, nausea, erythema multiforme, and eosinophilia have also been seen.

## Other Centrally Acting Spasmolytic Drugs

**Gabapentin** is an antiepileptic drug that has shown considerable promise as a spasmolytic agent in several studies involving patients with multiple sclerosis. Pregabalin is a new analog of gabapentin that may also prove useful.

**Progabide** and **glycine** have also been found in preliminary studies to reduce spasticity. Progabide is a $GABA_A$ and $GABA_B$ agonist and has active metabolites, including GABA itself.

**Glycine** is another inhibitory amino acid neurotransmitter. It appears to possess pharmacologic activity when given orally and readily passes the blood-brain barrier.

**Idrocilamide** and **riluzole** are newer drugs for the treatment of amyotrophic lateral sclerosis that appear to have spasm-reducing effects, possibly through inhibition of glutamatergic transmission in the central nervous system.

## References

Kisor DF, Schmith VD (1999). Clinical pharmacokinetics of cisatracurium besilate. *Clin Pharmacokinet* **36:** 27.

Krause T *et al.*, (2004). Dantrolene- a review of its pharmacology, therapeutic use and new developments. *Anaesthesia* **59:** 364.

Lee C (2001). Structure, conformation, and action of neuromuscular blocking drugs. *Br J Anaesth* **87:** 755.

Lopez JR et al., (1992). Effects of dantrolene on myoplasmic free [Ca2+] measured *in vivo* in patients susceptible to malignant hyperthermia. *Anesthesiology* **76:** 711.

Marshall CG, Ogden DC, Colquhoun D (1990). The actions of suxamethonium (succinyl-dicholine) as an agonist and channel blocker at the nicotinic receptor of frog muscle. *J Physiol (Lond)* **428:** 155.

Nolan KW, Cole LL, Liptak GS (2006). Use of botulinum toxin type A in children with cerebral palsy. *Phys Ther* **86:** 573.

Verrotti A *et al.,* (2006). Pharmacotherapy of spasticity in children with cerebral palsy. *Pediatr Neurol* **34:** 1.

# Part - III

# Drugs Affecting Central Nervous System

CHAPTER

# General Considerations of Central Nervous System

# 17

The CNS [brain and spinal cord (SC)] can be divided into its anatomical areas or its physiological function. The study of the drugs that can affect the brain and their varied mechanisms of action (MOA), compound the complexity of this system.

## Macroanatomy

The brain can be subdivided into its regions: cerebrum and its hemispheres, midbrainpons, medulla, thalamus, hypothalamus, cerebellum, and basal ganglia. As well, there are systems such as the limbic system and the reticular activating system.

A. **Cerebrum:** It is the largest and main portion of the brain with the outer layer, which covers the hemispheres, being the cerebral cortex which is made up of several layers of gray cells. The cortex receives information from the senses and directs the conscious movements of the body and therefore is perceived to be the thinking and reasoning part of the brain.

   Regions of the cortex can be classified according to:

   1. The modality of information processed (i.e., sensory, motor, auditory, olfactory, etc.)
   2. The anatomical area (frontal, temporal, parietal, occipital)
   3. By the geometrical relationship between cell types which serve to interconnect the systems *via* pathways in order to modulate information (i.e., between the cortical and subcortical systems).

B. **Brain Stem:** It is the rostral stem like portion of brain connecting the cerebral hemispheres with the SC and is comprised of the midbrainpons and medulla oblongata. The midbrain is just below the thalamus and contains a center for visual reflexes such as moving the head and eyes. The PONS is inferior to the midbrain and connects the cerebellum to the motor output from cortex and has the respiratory center. The medulla oblongata is the caudal part of the brainstem and contains centers that regulate the heart, vasculature, and respiratory system. It is also a point for central integration for coordination of reflexive actions such as swallowing and vomiting. It is also where the motor and sensory nerves crossover. The brainstem contains most of nuclei of the cranial nerves as well as the reticular activating system.

C. **Diencephalon-Thalamus and Hypothalamus:** Forms central core of brain and surrounds the 3$^{rd}$ ventricle. The thalamus lies deep within the center of the brain beneath the basal ganglia and above the hypothalamus. It functions as a relay station between the incoming sensory pathways and integrates these sensations on the way to the cortex. It also acts as a pathway between the basal ganglia and associative regions of the cortex. There is also a pathway to the hypothalamus. The hypothalamus lies below the thalamus at the base of the cerebrum. It is the principal integrating center for the entire autonomic nervous system. As well, it is important in vital functions such as regulation of body temperature, water balance, blood glucose levels, metabolism, and emotion. It directs many of the body's daily rhythms such as sleep and activity, appetite and digestion, sexual functions, and menstrual and reproductive cycles.

D. **Cerebellum:** It arises from the posterior pons and behind the cerebral hemispheres. It has projections to the motor cortex *via* the thalamus and to brainstem nuclei concerned with vestibular function. The three primary functions of the cerebellum include:

1. Aid in controlling axial muscles in posture and therefore balance and equilibrium, as well as coordinating hand and eye movements;
2. regulation of muscle tone and movement;
3. modulation of output of the motor cortex (especially rapid skeletal muscle activities such as typing, playing an instrument, and running). It functions to coordinate the motion of various muscles involved in voluntary movement-it operates below the level of our consciousness and assistin in the optimal coordination and performance of movements. It also plays a role in learning and memory.

Lesions to the cerebellum result in ataxia, reduced muscle tone, delayed initiation of movements, nystagmus, dysarthria, and oscillation at end movements.

E. **Basal Ganglia:** Are deep nuclei of the cerebrum and include the striatum (caudate nucleus and putamen) and globus pallidus. Brainstem nuclei closely associated with the basal ganglia are the substantia nigra and subthalamic nucleus. Many of the impulses from the basal ganglia are inhibitory and mediated by dopamine and gamma-aminobutyric acid (GABA). It is part of the extrapyramidal system (EPS) which complements the pyramidal system (voluntary). Diseases of the basal ganglia result in disorders of movement as well as posture dependent upon the area and specific neurotransmitters involved. For example, damage to the striatum where GABA is secreted results in random and continuous uncontrolled movements termed chorea. Destruction to the substantia nigra results in a loss of dopamine creating an predominance of acetylcholine (Ach) and results in movement disturbances such as tremors, bradykinesia, and dystonia.

F. **Limbic System:** Is the term for an combination of brain regions (hippocampus, amygdaloid complex, olfactory nuclei, basal ganglia, selected nuclei of the dienecephalon) which lie beneath the cerebral cortex and where a variety of complex emotional and motivational functions have been attributed. It seems to integrate emotional state with motor and visceral activities.

G. **Reticular Activating System:** It determines overall CNS activity level, thus it is essential for regulation of sleep, wakefulness, level of arousal, and coordination of eye movements. The neurons of the RAS are both excitatory and inhibitory with the primary neurotransmitter being Ach.

## Microanatomy of the Brain

The specific connections between neurons within or across the anatomical or functional divisions of the brain are essential to the brain's functions. Cells in the CNS are classified as either neurons or nonneuronal cells.

A. **Neurons:** Can be classified according to either function (sensory, motor, interneuron), location, or by the identity of the transmitter released.

B. **Nonneuronal Cells:**

1. Macroglia-is the most abundant supportive cell and includes astrocytes (plays a variety of metabolic supportive roles) and oligodendroglia (myelin-producing cells insulating the axon).
2. Microglia-related to macrophages and monocytes.
3. Cells of the cerebral vasculature and the CSF forming cells of the choroids plexus.
4. Meninges.

C. **Blood-Brain Barrier:** Permeability barrier between the CNS and Blood limiting the diffusion of substances into various regions of the CNS. It is as a result of the tight junction between the vascular endothelial cells of brain capillaries and secondarily to the neighbouring glial cells which further decrease permeability. The exception is in the areas around the posterior pituitary and the CTZ where it does not exist.

## Central Neurotransmitters

Neurotransmitters are chemical mediators which are released from nerve endings into the synaptic cleft once an action potential has been reached eliciting an influx of $Ca^{++}$ ions (a voltage dependent action). The neurotransmitter then reaches it target postsynaptic receptor site with the result being either direct excitation or inhibition or enhancing excitation or inhibition.

### Biogenic Amines

#### Dopamine

***Dopamine-precursor of norepinephrine*:** Approximately half of CNS content of catecholamines cells of the choroid plexus is dopamine with large amounts in the basal ganglia (especially caudate nucleus), olfactory tubercle, central nucleus of the amygdala, limbic system, and certain areas of the frontal cortex. There are 5 dopamine receptor subtypes: $D_1$ (and $D_5$) activate adenylyl cylclase, $D_2$ (and $D_3$ & $D_4$) inhibit adenylyl cyclase. Some $D_2$ receptors may also suppress $Ca^{++}$ currents and activate $K^+$ currents.

The brain contains several well-defined dopaminergic systems.

The most extensively studied are the nigrostriatal, mesolimbic, and mesocortical neuronal systems that originate in the midbrain and project to the striatum, limbic system, and cortex, respectively. These are involved in the control of locomotion, emotion, and cognition and have no direct role in the regulation of pituitary function. Neurons originating from arcuate nucleus (A12) and periventricular nucleus (A14), are relevant because they are directly involved in the control of prolactin (PRL) secretion.

Based on anatomical and functional studies, two dopaminergic systems that regulate PRL were initially identified: the tuberoinfundibular dopaminergic (TIDA) and tuberohypophysial dopaminergic (THDA).

Dopamine belong to a class of neurotransmitters known as catecholamines, which are structurally defined by a catechol ring and an amine side chain.

***Dopamine synthesis* (Fig 17-1):**

Dopamine is synthesized from the amino acid tyrosine; the majority of circulating tyrosine originates from dietary sources, but small amounts are derived from hydroxylation of phenylalanine by the liver enzyme phenylalanine hydroxylase. Blood-borne tyrosine is taken up into the brain by a low-affinity amino acid transport system and subsequently from brain extracellular fluid into dopaminergic neurons by high- and low-affinity amino acid transporters.

Tyrosine is converted to dopamine by the enzymes tyrosine hydroxylase (TH) and l-amino acid decarboxylase (AADC) also called dihydroxyphenylalanine (DOPA) decarboxylase (DDC). TH is the rate-limiting step in their biosynthetic pathway; the TH gene is localized to chromosome 11p in humans and encodes a single form of TH that can be alternatively spliced. The mRNA expression of the TH is abundant throughout the human mesencephalon. The mature enzyme is a soluble cytosolic protein composed of four subunits of approximately 60 kDa each. TH activity is the most critical factor that controls dopamine synthesis, and considerable efforts have been devoted to understanding activation/inactivation of this enzyme. The enzyme uses pyridoxal phosphate as a cofactor and can convert both DOPA to dopamine and 5-hydroxytryptophan to serotonin [5-hydroxytryptamine (5-HT)].

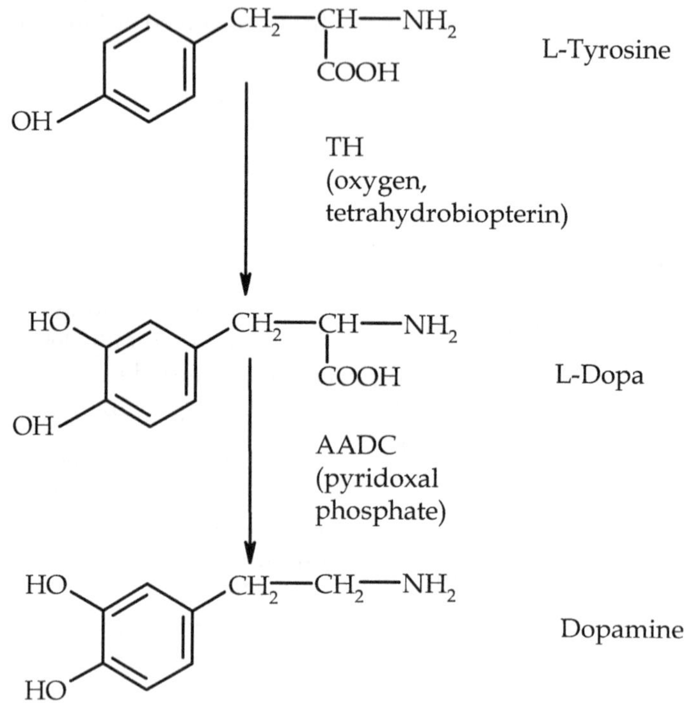


**Fig 17-1:** Dopamine synthesis

***Storage and Exocytosis* (Fig 17-2):**

In dopaminergic neurons, the neurotransmitter is transported from the cytoplasm to specialized storage vesicles at extremely high concentrations, 0.5–0.6 m, which is near its limit of solubility. Here the amine is concentrated to approximately at a 100- to 1000-times higher than the level in the cytosol.

It should be noted that dopamine can be synthesized and released from dendrites, in addition to terminal regions; however, in dendrites dopamine appears to be stored both in classical vesicles and in smooth endoplasmic reticulum.

Dopamine is translocated from the cytoplasm into the vesicles by the vesicular monoamine transporter (VMAT).

The function of the vesicles is 4-fold:

- To protect dopamine from enzymatic degradation by MAO,
- To minimize constitutive secretion by diffusion from the cells,
- To facilitate regulated release, and
- To enable rapid replenishment of depleted stores.

The life cycle of the vesicles includes:

- Targeting to the active zone of the presynaptic membrane,
- Docking,
- Fusion,
- Release of the vesicular content,
- Retrieval by endocytosis, and
- Refilling with the neurotransmitter.

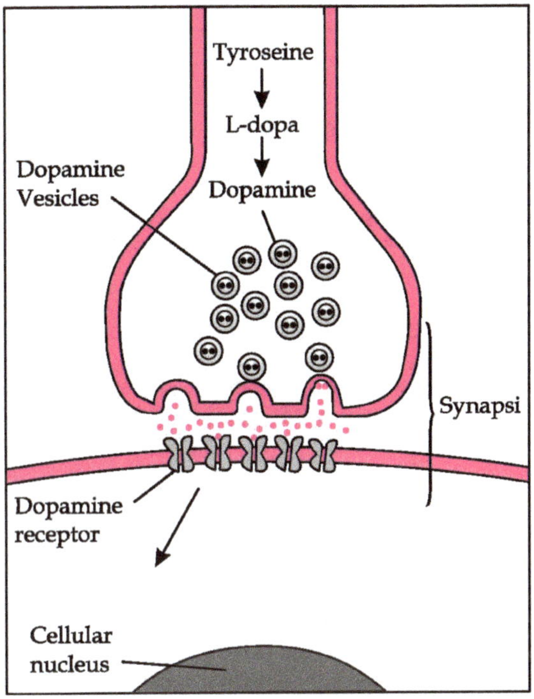


**Fig 17-2:** Exocytosis

Monoamines are stored primarily in small translucent ("clear") vesicles (50–100 nm in diameter) but are also present in large dense core vesicles (up to 500 nm in diameter), often co-sequestered with neuropeptides. The synaptic vesicle is a highly specialized structure whose membrane is composed of a lipid bilayer with embedded integral proteins that participate in vesicular trafficking, docking, and fusion. The vesicle membrane also contains an $H^+$-ATPase, which maintains the proton gradient that energizes VMAT and preserves an acidic intravesicular environment.

Each vesicle is filled with several thousand molecules of dopamine as well as other soluble constituents. Upon the arrival of an action potential, a change in membrane protein conformation allows the influx of calcium ions, which is a key part of the stimulus responsible for the fusion of vesicles with the neuronal membrane.

By the process of exocytosis, vesicles discharge their soluble contents into the synapse, the extent of dopamine release appears to be dependent on the rate and pattern of neuronal firing, and particularly interesting is the increased dopamine release in response to "burst-firing".

The docking mechanism involves a family of proteins termed soluble N-ethylmaleimide-sensitive factor (NSF) attachment proteins, Soluble NSF Attachment Protein (SNAP) receptors, Soluble NSF Attachment Protein REceptor (SNARE) complexes: v-SNAREs, designating vesicular-associated proteins, and t-SNAREs, designating target (plasma membrane) cognate complexes.

At least seven to eight proteins are essential for docking: vesicular synaptobrevin and synaptotagmin; SNAP-25 and syntaxin, which are located in both the vesicles and plasma membrane; and two soluble proteins, NSF and SNAP, which catalyze the disassembly of the SNAP-25-syntaxin-synaptobrevin complex during docking and fusion .

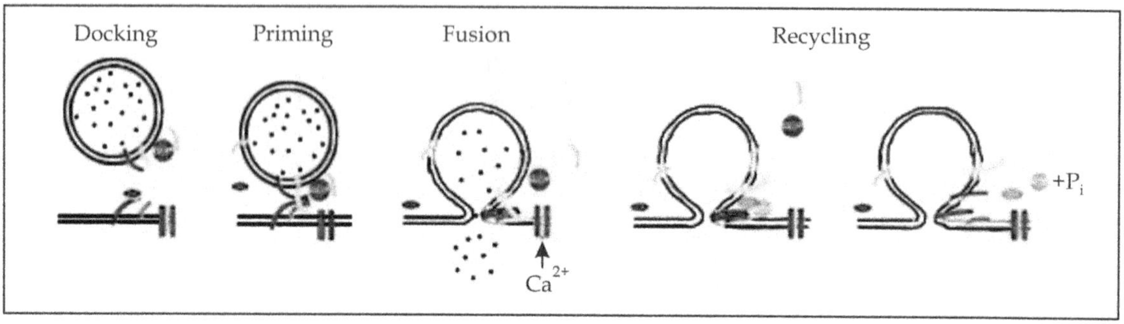


Stages and key proteins involved in vesicle membrane fusion. See text for a full explanation of the processes involved. The proteins are color coded: snaptobrevin (dark blue), synaptophysin (light blue), syntatin (red), nSec1 (brown), SNAP-25 (dark green), synaptotagtnin (yellow), Rab3A (dark red circle). Rabphifin-3A (pale green). $Ca^{2+}$ channel (megenta), NSF (pink) and α-SNAP (sky blue). $P_i$ inorganic phosphate.

**Fig 17-3:** The synaptic vesicle cycle

***The synaptic vesicle cycle*** **(Fig 17-3):**

Calcium is central to all aspects of exocytosis, including rapid fusion and unloading of the vesicles as well as recruitment and translocation of loaded vesicles.

Calcium influx occurs through voltage-gated calcium channels and leads to fusion of the synaptic vesicles with the plasma membrane and release of their content to the extracellular space. This is a much faster process than the relatively slow release of peptide or protein hormones from endocrine cells. In most neurons, dopamine is released into the synaptic cleft and binds to postsynaptic receptors. In contrast, the dopaminergic neurons of the hypothalamo-pituitary unit (with the exception of the dopaminergic neurons innervating the intermediate lobe of the pituitary) lack true synaptic contacts and are classified as secretory neurons. In this case, dopamine diffuses away from the terminals through the perivascular space and is transported by portal blood to distal pituitary target cells. The rate of dopamine release from secretory neurons appears to be slower than that from classical neurons.

It has been argued that the speed of neurotransmitter release is reciprocally related to the distance of its site of action, but the mechanism responsible for this feature is not clear. It is assumed that only a small fraction of docked vesicles can instantaneously release their cargo in response to calcium influx. These vesicles comprise the "fusion-ready" pool that undergoes a very rapid ATP-dependent fusion. The slower release phase is carried out by docked vesicles that exist in a different biochemical state and require priming to promote fusion.

These vesicles constitute a precursor pool that replenishes the rapid release pool. Priming is ATP dependent, involves the SNARE proteins, and is associated with production of phosphoinositides and protein phosphorylation. An even slower pool is composed of vesicles that are anchored to the cytoskeleton *via* actin-binding synapsins but are not docked to the membrane.When synapsins become phosphorylated in response to an influx of calcium, the vesicles detach from the cytoskeletal elements and can translocate to the active zone of the presynaptic membrane. However, vesicular translocation is too slow to account for the immediate calcium dependent exocytosis.

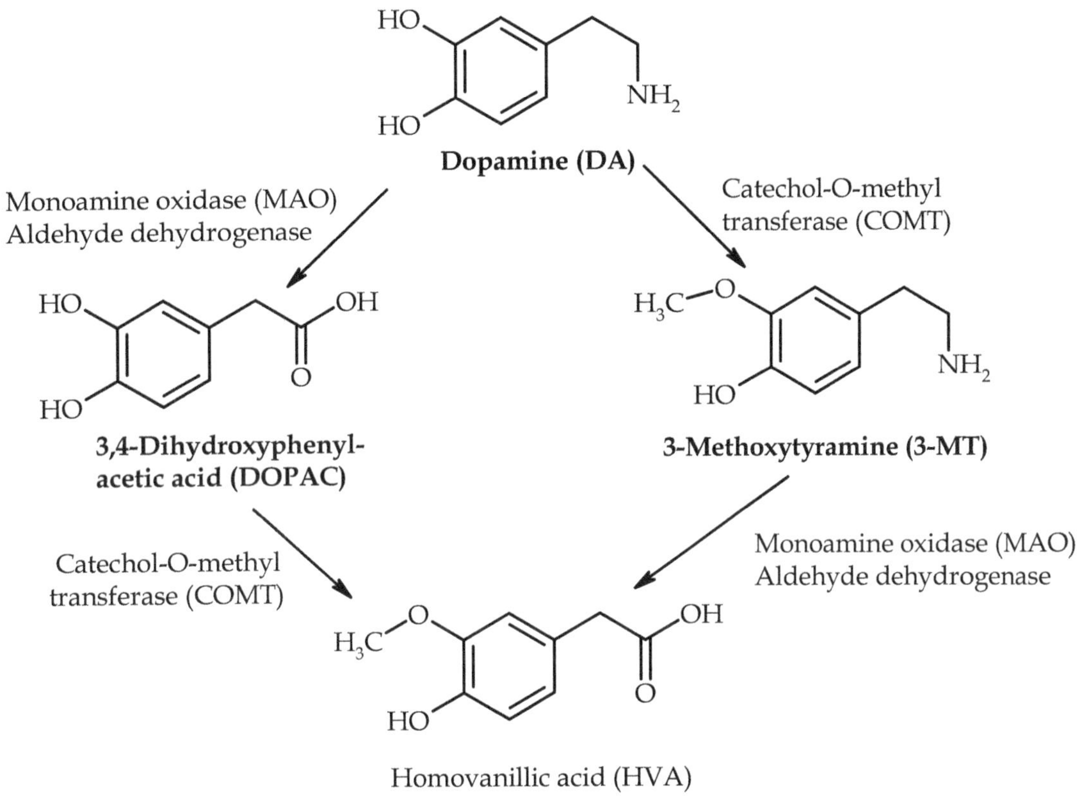


**Fig 17-4:** Inactivation and degradation of dopamine

***Inactivation and degradation of dopamine* (Fig 17-4):**

Dopamine is inactivated by:

1. Reuptake *via* the dopamine transporter
2. Metabolism
   I. Monoamine oxidase (MAO)
   II. Catechol-O-methyl transferase (COMT)

*I.* ***Reuptake:*** Reuptake is the process by which the released transmitter is brought back into presynaptic nerve terminals or is internalized by surrounding glial cells.

Reuptake of dopamine is mediated by two classes of transporters:

Dopamine transporter DAT, which transports dopamine from the extracellular to the intracellular space, and VMAT, which reloads dopamine into the vesicles. This is an energy dependent process. Sodium/ potassium ATPases use energy from ATP hydrolysis to create a concentration gradient of ions across the pre-synaptic membrane that drives the opening of the transporter and co-transport of sodium and chloride ions and dopamine from the synaptic cleft. Potassium ions binding to the transporter enable it to return to the outward position. Release of the potassium ions into the synaptic cleft equilibrates the ionic gradient across the pre-synaptic membrane. The dopamine re-uptake transporter is then available to bind another dopamine molecule for re-uptake.

*II.* ***Metabolism:*** The main enzymes responsible for the metabolism of dopamine are shown in the figure above. The principal locations of these metabolizing enzymes are listed in Table 17-1.

**Table 17-1:** Location of metabolizing enzymes

| Enzyme | Subtype | Cellular location | Subcellular location |
|---|---|---|---|
| MAO | A | Dopamine and norepinephrine neurons | Mitcohondria |
| MAO | B | Glia, serotonin neurons | Mitcohondria |
| COMT | high Km | Gilla | Soluble |
| COMT | low Km | Postsynaptic to dopamine neuron | Membrane-bound |
| PST | M | Postsynaptic to dopamine neuron | Cytosolic |

Catabolism is one of the effective mechanisms for dopamine inactivation. This involves multiple pathways that include oxidative deamination by monoamine oxidase (MAO), O-methylation by catechol-O-methyltransferase (COMT) and conjugation by sulfotransferases or glucoronidases. The preferred metabolic pathway at a given site depends on the compartmentalization of the metabolic enzymes. For example, MAO is located in the external membrane of the mitochondria and acts intracellularly, whereas COMT is associated with the external cell membrane and acts only extracellularly.

**I. MAO Synaptic vesicular monoamine transporter expression:**

Exists as two isoenzymes, A and B, with an apparent molecular mass of 60–63 Da each. The two MAO genes, each comprised of 15 exons, are located on the X-chromosome and appear to have been derived from the same ancestral gene. They differ in substrate specificity as well as selectivity for inhibitors.

MAO-A is more highly expressed in catecholaminergic neurons, whereas MAO-B is more abundant in serotonergic and histaminergic neurons and in glial cells. Deamination of dopamine by MAO produces dihydroxyphenylacetic acid (DOPAC). Determination of the ratio of DOPAC/ dopamine concentrations serves as a good method for estimating rapid changes in neuronal activity.

**II. COMT**

O-Methylation by COMT is primarily responsible for inactivation of circulating catecholamines. Consecutive conversion of dopamine by MAO and COMT yields homovanillic acid. The enzyme introduces a methyl group to the catecholamine, which is donated by S-adenosyl methionine (SAM). COMT is an intracellular enzyme located in the postsynaptic neuron. Any compound having a catechol structure, like catecholestrogens and catechol-containing flavonoids, are substrates of COMT.

***Receptors***

***Dopamine receptor subtypes* (Fig 17-5):**

***The dopamine D1-, D5-like receptors***

The $D_1$-like receptor family contains the $D_1$ and $D_5$ receptor subtypes and the $D_2$-like family contains the $D_3$ and $D_4$ subtypes. The $D_1$-like receptors are found throughout the brain and in blood vessels and smooth muscle. Dopamine $D_1$-like receptors are coupled to stimulatory G-proteins and they have a stimulatory effect on neurotransmission when bound by an agonist. Regions of the brain with a high density of $D_1$-like receptors tend have a low density of $D_2$-like receptors whereas regions of the brain with a low $D_1$-like receptor density have a high density of $D_2$-like receptors.

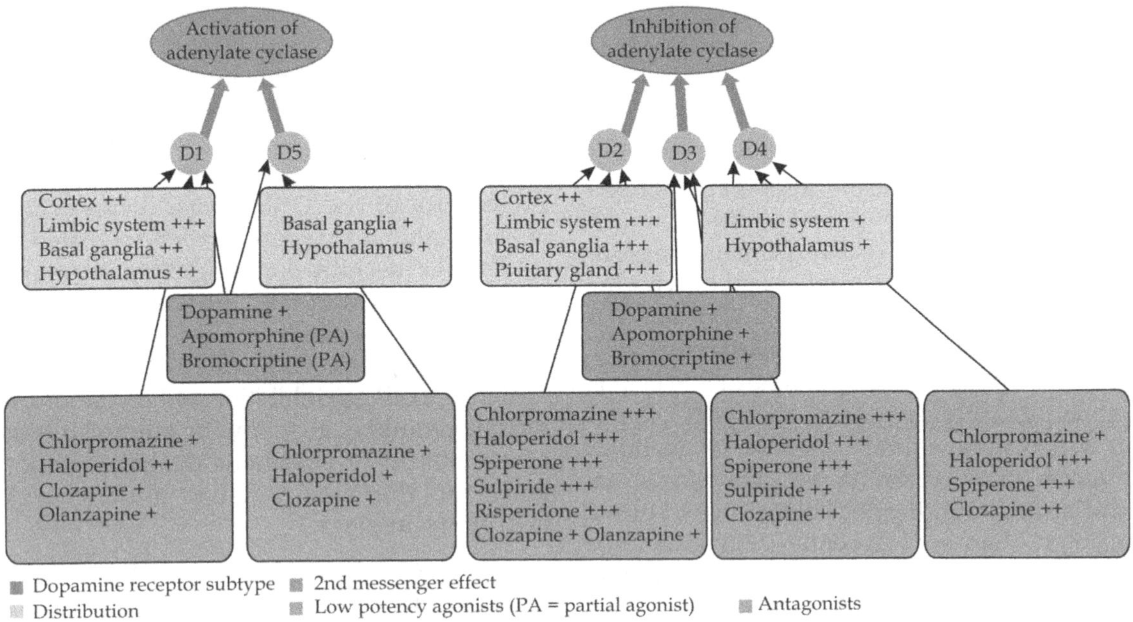


**Fig 17-5:** Types of dopamine receptors

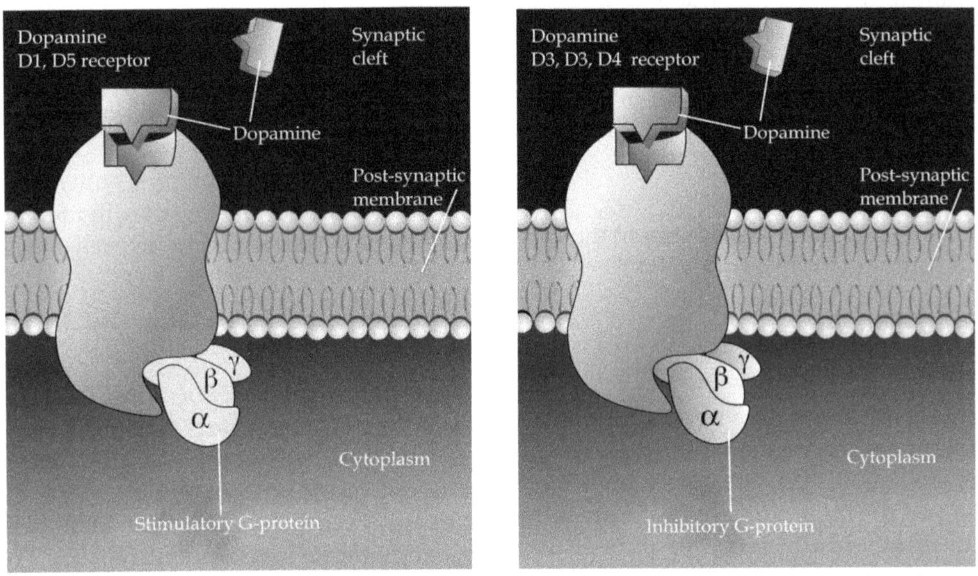


**Fig 17-6:** The dopamine $D_2$, $D_3$, $D_4$ receptor

The $D_2$-like family contains the $D_2$, $D_3$ and $D_4$ subtypes and the $D_1$-like receptor family contains the $D_1$ and $D_5$ receptor subtypes. The $D_2$-like receptors are found throughout the brain and in smooth muscle and presynaptic nerve terminals. Coupled to inhibitory G-proteins, dopamine $D_2$-like receptors have an inhibitory effect on neurotransmission when bound by an agonist. Many neuroleptic drugs are antagonists of the $D_2$ receptors.

***Norepinephrine*:** Relatively large amounts are located in hypothalamus and in certain zones of the limbic system (parts of amygdale and hippocampus) but is present in most brain regions (cerebral cortex, brain stem, cerebellum, and spinal cord) but in lower amounts. It is primarily an excitatory neurotransmitter but in selected areas in the CNS and PNS it has inhibitory effects.

***Epinephrine***: Epinephrine containing neurons are found in medullary reticular formation with some connections to the pontine region, diencephalic nuclei, and paraventricular nucleus of the dorsal thalamus. Also found in periaqueductal gray area and spinal cord.

***Serotonin***: (5-hydroxytryptamine or 5-HT)- It is primarily an inhibitory neurotransmitter, found in hypothalamus, limbic system, cerebellum, piriform cortex, cerebral cortex, choroids plexus, and retina. High concentration is found platelets. There are 14 receptor subtypes each of which is composed of a further set of subtypes.

***Histamine***: Most of histamine receptors are found in ventral posterior hypothalamus and extends to ascending and descending tracts in the brain. The histamine system is thought to function in regulating arousal, body temperature, vascular dynamics, the reticular activating system. There are 3 histamine receptor subtypes.

## Acetylcholine

Seems to be an excitatory transmitter in the CNS versus its inhibitory effects in the PNS.

## GABA and Glycine

### Introduction

Amino acids are among the most abundant of all neurotransmitters present within the central nervous system (CNS). Studies which have characterized the high-affinity uptake of amino acids, in either brain slices or subcellular fractions, support current dogma that the majority of neurons in the mammalian brain utilize either gamma amino butyric acid (GABA) as their primary neurotransmitters. In effect, GABA and glutamate serve to regulate the excitability of virtually all neurons in brain and, not surprisingly, therefore have been implicated as important mediators of many critical physiological as well as pathophysiological events that underlie brain function and/or dysfunction. Pharmacological studies utilizing drugs which selectively block or augment the actions of GABA or glutamate support the notion that these two neurotransmitters, by virtue of their often opposing excitatory and inhibitory actions, control, to a large degree, the overall excitability of the CNS. Thus, drugs which enhance inhibitory synaptic events mediated by GABA often decrease opposing excitatory events mediated by glutamate and vice versa. The behavioral consequences of such pharmacologically induced changes in the "balance" between inhibition and excitation are often profound (e.g., following administration of convulsant or anesthetic drugs which are known to alter GABAergic or glutamatergic neurotransmission).

GABA and glycine are arguably the most important inhibitory neurotransmitters in the brain and brainstem/spinal cord, respectively. These inhibitory amino acids are of particular interest to the neuropsychopharmacologist, because many commonly studied (and therapeutically useful) drugs work by selectively affecting these two neurotransmitter systems. What follows is a review of these two inhibitory amino acid neurotransmitters, with an emphasis on the important role they play in mediating the actions of a variety of neuro psychopharmacologic agents.

### GABA: Synthesis, Uptake, and Metabolism (Fig 17-7)

GABA is formed *in vivo via* a metabolic pathway called the GABA shunt. The initial step in this pathway utilizes ketoglutarate formed from glucose metabolism *via* the Krebs cycle. Ketoglutarate is then transaminated by α-oxoglutarate transaminase (GABA-T) to form glutamate, the immediate precursor of GABA. Finally, glutamate is decarboxylated to form GABA by the enzyme(s) glutamic acid decarboxylase (GAD). GAD is expressed only in GABAergic neurons and in certain peripheral tissues which are also known to synthesize GABA. Like most neurotransmitters, GABA is stored in synaptic vesicles and is released in a $Ca^{2+}$- dependent manner upon depolarization of the presynaptic membrane. Following release into synaptic cleft, GABA's actions are terminated principally by reuptake into presynaptic terminals and/or surrounding glia. GABA is also metabolized by GABA-T to form succinic semialdehyde. This transamination will regenerate glutamate when it occurs in the presence of ketoglutarate. Succinic semialdehyde is oxidized by succinic semialdehyde dehydrogenase (SSADH) to succinic acid which then re-enters the Krebs cycle.

The reuptake of GABA occurs *via* highly specific transmembrane transporters which have recently been shown to be members of a large family of $Na^+$-dependent neurotransmitter transporters. GABA uptake is temperature- and ion-dependent (both $Na^+$ and $Cl^-$ ions are required for optimal uptake). Affinity purification of the GABA transporter protein has recently led to its molecular cloning. The principal neuronal GABA transporter appears to be a 70 to 80 Da glycoprotein which, based on its deduced amino acid sequence, is predicted to contain 12 hydrophobic membrane-spanning domains. To date, at least two other GABA transporter cDNAs have been cloned. However, the physiological and pharmacological significance of this heterogeneity is unknown. Nonetheless, specific inhibitors of GABA uptake which directly bind to the transporter itself have been synthesized, and several have been shown to have anticonvulsant and/or antinociceptive properties in laboratory animals.

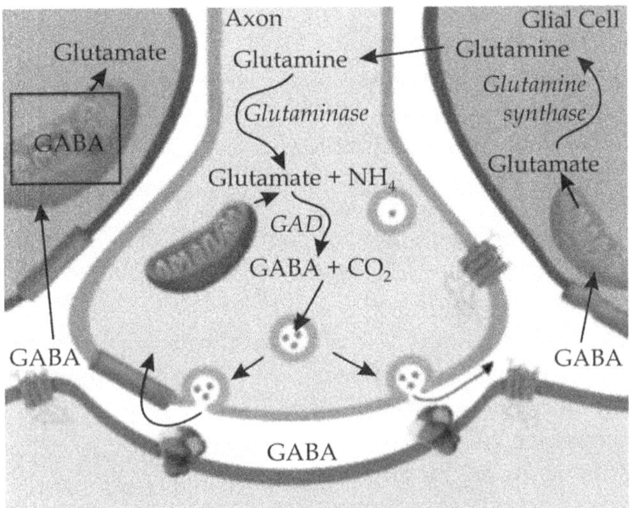


**Fig 17-7:** GABA synthesis and metabolism

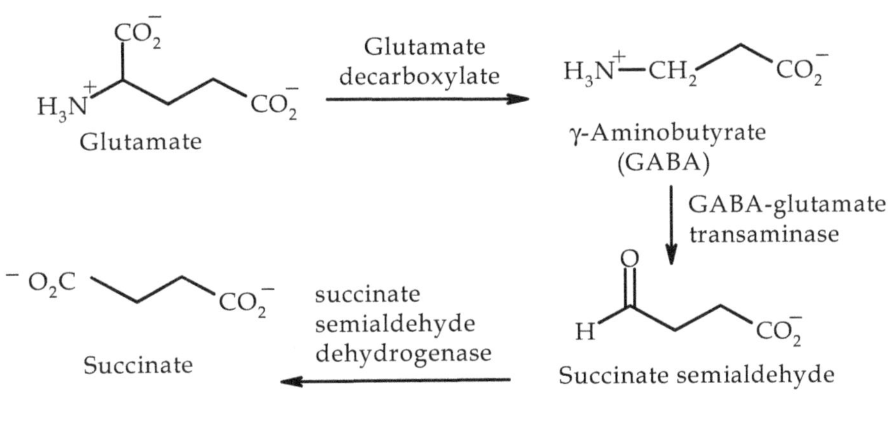

### GABA-A Receptors: Physiology to Pharmacology

Receptors for both inhibitory and excitatory amino acid neurotransmitters are either ionotropic (i.e., their activation results in enhanced membrane ion conductance) or metabotropic (i.e., their activation results in increased intracellular levels of secondary messenger) in nature. GABA-A receptors are ionotropic receptors leading to increased $Cl^-$ ion conductance, whereas GABA-B receptors are metabotropic receptors which are coupled to G proteins and thereby indirectly alter membrane ion permeability and neuronal excitability. Electrophysiological studies using voltage-clamp and single-channel recording techniques have yielded a rather detailed description and understanding of the operation of the GABA-A receptor-gated $Cl^-$ ion channel. Activation of the GABA-A receptor by agonist results in an increase in $Cl^-$ ion conductance *via* the receptor-gated ion channel or pore. This increase in $Cl^-$ ion conductance, which requires the binding and cooperative interaction of two molecules of GABA, is actually due to an increase in the mean open time of the $Cl^-$ ion channel itself. (GABA activates the GABA-A receptor at low micromolar concentrations, suggesting that it must be highly compartmentalized within nervous tissue). The increase in $Cl^-$ ion conductance observed following activation of GABA-A receptors results in a localized hyperpolarization of the neuronal membrane. This decrease in neuronal membrane "excitability" results in the inhibitory actions of GABA.

### GABA-A Receptor Agonists and Antagonists

GABA-Areceptors, like most receptors, can be defined by the drugs (and other ligands) which selectively bind to, and either stimulate or block, receptor activity. A variety of GABA receptor agonists have been discovered and have been shown to selectively activate GABA-A receptors. Muscimol, a GABA analogue isolated from the hallucinogenic mushroom *Amanita muscaria*, is one of the most selective and potent GABA agonists. Muscimol is also not a substrate for the GABA transporter, which makes it useful for electrophysiological and biochemical studies. Bicuculline is the prototypical and competitive and directly competes with GABA. Bicuculline reduces both the frequency and mean open time of the GABA-gated $Cl^-$ ion channel. Picrotoxin and other extremely potent convulsants such as t-butylbicyclo-phosphorothionate (TBPS) are noncompetitive GABA receptor antagonists which do not compete directly with GABA for its recognition site(s) but, instead, bind to a separate and distinct recognition site(s) associated with the receptor complex. Both classes of GABA-A receptor antagonists produce seizures when administered to laboratory animals. The affinity of cage convulsants such as TBPS for GABA-A receptors is so high that they have proven to be useful radioligands for measuring GABA-A receptors *in vitro* and for their subsequent biochemical and pharmacological characterization. These studies have revealed that GABA-A receptors have multiple allosteric binding sites for drugs which, when occupied, modulate (positively or negatively) the inhibitory actions of GABA.

### Benzodiazepines and Barbiturates Act at GABA-A Receptors (Fig 17-8):

While both benzodiazepines and barbiturates bind to GABA-A receptors to augment GABA-mediated responses, they do so in different ways. Barbiturates have dual actions to enhance GABA-A receptor-mediated $Cl^-$ ion conductance. At low (subanesthetic) concentrations, barbiturates augment the affinity of the GABA-A receptor for GABA and increase the mean channel opening time induced by GABA facilited acitivity. At higher (anesthetic) concentrations, barbiturates directly increase channel openings, even in the absence of GABA mematic activity. Benzodiazepines, on the other hand, have no direct effects on channel opening but only increase the affinity of the receptor for GABA as well as the frequency of GABA-activated channel openings. This is an important distinction because it means that benzodiazepines will markedly augment GABA's actions at low intrasynaptic GABA concentrations, but will have little to no effect at saturating concentrations of GABA (i.e., benzodiazepines "shift" the concentration–response curve for GABA slightly to the left). These differences undoubtedly contribute to the relatively low toxicity of benzodiazepines compared to barbiturates.

There is now considerable evidence that a number of other sedative-hypnotic-anesthetic

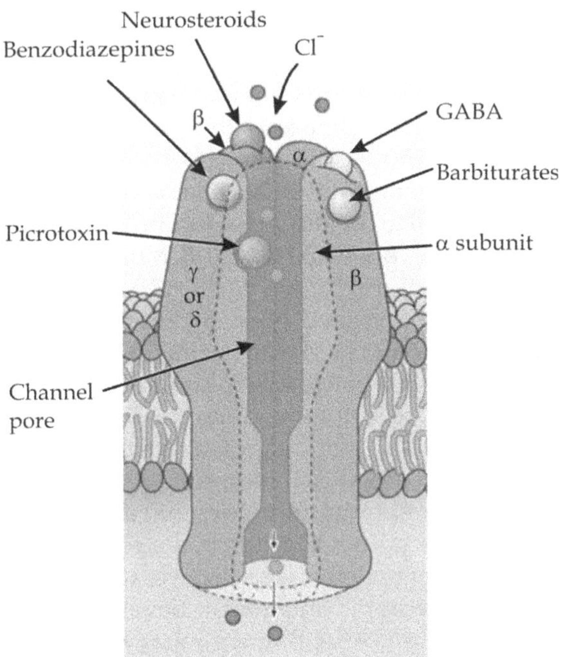


**Fig 17-8:** GABA receptors

drugs also interact with GABA-A receptors and at pharmacologically-relevant concentrations. Parenthetically, these studies (cited below) were among the first to suggest that the behavioral effects of alcohols and anesthetics were due, at least in part, to their "specific" actions at critical membrane protein targets, notably ligand-gated ion channels. (It had been widely assumed for over 100 years that the behavioral effects of alcohols and anesthetics were due to their "nonspecific" effects on membrane lipids).

Ethanol, one of the most commonly used (and abused) sedative-hypnotic agents, has been shown by several investigators to augment GABA-activated $Cl^-$ ion conductance in a variety of intact and isolated neuronal membrane preparations. To date, however, electrophysiological studies of ethanol's actions in augmenting GABA-activated $Cl^-$ ion conductance have yielded somewhat mixed results. More recent studies have generally confirmed that pharmacologically-relevant concentrations of ethanol (10–100 mM) weakly (but significantly) augment GABA-activated $Cl^-$ ion conductance as longer chain-length alcohols and general anesthetics do. Moreover, several imidazobenzodiazepine inverse agonists of the benzodiazepine receptor (see below) have been reported to antagonize the sedative/ataxic effects of ethanol further implicating the GABA-A receptor as one of the key central sites mediating at least some of ethanol's neuropharmacological effects. The effects of ethanol on GABA-A receptors, coupled with its more recently described actions in inhibiting glutamate (NMDA) receptor-mediated depolarizing events, likely contribute to the anxiolytic and sedative effects of alcohols.

### Agonists, Antagonists, and Inverse Agonists

Since the discovery of the benzodiazepine receptor (recognition site), a large number of benzodiazepine and nonbenzodiazepine drugs have been found to interact with these receptors—and in unexpected ways. In addition to those receptor ligands which augment GABA responses (now called agonists), two other broad classes of ligands have now been characterized. Selective antagonist flumazenil (imidazobenzodiazepine) binds with high affinity to GABA-A receptors but are devoid of intrinsic activity of their own. However, these antagonists completely block the actions of benzodiazepine receptor agonists in augmenting GABA-mediated responses. Selective antagonists like flumazenil also block (or reverse) the actions of inverse agonists. The latter are benzodiazepine receptor ligands which decrease GABA-activated $Cl^-$ ion conductance (by decreasing the frequency of channel openings). The GABA-A receptor can thus be positively or negatively modulated by compounds which range in activity from full agonists to full inverse agonists. Along this continuum like compounds with different degrees of intrinsic efficacy—that is, compounds with only partial agonist or inverse agonist actions. Behaviorally, full agonists have sedative - anesthetic properties, whereas full inverse agonists are convulsants. Partial benzodiazepine receptor agonists (now in development by several pharmaceutical companies) may prove to be effective anxiolytics, devoid of the sedative effects generally observed with full agonists. The fact that benzodiazepine receptor agonists reduce anxiety and that inverse agonists are profoundly anxiogenic, coupled with recent observations that the "sensitivity" of animals to inverse agonists can be altered (in some cases increased) by pharmacological or environmental factors, has prompted considerable speculation that GABA-A receptors are involved in at least some forms of human anxiety.

The large number of drug recognition sites associated with GABA-A receptors (which are clearly distinct from those which recognize GABA itself) have led several investigators to propose the existence of endogenous receptor ligands. Several such "candidate" ligands have been identified; however, with the possible exception of two, there is little compelling evidence at present that any interact with GABA-A receptors *in vivo*. One of these ligands is an endogenous peptide called diazepam-binding inhibitor (DBI) and was shown to interact with GABA-A receptors and to have anxiogenic properties (similar to inverse agonists). The other postulated endogenous ligand(s) include two natural steroid metabolites of progesterone and deoxycorticosterone (allopregnanolone and allotetrahydro-DOC). These neuroactive steroids bind with high affinity to GABA-A receptors and have "barbiturate-like" actions in augmenting GABA-mediated responses. The plasma and brain levels of these neuroactive steroids increase dramatically following exposure of rats to various stressors. Plasma allopregnanolone levels are also quite high during the third trimester of pregnancy, and they decrease dramatically following parturition. None of these putative natural ligands, however, have yet been unequivocally demonstrated to subserve any physiological function.

### GABA-B Receptors

While attempting to identify functional GABA receptors on peripheral nerve terminals, Bowery and Hudson described a bicuculline insensitive action of GABA in reducing the release of [3H] norepinephrine. Subsequently, these investigators extended their findings to the CNS, where it became clear that GABA could also potently inhibit the depolarization-induced release of [3H] norepinephrine from brain slices. GABA-A, It was apparent that many GABA-A receptor (bicuculline-sensitive) agonists were unable to mimic the actions of GABA-A in inhibiting neurotransmitter release—leading to the proposal to divide GABA receptors into two subtypes, GABA-A and GABA-B. Moreover, one compound, β-p-chlorophenyl-GABA (baclofen), which was designed to be a centrally active GABA analogue (and which is still marketed as an antispastic agent), was found to be inactive at GABA-A receptors but quite active at GABA-B receptors. Therefore, baclofen proved to be the first selective GABA-B receptor agonist and is still used extensively for characterizing GABA-B receptors. Phaclofen, the phosphonic derivative of baclofen, is a selective, albeit weak, GABA-B receptor antagonist. Several newer, more potent GABA-B antagonists have been discovered; however, the published data on these compounds are rather limited. Nonetheless, administration of GABA-B antagonists to laboratory animals does not result in the profound behavioral sequelae observed following administration of GABA-A receptor antagonists (e.g., seizures). This suggests that GABA-A receptors are tonically (and continuously) activated, whereas GABA-B receptors may only be activated under certain physiological conditions.

Activation of GABA-B receptors in many brain regions results in an increase in $K^+$ channel conductance with a resultant hyperpolarization of the neuronal membrane. This increase in $K^+$ conductance is often blocked by pretreatment with pertussis toxin, indicating that many postsynaptic GABA-B receptors are indirectly coupled to $K^+$ channels through an intervening G protein. There is considerable evidence that a large proportion of GABA-B receptors are coupled to G proteins, but there is also evidence that some presynaptic GABA-B receptors may be directly linked to $K^+$ channels. The fact that GABA-B receptors are coupled to G proteins may also explain, in part, the reported effects of GAB - B receptor agonists on $Ca^{2+}$ conductance and secondarily neurotransmitter release. Very little data is available on the structure of the GABA-B receptor. To date, attempts to clone the GABA-B receptor by microsequencing a portion of the purified protein or by expression cloning in oocytes have proven to be unsuccessful.

**Glycine: Synthesis and Uptake**

Glycine (Fig. 17-9) is the major inhibitory neurotransmitter in the brainstem and spinal cord, where it participates in a variety of motor and sensory functions. Glycine is also present in the forebrain, where it has recently been shown to function as a co-agonist at the N-methyl-D-aspartate (NMDA) subtype of glutamate receptor. In the latter, context glycine promotes the actions of glutamate, the major excitatory neurotransmitter of the NMDA receptor. Thus, glycine subserves both inhibitory and excitatory functions within the CNS.

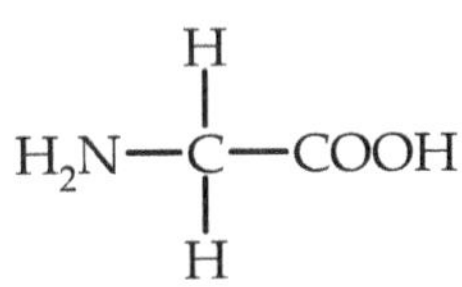

**Fig 17-9:** Glycine

Glycine is formed from serine by the enzyme serine hydroxymethyltransferase (SHMT). Glycine, like GABA, is released from nerve endings in a $Ca^{2+}$-dependent fashion. The actions of glycine are terminated primarily by reuptake *via* $Na^+/Cl^-$ dependent, high-affinity glycine transporters. The specific uptake of glycine has been demonstrated in the brainstem and spinal cord in regions where there are also high densities of inhibitory glycine receptors.

Recently, two glycine transporters have been cloned and shown to be expressed in the CNS as well as in various peripheral tissues. These glycine transporters are members of the large family of $Na^+/Cl^-$ dependent neurotransmitter transporters, and both share approximately 50% sequence identity with the GABA transporters discussed above. The deduced amino acid sequence of both cDNAs predicts the typical 12 transmembrane domains characteristic of these transporters. The two glycine cloned transporters have been named glycine transporter GLYT-1 and GLYT-2 in the order that they were reported. These transporter cDNAs are transcribed from the same gene and are quite similar in their 3′ nucleotide sequences. They differ in their 5′ noncoding regions as well as in the first 44 nucleotides of their coding sequence. Expression of GLYT-1 and GLYT-2 yield

**Table 17-2:** GABA receptors

| Category | Ligand-gated ion channel | G-protein coupled receptor | Ligand-gated ion channel |
|---|---|---|---|
| Subunits | α, β, ψ, δ, ε, π, θ | GBR-1, GBR-2 | N |
| Agoinsts | Muscimol, THIP | Baclofen | ---------------- |
| Antagonists | Bicuculline | Phaclofen | Baclofen |
| Desensitization | Yes | No | |
| Modulator | Benzodiazepines | Not yet identified | Zinc |
| Location | CNS | Interpenduncular nuclei | Retina |

transporters with similar kinetic and pharmacological properties. Interestingly, however, the distribution of GLYT-1 and GLYT-2 transcripts measured by *in situ* hybridization are different. GLYT-1 mRNA also closely parallels the distribution of the glycine receptor. These data suggest that GLYT-1 is primarily a glial glycine transporter whereas GLYT-2 is primarily a neuronal transporter. The mapping of both glycine transporter mRNAs, as well as the glycine receptor subunit mRNAs, confirm the importance of this neurotransmitter in the brainstem and spinal cord, but support a more widespread distribution in supraspinal brain regions than was previously suspected.

### *Glycine Receptors*

Inhibitory glycine receptors are blocked by the plant alkaloid strychnine, which was also first used to label glycine receptors in spinal cord membranes. Strychnine poisoning results in muscular contractions and tetany as a result of glycinergic disinhibition and over excitation. Electrophysiological studies primarily carried out in rodent spinal cord neurons have demonstrated that glycine activates $Cl^-$ ion conductance. Like GABA, this increase in $Cl^-$ ion conductance results in a hyperpolarization of the neuronal membrane and an antagonism of other depolarizing stimuli. Other α- and β- amino acids, including β-alanine and taurine, also activate glycine receptors, but with lower potency.

The glycine receptor was first successfully solubilized and purified by Betz and colleagues using affinity purification over an affinity matrix derivatized with aminostrychnine. The affinity-purified glycine receptor was shown to consist of two polypeptide subunits of approximately 48 kD (a) and 58 kD (b), respectively. Reconstitution of these polypeptide subunits into lipid vesicles resulted in functional receptors, and intramolecular cross-linking experiments suggested that the native glycine receptor is a pentameric structure. Photoaffinity labeling of the glycine receptor with [3H] strychnine revealed that both the strychnine and glycine binding sites are located on the 48-kD a subunit. Purification of the α-and β-receptor subunits was followed closely by their molecular cloning .

The deduced amino acid sequences of the α- and β-glycine-receptor subunits predict structures quite homologous to the subunits of other ligand-gated ion channels, including the GABA-A receptor. Each subunit has four hydrophobic membrane-spanning sequences, and each shares considerable sequence identity with the other. Several glycine-receptor α-subunit variants have now been identified ($\alpha_{1-4}$), and, not surprisingly, they differ in their pharmacological properties and level of expression. As mentioned, both the agonist and antagonist binding sites are located on the a subunit, but at different amino acids. Interestingly, glycine receptors comprised of α subunits are efficiently gated by taurine and β-alanine, whereas $\alpha_2$-containing receptors are not. The $\alpha_1$ and $\alpha_2$ genes are expressed in the adult and neonatal brain, respectively. Interestingly, the β-subunit transcript is expressed at relatively high levels in the cerebral cortex and cerebellum, where no a transcripts or specific [3H]strychnine binding sites have been observed. Coexpression of β subunits with a subunits (as opposed to homo-oligomeric α-subunit glycine receptors) results in glycine receptors with pharmacological properties quite similar to native glycine receptors. Nonetheless, the widespread distribution of β-subunit mRNA in brain suggests that other, perhaps strychnine-insensitive glycine receptor isoforms will be found.

Recently, the expression of α and α subunits has been shown to be developmentally regulated with a switch from the neonatal $\alpha_2$ subunit (strychnine-insensitive) to the adult $\alpha_1$ form (strychnine-sensitive) at about 2 weeks postnatally in the mouse. The timing of this "switch" corresponds with the development of spasticity in the mutant spastic mouse, prompting speculation that insufficient expression of the adult isoform may underlie some forms of spasticity.

## Amino Acids

Most common inhibitory and excitatory neurotransmitters in CNS.

Anatomy of the Glutamate System

1. Descending pathways from the cortical pyramidal cells
2. Descending pathways from cerebellum
3. Interconnections of limbic system (particularly, amygdala and hippocampus)

**Glutamate Synthesis (Fig 17-9):**

- Neurotransmitter pool derived from glucose and other precursors
- Glutamate, aspartate, glutamine and α-ketoglutatrate converted by **transaminases** (aminotransferases) to form each other
- Glutamine to Glutamate by **glutaminase**
- Glutamate to glutamine (in Astrocytes and Glial cells) by **glutamine synthetase** (glutamine then transported out of non-neuronal cells by $SN_1$ (a sodium/$H^+$ pump)

**Glutamate Release**

Excitatory synaptic transmission is mediated by glutamate, which is present in very high concentrations in excitatory synaptic vesicles (~ 100 mM). Glutamate is released into the synaptic cleft by $Ca^{2+}$-dependent exocytosis . The released glutamate acts on postsynaptic glutamate receptors and is cleared by glutamate transporters present on surrounding glia. In glia, glutamate is converted to glutamine by glutamine synthetase, released from the glia, taken up by the nerve terminal, and converted back to glutamate by the enzyme glutaminase. The high concentration of glutamate in synaptic vesicles is achieved by the vesicular glutamate transporter (VGLUT). These two excitatory amino acids (EAAs) are widely distributed throughout the mammalian CNS. Their administration leads to rapid depolarization of neurons and an increase in firing rate.

There are two distinct classes of *Excitatory amino-acid* (EAA )receptors: ionotropic receptors and metabotropic receptors. The ionotropic receptors directly gate ion channels, while the metabotropic receptors are coupled to intracellular G proteins.

**Glutamate Receptors (Fig 17-10)**

Receptors are named according to their sensitivity to the action of selective agonists. The best-characterized receptor is known as the NMDA (N-methyl-D aspartate) receptor,which directly gates a $Mg^{+2}$ cation channel that is also permeable to $Ca^{+2}$ and $Na^+$. Compounds that

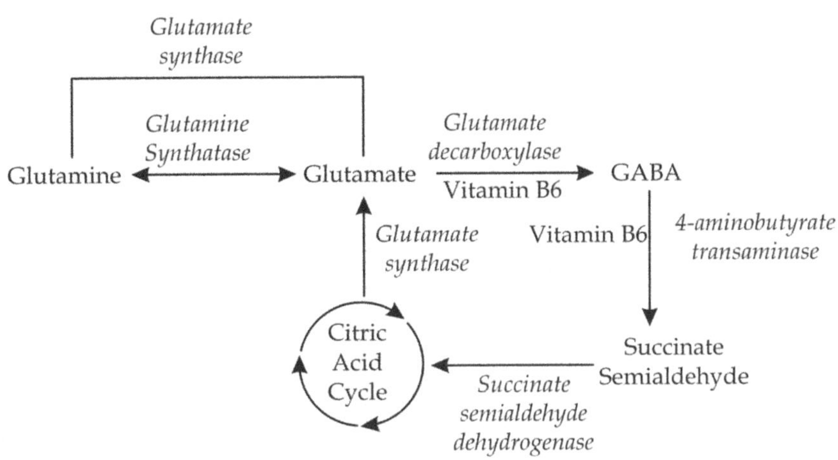


**Fig 17-10:** Synthesis of glutamate

block the NMDA receptor complex may attenuate the neuronal damage following anoxia, such as occurs during a stroke; much of the neuronal damage associated with strokes may be related to the release of glutamic acid, aspartic acid, or both. Similarly, neuronal damage may occur as a result of seizures, and this also may be related to excessive EAA release. Antagonists of the NMDA receptor complex are being studied for possible uses in strokes and other types of hypoxia.

The ionotropic receptors can be further divided into three subtypes based on the action of selective agonists: α-amino-3-hydroxy-5-methylisoxazole-4-propionic acid (AMPA), kainic acid (KA) and N-methyl-D-aspartate (NMDA). All of the ionotropic receptors are composed of four subunits. AMPA receptors, which are present on all neurons, are heterotetramers assembled from four subunits (GluR1-GluR4). The majority of AMPA receptors contain the GluR2 subunit and are permeable to $Na^+$ and $K^+$, but not to $Ca^{2+}$. Some AMPA receptors, typically present on inhibitory interneurons, lack the GluR2 subunit and are also permeable to $Ca^{2+}$.

Kainate receptors are not as uniformly distributed as AMPA receptors, being expressed at high levels in the hippocampus, cerebellum, and spinal cord. They are formed from a number of subunit combinations (GluR5-GluR7, and KA1 and KA2). Although KA1 and KA2 are unable to form channels on their own, their presence in the receptor changes the receptor's affinity and kinetics. Similar to AMPA receptors, kainate receptors are permeable to $Na^+$ and $K^+$ and in some subunit combinations can also be permeable to $Ca^{2+}$.

NMDA receptors are as ubiquitous as AMPA receptors, being present on essentially all neurons in the CNS. All NMDA receptors require the presence of the subunit NR1. The channel also contains one or two NR2 subunits (NR2A-D). Unlike AMPA and kainate receptors, all NMDA receptors are highly permeable to $Ca^{2+}$ as well as to $Na^+$ and $K^+$. NMDA receptor function is controlled in a number of intriguing ways. In addition to glutamate binding, the channel also requires the binding of glycine to a separate site. The physiologic role for glycine binding is unclear because the glycine site appears to be saturated at normal ambient levels of glycine. Another key difference between AMPA and kainate receptors on the one hand, and NMDA receptors on the other, is that AMPA and kainate receptor activation results in channel opening at resting membrane potential,

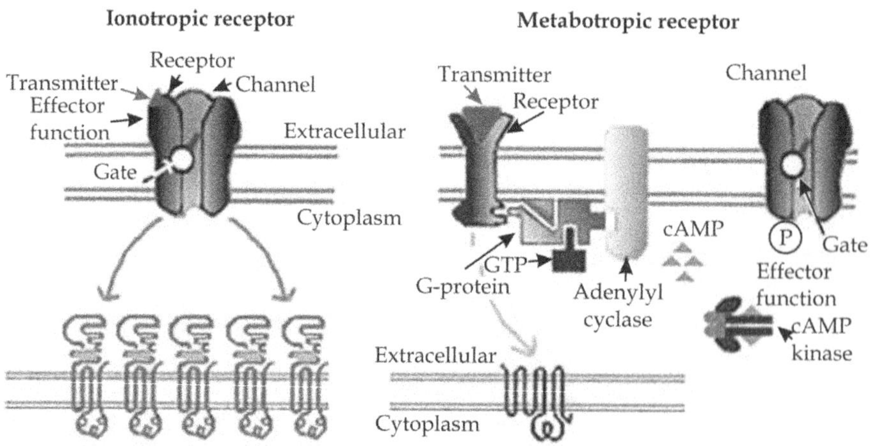


Ionotropic receptors and their associated ion channels form one complex (top). each iGluR is formed from the coaasembly of multiple (4-5) subunits

Metabotropic receptors are coupled to their associated ion channels by a second messenger cascade (top). each mGluR is composed of one polyperptide , which is coupled to a G-protein.

**Fig 17-11:** Glutamate receptors

whereas NMDA receptor activation does not. This is due to the voltage-dependent block of the NMDA pore by extracellular $Mg^{2+}$. When the neuron is strongly depolarized, as occurs with intense activation of the synapse or by activation of neighboring synapses, the $Mg^{2+}$ ion is expelled and the channel opens. Thus, there are two requirements for NMDA receptor channel opening: Glutamate must bind the receptor and the membrane must be depolarized. The rise in intracellular $Ca^{2+}$ that accompanies channel opening results in a long-lasting enhancement in synaptic strength that is referred to as long-term potentiation (LTP). The change can last for many hours or even days and is generally accepted as an important cellular mechanism underlying learning and memory.

The metabotropic glutamate receptors are G protein-coupled receptors that act indirectly on ion channels *via* G proteins. Metabotropic receptors (mGluR1-mGluR8) have been divided into three groups (I, II, and III). A variety of agonists and antagonists have been developed that interact selectively with the different groups. Group I receptors are typically located postsynaptically and are thought to cause neuronal excitation by activating a nonselective cation channel. These receptors also activate phospholipase C, leading to $IP_3$-mediated intracellular $Ca^{2+}$ release. In contrast, group II and group III receptors are typically located on presynaptic nerve terminals and act as inhibitory autoreceptors. Activation of these receptors causes the inhibition of $Ca^{2+}$ channels resulting in inhibition of transmitter release. These receptors are activated only when the concentration of glutamate rises to high levels during repetitive stimulation of the synapse. Activation of these receptors causes the inhibition of adenylyl cyclase and decreases cAMP generation.

The postsynaptic membrane at excitatory synapses is thickened and referred to as the postsynaptic density. This is a highly complex structure containing glutamate receptors, signaling proteins, scaffolding proteins, and cytoskeletal proteins. A typical excitatory synapse contains AMPA receptors, which tend to be located toward the periphery, and NMDA receptors, which are concentrated in the center. Kainate receptors are present at a subset of excitatory synapses, but their exact location is unknown. Metabotropic glutamate receptors (group I), which are localized just outside the PSD, are also present at some excitatory synapses.

## Neuropeptides (polypeptides)

(a) Substance P
(b) Vasopressin
(c) Oxytocin
(d) Somatostatin
(e) Glucagons
(f) Angiotensin II
(g) Atrial natriuretic peptide
(h) Enkephalins
(i) Endorphins

## Purine Nucleotides

### Overview of Purines

**Purines:** Adenosine and uridine di- and triphosphates have roles as extracellular signaling molecules. ATP is a component of the adrenergic storage vesicle and is released with catecholamines. Intracellular nucleotides may also reach the cell surface by other means and extracellular adenosine can result from cellular release or extracellular production from adenine nucleotides. These extracellular nucleotides and adenosine act on a family of purinergic receptors that is divided into two classes, $P_1$ and $P_2$. The $P_1$ receptors are GPCRs that interact with adenosine; two of these receptors ($A_1$ and $A_3$) couple to $G_i$ and two ($A_{2a}$ and $A_{2b}$) couple to $G_s$; methylxanthines antagonize $A_1$ and $A_3$ receptors. Activation of $A_1$ receptors is associated with inhibition of adenylyl cyclase, activation of $K^+$ currents, and in some instances, with activation of PLC, stimulation of $A_2$ receptors activates adenylyl cyclase. The $P_2$ class consists of a large number of $P_{2X}$ receptors that are ligand-gated ion channels, and of the $P_{2Y}$ receptors, a large subclass of GPCRs that couple to $G_q$ or $G_s$ and their associated effectors. The $P_{2Y14}$ receptor is expressed in the CNS, it interacts with UDP-glucose and may couple to $G_q$. The co-storage of ATP and catecholamines in adrenergic storage vesicles and their co-release from adrenergic nerves suggests that $P_{2Y}$ receptors in the synaptic region will be stimulated whenever a nerve releases catecholamine. There is *in vitro* evidence for synergistic $G_q$ ,$G_s$ crosstalk (enhanced β adrenergic response) when $\beta_2$ receptors and $G_q$-linked $P_{2Y}$ receptors are activated simultaneously. Although many of these receptors can be detected in brain, most of the current interest stems from pharmacological rather than physiological observations. Adenosine can act presynaptically throughout the cortex and hippocampal formation to inhibit the release of amine and amino acid transmitters. ATP-regulated responses have been linked pharmacologically to a variety of supracellular functions, including anxiety, stroke, and epilepsy.

### ATP as a Neurotransmitter (Fig 17-11)

The idea that such a workaday metabolite as ATP might be a member of the neurotransmitter elite was resisted for a long time, but it is now firmly established. ATP is a transmitter in the periphery, both as a primary mediator and as a co-transmitter in noradrenergic nerve terminals. The nucleotide is contained in synaptic vesicles of both adrenergic and cholinergic neurons, and it accounts for many of the actions produced by stimulation of autonomic nerves that are not caused by acetylcholine or noradrenaline . These effects include the relaxation of intestinal smooth muscle evoked by sympathetic stimulation, and contraction of the bladder produced by parasympathetic nerves. Burn stock and his colleagues have shown that ATP is released on nerve stimulation in a $Ca^{2+}$-dependent fashion, and that exogenous ATP, in general, mimics the effects of nerve stimulation in various preparations. Furthermore, the ATP receptor antagonist **suramin** (a drug developed many years ago for treating trypanosome infections) blocks these synaptic responses. Recent work has also shown ATP to function as a conventional 'fast' transmitter in the CNS and in autonomic ganglia . ATP is present in all cells in millimolar concentrations and is released, independently of exocytosis, if the cells are damaged (e.g., by ischaemia). ATP released from cells is rapidly dephosphorylated by a range of tissue-specific nucleotidases, producing ADP and, both of which produce a wide variety of receptor-mediated effects. Adenosine, produced following hydrolysis of ATP, exerts presynaptic inhibitory effects on the release of excitatory transmitters in the CNS and periphery.

### Purine Receptors (Fig 17-12)

There are two main types and subtypes are distinguished on the basis of their agonist and antagonist selectivity, as well as molecular structure .

- $P_1$ receptors (subtypes $A_1$, $A_2$ and $A_3$). These are GPCRs that respond to adenosine and are present in many

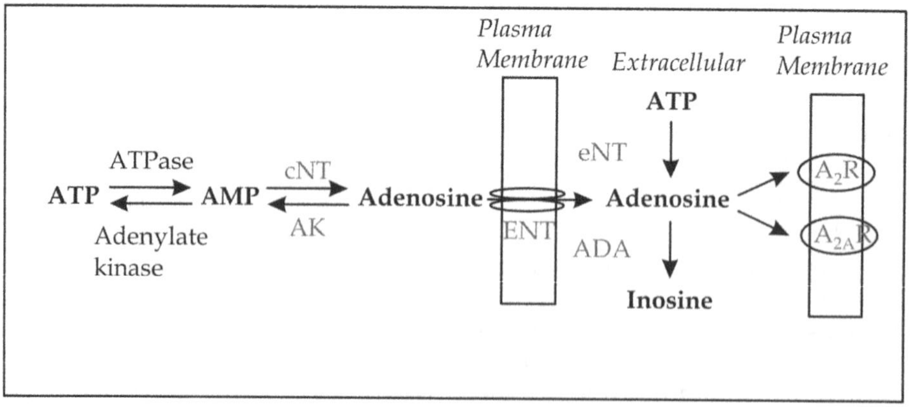


**Fig 17-12:** ATP Neurotransmitter

different tissues. They are linked to stimulation or inhibition of adenylate cyclase.

- $P_2$ receptors (subtypes $P_{2X}$ and $P_{2Y}$, each with several further subdivisions). These respond to ATP and/or ADP. $P_{2X}$ receptors are multimeric ionotropic receptors , whereas $P_{2Y}$ receptors are GPCRs coupled to adenylate cyclase or phosphoinositide metabolism.

## $P_2$ Receptors and Actions

$P_2$ receptors respond to various adenine nucleotides, generally preferring ATP over ADP or AMP. The role of ATP as a fast transmitter involves $P_{2X}$ receptors, of which seven subtypes have been identified. These occur as a variety of mixed (heteromeric) assemblies. Not all their functions are clear, but the following actions are generally agreed.

- $P_{2X1}$ receptors are expressed on various smooth muscle cells. ATP is a co-transmitter released by sympathetic nerves, and $P_{2X1}$ receptors are responsible for the initial contraction.
- $P_{2X2}$ receptors are expressed in many brain regions and mediate 'fast' transmission by ATP in the brain.
- $P_{2X3}$ receptors occur in nociceptive afferent neurons and may participate in pain associated with ATP released through tissue injury.
- $P_{2X7}$ receptors are unusual in that activation causes a large and non-selective increase in membrane permeability. They are expressed mainly by cells of the immune system, and they control the release of certain cytokines.

**Adenosine as a Mediator**

Adenosine differs from ATP in that it is not stored by and released from, secretory vesicles. Rather, it exists free in the cytosol of all cells and is transported in and out of cells mainly using a membrane transporter. Not much is known about the way in which this is controlled. Adenosine in tissues comes partly from this source and partly from extracellular hydrolysis of released ATP or ADP.

Adenosine produces many pharmacological effects, both in the periphery and in the CNS. Under less extreme conditions, variations in adenosine release may play a role in controlling blood flow and (through effects on the carotid bodies) respiration, matching them to the metabolic needs of the tissues.

Adenosine is destroyed or taken up within a few seconds of intravenous administration , but longer-lasting analogues have been discovered that also show greater receptor selectivity. Adenosine uptake is blocked by dipyridamole, a vasodilator and antiplatelet drug .

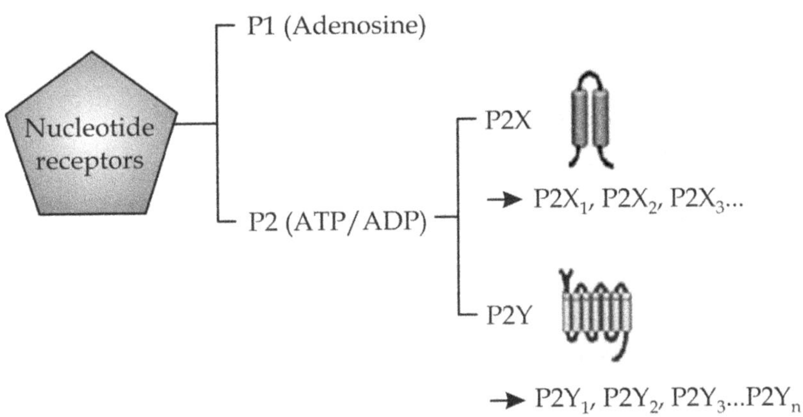


**Fig 17-13:** Purine receptors

Another area of growing interest is asthma. Adenosine has been identified as a potential mediator of cytokine release from mast cells, of hyperreactivity of vagal and other airway neurons, and other actions that may directly or indirectly contribute to the disease.

### Adenosine Receptors

The main effects of adenosine, and the receptors involved, are as follow.

- Vasodilatation, including coronary vessels ($A_2$), except in the kidney, where $A_1$ receptors produce vasoconstriction. Adenosine infusion causes a fall in blood pressure.
- Inhibition of platelet aggregation ($A_2$).
- Block of cardiac atrioventricular conduction ($A_1$) and reduction of force of contraction.
- Bronchoconstriction, especially in asthmatic subjects ($A_1$); the antiasthmatic effect of **methylxanthines** may partly reflect $A_1$ receptor antagonism.
- Release of mediators from mast cells ($A_3$): this contributes to bronchoconstriction.
- Stimulation of nociceptive afferent neurons, especially in the heart ($A_2$): adenosine release in response to ischaemia has been suggested as a mechanism of anginal pain. Carotid body afferents are also stimulated, causing reflex hyperventilation.
- Inhibition of transmitter release at many peripheral and central synapses ($A_1$). In the CNS, adenosine generally exerts a pre- and postsynaptic depressant action, reducing motor activity, depressing respiration, inducing sleep and reducing anxiety, all of which effects are the opposite of those produced by methylxanthines.
- Neuroprotection, in cerebral ischaemia, probably through inhibition of glutamate release through $A_1$ receptors.

### Pharmacological Aspects

#### *Uses of Adenosine*

Because of its inhibitory effect on cardiac conduction, adenosine may be used as an intravenous bolus injection to terminate supraventricular tachycardia. It is safer than alternative drugs such as β-adrenoceptor antagonists or verapamil, because of its short duration of action. Otherwise, adenosine is not used therapeutically, although longer-lasting $A_1$ receptor agonists might prove useful in various conditions (e.g., hypertension, ischaemic heart disease and stroke). Selective adenosine receptor antagonists could also have advantages over theophylline in the treatment of asthma.

#### *Drugs Acting on Purine Receptors*

Methylxanthines, especially analogues of theophylline, are $A_1/A_2$ receptor antagonists; however, they also increase cAMP by inhibiting phosphodiesterase, which contributes to their pharmacological actions independent of adenosine receptor antagonism. CNS stimulation by methylxanthines such as **caffeine** is partly a result of block of inhibitory $A_1/A_2$ receptors. Certain derivatives of theophylline are claimed to show greater selectivity for adenosine receptors over phosphodiesterase. $P_2$ receptors are blocked by suramin.

## Peptides

I. Peptides are the most common neurotransmitters in the hypothalamus.

II. They are all synthesized on ribosomes and are all inactivated by hydrolysis at the synapse.

III. Peptides are far more potent than other neurotransmitters, requiring only very small amounts to produce a profound effect.

IV. Opioid peptides include the endorphins, enkephalins and dynorphins. They are associated with pain relief and pleasure.

V. Cholecystokinin (CCK) seems to function in the production of satiety.

VI. Low doses of the peptide vasopressin have been shown to enhance learning in laboratory animals.

## References

Aizenman CD *et al.*, (2000). Use-dependent changes in synaptic strength at the Purkinje cell to deep nuclear synapse. *Prog Brain Res* **124:** 257.

Bredt DS, Nicoll RA (2003). AMPA receptor trafficking at excitatory synapses. *Neuron* **40:** 361.

Catterall WA *et al.*, (2003). Compendium of voltage-gated ion channels: Calcium channels. *Pharmacol Rev* **55:** 579.

Catterall WA, Goldin AL, Waxman SG (2003). Compendium of voltage-gated ion channels: Sodium channels. *Pharmacol Rev* **55:**575.

Clapham DE *et al.*, (2003). Compendium of voltage-gated ion channels: Transient receptor potential channels. *Pharmacol Rev* **55:** 591.

CHAPTER

# Neurodegenerative Diseases 18

## Introduction

Neurodegenerative diseases affect the central nervous system causing progressive nervous system dysfunction. These debilitating and incurable conditions are characterized by loss of neuronal cell function and are often associated with atrophy of the affected nervous system structures. An important subset of neurodegenerative disease concerns dementias associated with aging. Alzheimer's disease (AD) is the most common clinically recognized dementia in aging populations, and 43% of people 85 or older are thought to suffer from Alzheimer's in the United States. Parkinson's disease (PD), another common nervous system disorder associated with the elderly, affects 1-3% of the population over 60. United Nations population projections estimate a world population of 400 million people 80 years of age or older by the year 2050. Given the financial, social and personal impact of the burden of these diseases, determining causes, prevention and treatment has become a major focus of basic and clinical research.

Study of the etiology of neurodegenerative diseases shows association with genetic factors to be variable within populations for one disease state. Even in the case of Huntington's disease (HD), which is linked to a specific gene, how mutant Huntington's protein effects downstream symptoms of the disorder, including dementia, is not fully understood. The molecular basis of the effects of genetic variation, lifestyle and environmental factors including trauma and infection involves multiple signalling pathways. Neuropathlogical hallmarks of dementia include β-amyloid plaques and neurofibrillary tangles in AD, and Lewy body inclusions in PD. However, while protein aggregation clearly plays a role in neurodegenerative disease, there is evidence that these are signatures of neuronal damage and additional causative elements remain to be discerned. The role of inflammation is an active area of investigation, as is the role of nitric oxide signalling. The effects of these and other key events on transcriptional regulation and initiation of apoptosis and neurotoxicity continues to be intensively explored.

## Alzheimer's Disease

Alzheimer's disease (AD) is a progressive dementia affecting cognition, behaviour, and functional status with no known cause or cure. Patients eventually lose cognitive, analytical, and physical functioning, and the disease is ultimately fatal.

### Pathophysiology

The pathophysiology of Alzheimer disease is complex and multifactorial. Characteristic pathologic features include the accumulation of amyloid cerebral plaques and neurofibrillary tangles of abnormally insoluble tau, an axonal protein. Synaptic levels of acetylcholine decrease as a result of cholinergic neuron involvement. Many other factors may contribute to the pathophysiology, such as depletion of other neurotransmitters, loss of neural synapses, mitochondrial dysfunction, oxidative stress, inflammation, ischemia, insulin signalling, and cholesterol metabolism. Emerging treatments may be directed at these pathways.

## Symptoms

### General

The patient may have vague memory complaints initially, or the patient's significant other may report that the patient is "forgetful". Cognitive decline is gradual over the course of illness. Behavioral disturbances may be present in moderate stages. Loss of daily function is common in advanced stages.

### Symptoms

*Cognitive*

Memory loss (poor recall and losing items)

Aphasia (circumlocution and anomia)

Apraxia

Agnosia

Disorientation (impaired perception of time and unable to recognize familiar people)

Impaired Executive Function

*Noncognitive*

Depression, psychotic symptoms (hallucinations and delusions)

Behavioral disturbances (physical and verbal aggression, motor hyperactivity, uncooperativeness, wandering, repetitive mannerisms and activities, and combativeness)

### Functional

Inability to care for self (dressing, bathing, toileting, and eating)

## Treatment

### Nonpharmacological Therapy

Sleep disturbances, wandering, urinary incontinence, agitation, and aggression should be managed with behavioural interventions whenever possible.

On initial diagnosis, the patient and caregiver should be educated on the course of illness, available treatments, legal decisions, changes in lifestyle that will be necessary with disease progression, and other quality of life issues. The Alzheimer's Association recommends staying physically, mentally, and socially active, adopting a low-fat/low-cholesterol diet rich in dark vegetables and fruit, and managing body weight.

### Pharmacotherapy of Cognitive Symptoms

Managing blood pressure, cholesterol, and blood sugar may reduce the risk of developing AD and may prevent the worsening of dementia in patients with AD.

Current pharmacotherapeutic interventions are primarily symptomatic attempts to improve or maintain cognition.

### Cholinesterase Inhibitors and Memantine

**Cholinesterase inhibitors** and **memantine** are first-line therapy in early management of behavioural symptoms. Modest improvement may be achieved.

### Cholinesterase Inhibitors

No direct comparative trials have assessed the effectiveness of one agent over another. **Donepezil, Rivastigmine,** and **Galantamine** are indicated in mild to moderate AD, while Donepezil is also indicated in severe AD.

The most frequent adverse effects are mild to moderate GI symptoms (nausea, vomiting, and diarrhoea), urinary incontinence, dizziness, headache, syncope, bradycardia, muscle weakness, salivation, and sweating. Abrupt discontinuation can cause worsening of cognition and behavior in some patients. **Donepezil** (Aricept) is a piperidine derivative with specificity for inhibition of acetylcholinesterase rather than butyrylcholinesterase. **Rivastigmine** has central activity at acetylcholinesterase and butyrylcholinesterase sites, but low activity at these sites in the periphery.

**Galantamine** is a cholinesterase inhibitor that also has activity as a nicotinic receptor agonist.

**Tacrine** was the first cholinesterase inhibitor approved for the treatment of AD, but it has been replaced by safer drugs which are better tolerated.

### Other Drugs

**Memantine** (Namenda) blocks glutamatergic neurotransmission by antagonizing *N*-methyl-D-aspartate receptors, which may prevent excitotoxic reactions. It is used as monotherapy, and data suggest that when it is combined with a cholinesterase inhibitor, there is improvement in cognition and activities of daily living. It is indicated for treatment of moderate to severe AD. It is not metabolized by the liver, but is primarily excreted unchanged in the urine (half-life of elimination = 60 to 80 hours).It is usually well tolerated and side effects include constipation, confusion, dizziness, hallucinations, headache, cough and hypertension. It is initiated at 5 mg/day and increased weekly by 5 mg/day to the effective dose of 10 mg twice daily. Dosing must be adjusted in patients with renal impairment. Recent trials do not support the use of **estrogen** to prevent or treat cognitive decline. Evidence related to the role of **vitamin E** in preventing AD is mixed, and conclusions cannot be drawn at this time. Because of a significant incidence of side effects and a lack of compelling evidence, **Nonsteroidal antiinflammatory drugs** are not recommended for treatment or prevention of AD.

There is interest in the use of lipid-lowering agents especially the 3-hydroxy-3-methylglutaryl coenzyme A-reductase inhibitors, to prevent AD. **Pravastatin** and **lovastatin**, but not **simvastatin**, were associated with a lower prevalence of AD. Further study is needed before these agents can be recommended for this use. A metaanalysis indicated that EGb 761 (an extract of ***Ginkgo biloba***) may have some therapeutic effect at doses of 120 to 240 mg of the standard leaf extract twice daily. Because of limited efficacy data, the potential for adverse effects (e.g., nausea, vomiting, diarrhea, headache, dizziness, weakness, and hemorrhage) and the poor standardization of herbal products it is recommended that *Ginkgo biloba* be used only with caution. *Ginkgo biloba* should not be used in individuals taking anticoagulants or antiplatelet drugs, and should be use cautiously in those taking **nonsteroidal antiinflammatory drugs**. Although initial studies suggest potential effectiveness of **huperzine A**, it has not been adequately evaluated for treatment of AD.

### Pharmacotherapy of Noncognitive Symptoms

Pharmacotherapy is aimed at treating psychotic symptoms, inappropriate or disruptive behavior, and depression.

General guidelines are as follows:

1. Use reduced doses
2. Monitor closely
3. Titrate dosage slowly
4. Document carefully and
5. Periodically attempt to reduce medication in minimally symptomatic patients.

Psychotropic medications with anticholinergic effects should be avoided because they may worsen cognition.

### Antipsychotics

Antipsychotic medications have traditionally been used to treat disruptive behaviors and psychosis in AD patients. A metaanalysis showed that 17% to 18% of dementia patients showed a modest treatment response to atypical antipsychotics. Adverse events included somnolence, extrapyramidal symptoms, abnormal gait, worsening cognition, cerebrovascular events and increased risk of death. Typical antipsychotics may also be associated with a small increased risk of death, as well as more severe extrapyramidal effects and hypotension.

### Antidepressants

Depression and dementia have many symptoms in common and the diagnosis of depression can be difficult, especially later in the course of AD. Treatment with a selective serotonin reuptake inhibitor is usually initiated in depressed patients with AD. **Paroxetine** causes more anticholinergic side effects than the other **selective serotonin reuptake inhibitors**. **Venlafaxine** may also be used.

Although probably equally effective, the **tricyclic antidepressants** are usually avoided because of anticholinergic side effects.

**Miscellaneous Therapies**

**Carbamazepine**, mean dose 300 mg/day may improve psychosis and behavioral disturbance in AD patients.

**Oxazepam** and other benzodiazepines have been used to treat anxiety, agitation, and aggression, but they generally show inferior efficacy compared with antipsychotics. They can also worsen cognition, cause disinhibition and increase the risk of falls.

## Parkinson's Disease

Parkinson's disease (PD) has highly characteristic neuropathologic findings and clinical presentation, including motor deficits and in some cases mental deterioration.

### Pathophysiology

The two hallmark features in the substantia nigra pars compacta are loss of neurons and the presence of Lewy bodies. There is a positive correlation between the degree of nigrostriatal dopamine loss and severity of motor symptoms. PD is relatively asymptomatic until profound depletion (70% to 80%) of substantia nigra pars compacta neurons has occurred. Reduced activation of dopamine-1 and dopamine-2 receptors results in greater inhibition of the thalamus. Clinical improvement may be more related to restoring activity at the dopamine-2 receptor than at the dopamine-1 receptor. Loss of presynaptic nigrostriatal dopamine neurons results in inhibition of thalamic activity and activity in the motor cortex. Degeneration of nigrostriatal dopamine neurons results in a relative increase of striatal cholinergic activity, which contributes to the tremor of PD.

### Symptoms

**General features**

For clinically probable PD, the patient exhibits at least two of the following: resting tremor, rigidity or bradykinesia. Asymmetric onset (unilaterality) of these features is usual. Postural instability (difficulty with maintaining balance) is more common in advanced PD.

**Motor symptoms**

The patient experiences decreased manual dexterity, difficulty arising from seating position, diminished arm swing during ambulation, dysarthria (slurred speech), dysphagia (difficulty with swallowing), festinating gait (tendency to pass from a walking to a running pace), flexed posture (axial, upper/lower extremities), "freezing" at initiation of movement, hypomimia (reduced facial animation), hypophonia (reduced voice volume) and micrographia (diminution of handwritten letters/symbols).

**Autonomic and sensory symptoms**

The patient experiences bladder and anal sphincter disturbances, constipation, diaphoresis, fatigue, olfactory disturbance, orthostatic blood pressure changes, pain, paresthesia, paroxysmal vascular flushing, seborrhea, sexual dysfunction and sialorrhea (drooling).

**Mental status changes**

The patient experiences anxiety, apathy, bradyphrenia (slowness of thought processes), confusional state, dementia, depression, hallucinosis/psychosis (typically drug-induced) and sleep disorders (excessive daytime sleepiness, insomnia, obstructive sleep apnea and rapid eye movement sleep behavior disorder).

**Classification of anti-parkinsonism drugs**

*Anticholinergic Agents:* Benztropine, Biperiden, Trihexyphenidyl

*Dopamine Precursors:* Levodopa and Carbidopa

*Dopamine Receptor Agonists:* Apomorphine, Bromocriptine, Pergolide, Pramipexole, Ropinirole.

*Selective MAO inhibitors:* Selegiline, Rasagiline

*COMT inhibitors:* Entacapone, Tolcapone

*Others:* Amantadine

## Treatment

### Pharmacological Therapy

Monotherapy usually begins with a monoamine oxidase-B (MAO-B) inhibitor, or if the patient is young, a dopamine agonist. When additional relief is needed, the addition of levodopa (L-dopa) should be considered. With the development of motor fluctuations, addition of a catechol-O-methyltransferase (COMT) inhibitor should be considered to extend L-dopa duration of activity. For management of L-dopa-induced dyskinesias, the addition of amantadine should be considered.

### Anticholinergic Medications

Anticholinergic drugs can be effective for tremor and dystonic features in some patients but rarely show substantial benefit for bradykinesia or other disabilities. They can be used as monotherapy or in conjunction with other antiparkinsonian drugs. They differ little from each other in therapeutic potential or adverse effects.

Anticholinergic side effects include dry mouth, blurred vision, constipation and urinary retention. More serious reactions include forgetfulness, sedation, depression and anxiety. Patients with pre-existing cognitive deficits and the elderly are at greater risk for central anticholinergic side effects.

### Benztropine

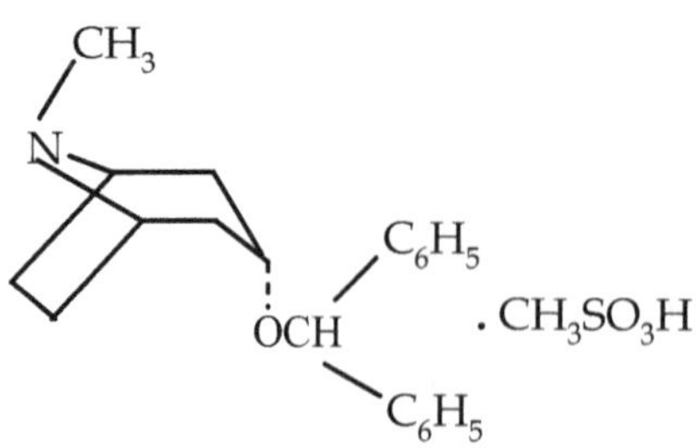


**Fig 18-1:** Structure of benztropine

Benztropine (Fig 18-1) is an anticholinergic agent used predominantly in the symptomatic therapy of Parkinson's disease and movement disorders. Benztropine has not been associated with serum enzyme elevations during treatment and must be a very rare cause of clinically apparent acute liver injury if it occurs at all. Benztropine is an anticholinergic agent that blocks the central cholinergic receptors helping to balance cholinergic transmission in the basal ganglia. Benztropine may also block dopamine reuptake and storage in central sites thus increasing dopaminergic activity. The exact mechanism(s) by which the anticholinergic agents are beneficial for symptoms of Parkinson's disease is unknown. They are used largely in early Parkinsonism and as adjunctive therapy with levodopa or more potent anti-parkinson's disease agents. Current indications include therapy of symptomatic Parkinson's disease as well as drug-induced extrapyramidal syndromes. Benztropine in parenteral forms is also used for therapy of acute dystonic reactions. Benztropine is available in tablets of 0.5, 1 and 2 mg and in liquid solution for injection (2 ml ampoules; 1 mg/ml) in generic forms and under the brand name of Cogentin. The recommended dose is 0.5 to 6 mg daily. Common side effects are due to its anticholinergic activity and include nervousness, drowsiness, confusion, tachycardia, blurred vision, constipation, dry mouth, nausea and urinary retention.

### Biperiden

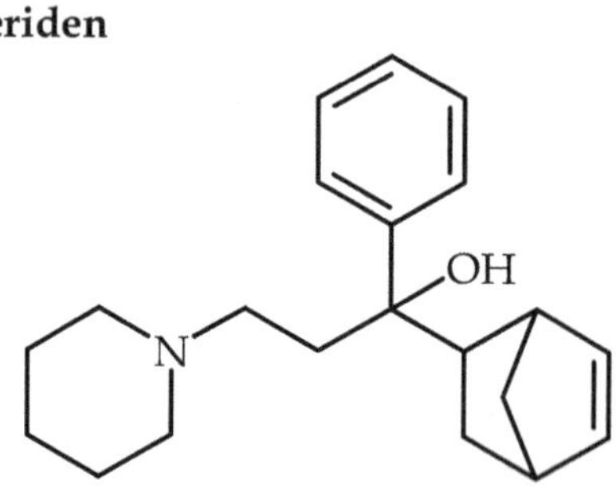


**Fig 18-2:** Structure of biperidin

Biperiden (Fig 18-2) is an oral anticholinergic agent used predominantly in the symptomatic therapy of Parkinson's disease and movement disorders. Biperiden has not been associated with serum enzyme elevations during treatment and may be a very rare cause of clinically apparent acute liver injury. Biperiden is an anticholinergic agent that blocks the central cholinergic receptors helping to balance cholinergic transmission in the basal ganglia. Biperiden may also block dopamine reuptake and storage in central sites thus increasing dopaminergic activity. The exact mechanism(s) by which the anticholinergic agents are beneficial for symptoms of Parkinson's disease is unknown. They are used largely in early Parkinsonism and as adjunctive therapy with levodopa or more potent anti-parkinson's disease agents. Current indications include therapy of symptomatic Parkinson's disease as well as spastic disorders and extrapyramidal disorders due to medications. Biperiden is available in tablets of 2 mg in generic forms and under the brand name of Akineton. The recommended dose is 2 mg three to four times daily. Common side effects are due to its anticholinergic activity and include nervousness, drowsiness, confusion, tachycardia, blurred vision, constipation, dry mouth, nausea and urinary retention.

**Trihexyphenidyl**

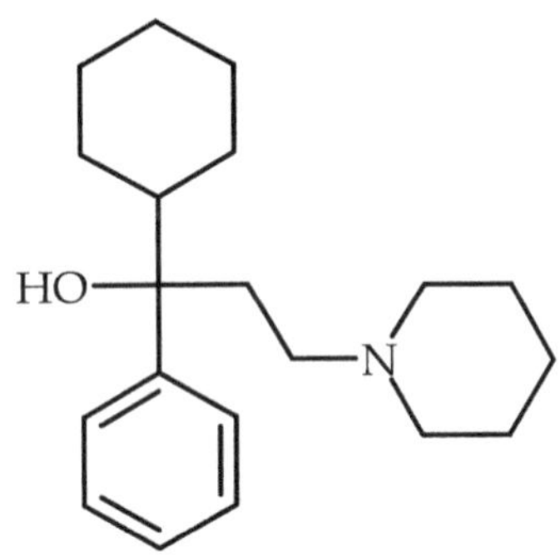


**Fig 18-3:** Structure of trihexyphenidyl

Trihexyphenidyl (Fig 18-3) is an oral anticholinergic agent used predominantly in the symptomatic therapy of Parkinson's disease and movement disorders. Trihexyphenidyl has not been associated with serum enzyme elevations during treatment, but has been implicated in rare cases of acute liver injury. Trihexyphenidyl is an anticholinergic agent that blocks the central cholinergic receptors helping to balance cholinergic transmission in the basal ganglia. Trihexyphenidyl may also block dopamine reuptake and storage in central sites thus increasing dopaminergic activity. The exact mechanism(s) by which the anticholinergic agents are beneficial for symptoms of parkinson's disease is unknown. They are used largely in early Parkinsonism and as adjunctive therapy with levodopa or more potent anti-parkinson's disease agents. Current indications include therapy of symptomatic Parkinson's disease as well as spastic disorders and extrapyramidal disorders due to medications. Trihexyphenidyl is available in tablets of 2 and 5 mg and as an elixir of 2 mg/5 ml in generic forms and formerly under the brand name Artane. The recommended dose is 2 to 5 mg three times daily. Common side effects are due to its anticholinergic activity and include nervousness, confusion, drowsiness, tachycardia, blurred vision, constipation, dry mouth, nausea and urinary retention.

**Levodopa and Carbidopa/Levodopa**

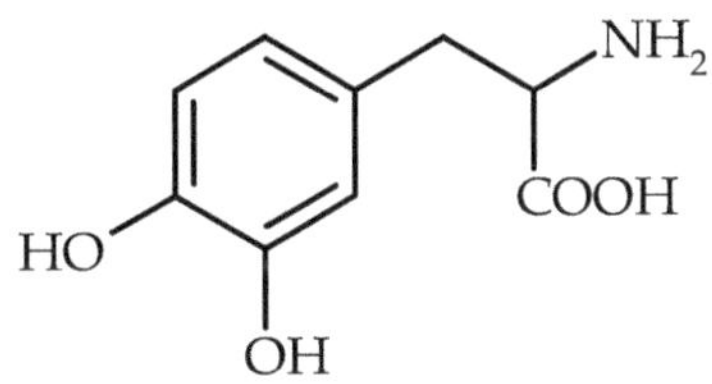


Levodopa

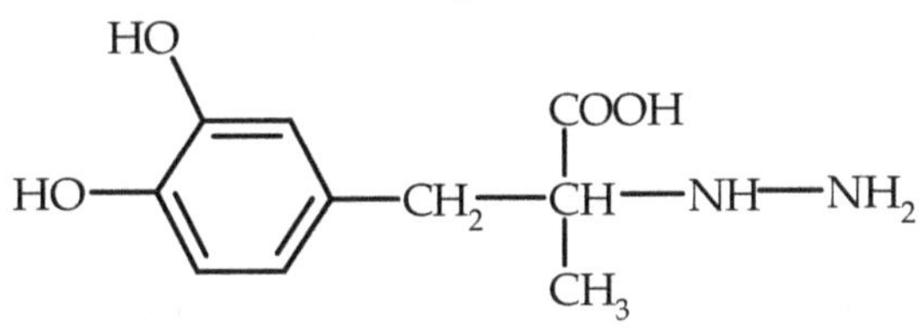


Carbidopa

**Fig 18-4:** Structure of Levodopa and Carbidopa

**L-dopa**, Fig 18-4 the most effective drug available, is the immediate precursor of dopamine. It crosses the blood-brain barrier, whereas dopamine does not. Ultimately, all PD patients will require L-dopa. The decision whether to start L-dopa as soon as the diagnosis is made or only when symptoms compromise social, occupational, or psychological well-being has generated controversy. In the CNS and elsewhere, L-dopa is converted by L-amino acid decarboxylase (L-AAD) to dopamine. In the periphery, L-AAD can be blocked by administering **carbidopa** or **benserazide**, which does not cross the blood–brain barrier Carbidopa therefore increases the CNS penetration of exogenously administered. L-dopa and decreases adverse effects (e.g., nausea, vomiting, cardiac arrhythmias, postural hypotension, vivid dreams) from peripheral L-dopa metabolism to dopamine.

Starting L-dopa at 300 mg/day (in divided doses) in combination with carbidopa often achieves adequate relief of disability. The usual maximal dose of L-dopa is 800 to 1,000 mg/day.

About 75 mg of carbidopa is required to effectively block L-AAD, but some patients may need more. Carbidopa/L-dopa is most widely used in a 25 mg/100 mg tablet, but 25 mg/250 mg and 10 mg/100 mg dosage forms are also available. Controlled-release preparations of carbidopa/L-dopa are available in 50 mg/200 mg and 25 mg/100 mg strengths. For patients with difficulty swallowing, an orally disintegrating tablet is available. If peripheral adverse effects are prominent, 25 mg carbidopa (Lodosyn) tablets are available.

There is marked intra- and intersubject variability in time to peak plasma concentrations after oral L-dopa. Meals delay gastric emptying, but antacids promote gastric emptying. L-dopa is absorbed primarily in the proximal duodenum by a saturable large neutral amino acid transport system. Large neutral amino acids (including high protein meals) can interfere with bioavailability.

L-dopa is not bound to plasma proteins, and the elimination half-life is about 1 hour. The addition of carbidopa can extend the half-life to 1.5 hours, and the addition of a COMT inhibitor (e.g., **entacapone**) can extend it to about 2 to 2.5 hours.

Long-term L-dopa-associated motor complications can be disabling. The most common of these are end-of-dose "wearing off" and "peak-dose dyskinesias". Ten percent of PD patients will develop involuntary movements.

"End-of-dose wearing off" is common and related to the increasing loss of neuronal storage capability for dopamine and the short half-life of L-dopa. Bedtime administration of a dopamine agonist or a sustained release formulation product (e.g., carbidopa/L-dopa CR, ropinirole CR, Rotigotine transdermal patch) can help reduce nocturnal off episodes and improve functioning upon awakening. "Delayed-on" or "no-on" can result from delayed gastric emptying or decreased absorption in the duodenum. Crushing the tablet of carbidopa/L-dopa and taking with a glass of water or using the orally disintegrating tablet formulation on an empty stomach can help. Subcutaneous apomorphine may also be used as rescue therapy.

"Freezing", a sudden, episodic inhibition of lower extremity motor function may be worsened by anxiety and may increase the risk of falls.

Dyskinesias are involuntary choreiform movements, usually involving the neck, trunk, and extremities. They are usually associated with peak striatal dopamine levels. Less commonly, dyskinesias also can develop during the rise and fall of L-dopa effects (the dyskinesias-improvement-dyskinesias or diphasic pattern of response).

"Off-period dystonia", sustained muscle contractions that occur more commonly in distal lower extremity (e.g., foot), occur often in the early morning hours. They may be treated with bedtime administration of sustained-release products, use of baclofen or selective denervation with botulinum toxin.

**Monoamine Oxidase - B Inhibitors**

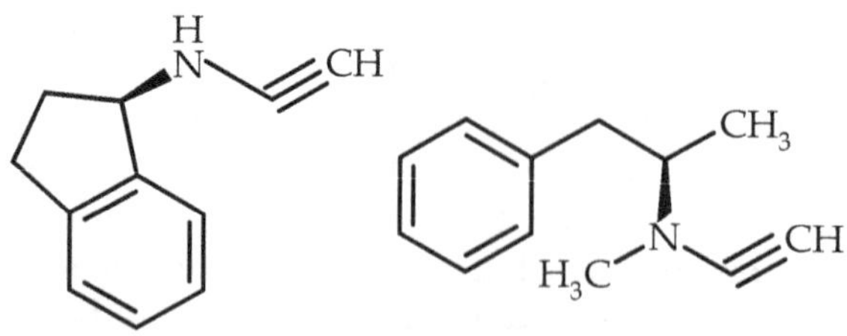


Rasagiline Selegiline

**Fig 18-5:** Structures of rasagiline and selegiline

### Rasagiline

Rasagiline (Fig 18-5) is an inhibitor of monoamine oxidase used as adjunctive therapy in combination with levodopa and carbidopa in the management of Parkinson's disease. Rasagiline has been associated with a low rate of serum enzyme elevations during treatment, but has not been linked to instances of clinically apparent acute liver injury. Rasagiline is a specific inhibitor of monoamine oxidase (MAO) type B which is a major enzyme in the pathway of dopamine and levodopa metabolism. As a result, rasagiline results in an increase in the bioavailability of levodopa enhancing and increasing the duration of its effects in Parkinson's disease. Rasagiline is available in tablets of 0.5 and 1 mg under the brand name of Azilect. Rasagiline is typically given in oral doses of 0.5 to 1 mg once daily alone or in combination with levodopa/carbidopa. Common side effects include headache, nausea, dizziness, agitation, delusions, insomnia, orthostatic hypotension, dry mouth, headache and gastrointestinal upset - most of which are attributable to enhanced dopaminergic effects. Rasagiline has been reported to cause serum enzyme elevations in a small proportion of patients treated long-term, although the abnormalities were usually mild and self-limiting. Rasagiline has not been implicated in cases of acute liver injury but such instances have been reported with other less specific MAO inhibitors.

### Selegiline

Selegiline is an inhibitor of monoamine oxidase used in the treatment of depression and as adjunctive therapy in combination with levodopa and carbidopa in the therapy of Parkinson's disease. Selegiline has been associated with a low rate of serum enzyme elevations during treatment, but has not been linked to instances of clinically apparent acute liver injury. Selegiline is a specific inhibitor of monoamine oxidase (MAO) type B which is a major enzyme in the pathway of dopamine and levodopa metabolism. As a result, selegiline results in an increase in the bioavailability of levodopa enhancing and increasing the duration of its effects in Parkinson's disease. Selegiline is also an antidepressant, its mechanism of action being inhibition of dopamine reuptake from the synaptic cleft. Selegiline is available in capsules and tablets of 5 mg and as a transdermal patch (6, 9 and 12 mg/24 hours) as generic and under the brand names of Carbex, Eldepryl and (transdermal) Emsam. Selegiline is typically given in oral doses of 10 mg daily in divided doses (for Parkinson's disease) and as a transdermal system in doses of 6 to 12 mg daily (for depression). Common side effects include headache, nausea, dizziness, agitation, delusions, insomnia, orthostatic hypotension, dry mouth, headache and gastrointestinal upset - most of which are attributable to enhanced dopaminergic effects. In higher doses, selegiline can also inhibit MAO A and, similar to the non-specific MAO inhibitors, cause increased susceptibility to dietary tyramine inducing hypertensive crises ("cheese effect"). Selegiline has been reported to cause serum enzyme elevations in up to 40% of patients treated long-term. Although the abnormalities were usually mild and self-limiting, they were persistent with continuation of treatment in some patients ultimately requiring drug discointuation. Selegiline has not been implicated in cases of acute liver injury, but such instances have been reported with other less specific MAO inhibitors.

### Catechol-*O*-Methyltransferase Inhibitors

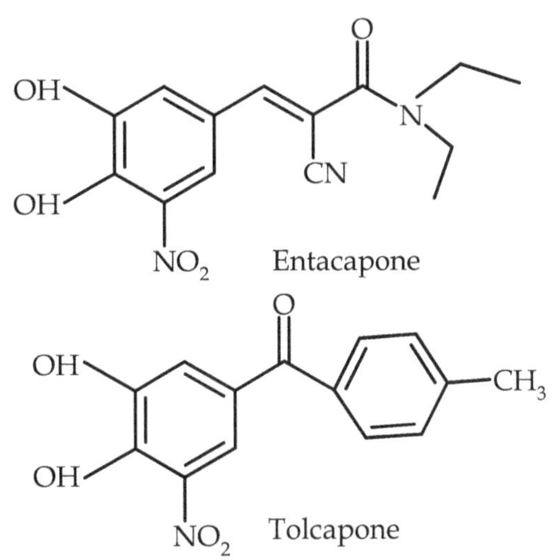


**Fig 18-6:** Structures of entacapone and tolcapone

### Entacapone

Entacapone (Fig 18-6) is a catechol-O-methyltransferase inhibitor used in the therapy of Parkinson's disease as adjunctive therapy in combination with levodopa and carbidopa. Entacapone has been associated with a low rate of serum enzyme elevations during treatment, but has yet to be implicated in cases of clinically apparent acute liver injury with jaundice. Entacapone is a specific inhibitor of cathechol-O-methyltransferase (COMT) which is a major enzyme in the pathway of levodopa metabolism. As a result, entacapone slows the metabolism of levodopa causing an increase in its bioavailability and duration of action. Entacapone inhibits COMT activity only peripherally unlike tolcapone which acts both peripherally and centrally. Entacapone is available in tablets of 200 mg under the brand name of Comtan. It is also available in several fixed dose combinations with carbidopa and levodopa under the brand name Stalevo. Entacapone is typically initiated in doses of 200 mg with each dose of levodopa/carbidopa to a maximum of 1200 mg daily. Common side effects include somnolence, dizziness, confusion, dyskinesia, vivid dreams, hallucinations, depression, fatigue, headache, diarrhea and gastrointestinal upset, side effects that are largely due to enhancement of the dopaminergic effects of levodopa. Entacapone therapy has been associated with serum aminotransferase elevations (> 3 times the upper limit of normal) in only 0.3-0.5% of patients which is similar or minimally higher than the rate in subjects receiving placebo. The elevations were usually transient and asymptomatic and rarely required dose adjustment. In preliminary clinical trials, there were no reports of clinically apparent serious liver injury with jaundice. Subsequently, isolated instances of hepatotoxicity have been reported, injury arising 2-6 weeks after starting entacapone with mild jaundice and cholestatic pattern of liver enzyme elevations, and rapid recovery on stopping. Immunoallergic and autoimmune features were not present. Thus, entacapone may rarely cause clinically apparent liver injury, but it has not been associated with the severe hepatitis and acute liver failure that characterized cases of tolcapone induced liver injury.

Entacapone is extensively metabolized by the liver and eliminated through biotransformation mostly by glucuronidation *via* UDP-glucuronosyl transferase. Polymorphisms of this enzyme have been linked to liver enzyme elevations during therapy but the relationship between dose, metabolism and liver injury due to entacapone has not been defined.

### Tolcapone

Tolcapone is a catechol-O-methyltransferase inhibitor used in the therapy of Parkinson's disease as adjunctive therapy in combination with levodopa and carbidopa. Tolcapone has been associated with serum enzyme elevations during treatment and with several instances of clinically apparent acute liver injury which can be severe and even fatal. Tolcapone is a specific inhibitor of cathechol-O-methyltransferase (COMT) which is a major enzyme in the pathway of levodopa metabolism. As a result, tolcapone slows the metabolism of levodopa and results in an increase in its bioavailability and duration of action. Tolcapone inhibits COMT activity both peripherally and in the central nervous system. Subsequent tolcapone was reintroduced but with requirements for monitoring of serum enzymes. Tolcapone is currently available in tablets of 100 and 200 mg under the brand name of Tasmar. Tolcapone is typically initiated in doses of 100 mg three times daily with adjustment upwards based upon tolerance and clinical effects to a maximum of 600 mg daily. Common side effects include somnolence, dizziness, confusion, dyskinesia, vivid dreams, hallucinations, depression, fatigue, headache, diarrhea and gastrointestinal upset, symptoms that are typical of dopaminergic stimulation and enhanced effects of levodopa.Tolcapone has been reported to cause serum aminotransferase elevations above 3 times the upper limit of normal in 1 to 5% of patients. While these abnormalities are usually asymptomatic and self-limiting, some persist if therapy is continued and resolved only with stopping tolcapone.

More importantly, tolcapone has been implicated in several cases of severe clinically apparent acute liver injury and at least three cases of death from acute liver failure. The onset of injury was insidious, arising 1 to 5 months after starting treatment. The pattern of serum enzyme elevations was hepatocellular and the clinical phenotype was acute viral hepatitis-like. Immunoallergic manifestations were not present, but some patients had autoantibodies of unclear significance. Because of these reports, regular monitoring of serum aminotransferase levels has been mandated (every 2-4 weeks for the first 6 months of treatment and as clinically indicated thereafter) during tolcapone therapy and treatment should be promptly discontinued if ALT or AST levels rise above twice the upper limit of the normal range or if signs or symptoms of liver injury are present. Tolcapone is metabolized extensively in the liver and undergoes glucuronidation prior to excretion. The hepatotoxicity of tolcapone is likely due to production of a toxic intermediate that overwhelms the usual protective mechanisms of excretion. Increased likelihood of hepatic injury due to tolcapone has been linked to variants of the gene that is responsible for glucuronidation: UDP-glucuronosyl transferase.

**Dopamine Agonists Fig 18-7**

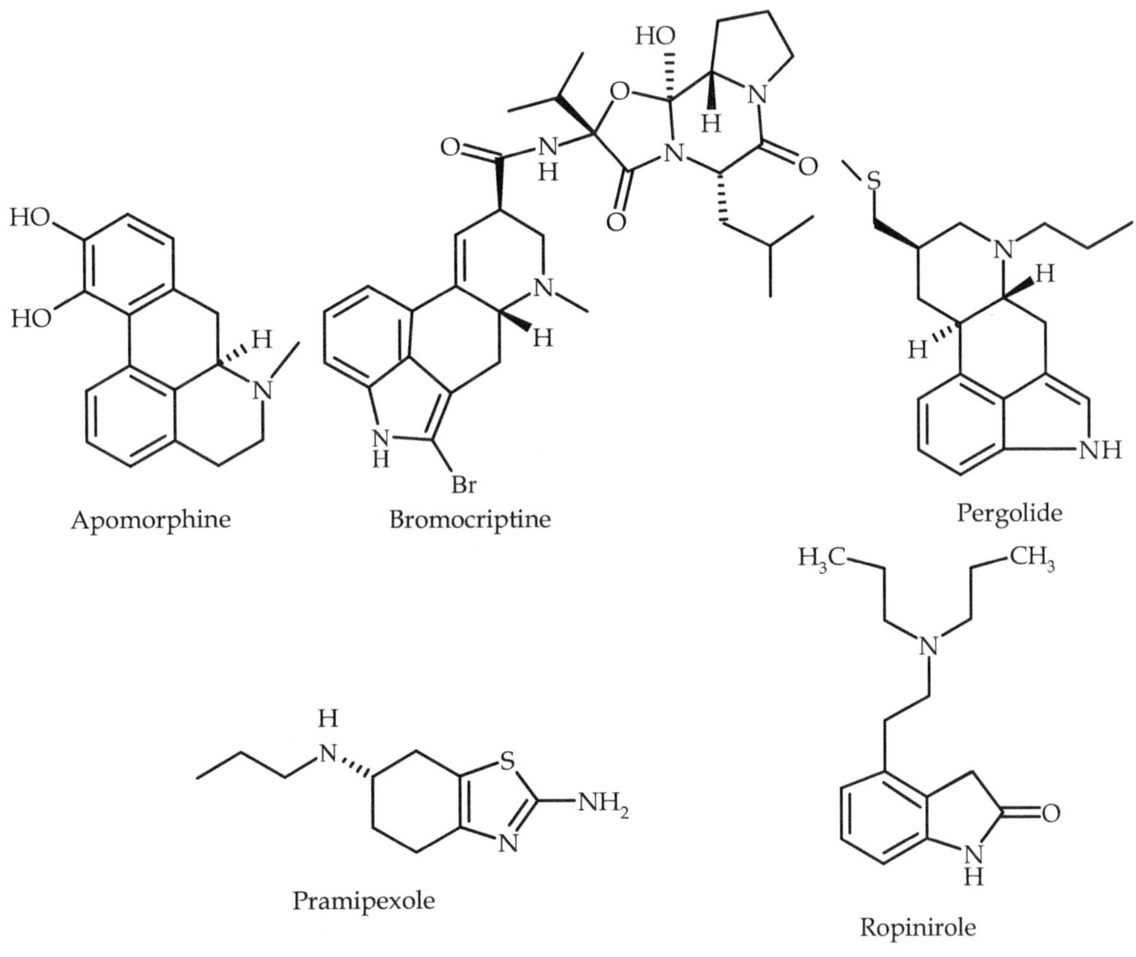


**Fig 18-7:** Structures of dopamine agonists

### Apomorphine

Apomorphine is a subcutaneously administered dopamine receptor agonist used predominantly in the therapy of hypomobility of advanced Parkinson's disease. The use of apomorphine has been limited, but it has not been associated with serum enzyme elevations during treatment nor has it been implicated in cases of acute liver injury. Apomorphine is a subcutaneously administered dopamine receptor agonist which has moderate affinity for the $D_2$, $D_3$ and $D_5$ class of dopamine receptors in the central nervous system and little activity against the $D_1$ class. It also has some alpha adrenergic activity. Current indications are for intermittent hypomobility of advanced Parkinson's disease. It is also used for acute dystonic reactions. Apomorphine is available in a liquid solution of 10 mg/ ml under the brand name Apokyn. It is given in 0.2 to 0.6 ml doses subcutaneously as needed up to 3 times daily. Apomorphine injections usually cause nausea and vomiting requiring antiemetics. It can cause hypotension, gastrointestinal upset, anxiety, confusion, dizziness, headache, hallucinations, vivid dreams and insomnia, symptoms typical of dopaminergic stimulation.

### Bromocriptine

Bromocriptine is an oral dopamine receptor agonist used predominantly in the therapy of Parkinson's disease, but which has other activities including inhibition of prolactin and growth hormone release which has led to its use in acromegaly, infertility and galactorrhea. Bromocriptine therapy is associated with low rate of transient serum enzyme elevations during treatment and has been implicated in rare cases of acute liver injury.Bromocriptine is a semisynthetic ergot alkaloid derivative which acts as a dopamine receptor agonist. Bromocriptine has strong agonist activity on the $D_2$ class of dopamine receptors and partial antagonist of the $D_1$ receptors in central nervous system. Current indications are the therapy of symptomatic Parkinson's disease as well as spastic disorders and extrapyramidal disorders caused by medications. Bromocriptine also has inhibitory activity on prolactin and growth hormone release, and its indications also include treatment of amenorrhea and galactorrhea related to hyperprolactinemia, female infertility, acromegaly, Cushing's syndrome and premenstrual syndrome. Bromocriptine is available in tablets of 2.5 mg and capsules of 5 mg in generic forms and under the brand name of Parlodel. The recommended dose for Parkinson's disease is 10 to 40 mg daily, but it must be introduced gradually and the dose titrated based upon tolerance and effect. In Parkinson's disease, it is usually used in combination with levodopa/carbidopa. Common **side effects** include profound hypotension (with the first dose phenomenon), somnolence, fatigue, vivid dreams, anxiety, confusion, hallucinations, delusions, depression, dizziness, headache, nausea and gastrointestinal upset, symptoms common with increased dopaminergic activity. Bromocriptine has been reported to cause serum aminotransferase elevations in a small proportion of patients, but these abnormalities are usually mild, asymptomatic and self-limiting. In rare instances, more marked elevations occur that may require dose modification or discontinuation and which can recur with rechallenge. In addition, bromocriptine has been implicated in a small number of cases of clinically apparent acute liver injury, but the clinical characteristics and typical pattern of enzyme elevations has not been characterized and case reports of hepatic injury due to bromocriptine have not been published. Thus, bromocriptine is a very rare cause of clinically apparent liver injury and has not been implicated in causing acute liver failure or chronic liver injury.Bromocriptine is rapidly removed from the serum by the liver largely by hydrolysis and excreted rapidly.

### Pergolide

Pergolide is an oral dopamine receptor agonist used predominantly in the therapy of Parkinson's disease. Pergolide therapy is associated with low rate of transient serum enzyme elevations during treatment and has been implicated in rare cases of acute liver injury. Pergolide is an ergot derivative similar to bromocriptine which acts as a dopamine receptor agonist. Pergolide, unlike bromocriptine, has agonist activity on both $D_1$ and $D_2$ dopamine receptors and acts directly on the substantia nigra. Pergolide was approved for use in the United States in 1988 and has been in use since in the therapy of symptomatic Parkinson's disease, usually in combination with levodopa/carbidopa. Pergolide is available in tablets of 0.05, 0.25 and 1.0 mg in generic forms and under the brand name of Permax. The typical initiating dose of pergolide is 0.05 mg once daily for the first 2 days with gradual increase thereafter based upon tolerance and effect. The average therapeutic dose in clinical studies was 3 mg per day given in 3 divided doses, common **side effects** include profound hypotension (with the first dose), somnolence, fatigue, vivid dreams, insomnia, anxiety, confusion, depression, dizziness, headache, nausea and gastro-intestinal upset. Pergolide has been reported to cause serum aminotransferase elevations in a small proportion of patients, but these abnormalities are usually mild, asymptomatic and self-limiting even without dose adjustment. In addition, pergolide has been implicated in a small number of cases of clinically apparent, acute liver injury, but the frequency, severity, clinical characteristics and typical pattern of enzyme elevations have not been characterized. Thus, pergolide is a very rare cause of clinically apparent liver injury. Pergolide is metabolized extensively by the liver and metabolic by products excreted rapidly in the urine.

**Pramipexole**

Pramipexole is a selective dopamine receptor agonist used in the therapy of Parkinson's disease. Pramipexole therapy is associated with a low rate of transient serum enzyme elevations during treatment, but has not been implicated in cases of clinically apparent acute liver injury. Pramipexole is synthetic, nonergot derivative dopamine receptor agonist that has selective activity for the $D_2$ class of dopamine receptors and little agonist activity for the $D_1$ class. For this reason, pramipexole may be better tolerated than bromocriptine or pergolide which have activity for both $D_1$ and $D_2$ receptors. Pramipexole was approved for use in the United States in 1997 for the therapy of symptomatic Parkinson's disease. Pramipexole is available in tablets of 0.125, 0.25, 0.5, 1 and 1.5 mg generically and under the brand name of Miraplex. It is used often but not always in combination with levodopa/carbidopa. Pramipexole is typically initiated in low doses (0.375 mg in 3 divided doses daily) with adjustment upwards based upon tolerance and clinical effects. The typical maintenance dose for Parkinson's disease is 1.5 to 4.5 mg daily in three divided doses. Pramipexole can be initiated more quickly than bromocriptine or pergolide, and does not cause the profound hypotension and nausea that are typical of the ergot derivatives. Common **side effects** include somnolence, fatigue, vivid dreams, anxiety, confusion, depression, dizziness, headache and gastrointestinal upset. Pramipexole has been reported to cause serum aminotransferase elevations in a small proportion of patients, but these abnormalities are usually mild, asymptomatic and self-limiting even without dose adjustment. Pramipexole has not been implicated in cases of clinically apparent acute liver injury which must be rare if it occurs at all.

**Ropinirole**

Ropinirole is a selective dopamine receptor agonist used in the therapy of Parkinson's disease. Ropinirole therapy is associated with low rate of transient serum enzyme elevations during treatment and has been implicated in rare cases of acute liver injury. Ropinirole is a synthetic, nonergot derivative dopamine receptor agonist that has selective activity for the $D_2$ class of dopamine receptors and little agonist activity for the $D_1$ class. For this reason, ropinirole may be better tolerated than bromocriptine or pergolide which act on both classes of dopamine receptors. Ropinirole was approved for use in the United States in 1997 for the therapy of symptomatic Parkinson's disease. Indications were later expanded to include restless legs syndrome. Ropinirole is available in tablets of 0.25, 0.50, 1, 2, 3, 4 and 5 mg under the brand name of Requip. Ropinirole is typically initiated in low doses with adjustment upwards based upon tolerance and clinical effects. In treatment of Parkinson's disease, the typical dose of ropinirole is 3 to 6 mg daily in three divided doses, often but not always in combination with levodopa/carbidopa. Ropinirole can be initiated more quickly than bromocriptine or pergolide and does not cause the profound hypotension and nausea that are typical of the ergot derivatives. Ropinirole is also approved for use in restless legs syndrome, typically starting at 0.25 mg daily, 1 to 3 hours before bedtime and increasing the dose slowly based upon tolerance and effect. Common **side effects** of ropinirole include somnolence, fatigue, vivid dreams, anxiety, confusion, depression, dizziness, headache and gastrointestinal upset, symptoms that are typical of dopaminergic stimulation. Ropinirole has been reported to cause serum aminotransferase or alkaline phosphatase elevations in a small proportion of patients, but these abnormalities are usually mild, asymptomatic and self-limiting even without dose adjustment. Ropinirole has been implicated in a small number of cases of acute liver injury, but the clinical characteristics and typical pattern of enzyme elevations has not been characterized. In one case report the time to onset was 2 months and the pattern of liver enzyme elevations was mixed and associated with marked jaundice. Immunoallergic and autoimmune features were not present. The injury resolved within 2 months of stopping. Thus, ropinirole can cause acute, clinically apparent liver injury with jaundice, but it is rare. Ropinirole is extensively metabolized in the liver, largely by the cytochrome P450 system (CYP 1A2) to inactive metabolites. Liver injury may be caused by production of a toxic or immunogenic intermediate of its metabolism.

**Amantadine**

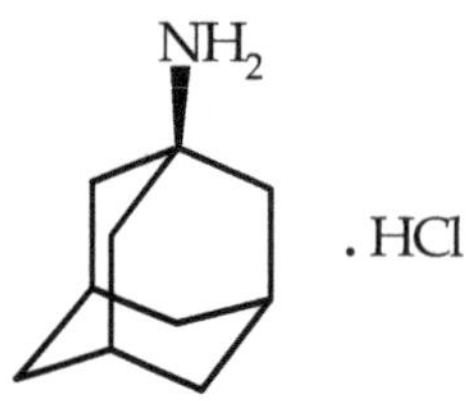


**Fig 18-8:** Structure of amantadine

Amantadine (Fig 18-8) is a primary amine that has both antiviral and dopaminergic activity and is used in the therapy of influenza A and management of Parkinson's disease. Amantadine has not been associated with clinically apparent liver injury. Amantadine is a cyclic primary amine that has antiviral and anti-parkinsonian activities. The anti-parkinsonian activity of amantadine appears to be due to its effects on release of dopamine in the substantia nigra. Amantadine is indicated for therapy of influenza A and in management of Parkinson's disease and extrapyramidal reactions. Amantadine is available as capsules or tablets of 100 mg and as oral syrup generically and under the brand name of Symmetrel. The recommended oral dose for influenza in adults is 200 mg daily until symptoms have resolved. The dose in Parkinson's disease is 100 to 300 mg daily in divided doses. Side effects include anxiety, dizziness, ataxia, confusion, fatigue, headache, insomnia, dry mouth and gastrointestinal upset. Despite widespread use, there is little evidence that amantadine when given orally causes liver injury, either in the form of serum enzyme elevations or clinically apparent liver disease. Amantadine has minimal hepatic metabolism and is excreted largely unchanged in the urine, factors which perhaps explain the absence of significant hepatotoxicity.

**Diet and Exercise**

If a person is taking L-dopa, their doctor may recommend adjusting the amount of protein in their diet, since protein may interfere with the absorption of the drug. Swimming, walking, physical therapy, and muscle strength exercises help to maintain muscle tone and strength and improve mobility. Full range of motion exercises improve balance, walking, and strength.

**Surgery**

Surgery is not performed as often since the discovery of L-dopa. Cryothalamotomy: a super cooled metal tipped probe is surgically inserted into the thalamus to destroy areas of the brain that are producing tremors.

- ***Pallidotomy:*** A portion of the brain, the globus pallidus, is lesioned. This may improve tremor, rigidity, and bradykinesia, possibly by interrupting the neural pathway between the globus pallidus and the corpus striatum or thalamus.

- *Deep brain stimulation (DBS):* Implantation of an electrical stimulator, similar to a cardiac pacemaker, to counteract the loss of dopamine producing cells in the substantia nigra. In contrast to the other two forms of surgery, DBS does not form permanent brain lesions.

## Huntington Disease

Huntington disease (HD) is a progressive neurodegenerative disorder with an established genetic origin and symptoms that are preferable to specific regions of brain disease.

Cellular and molecular techniques are rapidly elucidating the pathogenesis of the disorder and are leading to approaches designed to develop rational treatments. Thus, HD serves as a model for the future study of those psychiatric disorders in which abnormal brain function is thought to arise from predominantly genetic factors.

### Symptoms and Stages of HD

**Signs and Symptoms**

Because Huntington's disease affects the mind, body and emotions, symptoms often mimic other conditions. The general symptoms in early stages can include poor memory; difficulty in making decisions; mood changes such as increased depression, anger or irritability; a growing lack of coordination, twitching or other uncontrolled movements; difficulty in walking, speaking and swallowing. The order in which symptoms develop will vary from person to person. As the disease continues, the symptoms become progressively worse and lead to incapacitation.

**The different types of symptoms are**

***Physical symptoms:*** Physical symptoms include chorea (involuntary movements of the limbs, face and body). Chorea may lead to difficulty in walking, speaking and swallowing. Choking is a particular hazard, due to reduced ability to control the muscles of the tongue, neck and diaphragm. People often lose weight because they have difficulty in eating and burn more calories due to the continuous movement.

**The physical symptoms are:**

- Development of tics (involuntary movement) in the fingers, feet, face, or trunk
- Increased clumsiness
- Loss of coordination and balance
- Slurred speech
- Jaw clenching or teeth grinding
- Difficulty in swallowing or eating
- Continual muscular contractions
- Stumbling or falling

***Cognitive or Mental symptoms:*** Over time, these symptoms may progress to a stage where the person loses the ability to recognize familiar objects, people and places. Cognitive symptoms include a loss of drive and initiative. People with Huntington's disease may appear to be lazy or uninterested in life, spending days doing little, or neglecting personal hygiene. They may also lose the ability to organize themselves, as planning skills and ability to carry out more than one task at once deteriorate. In later stages, people may get memory loss and be less able to understand speech. Memory affected, but affected persons rarely lose their memory of family, friends and the immediate situation.

The following cognitive or mental symptoms as follows:

- Decreased concentration
- Forgetfulness and memory decline
- Poor judgment
- Difficulty making decisions or answering questions
- Difficulty driving

***Emotional symptoms:*** Initial emotional symptoms are usually slight and thus easy to misinterpret. Many conditions and life circumstances can trigger mood changes, so it is especially important to know what psychiatric signs may indicate Huntington's disease.

Depression, the most common psychiatric symptom of Huntington's disease will generally manifest as:

- Hostility/irritability
- Lack of energy
- Ongoing disinterest in life (lack of pleasure or joy)
- Bipolar disorder (manic-depression) in some Huntington's disease patients

Emotional symptoms include depression, not only because of the burden of having a progressive disorder, but also as a direct result of the damage to certain brain cells. People often become frustrated at being unable to work or carry out previously simple tasks. They also seem to behave stubbornly, probably due to a reduced ability to react flexibly and to understand the needs and emotions of others. People with Huntington's disease may also become more irritable and antisocial than usual. Such persons often become irritable, anxious and depressed that is why common causes of death include suicide and intercurrent infections.

A person with Huntington's disease may eventually begin to exhibit psychotic behavior such as:

- Delusions
- Hallucinations
- In-appropriate behavior (e.g., unprovoked aggression)
- Paranoia
- The outcome of Huntington's disease is invariably fatal; over a course of 15 to 30 years, the affected person becomes totally disabled and unable to communicate requiring full time care; death ensues from the complications of immobility.

## The Stages of HD

Though the pattern and severity of symptoms vary from person to person, the course of HD can be roughly divided into three stages.

1. Early in the disease, manifestations include subtle changes in coordination, perhaps some involuntary movements, difficulty thinking through problems, and often, a depressed or irritable mood. At this stage, medications are often effective in treating depression and other emotional symptoms. It is a good time to begin planning for the future. Financial plans should be made and legal documents (a Living Will, for example) drawn up.
2. In the middle stage, involuntary movements (chorea) may become more pronounced. A staggering gait can sometimes be mistaken for drunkenness (it can be helpful to carry documentation that clearly refers to a diagnosis of Huntington 's disease). Speech and swallowing will begin to be affected. It is important to consult a speech-language pathologist (speech therapist) who will be able to offer suggestions and strategies for improving communication and swallowing abilities. Likewise, occupational and physical therapists can develop programs to help maintain the highest level of functioning and thereby improve the quality of life. Thinking and reasoning skills will also gradually diminish. At this stage it may become increasingly difficult to hold a job and to carry out household responsibilities. Here again, simple strategies may be employed to help decrease frustration, increase functioning and prolong independence. For example, disorientation and short-term memory loss can be addressed by labelling drawers, maintaining a daily routine and posting a calendar listing appointments and events.
3. People with late-stage HD may have severe chorea, but more often have become rigid. Choking on food becomes a major concern, as does weight loss. At this stage people with HD are totally dependent on others for all aspects of care, can no longer walk and are not able to speak. Although cognitive abilities are severely impaired, it is important to remember that the person is generally still aware of his/her environment, remains able

to comprehend language and retains an awareness of loved ones and others. He/she may continue to enjoy looking at photographs and hearing stories of family and friends.

## Diagnosis

Genetic testing can diagnose Huntington's at every stage of the life cycle.

**There are three categories for testing:**

1. **Prenatal testing**, either amniocentesis (a sample of fluid from around the fetus), or chorionic villus sampling (CVS—a sample of fetal cells from the placenta) will indicate whether the baby has inherited the gene for Huntington's.
2. **Pre-symptomatic testing** is available to people who are at risk of inheriting Huntington's disease from a parent, but don't have symptoms and don't know whether or not they carry the gene.
3. **Confirmatory testing** determines whether a person showing what appear to be the symptoms of HD, actually has the disease. Neurological and psychological tests are also conducted to arrive at a conclusive diagnosis of Huntington's Disease.

Pre-symptomatic testing is usually requested or recommended when a parent is known to have or is suspected of having, Huntington's disease or an at-risk parent is still living, but doesn't know whether they carry the Huntington's gene.

# Juvenile Huntington's Disease

In approximately ten percent of cases, Huntington's disease affects children or adolescents. Children most often inherit the disease from their fathers (adult-onset HD is inherited from both parents with the same frequency). The symptoms of the juvenile form, or Westphal variant of HD are somewhat different from adult-onset HD. Initial symptoms usually involve slow, stiff and awkward walking and talking, choking, clumsiness and falling. Later, the child may become slow to respond and performance at school may become erratic. The course of the juvenile variant is generally more rapid than adult-onset HD.

## Symptomatic Treatment and Management

An integrated, multi-disciplinary approach focuses on the triad of:

Diet and supplements

Exercise

Spiritual and psycho-social support

This above program enhances quality of life for people living with Huntington's disease as well as for those at risk of developing Huntington's disease and may very likely delays the onset of symptoms. Foods known to nourish the brain, support memory and build overall immunity are especially recommended. Once Huntington's disease is confirmed, patients are encouraged to continue this approach, adding other health support therapies, as they become necessary including physical, occupational and speech therapy.

Most people with Huntington's disease eventually become physically and mentally disabled. As the disease progresses, long-term nursing home care may be necessary. Because Huntington's disease has no known cure, treatment is supportive, protective and aimed at relieving symptoms. It is extremely important for people with Huntington's disease to maintain physical fitness as much as possible, as individuals who exercise and keep active tend to do better than those who do not. No satisfactory treatment is available to stop or reverse Huntington's disease, but some approaches can control signs and symptoms. Medications are available to treat the symptoms of Huntington's disease. Treatments include medication, mental health care, other therapies (speech, swallowing and physical therapies) and family support.

**Medication:** No medications are approved by the Food and Drug Administration (FDA) to treat the symptoms of Huntington's disease. Physicians prescribe a number of medications to help control emotional and movement problems associated with Huntington's disease. Most drugs used to treat the symptoms of Huntington's disease have side effects such as fatigue, restlessness or hyperexcitability. Many drugs are being studied to determine if they slow the progression of Huntington's disease, but currently no drug has been recommended. To decrease chorea, tranquilizers such as dopamine antagonists, dopamine depletors or clonazepam. These drugs have side effects (such as worse balance, more difficulty swallowing and exacerbation of depression) that must be weighed against their benefits. SSRIs (Selective Seratonin Specific Re-uptake Inhibitors) antidepressants, mood stabilizers or neuroleptics may also be prescribed in coordination medications with psychiatric counselling to address psychological problems. Practical treatment for symptomatic Huntington's disease emphasizes the selective use of medications.

The symptomatic treatment of Huntington's disease may be outlined as follows:

**Dopamine antagonists:** Dopamine antagonists are effective in reducing the involuntary movements. Haloperidol, pimozide and sulpiride are the most frequently used dopamine antagonists in the treatment of movement disorders like chorea as observed in Huntington's disease.

**Presynaptic dopamine depletors:** Tetrabenazine is presynaptic dopamine depletors, which acts on neurons to deplete synaptic vesicles of dopamine and other monoamines. It causes the release of dopamine from synaptic vesicles and blocks its uptake into the vesicles. Tetrabenazine produces a decrease in the content and activity of dopamine, norepinephrine and serotonin in the brain. It also acts to block postsynaptic dopamine receptors. The central activity of tetrabenazine relative to its peripheral activity is greater than that of reserpine. It has been found to be useful in the treatment of chorea. The chorea may also be controlled by use of reserpine. Reserpine depletes cerebral dopamine by preventing intraneuronal storage, it is introduced in low doses (e.g., 0.25 mg daily) and daily dose is then built up gradually (e.g., by 0.25 mg every week) until benefit occurs or adverse effects in become troublesome.

**Antidepressants:** Depression can be treated effectively with standard antidepressants drugs like Fluoxetine that is effective treatment for both the depression and the irritability manifest in symptomatic Huntington's disease. Carbamazepine was found to be effective for depression. Several recent reports suggests that Olanzapine may also be helpful; the dose varies with the patient but 10 mg daily is often sufficient although doses as 30 mg daily are sometimes required. Some other antidepressants including sertraline and nortriptyline can also help to control depression and the obsessive compulsive rituals that some people with Huntington's disease develop. Medications such as lithium can also help to control extreme emotions and swings.

**Tranquilizers and antipsychotic drugs:** Tranquilizers as well as chlorpromazine, haloperidol and imipramine help control chorea movements but they can't stop mental deterioration. They also alleviate discomfort and depression, making the patient easier to manage. Antipsychotic drugs such as haloperidol and clozapine can help control movements, violent outbursts and hallucinations. Psychosis can be treated with atypical neuroleptics clozapine (50 to 600 mg/day), quetiapine (100 to 600 mg/day) and resperidone (2 to 8 mg/day). These medications control dyskinesias as well as traditional neuroleptics but have fewer extra pyramidal side effects. However, tranquilizers increase patient rigidity. Paranoia, delusional states and psychosis usually requires treatment with antipsychotic drugs but doses required often are lower than those usually used in primary psychiatric disorder. In individuals with predominantly rigid Huntington's disease, clozapine or carbamazepine may be more effective treatment of paranoia and psychosis. Haloperidol is started in a small dose, e.g., 1 mg twice daily and increased every 4 days depending on the response. If haloperidol is not helpful, treatment with increasing of perphenazine up to a total of about 20 mg daily.

In some instances, antipsychotic drugs may cause side effects that mimic the signs of Parkinson's disease including involuntary twitching in the face and body.

**Anxiolytic - Benzodiazepines:** Many patients of Huntington's disease exhibit worsening of involuntary movements because of anxiety or stress. In these situations, judicious use of sedative or anxiolytic benzodiazepines can be very helpful. Benzodiazepines may also be useful in alleviating aggressiveness or anxiety, but attention must be paid to unsteady gait, sedation and predisposition to aspiration while patients are taking these agents. Long-acting benzodiazepines are favored over short-acting ones because of the lesser potential for abuse and paradoxical excitation. Clomipramine and selective serotonin reuptake inhibitors may be beneficial in controlling obsessive-compulsive behavior associated with Huntington's disease, as is the case with other dementias.

**Anticonvulsants:** Individuals with Huntington's disease occasionally develop Myoclonus and seizures that can be controlled effectively with standard anticonvulsant drugs like clonazepam, valproic acid, or other anticonvulsants.

**Antibiotics:** Antibiotic may treat Huntington's disease. A common antibiotic holds promise as a treatment for Huntington's disease, a hereditary disorder for which there is no effective treatment or cure. In mice genetically engineered to develop a similar illness, Minocycline, an antibiotic used to treat some forms of acne and arthritis, slowed down the development of symptoms and death from the disease, researchers report. An enzyme called caspase-1 and a substance called nitric oxide are believed to be involved in Huntington's disease. Since the antibiotic minocycline targets this enzyme and another one involved in the release of nitric oxide, the researchers tested its effects in mice with a disease similar to Huntington's. Assuming that the drug does slow down Huntington's disease, it will probably be used in combination with other drugs that are developed to treat the disease.

**Miscellaneous:** No treatment is available to reverse, retard, or stop the relentless progression of Huntington's disease. However, several medications, including baclofen, idebenone and vitamin E have been studied in clinical trials with limited samples . Some clinical studies have involved using stem cells (the most basic form of cells from which others develop) to grow cells that can be transplanted into the brain of a person affected by the disease. This approach may eventually improve the outlook for those who possess the faulty Huntington gene. To control chorea movements without rigidity, choline may be prescribed. Institutionalization is usually necessary because of deterioration. Electro-convulsive therapy has been used for patients with severe depression associated with Huntington's disease. Although drug therapy for inappropriate sexual behavior is generally reserved as a last option, medroxyprogesterone may be useful. Scientific investigations using electronic and other technologies enable scientists to see what the defective gene does to various structures in the brain and how it affects the body's chemistry and metabolism. Laboratory animals are being bred in the hope of duplicating the clinical features of Huntington's disease so that researchers can learn more about the symptoms and progression of Huntington's disease. Investigators are implanting fetal tissue in rodents and nonhuman primates with the hope of understanding, restoring or replacing functions typically lost by neuronal degeneration in individuals with Huntington's disease. Related areas of investigation include excitotoxicity (over stimulation of cells by natural chemicals found in the brain), defective energy metabolism (a defect in the mitochondria), oxidative stress (normal metabolic activity in the brain that produces toxic compounds called here radicals) and tropic factors (natural chemical substances found in the human body that may protect against cell death).

**Mental health care:** The depression rate among people with Huntington's disease is very high and can be caused by the disease or the challenges it creates. The higher risk for suicide than in the general population and should be openly assessed.

**Other therapies:** Huntington's disease can impair speech, affecting ability to express complex thoughts. Speech therapy can help patients had better retain communication abilities and specialists in swallowing can help prevent choking. Physical therapy can help improve strength, gait and decrease the frequency or seriousness of falls.

**Family support:** Family members of people with Huntington's disease will also need help in coping with the stresses of the disease. Legal and social aid, home care services, recreation and work centers, group housing and institutional care are outside resources patients and their families may need to consider. The general health needs of a person with Huntington's disease are also important. Dieticians can advise on adequate calorie and nutrient intake. Social and psychiatric support can help with family relationships and antisocial behavior. Family therapy and genetic counselling are often useful for alleviating family conflict and stressors related to relationship losses. Behavioral treatment is likewise a useful strategy for minimizing social isolation and lack of social stimulation. In addition to its neurological and behavioral challenges, the care of patients with Huntington's disease is often complicated in the extended care setting by the emergence of multiple family issues. The emotional burden of Huntington's disease is significant for the spouse, children and other family members. By the time a patient with Huntington's disease reaches the extended care setting, the family usually emotionally and physically exhausted. Although some family members may feel relieved that they are no longer responsible for the direct care of the patient at home, some may also feel guilty of abandoning their loved ones to the extended care setting. To be able work effectively with the family of a patient with Huntington's disease, clinicians should be mindful of their own complex-emotions. Withdrawal from the patient or over involvement in the patient care is not uncommon. Clinicians should be sensitive to the family's need to make sense of their loved one's pathological behaviours and their general expectation that clinicians will provide simple medical explanations for the patient's symptoms. First step in working with family members of patients with Huntington's disease. Clinicians may have to work with hostile and dissatisfied relatives who in turn negatively affect the patient's behavior. Special attention must be paid to the children of patients with Huntington's disease. As with any dementing disorder, careful listening is the some may have significant difficulty accepting not only their parent's diagnosis but also the genetic risk they themselves carry. Genetic counselling should be offered and questions should be answered directly and clearly.

## References

Bottino CM (2005). Cognitive rehabilitation combined with drug treatment in Alzheimer's disease patients: a pilot study. *Clin Rehabil.* **19(8):** 861-869.

Doody RS (2001). Practice parameter: management of dementia (an evidence-based review). Report of the Quality Standards Subcommittee of the American Academy of Neurology. *Neurology.* **56(9):** 1154-1166.

Lang AE (2009). When and how should treatment be started in Parkinson disease?. *Neurology.* **72(7 Suppl):** S39-43.

Login I.S, M.J. Cronin and R.M. Macleod (1982). Tetrabenazine Has Properties of A Dopamine Receptor Antagonist. *Ann. Neurol.* **12:** 257-262.

Pletscher A, A. Brosi and K.F. Gey (1962). Benzoquinoline Derivatives: A New Class of Monoamine Decreasing Drugs with Psychiatric Action. *Int. Rev. Neurobiol.* **4:** 275-306.

Ranen NG, Lipsey JR, Treisman G, *et al.,* (1996). Setraline in the treatment of severe aggressiveness in Huntington's disease. *J Neuropsychiatry Clin Neurosci* **8:** 338-340.

Robert M.F (2000). Antibiotic Minocycline May Treat Huntington's Disease. *Nature Medicine* **6:** 797-801.

Rosenblatt A, Ranen N, Nance M, *et al.,* (1999). *A physician's guide to the management of Huntington's disease,* second ed. New York: Huntington's Disease Society of America.

Shoulson I (1992). Huntington's Disease. In Diseases of the Nervous System: Clinical Neurobiology, Eds. W.B. Saunders, Philadelphia, USA, pp: 1159-1168.

Standaert, G.D. and B.A. Young (2001). In The Pharmacological Basis of Therapeutics, Eds. J.G. Hardman, L.E. Limbird and A.G. Gilman, McGrawHill, Singapore, pp: 562-564.

Weaver FM, Follett K, Stern M, *et al.,* (2009). Bilateral deep brain stimulation *vs* best medical therapy for patients with advanced Parkinson disease: a randomized controlled trial. *JAMA*. **301(1):** 63-73.

Zesiewicz TA, Sullivan KL, Arnulf I, Chaudhuri KR, Morgan JC, Gronseth GS, et al., (2010). Practice Parameter: treatment of nonmotor symptoms of Parkinson disease: report of the Quality Standards Subcommittee of the American Academy of Neurology. *Neurology*. **74(11):** 924-31.

CHAPTER 19

# General Anaesthetics

**Definition:** Anesthesia (an = without, aisthesis = sensation)

Anesthesia is medication that attempts to eliminate pain impulse from reaching the brain. In general anesthesia this is accomplished by putting the patient asleep.

**General anesthesia**

A drug that brings about a reversible loss of all sensation and consciousness.

These drugs are generally administered by an anesthesiologist in order to induce or maintain general anesthesia to facilitate surgery and unpleasant procedure. General anesthetics depress the central nervous system. It causes immobility and muscle relaxant.

## Principle of General Anaesthesia

The practice of anesthesia is usually neither therapeutic nor diagnostic.

The development of new anesthetic agents have been driven by three general objectives

They are

Sustaining physiologic homeostasis during surgical procedure.

Minimize the potentially deleterious effects of anesthetic agent and technique.

Improving postoperative out comes.

## Stages of Anesthesia

The stages of anesthesia are shown in Fig 19-1.

**Stage I: Analgesia:** Start from beginning of anesthetic administration and last up to loss of consciousness, feels a dream like state, reflexes and respiration remain normal.

**Stage II: Stage of delirium:** From loss of consciousness to beginning of regular respiration. Apparent excitement is seen. Muscle tone increases. Jaws are tightly closed. Heart rate and blood pressure may rise.

**Stage III: Surgical anesthesia:** Extends from onset of regular respiration to cessation of spontaneous breathing. This has been divided into 4 planes:

Plane 1: This plane ends when eyes become fixed.

Plane 2: Loss of corneal and laryngeal reflexes.

Plane 3: Pupil starts dilating and light reflexes is slugish.

Plane 4: Dilated pupil, decrease muscle tone, BP falls.

**Stage IV: Medullary paralysis :** Respiratory and vasomotor control ceases.

The term 'potency' refers to the quantity of an inhalational anesthetic that must be administered to cause a desired effect such as general anesthesia and the standard index of inhalation anesthetics is the minimum alveolar concentration (MAC) which was proposed by Merkel and Eger in 1963.

MAC is defined as the alveolar concentration of anesthetic that prevents muscular movement in half the test subjects in response to a painful stimulus. It is usually expressed as a % but this assumes a normal sea level atmospheric pressure. As blood anesthetic gas levels are difficult to measure, end tidal levels of inhalant anesthetics are usually accepted as approximating to alveolar and therefore to blood gas tensions. The anesthetic potency of an inhaled agent is inversely related to MAC. MAC is also inversely related to the oil/gas partition coefficient (PC).

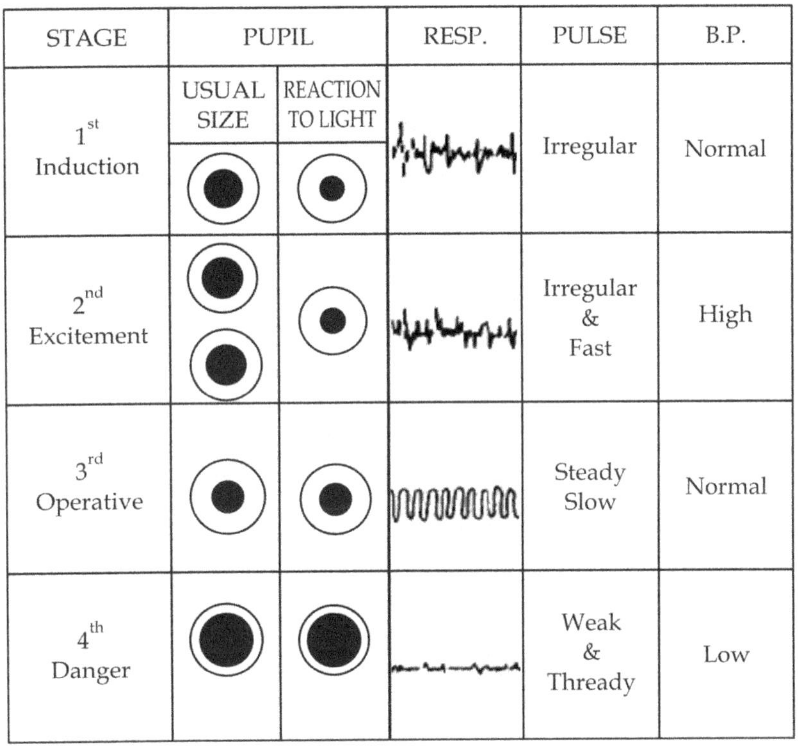


**Fig 19-1:** Stages of anesthesia

The partition coefficient is defined as the ratio of the amount of substance (e.g., inhalant) present in one phase (oil, blood etc.) compared with another (gas), the two phases being of equal volume and in equilibrium.

A blood gas PC of 0.5 means that the concentration of inhalant in the blood is half that present in the alveolar gas when the partial pressure of the anesthetic is identical at both sites. PC in an inhalation anesthetic is most commonly used to refer its solubility in a given solvent (e.g., oil, blood etc.). A very potent anesthetic (e.g., methoxyflurane) has a low MAC value and a high oil/gas PC, whereas a low potency agent (e.g., $N_2O$) has a high MAC and low oil/gas PC. In other words, an anesthetic with a high oil solubility (i.e., high oil/gas PC) is effective at a low alveolar concentration and has a high potency.

The anesthetic dose is commonly defined in terms of multiples of MAC (i.e., 1.5 times MAC or 1.5 MAC). Surgical depth is usually achieved at 1.2 to 1.5 times of MAC values. In a single species the variation in MAC values is generally small. Even between species the variation is not usually large. One exception is $N_2O$ where MAC in man is 104%, whereas in most animals close to 200%, making the agent far less effective in domestic animals. In man, MAC is greatly influenced by age in inverse relationship. MAC is also reduced by any sedative, analgesic or parental anesthetic agents which has been used.

**Factors to decrease MAC**

- Hypotension
- Anemia (PCV < 13%)
- Hypothermia
- Metabolic acidosis
- Hypoxia
- Premedicants
- Pregnancy
- Aging
- Hypothyroidism

**Factors to increase MAC**

- Increased body temperature
- Hyperthyroidism
- Hypernatremia
- Concurrent use of central nervous stimulant (e.g., Doxapram)

**Factors known not to affect MAC**

- Type of stimulation to test
- Duration of anesthesia
- Sex
- $PaCO_2$ (between 15-95 mmHg)
- Hypertension
- Potassium

## Theory of General Anaesthetics

### Lipid Theory

The Lipid theory for anaesthetics is shown in Fig 19-2.

The anesthetic action is correlated with the oil/gas coefficients. Higher the solubility of general anesthetics in oil greater is the anesthetics action.

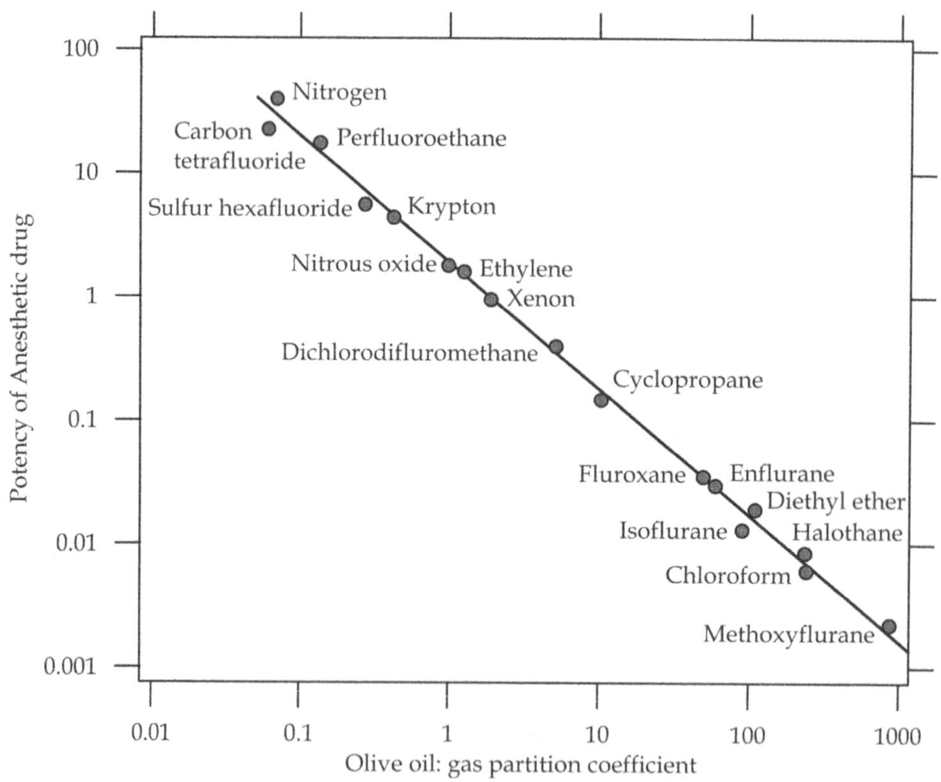


**Fig 19-2:** The Meyer – Overton theory for anaesthetics

MAC is the concentration necessary to prevent responding in 50% of population.

Blood gas partition coefficient

*Lower the Blood:* Gas partition coefficient the faster the induction and recovery.

**Other theories included**

***Binding theory:*** Anesthetics bind to hydrophobic portion of the ion channel

***Neuromodulator theory:*** Bind to cell-surface receptors. Increased $Cl^-$ flux (possible GABA mediation)

**Table 19-1:** Difference between general and local anaesthetics

| Description | General anesthetics | Local anesthetics |
|---|---|---|
| 1. Site of action | Central Nervous System | Peripheral Nerves and Spinal cord |
| 2. Area of body involved | Whole body | Restricted area |
| 3. Conciousness | Lost | Unaltered |
| 4. Major surgery | Preferred | Cannot be used |
| 5. Minor surgery | Cannot be used | Preferred |
| 6. Poor health patient | Risky | Safer |
| 7. Care of vital function | Essential | Usually not needed |

## Classification

The classification of inductio agents are shown in Fig 19-3.

General Anesthetics now divided into two classes

1. **Inhaled anesthetics**

    Nitrous oxide

    Halothane

    Enflurane

    Isoflurane

    Desflurane

2. **Intravenous anesthetics or induction agents**

***Barbiturates:*** Thiopental and Methohexital

***Opioids:*** Alfentanil, Meperidine, Fentanyl, Sufentanil (agonists)

***Benzodiazepine:*** Diazepam, Midazolam

**Miscellaneous agents**

*Etomidate* - Nonbarbiturate hypnotic agent without analgesic properties

*Droperidol* - Neuroleptic (Butyrophenone similar to Haloperidol) - combined with Fentanyl

*Ketamine* - Dissociative anesthetic

*Propofol* - New (1989) and unrelated to other intravenous anesthetic agents

Alpha$_2$ adrenergic agonists - Clonidine and others

## Intravenous Anesthetics or Induction Agents

The term intravenous anesthetic agent implies inducing anesthesia by drugs administered intravenously.

Advantages of i.v anesthesia include rapid and smooth induction of anesthesia, little equipment requirement (syringes, needles, catheters) and easy administration of drugs.

Disadvantages include difficult retrieval of drug once administered, less control of depth and duration of anesthesia, lack of ventilatory support and poor tolerability in debilitated, dehydrated or toxicated animals.

**The properties of an ideal i.v induction drug**

A number of properties, both physical and pharmacological (pharmacokinetic and pharmacodynamic) will be beneficial when designing our ideal intravenous anaesthetic drug.

**Physical properties**

Water soluble and stable in solution

Stable on exposure to light

Long shelf life

No pain on intravenous injection

Painful when injected into an artery

Non-irritant when injected subcutaneously

Low incidence of thrombophlebitis

Cheap

**Pharmacokinetic properties**

Rapid onset in one arm-brain circulation time

Rapid distribution to vascular tissue

Rapid clearance and metabolism

No active metabolites

**Pharmacodynamic properties**

High therapeutic ratio ( ratio of toxic dose : minimally effective dose )

Minimal cardiovascular and respiratory effects

No histamine release/hypersensitivity reactions

No emetic effects

No involuntary movements

No emergence nightmares

No hang over effect

No adrenocortical suppression

Safe to use in porphyria

**The following anesthetic agents are used :**

**Barbiturates**

Oxybarbiturate - pentobarbital and methohexital

Thiobarbiturates - thiopental and thiamylal

**Non-barbiturates**

Propofol

Etomidate

Alphaxalone

Propanidid

**Dissociatives**

Ketamine

Tiletamine (in Telazol®)

Mechanism of action of barbiturates and non-barbiturates intravenous anesthetics is believed to be *via* CNS depression by modulation of GABA-mediated neurotransmission.

**Properties of specific i.v induction drugs**

**Sodium Thiopental**

Thiopental (also referred to as thiopentone and pentothal) is a barbiturate, supplied as a hygroscopic (attracts moisture from the

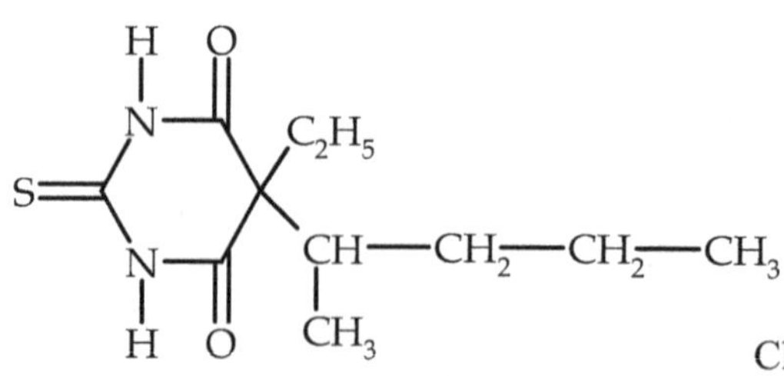

Thiopental

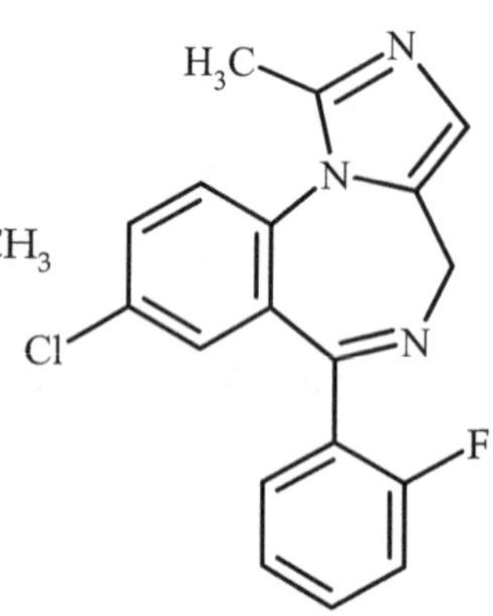

Midazolam

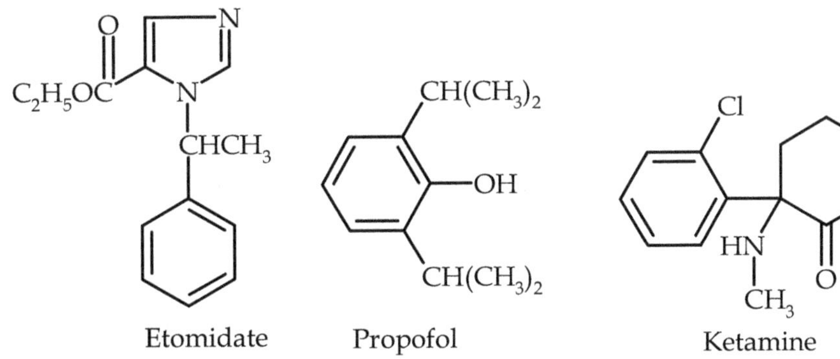


**Fig 19-3:** Intravenous anesthetics or induction agents

atmosphere) pale yellow powder. Ampoules commonly contain 500mg of sodium thiopental with 6% sodium carbonate in an inert atmosphere of nitrogen. Reconstituted with 20 ml of water this yields a 2.5% solution (25 mg/ml) with a pH of 10.8. The alkaline solution is bacteriostatic and safe to keep for 48 hours. The molecular structure of thiopental is based upon the barbiturate ring - as shown above. A sulphur atom at the carbon R2 position confers the short duration of action. A dose of 4-5 mg/kg of thiopental produces a smooth onset of hypnosis with good definitive endpoints within 30 seconds of intravenous injection. Recovery after a single dose is rapid due to redistribution and there is a low incidence of restlessness and nausea and vomiting.

Thiopental is 65-85% protein bound in plasma. Metabolism is slow and occurs in the liver. Excretion of metabolites occurs mainly in the urine. Following repeated doses or infusions of thiopental, metabolism follows zero order kinetics; this means that a constant amount of drug is being eliminated per unit time, irrespective of the plasma concentration. Some drugs are metabolized by first order kinetics, a constant fraction of drug is eliminated per unit time, i.e., dependant on plasma concentration. Zero order kinetics occur when the metabolic pathways become saturated leading to an accumulation of the active drug and delayed recovery. Thiopental directly depresses the contractile force of the heart, reducing cardiac output and blood pressure. There may be a compensatory increase heart rate. It also decreases venous tone, causing pooling of blood in the peripheral veins, increasing the degree of hypotension, particularly in patients who are hypovolaemic (e.g., following haemorrhage). Respiratory depression is common and a period of apnoea is usually seen following a bolus dose. Airway reflexes are well preserved in comparison with propofol; as a result it is unsuitable for use when inserting a laryngeal mask airway (LMA) which may cause coughing and laryngospasm. Histamine release can occur which may precipitate bronchospasm. Thiopental reduces cerebral blood flow, cerebral metabolic rate and oxygen demand. It has potent anticonvulsant properties. Following traumatic brain injury, infusion of thiopental to produce a "barbiturate coma" lowers intracranial pressure and may improve neurological outcome. This is however associated with significant accumulation, causing a prolonged effect with multiple complications. The porphyrias are a group of disease characterised by overproduction and excretion of porphyrins (intermediate compounds produced during haemoprotein synthesis). Acute attacks may be precipitated by drugs, stress, infection, alcohol, pregnancy and starvation. Thiopental may precipitate porphyria due to hepatic enzyme induction in susceptible patients, and hence it should be avoided.

### Propofol (2,6 di-isopropylphenol)

Propofol is usually presented as a 1 or 2% aqueous emulsion (tiny fat droplets in suspension, hence the white colour) containing soya oil, egg phosphatide and glycerol. It is isotonic to plasma and has a pH of 7.0 - 8.5. It can cause pain on injection into small veins. It is a short-acting general anaesthetic drug, with an onset of action of approximately 30 seconds. Recovery from anaesthesia is usually rapid. A smooth induction of anaesthesia usually follows a dose of 2-2.5 mg/kg. Propofol should be titrated against the response of the patient until the clinical signs show the onset of anesthesia. The best endpoint is loss of verbal contact with the patient. Following an i.v bolus, there is rapid equilibration between the plasma and the highly perfused tissue of the brain as described earlier. Plasma levels decline rapidly as a result of redistribution, followed by a more prolonged period of hepatic metabolism and renal clearance. The initial redistribution half-life is between 2 and 4 minutes. Moderate hepatic or renal impairment does not alter the pharmacokinetics of propofol. Propofol causes the most marked fall in blood pressure of all the induction drugs. This is mainly due to systemic vasodilatation. There may be an accompanying slight increase in heart rate. The fall in blood pressure is dose dependent and is most marked in the elderly and in shocked patients. This can be minimized by slow injection - avoiding inadvertent overdose. With the exception of ketamine, all induction drugs act on the respiratory centre to cause respiratory depression. This effect is the most profound with propofol and a period of apnoea is usually seen. Propofol also markedly reduces airway and pharyngeal reflexes, making it the ideal drug to use with the laryngeal mask. Propofol has been associated with epileptiform movements, that must not be confused with true seizure activity, on induction and recovery, but it is anticonvulsant in normal doses. It has also been shown to reduce cerebral blood flow, metabolic rate and intra-cranial pressure. An infusion of propofol is used commonly to provide sedation for adult patients undergoing minor procedures and on the intensive care unit. It is also the most commonly used drug to provide total intravenous anaesthesia, propofol infusion is contraindicated for sedation in children due to concerns regarding its safety. A "propofol infusion syndrome" has been described, effected children developing metabolic acidosis, lipidaemia, cardiac arrhythmias and an increased mortality.

### Etomidate

Etomidate is an imidazole ester. It is usually presented as a lipid emulsion or as a clear solution containing propylene glycol at a concentration of 2 mg/ml. Pain on injection is common and there is a high rate of thrombophlebitis in the post operative period. The standard induction dose is 0.3 mg/kg, and recovery is rapid due to redistribution to muscle and fat. Induction of anaesthesia can be accompanied by involuntary movements which may be mistaken for generalized seizure activity. Recovery is frequently unpleasant and accompanied by nausea and vomiting. It is rapidly metabolized by hepatic and plasma esterases to yield inactive metabolites. Excretion is predominantly urinary and the elimination half life varies from 1 - 5 hours. Etomidate causes the least cardiovascular depression of the i.v anaesthetic drugs, with only a small reduction in the cardiac output and blood pressure. In the past, etomidate was widely used to induce anesthesia in the shocked, elderly or cardiovascularly compromised patient. Etomidate causes transient apnoea, though less so than other drugs and can cause cough or hiccups. Post operative nausea and vomiting is common after etomidate administration. Etomidate inhibits 11-β-hydroxylase, an enzyme important in adrenal steroid production. A single induction dose blocks the normal stress-induced increase in adrenal cortisol production for 4-8 hours, and up to 24 hours in elderly and debilitated patients. Continuous infusion of etomidate for sedation in critically ill patients has been shown to increase mortality. Although no increase in mortality has been identified following a single dose during induction of anesthesia, the use of etomidate has declined in recent years due to a perceived potential morbidity.

### Ketamine

Ketamine is a derivative of phencyclidine, a dissociative drug formerly used as an anesthetic agent, which exhibited hallucinogenic and neurotoxic effects. A dissociative drug is one which reduces signals to the conscious mind from other parts of the brain, typically the senses. Ketamine can take the form of two stereo-isomers, R and S ketamine, as shown above. Stereoisomers are molecules in which the same atoms are bonded together in the same order, but they show a different 3D arrangement in space making them non-superimposable (they are often referred to as "mirror images" of each other). It is usually presented as a racemic mixture of the 2 stereo-isomers, but S ketamine has recently become available due to its more desirable pharmacological properties. Ketamine is prepared in a slightly acidic solution (pH 3.5–5.5) containing 10, 50 or 100 mg of ketamine per ml. Standard ampoules also contain a preservative which prevents intrathecal or epidural use. It is also available as a powder for reconstitution. Ketamine has hypnotic, analgesic and local anaesthetic properties. Its effects are mediated primarily by noncompetitive antagonism at the N-methyl-D-aspartate (NMDA) receptor in the brain and spinal cord. Other mechanisms of action of ketamine may include an interaction with opioid receptors, however naloxone does not antagonize the analgesic effects of ketamine in humans. Ketamine produces so-called 'dissociative' anaesthesia. This unique clinical state is characterised by catalepsy in which the eyes may remain open with a slow nystagmic gaze and the corneal and light reflexes remain intact. Varying degrees of hypertonus and occasional purposeful movements unrelated to painful stimuli can be seen, even during adequate surgical anaesthesia. Psychic sensations including alterations in mood state, floating sensations, vivid dreams and hallucinations are common during emergence from ketamine anaesthesia. These usually disappear on full wakening. Benzodiazepine premedication reduces this emergence delirium. As mentioned, the ketamine molecule exists in two stereo-isomers - R and S ketamine. These isomers exhibit pharmacological and clinical differences. S - ketamine is three times as potent as R-ketamine and the recovery time and psychomimetic sequelae are reduced. This may however be a consequence of the reduced dose requirement required with the more potent S-ketamine. Ketamine is unique amongst induction drugs in that it can be administered i.v, i.m, orally, nasally, rectally, and the preservative-free solution epidurally. The dose depends on the route of administration and the desired therapeutic effect. For induction of anaesthesia a dose of 0.5–1.5 mg/kg can be given i.v, or 4–10 mg/kg i.m. The onset of action is slower than other induction drugs (unconsciousness in 1-2 min for i.v use) and the end point may be difficult to judge with patients staring into the distance for a short period of time. The duration of action of a single dose is approximately 5-10 minutes. Ketamine is metabolised in the liver, and conjugated metabolites are excreted in the urine. The elimination half life is 2.5 hours. Ketamine has a unique combination of cardiovascular effects. Its administration, unlike other induction drugs, is usually associated with tachycardia, increased blood pressure and increased cardiac output. This makes ketamine useful in the shocked, unwell patient.

Ketamine has a minimal effect on central respiratory drive, although a transient decrease in ventilation can occur after bolus administration. This, coupled with the fact that the protective airway reflexes remain relatively preserved, makes ketamine the ideal anaesthetic drug to be used. It does however increase salivation which can lead to upper airway obstruction. Salivation can be reduced by premedication with antimuscarinic drug such as glycopyrrolate. Ketamine is a bronchial smooth muscle relaxant, and therefore has a special role in the patients with asthma. In the past, ketamine was thought to increase cerebral blood flow and intracranial pressure, thereby limiting its use in patients with a head injury. However, providing hypoventilation and hypercapnia are avoided, this does not occur and there is some evidence that ketamine may have some cerebral protective effects *via* its action on NMDA receptors. Ketamine is thought to be safe to use in porphyria.

### Midazolam

Strictly speaking not an intravenous induction drug, but because of its pharmacokinetics midazolam can be used to induce anaesthesia. Midazolam is a water soluble benzodiazepine. It comes as a clear solution, usually at a concentration of 2 mg/ml. Midazolam exhibits a form of isomerism known as tautomerism. In the ampoule, as an acidic solution, the molecule exists in an ionized form. At physiological pH the molecule changes to becomes a highly lipid soluble unionized ring, accounting for its rapid onset of action. It does not cause pain on injection. Like other benzodiazepines, midazolam acts at specific receptors closely allied to the $GABA_A$ receptor. Activation of the benzodiazepine receptor increases chloride influx to neuronal cells *via* the $GABA_A$ receptor, causing neuronal hyperpolarisation and the clinical effects seen. Midazolam is usually used for sedation at a dose range of 0.05-0.1mg/kg (IV). Its advantage in this setting is its short duration of action and amnesic properties. In children it is useful as premedication - 30 minutes preoperatively as an oral dose of 0.5 mg/kg. It can be used as a sole i. v induction drug, at a dose of 0.3 mg/kg, but its onset is slow, limiting its use. Its duration of action is around 30 minutes which is longer than that of the other induction drugs. It undergoes hepatic metabolism and renal elimination. In the elderly, the lower hepatic blood flow and metabolic activity result in a significantly prolonged half life. Midazolam has mild cardiovascular and respiratory depressant effects, so monitoring is important duration sedation. When used as a sole induction drug, midazolam causes apnoea in up to 70% of patients. The effects of midazolam can be reversed with flumazenil, a competitive benzodiazepine antagonist. This should be given by intravenous injection in 100 mcg increments and should act within 2 minutes. Flumazenil must be used cautiously, as it can cause agitation and seizures.

## Inhaled Anaesthetics

The inhaled anaesthetics are shown in Fig 19-4.

### Mode of Action

The molecular basis of inhalational anaesthesia is not fully understood. Historically, the first observation that had a significant impact was

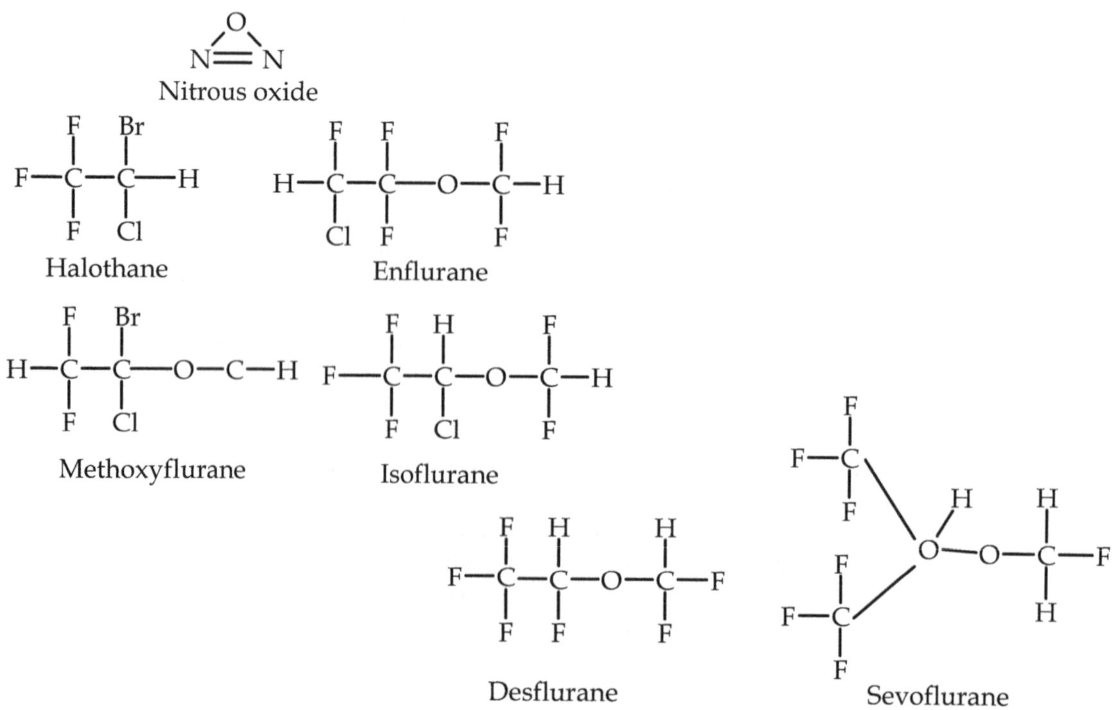


**Fig 19-4:** Inhalational anesthetics

the Meyer-Overton hypothesis which demonstrated that the potency (expressed as minimum alveolar concentration, MAC) of an anaesthetic agent increased in direct proportion to its oil: gas partition coefficient. This led to the interpretation that the site of action of general anaesthetics was the lipid bilayer of nerve membranes and that when a sufficient amount of drug was dissolved in this layer, and then anaesthesia occurred. There were several theories as to the molecular mechanism, but each with its own limitations. More recent research suggests that inhalational agents may act on specific membrane proteins and alter ion flux or receptor function. This is supported by the fact that anaesthetic Enantiomers (optical isomers) usually display different anaesthetic potencies in animals.

The prime candidates for protein targets are:

$GABA_A$ receptors - potentiation of GABA at this receptor occurs with halothane, isoflurane and sevoflurane.

Glycine receptors - these are often at the same CNS sites as the $GABA_A$ receptors and are of particular

**Nitrous Oxide ($N_2O$)**

$N_2O$ has a high MAC and is widely used in combination with other inhaled anaesthetic agents or with $O_2$. However, it interferes with DNA synthesis even after relatively brief exposure. It is manufactured by heating ammonium nitrate to 250 °C, and impurities are removed by passage through scrubbers, water and caustic soda:

$$NH_4NO_3 \rightarrow N_2O + 2H_2O$$

$N_2O$ is stored as a liquid in French blue cylinders with a gauge pressure of 51 bar at 20 °C. The gauge pressure does not give an indication of cylinder content until all the remaining $N_2O$ is in the gaseous phase. The filling ratio of the cylinders (defined as the mass of $N_2O$ in the cylinder divided by the mass of water that the cylinder could hold) is 0.75 in temperate regions, but reduced to 0.67 in tropical areas to avoid cylinder explosions. It has a critical temperature of 36.5 °C and its critical pressure is 72 bar.

**Effects**

*Respiratory*

Small fall in tidal volume that is offset by an increased respiratory rate.

*Cardiovascular*

Mild direct myocardial depression which is offset by an increase in sympathetic activity *via* its central effects. However, in patients with cardiac failure there may be a significant reduction in cardiac output.

*Central nervous system*

Cerebral blood flow (CBF) is increased. Concentration effect, second gas effect and diffusion hypoxia despite the low blood: gas solubility coefficient of $N_2O$ (it is about 20 times more soluble than $O_2$ and $N_2$). During induction with high concentrations of $N_2O$, the volume of $N_2O$ entering the pulmonary capillaries will be significantly greater than the volume of $N_2$ entering the alveolus. As a consequence, the volume of the alveolus decreases, thereby increasing fractional concentrations of the remaining gases. The concentration effect refers to the disproportionate rise in alveolar partial pressure and its high rate of approximation to the inhaled concentration. It is only seen with $N_2O$ as it is the only agent to be present in high enough concentration and occurs due to two processes. First, the concentrating effect of the rapid $N_2O$ uptake and second, increased ventilation as dead space gas is drawn into the alveolus to make up for the diminished volume. The second gas effect is a result of the concentration effect. Volatile agents given in combination with high concentrations of $N_2O$ will be concentrated resulting in a higher alveolar partial pressure and reduced induction time. Diffusion hypoxia is due to the reverse of the concentration effect. At the end of anaesthesia when $N_2O/O_2$ is replaced with $N_2/O_2$, the volume of $N_2O$ entering the alveolus from blood will be greater than the volume of $N_2$ entering the pulmonary capillaries resulting in dilution of all the alveolar gases including $O_2$. If supplemental $O_2$ is not given at this point, then diffusion hypoxia could result. As well as these effects seen across the alveolar membrane, $N_2O$ will cause a rapid expansion of any air filled spaces such as pneumothorax, vascular air embolus and luminal bowel gas.

### Adverse effects

$N_2O$ oxidises the cobalt ion in vitamin $B_{12}$, which prevents its action as the cofactor for methionine synthase. Methionine synthase also appears to be inhibited directly by $N_2O$. The result is reduced synthesis of methionine, thymidine, tetrahydrofolate and DNA. Exposure of only a few hours may result in megaloblastic changes in bone marrow, and prolonged exposure may result in agranulocytosis and neurological syndromes that resemble subacute combined degeneration of the cord due to chronic vitamin $B_{12}$ inactivation. Teratogenicity has been shown in rats, but not convincingly demonstrated in humans, although $N_2O$ is often avoided in the first trimester.

## Halothane

Halothane is unstable when exposed to light, corrodes certain metals and dissolves into rubber. It is presented with 0.01% thymol to prevent liberation of free bromine.

### Effects

#### *Respiratory*

Minute ventilation is depressed largely due to decreased tidal volume and the normal response to hypoxia and hypercarbia are blunted. It has a sweet non-irritant odour and may be used for gaseous induction. Halothane also dilates bronchioles and is useful in asthmatic patients.

#### *Cardiovascular*

Bradycardia is produced by increased vagal tone, depressed sinoatrial and atrio-ventricular activity. It also directly depresses the myocardium and systemic vascular resistance (SVR) is reduced. Halothane sensitizes the heart to catecholamines which may lead to arrhythmias and the quantity of adrenaline used for infiltration should be limited.

#### *Central nervous system*

Cerebral blood flow is increased more than any other volatile agent leading to significant increases in intra-cranial pressure (ICP). However, cerebral oxygen requirements are reduced.

### Metabolism

As much as 25% of halothane undergoes oxidative metabolism by hepatic cytochrome p450 to produce trifluoroacetic acid, $Br^-$ and $Cl^-$. However, when the liver becomes hypoxic, reductive metabolism predominates, producing $F^-$.

### Adverse effects

Hepatic damage can take one of two forms:

Reversible form - often subclinical and is associated with a rise in hepatic transaminases. This is probably due to hepatic hypoxia. Fulminant hepatic necrosis ('halothane hepatitis') – trifluoroacetyl chloride may behave as a hapten which binds to hepatic proteins and induces antibody formation. Diagnosis is by exclusion, and risk factors include: multiple exposures, obesity, middle age and female sex. Mortality is around 50-75%. The incidence in adults is 1 in 25000-35000. Halothane should be avoided if it has been given in the previous 3 months, if there is a past history of adverse reaction to halothane, or if there is pre-existing liver disease.

## Isoflurane

Isoflurane is widely used for maintenance of anaesthesia.

### Effects

#### *Respiratory*

Ventilation is depressed more than halothane, but less than Enflurane. Minute ventilation is decreased, respiratory rate and $PaCO_2$ are increased. It has a pungent smell and can cause upper airway irritability and breath-holding so gaseous induction is not recommended. However it does cause some bronchodilation.

*Cardiovascular*

The main effect is to reduce SVR resulting in compensatory tachycardia and only a small decrease in myocardial contractility.

Isoflurane may also have myocardial protective properties *via* its effects on ATP-dependent potassium channels.

*Central nervous system*

Of all the volatile agents, isoflurane produces the best balance of reduced cerebral oxygen requirement and minimal increase in CBF.

**Adverse effects**

Carbon monoxide may be produced by a reaction between the -$CHF_2$ group and dry soda lime (or baralyme). Enflurane and desflurane may also react in a similar manner.

**Enflurane**

Its use has decreased due to newer agents with more favourable profiles.

**Effects**

*Respiratory*

Causes more depression of ventilation than the other agents with a reduction in minute volume and increase in $PaCO_2$. The response to hypercarbia is blunted.

*Cardiovascular*

Heart rate increases, but cardiac output, contractility, systemic vascular resistance and blood pressure fall.

*Central nervous system*

High concentrations of enflurane in the presence of hypocarbia produce a 3Hz spike and wave pattern on the EEG consistent with petit mal activity. It is therefore usually avoided in epileptic patients. There is an increase in CBF and ICP to a degree in-between halothane and isoflurane.

**Metabolism**

Only 2% is metabolized by hepatic cytochrome P450. F- ions are produced, but rarely reach the concentration (> 40 mcmol.$l^{-1}$) known to produce reversible nephropathy. Even so, it is usually avoided in patients with renal impairment.

**Adverse effects**

Hepatic damage may occur.

**Desflurane**

Desflurane's relatively low boiling point (23.5 °C) makes it extremely volatile, however, since this temperature is close to ambient temperature in many theatre settings, full vapour saturation cannot be guaranteed if a conventional vaporizer is employed. Therefore, a Tec 6 vaporizer is used which heats the agent to 39 °C at a pressure of 2 atmospheres, ensuring full vapour saturation which enables a carefully regulated amount of vapour to be added to the fresh gas flow. Its low blood:gas partition coefficient results in fast onset and offset of action. These properties make it ideal for long procedures where rapid wake-up is important to assess the patient (e.g., after neurosurgery).

**Effects**

*Respiratory*

Similar respiratory effects to the other agents with a rise in $PaCO_2$ and a fall in minute ventilation. These effects are more pronounced than halothane, but less than isoflurane and enflurane. It has a potent odour and can cause coughing and breath holding and is not suitable for induction.

*Cardiovascular*

Effects are similar to isoflurane, but in concentrations above 1 MAC, desflurane may produce tachycardia and hypertension. Care should be taken in patients with ischaemic heart disease. Vascular resistance falls in the cerebral and coronary circulations.

**Metabolism**

Only 0.02% is metabolised.

**Sevoflurane**

**Effects**

*Respiratory*

Ventilation is depressed in a predictable manner with a rise in $PaCO_2$ and a fall in minute ventilation. Its pleasant odour and relatively low blood: gas partition coefficient make it particularly suitable for induction.

*Cardiovascular*

Heart rate and contractility are unchanged, but a fall in SVR leads to a reduction in blood pressure. Vascular resistance in the cerebral and coronary circulations is reduced.

*Central nervous system*

There is some evidence that children exhibit a higher incidence of post operative agitation and delirium compared with halothane.

**Metabolism**

Sevoflurane undergoes hepatic metabolism by cytochrome P450 (2E1) to a greater extent than all the other commonly used volatile agents apart from halothane. Hexafluoroisopropanol and inorganic F are produced, although renal adverse effects is not observed even when F plasma levels reach 50 mcmol.$l^{-1}$.

**Adverse effects**

When sevoflurane is administered in a circle system using soda lime or baralyme, a number of compounds are produced, named compounds A-E. Only compounds A and B are present in significant quantities. Animal studies extrapolated to humans suggest a human nephrotoxic threshold of 150-200 ppm but studies have shown that even with flow rates of 0.25 l.$min^{-1}$ for 5 hours, then the level of compound A produced peaks at less than 20 ppm and is not associated with renal impairment.

**Ether (Diethyl Ether)**

This is an inexpensive agent made from sugar cane (ethanol) that is still used in isolated settings in some countries. It is the volatile agent of choice when general anaesthesia is needed but no oxygen is available.

**Effects**

*Respiratory*

Ether stimulates respiration and when too much ether is given respiration becomes depressed before the heart. These effects make ether a relatively 'safe' anaesthetic agent and its continued use in some isolated settings in the developing world. It is a bronchodilator and may be used as the sole anaesthetic agent and is capable of producing good abdominal muscle relaxation. It stimulates salivation and is best used with an antisialogogue premedication. Ether is associated with a slow onset and a slow recovery. The vapour is unpleasant to breath initially and causes irritation of the bronchial tree which may slow down the induction of anaesthesia.

*Cardiovascular*

Cardiac output and blood pressure are usually increased due to its sympathomimetic effect mediated by adrenaline release.

*Other effects*

Ether has analgesic properties. The incidence of nausea and vomiting is higher with ether than with other agents. The frequency is related to the concentration of ether used and is lower when ether is given *via* an endotracheal tube during relaxant anaesthesia. Ether causes little uterine relaxation and it is especially useful for caesarean section (because the baby tolerates it and the uterus contracts well). It is better avoided in moderate or severe pre eclampsia because of its sympathomimetic activity.

**Adverse effects**

Ether is explosive when mixed with oxygen and is inflammable in air. It may be ignited by a flame or an electrical spark such as those produced by diathermy or static electricity. The ether vapour is inflammable within the patient (lungs, airway or stomach full of vapour) or outside the patient within 25 cm of the anaesthetic circuit. Scavenging must always be carried out (where possible) to avoid contact between heavy inflammable ether vapour and diathermy apparatus or other electrical devices that may spark. If the end of the scavenging tube is placed on the floor (away from any possible sources of ignition) then the heavy ether vapour will remain at floor level and the smell of the agent to the surgical and anaesthetic team reduced.

### Xenon

Xenon (Xe) is an inert, odourless gas that is present in minute quantities in the atmosphere and is produced by the fractional distillation of air. It has a high MAC and very low blood:gas partition coefficient resulting in a faster onset and offset of action than desflurane or $N_2O$. It also has significant analgesic properties and is not metabolised. The high cost of manufacture has limited its use to mainly that of a research agent.

**Table 19-2:** Effects of inhaled anaesthetics

| Effects | Halothane | Isoflurane | Enflurane | Desflurane | Sevoflurane |
|---|---|---|---|---|---|
| **Cardiovascular effects:** | | | | | |
| Contractility | ↓↓↓ | ↓ | ↓↓ | Minimal | ↓ |
| Heart rate | ↓↓ | ↑↑ | ↑ | ↑↑ | Nil |
| Systemic vascular resistance | ↓ | ↓↓ | ↓ | ↓↓ | ↓ |
| Blood pressure | ↓↓ | ↓↓ | ↓↓ | ↓↓ | ↓ |
| Splanchnic blood flow | ↓ | Unchanged | ↓ | Unchanged | Unchanged |
| Sensitization to catecholamines | ↑↑↑ | nil | ↑ | nil | |
| **Respiratory effects:** | | | | | |
| Respiratory rate | ↑ | ↑↑ | ↑↑ | ↑↑ | ↑↑ |
| Tidal volume | ↓ | ↓↓ | ↓↓↓ | ↓↓ | ↓ |
| $PaCO_2$ | Unchanged | ↑↑ | ↑↑↑ | ↑↑ | ↑ |
| **Other effects:** | | | | | |
| Cerebral blood flow | ↑↑↑ | ↑ | ↑ | ↑ | ↑ |
| Cerebral $O_2$ requirement | ↓ | ↓ | ↓ | ↓ | ↓ |
| **Other effects:** | | | | | |
| EEG | Burst suppression | Burst suppression | Epileptiform activity | Burst suppression | Burst suppression |
| Effect on uterus | Some relaxation | Some relaxation | Some relaxation | Some relaxation | Some relaxation |
| Potentiation of muscle relaxation | Some | Significant | Significant | Significant | Significant |
| Analgesia | So e | Some | Some | Some | Some |

# Preanaesthetic Medication

Use of the drugs prior to the administration of a general anaesthetic agent, with the important object of making anaesthesia safer and more agreeable to the patient.

## Objectives of Preanaesthetic Medication

Preanesthetic medications - drugs given generally prior to anesthesia (may be given during or after, as well) in order to:

Decrease anxiety without producing excessive drowsiness

Facilitate a rapid, smooth induction without prolonging emergence

Provide amnesia for the perioperative period

Relieve pre-and post-operative pain

Minimize undesirable side effects of anesthetics

**No drug can achieve all these objectives and needs combination of drugs used to achieve these objectives**

Sedatives/Anxiolytics

Opioid analgesics

Anticholinergic drugs

Antiemetics

Other drugs

**Classification: Pre-anaesthetic Medication**

1. **Sedatives/Anxiolytics**
   Benzodiazepines
   Barbiturates
   Butyrophenones
   Phenothiazines
   Chloral hydrate and Paraldehyde
2. **Opioid analgesics**
   Morphine
   Pethidine
   Buprenorphine
3. **Anticholinergic drugs**
   Atropine Sulphate
   Scopolamine (Hyoscine)
   Synthetic Anticholinergics - Glycopyrrolate
4. **Antiemetics**
   Phenothiazines (Promethazine and Trimeprazine)
   Cyclizine
   Trimethobenzamide
   Benzquinamide
   Metoclopramide
5. **Other drugs**
   $H_2$ Receptor Antagonists, Gastric Antacids and Omeprazole
   Other drugs for special problems

## Sedatives/Anxiolytics

**Decrease anxiety and apprehension**

Benzodiazepines

Barbiturates

Butyrophenones

Phenothiazines

Chloral hydrate & Paraldehyde

**Benzodiazepines**

Most widely used

Safety, muscle relaxant and less respiratory depression and amnesic effect

Useful for pt as well for the facilitation of anesthetic state

Diazepam most widely used - 5 to 10 mg orally or parenterally

Nitrazepam, Lorazepam, Midazolam

**Phenothiazines**

Antipsychotic drugs

Possess sedative, antiarrhythmic, antiemetic & antihistaminic properties

**MOA**: Blockade of $D_2$ receptors, other effects (blockade of alpha adrenoceptors, hitaminic ($H_1$) and 5-$HT_2$ receptors)

**Adverse effects:** Potentiate the effects of barbiturates and morphine → respiratory depression and arterial hypotension

Promethazine and trimeprazine ($H_1$ antagonists) are commonly employed

**Butyrophenones**

Antipsychotic drugs

Droperidol and Haloperidol

Similar actions like phenothiazine

**Barbiturates**

Low therapeutic index

Potent enzyme inducers: Drug interactions

Risk of physical dependence

Severe withdrawal syndrome

## Opioid Analgesics

**Relief of pre-operative and post-operative Pain**

Commonly employed drugs

Morphine (10 – 15 mg i.m)

Pethidine (50 – 100 mg i.m)

Buprenorphine (0.3 mg i.m)

Have sedative and analgesic properties

Buprenorphine has longer duration of action than morphine and pethidine.

Needed whenever there is existing pain or as an supplement to an anesthetic agent. Can be given before or at end of operation – without waiting for the patient to complain of pain

**Disadvantages**

Depress respiration and cause respiratory arrest

Morphine the tone of smooth muscle such as bronchial muscles and worsen the condition of having pulmonary insufficiency (emphysema, kyphoscoliosis).

Cause vasomotor depression, they decrease the ability of circulation to respond to stress, often delays awakening.

Morphine – induces vomiting and has an antidiuertic effect

Morphine – interfere with pupillary reactions, stages of anesthesia cannot be distinguished

Pethidine – produce tachycardia by its vagolytic action

Morphine and pethidine are histamine liberators

## Anticholinergic Drugs

Inhibition of parasympathetic nervous system.

Bronchial and salivary secretions can collect in the lungs and can predispose the infection and reflex laryngospasm.

Atropine Sulphate - an hr before operation (i.v or i.m-0.6 mg). Scopolamine (Hyoscine) - generally combined with morphine to block the vagal actions.

Decrease salivary and respiratory secretions and also prevent reflex parasympathetically induced hypotension, bradycardia, reflex laryngospasm and even cardiac arrest (Lessen the possibility of cardiac arrhythmias during the induction stage) due to blockade of cardiac vagal action and leads to tachycardia.

Synthetic Anticholinergics – Glycopyrrolate

- Long acting quaternary amine
- Less central actions
- Less tendency to cause excessive tachycardia

## Antiemetics– Antiemetic Effect

Phenothiazines such as Promethazine and Trimeprazine and help to prevent post operative nausea and vomiting (central dopaminergic blockade and antimuscarinic effects)

Other drugs such as Cyclizine (antihistaminic effect) 50 mg,

Trimethobenzamide 200 mg (Substituted Benzamide

Antiemetic like Metoclopramide, possesses $D_2$ Antagonist and

Mild anti- histaminic activity

Benzquinamide 25–50 mg (dopaminergic receptor blockade)

**Metoclopramide – dual MOA**

As Antiemetic

It has potent antiemetic and antinausea effect

Blocks $D_2$ receptors in CTZ of the medulla (area postrema)

Table 19-3: Preanaesthetic medications

| Drug classification | Generic name | Desired effect |
|---|---|---|
| **Benzodiazepines** | Diazepam<br>Midazolam | Reduce anxiety, sedation, amnesia, "Conscious sedation" |
| **Antihistamines** | Hydroxyzine | Sedation |
| **Opioid analgesics** | Morphine<br>Meperidine<br>Fentanyl<br>Remifentanil | Sedation to decrease tension, anxiety, and provide analgesia |
| **Phenothiazines** | Promethazine | Sedation, antihistaminic, antiemetic, decreased motor activity |
| **Anticholinergics** | Atropine<br>Glycopyrrollate | Inhibit secretion, bradycardia, vomiting, and laryngospasms |
| **GI Drugs** | Ondansetron<br>Cimetidine<br>Metoclopramide | Antiemetic,<br>decrease gastric acidity<br>decrease stomach contents |

As Prokinetic agent

It can selectively stimulate gut motor function

Blocks $D_2$ receptor in GIT and blocks the normal inhibitory effect of Dopamine on cholinergic smooth muscle stimulation— motility.

**Other Drugs**

$H_2$ receptor antagonists (Ranitidine) and gastric antacids (sodium citrate)

PPIs (Omeprazole), to prevent acid aspiration pneumonitis and Mendelson's syndrome

## References

Calvey TN, Williams NE (2001). Principles and Practice of Pharmacology for Anaesthetists, 4th ed. Blackwell Science.

Franks NP (2006). Molecular targets underlying general anaesthesia. *British Journal of Pharmacology* **147:** S72-81.

Peck TE, Hill SA, Williams M (2003). Pharmacology for Anaesthesia and Intensive Care, 2nd ed. Greenwich Medical Media Ltd.

Trapani G, *et al.*, (2000). Propofol in anesthesia. Mechanism of action, structure-activity relationships, and drug delivery. *Curr Med Chem* **7:** 249.

CHAPTER

# Sedative Hypnotics and Anxiolytic Drugs

# 20

**Anxiolytics:** Drugs which reduce anxiety and cause calm and quietness in the patient.

**Sedatives:** Drugs which produce sedation, calm and quietness in the patient.

**Hypnotics:** Drugs which produce sleep that resembles normal sleep.

**Hypnosis:** It is a subconscious condition in which the objective manifestations of the mind are more or less inactive, accompanied by abnormal sensitivity to stimulation.

## Sleep

A typical night sleep has several cycles. In a typical cycle there are 2 phases:

- N-REM phase of sleep (100 min)
- REM phase of sleep (20 min)

Total 2 hours, so 4 cycles in one night (8 hours sleep). REM means Rapid Eyeball Movement.

**N-REM sleep:** In this stage there is no movement of the eyeball. It has several stages:

In the beginning when the patient is awake, and the patient is in the zero stage.

When the patient is becoming drowsy, the patient enters into the stage-1 of N-REM sleep and then gradually passes through stages-2,3,4.

Stage-3 and 4 are the period when the sleep is the deepest. These 2 stages are very well marked in case of children. On the other hand in very old but normal person, there will be no stage-4 at all.

Dreaming is absent in stage-4 (which is also called slow wave sleep-SWS), there may be nightmares. BP, HR and respiratory rates are depressed in stage 3 and 4. Cortisol secretion is lower but pituitary GH secretion is high.

**REM sleep:** In this phase there is, movement of the eye (as if the person sees and follows the objects of dream) despite the fact that the muscles are more relaxed in this phase. REM sleep is also called the paradoxical sleep, because of EEG (electro-encephalogram) pattern which resembles awakened stage.

### Genesis of Sleep

The nor-adrenergic fibers arise from locus ceruleus of the brain. Hypo-activity of these nor-adrenergic fibers or reduction of availability of nor-adrenalin in this areas lead to excess sleep. Brain has also serotoninergic fibers. Excess serotonin (5HT) activity causes excess sleep and vice-versa. Excess activity of GABA in reticular activating system in the brain leads to sleep.

Hypnotics promote the sleep, but in hypnotic induced sleep the stage of N-REM sleep is prolonged whereas stage-3 and 4 of N-REM is reduced. REM is also reduced.

**Insomnia may be of:**

Longer latency to fall asleep after retiring to bed.

Inability to stay in sleep

Early awakening from sleep

The primary use of sedative–hypnotics and anxiolytic drugs is to encourage calmness (anxiolytics or sedatives) or to produce sleep (sedative–hypnotics). All people are subject to states of emotional tension and uneasiness. For otherwise healthy individuals, these occasions are usually sufficiently mild and short that pharmacological intervention is unnecessary. However, at times the symptoms of anxiety become quite discomforting and can interfere with a person's ability to function effectively. Anxiety almost invariably accompanies many medical and surgical conditions, and it is often a symptom of psychiatric illness. When the symptoms become intolerable or interfere with the treatment of the underlying disease and if counselling is not sufficient, drug treatment can be considered as a means of helping patients cope with their anxiety.

All central nervous system depressants have some ability to relieve anxiety. However, most of these drugs relieve symptoms of anxiety only at doses that produce noticeable sedation. Drugs used to produce sedation and relieve anxiety are consistently among the most commonly prescribed drugs. Whether they are prescribed too frequently remains a matter of controversy.

Insomnia includes a wide variety of sleep disturbances, such as difficulty in falling asleep, early or frequent awakenings, and remaining unrefreshed after sleep. Use of sedative-hypnotic drugs is one approach to the therapy of insomnia. Other measures include advice to avoid stimulants before retiring, maintenance of a proper diet, initiation of an exercise program, and avoidance of stressful or anxiety-provoking situations.

Most anxiolytic and sedative-hypnotic drugs produce dose dependent depression of central nervous system function. The ideal anxiolytic drug should calm the patient without causing too much daytime sedation and drowsiness and without producing physical or psychological dependence. Similarly, the ideal hypnotic drug should allow the patient to fall asleep quickly and should maintain sleep of sufficient quality and duration so that the patient awakes refreshed without a drug hangover. Also, both types of drugs should have very low toxicity and should not interact with other medications in such a way as to produce unwanted or dangerous effects.

## Classification

Benzodiazepines

Barbiturates (obsolete)

Zolpidem

Buspirone-also acts as a heterocyclis antidepressant

Glutethemide, Methypylore

Meprobamate

Chloral hydrate

## Azapirones

**Buspirone (Fig 20-1)** is the first example of a class of anxiolytic agents that can relieve some symptoms of anxiety in doses that do not cause sedation. Buspirone is structurally unrelated to existing psychotropic drugs.

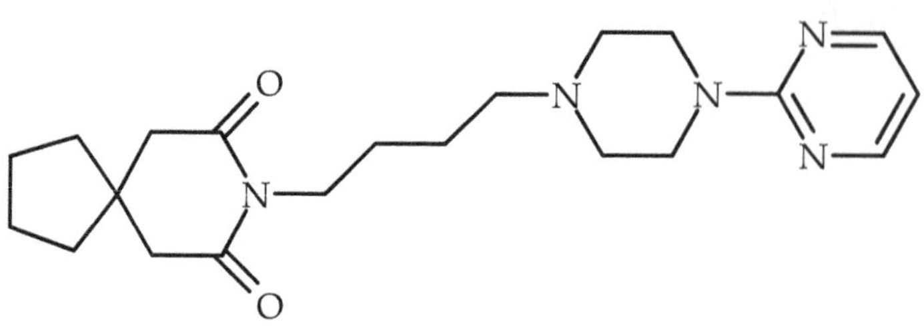

**Fig 20-1:** Buspirone

### Mechanism of action

Although Buspirone has been shown to interact with a number of neurotransmitter systems in the brain, it appears that its clinically relevant effects are mediated through interactions at the serotonin (5-hydroxytryptamine, 5-HT) 5-$HT_{1A}$ receptor, where it acts as a partial agonist.

### Pharmacological actions

Buspirone is as effective as the benzodiazepines in the treatment of general anxiety. However, the full anxiolytic effect of buspirone takes several weeks to develop, whereas the anxiolytic effect of the benzodiazepines is maximal after a few days of therapy. In therapeutic doses, buspirone has little or no sedative effect and lacks the muscle relaxant and anticonvulsant properties of the benzodiazepines. In addition, buspirone does not potentiate the central nervous system depression caused by sedative–hypnotic drugs or by alcohol, and it does not prevent the symptoms associated with benzodiazepine withdrawal.

### Pharmacokinetics

Buspirone is well absorbed from the gastro-intestinal tract, and peak blood levels are achieved in 1 to 1.5 hours; the drug is more than 95% bound to plasma proteins. Buspirone is extensively metabolized, with less than 1% of the parent drug excreted into the urine unchanged. At least one of the metabolic products of Buspirone is biologically active. The parent drug has an elimination half-life of 4 to 6 hours.

### Clinical uses

Buspirone is effective in general anxiety and in anxiety

### Adverse effects

Like the benzodiazepines, buspirone appears to be safe even when given in very high doses. The most common side effects are dizziness, light-headedness, and headache. Abuse, dependence, and withdrawal have not been reported and buspirone administration does not produce any cross-tolerance to the benzodiazepines. Buspirone has been reported to increase blood pressure in patients taking monoamine oxidase inhibitors, and it may increase plasma levels of haloperidol if co administered with that agent.

## Benzodiazepines

The benzodiazepines (Fig 20-2) constitute the most commonly used group of anxiolytics and sedative–hypnotics. Since the first member of this group, Chlordiazepoxide was introduced, many congeners have been marketed. Most of these drugs possess anxiolytic, sedative hypnotic and anticonvulsant properties. Thus, the clinical indications for specific benzodiazepines are not absolute and their uses overlap considerably.

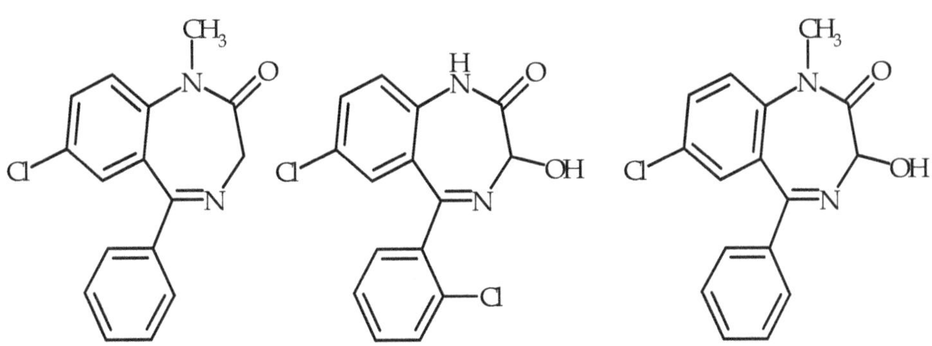

Diazepam Lorazepam Temazepam

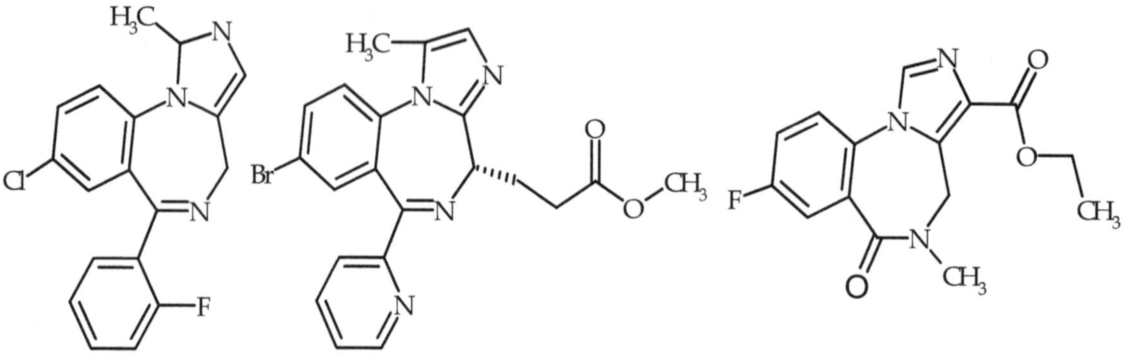

Midazolam Remimazolam Flumazenil

**Fig 20-2:** Benzodiazepines

### Chemistry

The basic chemical structure of the benzodiazepines consists of a benzene ring coupled to a seven-member heterocyclic structure containing two nitrogens (diazepine) at positions 1 and 4.

### Mechanism of action

The benzodiazepines bind with high affinity to specific macromolecules within the central nervous system. These benzodiazepine-binding sites (receptors) are closely associated with the receptors for α-aminobutyricacid (GABA), which is the major inhibitory neurotransmitter in the mammalian brain. Benzodiazepines potentiate GABAergic neurotransmission in essentially all areas of the central nervous system. This enhancement is thought to occur indirectly at the postsynaptic $GABA_A$ receptor complex.

The functional significance of this drug-receptor interaction is that the receptor complex regulates the entrance of chloride into the postsynaptic cells. The increase in chloride conductance mediated by GABA is intensified by the benzodiazepines. This facilitation of GABA-induced chloride conductance results in greater hyperpolarisation of these cells and therefore leads to diminished synaptic transmission.

Another chemical class of sedative-hypnotic drugs, the barbiturates also binds to receptors associated with the GABA-chloride ionophore, but these drugs appear to prolong rather than intensify GABA's effects.

In addition to the clinically useful benzodiazepines, which act as agonists at the benzodiazepine receptor, at least two other types of Ligands also interact with this binding site. These are the benzodiazepine receptor antagonists and the inverse agonists. For example, Flumazenil (Romazicon) is a receptor antagonist that selectively blocks the effects of other benzodiazepines at their binding sites.

### Pharmacological actions

Although it is widely claimed that the benzodiazepine drugs have a specific calming or anxiolytic effect, their most prominent and easily quantifiable action is central nervous system depression. In very low therapeutic doses, this depression manifests as relief of anxiety that is often accompanied by a feeling of sluggishness or drowsiness. As the dose is increased, the degree of depression is intensified such that muscle relaxation, hypnosis and a more intense central nervous system depression occur. This depression is related to the ability of these drugs to facilitate the inhibitory actions of GABA.

A significant advantage of the benzodiazepines over other central nervous system depressants (e.g., the barbiturates) is that they possess a much greater separation between the dose that produces sleep and the dose that produces death. This increased margin of safety has been one of the major reasons benzodiazepines have largely replaced the barbiturates and other types of sedative-hypnotics in the treatment of anxiety and insomnia. In addition, benzodiazepine administration is associated with few side effects.

**Pharmacokinetics**

Benzodiazepines are usually given orally and are well absorbed by this route. Since the benzodiazepines are weak bases, they are less ionized in the relatively alkaline environment of the small intestine and therefore most of their absorption takes place at this site. For emergency treatment of seizures or when used in anesthesia, the benzodiazepines also can be given parenterally. Diazepam and lorazepam are available for intravenous administration.

The distribution of the benzodiazepines from blood to tissues and back again is a dynamic process with considerable influence on the onset and duration of the therapeutic effects produced by these compounds. Those having greater lipid solubility tend to enter the central nervous system more rapidly and thus tend to produce their effects more quickly. Several of the benzodiazepines have therapeutic effects that are much shorter in duration than would be predicted based on their rates of metabolism and excretion, redistribution away from the central nervous system is of primary importance in terminating their therapeutic effects.

Although tissue redistribution of benzodiazepines may be an important means of terminating the actions of selected members of this class of drugs, many benzodiazepines do undergo extensive biotransformation. Metabolism takes place both by dealkylation (phase 1) and conjugation (phase 2) reactions. In many instances, dealkylation can results in the formation of pharmacologically active compounds. Indeed, most clinically available benzodiazepines are converted in the liver to one or more active metabolites. In several cases the active metabolites have a much longer half-life than the parent compound. In one case, acid hydrolysis in the stomach converts an inactive compound (clorazepate) to an active drug (nordazepam).

Since most of the benzodiazepines do undergo biotransformation, it is possible that changes in liver function may alter the duration of the therapeutic effect produced by these drugs. Despite the fact that few clinical studies have demonstrated serious toxicities associated with benzodiazepine administration in individuals with compromised liver function, prudence in the use of these compounds in the elderly and in individuals with liver disease seems advisable.

One of the great disadvantages associated with many of the sedative and hypnotic drugs (e.g., barbiturates, propanediol carbamates) which have now largely been replaced by the benzodiazepines, is the fact that those drugs are very effective inducers of hepatic drug-metabolizing enzymes. Since the benzodiazepines are only weak inducers of hepatic microsomal enzymes they cause relatively few clinically significant drug interactions related to metabolism of other drugs.

**Adverse effects**

Most adverse effects associated with use of the benzodiazepines are related to their ability to produce central nervous system depression. These include drowsiness, excessive sedation, impaired motor coordination, confusion and memory loss. These effects are most troublesome during the initial week or two of treatment. Subsequently, the patient becomes tolerant an these effects produce less difficulty. Although for most individuals these symptoms are mild, patients should be cautioned against engaging in potentially dangerous tasks such as operating machinery or driving a car during the initial treatment period.

Less common adverse effects include blurred vision, hallucinations and paradoxical reactions consisting of excitement, stimulation and hyperactivity. Also, a variety of gastrointestinal complaints occur, and blood dyscrasias have been reported, but these are rare. Benzodiazepine administration during pregnancy, delivery or lactation has the potential to have adverse effects on the fetus or newborn.

As with other central nervous system depressants, the effects of benzodiazepines are additive with those of ethanol. Patients should be warned that ethanol- containing beverages may produce a more profound depression when taken simultaneously with a benzodiazepine.

One of the major reasons for the popularity of the benzodiazepines is their relative safety. Overdoses with the benzodiazepines occur commonly, but fatal toxic occurrences are rare. Fatal intoxications are more likely in children, in individuals with respiratory difficulties and in individuals who have consumed another central nervous system depressant, such as alcohol. After an overdose, the patient begins a deep sleep that may last for 24 to 48 hours, depending on the dose. However, even with large overdoses, the patient can usually still be aroused.

Tolerance and dependence do occur with the use of benzodiazepines. Discontinuation of drug administration, particularly abrupt withdrawal, can be associated with a variety of symptoms, including rebound insomnia and rebound anxiety. The level of insomnia or anxiety may even exceed that which preceded the treatment. Usually, a gradual tapering of the dose until it is eventually discontinued lessens the likelihood of a withdrawal reaction, although in some individuals even this method of drug removal can result in anxiety, apprehension, tension, insomnia and loss of appetite. More severe symptoms may occur when an individual withdraws from a supratherapeutic dose, particularly if the drug has been taken for months or years. These symptoms can include, in addition to those already mentioned, muscle weakness, tremor, hyperalgesia, nausea, vomiting, weight loss and possibly convulsions.

## Clinical uses

### *Anxiety*

Anxiety disorders are among the most common forms of psychiatric illness. Anxiety often accompanies other psychiatric disease and such medical illnesses as angina pectoris, gastrointestinal disorders and hypertension. Anxiety that results from fear caused by an acute illness or a stressful event, such as a divorce or the loss of a loved one, is usually self-limiting and can be of relatively short duration. Other disorders that have anxiety as a component are not necessarily associated with a life event and may persist for considerable periods, even throughout the individual's life.

Both acute and chronic anxiety can be treated with benzodiazepines, although it is anticipated that for most anxiety disorders counselling will also play an important role. Benzodiazepines employed in the treatment of anxiety should be used in the lowest effective dose for the shortest duration so that they will provide maximum benefit to the patient while minimizing the potential for adverse reactions. For most types of anxiety, none of the benzodiazepines is therapeutically superior to any other. A benzodiazepine with a long half-life should be considered if the anxiety is intense and sustained. A drug with a short half-life may have advantages when the anxiety is provoked by clearly defined circumstances and is likely to be of short duration.

### *Insomnia*

All of the benzodiazepines will produce sedative–hypnotic effects of sufficient magnitude to induce sleep, provided that the dose is high enough. However, the aim in the treatment of sleep disorders is to induce sleep that is as close as possible to natural sleep so that the patient falls asleep quickly, sleeps through the night and has sleep of sufficient quality to awake refreshed.

Extensive sleep studies have been conducted with a variety of sedative-hypnotic drugs, and all of these drugs appear to alter the normal distribution of rapid eye movement (REM) and Non-REM sleep. Most of the older sedative-hypnotic agents markedly depress REM sleep. In contrast, when the benzodiazepines are used in appropriate doses, they depress REM sleep to a much smaller extent. As with treatment of anxiety, the choice of a particular benzodiazepine to treat a sleep disturbance is again generally based on pharmacokinetic criteria. While longer-acting compounds may ensure that a patient will sleep through the night, they also may cause cumulative effects resulting in daytime sluggishness or drug hangover. Shorter-acting compounds avoid the hangover problem, but their use may be associated with early awakening and an increase in daytime anxiety.

*Epilepsy and Seizures*

Nearly all central nervous system depressants have some capacity to suppress seizures by virtue of their depressant activity on the brain and spinal cord. Clonazepam and diazepam are two benzodiazepines that depress epileptiform activity and are used in the treatment of epilepsy and seizure disorders.

*Sedation, Amnesia and Anesthesia*

Benzodiazepines have the capacity to produce a calming effect and to cause anterograde amnesia, in which the patient cannot recall events that took place for some time after the drug was administered. Benzodiazepine-induced sedation and amnesia are deemed useful in the preparation of patients for anesthesia, surgery and other frightening or unpleasant medical and dental procedures and diagnostic tests.

*Muscle relaxation*

Benzodiazepines have the capacity to depress polysynaptic reflexes and have been shown to decrease decerebrate rigidity in cats and spasticity in patients with cerebral palsy. What is not clear is whether they can in humans, relax voluntary muscles in doses that do not cause considerable central nervous system depression. Nevertheless, benzodiazepines such as diazepam are often prescribed for patients who have muscle spasms and pain as a result of injury. In these circumstances, the sedative and anxiolytic properties of the drug also may promote relaxation and relieve tension associated with the condition.

*Alcohol and sedative-hypnotic withdrawal*

Withdrawal from alcohol or sedative-hypnotic drugs can be life threatening if physical dependence is present. Benzodiazepines, such as chlordiazepoxide (Librium) and diazepam (Valium) are sometimes used to lessen the intensity of the withdrawal symptoms when alcohol or sedative-hypnotic drug use is discontinued. Benzodiazepines are also employed to help relieve the anxiety and other behavioral symptoms that may occur during rehabilitation.

**Drug interactions**

When used with other sedative-hypnotics or alcohol, the benzodiazepines will produce additive central nervous system depression.

Many benzodiazepines are metabolized by the cytochrome P450 (CYP) enzyme designated CYP3A4. CYP3A4 is inhibited by grapejuice and by drugs such as ketoconazole, itraconazole, nefazodone, erythromycin and ritonavir. Co-administration of these substances along with a benzodiazepine may result in intensification and prolongation of the benzodiazepine effect. Conversely, rifampin, carbamazepine and phenytoin can induce the CYP3A4 enzyme and therefore their co administration can reduce the therapeutic effect of the benzodiazepines.

**Table 20-1:** Advantages of benzodiazepines (BDZ) over barbiturates

| Benzodiazepines | Barbiturates |
|---|---|
| High therapeutic index, safety margin is high | Low therapeutic index, narrow safety margin |
| Doesn't induce hepatic microsomal enzymes and so there is less dependence | Induce hepatic microsomal enzymes and more dependence is present |
| Doesn't alter normal sleeping pattern | Alters normal sleeping pattern |
| Doesn't produce morning hangover | Produces morning hangover |
| Less tolerance and dependence | More tolerance and dependence |
| Less cardio-respiratory failure | More cardio-respiratory failure |
| Has specific antidote-Flumazenil | No specific antidote |
| Slower elimination rate, so it has high efficacy | Low efficacy as there is rapid elimination |

***Disadvantages of benzodiazepines***

1. It produces amnesia.
2. Tolerance, dependence and withdrawal syndrome.
3. Formation of active metabolites.
4. Higher cost.
5. Additive adverse effect with other CNS depressant drugs like Alcohol.

## Barbiturates (Fig 20-3)

The Barbiturates are shown in Fig 20-3.

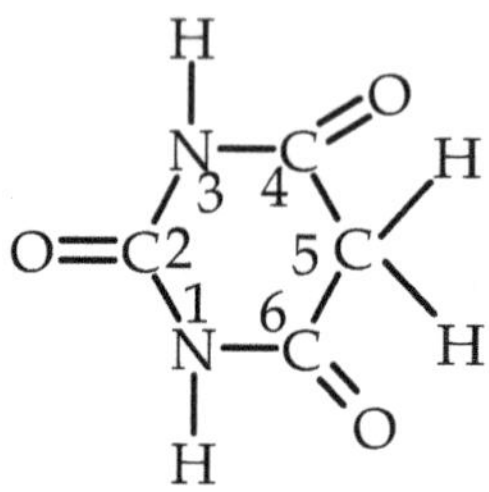

Barbituric acid

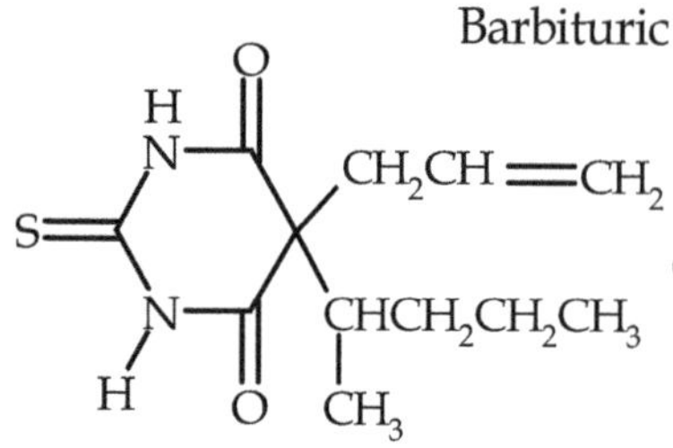

Thiamylal

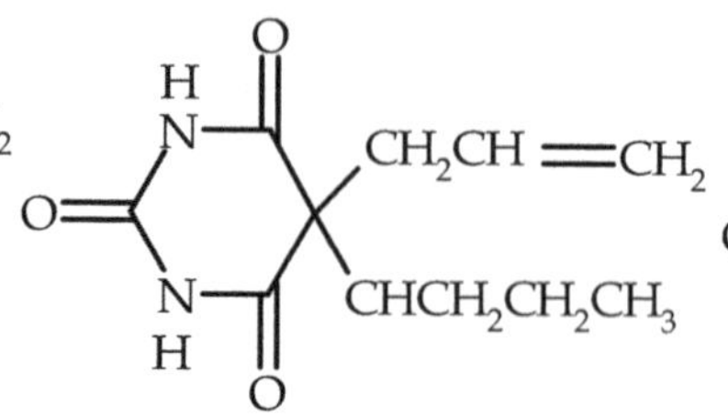

Secobarbital

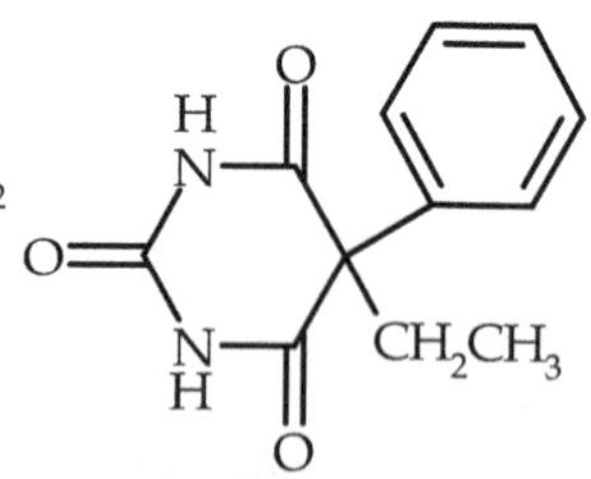

Phenobarbital

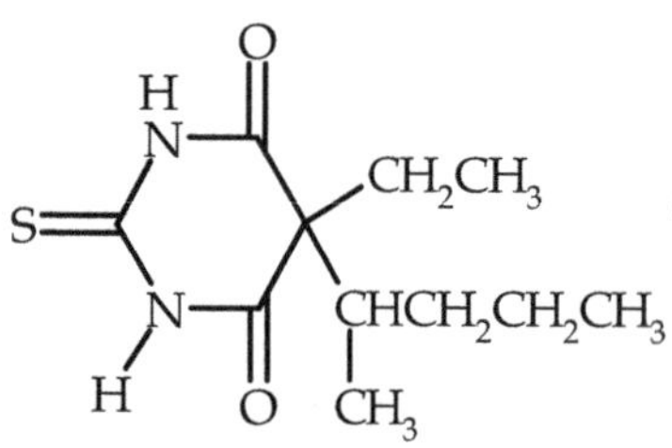

Thiopental

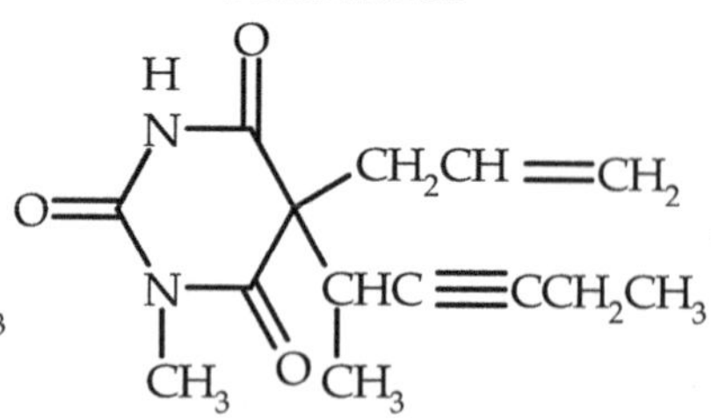

Methohexital

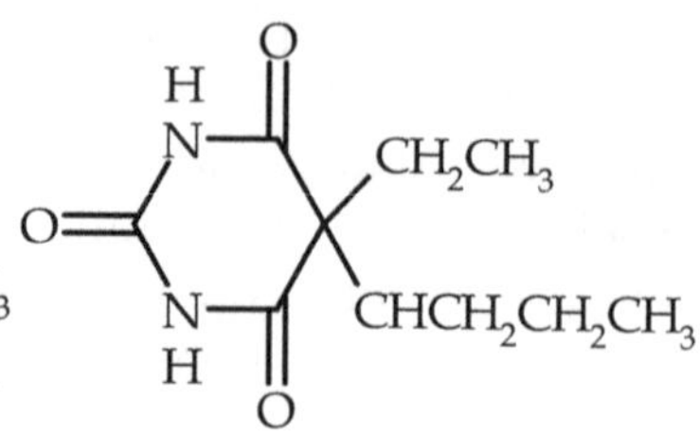

Pentobarbital

**Fig 20-3:** Barbiturates

These are the condensation of Urea + Malonic acid → Barbituric acid → Barbiturate (after adding radical), so it is a weak acid.

### Classification

| | |
|---|---|
| **Ultra short acting (30 min)** | Thiopentone sodium , Hexobarbitone , Methohexital |
| **Short acting (2 hr)** | Secobarbitone, Quinalbarbitone |
| **Intermediate acting (3-5 hr)** | Butobarbitone, Cyclobarbitone, Amylobarbitone, Pentobarbitone (anaesthetic), Allobarbitone |
| **Long acting (> 6 hr)** | Phenobarbitone, Barbitone, Methorbitone |

### Mechanism of action

Non-selective action. Barbiturates combine with the receptors on the GABA channel (not with the BDZ receptors) and facilitate the action of GABA by increasing the duration of GABA channel opening.

### Pharmacokinetics

Weak acid, so very quickly absorbed from the stomach and small intestine. Distributed throughout the body. Thiopentone sodium is used in anaesthesia as it is highly lipid soluble and rapidly enters into the CNS and very rapid onset of action. Redistribution from the CNS to other tissues (fat, skeletal muscle)- thiobarbiturates. Hepatic CYP450 system inducers. Not given with the oral contraceptives as there is therapeutic failure. Alkalization of the urine and increases excretion of drug by kidney by increasing ionization.

### Adverse effects

Coma, respiratory failure, circulatory failure, renal failure, allergic reaction , dependence and acute abuse-serious social and medical problem. Withdrawal symptoms begin in 8-36 hours

### Therapeutic uses

Used as anti-convulsant in epilepsy and seizure, to induce anaesthesia.

### Barbiturates are obsolete and unsuitable because

1. Low therapeutic index
2. Popular drug of social abuse
3. Physical dependence with more severe withdrawal symptom
4. Potent inducer of hepatic CYP450 system so many drug interactions
5. Action is non-selective
6. No antidote is available

### Phenobarbitone poisoning

*Signs and symptoms*

CNS depression

Respiratory depression

Cheyne stroke breathing-apnea followed by hyper-apnea

Oliguria

Renal dysfunction

***Treatment***

Immediate hospitalization in the ICU

Stomach wash by activated charcoal within 4 hours of poisoning

CVS resuscitation by 5% DA

Respiratory resuscitation by $O_2$

If the patient goes to shock, Dopamine is used to increase cardiac contractility

Forced alkaline diuresis-forced diuresis by mannitol and furosemide and alkalinity by $NaHCO_3$. So, the drug will be ionized and excreted through urine.

CNS stimulating agent-Bemegride

Haemodialysis

Monitoring of pulse, temperature, bp, respiratory rate and fluid input-output chart

## Other Benzodiazepine Receptor Agonists

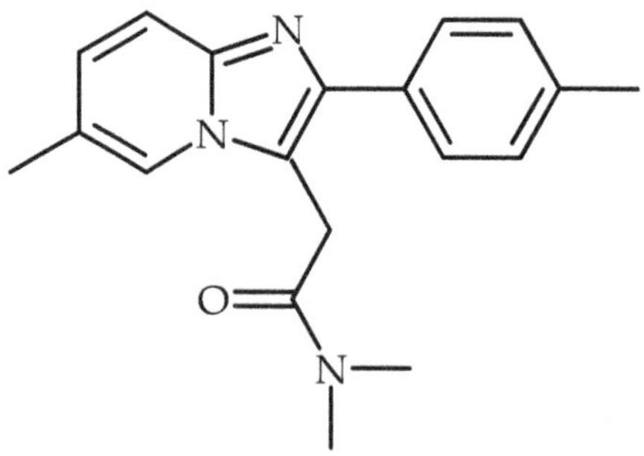


Zolpidem

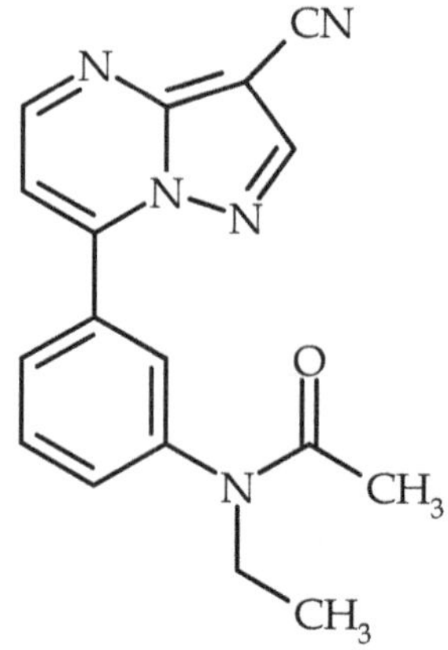


Zaleplon

**Fig 20-4 :** Benzodiazepine receptor agonists

The Benzodiazepine receptor agonists are shown in Fig 20-4.

Zolpidem (Ambien) and zaleplon (Sonata) are structurally unrelated to the benzodiazepines, but both drugs share pharmacological properties with the benzodiazepines. They bind to benzodiazepine receptors and facilitate GABA-mediated inhibition.

In usual sedative doses, zolpidem preserves deep sleep (stages 3 and 4) and has only minor and inconsistent effects on REM sleep. Compared with the benzodiazepines, zolpidem has relatively weak anxiolytic, anticonvulsant and skeletal muscle relaxant properties at therapeutic doses. Zolpidem has a rapid onset and a relatively short duration of action. It is well absorbed after oral administration, with approximately 70% bioavailability. It undergoes hydroxylation and oxidation to inactive metabolites in the liver. Its elimination half-life is approximately 2.5 hours, which is usually sufficient to provide for a normal 8 hours of sleep without daytime grogginess.

Principal side effects are gastrointestinal and central nervous system symptoms, including drowsiness, dizziness and diarrhea. Zolpidem may increase the depressant effects of other sedative drugs, such as the antipsychotics, tricyclic antidepressants and antihistamines.

There is less therapeutic experience with the newer zaleplon than with zolpidem. Zaleplon has a rapid onset and a half-life of approximately 1 hour. It is extensively metabolized by aldehyde dehydrogenase, so that less than 1% of a dose is excreted unchanged. Because of its rapid onset of action and short biological half-life, zaleplon is well suited for treatment of sleep onset insomnia. Its short half-life often does not ensure a full 8 hours of sleep.

## Sedatives and Anxiolytics with Other Major Uses

### Antihistamines

Several $H_1$ histamine antagonists (e.g., diphenhydramine, promethazine, and hydroxyzine) have been used as sedative-hypnotics, since they produce some degree of sedation. While this sedation is usually considered a side effect of their antihistaminic activity, in some cases the sedation is sufficient to allow the drugs to be used in the treatment of anxiety and sleep disturbances. For these drugs, the anxiolytic properties are thought to be a direct consequence of their ability to produce sedation.

Hydroxyzine hydrochloride (Atarax, Vistaril) is the antihistamine with the greatest use in the treatment of anxiety. It is often used to reduce the anxiety that is associated with anesthesia and surgery. It also produces sedation, dries mucous membranes (*via* an anticholinergic mechanism) and has antiemetic activity.

### β -Adrenoceptor Blocking Agents

β-Adrenoceptor antagonists, such as propranolol (Inderal) have been widely used in the treatment of cardiovascular diseases. These β -blockers also are useful in some forms of anxiety, particularly those that are characterized by somatic symptoms or by performance anxiety (stage fright). There is general agreement that β -blockers can lessen the severity and perhaps prevent the appearance of many of the autonomic responses associated with anxiety. These symptoms include tremors, sweating, tachycardia and palpitations.

### Antidepressants

Antidepressant drugs, such as the tricyclic antidepressants and the selective serotonin reuptake inhibitors (SSRIs) are very important for the treatment of psychotic depression. They have been shown to be effective when used in the treatment of several anxiety disorders, including general anxiety, obsessive-compulsive disorder and several phobias including agoraphobia. Because the SSRIs are less toxic than the tricyclic antidepressants, their use in the treatment of anxiety is safer and less likely to produce serious side effects.

## Older Sedative–Hypnotics and Anxiolytic Agents

Before the introduction of the benzodiazepines, a number of drugs from different chemical and pharmacological classes were used in the treatment of anxiety and insomnia. However, these drugs are more toxic and produce more serious side effects than do the benzodiazepines. Many also have significant abuse potential. Consequently, most of these compounds are no longer widely used. These drugs include the barbiturates (e.g., pentobarbital, amobarbital), carbamates (e.g., meprobamate), piperidinediones (e.g., glutethimide) and alcohols (e.g., ethchlorvynol).

Chloral hydrate (Noctec, Somnos) was developed in the late 1800,s and is still used as a sedative–hypnotic agent. It is a hydrated aldehyde with a disagreeable smell and taste that is rapidly reduced *in vivo* to trichloroethanol, which is considered to be the active metabolite. It produces a high incidence of gastric irritation and allergic responses, occasionally causes cardiac arrhythmias and is unreliable in patients with liver damage.

## Non-prescription Drugs

A wide variety of sedative–hypnotic products that do not require a prescription are available. Most of these over the counter products have antihistamines, such as pyrilamine, diphenhydramine or promethazine as the active ingredient. In most cases, the dose of the active ingredient is low and the preparations are safe.

Ethanol (ethyl alcohol) has central nervous system depressant properties and is widely used to relieve anxiety and produce sedation. Although some medical practitioners occasionally prescribe an alcoholic beverage for relieving minor anxiety and inducing sleep, individuals frequently self-medicate with ethanol. Many individuals who abuse alcohol may have started using it to relieve symptoms of central nervous system disorders, such as anxiety and depression.

Ethanol produces central nervous system depression over a wide range of doses. Its effects are additive or sometimes more than additive with other central nervous system depressants. Symptoms often associated with acute alcohol intoxication include increase in self- confidence, loss of inhibitions, euphoria and loss of judgment. With increasing doses motor and intellectual impairment become prominent.

Chronic abuse of ethanol leads to severe liver impairment.

## References

Doghramji PP (2001). Treatment of insomnia with zaleplon, a novel sleep medication. *Int J Clin Pract* **55:** 329-334.

Dooley M and Plosker GL. Zaleplon (2000). A review of its use in the treatment of insomnia. *Drugs* **60:** 413-445.

Yuan R, Flockhart DA, and Balian JD (1999). Pharmacokinetic and pharmacodynamic consequences of metabolism based drug interactions with alprazolam, midazolam and triazolam. *J Clin Pharmacol* **39:** 1109-1125.

Zohar J and Westenberg HG (2000). Anxiety disorders: A review of tricyclic antidepressants and selective serotonin reuptake inhibitors. *Acta Psychiatr Scand Suppl* **403:** 39-49.

CHAPTER

# Neuroleptics 21

## Introduction

### Schizophrenia

Schizophrenia represents a major mental illness, or possibly a group of Illnesses, manifested chiefly by disordered thought processes including disturbances in attention and associations. This leads to difficulties in communication, interpersonal relationships and reality testing. Studies indicate that schizophrenia occurs 4-times more frequently among biological relatives than in the general population.

### Symptoms

#### Positive Symptoms

Positive or florid, symptoms appear as an excess or distortion of everyday behaviour. They include psychotic features such as delusions or hallucinations, disorganised speech or thinking and chaotic or confused behaviour.

***Delusions*** are beliefs that usually involve a misinterpretation of perception or experience. For example, people may believe that they are religious figures or members of the royal family, they may believe they are being persecuted by the police or that a group of people are after them.

***Hallucinations*** can be experienced through any of the senses, but auditory hallucinations ('hearing voices') are most common. People hear voices in their head or they may believe that the television is speaking to them directly.

***Disorganised speech and thinking*** are characterised by losing track of conversations, changing from one topic to another unrelated topic or giving loosely or totally unrelated answers to questions. Similarly, thought processes may be jumbled and not follow any discernible sequence.

***Chaotic or disorganised behaviour*** may be expressed in a variety of ways, ranging from childishness to unpredictability and agitation. People may appear dishevelled or dress in an unusual manner, they may display inappropriate sexual behaviour or extreme agitation such as shouting and swearing for no apparent reason. One of the things that can be upsetting and distressing for both the individual and others, is that the individual may not be aware that their experience is not shared by others. The sense of their reality is such that they find it difficult when they encounter any difference in opinion on this matter.

#### Negative Symptoms

Negative symptoms appear as a decrease or loss of everyday functions. They include flattened affect, poverty of speech and loss of motivation.

***Flattened affect*** is loss of emotional expressiveness. A person's face may appear expression less, they may have poor eye contact and reduced body language.

***Poverty of speech*** also known as alogia, is manifested by loss of fluency in spoken communication. People are less likely to initiate conversations and replies to questions may be met with very brief responses.

***Loss of motivation*** or avolition, is characterised by difficulties in initiating or taking part in activities. The person may appear withdrawn and show no interest in participation. Acute schizophrenia is characterised primarily by positive symptoms while chronic schizophrenia is characterised primarily by negative symptoms.

Symptoms can start at any age, but most commonly occur in the late teens or early twenties. More or less equal numbers of young men and women develop schizophrenia, though women are usually four or five years older than men at the onset. It occurs in all cultures and its prevalence is much the same in every country.

## Types

Catatonic Type

Either in position or speech (imitating others); Very rare

Disorganized Type

Disturbance in behavior, speech and thought; Flat affect, eccentric

Paranoid Type

Delusions and auditory hallucinations; Cognitive functioning remains intact

Residual Type

Have been previously diagnosed but no longer show prominent symptoms; still have other symptoms

**Undifferentiated Type**

The etiology of schizophrenia is unclear. However, there is evidence that it results from abnormal neurotransmission systems in the brain, especially in the dopaminergic, serotonergic and glutamatergic systems. There is also evidence of extensive interactions among neurotrans-mission systems. For example, the serotonergic and glutamatergic systems can alter dopaminergic activity and drugs that may cause psychosis affect several systems (e.g., adrenergics increase norepinephrine; antidepressants increase norepinephrine, serotonin or both). Thus, schizophrenia probably results from imbalances and abnormal integration among several neurotransmission systems. In addition, illnesses or drugs that alter neurotransmission in one system are likely to alter neurotrans-mission in other systems. The dopaminergic, serotonergic and glutamatergic systems have been studied most.

# Theories of Schizophrenia

## Dopamine Hypothesis

The dopaminergic system has been more extensively studied than other systems, because schizophrenia has long been attributed to increased dopamine activity in the brain. Stimulation of dopamine can initiate psychotic symptoms or exacerbate an existing psychotic disorder. The importance of dopamine is further supported by two findings: (1) antipsychotic drugs exert their therapeutic effects by decreasing dopamine activity (i.e., blocking dopamine receptors) and (2) drugs that increase dopamine levels in the brain (e.g., bromocriptine, cocaine, levodopa) can cause signs and symptoms of psychosis. In addition to the increased amount of dopamine, dopamine receptors are also involved. Two groups of dopamine receptors have been differentiated, mainly by the effects of the dopamine–receptor complex on intracellular functions. The first group stimulates cellular functions, whereas the second group decreases cellular functions and alters the movement of calcium and potassium ions across neuronal cell membranes. The second group ($D_2$ receptors) is considered important in the pathophysiology of schizophrenia. Thus, at the cellular level, dopamine activity is determined by its interaction with various receptors and the simultaneous actions of other neurotransmitters at the same target neurons. In general, overactivity of dopamine in some parts of the brain is thought to account for the positive symptoms of schizophrenia and underactivity in another part of the brain is thought to account for the negative symptoms.

## Serotonin Hypothesis

The serotonergic system, which is widespread in the brain, is mainly inhibitory in nature. In schizophrenia, serotonin apparently decreases dopamine activity in the part of the brain associated with negative symptoms causing or aggravating these symptoms.

### Glutamate Hypothesis

The Glutamatergic neurotransmission system involves glutamate, the major excitatory neurotransmitter in the CNS. Glutamate receptors are widespread and possibly located on every neuron in the brain. They are also diverse and their functions may vary according to subtypes and their locations in particular parts of the brain. When glutamate binds to its receptors, the resulting neuronal depolarization activates signalling molecules (e.g., calcium, nitric oxide) within and between brain cells. Thus, glutamatergic transmission may affect every CNS neuron and is considered essential for all mental, sensory, motor and affective functions. Dysfunction of glutamatergic neurotransmission has been implicated in the development of psychosis. In addition, the glutamatergic system interacts with the dopaminergic and gamma-aminobutyric acid systems and possibly other neurotransmission systems. In people with schizophrenia, evidence indicates the presence of abnormalities in the number, density, composition and function of glutamate receptors. In addition, glutamate receptors are genetically encoded and can interact with environmental factors (e.g., stress, alcohol and other drugs) during brain development. Thus, glutamatergic dysfunction may account for the roles of genetic and environmental risk factors in the development of schizophrenia as well as the cognitive impairments and negative symptoms associated with the disorder.

## Definitions

*Neuroleptic*: Synonym for antipsychotic drug; originally indicated drug with antipsychotic effect but with neurologic (extrapyramidal motor) side effects.

*Typical neuroleptic:* Older agents fitting this description

*Atypical neuroleptic:* Newer agents: antipsychotic effect with reduced or no neurologic side effects

### Ideal Antipsychotic

Shows efficacy and effectiveness against all symptoms of schizophrenia.

Well tolerated with no or minimal side effects.

No or minimal drug-drug interactions.

Single dose.

Helps patients to function and enjoy a good quality of life.

Preserve brain tissue.

## Classification of Antipsychotic Drugs

**Typical antipsychotics**

Phenothiazines

E.g., Chlorpromazine, Fluphenazine, Thioridazine

Butyrophenones

E.g., Haloperidol, Droperidol

Thioxanthines

E.g., Thiothixene

**Atypical antipsychotics**

Benzamides

Remoxipride (investigational)

Diphenylbutylpiperazines

E.g., Pimozide

Dibenzodiazepines

### Distinction between 'typical' and 'atypical' groups is not clearly defined, but rests on:

Incidence of extrapyramidal side-effects (less in 'atypical' group)

Efficacy in treatment-resistant group of patients

Efficacy against negative symptoms

Antipsychotic drugs are derived from several chemical groups. These drugs may be broadly categorized as "typical," conventional or first-generation agents [phenothiazines and older nonphenothiazines, such as haloperidol (Haldol), with similar pharmacologic actions, clinical uses and adverse effects], or as "atypical" or second-generation agents, which can also be called newer nonphenothiazines.

## Mechanism of Action

Most antipsychotic drugs bind to $D_2$ dopamine receptors and block the action of dopamine. However, drug binding to the receptors does not account for antipsychotic effects because binding occurs within a few hours after a drug dose and antipsychotic effects may not occur until the drugs have been given for a few weeks. Manifestations of hyperarousal (e.g., anxiety, agitation, hyperactivity, insomnia, aggressive or combative behavior) are relieved more quickly than hallucinations, delusions and thought disorders. One view of the delayed effects is that the blockade of dopamine receptors leads to changes in the receptors and post receptor effects on cell metabolism and function. With chronic drug administration (i.e., chronic blockade of dopamine receptors), there is an increased number of dopamine receptors on postsynaptic and possibly presynaptic nerve cell membranes (up-regulation). Clozapine (Clozaril) and other atypical agents interact with dopamine, serotonin and glutamate receptors. Overall, the drugs re-regulate the abnormal neuro-transmission systems associated with psychosis.

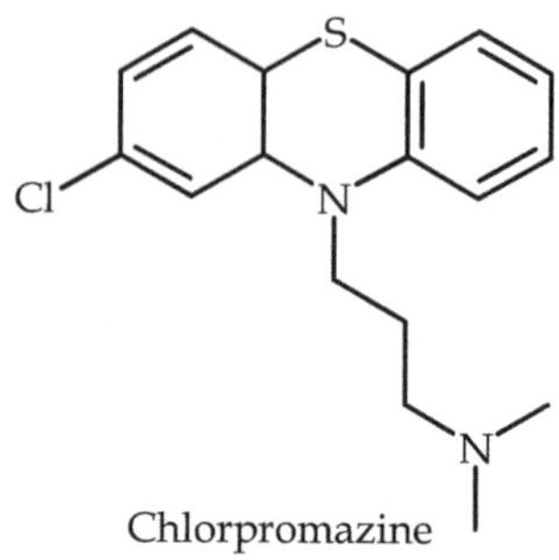

Chlorpromazine

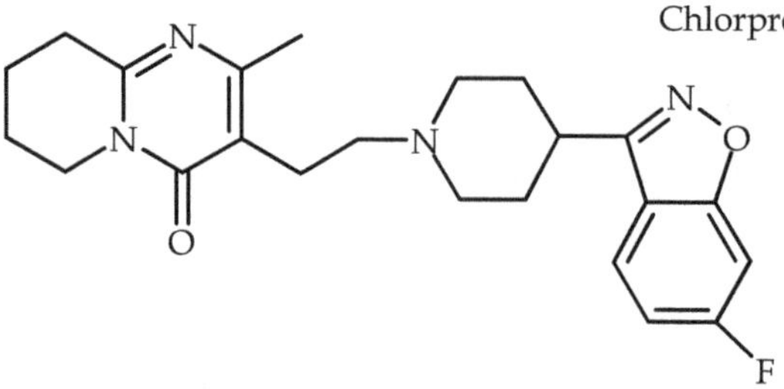

Risperidone

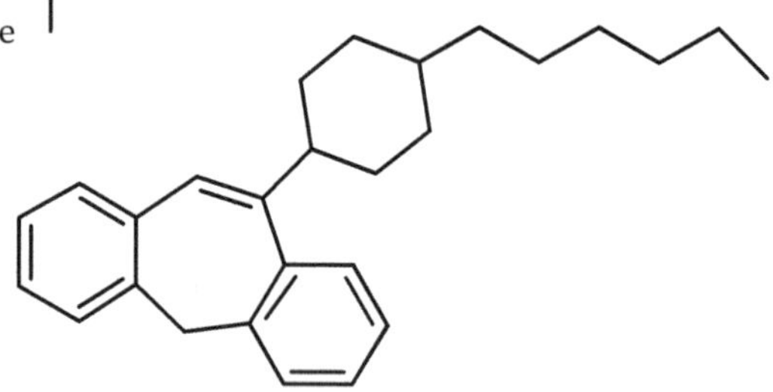

Ziprazidone

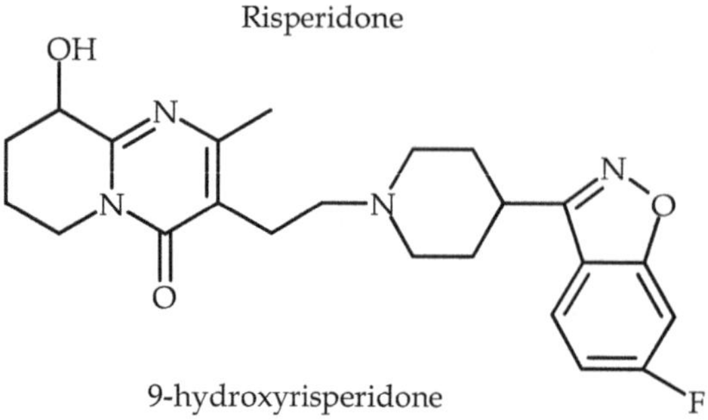

9-hydroxyrisperidone

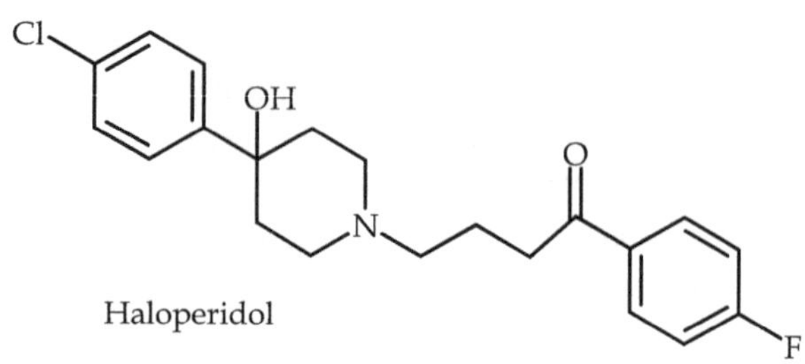

Haloperidol

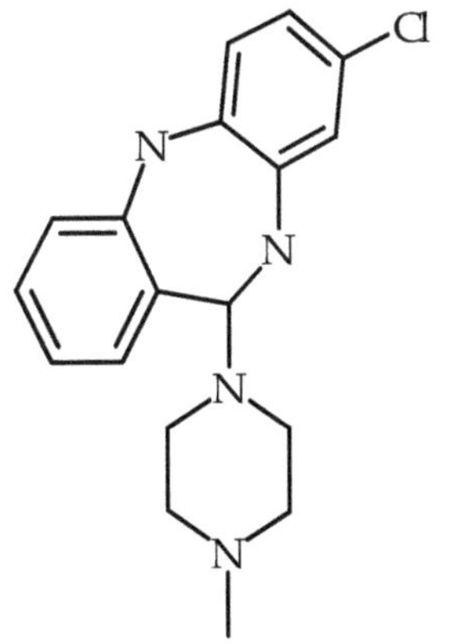

Clozapine

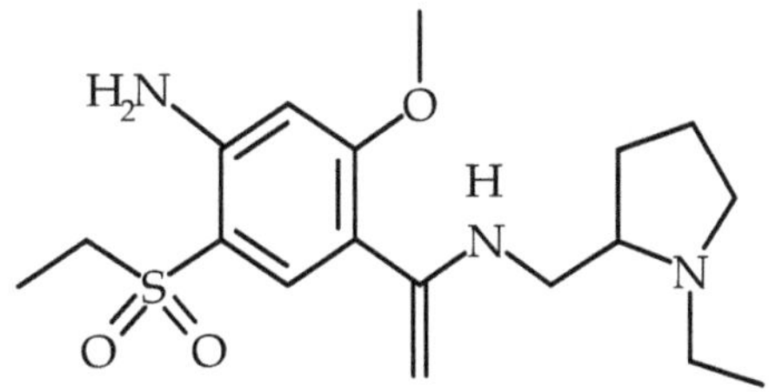

Amisulpride

**Fig 21-1:** Antipsychotics

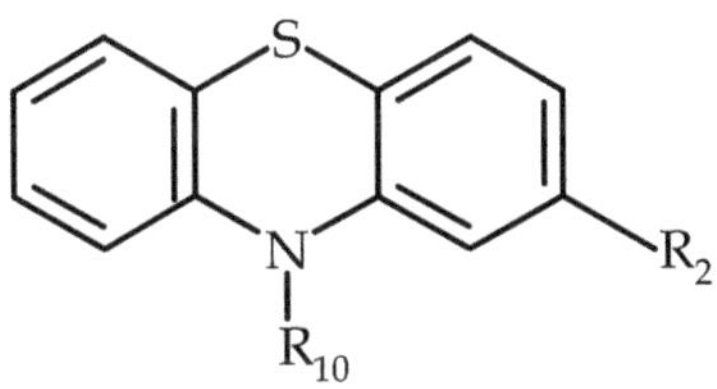

| | $R_2$ | $R_{10}$ |
|---|---|---|
| Promethazine (1) | H | —$CH_2\overset{*}{C}H(CH_3)N(CH_3)_2$ |
| Ethopropazine (2) | H | —$CH_2\overset{*}{C}H(CH_3)N(C_2H_5)_2$ |
| Trimeprazine (3) | H | —$CH_2\overset{*}{C}H(CH_3)CH_2N(CH_3)_2$ |
| Methotrimeprazine (4) | $OCH_3$ | —$CH_2\overset{*}{C}H(CH_3)CH_2N(CH_3)_2$ |
| Thioridazine (5) | $SCH_3$ | —$CH_2CH_2$— 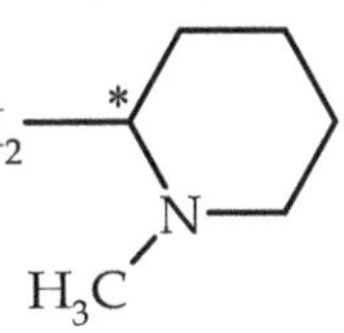 |

**Fig 21-2:** Phenothiazines

## Phenothiazines

The Phenothiazines are shown in Fig 21-2.

### Chlorpromazine

***Mechanism of action:*** Blockade of dopamine $D_1$ and $D_2$-like family receptors in the basal ganglia- $D_1$-like ($D_1$, $D_5$)- activate adenylate cyclase, $D_2$-like ($D_2$, $D_3$, $D_4$)- inhibit adenylate cyclase and also block Histamine and Muscarinic receptors.

## Pharmacologic Effects and Mechanism

Neuroleptics exert a significant influence upon CNS.

1. The main effect of neuroleptics upon the CNS is antipsychotic one. The antagonism of dopamine in the mesolimbic-mesocortical system is the basis of the therapeutic actions of the antipsychotic drugs. Displays of this action are elimination of delirium and hallucinations.
2. The sedative action is caused by blockade of M-cholinoceptors located in the limbic system and of the α -adrenoceptors of ascending part of the reticular formation. Displays of this action are drowsiness, impairment of psychomotor reactions, mental function and apathy.
3. In high doses neuroleptics exert hypnotic action.
4. The typical effect of these drugs is decrease of motor activity (central myorelaxation action).
5. These drugs inhibit the center of thermoregulation that leads to decrease of body temperature. After neuroleptic administration the poikilothermia develops (body temperature varies with the temperature of environment: when the temperature of environment lowers, the temperature of body lowers too).
6. Neuroleptics exert significant antiemetic action which is associated with blockade of $D_2$-receptors of trigger zone of the vomiting centre.
7. Neuroleptics have significant influence upon the endocrine sphere. Drugs increase the secretion of prolactin. Antipsychotics are used chronically and thus cause prolonged hyperprolactinemia. As a result, concern aroses over possible contribution to risk of carcinoma of the breast. Neuroleptics inhibit the release of growth hormone and reduce the secretion of corticotropin-releasing hormone and gonadotropines.
8. Neuroleptics decrease the activity of vasomotor center.
9. The one of manifestations of central action of neurolepticsis its ability to potentiate the action of some neurotropic drugs – general anaesthetics, hypnotic drugs and opioid analgetics.

Neuroleptics exert influence upon the peripheral innervation.

1. α-adrenoblocking action leads to the dilation of arteries. Phenothiazine derivatives have a direct negative inotropic action and antiarrhytmic effect on the heart. These drugs decrease the strength of cardiac contractions. Hypotension is usually accompanied by reflex tachycardia. Mean arterial pressure, peripheral resistance and stroke volume are decreased, while pulse rate is increased.
2. Antimuscarinic activities cause blurred vision, dry mouth and urinary retention. The tone and motility of gastrointestinal tract are decreased.
3. In local action neuroleptics cause significant irritation, which is superseded by anaesthesia.
4. Neuroleptics are spasmolitics of myotropic type of action.

## Pharmacokinetics

The phenothiazines are well absorbed after oral and parenteral administration. They are distributed to most body tissues and reach high concentrations in the brain. They are metabolized in the liver by the cytochrome P450 enzyme system; produce several pharmacologically active metabolites. Metabolites are excreted in urine. These drugs do not cause psychological dependence, but they may cause physical dependence manifested by withdrawal symptoms (e.g., lethargy, difficulty sleeping) if they are abruptly discontinued.

## Adverse Effects

***The extrapyramidal system (EPS)*** - the EPS is not a side-effect of antipsychotics, but needs to be mentioned before certain side effects. The EPS is a motor system composed of dopamine (DA) and acetylcholine (Ach) neurons which enjoy a reciprocal relationship. In some individuals when DA receptors are blocked, the balance in the system is disrupted, leading to side-effects.

***Acute neurological side-effects (acute EPS effects)*** occur secondary to $D_2$ receptor blockade in the EPS. These can appear on the first day of treatment and can take various forms of involuntary muscle spasm, particularly involving of the jaw, tongue, neck and eyes. A dramatic form is **Occulogyric crisis** – in which the neck arches back and the eyes roll upward. A potentially dangerous form is **Laryngospasm** – an early warning sign may be the patient's voice becoming higher pitched. Balance has been disturbed resulting in muscle spasm, and can be restored by acute treatment with oral or intramuscular injection of an anti-Ach drug- such as Benztropine (2 mg). The response is immediate and pleasing.

***Medium-term neurological side-effects*** are also due to $D_2$ blockade in the EPS.

***Akathisia*** usually occurs within the first few day of treatment and involves either a mental and/or motor restlessness. Mental restlessness presents as increasing distress and agitation. Motor restlessness usually affects the lower limbs, with shifting from one foot to the other while standing and constant crossing and uncrossing of the legs while sitting. This is a difficult condition to manage. Useful steps include lowering the dose of the antipsychotic (if possible), adding diazepam or propranolol, or adding an anticholinergic (none of these agents is dramatically effective).

***Parkinsonism*** usually occurs some days or weeks after the commencement of treatment. There is a mask-like face, rigidity of limbs, bradykinesia and loss of upper limb-swing while walking. Tremor and festinating gait are less common. The best management is reduction in dose of the antipsychotic (if possible) and the addition of an anticholinergic agent.

***Chronic neurological side-effects (late EPS effects)*** usually occur after months or years of continuous $D_2$ blockade. **Tardive dyskinesia (TD)** manifests as continuous choreoathetoid movements of the mouth and tongue, frequently with lip-smacking and may also involve the head, neck and trunk. Late EPS effects may continue after cessation of the typical antipsychotic.

***Neuroendocrine effects*** result from blockade of dopamine transmission in the infundibular tract. Prolactin levels rise, with most antipsychotic agents and extreme cases may cause galactorrhea, amenorrhoea and infertility.

***Neuroleptic malignant syndrome (NMS)*** is probably due to disruption of dopaminergic function, but the mechanism is not understood. Untreated, the mortality rate is 20% and immediate medical attention is mandatory. The symptoms include muscle rigidity, hyperthermia, autonomic instability and fluctuating consciousness. Renal failure secondary to rhabdomyolysis is a major complication and the cause of mortality.

***Anticholinergic side-effects*** include dry mouth, difficulty with micturition, constipation, blurred vision and ejaculatory failure. Anticholinergic delirium is a toxic confusional state; it usually occurs in patients taking a range of drugs directed at different symptoms and antipsychotics may play a role.

***Histamine blockade*** may produce severe sedation.

***Alpha adrenergic blockade*** may produce postural hypotension, cardiac arrhythmias and impotence.

***Dermatological side-effects*** include skin rash and photosensitivity.

***Weight gain*** is common with most typical antipsychotics.

## Therapeutic Uses

1. Treatment of schizophrenia is the primary indication for use of neuroleptics. Therapy is typically continued for at least a year after remissions are apparent.
2. Antipsychotics can also be employed to control disturbed behaviour in-senile dementia or Alzheimer's disease, since they

decrease confusion, agitation and hyperactivity.

3. Neuroleptics are also used for discontinuance of acute psychomotor excitement.
4. Most of these drugs also exhibit a strong antiemetic effect and can be used clinically for the treatment of vomiting (due to cancer chemotherapy, radiation therapy, different intoxications) and durable hiccup.
5. Droperidol in combination with opioid analgesics Fentanyl is used for neuroleptanaesthesia.
6. Neuroleptics may be used for premedication before general anaesthesia.
7. Neuroleptics which have the significant α-adrenoblocking properties (for example, aminazine) are used for interruption of hypertensive crises, for prevention of

**Table 21-1:** Adverse reactions of phenothiazines and their treatment

| Reaction | Features | Time of maximal risk | Proposed mechanism | Treatment |
|---|---|---|---|---|
| Acute dystonia | Spasm of muscles of tongue, face, neck, back; may mimic seizures; not hysteria | 1 to 5 days | Unknown | Antiparkinsonian agents are diagnostic and curative |
| Akathisia | Motor restlessness; not anxiety or "agitation" | 5 to 60 days | Unknown | Reduce dose or change drug, antiparkinsonian agents, benzodiazepines or propranolol may help |
| Parkinsonism | Bradykinesia, rigidity, variable tremor, mask facies, shuffling gait | 5 to 30 days | Antagonism of dopamine | Antiparkinsonian agents helpful |
| Neuroleptic malignant syndrome | Catatonia, stupor, fever, unstable blood pressure, myoglobinemia; can be fatal | Weeks; can persist for days after stopping neuroleptic | Antagonism of dopamine may contribute | Stop neuroleptic immediately, dantrolene or bromocriptine may help,antiparkinsonian agents not effective |
| Perioral tremor ("rabbit" syndrome) | Perioral tremor (may be a late variant of parkinsonism) | After months or years of treatment | Unknown | Antiparkinsonian agents often help |
| Tardive dyskinesia | Oral-facial dyskinesia; widespread choreoathetosis or dystonia | After months or years of treatment (worse on withdrawal) | Excess function of dopamine hypothesized | Prevention crucial; treatment unsatisfactory |

cardiogenic shock and treatment of acute pulmonary edema.

Many drugs have been claimed to be helpful for acute dystonia. Among the most commonly employed treatments are diphenhydramine hydrochloride, 25 or 50 mg intramuscularly, or benztropine mesylate, 1 or 2 mg intramuscularly or slowly intravenously, followed by oral medication with the same agent for a period of days to perhaps several weeks thereafter. Propranolol often is effective in relatively low doses (20-80 mg per day). Selective beta1-adrenergic receptor antagonists are less effective. Despite the response to dantrolene, there is no evidence of an abnormality of $Ca^{2+}$ transport in skeletal muscle; with lingering neuroleptic effects, bromocriptine may be tolerated in large doses (10-40 mg per day).

### Phenothiazines - Drug Interactions

Enzyme interactions with barbiturates (phenobarbital); phenytoin (Dilantin); carbamazepine (Tegretol) - reduce phenothiazine levels. Co-administration must be carefully monitored to prevent toxicity. SSRIs increases levels and may increase side effects.

## Nonphenothiazines

Nonphenothiazines include first-generation "typical" antipsychotics, which share many similarities to phenothiazines and second-generation "atypical" antipsychotics, which vary in relation to typical drugs and to each other.

### First-Generation "Typical" Antipsychotics

***Haloperidol*** (Haldol) is a butyrophenone used in psychiatric disorders. A related drug, droperidol, is used in anaesthesia and as an antiemetic. Haloperidol is a frequently used, potent, long-acting drug. It is well absorbed after oral or intramuscular (i.m) administration, is metabolized in the liver and is excreted in urine and bile. It may cause adverse effects similar to those of the phenothiazines. Usually, it produces a relatively low incidence of hypotension and sedation and a high incidence of extrapyramidal effects. Haloperidol may be used as the initial drug for treating psychotic disorders or as a substitute in clients who are hypersensitive or refractory to the phenothiazines. It also is used to treat some conditions in which other antipsychotic drugs are not used, including mental retardation with hyper kinesia (abnormally increased motor activity), Tourette's syndrome (a rare disorder characterized by involuntary movements and vocalizations) and Huntington's disease (a rare genetic disorder that involves progressive psychiatric symptoms and involuntary movements).

***Loxapine*** (Loxitane) is similar to phenothiazines and related drugs. It is recommended for use in only the treatment of schizophrenia.

***Molindone*** (Moban) differs chemically from other agents but has similar pharmacological actions.

***Pimozide*** (Orap) is approved only for the treatment of Tourette's syndrome in clients who fail to respond to haloperidol. Potentially serious adverse effects include tardive dyskinesia, major motor seizures and sudden death.

***Thiothixene*** (Navane) is used only for antipsychotic effects, although it produces other effects similar to those of the phenothiazines.

### Second-Generation "Atypical" Antipsychotics

In recent years, the "atypical" or newer nonphenothiazines have become the drugs of first choice. They have virtually replaced phenothiazines and related drugs except in clients doing well on older drugs and in the treatment of acute psychotic episodes. The atypical drugs have both similarities and differences when compared with other antipsychotic drugs and with each other. The main similarity is their effectiveness in treating the positive symptoms of psychosis; the main differences are greater effectiveness in relieving negative symptoms of schizophrenia and fewer resulting movement disorders (i.e., extrapyramidal symptoms such as acute dystonia, parkinsonism, akathisia and tardive dyskinesia). Although adverse effects are generally milder and more tolerable than with older drugs, clozapine may cause life-threatening agranulocytosis and some of these drugs have been associated with weight gain, hyperglycemia, diabetes and neuroleptic malignant syndrome.

***Clozapine*** (Clozaril), the prototype of the atypical agents, is chemically different from the older antipsychotic drugs. It blocks both dopamine and serotonin receptors in the brain. Clozapine is indicated for clients with schizophrenia, including those who have exhibited recurrent suicidal behavior.

Advantages of clozapine include improvement of negative symptoms, without causing the extrapyramidal effects associated with older antipsychotic drugs. However, despite these advantages, it is a second-line drug, recommended only for clients who have not responded to treatment with at least two other antipsychotic drugs or who have disabling tardive dyskinesia. The reason for the second-line status of clozapine is its association with agranulocytosis, a life-threatening decrease in white blood cells (WBCs), which usually occurs during the first 3 months of therapy. Weekly WBC counts are required during the first 6 months of therapy, if acceptable WBC counts are maintained, then WBC counts can be monitored every other week. In addition, clozapine is reportedly more likely to cause constipation, dizziness, drowsiness, hypotension, seizures, and weight gain than other atypical drugs.

***Olanzapine*** (Zyprexa) has therapeutic effects similar to those of clozapine, but adverse effects may differ. Compared with clozapine, olanzapine is more likely to cause extrapyramidal effects and less likely to cause agranulocytosis. Compared with the typical antipsychotics, olanzapine reportedly causes less sedation, extrapyramidal symptoms, anticholinergic effects, and orthostatic hypotension. However, it has been associated with weight gain, hyperglycemia, and initiation or aggravation of diabetes mellitus. The drug is well absorbed after oral administration, its absorption is not affected by food. A steady-state concentration is reached after approximately 1 week of once-daily administration. Olanzapine is metabolized in the liver and excreted in urine and feces.

***Quetiapine*** (Seroquel), like the other atypical agents, blocks both dopamine and serotonin receptors and relieves both positive and negative symptoms of psychosis. After oral administration, quetiapine is well absorbed and may be taken without regard to meals. It is extensively metabolized in the liver by the cytochrome P450 enzyme system. Clinically significant drug interactions may occur with drugs that induce or inhibit the liver enzymes, and dosage of quetiapine may need to be increased in patients taking enzyme inducers (e.g., carbamazepine, phenytoin, rifampin) or decreased in clients taking enzyme inhibitors (e.g., cimetidine, erythromycin). Common **adverse effects** include drowsiness, headache, orthostatic hypotension, and weight gain.

***Risperidone*** (Risperdal) also blocks both dopamine and serotonin receptors and relieves both positive and negative symptoms of psychosis. It is a frequently prescribed, first choice agent that is usually well tolerated. In a study that compared risperidone and olanzapine, researchers concluded that both drugs were well tolerated and effective in treating schizophrenia, but risperidone relieved positive symptoms, anxiety, and depression to a greater degree and caused less weight gain than olanzapine. Risperidone is well absorbed with oral administration. Peak blood levels occur in 1 to 2 hours, but therapeutic effects are delayed for 1 to 2 weeks. Risperidone is metabolized mainly in the liver by the cytochrome P450 2D6 enzymes and produces an active metabolite. Effects are attributed approximately equally to risperidone and the metabolite. Most (70%) of the drug is excreted in urine and some (14%) in feces.

**Adverse Effects:** Include agitation, anxiety, headache, insomnia, dizziness, and hypotension. Risperidone may also cause parkinsonism and other movement disorders, especially at higher doses, but is less likely to do so than the typical antipsychotic drugs.

***Ziprasidone*** (Geodon) is another atypical agent used to treat schizophrenia. It is effective in suppressing many of the negative symptoms such as blunted affect, lack of motivation and social withdrawal. It is contraindicated in people who are allergic to the drug; who are pregnant or lactating; who have a prolonged QT/QTc interval on electrocardiogram (ECG); or who have a history of severe heart disease. It must be used cautiously in people with impaired renal or hepatic function and cardiovascular disease. Because it may prolong the QT/QTc interval and cause torsades de pointes, a potentially fatal type of ventricular tachycardia, ziprasidone is probably not a drug of first choice. Ziprasidone is metabolized in the liver and excreted in urine. **Adverse effects** include cardiac dysrhythmias, drowsiness, headache, and nausea; weight gain is less likely than with other antipsychotic drugs.

***Aripiprazole*** (Abilify), the newest atypical drug, is approved for the treatment of schizophrenia and is the first in a new category of drugs called partial dopamine agonists. A partial agonist is a drug that has the ability to block a receptor if it is over stimulated and to stimulate a receptor if it is under stimulated. The beneficial effect of aripiprazole in patients with schizophrenia is proposed to involve a combination of partial agonist activity at $D_2$ and serotonin 5-HT receptors and antagonist activity at serotonin 5-HT receptors. Aripiprazole also affects alpha adrenergic receptors and histamine ($H_1$) receptors. Antagonism of alpha adrenergic receptors may account for the occurrence of **adverse effects** such as orthostatic hypotension. Aripiprazole may also cause neuroleptic malignant syndrome, tardive dyskinesia, weight gain, hyperglycemia and diabetes mellitus.

**Table 21-2:** Dosages of antipsychotics

| Generic/ trade name | Routes of administration and dosage ranges | Generic/ trade name | Adults |
|---|---|---|---|
| **Chlorpromazine** (Thorazine) | *Adults:* PO 200-600 mg daily in divided doses. Dose may be increased by 100 mg daily q 2-3 days until symptoms are controlled, adverse effects occur, or a maximum daily dose of 2 gm is reached. IM 25-100 mg initially for acute psychotic symptoms, repeated in 1-4 hours PRN until control is achieved.<br>*Elderly or debilitated adults:* PO one third to one half usual adult dose, increased by 25 mg daily q 2-3 days if necessary.<br>IM 10 mg q 6- 8 hr until acute symptoms are controlled.<br>Children PO, IM 0.5 mg/kg q 4-8 hr. Maximum IM dose, 40 mg daily in children under 5 y of age and 75 mg for older children. | **Loxapine** (Loxitane) | PO 10 mg twice a day initially, may be increased to 50 mg/d in severe psychoses; usual maintenance dose 20-60 mg/d; maximum dose, 250 mg/d<br>IM 12.5-50 mg q 4- 6 hr or longer, depending on response. Change to oral drug when symptoms controlled<br>*Elderly or debilitated adults:* One third to one half the usual adult dosage |

*Table 21-2 Contd...*

| Generic/ Trade Name | Routes of Administration and Dosage Ranges | Generic/ Trade Name | Adults |
|---|---|---|---|
| **Fluphenazine decanoate and enanthate** (Prolixin Decanoate; Prolixin Enanthate) | *Adults under 50 y:* IM; Sub-Q 12.5 mg initially followed by 25 mg every 2 weeks. Dosage requirements rarely exceed 100 mg q 2-6 wk.<br>*Adults over 50 y:* debilitated clients, or clients with a history of extra pyramidal reactions: 2.5 mg initially followed by 2.5-5 mg q 10-14 days<br>*Children:* No dosage established | **Molindone** (Moban) | PO 50-75 mg/d, increased gradually if necessary up to 225 mg/d, then reduced for maintenance; usual maintenance dose, 15-40 mg/d<br>*Elderly or debilitated adults*: One third to one half the usual adult dosage |
| **Fluphenazine hydrochloride** (Prolixin, Permitill) | *Adults:* PO 2.5-10 mg initially, gradually reduced to maintenance dose of 1-5 mg (doses above 3 mg are rarely necessary). Acute psychosis; 1.25 mg initially, increased gradually to 2.5-10 mg daily in 3-4 divided doses.<br>Elderly or debilitated adults: PO 1-2.5 mg daily, IM one third to one half the usual adult dose.<br>*Children:* PO 0.75-10 mg daily in children 5 to 12 y. IM no dosage established. | **Pimozide** (Orap) | PO 1-2 mg/d in divided doses initially, increased if necessary; usual maintenance dose, approximately 10 mg/d; maximum dose, 20 mg/d |
| **Perphenazine** (Trilafon) | *Adults:* PO 16-64 mg daily in divided doses. Acute psychoses: IM 5-10 mg initially, then 5 mg q 6 hr if necessary. Maximum daily dose, 15 mg for ambulatory clients and 30 mg for hospitalized clients<br>*Elderly or debilitated adults:* PO, IM one third to one half usual adult dose<br>*Children:* PO dosages not established, but the following amounts have been given in divided doses: ages 1-6 y, 4-6 mg daily; 6-12 y, 6 mg daily, over 12 y, 6-12 mg daily | **Thiothixene** (Navane) | PO 6-10 mg/d in divided doses; maximum 60 mg/d<br>Acute psychosis, IM 8-16 mg/d in divided doses; maximum 30 mg/d<br>*Elderly or debilitated adults:* PO, IM one third to one half the usual adult dosage |
| | | **Second-Generation, "Atypical" Drugs** | |
| | | **Aripiprazole** (Ability) | PO 10-15 mg once daily; maximum dose 30 mg/d |
| | | **Clozapine** (Clozaril) | PO 25 mg once or twice daily initially, increased by 25-50 mg/d, if tolerated, to 300-450 mg/d by end of 2nd wk |
| | | **Olanzapine** (Zyprexa) | PO 5-10 mg/d initially; given once daily at bedtime; increased over several weeks to 20 mg/d, if necessary |
| | | **Quetiapine** (Seroquel) | PO 25 mg bid initially; increased by 25-50 mg two or three times daily on second and third days, as tolera-ted, to 300-400 mg, in two or three divided doses on the fourth day. |

Aripiprazole is well absorbed orally, with or without food. It is 99% protein bound. It is metabolized in the liver by the CYP3A4 and CYP2D6 enzyme systems and has an active metabolite. Generally, no dosage adjustment for aripiprazole is required on the basis of hepatic or renal impairment. About 8% of the Caucasian population lacks the capacity to metabolize CYP2D6 substrates and therefore requires significantly lower doses of aripiprazole to avoid drug toxicity.

## References

Alexopoulos G, Streim J, Carpenter D and Docherty J (2004). Expert consensus panel for using antipsychotic drugs in older patients. *Journal of Clinical Psychiatry* **65(2):** 5-99.

American Academy of Child and Adolescent Psychiatry, Work Group on Quality Issues (2001). The practice parameter for the assessment and treatment of children and adolescents with schizophrenia. *Journal of the American Academy of Child & Adolescent Psychiatry* **40(7):** 4S-23S.

American Psychiatric Association (2000). Diagnostic and statistical manual of mental disorders (4th ed., text revision). Washington, DC: American Psychiatric Association.

Bhanji N, Chouinard G, and Margolese H (2004). A review of compliance, depot intramuscular antipsychotics and the new long-acting Injectable atypical antipsychotic risperidone in schizophrenia. *European Neuropsychopharmacology* **14(2):** 87-92.

Conley R. R and Mahmoud R (2001). A randomized double-blind study of risperidone and olanzapine in the treatment of schizophrenia or schizoaffective disorder. *American Journal of Psychiatry* **158:** 765-774.

Correll C, Leucht S and Kane J (2004). Lower risk for tardive dyskinesia associated with second-generation antipsychotics: A systematic review of 1-year studies. *American Journal of Psychiatry* **161(3):** 414-425.

Drug facts and comparisons. (Updated monthly). St. Louis: Facts and Comparisons. Freeman R (2003). Schizophrenia. *New England Journal of Medicine* **349(18):** 1738-1749.

CHAPTER

# Antidepressants 22

## Introduction

Major depression is one of the most common psychiatric disorders. At any given moment, about 3–5% of the population is depressed (point prevalence) and an estimated 10% of people may become depressed during their lives (lifetime prevalence). The symptoms of depression are often subtle and unrecognized both by patients and by physicians. Patients with vague complaints that resist explanation as manifestations of somatic disorders and those who might be simplistically described as "neurotic" should be suspected of being depressed.

Depression may be described as feeling sad, blue, unhappy, miserable or down in the dumps. Most of us feel this way at one time or another for short periods.

True clinical depression is a mood disorder in which feelings of sadness, loss, anger or frustration interfere with everyday life for weeks or longer.

## Causes for Depression

The exact cause of depression is not known. Many researchers believe it is caused by chemical changes in the brain. This may be due to a problem with the genes, or triggered by certain stressful events. More likely, it's a combination of both.

Some types of depression run in families. But depression can also occur if the person have no family history of the illness. Anyone can develop depression, even kids.

The following may play a role in depression:

Alcohol or drug abuse

Certain medical conditions, including underactive thyroid, cancer or long-term pain

Certain medications such as steroids

Sleeping problems

Stressful life events

## The Monoamine Theory

Adrenaline, Noradrenaline, Dopamine and 5-HT are neurotransmitters (Biogenic amines) presented in Noradrenergic, Serotonergic or Dopaminergic etc. neurons

Normally NA and 5 HT are in adequate numbers at post synaptic region

In Depression – Deficiency of NA or 5 HT or both

## Symptoms

Depression can change or distort the way the person see themself, their life and those around them.

People who have depression usually see everything with a more negative attitude. They cannot imagine that any problem or situation can be solved in a positive way.

Symptoms of depression can include:

- Agitation, restlessness and irritability

- Becoming withdrawn or isolated
- Difficulty concentrating
- Dramatic change in appetite, often with weight gain or loss
- Fatigue and lack of energy
- Feelings of hopelessness and helplessness
- Feelings of worthlessness, self-hate and guilt
- Loss of interest or pleasure in activities that were once enjoyed
- Thoughts of death or suicide
- Trouble sleeping or too much sleeping
- Depression can appear as anger and discouragement, rather than feelings of sadness
- If depression is very severe, there may also be psychotic symptoms, such as hallucinations and delusions

## Treatment

In general, treatments for depression include:

Medications called antidepressants

Talk therapy, called psychotherapy

## Classification

### Antidepressants

**MAO inhibitors**

*Irreversible:* Isocarboxazid, Iproniazid, Phenelzine and Tranylcypromine

*Reversible:* Moclobemide and Clorgyline

**Tricyclic antidepressants (TCAs):**

NA and 5 HT reuptake inhibitors – Imipramine, Amitriptylin, Doxepin, Dothiepin and Clomipramine

NA reuptake inhibitors – Desimipramine, Nortriptyline, Amoxapine

**Selective Serotonin reuptake inhibitors:** Fluoxetine, Fluvoxamine, Sertraline and Citalopram

**Atypical antidepressants:** Trazodone, Mianserin, Mirtazapine, Bupropion and Tianeptine

**Serotonin-Norepinephrine Reuptake Inhibitors:** Venlafaxine, Duloxetine

## Selective Serotonin Reuptake Inhibitors

Selective serotonin reuptake inhibitors, also known as SSRIs or serotonin boosters, are thought to work by correcting chemical imbalances in the brain. Normally, chemicals called neurotransmitters carry signals from one nerve cell to another. These chemicals are constantly being released and taken back up at the ends of nerve cells. Selective serotonin reuptake inhibitors act on one particular neurotransmitter, serotonin, reducing its re-entry into nerve cells and thus allowing serotonin to build up. Although exact mechanism how it works is not known, serotonin is involved in the control of moods, as well as other functions such as sleep, body temperature and appetite for sweets and other carbohydrates. Somehow, drugs that prevent the uptake of serotonin improve the moods of people with serious depression, obsessive compulsive disorder and some types of anxiety disorders.

Selective serotonin reuptake inhibitors are available only with a prescription and are sold in tablet, capsule and liquid forms. Commonly used selective serotonin reuptake inhibitors are fluoxetine (Prozac), paroxetine (Paxil), sertraline (Zoloft) and fluvoxamine (Luvox).

### Mechanism of Action

SSRIs are believed to act by inhibiting the reuptake of serotonin after being released in synapses. How much an individual will respond to this, however, also depends on genetics. In addition, several other mechanisms are suggested for the desired effect, e.g., neuroprotection and anti-inflammatory and immunomodulatory factors. Taken together, SSRIs has several advantages compared with tricyclic antidepressants (TCAs) and 5-HT-prodrugs. However, the latter might be required in addition to SSRIs in certain situations.

## Pharmacokinetics

All of the SSRIs are well absorbed after oral administration. Peak levels are seen in approximately 2 to 8 hours on average. Food has little effect on absorption (except with sertraline, for which food increases its absorption). Only sertraline undergoes significant first-pass metabolism. All of these agents are well distributed, having volumes of distribution far in excess of body weight . The majority of SSRIs have plasma half-lives that range between 16 and 36 hours. Metabolism by P450-dependent enzymes and glucuronide or sulfate conjugation occur extensively. Fluoxetine differs from the other members of the class in two respects. First, it has a much longer half-life (50 hours) and is available as a sustained-release preparation allowing once-weekly dosing. Second, the metabolite of the S-enantiomer, S-norfluoxetine, is as potent as the parent compound. The half-life of the metabolite is quite long, averaging 10 days. Fluoxetine and paroxetine are potent inhibitors of a hepatic cytochrome P450 isoenzyme (CYP2D6) responsible for the elimination of tricyclic antidepressant drugs, neuroleptic drugs and some antiarrhythmic and $\alpha_2$-adrenergic antagonist drugs. Other cytochrome enzymes (CYP2C9/19, CYP3A4, CYP1A2) are involved with SSRIs metabolism and may also be inhibited to various degrees by the SSRIs and thus, may affect the metabolism of multiple medications.

Excretion of the SSRIs is primarily through the kidneys, except for paroxetine and sertraline, which also undergo fecal excretion (35 and 50 percent, respectively). Dosages of all of these drugs should be adjusted downward in patients with hepatic impairment.

## Therapeutic Uses

Selective serotonin reuptake inhibitors are used to treat serious, continuing depression that interferes with a person's ability to function. Like other antidepressant drugs, they help reduce the extreme sadness, hopelessness and lack of interest in life that are typical in people with depression. Selective serotonin reuptake inhibitors also are used to treat panic disorder, obsessive compulsive disorder (OCD) and have shown promise for treating a variety of other conditions, such as premenstrual syndrome, eating disorders, obesity, self-mutilation and migraine headache.

## Adverse Effects

The most common side effects are anxiety and nervousness (reported by 5-13% of people taking various SSRIs), tremor (5-14%), trouble sleeping (2-8%), tiredness or weakness (4-15%), nausea (11-26%), diarrhea (11-26%), constipation (1-8%), loss of appetite (3-18%), weight loss (1-13%), dry mouth (10-22%), headache (1-5%), sweating (5-9%), trouble urinating (1-2%) and decreased sexual ability (8-15%).

More serious side effects are possible, but extremely rare. People taking SSRIs who notice unusual joint or muscle pain, breathing problems, chills or fever, excessive excitement, fast talking or actions that are out of control or mood swings should contact their doctors. People who develop skin rashes or hives after taking an SSRIs should stop taking the medication and contact their doctors as soon as possible. Other rare side effects may occur.

Side effects may continue for some time after treatment with this medicine ends. How long the effects continue depends on how long the drug was taken and how much of it was used. In most cases, doctors recommend that patients taper off SSRIs rather than abruptly stopping them, because of the risk of developing a condition known as SSRIs discontinuation syndrome. This syndrome can mimic serious illness. People who experience agitation, confusion, or restlessness, dizziness or light-headedness, vision problems, tremor, sleep problems, unusual tiredness or weakness, nausea and vomiting or diarrhea, headache, excessive sweating, runny nose or muscle pain for more than a few days after stopping or tapering an SSRI.

## Drug Interactions

SSRIs may interact with other medicines. When this happens, the effects of one or both of the drugs may change or the risk of side effects may be greater. Among the drugs that may interact with SSRIs are:

Central nervous system (CNS) depressants such as medicine for allergies, colds, hay fever, and asthma; sedatives; tranquilizers, analgesics, muscle relaxants, medicine for seizures, barbiturates and anaesthetics.

*Anticoagulants*

Monoamine oxidase inhibitors (MAOIs) such as Nardil or Parnate, used to treat conditions including depression and Parkinson's disease.

*Antiseizure drug phenytoin (Dilantin)*

The food supplement (and sleep aid) tryptophan, which has been withdrawn from the United States market, but may be found in some herbal preparations

*Digitalis and other heart medicines*

St. John's wort (*Hypericum perforatum*) is a herb used in Europe and the United States to relieve mild-to-moderate symptoms of depression. Research indicates that it acts as an SSRI and not as an MAO inhibitor, as previously believed. People who are using St. John's wort to relieve depression should not take a prescription SSRI at the same time.

# Serotonin-Norepinephrine Reuptake Inhibitors

Serotonin-norepinephrine reuptake inhibitors (SNRIs) were first introduced in the mid-1990s. This class of antidepressants works by inhibiting the reabsorption of not one but two important brain chemicals: serotonin and norepinephrine. That's why these drugs are sometimes called dual reuptake inhibitors or dual-acting antidepressants.

## Types of SNRIs

There are currently three SNRIs on the market. The generic names are listed below with their brand-name counterparts in parentheses.

Desvenlafaxine (Pristiq)
Duloxetine (Cymbalta)
Venlafaxine (Effexor, Effexor XR)

## Mechanism of Action

Depression is associated with low levels of certain brain chemicals. These chemicals, which are collectively called neurotransmitters, carry messages between brain cells. Certain neurotransmitters including serotonin and norepinephrine are known to affect mood. Serotonin is sometimes called a "feel good" chemical because it is associated with positive feelings of well-being. Norepinephrine is related to alertness and energy. SNRIs increase the amount of available serotonin and norepinephrine in the brain by blocking the reabsorption of those neurotransmitters.

## Adverse Effects

**Possible side effects include**

Nausea, changes in appetite, muscle weakness, tremor, agitation , heart palpitation increased blood pressure and heart rate, difficulty urinating, dizziness, excessive sweating, sexual dysfunction (inability to maintain an erection or orgasm), constipation.

# Atypical Antidepressants

Atypical antidepressants are called atypical because they don't fit into other classes of antidepressants. They are each unique medications that work in different ways from one another.

## Mechanism of Action

Atypical antidepressants ease depression by affecting chemical messengers (neurotransmitters) used to communicate between brain cells. Most antidepressants work by changing the levels of one or more of these naturally occurring brain chemicals.

Like other types of antidepressants, atypical antidepressants affect neurotransmitters including dopamine, serotonin and norepinephrine. Changing the balance of these chemicals seems to help brain cells send and receive messages, which in turn boosts mood.

## Atypical Antidepressants Approved to Treat Depression

**Atypical antidepressants approved include:**

Bupropion (Wellbutrin, Wellbutrin SR, Wellbutrin XL)

Mirtazapine (Remeron, Remeron SolTab)

Nefazodone

Trazodone (Oleptro)

## Adverse Effects of Atypical Antidepressants

Because each atypical antidepressant is unique, side effects and other characteristics of each one is different.

**Bupropion:** Side effects can include:

Anxiety, restlessness or agitation, confusion, constipation, dry mouth, headache increased, irregular heartbeat, insomnia, nausea, sore throat, tremor.

**Mirtazapine:** It is generally taken before bed because it can make you sleepy. Like bupropion, mirtazapine may help counter sexual side effects caused by another antidepressant.

*Side effects can include:*

Constipation, dizziness or light-headedness, dry mouth, increased appetite, increased cholesterol, increased or decreased blood pressure, low white blood cell count, sleepiness, weakness, weight gain.

**Nefazodone:** It may help ease anxiety as well as depression. Nefazodone can make the person sleepy. It seems less likely to cause sexual side effects than do some other antidepressants.

*Side effects can include:*

Blurred vision, confusion, constipation, dizziness or light-headedness, low blood pressure, nausea, sleepiness, weakness.

**Trazodone:** It is a weak antidepressant that causes sleepiness and can help with anxiety. Like mirtazapine, it's usually taken at bedtime. It may be prescribed along with other antidepressants to help with sleep.

*Side effects can include:*

Sleepiness, headache, dry mouth, dizziness or light-headedness, nausea, fatigue, diarrhea, constipation, insomnia, low blood pressure, confusion, blurred vision, irregular heartbeat.

# Tricyclic and Tetracyclic Antidepressants

Tricyclic and tetracyclic antidepressants were among the earliest antidepressants developed. They're effective, but have generally been replaced by antidepressants that cause fewer side effects.

## Mechanism of Action

Tricyclic and tetracyclic antidepressants, also called cyclic antidepressants, ease depression by affecting chemical messengers in the brain (neurotransmitters). These naturally occurring brain chemicals are used to communicate between brain cells.

Cyclic antidepressants block the absorption (reuptake) of the neurotransmitters serotonin (ser-oh-TOE-nin) and norepinephrine (nor-ep-ih-NEF-rin), making more of these chemicals available in the brain. This seems to help brain cells send and receive messages, which in turn boosts mood. These antidepressants also affect other chemical messengers, which can lead to a number of side effects.

## Cyclic Antidepressants Approved to Treat Depression

Tricyclic and tetracyclic antidepressants approved by the Food and Drug Administration to treat depression, with their generic names followed by brand names in parentheses, include:

Amitriptyline

Amoxapine

Desipramine (Norpramin)

Doxepin

Imipramine (Tofranil, Tofranil-PM)

Maprotiline

Nortriptyline (Pamelor)

Protriptyline (Vivactil)

Trimipramine (Surmontil)

## Adverse Effects of Tricyclic Antidepressants

**Side effects of cyclic antidepressants include:**

Drowsiness, dry mouth, blurred vision, constipation, urinary retention, dizziness, delayed orgasm and low sex drive, particularly in men, increased heart rate, disorientation or confusion, low blood pressure, which can cause light-headedness, increased appetite, weight gain, fatigue, headache, sensitivity to sunlight, nausea, seizures (particularly with maprotiline).

# MAO Inhibitors

MAO stands for Monoamine Oxidase, which is an enzyme responsible for metabolizing neurotransmitors such as seratonin and norepinephrine. This family of prescription medications are used primarily for treating depression, although one MAO Inhibitor, selegeline, is used to treat Parkinson's Disease.

***The 4 MAO Inhibitors currently available and used to treat depression are:***

Isocarboxazid (Brand name **Marplan**)

Phenelzine (Brand name **Nardil**)

Tranylcypromine (Brand name **Parnate**)

Selegeline (Brand name **Emsam**, a transdermal patch)

MAO inhibitors are only available by prescription.

## Mechanism of Action

MAO inhibitors (also called MAOI's) work by interfering with the enzyme responsible for metabolizing serotonin, epinephrine, dopamine and norepinephrine. By binding to this enzyme they effectively increase the concentration of these neurotransmitters which in turn causes changes within specific areas of the CNS (central nervous system). These changes have been shown to result in a decrease in symptoms associated with depression.

## Risks are Associated with MAO Inhibitors

MAO inhibitors prevent MAO from metabolizing these important neurotransmitters. However, they are so effective, that they can also create problems, particularly with certain over-the-counter cold remedies and specific food items.

## Medications to Avoid

Because MAO inhibitors increase norepinephrine (a powerful blood vessel constrictor) it is important that patients taking one of these products do NOT ingest any other medication which could potentially increase norepinephrine levels even further. The consequences of such a combination could be, in some cases, fatal.

**Such medications include:**

Pseudoephedrine (A nasal decongestant, now only available "behind the counter" in a pharmacy, but very commonly included in cold remedies)

Phenylephrine (A decongestant used in place of pseudoephedrine in many cough/cold products)

Amphetamine or Dextroamphetamine [Often used, by prescription to treat *Attention deficit hyperactivity disorder* (ADHD)]

Naphazoline and Oxymetazoline (In nasal sprays)

Isometheptene (ingredient in the prescription drug Migranal)

Methylphenidate (also known as Ritalin)

Meperidine (the ingredient in prescription Demerol, for pain)

Eye drops with decongestants should also be avoided

## Foods to Avoid

Monoamine oxidase also exists in our intestinal tract and aids in the breakdown of a substance known as Tyramine. MAO inhibitors interfere with this process, and will allow large amounts of tyramine (from foods or beverages containing tyramine) to enter the the blood stream and contribute to a sequence of events that could lead to a hypertensive crisis (ie a very dramatic, potentially fatal, elevation of the blood pressure).

Therefore, patients on MAO inhibitors must completely avoid foods and beverages which contain significant amounts of tyramine. These include, but are not limited to:

Aged cheese and meats
Smoked meats or pickled meats
Liver
Anchovies
Pepperoni
Salami
Raisins
Caffeine should be used sparingly
Avoid wine, sherry, beer, and hard liquor

## Adverse Effects

Severe and often unpredictable side effects due to drug-food and drug-drug interactions limit the widespread use of MAO inhibitors. For example, tyramine which is contained in certain foods, such as aged cheeses and meats, chicken liver, pickled or smoked fish such as anchovies or herring, and red wines, is normally inactivated by MAO in the gut.

Individuals receiving an MAO inhibitor are unable to degrade tyramine obtained from the diet. Tyramine causes the release of large amounts of stored catecholamines from nerve terminals, resulting in occipital headache, stiff neck, tachycardia, nausea, hypertension, cardiac arrhythmias, seizures and possibly stroke.

Patients must therefore be educated to avoid tyramine-containing foods. Phentolamine or Prazosin are helpful in the management of tyramine-induced hypertension. Other possible side effects of treatment with MAO inhibitors include drowsiness, orthostatic hypotension, blurred vision, dry mouth, dysuria and constipation.

The MAO inhibitors and SSRIs should not be co administered due to the risk of the life-threatening serotonin syndrome. Both types of drugs require washout periods of at least 2 weeks before the other type is administered, with the exception of Fluoxetine, which should be discontinued at least 6 weeks before a MAO inhibitor is initiated. Combination of MAO inhibitors and bupropion can produce seizures.

## References

American Psychiatric Association (2000). APA practice guideline for major depressive disorder in adults (revision). *Am J Psychiatry* **157:** 1.

Anderson IM, Tomenson BM (2000). Selective serotonin reuptake inhibitors versus tricyclic antidepressants: A meta-analysis of efficacy and tolerability. *J Affect Disord* **58:** 19.

Berton O, Nestler EJ (2006). New approaches to antidepressant drug discovery: Beyond monoamines. *Nat Rev Neurosci* **7:** 137.

Bradberry SM *et al.,* (2005). Management of the cardiovascular complications of tricyclic antidepressant poisoning: Role of sodium bicarbonate. *Toxicol Rev* **24:** 195.

Briley M (2003). New hope in the treatment of painful symptoms in depression. *Curr Opin Investig Drugs* **4:** 42.

Duman RS, Heninger G, Nestler E (1997). A molecular and cellular theory of depression. *Arch Gen Psychiatry* **54:** 597.

Ernst CL, Goldberg JF (2003). Antidepressant properties of anticonvulsant drugs for bipolar disorder. *J Clin Psychopharmacol* **23:** 182.

Esposito E (2006). Serotonin-dopamine interaction as a focus of novel antidepressant drugs. *Curr Drug Targets* **7:** 177.

Geddes JR, *et al.,* (2003). Relapse prevention with antidepressant drug treatment in depressive disorders: A systematic review. *Lancet* **361:** 653.

CHAPTER

# 23 Antiepileptic Drugs

## Introduction

*Convulsions*: Sudden attack of involuntary muscular contractions and relaxations.

*Seizures:* Abnormal central nervous system electrical activity.

*Epilepsy:* A group of recurrent disorders of cerebral function characterized by both seizures. It may be associated with convulsion.

## Pathophysiology

Current theories try to explain the mechanism(s) for the abnormally increased propensity of the brain to develop excessive discharges of cerebral neurons. The early theory according to which disruption of the normal balance between excitation and inhibition in the brain results in seizure generation, may be an over simplification. Cortical networks that generate oscillations, on which inhibitory neurons, neuronal communication (e.g., synaptic transmission), and intrinsic neuronal properties (e.g., ability of a neuron to maintain burst firing) are dependent, are thought to be crucial elements of seizure generation. The occurrence of epileptic activity may be an emergent property of such oscillatory networks. Transition from normal behavior to a seizure behavior may be caused by a number of factors including greater spread and neuronal recruitment secondary to a combination of enhanced connectivity, enhanced excitatory transmission, a failure of inhibitory mechanisms, and changes in intrinsic neuronal properties.

## Types of Seizures

**Seizures have been categorized by:**

Site of origin

Etiology

Electrophysiological correlation

Clinical presentation

**Seizures have been classified into two broad groups:**

Partial (or focal)

Generalized

### Partial Seizures

In partial seizures, the seizure happens in, and affects, just one part of the brain. This could be any part of the brain, and what happens to the person depends on which part of the brain is affected and how big the affected area is.

**Simple partial seizures**

If the area of the brain affected by the seizure is small, this is called a simple partial seizure (SPS). The person will be awake and aware during the seizure and will remember what happened to him/her.

Temporal lobe SPS are the most common type of SPS. Symptoms can include:

- An 'epigastric rising sensation'
- A flashback of memory
- A sudden, intense feeling of fear or joy
- A funny taste or smell

Frontal lobe SPS can be harder to put into words. Some people experience:

- Strange movements
- A feeling of a wave going through the head or body
- Stiffness or jerking of part of the body that might start in one place, for example the face and spread to other parts of the body.

Parietal lobe SPS often include strange sensations such as

- Numbness or tingling
- Burning sensations or a feeling of heat
- A feeling that part of the body, an arm or leg, is bigger or smaller than they really are.

Occipital lobe SPS involve visual sensations, such as:

- Distortion or loss of vision
- Seeing flashing lights or coloured shapes
- Seeing people or objects that are not there (hallucinations)

**Complex partial seizures**

Complex partial seizure (CPS) is a partial seizure with impaired consciousness. The focus is on temporal lobe. These seizures affect three things - the person's awareness (they will be only partly conscious), their accessibility (they may not be able to respond) and their memory (they may not remember most or all of the seizure).

Temporal lobe CPS is the most common CPS. Often people experience:

- Automatisms such as lip-smacking or chewing movements or rubbing, stroking or fiddling with their hands; or
- Looking from one side to another in a confused way

This type of CPS usually lasts around 2–3 minutes (about the length of a song on the radio) and then it takes the person 5–10 minutes to come around. They are often confused.

Frontal lobe CPS are often much shorter then temporal lobe CPS, usually lasting about 15–30 seconds (about as long as a TV advertisement). During the seizures the person might:

- Make strange postures with their arms or legs; or
- Make juddering movements

Afterwards the person will usually recover quite quickly.

## Generalised Seizures

In generalised seizures the seizure affects all of the brain all at once. Generalised seizures affect the person's consciousness so that they lose consciousness, even just for a few seconds. Because of this, after the seizure, they will have no memory of the seizure.

**Tonic clonic seizures (GTCS or Grand mal seizures)**

These are the seizures that we usually think of as epilepsy. There are two parts to this seizure. In the tonic part, all the muscles in the person's body 'contract' and go stiff. If they are standing up they will fall down. Because the muscles around the chest go stiff, this pushes air out of the lungs and the person may cry out. Also they might bite their tongue as the seizure starts.

The next part of the seizure is the clonic, jerking or convulsing part. This might last for a couple of minutes. The muscles go stiff and then relax, stiff and relax repeatedly. This makes the person's arms and legs jerk. Often the person's breathing is affected. They might grunt or snort or sound as if it is difficult to breathe and they may go very pale in colour or slightly blue around the lips. This is because the muscles around the rib cage that help us to breathe are contracting and relaxing too.

The seizure stops when all the jerking stops. The person will then relax and go floppy, and start to breathe normally again. They might feel tired and sleepy. They might also be confused, have a headache and want to sleep. Some people say it feels like they have run a marathon in a couple of minutes - that's how tired they are.

**Tonic seizures (GTS )**

Tonic seizures happen when all the muscles in the person's body go stiff. They become rigid and will fall down, usually backwards, a bit like a tree being cut down. These seizures tend to be very quick and the person comes round from them quickly.

**Atonic seizures (Akinetic seizures )**

Atonic seizures are the opposite of tonic seizures and all the muscles in the body suddenly go floppy. When this happens the person will fall down, usually forwards (like a puppet whose strings have been cut). These seizures are also called 'drop attacks' as they cause the person to suddenly drop to the ground. Like tonic seizures the person usually recovers quickly, but they may hurt themselves when they fall. There is no convulsion.

**Myoclonic seizures**

'Myoclonic' means 'muscle jerk', which describes what happens during these seizures. Usually the arms or leg will briefly jerk, although it can be the head or trunk (top half of the body). These jerks are similar to the jerks we all have just as we are falling off to sleep (hypnagogic jerk), but they happen at other times during the day, often during the first few hours after waking-up. Usually the person recovers quickly.

**Absence seizures (Petit mal epilepsy)**

Absences are brief seizures where the person is 'absent' for a couple of seconds, going blank and staring. The seizures can be quite subtle and hard to see, as there may be no obvious movement. If the person is talking, they will usually pause in the middle of what they are saying, but if they are walking around they might carry on walking. During the seizures they are unconscious .

Absences tend to be more frequent in children, but can still happen in adults. Some children can have multiples of absences every day, which can cause a lot of disruption to their life.

Absences can be confused with daydreaming. If someone talk to person who is daydreaming, they will usually respond but this is not so with absences. Also, if the 'blank spells' happen when the person is doing something they enjoy, such as talking or playing a game, then they are less likely to be daydreaming.

Some absences last longer than a few seconds and involve some movement of the body, such as jerking of the shoulders. These seizures are known as atypical absences and tend to happen in people with learning disabilities, who may have other types of seizures as well.

**Secondarily generalised seizures**

Sometimes a partial seizure can become a generalised seizure and is called a secondarily generalised seizure (as it starts out as a partial seizure and becomes generalised seizure). The most common type of generalised seizure to happen in this case is a tonic clonic seizure.

As the seizure starts as a simple or complex partial seizure, the person might be aware that the seizure has started, but as it becomes generalised, they will lose consciousness. Untreated or irregularly treated partial seizures may become secondarily generalised. Some may even produce status epilepticus.

## Causes for Acute Seizures

Trauma, encephalitis, drugs, birth trauma, withdrawal from depressants, high fever, hypoglycemia, extreme acidosis, extreme alkalosis, hyponatremia, hypocalcemia.

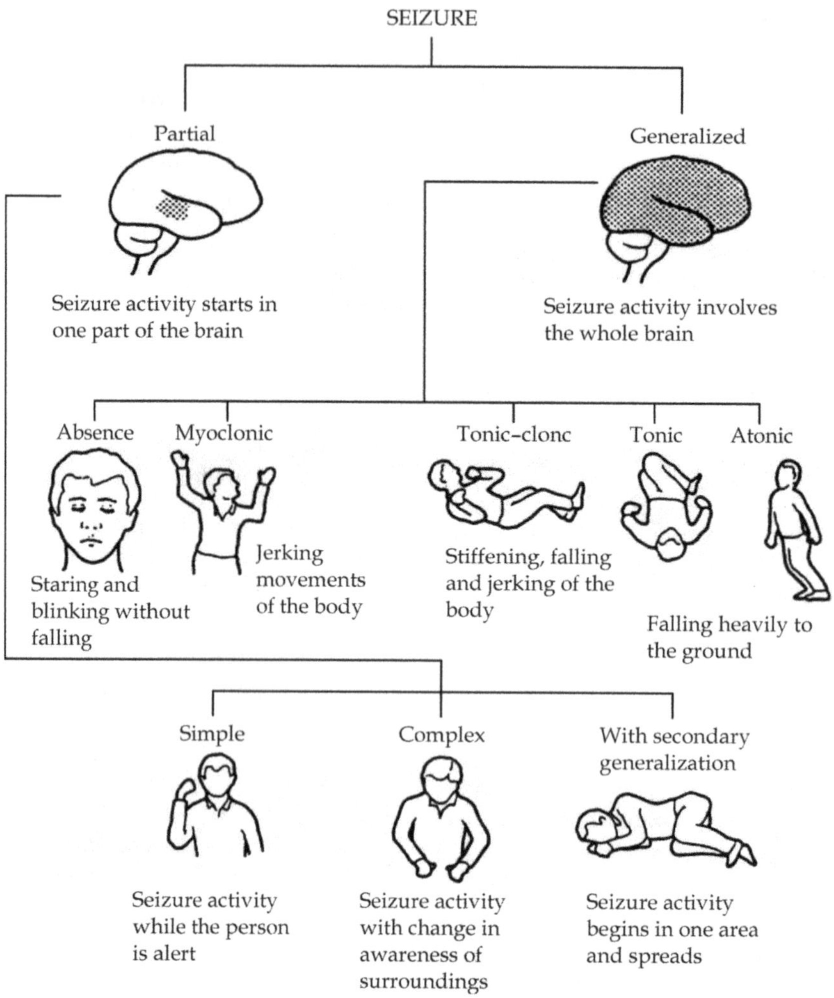


**Fig 23-1:** Classification of seizures

## Treatment

Try to find a cause (e.g., fever, head trauma, drug abuse).

Recurrent seizures that cannot be attributed to any cause are seen in patients with epilepsy.

Therapy is aimed at control of seizures.

Drugs do not cure.

The type of seizure determines the choice of drug!

More than 80% of patients with epilepsy can have their seizures controlled with medications.

Monotherapy with antiepileptic drugs.

Dose gradually increased until seizures are controlled or adverse effects become unacceptable.

Multiple-drug therapy may be required.

Achieve steady-state kinetics.

Monitor plasma drug levels.

Avoid sudden withdrawal.

## Strategies

Modification of ion conductances.

Increase inhibitory (GABAergic) transmission.

Decrease excitatory (Glutamatergic) activity.

**Table 23-1:** Drugs used to treat different types of seizures

| Seizure disorder | Drugs |
|---|---|
| Tonic-clonic (Grand mal)<br>Drug of choice | Carbamazepine or<br>Valproate or<br>Phenytoin or<br>Phenobarbital |
| Alternatives: | Topiramte<br>Lamotrigine (as adjunct or alone)<br>Gabapentin (as adjunct) |
| Partial (simple or complex)<br>Drug of choice | Carbamazepine or Topiramte or<br>Phenytoin or<br>Valproate |
| Alternatives: | Phenobarbital<br>Lamotrigine (as adjunct or alone)<br>Gabapentin (as adjunct ) |
| Absence (petit mal)<br>Drug of choice | Valproate or<br>Ethosuximide |
| Alternatives: | Clonazepam<br>Lamotrigine |
| Myoclonic, Atonic<br>Drug of choice | Valproate |
| Alternatives: | Clonazepam |
| Status Epilepticus<br>Drug of choice | Diazepam, i.v.<br>or Phenytoin, i.v. or Valproate<br>Fosphenytoin |
| Alternatives: | Phenobarbital, i.v |
| Febrile Seizures<br>* Preferred | Diaze pam, rectal*<br>Diazepam ,i.v<br>Clonazepam |

## Classification of Antiepileptics

The classification of Antiepileptics are shown in Fig 23-11.

**By acting on the neuronal membrane action potential:**

1. *Membrane stabilization:* Phenytoin; Carbamazepine: Phenobarbital; Lamotrigine; Topiramate, Zonisamide.
2. *Prolong refractory period:* Ethosuximide, Valproate

**By enhancement of GABA neurotransmissions:**

1. *Inhibit GABA catabolism (inhibit GABA transaminase) :* Valproate; Vigabatrin
2. *Inhibit re-uptake of GABA:* Tiagabine
3. *Analog of GABA:* Gabapentin
4. *Increase the activity of GABA:* Phenobarbitone; Topiramate; Gabapentin
5. *By antagonizing the action of Aspartate and Glutamate:* Lamotrigine

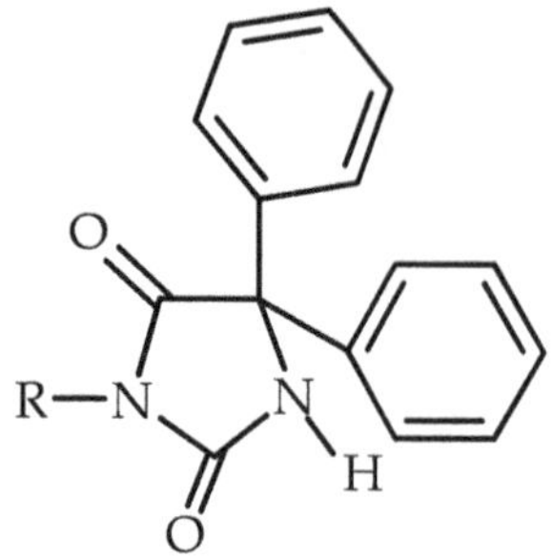

$R = H_2$ Phenytoin

$R = CH_2OPO_3^{2-}$ Fosphenytoin

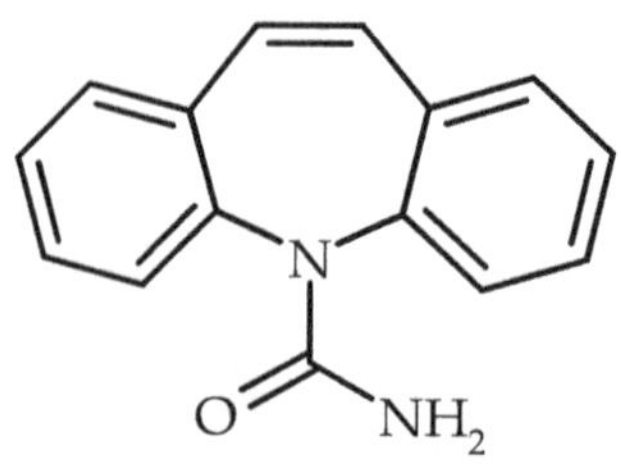

Carbamazepine

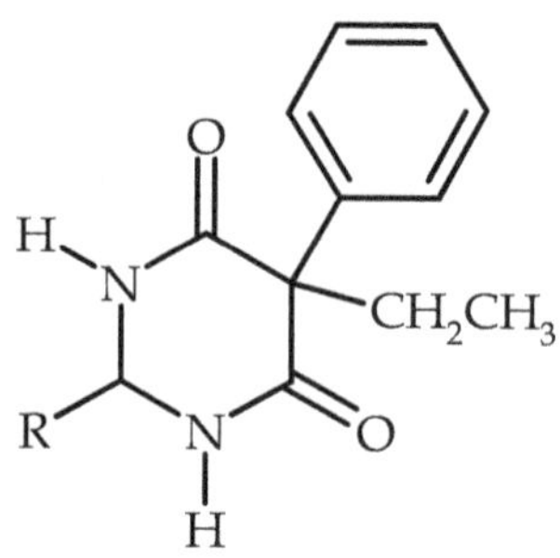

R=H, Primidone

R =O, Phenobarbital

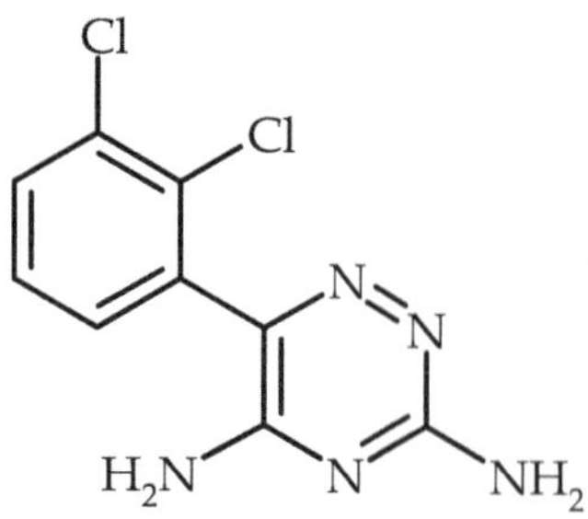

Lamotrigine

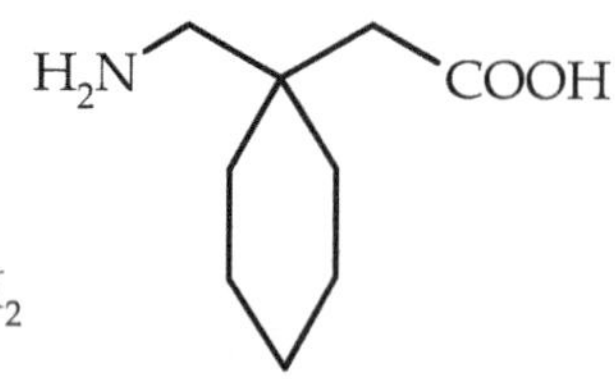

Gabapentin

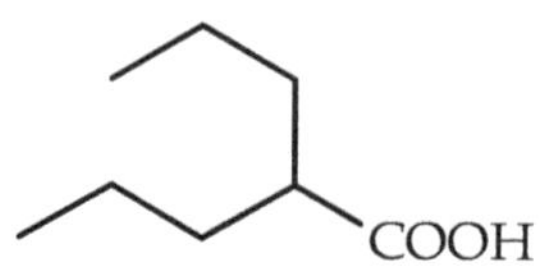

Valproic acid

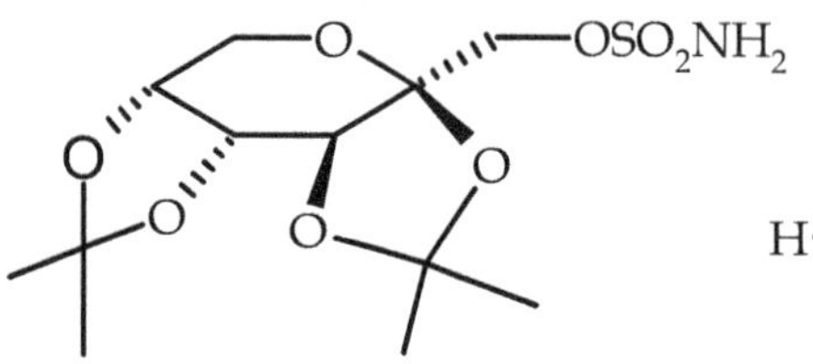

Topiramate

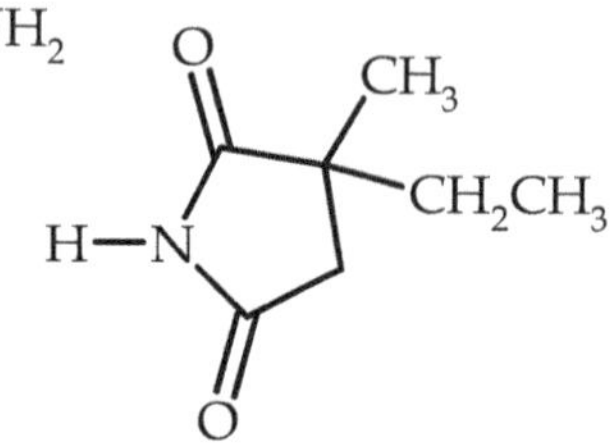

Ethosuximide

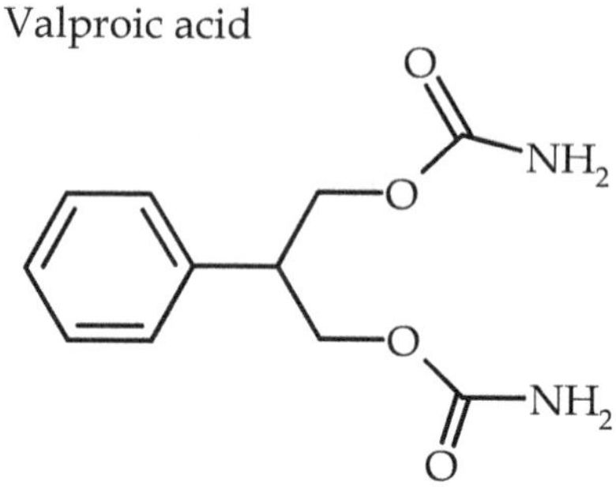

Felbamate

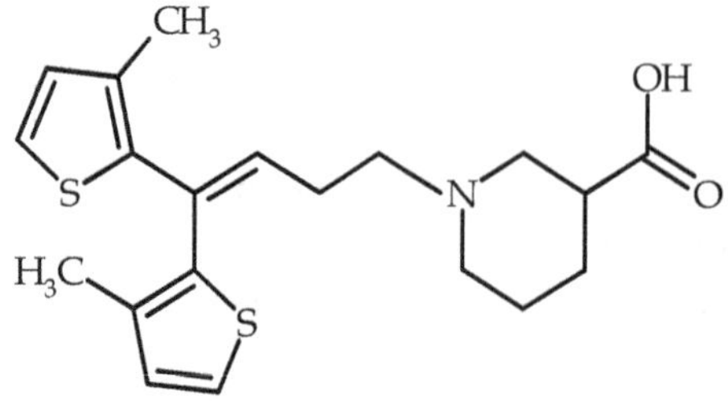

Tiagabine

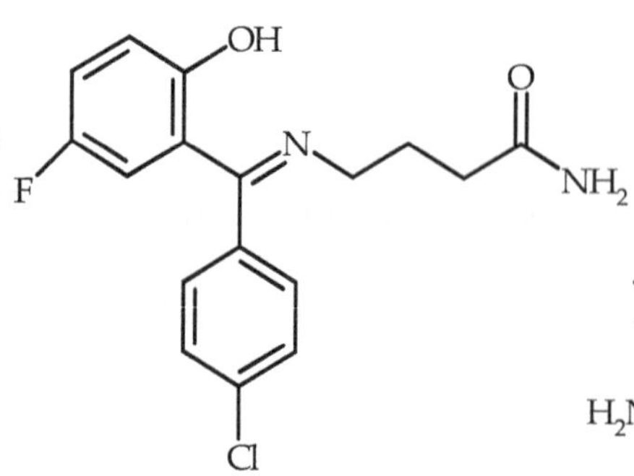

Progabide

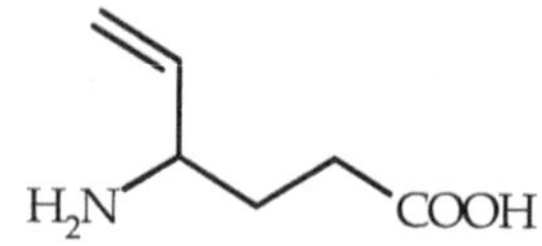

Vigabatrin

**Fig 23-2:** Antiepileptic drugs

## Sodium Channel Blocking Agents

Drugs sharing this mechanism include Phenytoin (Dilantin), Carbamazepine (Tegretol), Oxcarbazepine (Trileptal), Topiramate (Topamax), Valproic acid (Depakene), Zonisamide (Zonegran) and Lamotrigine (Lamictal). All of these agents have the capacity to block sustained high-frequency repetitive firing (SRF) of action potentials.This is accomplished by reducing the amplitude of sodium-dependent action potentials through an enhancement of steady-state inactivation. The sodium channel exists in three main conformations: a resting (R) or activatable state, an open (0) or conducting state and an inactive (I) or non activatable state. The anticonvulsant drugs bind preferentially to the inactive form of the channel. Because it takes time for the bound drug to dissociate from the inactive channel, there is time dependence to the block. Since the fraction of inactive channels is increased by membrane depolarization as well by repetitive firing, the binding to the I state by antiepileptic drugs can produce voltage, use and time dependent block of sodium-dependent action potentials.

### Phenytoin

Phenytoin is a valuable agent for the treatment of generalized tonic–clonic seizures and for the treatment of partial seizures with complex symptoms.

**Mechanism of action**

Membrane stabilization by blocking $Na^+$ and $Ca^{+2}$ influx into the neuronal axon or inhibits the release of excitatory amino acids *via* inhibition of calcium influx.

**Pharmacokinetics**

An understanding of absorption, binding, metabolism and excretion is more important for phenytoin than it is for most drugs. Following oral administration, phenytoin absorption is slow but usually complete and it occurs primarily in the duodenum. Phenytoin is highly bound (about 90%) to plasma proteins, primarily plasma albumin. Since several other substances can also bind to albumin, phenytoin administration can displace (and be displaced by) such agents as thyroxine, triiodothyronine, valproic acid, sulfafurazole and salicylates.

Phenytoin is one of very few drugs that may display zero-order (or saturation) kinetics in its metabolism. At low blood levels the rate of phenytoin metabolism is proportional to the drug's blood levels (i.e., first-order kinetics). However, at the higher blood levels usually required to control seizures, the maximum capacity of drug-metabolizing enzymes is often exceeded (i.e., the enzyme is saturated) and further increases in the dose of phenytoin may lead to a disproportionate increase in the drug's blood concentration. Since the plasma levels continue to increase in such a situation, steady-state levels are not attained and toxicity may ensue.

**Dose:** 300-400 mg/day

**Clinical uses**

Used for partial seizures and generalized tonic-clonic seizures. But not effective for absence Seizures. Also can be used for treatment of ventricular fibrillation.

**Adverse effects**

Acute adverse effects seen after phenytoin administration usually result from overdosage. They are generally characterized by nystagmus, ataxia, vertigo, and diplopia (cerebellovestibular dysfunction). Higher doses lead to altered levels of consciousness and cognitive changes. A variety of idiosyncratic reactions may be seen shortly after therapy has begun. Skin rashes, usually morbilliform in character, are most common. Exfoliative dermatitis or toxic epidermal necrolysis (Lyell's syndrome) has been observed but is infrequent. Other rashes occasionally have been reported, as have a variety of blood dyscrasias and hepatic necrosis. The most common side effect in children receiving long-term therapy is gingival hyperplasia or overgrowth of the gums (occurs in up to 50% of patients). Hirsutism also is an annoying side effect of phenytoin, particularly in young females. Thickening of subcutaneous tissue, coarsening of facial features and enlargement of lips and nose (hydantoin facies) are often seen in patients receiving long-term phenytoin therapy. Peripheral neuropathy and chronic cerebellar degeneration have been reported, but they are rare. There is evidence that phenytoin is teratogenic in humans, but the mechanism is not clear. However, it is known that phenytoin can produce a folate deficiency, and folate deficiency is associated with teratogenesis.

**Pharmacokinetic interactions**

Inhibitors of liver enzymes elevate its plasma levels e.g., Chloramphenicol, INH, etc. Inducers of liver enzymes reduce its plasma levels e.g., Carbamazepine; Rifampicin. Coadministration of the following drugs can result in elevations of plasma phenytoin levels in most patients: cimetidine, chloramphenicol, disulfiram, sulthiame and isoniazid (in slow acetylators). Phenytoin often causes a decline in plasma carbamazepine levels if these two drugs are given concomitantly. Ethotoin and mephenytoin are congeners of phenytoin . They are not widely used.

## Carbamazepine

**Mechanism of action**

Its mechanism of action and clinical uses are similar to that of phenytoin. However, it is also commonly used for treatment of mania and trigeminal neuralgia.

**Pharmacokinetics**

Carbamazepine has become a major drug in the treatment of seizure disorders. It has high efficacy, is well tolerated by most patients and exhibits fewer long-term side effects than other drugs. Oral absorption of carbamazepine is quite slow and often erratic. Its half-life is reported to vary from 12 to 60 hours in humans. The development of blood level assays has markedly improved the success of therapy with this drug, since serum concentration is only partially dose related. Carbamazepine is metabolized in the liver and there is evidence that its continued administration leads to hepatic enzyme induction. Carbamazepine10,11-epoxide is a pharmacologically active metabolite with significant anticonvulsant effects of its own. Carbamazepine is an effective agent for the treatment of partial seizures and generalized tonic–clonic seizures; its use is contraindicated in absence epilepsy.

**Dose:** 200-800 mg/day (given BID as sustained release form)

**Adverse effects**

Like most of the agents that block sodium channels, side effects associated with carbamazepine administration involve the central nervous system (CNS). Drowsiness is the most common side effect, followed by nausea, headache, dizziness, incoordination, vertigo, and diplopia. These effects occur particularly when the drug is first taken, but tolerance often develops over a few weeks. There appears to be little risk of cognitive impairment with carbamazepine. Carbamazepine causes a variety of rashes and other allergic reactions including fever, hepatosplenomegaly and lymphadenopathy, but the incidence of serious hypersensitivity reactions is rare. Systemic lupus erythematosus can occur, but discontinuation of the drug leads to eventual disappearance of the symptoms. Idiosyncratic hematological reactions to carbamazepine may occur, but serious blood dyscrasias are rare. Carbamazepine has been shown to exacerbate or precipitate seizures in some patients, particularly those exhibiting generalized atypical absences. While the number of side effects may be fairly large, most are not serious and can be managed. Severe adverse reactions occur less commonly than with phenytoin and similar drugs.

**Therapeutic use**

Carbamazepine is also useful in the treatment of trigeminal neuralgia and is an effective agent for the treatment of bipolar disorders .

### Drug interactions

Most of the drug interactions with carbamazepine are related to its effects on microsomal drug metabolism. Carbamazepine can induce its own metabolism (autoinduction) after prolonged administration, decreasing its clearance rate, half-life and serum concentrations. The possibility of autoinduction requires the clinician to reevaluate the patient's blood levels after a month of carbamazepine therapy. The autoinduction phenomenon is over in about a month. Carbamazepine also can induce the enzymes that metabolize other anticonvulsant drugs, including phenytoin, primidone, phenobarbital, valproic acid, clonazepam and ethosuximide, and metabolism of other drugs the patient may be taking. Similarly, other drugs may induce metabolism of carbamazepine; the end result is the same as for autoinduction and the dose of carbamazepine must be readjusted. A common drug–drug interaction is between carbamazepine and the macrolide antibiotics erythromycin and troleandomycin. After a few days of antibiotic therapy, symptoms of carbamazepine toxicity develop; this is readily reversible if either the antibiotic or carbamazepine is discontinued. Cimetidine, propoxyphene and isoniazid also have been reported to inhibit metabolism of carbamazepine. It is essential to monitor blood levels and adjust the dose if necessary whenever additional drugs are given to patients taking carbamazepine.

## Oxcarbazepine

Oxcarbazepine is chemically and pharmacologically closely related to carbamazepine, but it has much less capacity to induce drug-metabolizing enzymes. This property decreases the problems associated with drug interactions when oxcarbazepine is used in combination with other drugs. The clinical uses and adverse effect profile of oxcarbazepine appear to be similar to those of carbamazepine.

## Lamotrigine

### Mechanism of Action

Inhibits excitatory amino acid release (glutamate and aspartate) by blockade of Na channels. Its primary mechanism of action appears to be blockage of voltage dependent sodium channels, although its effectiveness against absence seizures indicates that additional mechanisms may be active.

### Pharmacokinetics

Lamotrigine is almost completely absorbed from the gastrointestinal tract and peak plasma levels are achieved in about 2 to 5 hours. The plasma half-life after a single dose is about 24 hours. Unlike most drugs, lamotrigine is metabolized primarily by glucuronidation. Therefore, it appears likely that lamotrigine will not induce or inhibit cytochrome P450 isozymes, in contrast to most anti epileptic drugs.

### Clinical use

Lamotrigine has a broad spectrum of action and is effective in generalized and partial epilepsies.

### Adverse effects

Severe skin rashes appear to be the major concern with lamotrigine use. The incidence of rash is greater in children than in adults. Other adverse effects are similar to those of drugs with the same mechanism of action, such as cerebello vestibular changes leading to dizziness, diplopia, ataxia and blurred vision. Disseminated intravascular coagulation has been reported.

## Zonisamide

It is effective in partial complex and generalized tonic–clonic seizures and also appears to be beneficial in certain myoclonic seizures.

### Pharmacokinetics

It has a long half-life (about 60 hours) and requires about 2 weeks to achieve steady-state levels. Well absorbed from GIT (100%) and

Protein binding 40%. Extensively metabolized in the liver. No effect on liver enzymes.

### Adverse effects

It causes cerebellovestibular side effects similar to those of most other AEDs sharing its mechanism of action. In addition, it appears to cause an increased incidence of kidney stones.

### Clinical uses

Add-on therapy for partial seizures.

## Topiramate

### Mechanism of action

Blocks sodium channels (membrane stabilization) and also potentiates the inhibitory effect of GABA.

### Pharmacokinetics

Well absorbed orally (80%). Food has no effect on absorption. Has no effect on microsomal enzymes. 9-17% protein bound (minimal). Mostly excreted unchanged in urine. Plasma $t_{1/2}$ 18-24 hr.

### Adverse effects

Topiramate causes a higher incidence of CNS related side effects (primarily cognitive slowing and confusion) than other drugs. It does not appear to cause a significant incidence of rashes or other hypersensitivity reactions; however, a significantly higher incidence of kidney stones has been observed in persons receiving topiramate than in a similar untreated population.

### Clinical use

Recently, this drug become one of the safest antiepileptics which can be used alone for partial and generalized tonic-clonic and absence seizures. Topiramate is most useful in patients with generalized tonic–clonic seizures and those with partial complex seizures.

## Sodium Valproate or Valproic Acid

Although it is marketed as both valproic acid (Depakene) and as sodium valproate (Depakote), it is the valproate ion that is absorbed from the gastrointestinal tract and is the active form.As with several other AEDs, it is difficult to ascribe a single mechanism of action to valproic acid. This compound has broad anticonvulsant activity, both in experimental studies and in the therapeutic management of human epilepsy.

### Mechanism of action

May be due to increase in GABA content of the brain (inhibits GABA–transaminase and succinic semialdehyde dehydrogenase). Valproic acid has been shown to block voltage-dependent sodium channels at therapeutically relevant concentrations. In several experimental studies, valproate caused an increase in brain GABA; the mechanism was unclear. There is evidence that valproate may also inhibit T-calcium channels and that this may be important in its mechanism of action in patients with absence seizure (Petit mal epilepsy).

### Pharmacokinetics

Valproic acid is well absorbed from the gastrointestinal tract and is highly bound (~90%) to plasma protein and most of the compound is therefore retained within the vascular compartment. Valproate rapidly enters the brain from the circulation; the subsequent decline in brain concentration parallels that in plasma, indicating equilibration between brain and capillary blood. A large number of metabolites have been identified, but it is not known whether they play a role in the anticonvulsant effect of the parent drug. Valproic acid inhibits the metabolism of several drugs, including phenobarbital, primidone, carbamazepine and phenytoin, leading to an increased blood level of these compounds. At high doses, valproic acid can inhibit its own metabolism. It can also displace phenytoin from binding sites on plasma proteins, with a resultant increase in unbound phenytoin and increased phenytoin toxicity. In this instance, the dosage of phenytoin should be adjusted as required. These examples reinforce the need to determine serum anticonvulsant levels in epileptic patients when polytherapy is employed. Valproic acid has become a major AED against several seizure types.

### Adverse effects

The most serious adverse effect associated with valproic acid is fatal hepatic failure. Fatal hepatotoxicity is most likely to occur in children under age 2 years, especially in those with severe seizures who are given multiple anticonvulsant drug therapy. The hepatotoxicity is not dose related and is considered an idiosyncratic reaction; it can occur in individuals in other age groups, and therefore, valproic acid should not be administered to patients with hepatic disease or significant hepatic dysfunction or to those who are hypersensitive to it.

Valproic acid administration has been linked to an increased incidence of neural tube defects in the fetus of mothers who received valproate during the first trimester of pregnancy. Patients taking valproate may develop clotting abnormalities. Valproic acid causes hair loss in about 5% of patients, but this effect is reversible. Transient gastrointestinal effects are common, and some mild behavioral effects have been reported. Metabolic effects, including hyperglycemia, hyperglycinuria and hyperammonemia, have been reported. An increase in body weight also has been noted. Valproic acid is not a CNS depressant, but its administration may lead to increased depression if it is used in combination with phenobarbital, primidone, benzodiazepines or other CNS depressant agents.

### Therapeutic use

It is highly effective against absence seizures and myoclonic seizures. In addition, valproic acid can be used either alone or in combination with other drugs for the treatment of generalized tonic-clonic epilepsy and for partial seizures with complex symptoms.

## Drugs that Primarily Enhance the Action of GABA

A major effort has been directed to the search for agents that can mimic, facilitate, prolong or enhance the actions of GABA, with the expectation that such compounds will likely be beneficial in the treatment of convulsive disorders.

## Benzodiazepines

Several benzodiazepines are used in the management of epileptic seizures, although only a few are approved for the treatment of seizure disorders. Since the benzodiazepines share many properties, they will be discussed as a class; individual members will be mentioned for specific indications.

### Mechanism of action

The primary action of the benzodiazepines as anticonvulsants is to enhance inhibition through their interaction with the GABA receptor at the benzodiazepine binding site. However, there appears to be an additional action of benzodiazepines, blocking voltage-dependent sodium channels. This effect is not seen at usual doses but is likely a factor in their use in the treatment of status epilepticus .

### Pharmacokinetics

Benzodiazepines are well absorbed and the oral route is preferred in most situations. In the treatment of status epilepticus, the preferred route is usually intravenous. Benzodiazepines are extensively metabolized by the microsomal drug-metabolizing system; frequently an active compound is broken down to another agent that is also active pharmacologically. This is the reason for the long duration of action of several benzodiazepines.

### Adverse effects

Drowsiness occurs readily and unfortunately is usually a problem at therapeutic doses. The other limiting side effect of the benzodiazepines is the rapid development of tolerance to their anticonvulsant effects. Although all of the benzodiazepines are similar, certain ones are employed more for the treatment of seizure disorders.

### Therapeutic use

Their major usefulness is in the treatment of absence, myoclonic, and atonic seizures and in the emergency treatment of status epilepticus. Clonazepam was the first benzodiazepine approved specifically for the treatment of convulsive disorders. Clonazepam is a very long acting compound with potent anticonvulsant activity. Unfortunately, sedation and tolerance tend to limit its usefulness. Drooling and hypersalivation may be troublesome in children and in infants. Lorazepam is the benzodiazepine of choice for emergency treatment of status epilepticus, serial seizures and prolonged seizures and for prophylaxis of febrile seizures. The intravenous route is preferable for emergency treatment. Clorazepate dipotassium is approved as an adjunct in the treatment of partial complex seizures. It appears to be useful, especially in patients with high seizure frequencies and psychic disturbances.

## Vigabatrin

### Mechanism of action

Vigabatrin (Sabril) is a relatively specific irreversible inhibitor of GABA-transaminase (GABA-T), the major enzyme responsible for the metabolism of GABA in the mammalian CNS. As a result of inhibition of GABA-T, there is an increase in the concentration of GABA in the brain and consequently an increase in inhibitory neurotransmission.

### Pharmacokinetics

Vigabatrin is well absorbed orally and is distributed to all body systems. The major route of elimination for vigabatrin is renal excretion of the parent compound; no metabolites have been identified in humans. Not bound to proteins, not metabolized and excreted unchanged in urine. Plasma half life is 4-7 hr.

### Adverse effects

Visual field defects, psychosis and depression (limits its use).

### Therapeutic uses

At present, the primary indication for vigabatrin is in the treatment of patients with partial seizures, but it appears to be an effective and generally well tolerated antiepileptic medication for other seizure types as well.

## Tiagabine

### Mechanism of action

Tiagabine (Gabitril) blocks the reuptake of GABA into neurons and glia, thereby resulting in higher levels of GABA in the synaptic cleft. The ability to increase GABA concentrations is presumed to be involved in the effectiveness of tiagabine in the treatment of seizure disorders.

### Pharmacokinetics

Bioavailability > 90%. Highly protein bound (96%). Metabolized in the liver and has Plasma $t_{1/2}$ 4 -7 hr.

### Adverse effects

Adverse effects of tiagabine administration include dizziness, somnolence, nervousness, nausea and confusion.

### Therapeutic use

It is primarily used in the treatment of partial complex seizures.

## Phenobarbital and Primidone (Mysoline)

Phenobarbital and primidone are quite similar both chemically and pharmacologically and much of the anticonvulsant activity of primidone may be ascribed to its metabolic conversion to phenobarbital. As would be expected in such a case, the clinical indications for the two compounds are very similar. There is some indication that primidone may be more effective in the treatment of partial seizures with complex symptoms, but the evidence is not compelling.

### Mechanism of action

The primary mechanism of action of phenobarbital is related to its effect of facilitating GABA inhibition. By binding to an allosteric site on the GABA-benzodiazepine receptor, hence by prolonging the opening of the chloride channels, phenobarbital enhances GABA's inhibitory activity. At somewhat higher concentrations, phenobarbital can block sodium channels, similar to drugs previously discussed, and may block excitatory glutamate responses.

### Pharmacokinetics

Phenobarbital is effective orally and is distributed widely throughout the body. It is metabolized by microsomal drug-metabolizing enzymes, but up to 50% of the parent drug is excreted unchanged by the kidneys. Primidone is metabolized to phenobarbital and phenylethylmalonamide. The latter metabolite has anticonvulsant activity, but most of the anticonvulsant efficacy of primidone is due to the phenobarbital that is produced.

### Adverse effects

The major untoward effect of phenobarbital and primidone, when used as anticonvulsants, is sedation. Another side effect of considerable importance, particularly in children, is a possible disturbance in cognitive function. Even when the serum concentration is within the therapeutic range, apparently the ability to concentrate and perform simple tasks is decreased.

### Therapeutic uses

At present, phenobarbital and primidone are considered as alternative drugs for the treatment of partial seizures and for generalized tonic-clonic epilepsy. They are judged to be less effective than carbamazepine and phenytoin.

### Drug interactions

Phenobarbital and primidone are classic agents capable of inducing microsomal drug-metabolizing enzymes and this fact must be considered when using either drug singly or in combination with other agents. Consequently, many interactions can occur between phenobarbital and primidone and a variety of other drugs, and it is necessary, therefore to monitor drug blood concentrations to ensure that therapeutic levels of all administered agents are being maintained.

## Agents that Block T-Calcium Channels

### Ethosuximide

It is now generally accepted that the specific antiepileptic action of ethosuximide (and the older agent trimethadione, no longer employed) against absence epilepsy is its ability to reduce the low-threshold calcium current (LTCC) or T (transient) current. These currents underlie the 3-Hz spike wave discharges that are characteristic of absence epilepsy. A blockade of T-calcium current is likely also to be a mechanism used by valproic acid. The only clinical use for ethosuximide (Zarontin) is in the treatment of absence epilepsy. If absence attacks are the only seizure disorder present, Ethosuximide alone is effective. If other types of epilepsy are present, ethosuximide can be readily combined with other agents. For the most part, ethosuximide is a safe drug. Most of the **side effects** are dose related and consist of nausea, gastrointestinal irritation, drowsiness, and anorexia.

## Agents whose Mechanism of Action is not Known

### Felbamate

Felbamate (Felbatol) was introduced with the expectation that it would become a major drug in the treatment of epilepsy. Felbamate exhibited few manifestations of serious toxicity in early clinical trials. Soon after its introduction, however, it became apparent that its use was associated with a high incidence of aplastic anemia. Consequently, felbamate is indicated only for patients whose epilepsy is so severe that the risk of aplastic anemia is considered acceptable. While its mechanism of action has not been clearly established, felbamate shows some activity as an inhibitor of voltage-dependent sodium channels in a manner similar to that of phenytoin and carbamazepine. Felbamate also interacts at the strychnine-insensitive glycine recognition site on the NMDA receptor–ionophore complex. Whether this effect is important to its anticonvulsant activity is not clear.

### Gabapentin

Gabapentin (Neurotonin) was initially designed to be a rigid analogue of GABA. When it was discovered to have antiepileptic properties, it was assumed that thisactivity was related to a

GABAergic mechanism. However, subsequent studies have failed to show any GABAergic activity of gabapentin. Although it has not yet been possible to ascribe any definite mechanism to its antiepileptic activity, there is recent evidence that it may function as an agonist at GABA receptors in the brain. Gabapentin is recommended as adjunctive therapy in the treatment of partial seizures in adults. When used with other drugs, it appears to be an effective AED, it is usually not effective when employed alone for patients with severe seizures. Gabapentin is generally well tolerated, with somnolence, dizziness, and ataxia the most commonly reported adverse effects. A low incidence of potentially serious side effects and no significant allergic reactions have been reported.

## Levetiracetam

Levetiracetam (Keppra) has recently been approved for the treatment of partial-onset seizures. It appears to be safe and effective; its exact therapeutic profile has yet to be determined. It does not appear to share any of the mechanisms of action of agents that have been discussed to this point. It does have a highly specific brain binding site, but the significance of this observation to its mechanism of action has not been elucidated.

## Anticonvulsant Drugs and Pregnancy

The treatment of epileptic pregnant women poses particularly difficult questions.

There is good evidence of an increased risk of congenital malformations in infants born of women taking antiseizure medication during pregnancy, although most such women give birth to normal infants. Because most patients are taking multiple medications and congenital malformations can occur even without medication, it is difficult or impossible to demonstrate a cause and effect relationship for most agents. In some cases the evidence is clearer. Valproic acid has been known to cause spina bifida in a small percentage of cases. Phenytoin has also long been implicated in causing birth defects and a specific fetal hydantoin syndrome has been suggested. The most common abnormality seen in children of mothers receiving antiepileptic therapy is cleft palate. Withdrawal of medication from an epileptic pregnant woman is not without its hazards, to the patient and possibly to the fetus. It is not clear whether maternal seizures can directly affect the fetus. If it is feasible, the physician should prescribe only one drug at the lowest effective dosage to minimize teratogenic risks. The U. S. Food and Drug Administration has developed a use-in-pregnancy rating system that attempts to provide physicians with information that they can use to evaluate the risk to the fetus compared to the benefit to the patient.

This Classification uses five categories:

(A) Controlled studies show no risk;

(B) No evidence of risk to humans;

(C) Risk cannot be ruled out;

(D) Positive evidence of risk; and

(E) Contraindicated in pregnancy.

Using this Classification, during pregnancy all approved Antiepileptic drugs are in category C except carbamazepine, which is in category D. Neither phenytoin nor valproic acid is classified, but both have black box warnings regarding teratogenicity. A deficiency of folate during gestation has been associated with abnormal fetal growth and development. Since most Antiepileptic drugs cause some degree of folate deficiency, it is considered worthwhile to administer folate daily as a supplement during the period of organogenesis in the first trimester. Another concern in infants of mothers with epilepsy is a serious hemorrhagic disorder that is associated with high (25–35%) mortality. This probably results from the finding that many antiepileptic drugs can act as competitive inhibitors of vitamin K–dependent clotting factors. The competitive inhibition can be overcome by the administration of oral vitamin K supplements to the mother during the last week or 10 days of pregnancy.

## Treatment of Febrile Seizures

Convulsions associated with fever often occur in children 3 months to 5 years of age. Epilepsy later develops in approximately 2 to 3% of children who exhibit one or more such febrile seizures. Most authorities now recommend prophylactic treatment with anticonvulsant drugs only to patients at highest risk for development of epilepsy and for those who have multiple recurrent febrile seizures. Phenobarbital is the usual drug, although diazepam is also effective. Phenytoin and carbamazepine are ineffective and valproic acid may cause hepatotoxicity in very young patients.

## Treatment of Status Epilepticus

Status epilepticus is a continuous seizure state that can prove fatal unless the convulsions are terminated. It is a leading cause of death in epileptic patients and must be considered a medical emergency. The choice of drug may not be as important as establishing and correcting the cause of the seizures, maintaining vital functions, and beginning drug treatment as soon as possible. Virtually any general CNS depressant, including general anesthetics, can be used to terminate the seizure state. The pharmacological treatment of choice at present consists of intravenous infusion of either diazepam or lorazepam or fosphenytoin. Fosphenytoin (Cerebyx) is a prodrug that is highly soluble in intravenous solutions without solubilising agents and is supplied in vials for intravenous use.

Fosphenytoin is converted to phenytoin following parenteral administration. It is very effective in terminating seizures and will stop most status epilepticus episodes and provide long-term control without any decreased level of consciousness. All of these drugs should be administered slowly to avoid respiratory depression and apnea.

### References

Adkins JC and Noble S (1998). Tiagabine: A review of its pharmacodynamic and pharmacokinetic properties and therapeutic potential in the management of epilepsy. Drugs **55:** 437-460.

Bertrand S, *et al.*, (2001). The anticonvulsant, antihyperalgesic agent gabapentin is an agonist at brain gamma aminobutyric acid type B receptors negatively coupled to voltage-dependent calcium channels. *J Pharmacol Exper Therap* **298:** 15-24.

Ferrendelli JA (2001). Concerns with antiepileptic drug initiation: Safety, tolerability, and efficacy. *Epilepsia* **42:** 28-30.

Leppik IE (2001). Issues in the treatment of epilepsy. *Epilepsia* **42:** 1-6.

Treiman DM. GABAergic mechanisms in epilepsy. *Epilepsia* **42:** 8-12.

CHAPTER

# Opioid Analgesics 24

## Introduction

The drugs used to alleviate moderate to severe pain are either opiates (derived from the opium poppy) or opiate-like drugs (synthetic drugs). These drugs are together as opioids. Morphine, the prototypical opioid agonist, has long been known to relieve severe pain with remarkable efficacy. The opium poppy is the source of crude. It remains the standard against which all drugs that have strong analgesic action are compared. These drugs are collectively known as opioid analgesics and include not only the natural and semisynthetic alkaloid derivatives from opium but also include synthetic surrogates, other opioid-like drugs whose actions are blocked by the nonselective antagonist Naloxone, plus several endogenous peptides that interact with the several subtypes of opioid receptors.

**Examples:**

Opiates: morphine, codeine.

**Opiate-Like Drugs:** Fentanyl, meperidine, methadone.

See below, the structures of some Opioid analgesic drugs and derivatives.

The basic structure of morphine (Fig. 24-1) can be altered in rather minor ways that drastically change the effects of the drug. Acetylation of the hydroxyl groups leads to the synthesis of heroin (diacetylmorphine), which has a much greater ability to pass the blood-brain barrier. In the brain, however, heroin is converted to morphine and monoacetyl morphine. Some researchers attribute heroin's potent analgesic effects and rapid onset of action solely to its conversion to morphine. Others contend that heroin produces analgesic effects distinct from the conversion to morphine and thus should be considered as a therapeutically useful analgesic. Morphine is glucuronidated in the liver at the phenolic hydroxyl group (C). Protection of that group with a methyl group, as occurs in codeine and other codeine derivatives such as oxycodone, renders the molecule less susceptible to glucuronidation and decreases the first-pass effect in the liver. It is for this reason that codeine and its derivatives retain activity following oral administration to a greater degree

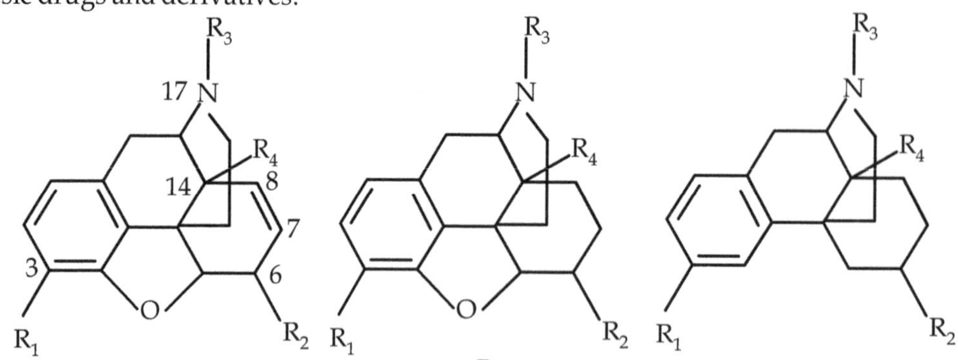


A B C

| Generic name | Template | $R_1$ | $R_2$ | $R_3$ | $R_4$ |
|---|---|---|---|---|---|
| Morphine | A | $-OH$ | $-OH$ | $-CH_3$ | $-H$ |
| Codeine | A | $-OCH_3$ | $-OH$ | $-CH_3$ | $-H$ |
| Heroin | A | $-OCOH_3$ | $-OCOCH_3$ | $-CH_3$ | $-H$ |
| Hydrocodone | B | $-OCH_3$ | $=O$ | $-CH_3$ | $-H$ |
| Oxycodone | B | $-OCH_3$ | $=O$ | $-CH_3$ | $-OH$ |
| Dihydrocodcine | B | $-OCH_3$ | $=OH$ | $-CH_3$ | $-OH$ |
| Hydromorphone | B | $-OH$ | $=O$ | $-CH_3$ | $-OH$ |
| Oxymorphone | B | $-OH$ | $=O$ | $-CH_3$ | $-OH$ |
| Levorphanol | C | $-OH$ | $-H$ | $-CH_3$ | $-OH$ |
| Butorphanol | C | $-OH$ | $-H$ | $-CH_2-$ 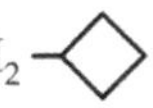 | $-OH$ |
| Nalbuphine | B | $-OH$ | $-OH$ | $-CH_2-$  | $-OH$ |
| Buprenorphine | B | $-OH$ | $-OCH_3$ | $-CH_2-$ 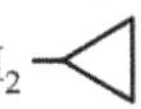 | $-OH$ |
| Naloxone | B | $-OH$ | $=O$ | $-CH_2CH{=}CH_2$ | $-OH$ |
| Naltrexone | B | $-OH$ | $=O$ | $-CH_2-$ 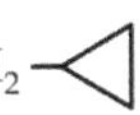 | $-OH$ |
| Nalmefene | B | $-OH$ | $=CH_2$ | $-CH_2-$ 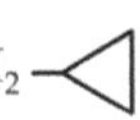 | $-OH$ |

**Fig 24-1:** Opioid analgesics

than does morphine. However, the glucuronidation of morphine at the hydroxyl moiety on C leads to an active metabolite, morphine-6-glucuronide, which contributes to the activity of morphine and extends its duration of action.

## Endogenous Opioids

The endogenous opioids are naturally occurring peptides that are the products of four known gene families. The gene responsible for the production of the endomorphins, a new class of endogenous opioids, has yet to be identified. The enkephalins, the first opioid peptides identified, were first discovered in the brain and were therefore given the name enkephalin, which means from the head. The dynorphins were so named because they were thought to be dynamic endorphins, having a wide range of activities in the body, a hypothesis that has proved to be accurate. The endogenous opioids have been implicated in the modulation of most of the critical functions of the body, including hormonal fluctuations, thermoregulation, mediation of stress and anxiety, production of analgesia and development of opioid tolerance and dependence. The endogenous opioids maintain homeostasis, amplify signals from the periphery to the brain and serve as neuromodulators of the body's response to external stimuli. As such, the endogenous opioids are critical to the maintenance of health and a sense of well-being.

## Enkephalins, Endorphins, Dynorphins, Endomorphins

**Enkephalins**

Met-Enkephalin ( Tyr-Gly-Gly-Phe-**Met** )

Leu-Enkephalin ( Tyr-Gly-Gly-Phe-**Leu)**

**Endorphins:** α-neoendorphin (**Tyr-Gly-Gly-Phe-Leu-Arg-Lys-Tyr-Pro**-Lys)

β-neoendorphin (**Tyr-Gly-Gly-Phe-Leu-Arg-Lys-Tyr-Pro)**

β-h-endorphin [**Tyr-Gly-Gly-Phe**-Met-Thr-Ser-Glu-Lys-Ser-Gln-Thr-Pro-Leu-Val-Thr-leu-Phe-Lys-Asn-Ala-Ile-Ile-Lys-Asn-Ala-Tyr-Lys-Lys-Gly-Glu (31-Residues) ]

**Dynorphins:** Dynorphin A ( **Tyr-Gly-Gly-Phe-Leu**-Arg-Arg-Ile-Arg-Pro-Lys-Leu-Lys-Trp-Asp-Asn-Gln )

Dynorphin B ( **Tyr-Gly-Gly-Phe-Leu**-Arg-Arg-Gln-Phe-Lys-Val-Val-Thr)

**Endomorphins:** Endomorphin 1 ( Tyr-Pro-Trp-Phe-$NH_2$)

Endomorphin 2 ( Tyr-Pro-Phe-Phe-$NH_2$)

Endogenous opioid peptides are derived from precursor peptides (proopiomelanocortin [POMC]) by proteolytic cleavage of POMC. POMC present in high level in the CNS (arcuate nucleus, limbic, brain stem, spinal cord). Enkephalins activate mu (μ) and delta (δ) opioid receptors. Enkephalins have slightly higher affinity for the δ than for the opioid μ receptor. Endomorphins have very high affinity for the μ opioid receptor.

# Opioid Receptors

Recently, a number of previously hypothesized opioid receptors have been cloned (μ, δ, and κ). The α-receptor, once thought to be an opioid receptor, is a nonopioid receptor that mediates some of the dysphoric effects of the opioids. The cloned opioid receptors are members of the large superfamily of G protein–coupled receptors. Subtypes of the receptors have been proposed. It has been shown that $\mu_1$-receptors mediate the analgesic and euphoric effects of the opioids and physical dependence on them, whereas $\mu_2$-receptors mediate the bradycardiac and respiratory depressant effects. δ-receptors, of which at least two subtypes have been identified pharmacologically, mediate spinal analgesic effects and have been implicated in the modulation of tolerance to μ-opioids. Three κ -opioid receptors have been identied and are thought to mediate spinal analgesia, miosis, sedation and diuresis. Opioid receptors and their precursor mRNAs are distributed throughout the brain and spinal cord. High levels of opioid binding have been found in the ascending pathways for nociceptive transmission, including the dorsal horn of the spinal cord and in particular the substantia gelatinosa, lamina II. Other ascending tracts with high levels of binding include the spinothalamic tracts to the subcortical regions and limbic areas of the brain responsible for the discriminative and sensory aspects of pain and the euphoric effects of the drugs. Limbic areas, including cortical sites and the amygdala are involved in the anxiolytic effects of the drugs. Binding in the thalamus and hypothalamus is also very high. Binding in the hypothalamus is linked to the modulation of hormone release and to thermoregulation by the opioids and opioid peptides. Some descending pathways possess high levels of opioid receptors believed to be linked to the analgesic effects of the drugs. In addition, the receptor binding in medullary pathways has been linked to inhibitory neurotransmitter release in the dorsal horn. Opioid binding at medullary sites is consistent with the respiratory depressant effects of the drugs. Binding in the nucleus accumbens and the resultant release of dopamine by the μ and δ opioids is linked to the development of physical dependence. However, the κ opioids, which also bind extensively in the nucleus accumbens are linked to a decrease in dopamine release, possibly explaining their lower abuse liability. The localization of different receptor subtypes within different-size fiber pathways has been established. The μ and δ receptors appear associated with the large-diameter fibers, while the k receptors appear to be located in the small to medium-size fiber bundles of the dorsal root ganglia. Such differences may explain the modulation of specific types of nociceptive stimuli by the different opioid agonists and opioid peptides.

## Mechanism of Opioid Receptor Function

1. μ, δ and κ are functionally coupled to pertussis toxin sensitive heterotrimeric G proteins (Gi) to inhibit adenylyl cyclase activity.
2. Activates receptor-activated $K^+$ currents which increase $K^+$ efflux (hyperpolarisation) reduces voltage-gated $Ca^{2+}$ entry.
3. Hyperpolarisation of membrane potential by $K^+$currents and inhibition of the $Ca^{2+}$ influx prevents neurotransmitter release and pain transmission in varying neuronal pathways.

## Classification of Opioid Analgesic Drugs

1. ***Strong agonists:*** Morphine (half life 4 hr)

   Meperidine (half life 2 hr)

   Methadone-long acting (half life 24 hrs)

   Heroin (2 hr; 3-fold increase in potency)

   Fentanyl (5 to 45 min, anesthetic)

   Oxycodone (4 hr)
2. ***Moderate agonists:*** Propoxyphene

   Codeine

   Hydrocodone
3. ***Mixed agonist-antagonists:*** Pentazocine-agonist on δ receptor and weak antagonist at μ and μ receptor

   Nalbuphine-similar to Pentazocine but potent antagonist at μ receptor

   Buprenorphine-lipophilic, about 0.4 mg equivalent to 10 mg morphine, partial μ agonist and antagonist at kappa receptor.
4. *Antagonists:*

   **Naloxone-**It rapidly displaces bound opioids from receptor within 30 sec of i.v injection, reverses the respiratory depression and coma due to heroin overdose, competitive antagonist for μ, δ and κ receptors with a 10-fold higher affinity for receptor .

   **Naltrexone-**longer duration of action than naloxone, a single oral dose blocks the effects of injected heroin (48 hr).

**Table 24-1:** Selectivity of opioid drugs and peptides for different receptors

| Compound | μ | δ | κ |
|---|---|---|---|
| *Agonists* | | | |
| Morphine | +++ | | + |
| Methadone | +++ | | + |
| Meperidine | ++ | + | + |
| Codeine | + | + | + |
| Etorphine | +++ | +++ | +++ |
| Fentanyl | +++ | | |
| Sufentanil | +++ | + | + |
| *Endogenous peptides* | | | |
| Met-enkephalin | ++ | +++ | |
| Leu-enkephalin | ++ | +++ | |
| β-Endorphin | +++ | +++ | |
| α-Neoendorphin | + | + | +++ |
| Dynorphin A | ++ | | +++ |
| Antagonists | | | |
| Naloxone | --- | - | -- |
| Naltrexone | --- | - | -- |
| Mixed aganists/antagonists | | | |
| Pentazocine | - | | + |
| Nalbuphine | -- | | ++ |
| Buprenorphine | ++ | | -- |

## Pharmacokinetics

Most of the opioids are well absorbed from the GI tract in addition to being absorbed following transcutaneous administration. As described previously, the first-pass effect on drugs like morphine, which have a free hydroxyl group in position 3, is glucuronidation by the liver. In the case of morphine, the conjugation to glucuronide decreases the oral bioavailability of the drug. Following absorption, the drugs distribute rapidly to all tissues, although the distribution is limited by their lipophilicity. Fentanyl (highly lipophilic) distributes to the brain rapidly but also remains in fat, which serves as a slow-releasing pool of the drug. Certain of the drugs, notably methadone and fentanyl, have long half-lives inconsistent with their duration of action. This discrepancy is due to accumulation in various tissue and plasma reservoirs and redistribution from the brain to these reservoirs. Heroin passes readily into the brain. Codeine passes into the brain more readily than morphine, which is slow in crossing the blood-brain barrier. The drugs cross readily into fetal tissues across the placenta and therefore should be used with care during pregnancy and delivery. Moreover, glucuronidation by the fetus is slow, increasing buildup of the drugs and increasing their half-life in the fetus. The majority of their metabolites are inactive with a few notable exceptions, such as morphine-6-glucuronide, which produces an analgesic effect; normeperidine and norpropoxyphene, which produce excitatory but not analgesic effects; and 6-α-naltexol, which is less active than naltrexone as an antagonist but prolongs the action of naltrexone. Excretion of the metabolites requires adequate renal function, since excretion by routes other than the urine are of minor importance.

## Cellular Mechanisms of Action

Opioid receptors are members of the G protein superfamily of receptors. Drug-induced interaction with these receptors is associated with a decrease in activation of the enzyme adenylyl cyclase and a subsequent decrease in cyclic adenosine monophosphate (cAMP) levels in the cell. Binding of opioids to their receptors produces a decrease in calcium entry to cells by decreasing the phosphorylation of the voltage operating calcium channels and allows for increased time for the channels to remain closed. In addition, activation of opioid receptors leads to potassium efflux and the resultant hyperpolarization limits the entry of calcium to the cell by increasing the negative charge of the membrane to levels at which these calcium channels fail to activate. The net result of the cellular decrease in calcium is a decrease in the release of dopamine, serotonin and nociceptive peptides, such as substance P resulting in blockage of nociceptive transmission.

## Pharmacological Effects

### Analgesia

Opioid agonists interact with receptors in the brain and in the spinal cord. The initial binding of opioids in the brain causes the release of the inhibitory neurotransmitter serotonin, which in turn induces inhibition of the dorsal horn neurons. Both the brain and the spinal cord are required for the production of a maximal analgesic effect following systemic administration of opioids, although analgesia can be elicited by spinal administration only. In the spinal cord, morphine inhibits the release of most nociceptive peptides. Morphine also affects descending noradrenergic pathways. Norepinephrine release in response to opioid administration results in an analgesic effect at the spinal level. Opioids have profound effects upon the cerebrocortical regions that control the somatosensory and discriminative aspects of pain. Thus, the opioids suppress the perception of pain by eliminating or altering the emotional aspects of pain and inducing euphoria and sleep with higher doses. Patients become inattentive to the painful stimuli, less anxious and more relaxed. Disruption of normal REM sleep occurs with opioid administration. In addition, opioids depress polysynaptic responses but can increase monosynaptic responses and lead to convulsant effects in high doses. In patients with chronic pain, the euphoric effect of opioids, mediated by the μ-receptor is usually blunted. Some patients feel a dysphoric effect upon the administration of opioids, which is most likely mediated by the σ-receptor.

### Medullary effects

Opioids depress respiration *via* the $\mu_2$-receptor at the level of the medulla and thereby increase $PCO_2$. Opioids reduce respiration, an effect that is fatal in the case of overdose, by a dual action. The opioids decrease both the sensitivity of the medulla to carbon dioxide concentrations and the respiratory rate. Cardiovascular function and the response to hypoxia are not compromised. Tolerance to the respiratory depressant effects of the opioids does not appear to occur, while tolerance to the emetic effects of the opioids occurs upon repeated administration. The area postrema chemoreceptor trigger zone of the medulla mediates opioid-induced vomiting.

### Miosis

Miosis or constriction of pupil is due to disinhibition of the Edinger-Westphal nucleus in the cortex resulting in increased pupillary constrictor tone. No tolerance develops to this effect.

### Hypothalamic effects

The opioids have pronounced effects on the release of hormones from both the pituitary and the hypothalamus. Stimulation of some of the opioid receptors in hypothalamic nuclei decrease the release of dopamine, thus increasing release of prolactin. Opioids bind in the supraoptic nuclei of the hypothalamus and increase the release of antidiuretic hormone (vasopressin).

### GI effects

Morphine and most other opioids produce some degree of constipation by increasing sphincter tone and decreasing gastric motility. Such an effect is uncomfortable for patients required to take opioids chronically. Tolerance to the constipative effects of the opioids does not generally occur. In addition, the decrease in gastric motility increases gastric emptying time and reduces absorption of other drugs. The constriction of sphincters, especially the bile duct, may result in increased pain in certain patients with biliary colic or other GI distress. Constriction of the urinary sphincter can lead to painful urine retention in some patients. The effects of opioids on the GI tract are largely mediated by the parasympathetic release of acetylcholine. All of the opioid receptors have been shown to mediate such GI effects.

### Immune function and histamine

Opioids induce the release of histamine, which leads to the itching sensation associated with use and abuse of opioids. Bronchiolar constriction is possible. Opioids are also immunosuppressive, having effects on the T helper and T-suppressor cells.

### Antitussive effects

The opioids block cough by a mechanism that is not yet understood. No stereoselectivity of the opioids for blockade of the cough reflex has been shown. Thus, the isomers of opioids, such as dextrorphan, are as efficacious as the L-isomers as antitussives. This lack of stereoselectivity prompted the development of the D-isomers of opioids as antitussives since they are devoid of the dependence liability of L-isomers. Certain of the opioids, such as propoxyphene and meperidine are relatively devoid of antitussive effects.

## Tolerance and Physical Dependence

All of the opioid agonists produce some degree of tolerance and physical dependence. The biochemical mechanisms underlying tolerance and physical dependence are unclear. It is known, however, that intracellular mechanisms of tolerance to opioids include increases in calcium levels in the cells, increased production of cAMP, decreased potassium efflux, alterations in the phosphorylation of intracellular and intranuclear proteins and the resultant return to normal levels of release of most neurotransmitters and neuromodulators. Tolerance to the analgesic effects of opioids occurs rapidly, especially when large doses of the drugs are used at short intervals. However, tolerance to the respiratory depressant and emetic effects of the opioids occurs more slowly. The miotic and constipative effects of the opioids rarely show tolerance. Tolerance to one opioid usually renders a patient cross-tolerant to other opioids but not to drugs of otherclasses. Within the opioid class of drugs, certain drugs with high intrinsic activity (e.g., fentanyl) appear to lack cross-tolerance to opioids of lower intrinsic activity (e.g., morphine), an effect thought to be related to the change in receptor number induced by the chronic opioid administration. Theoretically, a drug with high intrinsic activity would need to occupy fewer receptors to exert an effect and would be less affected by changes in receptor number, which occurs upon chronic administration of drugs with lower intrinsic activity. The cessation of opioid drug administration leads to an observable abstinence syndrome. In the case of the opioids, signs of withdrawal include chills, fever, sweating, yawning, vomiting, diarrhea, nausea, dizziness, and hypertension. The onset of symptoms occurs 6 to 12 hours after the last drug dose (depending on the kinetics of the drug) and continues for several days, with most of the signs of withdrawal ending by 72 hours after the last dose of the drug. However, signs of withdrawal including restlessness, anxiety, and drug craving may be detectable for 6 months to 1 year after cessation of drug use. In general, the effects observed upon withdrawal from a drug are opposite to those observed when the person is taking the drug and such is the case with the opioids. The degree of dependence is generally reflected by the severity of withdrawal signs. In addition, drugs with long half-lives such as methadone, produce a gradual and prolonged withdrawal. The use of methadone replacement for heroin is based upon the pharmacokinetics of methadone. The longer onset and duration of action and the oral bioavailability render the drug useful for the treatment of opioid addiction by decreasing the rapid highs and lows associated with fast-onset, short-duration drugs such as heroin.

Drugs with a short duration of action produce a more rapid onset of withdrawal signs. A derivative of methadone, L-α-acetyl-methadol (LAAM) has been approved for the treatment of opioid addiction. In some addicts whose degree of tolerance is not known, the patient is first given methadone to stabilize the withdrawal signs and is then switched to LAAM. LAAM has an advantage over methadone in that it has a longer duration of action. Dosing is required only three times per week in most addicts to prevent withdrawal. Babies born to opioid-addicted women also exhibit withdrawal signs, but because of the slower metabolism of opioids in the newborn, the withdrawal signs are more protracted. The babies are often treated with the opium preparation paregoric to reduce withdrawal signs.

## Morphine

### Clinical uses

Morphine remains the standard by which other analgesic drugs are compared. The predominant effects of morphine are at the μ-opioid receptor, although it interacts with other opioid receptors as well. Morphine is indicated for the treatment of moderate to severe and chronic pain. It is useful preoperatively for sedation, anxiolytic effects and to reduce the dose of anesthetics. Morphine is the drug of choice for the treatment of myocardial infarction because it decreases heart rate and causes vasodilation. In addition, morphine is the most commonly used drug for the treatment of dyspnea associated pulmonary edema. It is thought that morphine reduces the anxiety associated with shortness of breath and decreases the cardiac preload and afterload. The use of morphine *via* the oral route has drawbacks because of its first-pass effect; however, oral morphine has been recommended for use in cancer patients for its ease of administration. In particular, the long acting preparations of morphine, such as MS-Contin and Ora morph, are described as the cornerstone of pain treatment in cancer patients, either alone or in combination with nonopioids. Morphine is the most commonly used analgesic drug administered *via* the epidural route because it is potent, efficacious and hydrophilic. The more hydrophilic the drug, the slower the onset and the longer the duration of action following epidural administration. Single-dose or continuous infusion of morphine is used to provide pain relief in thoracic and abdominal surgical patients and in cancer patients at high risk for developing side effects associated with systemic opioids. Since morphine does not produce anesthesia *via* the epidural route, the patient is able to move about normally; motor function is preserved. The drawback to epidural use of morphine is that certain types of pain are relatively unresponsive, such as that associated with visceral stimuli, as in pancreatitis and neuropathic pain from nerve deafferentation. In addition, patients can develop respiratory depression and nausea from the rostral flow of the drug to Medullary centers, although the effects are much less severe than those observed following the systemic administration of the drug and can be alleviated by elevation of the head of the patient at a 30-degree angle. Patients may also itch because of histamine release. Patient-controlled analgesia (PCA) is an alternative method of administration of morphine. The use of an indwelling catheter allows the patient to administer the drug at frequent intervals for pain relief. PCA systems allow patients the freedom to assess the need for their own analgesia and to titrate a dose tailored to their needs. Dependence is rarely observed in patients using PCA for acute pain management.

**Adverse effects and contraindications**

The opioids generally have a high level of safety when used in therapeutic dosages. However, there are several notable exceptions. Morphine and other opioids are contraindicated in patients with hypersensitivity reactions to the opioids. In addition, morphine should not be used in patients with acute bronchial asthma and should not be given as the drug of first choice in patients with pulmonary disease, because it has antitussive effects that prevent the patient from clearing any buildup of mucus in the lungs. Opioids with less antitussive effects, such as meperidine, are better for such situations. When used *via* the epidural route, the site for injection must be free of infection. In addition, the use of corticosteroids by the patient should be halted for at least 2 weeks prior to the insertion of the catheter to prevent infection, since morphine increases the immunosuppressive effects of the steroids.

Opioids are contraindicated in head trauma because of the risk of a rise in intracranial pressure from vasodilation and increased cerebrospinal fluid volume. In addition, in such patients the onset of miosis following opioid administration can mask the pupillary responses used diagnostically for determination of concussion. The clearance of morphine and its active metabolite, morphine-6-glucuronide depends on adequate renal function. The elderly are particularly susceptible to accumulation of the drugs, hence respiratory depression and sedation. Morphine, like all opioids, passes through the placenta rapidly and has been associated with prolongation of labor in pregnant women and respiratory depression in the newborn. Morphine and other opioids exhibit intense sedative effects and increased respiratory depression when combined with other sedatives, such as alcohol or barbiturates. Increased sedation and toxicity are observed when morphine is administered in combination with the psychotropic drugs, such as chlorpromazine and monoamine oxidase inhibitors, or the anxiolytics, such as diazepam. Respiratory depression, miosis, hypotension, and coma are signs of morphine overdose. While the i.v administration of naloxone reverses the toxic effects of morphine, naloxone has a short duration of action and must be administered repeatedly at 30 to 45 minute intervals until morphine is cleared from the body.

# Other Opioids

## Meperidine or Pethidine

Meperidine (Demerol) is a synthetic opioid structurally unrelated to morphine.

**Mechanism:** It binds to μ receptors with some binding at k receptors.

**Actions:** It causes respiratory depression similar to morphine but has no significant cardiovascular effect when given orally. I.v administration produces a decrease in PVR resulting in increased peripheral blood flow. It causes papillary dilation *via* an atropine –like effect.

**Therapeutic uses:** Severe acute pain, it lacks anti-tussive activity and produces less smooth muscle contraction/ spasm than morphine.

**Pharmacokinetics:** It is well absorbed form the GI tract; it is most often given i.m. It has a shorter duration of action than morphine (2-4 hours). It is demethylated in the liver and excreted in the urine.

**Adverse effects:** With large repeated doses normeperidine (demethylated meperidine) accumulates causing anxiety, muscle tremors and convulsions. It causes papillary dilation (*vs.* miosis with morphine) in large doses. There is cross-tolerance with other opioids.

## Methadone

This is a synthetic orally effective opioid that is equipotent to morphine but induces less euphoria and has a longer duration of action.

**Mechanism of action:** Methadone binds to the μ receptors.

**Actions:** Methadone is well absorbed orally and is an equipotent analgesic to morphine. It causes miosis, respiratory depression, biliary spasm and constipation just like morphine.

**Therapeutic uses:** It is used for controlled withdrawal from heroin and morphine. Methadone is itself addictive but the withdrawal syndrome is somewhat milder but more protracted than with other opioids.

**Pharmacokinetics:** Readily absorbed orally it is highly protein bound so remains in tissues for a prolonged period. It is transformed in the liver and excreted by the urine as mostly inactive metabolites.

**Adverse effects:** Similar to morphine particularly the risk of addiction

## Fentanyl

Chemically related to meperidine. Fentanyl has 100 times the analgesic potency of morphine. It has a rapid onset of action and a short duration (15-30 minutes). It can be used i.v, epidural or Intrathecal. Transmucosal and Transdermal preparations are available. Fentanyl is metabolized to an inactive metabolite by the cytochrome P4503A4 system. Drug metabolites are eliminated through the urine. Like morphine fentanyl causes miosis (*vs.* mydriasis). A particular risk of the transmucosal or transdermal routes is respiratory depression, these delivery routes create a reservoir of drug in the skin or mucosa.

Sufentanil, alfentanil and remifentanil are related to fentanyl they differ in their potency and metabolic disposition. Sufentanil is even more potent than Fentanyl.

## Heroin

Heroin is produced by the diacetylation of morphine which results in a threefold increase in its potency. The acetylation allows it to cross the BBB much more rapidly yielding a more pronounced euphoria. It may be used i.v or smoked, both allow for rapid distribution, heroin is metabolized to morphine. There is no medical indication for its use in the US.

## Codeine

This is a much less potent analgesic than morphine, it produces less euphoria and has much lower abuse potential and rarely produces physical dependence.

It is an effective oral analgesic. It does possess significant antitussive effects at sub analgesic doses.

Codeine is often formulated with either acetaminophen, aspirin or ibuprofen; care but be exerted when these are used with over the counter analgesic to avoid overdose with the non-opioid agent.

A synthetic congener of codeine Dextromethorphan lacks analgesic properties is an effective antitussive available without prescription.

## Oxycodone

This is a semisynthetic derivative of morphine that is orally active; it too is formulated with over-the-counter analgesics. It is metabolized in the liver and excreted *via* the kidney. Controlled release forms of oxycontin requiring once or twice a day dosing are effective for chronic pain. Crushing these pills disrupts the sustained release mechanism resulting in acute intoxication consistent with opiate overdose.

**Hydrocodone** is a semi-synthetic opioid derived from two of the naturally occurring opiates, codeine and tebaine. Hydrocodone is an orally active narcotic analgesic and Antitussives. It is commonly available in tablet, capsule and syrup form and is often compounded with other analgesics like acetaminophen or ibuprofen.

### Propoxyphene

This is a derivative of methadone, it is used for mild to moderate pain; it has ~1/2 the potency of codeine.

It is often formulated with another over-the-counter analgesic. The combination has greater effect than either drug alone.

Toxic doses may produce cardio and pulmonary toxicity particularly when taken in combination with alcohol and/or sedatives in addition to CNS depression. Opioid antagonists can reverse the pulmonary and CNS effects but not the cardiotoxicity.

## Mixed Agonist-Antagonist and Partial Agonists

### Buprenorphine

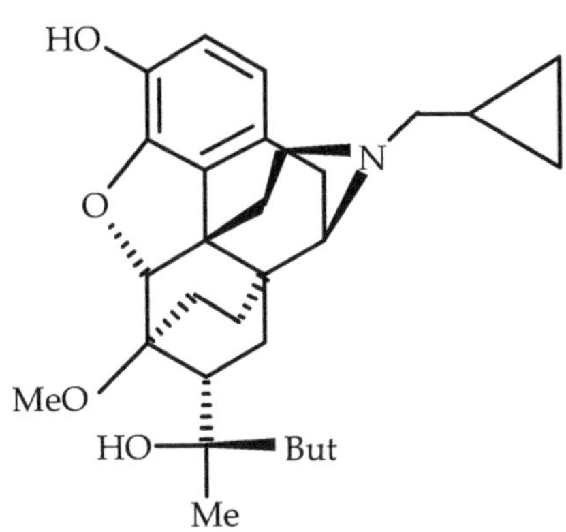


**Fig 24-2:** Buprenorphine

**Mechanism of action**

Buprenorphine (Fig 24-2) is a thebaine derivative with powerful analgesia approximately 25 to 40 times as potent as morphine, and its analgesic effect is due to partial agonist activity at μ-opioid receptors, i.e., when the molecule binds to a receptor, it is only partially activated in contrast to a full agonist such as morphine. Buprenorphine also has very high binding affinity for the μ receptor such that opioid receptor antagonists (e.g., naloxone) only partially reverse its effects. This agent is a partial agonist at μ receptors producing morphine-like effects in naïve users but precipitating withdrawal in morphine dependents.

### Pharmacokinetics

Buprenorphine is metabolised by the liver, via the CYP3A4 isozyme of the cytochrome P450 enzyme system, into norbuprenorphine (by *N*-dealkylation) and other metabolites. The metabolites are further conjugated with glucuronic acid. Eliminated mainly through excretion into the bile. The elimination half-life of buprenorphine is 20–73 hours (mean 37). Due to the mainly hepatic elimination there is no risk of accumulation in patients with renal impairment and in the elderly. Buprenorphine main active metabolite, norbuprenorphine, is a μ-opioid, δ-opioid and nociceptin receptor full agonist, as well as a κ-opioid receptor partial agonist.

**Administration**

Buprenorphine hydrochloride is administered by intramuscular injection, intravenous infusion, *via* Transdermal patch, or as a sublingual tablet. It is not administered orally, due to very high first pass metabolism.

**Dose**

To treat opioid addiction in higher dosages (> 2 mg).

To control moderate pain in non-opioid tolerant individuals in lower dosages (~200 μg), half life - 37 hours.

### Adverse effects

Respiratory depression not reversible by naloxone, hypotension and nausea.

### Therapeutic uses

Its main use is in opioid detoxification as its withdrawal syndrome appears less severe and of shorter duration than methadone. It is available outside of the specialized clinic allowed to dispense methadone for opiate withdrawal.

## Antagonists

Opioid antagonists bind with high affinity to the μ, κ and δ receptors. In normal individuals these agents produce no effect but in those with opiates present they induce an acute withdrawal syndrome.

### Naloxone

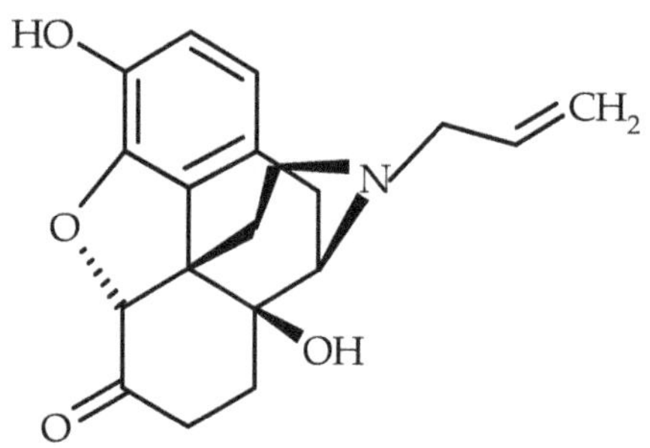


**Fig 24-3:** Naloxone

Naloxone (Fig 24-3) is a drug used to counter the effects of opioid overdose, for example heroin or morphine overdose. Naloxone is specifically used to counteract life-threatening depression of the central nervous system and respiratory system. Naloxone is also experimentally used in the treatment for congenital insensitivity to pain with anhidrosis (CIPA).

### Mechanism of action

Naloxone has an extremely high affinity for μ-opioid receptors in the central nervous system. Naloxone is a μ-opioid receptor competitive antagonist, and its rapid blockade of those receptors often produces rapid onset of withdrawal symptoms. Naloxone also has an antagonist action, though with a lower affinity, at κ- and δ-opioid receptors.

### Pharmacokinetics

1. Naloxone is administered parenterally. Although it is relatively well absorbed after oral administration, it undergoes extensive first-pass metabolism, making this route of delivery ineffective.
2. After intravenous (i.v) administration, naloxone is rapidly distributed throughout the body. It is highly lipophilic and readily crosses into the brain. Onset of action after i.v dosing is within 2 minutes, and is only slightly longer with intramuscular (i.m), subcutaneous, or endotracheal administration.
3. Duration of action is dependent on route and dose. I.v dosing typically provides a duration of action of 20 to 60 minutes. i.m use produces a longer effect than i.v administration, but absorption from this route is erratic.
4. Metabolism - Naloxone is hepatically metabolized, primarily through conjugation to naloxone-3-glucuronide.
5. Elimination - The elimination half-life in adults is approximately 60 minutes.

Naloxone is most commonly injected intravenously for fastest action. The drug generally acts within a minute, and its effects may last up to 45 minutes. It can also be administered *via* intramuscular or subcutaneous injection. Use of a wedge device (nasal atomizer) attached to a syringe to create a mist delivering the drug to the nasal mucosa may also be utilized, although this solution is more likely utilized outside of a clinical facility. Half life is 30-81 minutes.

### Dosage

Infants - 0.1 mg/kg, children from birth to 5 years of age or 20 kg of body weight

Children - 2.0 mg, 5 years of age or weighing more than 20 kg/bw

Pediatric - Ranging from 0.005 to 0.4 mg/kg

### Adverse effect

Possible side effects include - change in mood, increased sweating, nausea, nervousness, restlessness, trembling, vomiting, allergic reactions such as rash or swelling, dizziness, fainting, fast or irregular pulse, flushing, headache, heart rhythm changes, seizures, sudden chest pain

### Naltrexone

Used in the treatment of alcohol dependence and for the blockade of the effects of exogenously administered opioids.

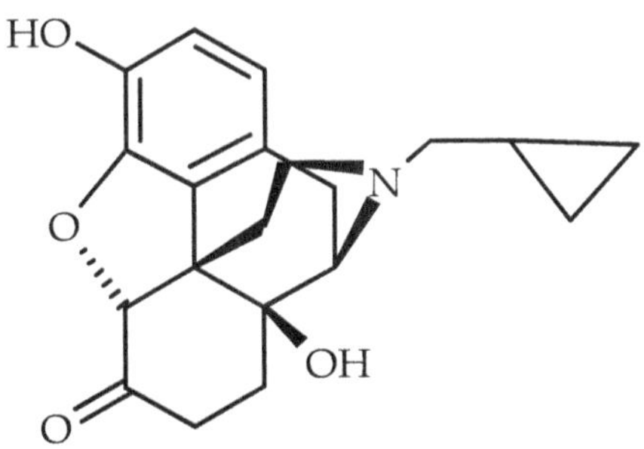


**Fig 24-4:** Naltrexone

### Mechanism of action

Naltrexone (Fig 24-4) binds to the opioid μ receptor antagonistically, thereby preventing conventional opiate (heroin, morphine) drugs from binding and inducing opioid neural responses. The mechanism of action of naltrexone in alcoholism is not understood, however, involvement of the endogenous opioid system is suggested by preclinical data. Naltrexone competitively binds to such receptors and may block the effects of endogenous opioids.

### Pharmacokinetics

Absorption - well absorbed orally, naltrexone is subject to significant first pass metabolism with oral bioavailability estimates ranging from 5 to 40%. Protein Binding - 21% bound to plasma proteins over the therapeutic dose range. Metabolism - Hepatic. Naltrexone is metabolised mainly to 6β-naltrexol by the liver enzyme dihydrodiol dehydrogenase. Other metabolites include 2-hydroxy-3-methoxy-6β-naltrexol and 2-hydroxy-3-methoxy-naltrexone. These are then further metabolised by conjugation with glucuronide. Half life is 4 hours for naltrexone and 13 hours for the active metabolite 6 beta-naltrexol.

Oral - The initial dose of Nalorex should be 25 mg (half a tablet) followed by 50 mg (one tablet) daily. A three-times-a-week dosing schedule may be considered if it is likely to result in better compliance e.g., 100 mg on Monday, 100 mg on Wednesday and 150 mg on Friday.

### Adverse effect

High doses of naltrexone produce salivation, depression/reduced activity, tremors and convulsions.

## References

Angst MS, Clark JD (2006). Opioid-induced hyperalgesia. Anesthesiology **104:** 570.

Basbaum AI, Jessel T (2000). The perception of pain. In Kandel ER *et al.*, (editors): Principles of Neural Science, 4th ed, McGraw-Hill.

Basbaum AI, Woolf CJ (1999). Pain. *Curr Biol* **9:** R429.

Benedetti C, Premuda L (1990). The history of opium and its derivatives. In: Benedetti C *et al.*, (editors): *Advances* in Pain Research and Therapy vol 14. Raven Press.

Bolan EA, Tallarida RJ, Pasternak GW (2002). Synergy between mu opioid ligands: Evidence for functional interactions among mu opioid receptor subtypes. *J Pharmacol Exp Ther* **303:** 557.

Bonci A, Williams JT (1997). Increased probability of GABA release during withdrawal from morphine. *J Neurosci* **17:** 796.

Daniels DJ, *et al.*, (2005). Opioid-induced tolerance and dependence in mice is modulated by the distance between pharmacophores in a bivalent ligand series. *Proc Natl Acad Sci USA* **102:** 19208.

Davis MP, Walsh D (2001). Methadone for relief of cancer pain: A review of pharmacokinetics, pharmacodynamics, drug interactions and protocols of administration. *Support Care Cancer* **9:** 73.

CHAPTER

# 25

# CNS Stimulants

## Introduction

Central nervous system (CNS) stimulation is the primary action of a diverse group of pharmacological agents and an adverse effect associated with the administration of an even larger group of drugs. CNS stimulation consists of a range of behaviours including mild elevation in alertness, increased nervousness and anxiety, and convulsions.

Although the use of CNS stimulants (also known as analeptics or convulsants) has declined, certain compounds within this category do possess some clinical utility. Historically, general CNS stimulants were used primarily as respiratory stimulants in the treatment of acute over dosage with CNS depressants (e.g., barbiturates).

Several factors have contributed to the almost complete lack of use of CNS stimulants in this clinical situation.

First, since the stimulants were not specific antagonists of the depressant agents, they frequently were not effective in reversing severe pharmacologically induced CNS depression.

Second, the duration of action of the CNS stimulant was generally shorter than that of the depressant.

Third, the dose of most CNS stimulants required to reverse severe CNS depression was quite close to the dose that produced convulsions and cardiac arrhythmias. In such cases, the CNS stimulant often exacerbated the clinical picture by producing severe life threatening complications. Another factor contributing to the decline in CNS stimulant use for drug-induced CNS depression has been the development of generally safer procedures for patient management. Supportive measures (e.g., maintenance of a patient airway, elevation of low blood pressure) often provide greater benefit to the patient than does the use of analeptic drugs.

## Classification

Compounds that possess as their primary action the stimulation of the CNS can be divided into three major categories based on either their proposed mechanism of action or their chemical structure.

**Table 25-1:** Classification of CNS stimulants

| Analeptic Stimulants | Psychomotor Stimulants | Methylxanthines |
|---|---|---|
| Doxapram | Amphetamine | Caffeine |
| Nikethamide | Methamphetamine | Theophylline |
| Pentylenetetrazole | Methylphenidate | Theobromine |
| Strychnine | Pemoline | |
| Picrotoxin | Ephedrine | |
| Bicuculline | Phentermine | |
| | Fenfluramine | |
| | Phenylpropanolamine | |

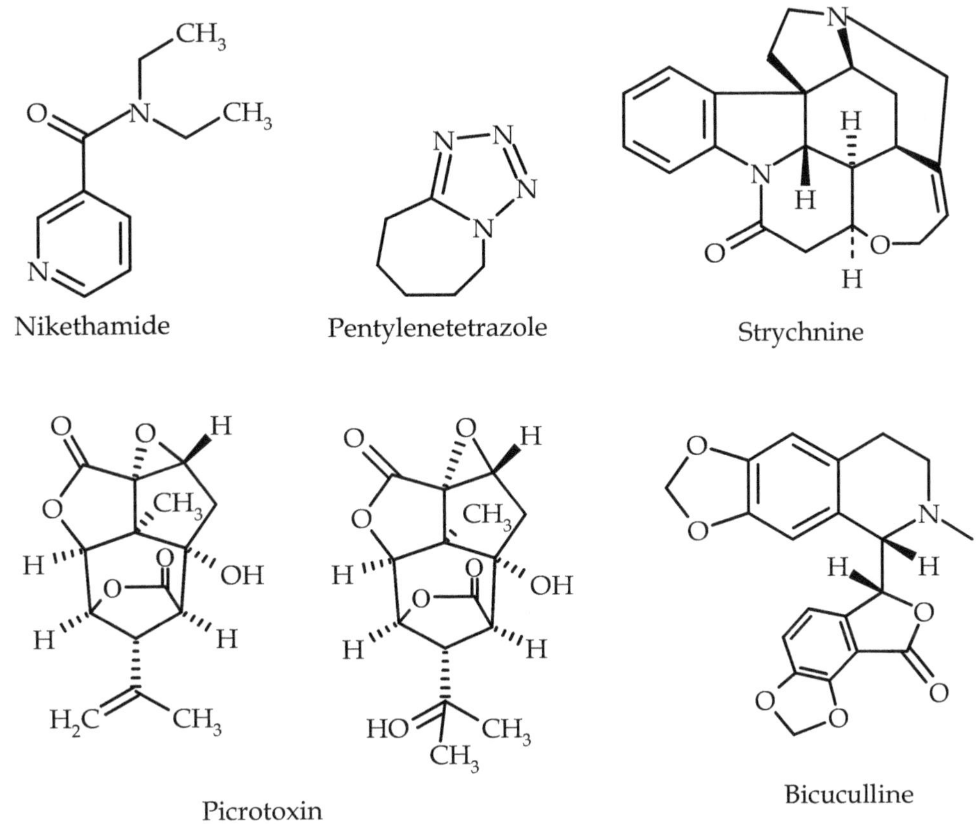


**Fig 25-1:** Analeptic stimulants

## Analeptic Stimulants

The analeptic stimulates are shown in Fig 25-1.

## Mechanism of Action

Perhaps the most unifying concept concerning the mode of action of these agents comes from studies of the GABA (gamma-aminobutyric acid) receptor–chloride ionophore interaction. It has long been recognized that the inhibitory action of many amino acid neurotransmitters (e.g., GABA) involves an increase in chloride conductance. Thus, GABA and other inhibitory amino acids actively promote an increase in chloride influx by activation of the chloride channel in the neuronal membrane. An increase in chloride conductance generally leads to membrane hyperpolarization and a reduction in the probability of action potential generation (i.e., inhibition of neuronal activity). With GABA in particular, the interaction appears to occur through specific membrane-associated GABA-A receptors that form an integral part of the chloride channel. The chloride channel appears to contain other regulatory sites with high affinity for such agents as the benzodiazepines, picrotoxin, alcohol, neuroactive steroids and the barbiturates.

Chloride movement across neuronal membranes can be regulated at this ion channel by at least three distinct molecular entities: (1) a GABA-binding site, (2) a benzodiazepine-binding site and (3) a picrotoxin-binding site. GABA and other agonists open the chloride channel (i.e., increase chloride conductance). Benzodiazepine-induced facilitation of GABA-mediated increases in chloride conduction are antagonized by pentylenetetrazole and possibly by the methylxanthines, while picrotoxin closes the chloride channel. Other agents that appear to promote chloride conductance through this channel include the barbiturates and alcohol.

The existence of the chloride channel as a major site of drug action permits a single molecular event (control of chloride ion movement) to be involved in the mechanism of action of a diverse class of agents.

Strychnine is an analeptic stimulant with a well defined mechanism of action that is unrelated to interaction with GABA receptors or other sites that modulate the activity of the chloride ionophore. Strychnine appears to be a specific competitive postsynaptic antagonist of glycine. Glycine, like GABA, is a known inhibitory transmitter in the mammalian CNS. Whereas GABA is likely to be more important in the brain, glycine is more important in the spinal cord. Glycine mediates inhibition of spinal cord neurons and is intimately involved in the regulation of spinal cord and brainstem reflexes.

## Pharmacokinetics

Most analeptic stimulants can be absorbed orally and have short durations of action. The pharmacological effect of most of these compounds is terminated through hepatic metabolism rather than renal excretion of unchanged drug.

## Clinical Uses

As indicated, most of the analeptic stimulants were used as pharmacological treatments for overdosage of CNS depressants.

Doxapram (Dopram) is sometimes used to counteract postanesthetic respiratory depression and as an aid in chronic obstructive pulmonary disease.

Pentylenetetrazole (Metrazol) was used experimentally on rare occasions to "activate" the electroencephalogram.

Strychnine is used almost exclusively in animal studies as a tool for studying CNS mechanisms because it is a relatively specific glycine antagonist.

### Adverse Effects

These agents produce convulsions that can be followed by coma and death. Convulsions produced by this class of agents (with the exception of strychnine) are usually tonic–clonic and are uncoordinated.

In some cases, the convulsions are preceded by marked stimulation of respiration, tachycardia and excessive pressor effects.

Under the influence of strychnine, all sensory stimuli produce exaggerated responses.

Diazepam and clonazepam appear to be moderately effective in preventing strychnine convulsions and either of these is the agent of choice.

Barbiturates are often used to treat overdoses of all of the analeptic stimulants.

## Psychomotor Stimulants

The Psychomotor Stimulants are shown Fig. 25-2.

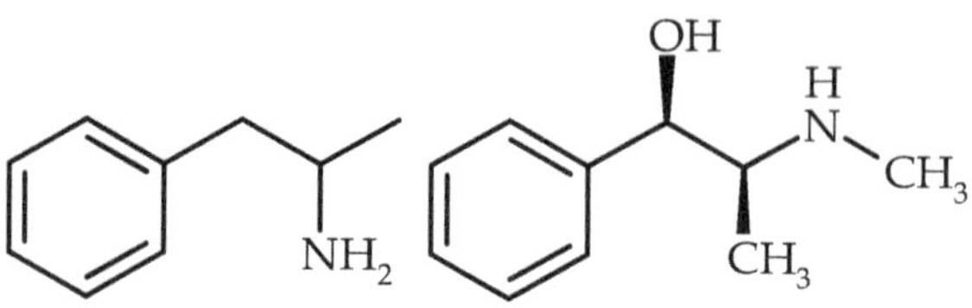


Amphetamine Ephedrine

**Fig 25-2:** Psychomotor stimulants

### Mechanism of Action

There is good evidence that the facilitation of peripheral sympathetic nervous system transmission produced by the amphetamines also occurs in the CNS. The possibility that amphetamines act indirectly (i.e., by releasing monoamines) at monoaminergic synapses in the brain and spinal cord seems likely. However, amphetamine has effects beyond displacement of catecholamines; these include inhibition of neuronal amine uptake, direct stimulation of dopamine and serotonin receptors, antagonism of catecholamine action at certain subtypes of adrenoceptors, and inhibition of monoamine oxidase.

## Pharmacokinetics

The primary important psychomotor stimulants are amphetamine (Adderall, Benzedrine, Dexedrine), methamphetamine (Desoxyn) and methylphenidate (Concerta, Ritalin, Metadate, Methylin). All of these compounds are well absorbed after oral administration, leaving injectable forms with few legitimate applications. Although several catabolic pathways metabolize the amphetamines, a considerable portion of untransformed drug is excreted in the urine. Thus, it is possible to ion-trap this weak organic base by acidifying the urine, thereby reducing its reabsorption in the renal tubules and enhancing its clearance.

## Clinical Uses

The therapeutic indications for the psychomotor stimulants are quite limited. They are beneficial in the treatment of the hyperkinetic syndrome (attention deficit hyperactivity disorder with minimal brain dysfunction).

This is generally a childhood disease characterized by hyperactivity, inability to concentrate, and impulsive behavior. Amphetamines and the more extensively used methylphenidate paradoxically are quite effective in calming a large proportion of children with this disorder. Pemoline (Cylert) is also used in the treatment of attention deficit disorder with hyperkinetic behavior.

Narcolepsy is another medically recognized indication for the use of the psychomotor stimulants. This disorder is characterized by sleep attacks, particularly during the day, sudden loss of muscle tone (cataplexy), sleep paralysis and vivid visual and auditory nightmares that may persist into the waking state. Drugs that influence the central action of adrenomimetic amines remarkably affect narcolepsy. Monoamine oxidase inhibitors (e.g., selegiline) and amphetamines are both quite effective in preventing sleep attacks and improving cataplexy.

Previously, another use of the amphetamines and other centrally acting adrenomimetics has been in the management of obesity and weight reduction. Although the amphetamines have a significant anorexic effect, tolerance to this action develops within a few weeks. In addition, insomnia restricted their use during the latter part of the day.

Fenfluramine (Pondimin) and phentermine (Adipex-P, Fastin) are anorexigenic drugs that produce depression of the CNS and at one time were used (Fen-phen) in the treatment of obesity. Sibutramine (Meridia) is also available for the treatment of obesity.

## Adverse Effects

The acute effects of psychomotor stimulant overdoses are related to their CNS stimulant properties and may include euphoria, dizziness, tremor, irritability and insomnia. At higher doses, convulsions and coma may ensue. These drugs are cardiac stimulants and may cause headache, palpitation, cardiac arrhythmias, anginal pain and either hypotension or hypertension. Dextro amphetamine produces somewhat less cardiac stimulation. Chronic intoxication, in addition to these symptoms, commonly results in weight loss and a psychotic reaction that is often diagnosed as schizophrenia. These agents produce addiction, including psychological dependence, tolerance, and physical dependence. Psychic dependence also has been seen following high doses of methylphenidate. The abstinence syndrome seen after abrupt discontinuation of amphetamines is neither as dramatic nor as predictable as that observed during withdrawal from the barbiturates or opioids. With the amphetamines, the abstinence syndrome consists primarily of prolonged sleep, fatigue, and extreme hunger (hyperphagia).

## Xanthines

The compounds known as xanthenes (Fig 25-3), methylxanthines, or xanthine derivatives constitute a particularly interesting class of drugs. The Xanthines are clearly CNS stimulants, although not all have this characteristic equally.

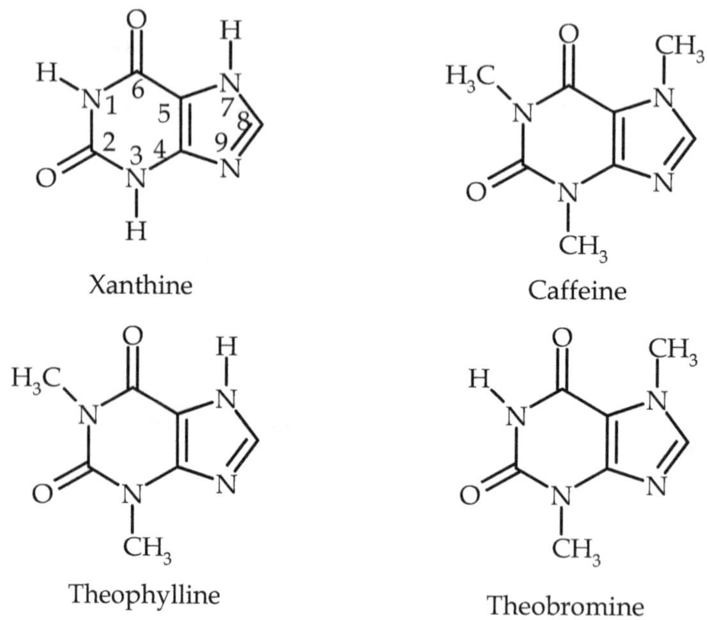


**Fig 25-3:** Xanthine Drugs

## Pharmacokinetics

Three xanthines are pharmacologically important: caffeine, theophylline and theobromine. All three alkaloids, which occur naturally in certain plants, are widely consumed in the form of beverages (infusions or decoctions) derived from these plants. Coffee primarily contains caffeine (about 100–150 mg per average cup); tea contains caffeine (30–40 mg per cup) and theophylline; and cocoa contains caffeine (15–18 mg per cup) and theobromine. Cola drinks also contain significant amounts of caffeine (about 40 mg/12 oz). The xanthines are readily absorbed by the oral and rectal routes. Although these agents can be administered by injection (aminophylline is a soluble salt of theophylline), intravascular administration is indicated only in status asthmaticus and apnea in premature infants. Intramuscular injection generally produces considerable pain at the injection site. The compounds are extensively metabolized, primarily to uric acid derivatives. There is, however, no indication that methylxanthines aggravate gout.

## Mechanism of Action

The mechanism of action of methylxanthine-induced stimulation of the CNS has been the subject of much investigation, and at least two other possible mechanisms of action of the methylxanthines have been suggested. The first derives from the ability of the methylxanthines to act as antagonists of the naturally occurring compound adenosine, a substance that can inhibit both neuronal activity and behavior through direct postsynaptic action on neurons and through indirect action involving presynaptic inhibition of neurotransmitter release. The A1 subtype of the purine receptors mediates these actions of adenosine. Thus, as an equilibrium-competitive antagonist of adenosine, the methylxanthines may produce excitation either by direct blockade of inhibitory effects of adenosine at the neuron or by an antagonism of the presynaptic inhibitory effect of adenosine on the release of an excitatory substance (e.g., acetylcholine). Another suggested mechanism of action involves the chloride channel. As discussed previously, the chloride channel is intimately associated with neuronal inhibition and its activity appears to be modulated at many different sites.

## Clinical Uses

### Central nervous system

Xanthines, primarily as the intramuscularly administered combination of caffeine and sodium benzoate, have been used in the treatment of CNS depressant overdosage. Black coffee has been used to physiologically antagonize alcohol intoxication, although many physicians believe that this ineffective therapy simply produces a wide-awake drunk.

### Diuresis

All the xnthines, but especially theophylline, are capable of producing some degree of diuresis in humans.

### Bronchial asthma

Theophylline is frequently used as a bronchodilator in the treatment of asthma. Caffeine as the citrate salt (Cafcit) is used for the short-term management of apnea in premature infants (28–33 weeks of gestational age).

### Cardiac uses

Theophylline, given as the soluble ethylenediamine salt aminophylline, offers some help in relieving the paroxysmal dyspnea that is often associated with left heart failure. A major portion of its efficacy may be due to the relief of bronchospasm secondary to pulmonary vascular congestion. Theophylline increases myocardial contractile force and has occasionally been used in the treatment of refractory forms of congestive heart failure.

### Miscellaneous uses

Xanthines (usually caffeine) are frequently combined with aspirin in the treatment of headaches. In combination with an ergot derivative, Methylxanthines have been used to treat migraine. These effects are likely due to their ability to produce vasoconstriction of cerebral blood vessels. Aminophylline is useful in the relief of pain due to acute biliary colic.

## Adverse Effects

Toxicity associated with the methylxanthines usually takes the form of nervousness, insomnia, and in severe cases, delirium. Cardiovascular stimulation is seen as tachycardia and extrasystoles. Excessive respiratory stimulation may occur and diuresis may be prominent. The intravenous administration of aminophylline (or theophylline) may present some problems if the drug is given too rapidly. In such cases, severe headache, hypotension and palpitation accompany drug administration. Subsequently the patient may show signs of excessive CNS stimulation, shock and even death.

## Abuse of Xanthines

The use of some xanthine-containing beverages is customary in most cultures and moderate use of such beverages does not appear to cause problems in most people. There is little question, however, that such use is habituating. For example, it has been observed that chronic coffee drinkers who suddenly abstain frequently have headaches and a general feeling of fatigue that may last for several days. Although it has not been established that these symptoms constitute any kind of abstinence syndrome, it remains a possibility. There is no good evidence for the development of tolerance to the CNS stimulant effects of caffeine.

## Drug Interactions

An interaction of potential clinical significance involves the xanthines and the coumarin anticoagulants. Xanthines by themselves shorten clotting time by increasing tissue prothrombin and factor V and in this regard may be expected to antagonize the effectiveness of oral anticoagulants. However, the usual therapeutic doses of xanthine cause no signficant effect on the patient's response to oral anticoagulants.

## References

Daval J-l, Nehling A, and Nicholas F (1991). Physiological and pharmacological properties of adenosine: Therapeutic implications. *life sci* **49:** 1435-1453.

Linden J. Structure and function of A1 adenoreceptors. *FASEB J* **5:** 2668-2676.

Seighart W (1995). Structure and pharmacology of gamma aminobutyric acid a receptor subtypes. *Pharmacol rev* **47:** 181-234.

CHAPTER

# Drug Dependence and Drug Abuse 26

**Drug Dependence:** It is a State when drug-taking becomes compulsive, taking precedence over other needs. Synonym - substance dependence

**Drug Addiction:** Is not clearly defined but implies a physical dependence, however, sometimes it is used as a synonym to drug (substance) dependence

**Drug Abuse:** More general term, includes recurrent use of any illegal/harmful substance, e.g., in sport

**Tolerance:** The decrease in a pharmacological effect on repeated administration of the drug imply the need to increase the dose to reach the pharmacological effect of the same intensity.

**Withdrawal (Syn. Abstinence) Syndrome:** Adverse effects, both psychological and physical, of stopping taking a drug. Distinguish commonly observed rebound phenomenon from the true dependence.

**Rewarding Effect:** Important and common feature of psychoactive addictive substances.

The phrases substance abuse and drug abuse are often applied to the use of an illegal or illicit chemical substance (e.g., LSD, heroin). However, these terms may be applied when a legally obtainable medication is used excessively and for unintended purposes or is diverted to someone else's use. Also, some legal substances (e.g., nicotine, alcohol) are used to the detriment of the individual. Inappropriate use, or abuse, is the excessive self-administration of any substance for nonmedical purposes. An additional aspect of drug abuse is the production of hazardous or harmful effects to the individual and/or to society. The etiology of substance abuse is a complicated phenomenon that is sometimes a function of genetics, socioeconomic status, education, peer pressure, thrill seeking, or experimenting behavior and sometimes an inappropriate attempt at self-medication to treat a real or perceived disease state. It is also clear that drug abuse is a function of the pharmacology of each drug. Almost all abused substances produce an effect on the brain that is perceived as desirable and will initiate drug-seeking behavior.

The professionals in the drug abuse field have such diverse backgrounds that adopting a common terminology for terms such as addiction and dependence has been difficult. These terms are best defined in the context of the pattern and consequences of drug use. Regardless of the characteristics of the drug-induced intoxication, the properties of the drug that are responsible for drug-seeking behavior are often referred to as the reinforcing properties. These drugs produce effects that are so desirable that the user is compelled to obtain more of the drug. Recurrent abuse of a drug may properly be termed an addiction when the individual becomes so obsessed with constantly obtaining and using a drug that it becomes a primary goal and disrupts the ability to function in family, social or career settings. Typically, especially during the initial stages of drug addiction, the primary reinforcing property is the production of euphoria, a term indicating anything from happiness or pleasantness to an excitement resembling sexual orgasm. Euphoria is considered to be a positive reinforcing property, one that the individual would desire or seek. The evaluation of drugs for their reinforcing properties is an assessment of their abuse potential. The craving or desire to obtain additional drug, especially when it is not available, was at one time termed psychological addiction or psychological dependence, though today these terms are not necessarily descriptive or specific. The term addiction should be used to describe recurrent drug abuse, while the term dependence refers to another state, a function of drug use, not drug craving. Addiction has also been used to describe recurrent substance abuse by individuals who realize it is harmful to their health but cannot fulfill their desire to stop, such as with tobacco.

Chronic use of a drug over a long period sometimes produces a state of tolerance that may be classified as pharmacokinetic, pharmacodynamic or behavioral. The degree of tolerance is generally proportional to the drug dose and the duration of use. In some cases, partial or complete tolerance to the euphoric effect of the drug develops. However, tolerance to many of the other acute effects also generally develops. Termination of drug abuse may create a condition of drug abstinence, which coincides with the emergence of a measurable physical syndrome. This abstinence syndrome is an indication of dependence, is often referred to as drug withdrawal and was once termed physical dependence to distinguish it from psychological dependence. It is assumed that adaptation, or tolerance, to repeated administration of drug is responsible for physical dependence. Generally, the severity of the abstinence syndrome or level of dependence is proportional to the degree of tolerance attained. However, the relationship between tolerance and dependence has not been fully resolved; tolerance and dependence can occur separately. Epidemiological studies indicate that most individuals who abuse any one drug often also abuse, or co-abuse, other drugs during the same period. Polydrug abuse complicates conclusions drawn from epidemiological and clinical studies. One reason for co-abuse of drugs relates to similarities in pharmacological effects. In these cases, once tolerance to the primary drug develops, the individual also has cross-tolerance to related classes of drugs. For example, the development of tolerance to one CNS depressant, such as barbiturates, anxiolytic agents or alcohol, simultaneously produces some degree of tolerance to the other depressants. Users may attempt to ameliorate selected drug effects by coabuse of drugs with opposite pharmacological profiles. Drugs of abuse are derived from numerous chemical classes, and therefore, it is not surprising that they produce distinctive pharmacological effects.

## Opioids

For centuries opium was used for both medicinal and recreational purposes. Derived from the poppy *Papaver somniferum*, it contains numerous opiates, the primary one of which is morphine. The term opiate has largely been replaced by opioid, which represents all compounds with morphine like activity and includes morphine, morphine derivatives and peptides. These drugs are frequently referred to as narcotics, a Greek term for stupor, which is scientifically obsolete. Even in its early history, opium presented a problem when it was smoked or taken orally. The introduction of the hypodermic needle and syringe, however, drastically enhanced the euphoric properties of opioids and thereby altered their abuse liability. In addition, the synthesis of heroin resulted in an opioid that was more potent than morphine and ideally suited for intravenous administration.

### Extent and Pattern of Abuse

The abuse of opioids falls into two distinct categories of users, those who initiate use solely for recreational purposes and those who become physically dependent as a result of being treated medically with opioids. The primary use of opioids is for the control of moderate to severe pain. However, few patients receiving opioids for pain management become dependent. Furthermore, dependence is less likely if opioids are used judiciously. Acute pain can be controlled with opioids such as hydromorphone or oxycodone, which have a rapid onset and short duration of action. In contrast, chronic pain is better treated with opioids such as methadone or morphine (e.g., Duramorph, MS Contin), which are less likely to produce euphoria because of their slow onset of action. Dependence in patients is most likely to occur in those with pain of unexplained or poorly defined etiology. Avoiding long-term use of opioids in this population reduces the risk of developing dependence. Development of dependence should not be a consideration in the management of terminal cancer pain. The primary illicit opioid is heroin (diacetyl-morphine),which was once used almost exclusively by the intravenous route. In recent years, the purity of street heroin has risen to levels that allow it to be smoked or snorted.

## Pharmacological Aspects

First-time users frequently experience unpleasant, or dysphoric, effects that may include nausea and vomiting. The frequent user experiences a rush, or warm flushing feeling, in the skin and lower extremities that is often equated with sexual orgasm. This intense euphoria lasts for one to several minutes and is followed by sedation, relaxation and tranquility lasting up to an hour. This latter period is sometimes called being on the nod. All effects have largely dissipated within 3 to 5 hours, which requires the user to inject at frequent intervals. Pharmacokinetics plays a very important role in the manner in which opioids are abused. Morphine and many of its derivatives are slowly and erratically absorbed after oral administration, which makes this route suitable for long-term management of pain but not for producing euphoria. In addition, opioids undergo considerable first-pass metabolism, which accounts for their low potency after oral administration. Heroin is more potent than morphine, although its effects arise primarily from metabolism to morphine. The potency difference is attributed to heroin's greater membrane permeability and resultant increased absorption into the brain.

## Tolerance and Dependence

Tolerance to the unpleasant effects experienced by some individuals at the initiation of opioid use develops readily. Significant tolerance also occurs to the analgesic, respiratory depressant, emetic and euphoric effects, although it develops somewhat more slowly to respiratory depression. Little tolerance to the GI effects and miosis develops. Cross-tolerance occurs with all known opioid analgesics. Opioid tolerance develops more quickly and to a greater extent than it does for most other drugs of abuse. The lethal opioid dose can be 20-fold higher in a tolerant individual than in a neophyte. Tolerance develops within a few days if potent opioids are given at frequent intervals, such as every 4 to 6 hours. Development of tolerance requires several weeks if the opioid is given only twice a day. The continued use of opioids results in the development of physical dependence, as demonstrated by the appearance of a characteristic abstinence syndrome upon interruption or cessation of use. The symptoms of withdrawal include hyperactivity, anxiety, restlessness, yawning, diarrhea, vomiting, chills, fever, lacrimation and runny nose. Piloerection (gooseflesh or cold turkey), mydriasis, increased blood pressure and heart rate and hyperpyrexia may be observed. Tremors, abdominal cramps and muscle and joint pains may be present. Drug craving is an important feature of opioid withdrawal. In contrast to some other drugs of abuse, withdrawal is not life threatening.

## Treatment of Opioid Dependence

Although the ultimate goal of treatment program is to achieve drug-free status as quickly as possible, it is rarely achieved without pharmacotherapy. The most commonly used strategy is to switch the patient from a short-acting opioid, such as heroin, to a long-acting agonist, such as methadone. It is easier to withdraw patients from methadone because it produces a protracted withdrawal syndrome that is less intense than that produced by heroin. Opioid antagonists, such as naltrexone, provide another treatment option in that addicts who are completely withdrawn from an opioid can be maintained on antagonists that will block the pleasurable effects of subsequent injections of heroin. Mixed opioid agonist- antagonists show promise in that they have sufficient agonist effects to reduce craving while at the same time exhibiting antagonist properties.

## Stimulants

A variety of drugs in distinct pharmacological and chemical classes can be considered under the broad classification as stimulants. Xanthines and methylxanthines constitute a weak class of stimulants that includes caffeine, theophylline (aminophylline) and theobromine. Caffeine is freely available in coffee, colas and certain over-the-counter pills. A low degree of tolerance develops to some of their effects and a mild withdrawal syndrome is observed following immediate cessation of their repeated use. The primary class of stimulants for which there is a tremendous addiction problem is the sympathomimetic stimulants, which include cocaine, amphetamine, methamphetamine (Desoxyn), methylphenidate (Ritalin) and phenmetrazine.

### Extent and Pattern of Abuse

Sympathomimetic stimulant drugs have very high abuse potential. They are typically used repeatedly for a short period during which time the user escalates the dose to greater and greater levels to attain the desired degree of euphoria. Extended uninterrupted use of stimulants for 24 to 72 hours is often referred to as a run and usually ends in a crash (24–36 hours of sleep) once the individual is exhausted physically. Besides illicit sources of stimulants, approximately 5 billion doses of these drugs are prescribed per year and there appears to be a significant degree of abuse *via* prescription diversion. While some stimulants, such as amphetamine and methylphenidate, are taken orally, others are either volatilized for inhalation or snorted as the solid (nasal insufflation). It is necessary to convert cocaine and methamphetamine to their free base so that they can be volatilized. Methamphetamine and cocaine are also abused *via* the intravenous route.

### Pharmacological Aspects

Most of the sympathomimetic stimulants exhibit similar pharmacological properties, differing primarily in the magnitude of their effects. Acute drug administration produces feelings of euphoria, elation and alertness. Intravenous injections of cocaine and amphetamine can produce a very intense rush of sensations that resemble sexual orgasm. At small doses cognition increases and mood is elevated. As the dose of drug escalates during a run, the overall activity of the individual changes from task performance to one generally characterized by stereotypical movements. The person starts performing certain behaviors repeatedly. Some grind or gnash their teeth. Many continuously touch or pick at their face or extremities. At this stage the individual becomes suspicious and may develop anxiety or paranoia. Acute toxic paranoid psychosis can develop, but it usually requires a longer period of abuse than a single acute session. Besides stimulating the CNS, these drugs activate the autonomic nervous system. Individuals have tachycardia, hypertension and possibly arrhythmias. Autonomic hyperactivity is also expressed as hyperthermia and mydriasis. More serious effects include the possibility of myocardial infarction, cerebrovascular hemorrhage, seizure and death.

### Mechanism of Action

In brief, the most commonly abused of these drugs, such as cocaine, work primarily as indirect agonists of the catecholamine neuro-transmitter systems *via* inhibitory actions upon the transmitter reuptake system. Considerable evidence supports a role for dopamine in mediating the rewarding effects of cocaine. There is also evidence that blockade of serotonin uptake may contribute to cocaine's actions.

## Tolerance and Dependence

Tolerance to stimulants develops fairly rapidly, even in the therapeutic dose range. It is the rapid development of tolerance that leads to the escalation of dose during drug abuse runs.

## Other Adverse Effects of Chronic Abuse

Chronic stimulant abuse alters the personality of the abuser. These and related changes are the result of neurotoxicity and are not characterized as either acute drug effects or withdrawal signs. Individuals have delusions of being pursued or persecuted and therefore become suspicious and paranoid. They become self-occupied and hostile toward others. Long-term abuse can produce toxic psychosis that closely resembles schizophrenia and must be treated with neuroleptic drugs (haloperidol, chlorpromazine). This psychosis can develop even within 1 to 2 weeks if the person is on a run of very high doses of stimulants.

## Nicotine

### Pharmacological actions

The behavioral effects of nicotine have been defined as both stimulant and depressant, effects that are influenced by the present mental status and expectations of the smoker. Smokers may feel alert and relaxed. Nicotine produces myriad effects on the central nervous system (CNS), almost all of which appear to be mediated through nicotinic receptors. Additionally, nicotine influences multiple neuronal systems. One of its most prominent effects is stimulated release of dopamine, particularly in the nucleus accumbens, which is a major component of the reward system. Nicotine also stimulates the release of endogenous opioids and glucocorticoids.

### Tolerance and Dependence

Tolerance to nicotine's effects develops rapidly and most likely involves multiple processes, although the pattern and extent of tolerance development is not identical for all of nicotine's effects. It has been proposed that rapid tolerance or desensitization occurs to the behavioral or reinforcing effects of nicotine. These effects are of such a short duration that a smoker continually cycles between a sensitized and desensitized state. This notion is consistent with the fact that drugs with high abuse liability have a rapid onset and short duration of action. Regardless of the mechanism of tolerance, nicotine is a highly addicting drug. Even though most individuals are unaware of nicotine's reinforcing properties when smoking, many individuals feel intense, long-lasting craving when attempting to stop. Although most smokers wish to quit, only about one-third attempt to do so each year.

# Sedative–Hypnotics

The CNS depressants include barbiturates, nonbarbiturate sedatives and the benzodiazepines. As the medical use of barbiturates decreased, primarily because of their high addiction liability and the danger of acute lethality, the use of the benzodiazepine anxiolytics increased. The most commonly abused barbiturates are secobarbital, pentobarbital and amobarbital. Phenobarbital is not generally abused, because of its slow onset of action. The most commonly abused anxiolytics include diazepam, chlordiazepoxide, midazolam, lorazepam and flurazepam. These drugs are readily attainable from illicit sources.Abused nonbarbiturate sedatives include glutethimide and meprobamate.

## Pharmacological Aspects

CNS depressants, including barbiturate, benzodiazepine, and ethanol, produce a similar intoxication. These drugs are abused for their euphoric effects and as a means to reduce anxiety and limit insomnia. As the dose of depressant increases, along with the degree of intoxication, the effects progress from anxiety reduction and muscle relaxation to motor impairment and unconsciousness. The difference between the classes of drugs is primarily dose responsiveness. Intoxication progresses from mild to severe over a relatively narrow dose range in the case of the barbiturates.

The benzodiazepine dose–response curve is such that more increase in dosage is necessary to make such a transition. Thus, the benzodiazepines are a safer class of depressant drugs. The acute effects of depressants can include euphoria, anxiety reduction, anticonvulsant activity, sedation, ataxia, motor incoordination, impaired judgment, anesthesia, coma and respiratory depression resulting in death. The benzodiazepines are rarely involved in lethality, but all CNS depressants enhance the effects of other depressant drugs. The physiological effects of high-dose depressants include miosis, shallow respiration and reduction in reflex responses.

### Tolerance and Dependence

Tolerance to many of the effects of the depressants develops. Unlike opioids, barbiturate and benzodiazepine tolerance develops slowly. Also, tolerance is incomplete in some instances or does not influence some pharmacological effects. One such exception is the lack of tolerance to barbiturate lethality. The lethal dose in a tolerant individual is not much different from that of the general population. Cross-tolerance develops to some degree between the depressant classes of drugs. Dependence on benzodiazepines, as evidenced by a withdrawal syndrome, can develop to large doses of drugs. Mild dependence is produced at therapeutic doses. Individuals report some craving for drug during withdrawal from benzodiazepines, but the level is not as great as among those who abuse alcohol. Once the withdrawal syndrome has dissipated, the abusers of benzodiazepines are not as likely to resume drug consumption as are alcoholics. Withdrawal signs appear to be more likely following chronic exposure to short acting benzodiazepines, such as alprazolam (half-life of less than 15 hours) or lorazepam than long-acting drugs. Despite gradual dose reduction, individuals may have anxiety attacks, confusion, agitation, restlessness, sweating, clouded sensorium, heightened sensory perception, perceptual disturbances, sleep disruption, muscle cramps, muscle twitches, and tremors; 2% of addicts may have a seizure during withdrawal. Withdrawal signs peak the second day after abrupt withdrawal and last for at least 5 to 7 days. Withdrawal symptoms following long-acting benzodiazepines (diazepam, clorazepate) peak during the second week of abstinence. In contrast to alcohol and the barbiturate sedatives, withdrawal from benzodiazepines is not life threatening.

## Ethanol

Ethanol is the most widely abused drug in the world. There are more than 10 million alcoholics in the United States alone. Excessive consumption of alcoholic beverages has been linked to as many as half of all traffic accidents, two-thirds of homicides, three-fourths of suicides and it is a significant factor in other crimes, in family problems and in personal and industrial accidents. The annual cost to the American economy has been estimated to exceed $100 billion in lost productivity, medical care, and property damage. Alcoholism has been difficult to define because of its complex nature. A person is generally considered an alcoholic, however, when his or her lifestyle is dominated by the procurement and consumption of alcoholic beverages and when this behavior interferes with personal, professional, social or family relations. A light drinker generally is defined as one who consumes an average of one drink or less per day, usually with the evening meal; a moderate drinker is one who has approximately three drinks per day; and a heavy drinker is one who has five or more drinks per day (or in the case of binge drinkers, at least once per week with five or more drinks on each occasion).

### Chemistry

Ethanol (ethyl alcohol, alcohol) is a simple organic molecule composed of a single hydroxyl group and a short two-carbon aliphatic chain, $CH_3CH_2OH$. The hydroxyl and ethyl moieties confer both hydrophilic and lipophilic properties on the molecule. Therefore, ethanol is an amphophile, a property important to its pharmacological activity.

## Absorption, Distribution, Metabolism and Excretion

After oral administration, ethanol is almost completely absorbed throughout the gastrointestinal tract. The rate of absorption is largely determined by the quantity consumed, the concentration in the beverage, the rate of consumption and the composition of the gastric contents. Eating food before or during drinking retards absorption, especially if the food has a high lipid content. After absorption, ethanol is distributed throughout body water. In organs with high blood flow, such as the brain, liver, lungs and kidney, equilibrium occurs rapidly. Conversely, in organs with low blood flow, such as muscle, equilibrium occurs more slowly. Ethanol readily passes through the blood-placental barrier into the fetal circulation. Although the concentration of ethanol in the blood can be quite predictable, measurements of blood ethanol, especially when the concentrations are rising, may lead to erroneous conclusions, since the values obtained can underestimate the concentration of ethanol in the brain. This fact can confound legal proceedings in drunk-driving cases where blood ethanol concentrations are considered an accurate and legally acceptable determinant of the amount of ethanol consumed. Ethanol is metabolized primarily in the liver by at least two enzyme systems. The best-studied and most important enzyme is zinc dependent: alcohol dehydrogenase. The rate of metabolism catalyzed by alcohol dehydrogenase is generally linear with time except at low ethanol concentrations and is relatively independent of the ethanol concentration (i.e., zero-order kinetics). In adults, ethanol is metabolized at about 10 to 15 ml/hour. Since metabolism of ethanol is slow, ingestion must be controlled to prevent accumulation and intoxication. There is little evidence that chronic ingestion of ethanol leads to a significant induction of alcohol dehydrogenase, even in heavy drinkers. Some populations, most notably East Asians, exhibit an unusual response after drinking ethanol. The symptoms include facial flushing, vasodilation, and tachycardia. These individuals apparently have a genetic deficiency of the enzyme aldehyde dehydrogenase, which leads to an accumulation of acetaldehyde even after they drink relatively small amounts of ethanol. If drugs such as metronidazole, griseofulvin, quinacrine, the hypoglycemic sulfonylureas, phenothiazines and phenylbutazone are coadministered with ethanol, a similar accumulation of acetaldehyde may occur. In addition to alcohol dehydrogenase, ethanol can be oxidized to acetaldehyde by the microsomal mixed function oxidase system (cytochrome P450 2EI). Although this microsomal ethanol-oxidizing system probably has minor importance in the metabolism of ethanol in humans, it may be involved in some of the reported interactions between ethanol and other drugs that are also metabolized by this system. Microsomal mixed-function oxidases may be induced by chronic ethanol ingestion. Because ethanol is metabolized in the liver, it can interfere with the metabolism of other drugs by blocking microsomal hydroxylation and demethylation. Drug classes whose metabolism is most affected include the barbiturates, coumarins, and anticonvulsants, such as phenytoin.Liver damage resulting from chronic abuse of ethanol can impair metabolism of a variety of drugs. Normally, 90 to 98% of an ingested dose of ethanol is metabolized by the liver. Most of the remaining 2 to 10% is excreted unchanged in the urine and expired air. The ethanol content in the urine is normally about 130% of the blood concentration and is quite constant; the expired air contains about 0.05% of the blood ethanol level, a concentration that also is remarkably consistent.

## Mechanism of Action

A great deal of attention has been focused on a class of proteins termed the ligand-gated ion channels as being important to the mechanism of action of alcohol. These integral membrane proteins function as gates or pores that allow the passage of certain ions into and out of neurons upon binding of the appropriate neurotransmitter. This flux of ions largely determines the degree of neuronal activity. Two distinct types of ligand-gated ion channels are particularly sensitive to concentrations of alcohol that produce intoxication and sedation. These are the Gamma-aminobutyric acid (GABA) chloride ionophore and the N-methyl-D-aspartate (NMDA) subtype of glutamate receptor. The GABA–chloride ion channel reduces neuronal activity by hyperpolarizing the neurons, while activation of the NMDA receptor causes neuronal depolarization or excitation. Alcohol has been shown to increase chloride flux through the GABA-A receptor and reduce calcium flux through the NMDA receptor. These actions result in powerful suppression of nerve cell activity, which is consistent with the depressant actions of alcohol in the brain.

## Pharmacological Actions on Central Nervous System

Alcohol is primarily a CNS depressant and the degree of depression is directly proportional to the quantity of ethanol consumed. However, behavioral stimulation can be found after ingestion of small amounts of ethanol. This stimulation is expressed as decreased social and psychological inhibition and is most likely the result of a depression of inhibitory pathways in the brain with release of cortical activity. The behavioral and physiological effects are associated with different blood ethanol concentrations. As the blood ethanol concentration begins to increase, behavioral activation, characterized by euphoria, talkativeness, aggressiveness and loss of behavioral control, generally precedes the overt CNS depression induced by ethanol. At progressively higher blood ethanol concentrations, the stage of relaxation is transformed into decreased social inhibitions, slurred speech, ataxia, decreased mental acuity, decreased reflexive responses, coma and, finally, death resulting from respiratory arrest. In moderation, however, there is no evidence that the judicious use of small amounts of alcoholic beverages (e.g., a glass of wine with meals) is permanently harmful.

## Other Body Systems

In general, ethanol in low to moderate amounts, is relatively benign to most body systems. A moderate amount of ethanol causes peripheral vasodilation, especially of cutaneous vessels and stimulates the secretion of salivary and gastric fluids; the latter action may aid digestion. On the other hand, ethanol consumption in high concentrations, as found in undiluted spirits, can induce hemorrhagic lesions in the duodenum, inhibit intestinal brush border enzymes, inhibit the uptake of amino acids and limit the absorption of vitamins and minerals. In addition, ethanol can reduce blood testosterone levels, resulting in sexual dysfunction. Ethanol is a diuretic. This effect may be caused by its ability to inhibit secretion of antidiuretic hormone from the posterior pituitary, which leads to a reduction in renal tubular water reabsorption. The large amount of fluid normally consumed with ethanol also contributes to increased urine production.

## Adverse Effects

### Acute ethanol intoxication and hangover

Ethanol intoxication is probably the best-known form of drug toxicity. Intoxicated individuals are a threat to themselves and others, particularly if they attempt to drive or operate machinery. Although death can result from ethanol overdose, usually the patient lapses into a coma before ingesting lethal quantities. Ethanol intoxication is sometimes mistakenly diagnosed as diabetic coma, schizophrenia, overdosage of other CNS depressant drugs, or skull fracture. An additional feature commonly associated with excessive ethanol consumption is difficulty in regulating body temperature. Hypothermia frequently results, with body temperature falling toward that of the ambient environment. This problem can be particularly severe in the elderly, who normally have difficulty regulating their body temperature. One of the consequences of ethanol intoxication is the hangover, a condition characterized by headache, nausea, sweating and tremor. Although unpleasant, a hangover is not dangerous, even though the person having one may feel otherwise.

## Treatment for Acute Intoxication

Generally, no treatment is required for acute ethanol intoxication. Allowing the individual to sleep off the effects of ethanol ingestion is the usual procedure. Hangovers are treated similarly; that is, no effective remedy exists for a hangover, except for controlling the amount of ethanol consumed. Sometimes ethanol overdose is a medical emergency. For example, prompt treatment is required if the patient is in danger of dying of respiratory arrest, is comatose, has dilated pupils, is hypothermic, or displays tachycardia.Treatment for severe ethanol overdose is generally supportive. Increased intracranial pressure can be relieved by intravenous administration of hypertonic mannitol. Hemodialysis can accelerate the removal of ethanol from the body. Stimulants of ethanol metabolism, such as fructose, are not sufficiently effective and use of analeptics is not recommended because of the possibility of precipitating convulsions.

## Alcoholism

Alcoholism is among the major health problems in most countries. Dependence on ethanol, as with other addictive drugs, is expressed as drug-seeking behavior and is abrupt cessation of drinking. The ethanol withdrawal syndrome is characterized by tremors, seizures, hyper-thermia, hallucinations and autonomic hyperactivity. A number of organs are affected adversely by chronic ethanol use, the result of a direct cytotoxic action. Hepatic fatty infiltration and cirrhosis are common in alcoholics; cancer may develop in advanced stages of hepatic disease. Ethanol produces a number of depressant effects on the myocardium. Atrial arrhythmias and ventricular tachycardia may arise from chronic ethanol use. A serious clinical entity, alcoholic cardiomyopathy, has also been described. A high rate of ethanol consumption can lead to inhibition of gastric secretion and irritation of the gastric mucosa. Ethanol irritates the entire gastrointestinal tract, which may lead to constipation and diminished absorption of nutrients. Other pathological effects include pancreatitis and peripheral neuropathy. Severe gonadal failure is often found in both men and women, accompanied by low blood levels of sex hormones.

A variety of pathological problems involving the CNS have been described in chronic alcoholics, the main ones being Wernicke's encephalopathy and Korsakoff's psychosis. Brain damage from chronic ethanol consumption can be especially severe in the elderly and may accelerate aging. Ethanol readily passes across the placenta and into the fetal circulation. The fetal alcohol syndrome has three primary features: microcephaly, prenatal growth deficiency and short palpebral fissures. Other characteristics include postnatal growth deficiency, fine motor dysfunction, cardiac defects and anomalies of the external genitalia and inner ear. A definite risk of producing fetal abnormalities occurs when ethanol consumption by the mother exceeds 3 oz daily, the equivalent of about six drinks.

### Treatment for alcoholism

The immediate concern in the treatment of alcoholics is detoxification and management of the ethanol withdrawal syndrome. Once the patient is detoxified, long term treatment requires complete abstinence, psychiatric treatment, family involvement and frequently support from lay organizations such as Alcoholics Anonymous. One pharmacological approach is aversion therapy using drugs such as disulfiram to associate drinking ethanol with unpleasant consequences. If ethanol is taken after disulfiram administration, blood acetaldehyde concen-trations increase 5 to 10 times, resulting in vasodilation, pulsating headache, nausea, vomiting, severe thirst, respiratory difficulties, chest pains, orthostatic hypotension, syncope, and blurred vision. In certain cases, marked respiratory depression, cardiac arrhythmias, cardiovascular collapse, myocardial infarction, acute congestive heart failure, unconsciousness, convulsions and sudden death have been discuss about alcohol withdrawl syndrome reported. Despite these potentially severe consequences, disulfiram is prescribed for some alcoholic patients. Another pharmacological approach is the use of anticraving drugs, for example serotonin uptake inhibitors, dopaminergic agonists and opioid antagonists. The only treatment that has shown considerable promise is one that uses the opioid antagonist naltrexone.

## Marijuana

The hemp plant, or cannabis (*Cannabis sativa*), continues to be the most frequently abused illicit substance in America. The dried leaves and flowering tops of the plant are referred to as marijuana and it is typically smoked in pipes or rolled as cigarettes. It also may be consumed in baked goods. Hashish is a solid black resinous material obtained from the leaves of the plant and is usually smoked in a pipe.

### Chemistry

The major psychoactive constituent in marijuana use is tetrahydrocannabinol (THC), the prototypical cannabinoid. Although marijuana contains a large number of cannabinoids, they lack behavioral activity with the exception of cannabinol, which is approximately onetenth as potent as THC. The THC content in hashish is more than double that in marijuana.

### Pharmacokinetic Aspects

THC is readily absorbed when marijuana is smoked. Pharmacological effects are produced rapidly and generally peak within 30 minutes of the onset of smoking. The dynamics of smoking (number of puffs, spacing, hold time and lung capacity) substantially influence how much drug is absorbed. Although oral ingestion of marijuana produces similar pharmacological effects, 9-THC is absorbed more slowly than by smoking. Impairment on various performance measures related to driving skills has been demonstrated immediately following marijuana smoking and up to 24 hours thereafter. Generally, behavioral and physiological effects return to baseline levels 4 to 6 hours after usage. Blood concentrations of 9-THC peak prior to drug-induced effects. This time discordance between blood concentrations of 9-THC and effects has made it difficult to establish a meaningful relationship between blood concentrations and effects. 9-THC is rapidly distributed to all tissues despite being tightly bound by plasma proteins. 9-THC is a highly lipophilic substance and so accumulates in tissue high in lipid content. Traces of 9-THC have been found in adipose tissue more than 30 days after the subject smoked a single joint. The terminal half-life of 9-THC in plasma ranges from 18 hours to 4 days.

### Mechanism of Action

A cannabinoid receptor identified in the brain of several species, including humans, is termed CB1. It is one of the most abundant receptors in the CNS and its distribution within the brain reflects the pharmacological effects produced by 9-THC. High receptor densities in the extrapyramidal motor system and the cerebellum are consistent with the actions of cannabinoids on many forms of movement. The effects of cannabinoids on cognition and memory may be due to the relatively dense receptor populations in the hippocampus and cortex. The presence of cannabinoid receptors in the ventromedial striatum and nucleus accumbens suggests an association with dopamine neurons hypothesized to mediate brain reward.

### Pharmacological Actions on Central Nervous System

Marijuana produces a distinctive behavioral syndrome that is easily distinguished from that of most other drugs. The most prominent feature is the initial period of euphoria, or high, which has been described as a sense of well-being and happiness. Euphoria is frequently followed by a period of drowsiness or sedation. Perception of time is altered, along with distortions in both hearing and vision. However, illusions and hallucinations occur infrequently. The subjective effects also include dissociation of ideas. The subjective effects of marijuana vary from individual to individual as a function of dose, route of administration, the experience and expectation of the subjects and individual vulnerability to certain psychoactive substances. Motor coordination also may decrease, especially in situations requiring highly complex motor skills, such as flying an airplane and driving an automobile. Increased appetite is frequently attributed to smoking marijuana. Cannabinoids are effective antiemetics, particularly in treating emesis arising during chemotherapy. 9-THC has been reported to be as effective as codeine as an analgesic, although pronounced behavioral effects occur with analgesic doses.

## Other Organ Systems

The most consistent pharmacological effect produced by marijuana is tachycardia, which is closely associated with the blood levels of 9-THC. There is relatively little effect on blood pressure unless large quantities of marijuana are smoked, in which case there can be marked orthostatic hypotension. Cannabinoids are also vasodilatory, which results in the characteristic conjunctival reddening following marijuana smoking. They also reduce intraocular pressure and are capable of producing bronchodilation.

## Adverse Effects

Marijuana is unique among drugs of abuse in that there have been no credible reports of fatal overdose. The most prominent effect of acute marijuana use is intoxication, which can impair the cognitive and motor skills needed to complete complex tasks. Anxiety and panic reactions are occasionally reported in inexperienced users or following use of large quantities of marijuana. 9-THC causes its greatest effects on short-term memory, as measured in free-recall tasks. Marijuana does not affect the retrieval of previously learned facts. In contrast to alcohol, there is no residual hangover from a single use of high quantities of marijuana. Heavy marijuana smoking produces bronchitis, and some individuals have evidence of precancerous lung conditions. However, definitive evidence of the relationship between marijuana smoking and the incidence of lung cancer is lacking. Tolerance develops to many of 9-THC's effects in heavy marijuana users. Although chronic cannabis use does not result in severe withdrawal symptoms, numerous reports attest to development of dependence in subjects taking high doses of THC for several weeks. The most prominent symptoms were irritability and restlessness; others included insomnia, anorexia, increased sweating and mild nausea. Cessation of mild or moderate use of marijuana, however, does not produce a withdrawal syndrome.

# Hallucinogens

The term hallucinogen is often used to describe a drug that produces a change in sensory perception, usually either visual or auditory. Drugs commonly assigned to this class include lysergic acid diethylamide (LSD), mescaline (derived from the *Peyote cactus*) and psilocybin (derived from a mushroom). However, this rather limited definition fails to include the other prominent property of this class of drugs, which is a change in thought and mood. For this reason the term is sometimes used interchangeably with psychedelic or psychotomimetic, the latter term representing the CNS effects beyond the hallucination itself. Most literal definitions of the term hallucinogen are inadequate, but it should be used to signify substances that consistently produce changes in sensory perception, thought, and mood. An hallucinogen is a drug that reliably produces alterations in perceptions as a primary effect. Drugs that should not be included are those that produce alterations in sensory perception only at toxic doses (e.g., antimuscarinic agents, antimalarials, and opioids) and fail to produce these effects in all individuals. This does not preclude a drug's being classified as an hallucinogen if it has other properties as well. Several drugs that reliably alter mood at low doses and produce altered sensory perceptions at slightly higher doses are close chemical analogues to the CNS stimulant class of drugs. These drugs that also reliably produce differing degrees of CNS stimulation in a dose responsive fashion include phencyclidine (PCP), methylene-dioxymethamphetamine (MDMA) and methylenedioxyaphetamine (MDA). The hallucinogens generally fall into two chemicalclasses. The indole alkylamines include LSD, psilocybin, psilocin, dimethyl-tryptamine (DMT) and diethyltryp-tamine (DET) all of which are structurally similar to serotonin. The other chemical subclass of hallucinogens contains phenylethylamine derivatives such as mescaline, MDMA, MDA, and DOM (dimethoxymethyl amphetamine). A related stimulatory hallucinogen, PCP, is a piperidine analogue that produces unique effects.

## Extent and Pattern of Abuse

LSD is very potent and produces both CNS and peripheral effects. Because of the rapid tolerance produced with these drugs, the typical abuser does not use the drug on a daily basis. Generally, a hallucinogen is abused approximately once per month. Illicit PCP abuse began in the 1960s, primarily by oral ingestion. However, its use was limited because PCP frequently produced dysphoria, which was unpredictable.

## Pharmacological Aspects

The effects of LSD may be observed for 8 hours. The specific acute effects of a drug like LSD include euphoria, depersonalization, enhanced awareness of sensory input, alterations in the perception of time or space or body image and to some extent, minor stimulant effects. Sometimes the dreamlike quality of the experience produces relaxation, good humor and a sense of wonder or euphoria. Often the effect is a function of expectation and environmental conditions. Someone who is anxious about the use of the hallucinogen may have drug-induced anxiety, panic, or even paranoid ideation. The loss of individuality can be perceived as a disintegration of the person and can lead to a panic attack. Even if the drug experience initially is euphoric, tremendous mood swings can occur and suddenly plunge the abuser into emotions of great anxiety or terror. These negative phenomena are not always precipitated by an unexpected or sudden frightful event but can be a function of the labile mood induced by the drug. The visual hallucinations are often composed of extremely vivid colors of geometric patterns, such as cones, spirals, or cobweb-like structures. Other types of hallucinations are possible. A true hallucination involves the belief by the individual that the (altered) sensations and perceptions actually represent reality. However, generally the person abusing LSD and related drugs retains the ability to test reality versus illusion and knows that the experience is not real. Thus, the typical drug-induced hallucinatory state would be more appropriately termed a pseudohallucination, though real hallucinations are possible. The subjective or psychotomimetic changes are those considered to be changes in mood. These effects are somewhat more and variable than the hallucinatory effects or changes in sensory perception. Though these effects can occur with LSD, they seem to be more common with other specific hallucinogens, such as MDMA and MDA. MDMA (XTC, or ecstasy) possesses hallucinogenic activity similar to that of mescaline but also produces stimulant activity similar to that of amphetamine. Initially MDMA produces euphoria, increases the ability to communicate with others, increases the degree of intimacy one feels toward others in the surroundings, increases self-esteem and mood, and generally appears reduce perceived intensity of psychological problems. Hallucinatory activity occurs at higher doses. One residual effect of abuse is the MDMA hangover, which is the occurrence on the second day after abuse of drowsiness and sore jaw muscles along with other possible side effects due to the stimulant properties of the drug. MDA, which is similar to MDMA, has been termed the love drug because it produces a feeling of closeness to others. Typically, a dose of 75 mg produces the primary psychotomimetic effects, while a dose of 150 mg produces LSD-like effects, and a dose of 300 mg produces amphetamine like CNS stimulation. The amphetamine like stimulation of the CNS and periphery is prominent with both MDA and MDMA. To a lesser degree this stimulation also occurs with LSD. The effects that can be produced by stimulatory doses of hallucinogens include tachycardia, hypertension and arrhythmias. PCP is unique in terms of its hallucinogenic properties and its other pharmacological effects. It possesses CNS stimulatory actions, but it is also a dissociative anesthetic. It induces a wide variety of psychotomimetic and hallucinatory effects during emergence from anesthesia. Because it possesses CNS stimulant properties comparable with those of amphetamine, it does not produce depression of the cardiovascular system like other anesthetics, though it does depress the respiratory system. At a low dose, individuals believe they are thinking and acting rapidly and efficiently. The general mood is happiness, though (especially at higher doses) the individual can vacillate between euphoria and depression. It primarily produces auditory hallucinations. At higher doses the stimulatory effects are more pronounced and the likelihood of tremendous mood swings more likely. At near anesthetic doses, it produces more typical depressant effects, including motor incoordination, catalepsy, vacant stare, or even amnesia. Coma is produced subsequent to respiratory depression.

## Tolerance and Dependence

Tolerance to the effects of hallucinogens develops rapidly. A high degree of tolerance can be produced after as few as three to four daily doses of drug. Generally, the abuser self-imposes the requirement for a 2- to 3-day drug-free period before another drug session. Additionally, there is a tremendous degree of cross-tolerance between the hallucinogens, so other LSD-like hallucinogens cannot be abused during the drug-free period either. One danger with the stimulant subclass of hallucinogens is rapid development of tolerance to some of their effects while the stimulatory properties remain and produce various side effects. Despite the apparent overlap of effects with stimulant drugs, however, there is no cross-tolerance with the CNS stimulants such as amphetamine. There are no observable physical withdrawal signs during drug abstinence, nor is there a tremendous craving for drug during the drug-free period. Therefore, clearly no dependence is attributed to the hallucinogens. Though there is an abuse potential with this class of drug and individuals express drug-seeking behavior, there does not seem to be the magnitude of craving found with other drug classes, such as the CNS stimulants.

## Treatment Strategies

The difference between the abused and the lethal dose of LSD is very large, so little pharmacological intervention is necessary. Treatment involves limiting external stimuli and placing the individual in a safe environment. Treatment of PCP intoxication also involves limiting external stimuli, minimizing lighting, noise and unnecessary physical contact. The life-threatening nature of PCP overdose, however, may require symptomatic treatment of respiratory depression by artificial respiration or use of neuroleptics to control violent rage or panic anxiety.

## Mechanism of Action

Hallucinogens disorganize neural function in the CNS. The structural similarities between the indole hallucinogens and the endogenous neurotransmitter serotonin led to the hypothesis that a primary mechanism of action for the hallucinogens is the activation of the $5HT_2$-receptor. LSD acts directly on this receptor as an agonist. Other drugs, such as MDM, induce the release of endogenous serotonin, which activates the serotonin receptor.

# Inhalants

Volatile chemicals and gases that produce behavioral effects are subject to abuse. These agents represent a broad range of chemical classes but in general can be classified as gases, volatile organic solvents and aliphatic nitrites. Inhalant abuse differs from that of many other drugs in that it is confined primarily to juveniles and young adults. The use of gases is primarily confined to nitrous oxide by young medical professionals who have ready access to this agent. It produces short-lived mild intoxication that typifies the early stages of anesthesia. Deaths occur occasionally by individuals inhaling nitrous oxide alone. Volatile organic solvents are usually aliphatic and aromatic hydrocarbons. They include substances such as gasoline, paint and lacquer thinners, lighter fluid, degreasers (methyl chloride and methylene chloride) and the solvents in airplane glue, typewriter correction fluid, and bathroom deodorizers. These agents produce a sense of exhilaration and light-headedness. Judgment and perception of reality are impaired and hallucinations may be produced. The mechanism by which inhalants produce their behavioral effects are poorly understood, but there are some indications that their actions are similar to those of other centrally acting depressants, including alcohol. Toxicity depends on the properties of the individual solvents. The consequences of inhaling these substances can be severe, for they have been implicated in producing cancer, cardiotoxicity, neuropathies and hepatotoxicity.

## Designer Drugs

In an effort to avoid federal regulations, chemists in clandestine laboratories adopted the strategy of synthesizing analogues of controlled substances. Although these drugs are technically not illegal until scheduled, the consequences of their abuse are unpredictable and in some instances lethal. Efforts to make synthetic heroin led to the synthesis of at least six chemicals that are structurally similar to fentanyl. These agents gained considerable attention because their increased potency over fentanyl and heroin led to a rash of overdoses and numerous deaths. The two derivatives are referred to as China White and are 900 and 1,100 times as potent as morphine. Meperidine has also been used as a template for preparing synthetic heroin, the end product being 1-methyl-4-propionoxy-4-phenylpiperidine (MPPP).However, MPPP is sometimes contaminated with the side reaction product 1-methyl,4-phenyl-1,2,3,6-tetrahydropyridine (MPTP), which produces a parkinsonian syndrome through nigrostriatal lesions. Several substituted derivatives of amphetamine have also been called designer drugs. The most widely known of this group is the hallucinogen MDMA (ecstasy).

## Anabolic Steroids

Historically, drugs used to increase the ability of an athlete to perform in a given sport included the use of stimulants to diminish the onset of fatigue or opiates to diminish the pain of exertion. Recently, abuse of anabolic-steroids (derivatives of testosterone) has increased. They are used to increase muscle size and definition (in the case of body-building competitors) and are sometimes co-abused with other growth enhancers, such as human growth hormone. In sports in which mass, physical size, or even total strength (a function of total muscle mass) is important, the abuse of anabolic steroids provides a shortcut to attainment of the physical stature that might otherwise require much more extensive training and exercise. However, it is a misconception to believe that anabolic steroid abuse is limited to professional athletes and body builders. There is clear evidence that these drugs are abused by adult men and women who are not athletes, who are blue-collar and white-collar workers and by male and female athletes at the college, high school, and junior high school levels.

## References

Maskos U, *et al.*, (2005). Nicotine reinforcement and cognition restored by targeted expression of nicotinic receptors. *Nature* **436:** 103.

Morton J.Ecstasy (2005). Pharmacology and neurotoxicity. *Curr Opin Pharmacol* **5:** 79.

Nichols DE (2004). Hallucinogens. *Pharmacol Ther* **101:** 131.

Snead OC 3rd, Gibson KM (2005). Gamma-hydroxybutyric acid. *N Engl J Med* **352:** 2721.

Sulzer D, *et al.*, (2005). Mechanisms of neurotransmitter release by amphetamines: A review. *Prog Neurobiol* **75:** 406.

CHAPTER 27

# Local Anaesthetics

## Introduction

Local anaesthetic agents can be defined as drugs which are used clinically to produce reversible loss of sensation in a circumscribed area of the body. At high concentrations, many drugs that are used for other purposes possess local anaesthetic or membrane stabilising properties. These include beta-adrenoceptor antagonists, opioid analgesics, anticonvulsants and antihistamines.

Most of the clinically useful local anaesthetic agents consist of an aromatic ring linked by a carbonyl containing moiety through a carbon chain to a substituted amino group.

## Chemistry

The basic chemical structure (Fig 27-1) of a local anesthetic molecule consists of 3 parts:

1. Lipophilic group- an aromatic group, usually an unsaturated benzene ring.
2. Intermediate bond- a hydrocarbon connecting chain, either an ester (-CO-) or amide (-HNC-) linkage. The intermediate bond determines the classification of local anesthetic.
3. Hydrophilic group- a tertiary amine and proton acceptor.

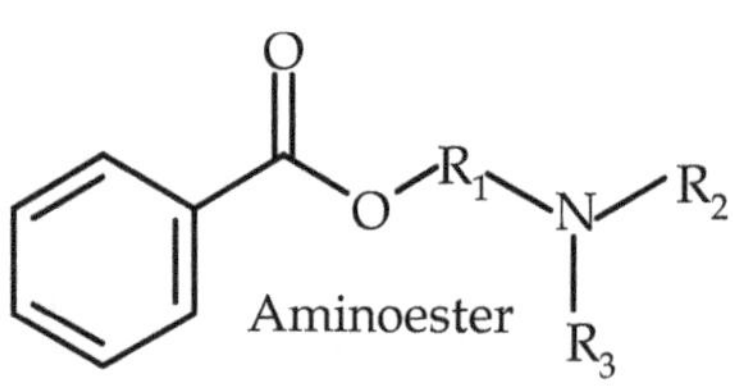

Aminoester

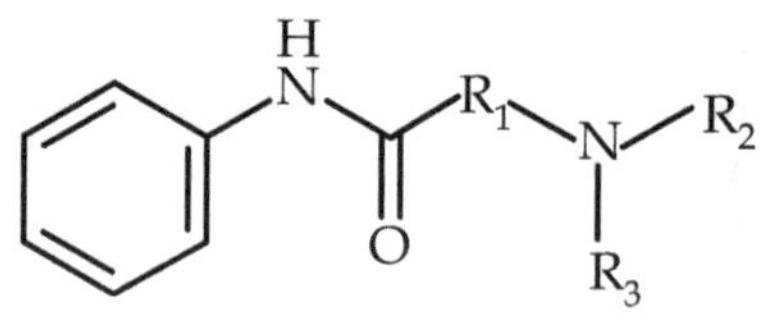

Aminoamide

**Fig 27-1:** Basic structures of local anaesthetics

## Classification

The classification of local anaesthetics are shown in Fig 27-2.

There are 2 classes of local anaesthetic drugs defined by the nature of the carbonyl-containing linkage group. Include classification with regard to duration of action.

**Esters**

- Benzocaine
- Chloroprocaine
- Cocaine
- Procaine
- Cyclomethycaine
- Dimethocaine/Larocaine
- Piperocaine
- Propoxycaine
- Procaine/Novocaine
- Proparacaine
- Tetracaine/Amethocaine

**Amides**

- Articaine
- Bupivacaine
- Cinchocaine/Dibucaine
- Etidocaine
- Levobupivacaine
- Lidocaine/Lignocaine

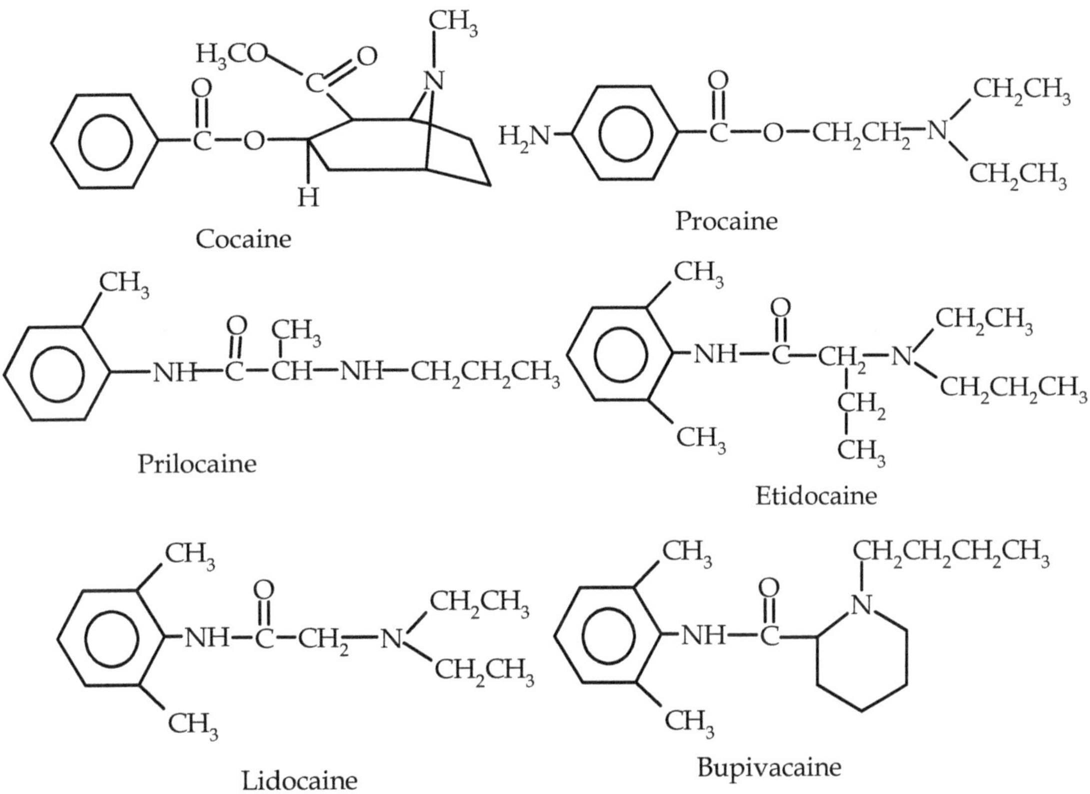


**Fig 27-2:** Local anaesthetics

- Mepivacaine
- Prilocaine
- Ropivacaine
- Trimecaine

## Combinations

**Local anesthetics mixed with other local anesthetics include**

- Lidocaine/prilocaine (EMLA)

**Local anesthetics and vasoconstrictors:** Vasoconstrictors increase the duration of local anesthesia by constricting the blood vessels, thereby safely concentrating the anaesthetic agent for an extended duration, as well as reducing hemorrhage. Examples include: Prilocaine hydrochloride and epinephrine.

There are important practical differences between these two groups of local anaesthetic agents. Esters are relatively unstable in solution and are rapidly hydrolysed in the body by plasma cholinesterase (and other esterases). One of the main breakdown products is para-amino benzoate (PABA) which is associated with allergic phenomena and hypersensitivity reactions. In contrast, amides are relatively stable in solution, are slowly metabolised by hepatic amidases and hypersensitivity reactions to amide local anaesthetics are extremely rare.

## Mechanism of Action

All local anesthetics are membrane stabilizing drugs; they reversibly decrease the rate of depolarization and repolarisation of excitable membranes (like nociceptors). Local anaesthetics cause reversible interruption of the conduction of impulses in peripheral nerves. The primary electrophysiological effect of these compounds is to cause a local decrease in the rate and degree of depolarisation of the nerve membrane such that the threshold potential for transmission is not reached and the electrical impulse is not propagated down the nerve. There is no effect on the resting or threshold potential, although the refractory period and repolarisation may be prolonged. These effects are due to blockade of sodium channels, thereby impairing sodium ion flux, across the membrane.

Most local anaesthetic agents are tertiary amine bases (B) that are administered as water soluble hydrochlorides (B.HCl). After injection, the tertiary amine base is liberated by the relatively alkaline pH of tissue fluids:

$$B.HCl + HCO_3 \rightleftharpoons B + H_2CO_3 + Cl^-$$

In tissue fluid the local anaesthetic will be present in both an ionised ($BH^+$) and non-ionised form (B); their relative proportions will depend on the pH of the solution and the pKa of the individual drug. The non-ionised base (B) then

**Table 27-1:** Pharmacological effects and clinical uses of local anaesthetics

| Anaesthetic agents | Ester or Amide | Onset of action | Duration of action | Clinical use | Properties |
|---|---|---|---|---|---|
| Procaine | Es e | Slow | Short | Limited.<br>Vascular spasm.<br>Diagnostic procedures. | Vasodilation.<br>Allergenic. |
| Amethocaine | Ester | Slow | Long | Topical anaesthesia.<br>Spinal anaesthesia. | High systemic toxicity. |
| Chloro-procaine | Ester | F st | Short | Peripheral anaesthesia.<br>Obstetric extradural blocks. | Low systemic toxicity. |
| Mepivacaine | Amide | Fast | Moderate | Infiltration.<br>Peripheral nerve blocks. | Versatile.<br>Moderate Vasodilation. |
| Prilocaine | Amide | Fast | Moderate | Infiltration.<br>Intravenous regional anaesthesia.<br>Peripheral nerve blocks. | Methaemo-globinaemia at high doses. Least systemic toxicity of amides. |
| Bupivacaine | Amide | Moderate | Long | Infiltration.<br>Peripheral nerve blocks.<br>Extradural and spinal blocks. | Separation of sensory & motor blockades. |
| Etidocaine | Amide | Fast | Long | Infiltration.<br>Peripheral nerve blocks.<br>Extradural blocks. | Profound motor blockade. |
| Lignocaine | Amide | Fast | Moderate | Infiltration /Topical.<br>Intravenous regional anaesthesia.<br>Peripheral nerve blocks.<br>Extradural and spinal blocks. | Most versatile agent. Moderate Vasodilation. |

diffuses through the nerve sheath, perineuronal tissues and the neuronal membrane, to reach the axoplasm where it partially ionises again:

$$B + H^+ \rightleftharpoons BH^+$$

In the ionised form $BH^+$, the local anaesthetic enters the sodium channel (from the interior of the nerve fibre) and either occludes the channel or combines with a specific receptor within the channel that results in channel blockade.

In clinical practice, local anaesthesia may be influenced by the local availability of free base (B), as only the unionised portion can diffuse through the neuronal membrane. Thus, local anaesthetics are relatively inactive when injected into tissues with an acid pH (e.g., pyogenic abscess) which is presumably due to reduced release of free base.

## Various Techniques of Local Anesthesia

Local anesthetics can block almost every nerve between the peripheral nerve endings and the central nervous system. The most peripheral technique is topical anesthesia to the skin or other body surface. Small and large peripheral nerves can be anesthetized individually (peripheral nerve block) or in anatomic nerve bundles (plexus anesthesia).

## Clinical Techniques Include

### Topical anaesthesia

Local anaesthetics may be applied to the skin, the eye, the ear, the nose and the mouth as well as other mucous membranes. In general, cocaine, amethocaine, lignocaine and prilocaine are the most useful and effective local anaesthetics for this purpose. When used to produce topical anaesthesia, they usually have a rapid onset of action (5-10 mins) and a moderate duration of action (30-60 mins). Cocaine is a potent vasoconstrictor and is useful in the reduction of bleeding as well as topical anaesthesia. Other local anaesthetic agents may be absorbed in significant amounts particularly after topical application to the more vascular areas, and fatalities have occurred after application of these agents to mucosal surfaces.

Absorption of local anaesthetics through intact skin is usually slow and unreliable and high concentrations (e.g., 20% benzocaine or 40% lignocaine) are required.

### Infiltration anaesthesia

Infiltration techniques are used to provide anaesthesia for minor surgical procedures. Amide anaesthetics with a moderate duration of action are commonly used (lignocaine, prilocaine and mepivacaine). The site of action is at unmyelinated nerve endings and onset is almost immediate. The duration of local anaesthesia is variable. Procaine has a short duration of action (15-30 min), while lignocaine, mepivacaine and prilocaine have a moderate duration of action (70-140 min). Bupivacaine has the longest duration of action (approximately 200 min). The addition of adrenaline (1 in 200,000) will increase the quality and prolong the duration of anaesthesia.

### Conduction anaesthesia

Conduction anaesthesia can be divided into minor nerve blockade (e.g., ulnar, radial or intercostal) and major blockade of deeper nerves or trunks with a wide dermatomal distribution (e.g., brachial plexus blockade). For each individual agent the duration of anaesthesia will be determined more by the total dose of the drug rather than the volume or concentration of drug used.

When amide local anaesthetics are used to produce minor nerve blockade, they have a relatively rapid onset of action (5-10 min). Lignocaine, mepivacaine and prilocaine have a moderate duration of action (1-2 hr), while bupivacaine and etidocaine produce local anaesthesia for 2-6 hr.

In major nerve blockade the onset is more variable, mainly due to anatomical factors which can delay or restrict the access of the local anaesthetic to its site of action. In general lignocaine, mepivacaine and prilocaine have a faster onset of action (10-15 min) than bupivacaine (15-30 min). Analgesia persists for 3-4 hr with lignocaine, prilocaine and mepivacaine, but up to 10 hr with bupivacaine.

**Extradural anaesthesia**

Local anaesthetic solutions are deposited in the epidural space between the dura mater and the periosteum lining the vertebral canal. The epidural space contains adipose tissue, lymphatics and blood vessels. The injected local anaesthetic solution produces analgesia by blocking conduction at the intradural spinal nerve roots.

The quality and extent of the blockade produced by each agent is determined by the volume as well as the total dose of the drug. The spread of local anaesthetic solutions may be more extensive in pregnant women as the volume of the potential space is reduced by venous engorgement in the epidural space. Enhanced effects may also be seen in the elderly and in patients with arteriosclerosis due to impairment of vascular absorption from the epidural space.

Bupivacaine (0.5%) or lignocaine (1.5-2.0%) are usually used to produce extradural anaesthesia. Repeated administration of lignocaine or mepivacaine into the epidural space may result in a diminished response with each subsequent dose (tachyphylaxis). This may be due to local changes in pH due to the relative acidity of these solutions. The reduction in pH may reduce the amount of free base available for diffusion across the neuronal membrane.

**Spinal anaesthesia**

The introduction of local anaesthetic solutions directly into the cerebrospinal fluid (CSF) produces spinal anaesthesia. The local anaesthetics do not have to cross tissue or diffusion barriers and also the central attachments of the ventral and dorsal nerve roots are unmyelinated, which allows rapid uptake of the free base. There is a faster onset of action and a smaller dose is required. Spinal anaesthesia produces a similar clinical effect with a dose approximately ten times smaller than that needed for extradural anaesthesia.

Solutions of amethocaine (0.2%), lignocaine (5%), prilocaine (5%) bupivacaine (0.5%) and mepivacaine (4%) are commonly used to produce spinal anaesthesia. Prilocaine and Mepivacaine have a slightly longer duration of action than lignocaine; bupivacaine has the longest duration of action.

**Intravenous Local Anaesthesia**

Intravenous regional anaesthesia (IVRA) is a useful method of providing analgesia for minor surgical procedures. The local anaesthetic agent is injected into a vein of a limb that has been previously exsanguinated and occluded by a tourniquet. The site of action is probably the unmyelinated nerve fibres, reached by retrograde spread in the vascular bed. The onset of action is almost immediate.

Lignocaine or prilocaine are commonly used and systemic blood levels of these agents are unlikely to be significant if the tourniquet is released more than 15 min after injection.

Bupivacaine and etidocaine should never be used for IVRA! They are significantly protein bound and once the tourniquet is released there is a risk of cardiotoxicity. Several deaths have been reported during IVRA with bupivacaine.

## Pharmacokinetics

It is well established that systemic absorption of local anesthetics correlates positively with the vascularity of the injection site (i.e., intravenous > tracheal > intracostal > paracervical > epidural

> brachial plexus > sciatic > subcutaneous). The spinal cord meninges influence distribution of local anesthetics from the epidural and subarachnoid spaces. Intact skin is a near complete barrier to local anesthetic penetration. In the latter case, special local anesthetic formulations (e.g., EMLA cream – a eutectic mixture of lidocaine and prilocaine) or delivery methods (e.g., electrophoresis) are employed to facilitate transcutaneous transfer. The large number of different injection sites used by pain physicians (e.g., epidural, intrathecal, intrapleural, intraarticular, intramuscular, perineural, topical) and the variety of dosing methods (e.g., single shot, continuous infusion, intermittent infusion) make more than superficial discussion of the distribution kinetics of local anesthetics from injection sites beyond the scope of this review.

Aminoester-linked local anesthetics are hydrolyzed by esterases in tissues and blood. Aminoamide-linked local anesthetics are biotransformed primarily in the liver by cytochrome P450 enzymes. Metabolites may retain local anesthetic activity and toxicity potential, albeit usually at lower potency than the parent compound.

Vasoconstrictors [e.g., epinephrine 1 : 400 000 (2.5 mg/ml)] are used to reduce absorption of local anesthetics into the systemic circulation. The value of doing so depends on vascularity of injection site and specific local anesthetic agent, which – among other considerations – vary in terms of intrinsic vasoactivity. The value of adding sodium bicarbonate to solutions to enhance speed of onset of local anesthetics also depends on injection site as well as physiochemical properties of the various local anesthetics. Addition of sodium bicarbonate increases the pH of solutions, which increases the ratio of uncharged to charged molecules. This increases the number of local anesthetic molecules in the form that most readily passes through biologic membranes. Hyaluronidase (tissue-spreading factor) is sometimes added to local anesthetic solutions to facilitate spread of solution at the injection site, thereby affecting speed of onset and extent of a block. This appears only to be useful when local anesthetic is injected behind the eyes in preparation for ophthalmologic surgery. Hyaluronidase may be injected with local anesthetic during epidural neurolysis to treat pain with positive benefit.

## Adverse Effects

### Localized Adverse Effects

The local adverse effects of anaesthetic agents include neurovascular manifestations such as prolonged anesthesia (numbness) and paresthesia (tingling, feeling of "pins and needles", or strange sensations). These are symptoms of localized nerve impairment or nerve damage.

### General Adverse Effects

General systemic adverse effects are due to the pharmacological effects of the anaesthetic agents used. The conduction of electric impulses follows a similar mechanism in peripheral nerves, the central nervous system, and the heart.

### Central Nervous System

Depending on local tissue concentrations of local anesthetics, there may be excitatory or depressant effects on the central nervous system. At lower concentrations, a relatively selective depression of inhibitory neurons results in cerebral excitation, which may lead to generalized convulsions. A profound depression of brain functions occurs at higher concentrations which may lead to coma, respiratory arrest and death. Such tissue concentrations may be due to very high plasma levels after intravenous injection of a large dose. Another possibility is direct exposure of the central nervous system through the CSF, i.e., overdose in spinal anesthesia or accidental injection into the subarachnoid space in epidural anesthesia.

## Cardiovascular System

The conductive system of the heart is quite sensitive to the action of local anaesthetic

**Treatment of overdose: "Lipid rescue"**

There is evidence that intralipid, a commonly available intravenous lipid emulsion, can be effective in treating severe cardiotoxicity secondary to local anaesthetic overdose.

## Hypersensitivity/Allergy

Adverse reactions to local anesthetics (especially the esters) are not uncommon, but true allergy is very rare. Allergic reactions to the esters are usually due to sensitivity to their metabolite, para-amino benzoic acid (PABA), and does not result in cross-allergy to amides. Therefore, amides can be used as alternatives in those patients. Non-allergic reactions may resemble allergy in their manifestations. In some cases, skin tests and provocative challenge may be necessary to establish a diagnosis of allergy. There are also cases of allergy to paraben derivatives, which are often added as preservatives to local anaesthetic solutions.

## Methemoglobinemia

The systemic toxicity of prilocaine is comparatively low, however its metabolite, o-toluidine, is known to cause methemoglobinemia. As methemoglobinemia reduces the amount of haemoglobin that is available for oxygen transport, this side effect is potentially life-threatening. Therefore dose limits for prilocaine should be strictly observed. Prilocaine is not recommended for use in labor pains or infants.

# Specific Uses

## Acute Pain

Acute pain may occur due to trauma, surgery, infection, disruption of blood circulation or many other conditions in which there is tissue injury. In a medical setting it is usually desirable to alleviate pain when its warning function is no longer needed. Acute pain can often be managed using analgesics. However, conduction anesthesia may be preferable because of superior pain control and fewer side effects. For purposes of pain therapy, local anaesthetic drugs are often given by repeated injection or continuous infusion through a catheter. Low doses of local anaesthetic drugs can be sufficient so that muscle weakness does not occur and patients may be mobilized.

**Some typical uses of conduction anesthesia for acute pain are:**

Labor pain (epidural anesthesia)

Postoperative pain (peripheral nerve blocks, epidural anesthesia)

Trauma (peripheral nerve blocks, intravenous regional anesthesia, epidural anesthesia)

## Chronic Pain

Chronic pain of more than minor intensity is a complex and often serious condition that requires diagnosis and treatment by an expert in pain medicine. Local anesthetics can be applied repeatedly or continuously for prolonged periods to relieve chronic pain, usually in combination with medication such as opioids, NSAIDs and anticonvulsants.

## Surgery and Dentistry

Virtually every part of the body can be anesthetized using conduction anesthesia. However, only a limited number of techniques are in common clinical use. Sometimes conduction anesthesia is combined with general anesthesia or sedation for the patient's comfort and ease of surgery. Typical operations performed under conduction anesthesia include:

Dentistry (surface anesthesia, infiltration anesthesia or intraligamentary anesthesia during restorative operations or extractions, regional nerve blocks during extractions and surgeries.

Eye surgery (surface anesthesia with topical anesthetics, retrobulbar block)

ENT operations, head and neck surgery (infiltration anesthesia, field blocks, peripheral nerve blocks, plexus anesthesia)

Shoulder and arm surgery (plexus anesthesia, intravenous regional anesthesia)

Heart and lung surgery (epidural anesthesia combined with general anesthesia)

Abdominal surgery (epidural/spinal anesthesia, often combined with general anesthesia)

Gynaecological, obstetrical and urological operations (spinal/epidural anesthesia)

Bone and joint surgery of the pelvis, hip and leg (spinal/epidural anesthesia, peripheral nerve blocks, intravenous regional anesthesia)

Surgery of skin and peripheral blood vessels (topical anesthesia, field blocks, peripheral nerve blocks, spinal/epidural anesthesia)

### Other Uses

Topical anesthesia, in the form of lidocaine/prilocaine (EMLA) is most commonly used to enable relatively painless venipuncture (blood collection) and placement of intravenous cannulae. It may also be suitable for other kinds of punctures such as ascites drainage and amniocentesis.

Surface anesthesia also facilitates some endoscopic procedures such as bronchoscopy (visualization of the lower airways) or cystoscopy (visualization of the inner surface of the bladder).

## Factors Affecting Local Anaesthetic Activity Clinically

### Dose

An increase in the dose of a local anesthetic will increase the likelihood of a successful block by producing a solid and long lasting anesthetic while decreasing the time to onset. An increase in the volume of local anesthetic using the same dose of local anesthetic does not appear to be beneficial in the clinical setting with the exception of the spread associated with epidural anesthesia.

### Addition of Vasoconstrictors

Epinephrine is the most commonly used vasoconstrictor. The usual dose and concentration is 5 mcg/ml or 1:200000. Norepinephrine and phenylephrine have been used as vasoconstrictors but do not exhibit properties that make them superior to epinephrine. Epinephrine acts to decrease lidocaine, bupivacaine, mepivacaine ropivacaine vascular absorption, reduces blood concentration of local anesthetics and decreases the risk of toxicity thus allowing more local anesthetic molecules to reach the nerve membrane. As more molecules reach the nerve membrane, there is an increase in the depth and duration of local anesthetic blockade. Epinephrine prolongs the duration of blockade for most short to moderate acting local anesthetics. The addition of epinephrine for neuraxial blockade has the added benefit of activating endogenous analgesic mechanisms through α-Adrenergic receptors. This may increase the intensity of analgesic action. The addition of vasoconstrictors is controversial. Some advocate that vasoconstrictors may result in nerve injury due to decreased blood flow.

Epinephrine containing local anesthetics should never be injected into end organs such as ears, nose, penis, fingers or toes. Epinephrine may cause vasoconstriction and subsequent necrosis of tissue.

## Site of Injection

The anatomical location of blockade influences onset and duration. Location affects the rate of diffusion, vascular absorption, and the amount of local anesthetic administered. Subarachnoid blockade exhibits the most rapid onset and shortest duration of action. Rapid onset, within the subarachnoid space, occurs because nerve roots are not covered with a sheath. The short duration of action is related to the small dose and volume of local anesthetic used to produce anesthesia. Brachial plexus blockade, in contrast, has slower onset and longer duration of action. Local anesthetics are deposited in the sheath around the brachial plexus. Diffusion must take place before reaching the site of action. The long duration of action is related to slow vascular absorption, large doses and increased exposure of neural tissue to local anesthetics.

## Carbonation and pH Adjustment

In the isolated nerve, adding carbon dioxide to the local anesthetic solution accelerates the onset on blockade. This is a result of an increase in the base from of the local anesthetic, direct effect of $CO_2$ on the nerve, and a decrease in the local pH. Clinically results are mixed. Sodium bicarbonate may also accelerate the onset of action. The addition of bicarbonate increases the pH, which in turn, increases the amount of local anesthetic in the uncharged base form. This theoretically accelerates the rate of diffusion across the sheath and membrane, resulting in a faster onset. Controversy exists concerning the clinical utility of pH adjustment. Studies remain ambiguous concerning the use of sodium bicarbonate to improve the speed of local anesthetic induced anesthesia.

## Mixtures of Local Anesthetics

Clinicians occasionally will combine local anesthetics to achieve quick onset and long duration. Often the clinician will combine a local anesthetic with a fast onset with a local anesthetic that has a long duration of action to achieve this goal. Clinical trials have yielded mixed results. Chloroprocaine and bupivacaine, in the brachial plexus region, have achieved a quick onset/prolonged duration. However, when used for epidural anesthesia it was found that the duration of action was shorter than if bupivacaine was administered alone. Clinically there are few advantages to this technique. It should be noted that when mixing local anesthetics the risk of toxicity remains. Care should be exercised not to exceed the maximum dose. Toxicities of local anesthetics are not independent, but additive! A solution containing 50% of the toxic dose of local anesthetic A and 50% of the toxic dose of local anesthetic B, will have the same implications as 100% of the toxic dose of either local anesthetic alone.

## Pregnancy

Hormonal changes during pregnancy are primarily responsible for the enhanced potency of local anesthetics. Mechanical factors such as dilated epidural veins, which decrease the volume of the epidural or subarachnoid space, may play a minor role in later stages of pregnancy. The spread and depth of epidural/ spinal anesthesia is greater in the pregnant patient when compared to the patient who is not pregnant. It has been found that the spread of local anesthetics are more extensive with epidural anesthesia as early as the first trimester. There is a correlation between progesterone levels and the mg per segment requirement of lidocaine required for the parturient. Based on current research, the dose of local anesthetics should be reduced for the pregnant patient by 30%, regardless of the trimester of pregnancy.

## Medication Interactions with Local Anesthetics

**Ester local anaesthetics:** Succinylcholine- may potentiate the effects since both are dependent on pseudocholinesterase for metabolism.

**Ester local anaesthetics:** Cholinesterase inhibitors such as neostigmine and pyridostigmine can lead to a decrease in the metabolism of ester local anesthetics.

**Ester local anaesthetics:** Decreased pseudocholinesterase activity during pregnancy and postpartum period.

**Local anesthetics in general:** Opioids and alpha adrenergic agonists potentiate the analgesic effects of local anesthetics.

**Local anesthetics in general:** Potentiate the effects of non-depolarizing muscle relaxant blockade.

**Chloroprocaine (epidural):** May interfere with the analgesic effects of subarachnoid opioids.

**Lidocaine:** Cimetidine and propranolol decrease hepatic blood flow and lidocaine clearance. This acts to increase the risk of systemic toxicity.

## References

Arnold Stern (2002). Pharmacology: Pre Test self-assessment and review. New York: McGraw-Hill, Medical Pub. Division. ISBN 0-07-136 704-7.

Litz RJ, Popp M, Stehr SN, Koch T (2006). Successful resuscitation of a patient with ropivacaine-induced asystole after axillary plexus block using lipid infusion. *Anaesthesia* **61(8):** 800-1. DOI:10.1111/j.1365-2044. 2006. 04740. x. PMID 16867094.

Pretreatment or resuscitation with a lipid infusion shifts the dose-response to bupivacaine-induced asystole in rats. *Anesthesiology* **88(4):** 1071-5.

Yagiela JA (1995). Vasoconstrictor agents for local anesthesia. *Anesth Prog* **42(3-4):** 116-20. PMC 2148913. PMID 8934977.

CHAPTER 28

# Dugs used in Myasthenia Gravis

MG, or myasthenia gravis, is an autoimmune condition. It concentrates on the "neuromuscular junction," which serves as the nerve and muscle's interface. Muscle tissue's neurotransmitter receptors are blocked, altered, or destroyed in MG by antibodies. People with myasthenia grow feeble because their muscles are unable to receive the signal to contract. Voluntary muscular weakness brought on by MG gets worse with activity and gets better with rest.

The major symptoms of MG change over time, vary in intensity, and appear in numerous combinations. Droopy eyes, double or hazy vision, weakened arms, hands, neck, face, or legs, and excessive weariness are some symptoms that may be present. When MG is severe, it can make it difficult to chew, smile, swallow, speak, or breathe.

## Medications

To treat MG, two different types of drugs are employed. One class of enzymes—anticholinesterases—temporarily eases MG symptoms. Immunosuppressants are another class that targets the disease's root cause. These medications prevent the body from initially harming the neuromuscular junction by inhibiting the immune system. Treatments that inhibit the immune system may have harmful adverse effects.

One of these drugs or a mix of them may be recommended by doctors. Finding the right drug and dosage for a certain patient might frequently take some time.

## Anticholinesterase Medication

Because they have few long-term negative effects, this is usually the first medicine recommended. It also has the fastest acting of all medications. These medications stop the chemical messenger acetylcholine, which is responsible for muscular contractions, from degrading. Muscle strength normally increases with acetylcholine intake. Anticholinesterase medications may partially or totally alleviate MG symptoms in some people, even though they do not directly combat the aberrant immune system response in MG.

Pyridostigmine bromide is the type of drug of this kind that is most frequently prescribed (Mestinon). It is offered in a time-release form and is accessible as a tablet or liquid. The duration and speed of the various kinds' efficacy varies.

It is advisable to take acetylcholinesterases with a bland diet, such as crackers, applesauce, or yoghurt, as they can cause stomach cramps and diarrhoea. Other typical adverse effects include sweating, cramping, and twitching of the muscles. When medication is used in excess, these symptoms can occasionally manifest.

## Immunosuppressant Medications

Immunosuppressants assist in preventing your body from generating the dangerous antibodies that initially cause MG weakness. Additionally, they decrease the body's ability to produce healthy antibodies, leaving you more vulnerable to illness and infection.

These medications should only be used under the close supervision of a doctor because they may have serious negative effects.

## Prednisone

For the majority of people with myasthenia, prednisone dramatically reduces MG symptoms. Although this medication doesn't work as quickly as anticholinesterases, it does so more quickly than other immunosuppressants and is less expensive. It is similar to the organic hormones that the cortex of the human adrenal gland produces. Prednisone can be quite useful in treating myasthenia, but there is a chance that it will have negative side effects. The severity of these side effects is influenced by the dosage and duration of prednisone treatment. There are several less frequent adverse effects as well, such as a variety of sleep disorders, mood swings, weight gain, fluid retention, decreased infection resistance, increased susceptibility to diabetes, high blood pressure, osteoporosis, glaucoma, cataracts, and stomach ulcers. With the use of other medications, the majority of these adverse effects can be avoided or managed. Additionally, it is crucial to "eat well," adhering to a diet that is well-balanced, high in potassium and calcium and low in salt, fat, and cholesterol. For starters, this can help prevent bone thinning, lessen fluid retention, and reduce weight gain. Prednisone prevents the body from producing adrenal hormones normally. To "reawaken" the body's natural hormones, prednisone medication must be weaned off gradually rather than abruptly.

- **Other immunosuppressant medications.** MG is treated with a variety of other drugs. Many were first created for people undergoing organ transplants or for the treatment of other immune-related disorders. These include tacrolimus (Prograf), azathioprine (Imuran), mycophenylate mofetil (CellCept), cyclosporine (Sandimmune, Neoral), and cyclophosphamide (Cytoxan, Neosar). If one of these drugs proves beneficial for a myasthenic, prednisone may no longer be required or the dosage may be reduced. The administration of these drugs is challenging. Each medicine has its own set of adverse effects and drug interactions, the dosage varies from person to person, and they can take months to start working.
- **Monoclonal antibody therapies.** These more recent and pricey medicines target highly certain immune system parts. Every six months, a series of IV infusions of rituximab (Rituxan), which is particularly helpful in treating the MuSK type of MG. By decreasing B-lymphocytes, the medication suppresses the immune system. Eculizumab (Soliris) is administered every two weeks after a course of four weekly infusions to treat generalised MG. This therapy protects the neuromuscular junction against immune system harm, necessitates additional safety measures, and can be combined with other therapies.

## Thymectomy

The thymus gland is surgically removed during a thymectomy. The thymus, which is situated in the upper chest behind the breast bone and is crucial for the immune system's development, is aberrant in nearly half of those with MG. Thymomas or tumours can grow on the thymus gland in some people. Thymomas are typically benign, however they can occasionally turn cancerous.

For people with thymomas and the majority of patients under 60 with moderate to severe generalised myasthenia, doctors advise thymectomies. Surgery can lessen MG symptoms and even cure some people, according to the National Institute of Neurological Disorders and Stroke, presumably by resetting the immune system. However, the timing of this improvement after surgery is variable and could take months or even years.

## Intravenous Immune Globulin (IVIg)

Rapidly deteriorating MG may be treated with immune globulin treatment. A human blood product called immune globulin is created from several thoroughly vetted donors. IVIg therapies appear to temporarily alter the immune system by supplying the body with normal antibodies from donor blood. The majority of people experience MG weakness that gets better within a week of treatment and lasts for a few weeks or months. IVIg treatments are costly and provide MG symptom relief only temporarily while waiting for longer acting immune modifying therapies to take action.

The speed at which the medication is taken is frequently correlated with side effects, such as headache or allergic reactions. This can be improved by reducing the infusion rate. To maintain the therapeutic effect, IVIg infusions may be repeated every month.

## Plasmapheresis

The process of "plasma exchange," also known as plasmapheresis, involves removing both "good" and "bad" antibodies from the blood. Blood is gradually removed from the body over the course of several hours using a special intravenous line. Plasma containing antibodies is then separated off, and the antibody-free blood is then returned to the body along with an albumin-like blood product to make up for some of the proteins lost during the procedure. The respite it offers is typically just transitory because this medication has no effect on the body's capacity to produce further antibodies.

Patients who need to gain strength prior to surgery or who have severe MG symptoms can benefit from plasmapheresis. For people who don't respond to other treatments, it is also occasionally administered. An individual typically becomes stronger after a few days of plasma exchange; the therapeutic advantage typically lasts two to three weeks. A series of treatments spread out over a period of two weeks are typically required because the benefits are frequently transient.

Large amounts of blood are removed during plasmapheresis, which can cause blood pressure to drop and cause dizziness or near-fainting. When a patient receives donor blood products or plasma, allergic reactions—from fever, chills, and rash to severe decreases in blood pressure—can take place. Immunoglobulin IV injection may also result in this.

CHAPTER

# Nootropics 29

Nootropics, commonly referred to as "smart medications," are a diverse set of substances that primarily activate cognitive processes including memory and learning, particularly when these processes are compromised. They essentially disrupt the central nervous system's (CNS) neuronal cells' metabolism. The name is made up of the Greek words tropein, which means to lead, and nöos, which means thinking.

## Mechanisms of Action

Nootropics boost the brain's supply of glucose and oxygen, provide antihypoxic effects, and shield brain tissue from neurotoxicity rather than acting directly by releasing neurotransmitters or acting as receptor ligands. They also promote the creation of neuronal proteins and nucleic acids and influence the metabolism of phospholipids in neuronal membranes. It has been discovered that some nootropics have an anti-aggregation impact, influence the removal of oxygen free radicals, and enhance erythrocyte flexibility. These compounds are metabolically active, however the majority of nootropics take a while to start working after a single dose and usually need repeated administration.

## Indications

Nootropics are used to treat memory, consciousness, and learning impairments in acute or subacute circumstances. They are advised for brain injury that is already present and showing symptoms like memory loss, mental retardation, and changes in the nature of awareness. The name of this ailment is acute psychoorganic syndrome (POS). In most situations, it can be reversed, but in rare circumstances, dementia might develop. Acute POS may result from a stroke, brain injury, infection, or drunkenness (alcohol, drugs with central anticholinergic effect, or carbon monoxide). Delirium tremens also falls under the POS category. Other symptoms may include persistent cognitive issues including mental retardation or memory loss. In these situations, nootropics are frequently administered, but their efficacy, particularly in cases of more severe dementia, is debatable. When there is merely a slowing of brain function without the onset of dementia, known as benign senescent forgetfulness, they appear to be more beneficial in patients with moderate cognitive impairments. Nootropics are occasionally used to treat attention and memory issues brought on by weariness and fatigue. They are also utilised by patients with encephalopathy and children with minimal brain dysfunction syndrome, and their impact on myalgic encephalomyelitis (chronic fatigue syndrome) has also been studied. Nootropics are given to people with Alzheimer's disease, schizophrenia, hyperkinetic disorder, or senile dementia as cognitive enhancers.

## Side Effects

Side effects of nootropics are uncommon and are rarely serious. In addition to individual intolerance, an increase in activity in the undesired direction, a sleep disorder, or an increase in libido may occasionally occur . Nootropics are contraindicated in hypersensitivity, pregnancy, and lactation.

- **Classical Nootropic Compound:**

### Deanol

2-(Dimethylamino)ethan-1-ol is the name of the compound. In the human brain, the substance is physiologically present. Deanol is frequently promoted as a natural nutritional supplement. DMAE is frequently found in dietary supplements as tartaric acid salts (bitartrate salt). Fish, particularly salmon and shellfish, can also provide small quantities, especially in little amounts. Deanol is a choline precursor that enables the brain to produce acetylcholine, the main neurotransmitter involved in memory and learning, at the highest possible level. In vivo rat tests, dimethylaminoethanol pyroglutamate elevated choline and acetylcholine extracellular levels in the prefrontal cortex of the brain.

It also enhanced spatial memory and lessened memory deficiencies brought on by scopolamine. Rats' working memory performance in the radial arm maze was considerably improved by dimethy laminoethanol cyclohexyl carboxylate fumarate. Humans who took supplements including vitamins, minerals, and substances containing DMAE for three months demonstrated improved alertness, focus, and mood in general, per electroencephalogram (EEG) examination. Additionally, DMAE enhanced sleep quality and promoted lucid dreams. Its administration has been studied in patients with minimal brain dysfunction syndrome and child hyperkinetic syndrome. The recommended daily dose of DMAE bitartrate is 500–2000 mg. It is not advised for use in those who are pregnant, nursing, or have schizophrenia.

### Meclofenoxate

The carbohydrate exchange is carried out by the meclofenoxate molecule, a 4-chlorophenoxyacetic acid that resembles the indoleacetic acid present in plant cells as a natural auxin. The previously mentioned 2-(dimethylamino)ethan-1-ol, also known as deanol, makes up the second portion of the molecule. When given parenterally, meclofenoxate is well absorbed. In vivo, it markedly boosted CNS choline levels (in rats). This rise in choline was accompanied by a rise in acetylcholine levels in the hippocampus. Thus, although it appears to be nearly twice as efficient as deanol, its effects on the levels of choline and acetylcholine in the brain are comparable.

Meclofenoxate was given orally to rats (100 mg/kg, daily for 37 days) to significantly lower proinflammatory mediator levels, improve memory impairment, and improve neuronal damage.

### Nicergoline

Since 1970, the ergot alkaloid nicergoline, sometimes known as nicergoline, has been employed in clinical settings. Nicergoline was first created as a vasodilator for the treatment of cerebrovascular diseases. Current clinical applications include the treatment of vascular or degenerative diseases marked by affective, behavioural, and somatic disorders, as well as cognitive impairment with diminished cognition. It is specifically used for memory loss, diminished alertness, attention, mood swings, weariness, dizziness, and abnormalities of the vestibular and cochlea.

Nicergoline's effects are diverse. It provided in vitro protection against -amyloid toxicity for cultured neurons. Nicergoline has been found to increase the function of cholinergic and catecholaminergic neurotransmitters in rats in vivo and to be an efficient medication for minimising neuronal susceptibility caused by experimentally induced nerve growth factor deficiency. It boosted metabolic activity (resulting in enhanced oxygen and glucose utilisation), prevented platelet aggregation, increased arterial blood circulation, and had neurotrophic and antioxidant activities in rats in vivo. Additionally, nicergoline improved cognitive performance in Alzheimer's disease rat models. Vasodilation and increased cerebral blood flow were caused with nicergoline. Additionally, vascular dementia patients have shown it to be effective. On many levels of cerebral, systemic, and cardiac hemo dynamics in ischemic stroke patients, nicergoline shown a comprehensively favourable effect. According to an electroencephalogram/event related potential (EEG/ERP) mapping study, nicergoline improved alertness and information processing at the neurophysiological level in patients with multi-infarct dementia and Alzheimer's disease, which resulted in clinical improvement at the behavioural level in both degenerative and vascular dementia. 30 to 60 mg should be taken each day. Rare side effects typically include headache, nausea, dizziness, diarrhoea, and fainting. It is not advised to take nicergoline during pregnancy or lactation due to the lack of experience with it in pregnant women.

**Piracetam :** Piracetam is known chemically as 2-(2-oxopyrrolidin-1-yl)acetamide. It is a cyclic derivative of acetamide and gamma-aminobutyric acid (GABA). Piracetam is believed to affect brain neurotransmission via altering ion channels ($Ca^{2+}$ and $K^+$), which results in a generalised increase in neuronal excitability. Through muscarinic receptors, it improved the action of the neurotransmitter acetylcholine. In rat models, it also altered N-methyl-D-aspartate receptors, causing an increase in cell membrane permeability. Additionally, piracetam has been shown to enhance oxygen consumption in the brain, as well as adenylate kinase activity in vivo in the rat brain, which is related to adenosine triphosphate metabolism. Cytochrome b5 is engaged in the mechanism of electron transfer in mitochondria, where it also improves permeability, and it appears to promote its synthesis. It reduced the severity of the nerve cell damage brought on by hypoxia, enhanced interhemispheric communication, and increased glucose metabolism in the rat brain. Piracetam has undergone testing for the treatment of alcohol withdrawal symptoms, stroke, unconsciousness, and the prevention of alcohol-induced hypoxia. Additionally, it enhanced rat models with xenobiotic-affected brain function. Piracetam has a very good tolerance and very occasionally causes adverse effects like insomnia, irritability, increased libido, and problems with sexual function.

- **Substances Increasing Brain Metabolism:**

The lesser periwinkle, Vinca minor, contains the vincamine alkaloid, which is the source of vinpocetine, a semi-synthetic derivative. Vinpocetine acts as a potent blocker of voltage-gated sodium channels, a selective inhibitor of $Ca^{2+}$/calmodulin-dependent cyclic nucleotide phosphodiesterase type I, inhibits platelet aggregation, lowers blood viscosity, vasodilates cerebral arteries, and boosts cerebral blood flow, according to ex vivo experiments. Ex vivo, vinpocetine improved brain cell tolerance to hypoxia and increased glucose and oxygen consumption through brain tissue.

To avoid having a hypersensitive reaction to it, it is advised that consumers only take 2–5 mg the first time. The amount can subsequently be increased to 10–30 mg per day, which, albeit infrequently, may result in adverse effects like nausea, dry mouth, dizziness, headache, and heartburn. Vinpocetine use is not advised during nursing or while pregnant.

- **Cholinergics**

These substances frequently contain acetylcholine precursors or cofactors in their composition. The main mediator in operations including memory, thought, counting, and attention is acetylcholine. Acetyl-L-carnitine, a source of acetylcholine precursors, as well as acetyl, choline, lecithin, and pyrrolidine derivatives are significant members of this group. Only its well-known representative, phosphatidylcholine (lecithin), is explained in more detail because it is classified as a cognitiv e chemical that predominantly affects cholinergic transmission in the brain.

Phosphatidylcholine (Lecithin) (Lecithin) Phosphatidylcholine is a member of the class of substances known as phospholipids, which make up the majority of the lipids in cell membranes. Commercial lecithin is an oil-based combination of these phospholipids. Phosphatidylcholine, phosphatidylethanolamine, phosphatidylserine, phosphatidylinositol, and phosphatidylglycerols are the next most prevalent ingredients in supplements that contain lecithin. Palmitic, oleic, and linoleic acids are examples of fatty acids that are ester bonded to phosphatides and found in lecithin.

Soybean and sunflower oils are the main sources of lecithin used in commercial products today. Additionally, lecithin can be found in nut kernels, whole grain products, liver, and egg yolk. As a precursor for the synthesis of acetylcholine, choline is slowly released from lecithin in accordance with the proposed mechanism of action. Lecithin's method of action seems to be obvious, yet clinical trial results on its efficacy were less than convincing. An in vivo experiment's findings revealed that giving phosphatidylcholine to mice with a dementia model boosted acetylcholine levels in the brain and enhanced memory.

## References

Giurgea, C.; Salama, M. Nootropic drugs. Prog. Neuro-Psychopharmacol. 1977, 1, 235–247.

Schifano, F.; Catalani, V.; Sharif, S.; Napoletano, F.; Corkery, J.M.; Arillotta, D.; Fergus, S.; Vento, A.; Guirguis, A. Benefits and Harms of 'Smart Drugs' (Nootropics) in Healthy Individuals. Drugs 2022, 82, 633–647.

Vyas, S.; Kothari, S.; Kachhwaha, S. Nootropic medicinal plants: Therapeutic alternatives for Alzheimer's disease. J. Herb. Med. 2019, 17, 100291.